OXFORD JUNIOR ENCYCLOPAEDIA

VOLUME XI
THE HOME

OXFORD JUNIOR ENCYCLOPAEDIA

GENERAL EDITORS
LAURA E. SALT AND ROBERT SINCLAIR
ILLUSTRATIONS EDITOR: HELEN MARY PETTER

VOLUME XI
THE HOME

DOMI NUS ILLU MINA TIO MEA

OXFORD UNIVERSITY PRESS

Oxford University Press, Amen House, London E.C.4

GLASGOW NEW YORK TORONTO MELBOURNE WELLINGTON
BOMBAY CALCUTTA MADRAS KARACHI KUALA LUMPUR
CAPE TOWN IBADAN NAIROBI ACCRA

FIRST PUBLISHED 1955
REPRINTED 1956, 1957

PRINTED IN GREAT BRITAIN
AT THE UNIVERSITY PRESS, OXFORD
BY CHARLES BATEY, PRINTER TO THE UNIVERSITY

PREFACE

IN authorizing the preparation of this work the Delegates of the Oxford University Press had foremost in mind the need to provide a basic book of reference for school libraries. In form it was to be a genuine encyclopaedia, in treatment and vocabulary suitable for the young reader. To many children (and indeed to many adults) reading is not a natural activity: they do not turn to books for their own sake. But they can be trained to go to books for information which they want for some particular purpose—and thus, very often, to form a habit which will be of lifelong value. Their capacity to read continuously for any length of time being limited, they can absorb knowledge better if they get it in small quantities: therefore they will often read reference books when they may reject the reading of more extended matter. Again, it is probably true to say of such readers that their approach is from the particular to the general, and from the application to the principle, rather than the reverse, that their main interest is in the modern world around them, and that since they are not very good at conceiving things outside their own experience, their capacity for grasping abstract ideas is limited. On the other hand, once their interest is aroused, they will often pursue a subject to remarkable lengths, so long as its development is logical and the treatment avoids dullness.

But such generalizations can easily be overdone: many children using the books will not be of this type. Moreover, it was evident from the first that a project involving so great an amount of work, however exactly it might meet its principal mark, would be fully justified only if it could be of service to a far wider circle of readers. Even for the age-group first in mind, anything like 'writing down to children' must plainly be taboo—but clear exposition and simple language are no bad qualities in writing for any audience. Here, then, it seemed was the opportunity to provide a work of reference suitable for many readers to whom the large, standard encyclopaedias are too heavy and technical, and the popular alternatives for the most part neither sufficiently complete nor authoritative. The fact that the plan allowed for an exceptionally large proportion of illustrations to text (between one-quarter and one-third of the total space) is an advantage to any reader, since pictures may, in many instances, save whole paragraphs of involved explanation. With these secondary aims well in mind, then, the General

Editors have ventured to hope that the encyclopaedia may find usefulness not only among certain younger children, but also among older students in clubs, libraries, and Young People's Colleges, and even to no small extent among their parents and other adults who may wish for a simple approach to some unfamiliar or forgotten subject.

SCOPE AND EMPHASIS. Within certain limits the OXFORD JUNIOR ENCYCLOPAEDIA purports to be reasonably comprehensive, though (in common with all general encyclopaedias) not exhaustive. Chief among these limits is that matter already easily available in school textbooks is included only so far as its presence is necessary for the proper understanding of the subject under discussion. Thus, although an immense field of history is surveyed, it will be found mainly under headings dealing with its effects, or in the biographies of those who lived to make it. Purely technical or scientific subjects, also, are omitted except when they have some general interest. In natural history and kindred studies the immense variety of forms necessarily led at times either to their treatment by groups or to their omission on purely arbitrary decisions as to which species would, in all probability, never be looked for, or because there was nothing particularly interesting to say of them. In point of general balance the stress is laid rather on the modern world, though due space is given to the factors which have shaped it, no less than to those which are changing it.

ARRANGEMENT. The encyclopaedia is planned to consist of twelve volumes. Each is arranged alphabetically within itself, and each deals with a particular range of related subjects. Within its terms of reference, then, each volume is virtually self-contained, and, owing to the great number of single-line cross-references, can well be used alone. This arrangement, which has several incidental advantages (as of production, in difficult times, and of prompt revision later), arose mainly from one consideration. If articles were to be kept really short—and, in fact, few approach and almost none exceeds 2,000 words—many subjects could be dealt with comprehensively only by referring the reader to other relevant articles—itself a desirable thing to do. It was clearly preferable for these to be under his hand, rather than be dispersed through any of the twelve volumes at the caprice of the alphabet. This the present arrangement achieves to a great extent. If it has led to a small amount of overlapping, that again is not without its advantages.

The cross-references play an indispensable part in the make-up of the encyclopaedia. They are of two kinds: references in the text to further articles amplifying the particular point under review, and references at the end of an article to others taking the whole subject farther. Therefore, a reader looking up any wide subject, such as FURNITURE, and following up its cross-references either in the text or at the end of the article, can discover under what main headwords the subject is treated. These, again, will refer him to any subsidiary articles, as also, in many cases, to those of a complementary nature. Thus he may be guided either from the general to the particular or vice versa. It is believed that the titles of the twelve volumes (see p. xii), in conjunction with their sub-titles, will usually lead the reader straight to the volume containing the information he wants. If not, he will need to consult the general index volume, which serves as a guide to the whole encyclopaedia. In selecting headwords, the rules generally followed have been to prefer the familiar, or even the colloquial, reserving the technical alternative for a single-line entry, and to group narrow subjects under a headword of wider scope. Thus, for ANTIBIOTICS, *see* DRUGS; for CARBOHYDRATES, *see* NUTRITION, section 6; for CHICKEN POX, *see* INFECTIOUS DISEASES; for SMOCKING, *see* NEEDLEWORK, DECORATIVE; and for CRINOLINES, *see* FOUNDATION GARMENTS.

L. E. S., R. S.

OXFORD, 1955

LIST OF CONTRIBUTORS

VOLUME EDITOR
Winifred Davin

PRINCIPAL CONTRIBUTORS

Houses

J. M. Richards, A.R.I.B.A.

Interior Decoration

Margaret S. Macdonald-Taylor, A.R.C.A., Hon. A.R.I.B.A., formerly Tutor, School of Architecture, Royal College of Art.

Furniture

John Lowe, B.A. (Oxon.), Assistant Keeper, Department of Woodwork, Victoria and Albert Museum.

Costume

Christina Hole.

Personal Decoration

James Laver, C.B.E., Hon. R.E., F.R.S.A., F.R.S.L., Keeper of Prints and Drawings, Victoria and Albert Museum.

Social History

Asa Briggs, M.A., B.Sc. (Econ.), Professor of Modern History, University of Leeds.

J. R. Hale.

Household Crafts

Joan E. Walley, B.Sc., Queen Elizabeth College, University of London.

Foods and Cooking

Elizabeth Mason, B.Sc. (N.Z.), B.A. (Cantab.).

Nursery

R. S. Illingworth, M.D., F.R.C.P., D.P.H., D.C.H., Professor of Child Health, University of Sheffield.

Edna Balint, B.Sc., Ph.D., Senior Lecturer in Child Development, Institute of Education, University of London.

Medicine and Health

F. N. L. Poynter, B.A., F.R.S.L., F.L.A., Librarian, Wellcome Historical Medical Library.

OTHER CONTRIBUTORS

H. Andrews, B.Sc., A.R.I.C., Building Research Station, Department of Scientific and Industrial Research.

J. Balfour Kirk, C.M.G., M.B., Ch.B., F.R.C.P.

D. T. Bartlett.

W. J. Bishop, F.L.A., Consulting Librarian, Royal College of Obstetricians and Gynaecologists; formerly Librarian, Wellcome Historical Medical Library.

Rev. G. W. Butterworth, Litt.D.

A. M. Cooke, D.M., F.R.C.P.

D. Stirling Craig, A.R.I.B.A., A.M.T.P.I., A.A.Dipl., Architectural Association School of Architecture; formerly Senior Architect, Stevenage Development Corporation.

Leslie H. Daiken, Founder and Hon. Chairman, The Toy Museum.

Douglas Findlay, M.D. (McGill).

Wilma George, M.A.

S. S. B. Gilder, M.B., B.S.

I. F. Grant, LL.D.

David Hawkes, M.A., Lecturer in Chinese, University of Oxford.

Alan Hodge, joint Editor, *History Today*.

G. A. Holmes, Tutor, St. Catherine's Society, Oxford.

Constance Howard, A.R.C.A., Goldsmith's School of Art, London.

Noel Hughes, M.A. (Oxon.).

K. D. Keele, M.D., F.R.C.P.

MICHAEL KIRKBY, M.A. (Oxon.), Assistant Curator, Castle Museum, York.

GEOFFREY LAPAGE, M.D., M.A., M.Sc., formerly Lecturer in Animal Pathology, University of Cambridge.

F. J. M. LAVER, B.Sc., M.I.E.E.

ELEANOR MACDONALD, M.B.E., B.A., Director, J. & E. Atkinson Ltd., London.

D. G. C. MACNABB, M.A., Fellow and Lecturer in Philosophy, Pembroke College, Oxford.

BRIDGET MASON.

D. M. McCALLUM, B.Phil., M.A., Tutor, University of Oxford Delegacy for Social Training.

LILIAN McCREA.

J. M. MOGEY, Lecturer in Sociology, University of Oxford.

IONA OPIE.

A. C. PALLOT, M.B.E., B.Sc. (Eng.), M.I.C.E., M.I.H.V.E. formerly Superintending Engineer, Ministry of Works and Department of Scientific and Industrial Research.

H. H. PRICE, M.A., F.B.A., Wykeham Professor of Logic, University of Oxford.

A. HINGSTON QUIGGIN.

I. G. ROBERTSON, Senior Assistant Keeper, Department of Fine Art, Ashmolean Museum, Oxford.

IVAN M. SHARMAN, Ph.D., F.R.I.C., Dunn Nutritional Laboratory, University of Cambridge and Medical Research Council.

CONSTANCE SPRY, O.B.E., Chairman, Constance Spry Ltd., London.

G. L. TAYLOR, M.A., Assistant Keeper, Department of Fine Art, Ashmolean Museum, Oxford.

A. L. TOWNSEND, Oxford Technical College.

R. R. WILLCOX, M.D.

O. L. ZANGWILL, M.A., Professor of Experimental Psychology, University of Cambridge.

Assistant General Editor: A. T. G. POCOCK

ACKNOWLEDGEMENTS

THE EDITORS wish to thank all those who have helped in any way in compiling this volume. They are particularly indebted to G. T. Hollis, Hon. M.A. (Oxon.), Editor, Oxford Medical Publications, and T. K. Derry, M.A., D.Phil. (Oxon.), for reading the proofs; to Jean Banister, M.A., Fellow and Tutor in Physiology, Somerville College, Oxford, for help with both text and illustrations of the physiology section; to Mrs. E. Griffith for the use of drawings from *Plain Needlework*; and to the Ashmolean Museum and Pitt Rivers Museum, Oxford, the Victoria and Albert Museum and the National Buildings Record, London, for help with illustrations.

COLOUR PLATES

PLAN OF VOLUMES

HOW TO USE THIS BOOK

THIS VOLUME is one of twelve, each on a separate subject, the whole set forming what is called an encyclopaedia, or work from which you can find out almost anything you want to know. (The word comes originally from the Greek *enkuklios*, circular or complete, and *paideia*, education.) Each of the twelve volumes is arranged alphabetically within itself, as twelve dictionaries would be.

The difference between a dictionary and an encyclopaedia is that while the first gives you no more than the meanings and derivations of words, the second tells you a very great deal more about their subjects. For instance, from a dictionary you could learn that a FARTHINGALE is a hooped petticoat, and little more; but an encyclopaedia will tell you that farthingales are foundation garments made of whalebone hoops and worn by 16th-century ladies to make their dresses spread out, that later forms of them were called 'cartwheels', and other interesting facts. Then a dictionary contains nearly every word in the language; but an encyclopaedia deals only with words and subjects about which there is something interesting to be said, beyond their bare meanings. So you should not expect to find every word in an encyclopaedia—every subject is there, but not every word.

To find any subject, you have first to decide in which of the twelve volumes it comes. Each of these has a title as well as a number, and also a list of general subjects to make the title clearer. All these are set out in the Plan of Volumes on the opposite page. Very often you will be able to tell from the title alone which volume contains the information you need; but if not, the list of sub-headings on the plan opposite will help to direct you. For example, if you want to find out about an animal or plant, you would look it up in Volume II, Natural History; but if you wanted to know how that animal or plant is used in something like farming, fishing, or trapping, you would find it in Volume VI. If your subject were something in nature that does not have life—such as the sun, or a particular country or river, or a kind of stone—you would find it in Volume III, with tides, earthquakes, the weather, and many other things. Matters connected with communication of any kind—of people, or goods, or even of ideas—are in Volume IV. So you would look there for languages and printing and broadcasting as well as for ships and trains and roads. But if it is the engineering side of any of these things that interests you, Volume VIII, Engineering, is the place to try. Business and trade are in Volume VII; and how we are governed and protected by the State, the law, and the armed forces is in Volume X. All kinds of sport and games, as well as acting, dancing, concerts, and musical instruments, are in Volume IX. The titles of Volumes V and XII, Great Lives and The Arts, explain themselves; and a rather fuller account of the volume you are reading now, THE HOME, is given on page xv.

To find your subject in the volume, think of its ordinary name, and then look it up as though you were using a dictionary—the As on the first page and the Zs (if there are any) on the last. If you cannot find it, try a more general word. For instance, if you want to read about BROOCHES and cannot find it under its name (as you cannot), try either DRESS FASTENINGS or JEWELLERY —either of which will lead you to it. As you read any article, you will probably come across the title of other articles in some way connected with what you are reading. You will know that they are titles of other articles because they will be printed in capital letters. Either they will be followed by (q.v.) in brackets (this is short for the Latin *quod vide*, and means 'which see'), or else they themselves will be in brackets, with the word *see* in front of them. You can look up these other articles at once if you want to know more about the particular point dealt with, or you can save them up until you have finished the article you are reading. At the end of any article you may find the words 'See also', followed by one or more titles in small capital letters. If you look these titles up, they will tell you still more about the subject that interests you. These last 'cross-references' are very useful if you want to look up a particularly wide subject (such as HOUSES or COSTUME), because they show you at once the titles of all the main articles dealing with it. You can then decide for yourself which to read.

WHAT YOU WILL FIND IN THIS VOLUME

THIS VOLUME IS ABOUT PEOPLE'S HOMES AND HOME LIFE: HOW PEOPLE LIVE,
DRESS, EAT, AND BRING UP THEIR CHILDREN

HOUSES. From the earliest times men and women have made homes,
ranging from PRIMITIVE DWELLINGS of mud and branches to elaborate CASTLES
and PALACES; and through the ages different types of HOUSES have developed
in different parts of the world. This volume describes how houses were
grouped for protection and convenience into VILLAGES and TOWNS, and were
subdivided into specialized ROOMS; and how the various parts of the house
developed—the ROOFS and WALLS, the WINDOWS, STAIRCASES, CHIMNEYS, and
FIREPLACES. It also gives an account of the FURNITURE of the house, its
INTERIOR DECORATION, and its HEATING, LIGHTING, SANITATION, and WATER
SUPPLY.

HOUSECRAFT AND HOUSEHOLD EQUIPMENT. Various crafts and
skills are necessary for successful HOUSEKEEPING, and these are described in
articles such as HOUSEWORK and LAUNDRY, HOUSEHOLD REPAIRS, NEEDLEWORK
and MENDING, and HOUSEHOLD BUDGET. The varied equipment needed in the
home—household LINEN, CLEANING MATERIALS, KITCHEN UTENSILS, and RE-
FRIGERATOR—is explained, as is also the development through the ages of
TABLE DISHES and GLASS, JUGS AND VESSELS, and TABLE-WARE.

FOOD AND COOKING. One of the most important household crafts is
COOKING, aided by a proper understanding of FOOD VALUES and NUTRITION.
This involves a knowledge of basic cooking methods such as BAKING and
STEAMING and of the making of SAUCES, SOUPS, SWEETS, or PASTRY; and also a
knowledge of how to prepare foods such as CHEESES, EGGS, FISH, VEGETABLES,
and MEAT. There is a section on ALES AND BEERS, WINES AND SPIRITS, and other
drinks, and there are articles on the history of FOOD, on INVALID COOKERY,
and on FOOD STORAGE and FOOD PRESERVATION.

CLOTHES AND PERSONAL DECORATION. The purpose of CLOTHES
is discussed, and there is a fully illustrated history of COSTUME, with special
articles on fashions through the ages in CHILDREN'S CLOTHES, UNDERCLOTHES,
BOOTS AND SHOES, HAIRDRESSING, JEWELLERY, and so on. PRIMITIVE COSTUME

and costume in different parts of the world are described, and there are more technical articles on DRESSMAKING, TAILORING, and DRESS DESIGN.

THE NURSERY. The history and modern practice of this important part of the home is fully dealt with, and there are articles on the upbringing of CHILDREN, the part played by LULLABIES and STORY-TELLING in the NURSERY, and the significance of PLAY. Factual accounts are given of the REPRODUCTIVE SYSTEM in humans, of BIRTH, and of the care and feeding of BABIES.

HEALTH AND ILLNESS. An important function of the home is to safeguard the health of its members and to care for them in illness, and for this the techniques of FIRST AID and HOME NURSING are valuable, together with some knowledge of PSYCHOLOGY, human physiology, and the more common human ailments. This volume, therefore, gives an account of human ANATOMY and descriptions of, for example, the working of the DIGESTIVE SYSTEM and the NERVOUS SYSTEM, the function of the HEART and KIDNEYS, the structure of the BRAIN and EYE, the part played by the ENDOCRINE GLANDS and other organs. It shows how the science of MEDICINE, the skill of modern SURGERY, and the excellence of modern NURSING all unite to overcome physical and mental ills.

FAMILY LIFE. The home provides for most people a vitally important SOCIAL ENVIRONMENT, which very greatly influences their behaviour. This volume, therefore, discusses such subjects as INTELLIGENCE and MEMORY; describes the social rules which have grown up to govern ETIQUETTE, TABLE MANNERS, and ENTERTAINMENT, and the customs connected with FAMILY FESTIVALS and giving of PRESENTS; and shows how the various FAMILY WELFARE SERVICES help to safeguard MARRIAGE and to ensure the happiness of FAMILY LIFE.

The words in capitals are the headings of some of the general articles

A

ADOLESCENCE, *see* LIFE CYCLE.

ADOPTION. This is an old and respected practice. The Old Testament tells how Moses was taken from the bulrushes and adopted by Pharaoh's daughter. For centuries people have been taking in and bringing up orphans, abandoned children, or the children of friends and relatives. Usually the motive is the welfare of the children, but at some periods, notably during the Roman Empire, noble families which were dying out relied on adopting children—or even co-opting young men—in order to ensure the survival and continuing fame of the family name.

In modern Europe the first motive has usually been the children's welfare, and the adopted children have usually grown up happily in new homes. But there were exceptions. Cases where children were abandoned or ill-treated and abused increased with the coming of the Industrial Revolution and the growth of cities, and sometimes, in 19th-century London, for example, abandoned children were found and brought up by unscrupulous people who trained them in various forms of crime. Dickens has portrayed in *Oliver Twist* a group of young criminals of this kind and their master.

To prevent such abuses, several Acts of Parliament were passed in the present century; for example, the Children Act of 1948 and the Adoption Act of 1950 (*see* CHILD WELFARE, Vol. X). Under the latter Act there can be no legal adoption without an order by a magistrate's court. By legal adoption the adopted child becomes the legitimate child of the adopters, taking their surname, which is put on his birth certificate.

Adoption not only provides new parents and a stable background for children who need them, but also provides children for childless people who desire them. Such people generally apply either to their Local Authority or to an adoption society. An adoption society is a charitable organization whose function is to bring adopters and children together, and whose activities are regulated by law. When the society, after detailed inquiries about would-be adopters, is satisfied that they are likely to be suitable parents, the child is sent to live with these parents for at least 3 months. During this time the Children's Officer of the Local Authority visits the home to make sure that it is satisfactory. Only at the end of this trial period is the Adoption Order made by the magistrate. Once made it is irrevocable; that is to say, the natural parents cannot reclaim the child nor the adopters disclaim him.

Adoption raises certain problems. If a natural mother gives up a child, whether because of illegitimacy or for some other reason, she experiences a denial of her maternal instincts which is psychologically damaging to her. The adopters have to come to terms with their feelings about the child's background and their fears of inherited tendencies, and they must decide how and when to tell him of his adoption. It is the accepted practice now for the child to learn it from his parents at an early age—often at first in the form of a story—rather than from another source later on. The knowledge that his new parents wanted him and chose him will make up for the rest.

The adoption society has the difficult task of finding the home which will best suit each individual child. Great care has to be taken in this matter, since once a child has begun to live with his would-be adopters, he will be upset if he is moved again. In this, as in other matters connected with adoption, there is still much research to be done.

The average annual number of adoptions in

England and Wales is at present about 14,000. There are many more people who would like to adopt children than there are children available to be adopted.

See also Vol. X: CHILDREN'S HOMES.

ALCOHOL, *see* ALES AND BEERS; WINES AND SPIRITS. *See also* Vol. VII: BEER BREWING; WHISKY DISTILLING.

ALES AND BEERS. The alcoholic fermentation of grain to produce beer (*see* BEER BREWING, Vol. VII) has been practised for thousands of years in many countries, the earliest records of brewing coming from Egypt where a drink called 'hequ' or 'hequp' was brewed. Although beer was also known in ancient Greece, it was more common in the northern countries of Europe where corn would grow but not the vine. In these countries it was the usual drink with meals for many centuries before the introduction of tea or coffee (*see* HOT DRINKS).

The Anglo-Saxons used both words 'beer' and 'ale', though what was the difference between the two drinks is not clear. When Hops (q.v. Vol. VI) were first introduced 5 centuries ago, 'beer' was the name of the brew with hops, and 'ale' that without hops. Today the usage of 'beer', 'ale', 'light', 'dark', and 'bitter' varies

Ashmolean Museum

'BEER STREET'. ENGRAVING BY WILLIAM HOGARTH (1697–1764)

This engraving shows how happy people could be if they drank only beer rather than gin, which led to much drunkenness and misery in the 18th century. Everyone is friendly and prosperous, and the pawnbroker has closed down

from one district to another, and even from one public house to the next in the same city. There is a distinction between 'draught', drawn from the cask, and 'bottled', which explains itself. The words 'light' and 'dark' in England usually indicate the colour, but in Scotland brews are described as 'light' and 'heavy' according to their specific gravity—darker-coloured beers with a low specific gravity may be called 'light', exactly opposite from the usage in southern England.

Apart from the use of hops, the differences in beer were originally differences of strength. In the time of Elizabeth I there were mainly two grades, single and double, the former often being referred to as 'small beer'. 'Double double beer', 'dagger ale', and 'sharp and strong' were also sold. In the early 18th century there were three main types: ale, beer, and 'twopenny', the latter being a small beer sold at 4*d*. per quart. A mixture of these called 'harf and harf' was popular with London market porters, and was subsequently produced under the name of 'entire' or 'entire butt', and later called 'porter'. Other differences developed due to the various kinds

Ashmolean Museum

A SILVER-GILT BEER TANKARD, 1574

of local water used in brewing. Thus London and Dublin became famous for porter and stout, the latter, made from roasted malt, being dark brown, while Burton upon Trent was noted for 'bitter', a very dry draught ale with plenty of hops. Ales with a very high alcoholic content were produced, and were given such names as barley wine and stingo. Lager was a Continental medium beer with a smaller hop content than the English beer.

Various special drinks were made from ale and beer—spiced beer by adding spices and other ingredients, and mulled ale by heating. The 'wassail bowle' contained hot strong ale to which sugar, spices, and roasted apples had been added; 'lamb's wool' was a similar drink. 'Braggart' contained cinnamon, honey, cloves, and ginger; and 'flip', described as 'a yard of flannel', was hot spiced beer to which beaten-up eggs had been added. 'Buttered ale' is self-explanatory. Today such mixed drinks are almost unknown, the only one generally drunk being 'shandy gaff', a mixture of beer with ginger beer or lemonade. A less common one is 'black velvet', a mixture of champagne and stout.

See also WINES AND SPIRITS; COLD DRINKS.
See also Vol. VII: BEER BREWING; BOTTLING (BEER); MALTING.

ALLERGIC DISEASES. The word 'allergy' was coined in 1906 by Professor Clemens von Pirquet of Vienna to describe a special state of exceptional sensitiveness of the body to certain substances brought into contact with it. This term has now become a part of everyday speech, and when we say that we are 'allergic' to something we mean that we 'react' to it in a more or less violent manner. People who are allergic in the medical sense oddly enough are hypersensitive to things which cause no reaction in ordinary people. Allergy is an important factor in medicine because most people have experienced it at some time during their lives—indeed, it is thought that about 10% of the population show more or less permanent manifestations of allergic disease.

Allergy takes an infinite number of forms, but in all of them an abnormal reaction is provoked by minute quantities of the particular 'allergen', or offending substance. A true allergen is always a 'protein'—a complex substance which forms an essential part of animal and plant tissues (*see* FOOD VALUES). The allergen releases in the body a substance called 'histamine', which acts like a poison. The principal allergic diseases are asthma, hay-fever, nettle-rash, and many other skin troubles; eczema and migraine (sick headache) are sometimes also allergic states. One of the most striking facts about allergy is that the abnormal reaction is produced only by a particular substance or group of substances. Thus, hay-fever, which is one of the commonest of the allergic diseases, is usually caused by the inhalation of the pollens of trees, grasses, and weeds; but a person who is sensitive to oak pollen may not be sensitive to elm pollen; some may react to couch grass, while others are not at all affected by couch grass but react to corn or barley. Some people are allergic to various flowers—even the smelling of a rose may produce headache, itchiness, inflammation of the eyes, and sneezing. Pollen allergy makes its appearance at certain fixed seasons; in England the pollen cloud is at its height from the middle of May to the middle of July, and this is the time at which sufferers have their annual bouts of hay-fever or 'summer catarrh'. Asthma, one of the most distressing of allergic diseases, is often provoked by contact with cats, dogs, or horses, the allergen being the dandruff in the animal's hair or fur.

The skin manifestations of allergy are very important. An attack of nettle-rash brings up weals on the skin, accompanied by itching and stinging. The eruption may be caused not only by certain plants, but also by light, heat, and cold, by contact with hair or fur, and by foods such as shellfish, mushrooms, cucumbers, and strawberries. Each individual victim to nettle-rash has his own nettle-rash allergen. Contact dermatitis (inflammatory disease of the skin) is an important problem in industry, because many people are sensitive to various woods, metals, and oils. This is not always a true allergy but sometimes a trouble caused by a local chemical irritation of the skin.

Many people react abnormally to certain drugs. A normal dose of aspirin, quinine, or some other medicine is followed by the appearance of skin rashes and other untoward signs and symptoms. Some people have such reactions to plasters, or ointments, or even to such apparently harmless things as spectacle frames. In some cases hypersensitivity seems to be inherited, but in others it is acquired. The exact mechanism by which it is brought about is very complicated; it may be briefly described as a disturbance of the natural mechanism whereby we acquire 'immunity' from a particular disease after overcoming a first attack of that disease.

In treating a case of allergy the doctor first has to identify the allergen that is causing the trouble. This can often be done by 'patch tests' —the application of extracts of pollens and other allergens to the skin. The offending substance produces a local allergic reaction by which it can be identified. The next step is to 'desensitize' the patient by injecting a number of small doses of his particular allergen in an attempt to build up resistance or immunity. In cases of food allergy, when the allergen is usually easily identified, the obvious course is to abstain from the particular food.

Of recent years, doctors have used drugs called 'anti-histamines' which neutralize the histamines released by the allergen. These drugs deal effectively with an attack, but are not cures as desensitization may be.

ANAEMIA, *see* BLOOD.

ANAESTHETICS. Anaesthesia in any part of the body means a loss of sensation, either permanently or temporarily, in that part. The term is more generally used to describe the artificially produced loss of sensation which makes a surgical operation painless.

Crude attempts at anaesthesia were made in ancient times, patients about to undergo an operation being stupefied with wine or with the juices of narcotic plants (*see* SURGERY, HISTORY OF). In 1846 an American dentist, W. T. Green Morton, introduced an anaesthetic in the form of a sulphuric ether vapour, and towards the end of that year not only did he successfully extract the tooth of a patient who had inhaled this vapour, but a surgeon, J. C. Warren, removed a tumour from a patient's neck at the Massachusetts General Hospital. On 21 December of that year the first operation under ether in Britain was performed by Robert Liston at University College Hospital, London. Sir James Young Simpson introduced chloroform as an alternative to ether in 1847, and for a time it superseded ether. Experience showed that both had certain disadvantages, and other anaesthetic agents were sought. Today new materials and methods are constantly being introduced to keep the science of anaesthesia abreast of advances in other branches of medicine and surgery.

There are two main kinds of anaesthesia: general and local. A patient to whom a general anaesthetic is administered loses consciousness, while a local anaesthetic affects only the area of operation, the patient remaining fully conscious. Cocaine, a drug extracted from the leaves of the coca shrub and the most commonly used local anaesthetic, was introduced in 1879. It is administered by injection. The main methods of giving a general anaesthetic are by inhalation, by an injection into a vein or into the spine, or by an enema.

In the early days of anaesthetics they were often administered by any assistant who happened to be available, or by the surgeon performing the operation. Inevitably there were accidents, patients receiving too little or too much anaesthetic, and even sometimes fatal overdosages. It was soon recognized, however, that this new branch of medicine needed specialists, and now the anaesthetist is an important member of the surgical team. During an operation it is his duty to keep a careful watch on the patient's pulse and respiration and to be ready to use oxygen and other restorative measures in case of collapse. Modern operations sometimes take hours to perform, and the anaesthetist has to ensure that the patient is able to withstand the strain upon his physical resources. An operation is made much less mentally trying to a patient by the modern custom of giving him, before he leaves the ward for the operating theatre, an injection which soothes him and induces a feeling of drowsiness.

In pre-anaesthetic days the surgeon had to concentrate on speed, his main concern being to end the patient's ordeal as quickly as possible; but the introduction of anaesthesia has widened the scope of surgery enormously. An operation is no longer a desperate procedure undertaken as a last resort, but a carefully planned undertaking to remedy structural or functional defects.

See also MEDICINE; SURGERY, HISTORY OF; SURGERY, MODERN.

ANATOMY. Anatomy, a word of Greek origin, signifies the cutting up, or dissection, of bodies with a view to revealing the structure of the parts in relation to the whole. The field of anatomy therefore covers: (1) the body as a whole—its form, shape, and symmetry; (2) the structure of its organs in all their detail, for example, the kidneys, heart, and brain, and the way

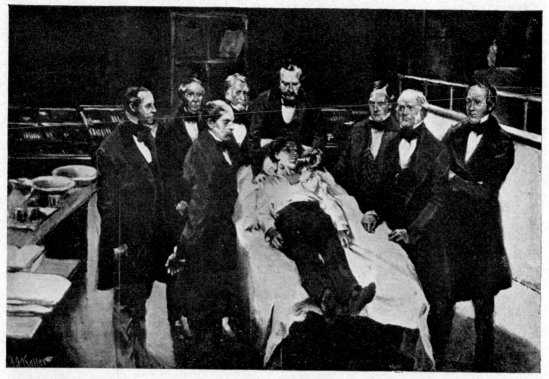

THE FIRST PUBLIC DEMONSTRATION OF SURGICAL ANAESTHESIA, WHICH TOOK PLACE IN BOSTON, U.S.A., IN 1846

in which they are arranged in systems as part of the whole body; (3) the structure of 'tissues', such as the muscle and nerve, which are the essential body-materials, from which special organs are derived; (4) the cells of which tissues are composed—these have to be studied under the microscope.

The shape of parts in relation to their function is often very significant. Roundness, for example, whether in a jellyfish or in a blood-cell, is suitable only to a sluggish existence, but the elongated shape of a bird or man aids rapid movement. Artists who study the body's shapely proportions and the attitudes of the limbs have played a noteworthy part in the history of scientific anatomy—for example, such men as Leonardo Da Vinci and Albrecht Dürer (qq.v. Vol. V).

The scientific study of anatomy reveals that the general structure of the human body has much in common with that of apes and earlier mammals from which man has evolved (see Evolution, Vol. I). In all these animals the organs are grouped into various systems, each making an important contribution to the life of the body

as a whole. The Digestive System (q.v.) consists of a long, complex tube, which begins at the mouth and passes through the body to emerge at the anus, and into which flow a variety of digestive juices, some from little glands in the wall of the tube, some from special organs such as the liver. These juices break down the food into simple substances, which may then be absorbed into the blood. The cardiovascular system, consisting of the Heart (q.v.) and blood-vessels, receives the blood carrying the digested food, and distributes it to all the tissues and organs of the body (see Blood, Circulation of). The heart also pumps the blood through the lungs, where it gathers oxygen from the air and loses waste gases. The respiratory system (see Respiration) consists of the apparatus necessary for supplying oxygen to the blood; the ribs, lungs, and diaphragm are the most important parts. The need of the cells for oxygen is even more urgent than their need for food: indeed, the body will die in a few minutes if it is deprived of oxygen, but can survive starvation for some days or even weeks. Living cells make waste products which are poisonous to the body, and their disposal is the work of the excretory system. Unwanted food is passed out of the body; the KIDNEYS (q.v.) collect poisonous substances in the blood and pass them in urine down

The female produces minute eggs in the ovaries, whence they travel along a tube to the womb or uterus. If an egg is fertilized by a male sperm, a new being is created, which will grow in

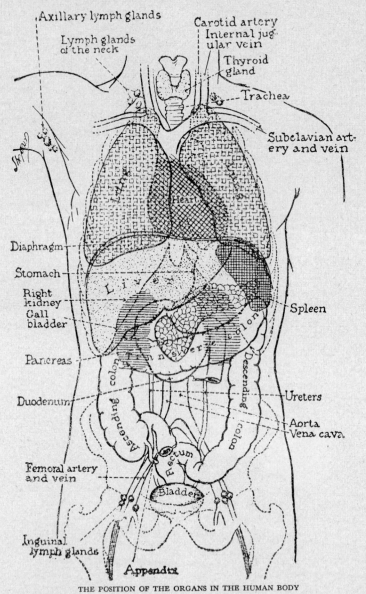

THE POSITION OF THE ORGANS IN THE HUMAN BODY

The small intestine (*see* p. 101) is cut away to show the organs beneath it.
From Logan Clendening, *The Human Body*, Alfred Knopf

to the bladder, from where they are evacuated. The REPRODUCTIVE SYSTEM (q.v.) in the male begins with the testes which make sperms. These are carried by a special duct to the root of the penis, the male sex-organ, which ejects them.

the womb until ready to come out into the world.

Man, like other animals but unlike plants, moves from place to place to search for food and to avoid danger. This is the purpose of the locomotor system, which consists of BONES AND JOINTS and MUSCLES (qq.v.). All these organs are regulated so that they work smoothly through the NERVOUS SYSTEM (q.v.), consisting of the BRAIN (q.v.) in the skull and the spinal cord which runs down the back inside the backbone.

An understanding of the anatomy of a part of the body involves not only a knowledge of its structure in adult man, but a comparison of it with corresponding parts in other animals. This often reveals deep resemblances of form beneath superficial differences. This study, known as comparative anatomy, brings to light such fascinating resemblances as those between the wing of a BAT (q.v. Vol. II) and the human hand. Different anatomical patterns have appeared all through the long ages of life on this earth as shown by the changing forms of fossils. Similar changes occur during the growth of the individual from the egg, the subject of embryology. Human anatomy includes all these different aspects.

So far we have mentioned only the anatomy of healthy organs. Disease alters these patterns, an alteration which can be understood only by someone who has a thorough knowledge of normal anatomy. This field, known as 'morbid anatomy', was first explored by an Italian anatomist, Morgagni, in the 18th century, and later developed by the great British surgeon, JOHN HUNTER (q.v. Vol. V). Surgeons need particular knowledge of those parts of the body concerned in operations, a study called 'surgical anatomy'.

Anatomy is largely concerned with the structure of organs, which are well-defined parts of the body possessing particular functions and each working with some degree of independence. The specialized structure of an organ is closely linked with its special function, as the HEART and BRAIN (qq.v.) exemplify well. The function of the heart has been adequately explained by its anatomy, but many parts of the brain play roles in the life of the body which are not yet understood. The anatomist, it is clear, though primarily concerned with the structure of organs, cannot avoid the study of their function, that is, 'physiology'.

Different organs have come into being through the differentiation of simple structures. The kidney, for example, is an organ which in a human being takes on many duties performed by the 'contractile vacuole' in the simple

AMOEBA (q.v. Vol. II). Such specialization, though it brings relative independence, also brings a need for further control to ensure that the unity of organs which comprise the whole body is maintained. Certain organs are specially devoted to this 'integration' in the human body. Within cells enzymes control the rate of chemical change. Tissue changes are governed by the ENDOCRINE GLANDS (q.v.). The circulating blood itself provides a constant physical and chemical environment to the organs of the body. The nervous system makes possible rapid coordination between sensation and movement. The brain of man, with its power of MEMORY (q.v.) and judgement, casts its integrating faculty over past and future in a way which makes it the dominant organ of the body.

The study of tissues came later in the history of anatomy than the dissection of organs. It was a Frenchman, Bichat, who in 1801 first concentrated attention on the materials of which organs are made—tissues such as muscle and nerve. In muscle the constituent cells possess great powers of shortening and lengthening as they contract or relax, a process very evident in the biceps muscle of the arm or in the heart. 'Epithelial' tissues form linings of varied nature, sometimes dry like the SKIN (q.v.), sometimes moistened by the secretions of mucous glands, as in the nose. Nervous tissue consists of cells, called 'neurones', provided with particularly long processes which run to all parts of the body conveying electrical impulses at speed. The supporting scaffolding of the body is the connective tissue which plays a variable part, in some places providing hard elastic tissue such as cartilage, in others a fluid such as the blood itself.

The increasing power of the microscope has made it possible to study the inner structure of cells—indeed, even to discover their actual molecular structure.

See also Vol. II: ANATOMY (Animal).

ANTIBIOTICS, see DRUGS.

ANTISEPSIS AND ASEPSIS. Antisepsis means destroying germs by applying chemicals such as carbolic acid, boracic acid, phenol, or iodine. Asepsis means keeping the germs away. Antisepsis and asepsis are both achieved by means of sterilizing agents, but there is a subtle distinction between the two processes as applied to surgery. The aim of antisepsis is to destroy germs already

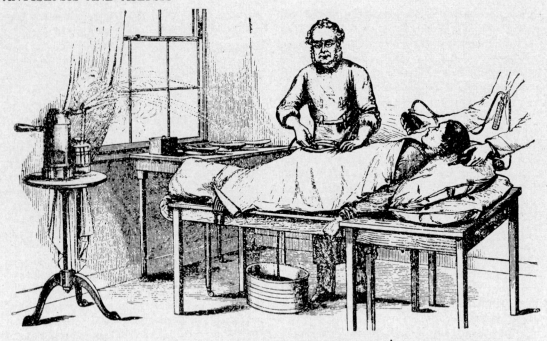

AN OPERATION PERFORMED WITH ONE OF THE EARLIEST FORMS OF LISTER'S ANTISEPTIC SPRAY

present in a wound or its surrounding tissues; that of asepsis is to prevent their access to or near the wound by preliminary sterilization of the air, the surgeon's hands and instruments, the dressings, and every other possible source of contamination.

The antiseptic system was introduced into surgery by Lord LISTER, who worked on the discoveries of the great French scientist Louis PASTEUR (qq.v. Vol. V). Before the time of Pasteur and Lister the mortality by surgical operations was appallingly high, not through lack of surgical skill but through post-operation infection (*see* SURGERY, HISTORY OF). The existence of germs had long been an established fact, but it was not until the 1860s that Pasteur demonstrated how germs could bring about changes in organic matter and could so cause disease. Lister, having read Pasteur's papers, reasoned that if, as the French scientist asserted, germs were universally present in the air, they were probably the cause of infection and septicaemia in living tissues exposed at operation. If the germs were killed or prevented from reaching the living tissue, there would be no infection.

Lister's introduction of antiseptics brought about the greatest revolution in the history of surgery. At first he used pure carbolic acid, but this was found to be too strong and to need dilu-

tion. As next worked out by Lister, operations took place under a cloud of carbolic acid vapour, all instruments and the operator's hands being disinfected with carbolic acid, the wound cleaned with the same preparation, and dressed with carbolized gauze and cotton wool. Later on Lister discarded the spray since, if hands, instruments, and dressings were disinfected, the spray was not necessary.

Although the results achieved by 'Listerism', as it was called, were sufficiently striking to ensure the adoption of the method in all surgical clinics, there were a number of drawbacks. It was found that antiseptics sufficiently strong to kill germs also often damaged the tissues of the human body. Hence there arose the aseptic method, the keeping of wounds free from all contact with germs. The air of a modern operating theatre is specially conditioned, and all instruments and dressings are sterilized beforehand by superheated steam. The surgeon and his assistants, the anaesthetist, and the nurses wear sterilized gowns, rubber gloves, caps, and masks. The skin of the patient is treated with antiseptics such as alcohol, iodine, or picric acid. In addition to the long-established methods of sterilization by boiling water or steam, by dry heat, or by germicides such as carbolic, there are now available the new drugs—the sulphonamides

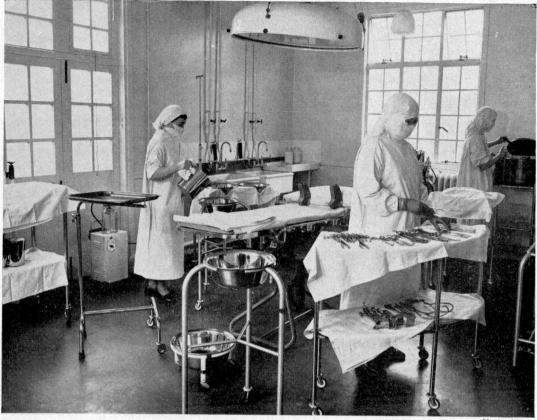

Nursing Mirror

PREPARING FOR AN OPERATION IN A THEATRE AT THE FULFORD MATERNITY HOSPITAL, YORK

The nurses, in their sterilized clothes, gloves, and masks, are sterilizing the instruments in the sterilizer on the right before laying them ready for the surgeon. The floor, walls, and furniture of the theatre are made of materials which do not harbour dirt

and antibiotics such as penicillin (*see* DRUGS). These do not necessarily kill germs, but they prevent their growth and multiplication, making it easy for the natural defences of the body to deal with them. Also, though they can be used locally, they can be given by mouth or by injection; in the latter case they are carried by the blood-stream to the seat of infection.

See also SURGERY, MODERN.

ARTHRITIS, *see* BONES AND JOINTS; ORTHO-PAEDICS.

ARTIFICIAL RESPIRATION, *see* FIRST AID.

ASPICS, *see* JELLIES AND ASPICS.

ASTHMA, *see* ALLERGIC DISEASES.

B

BABIES, CARE OF. For hundreds of years it was the strange practice in many countries to wrap babies in swaddling clothes from the time of birth to about the end of the first year. These clothes kept their arms and legs fastened tightly down so that they could not move, the idea being that the baby's fragile bones needed this support to ensure their growing straight and not bowed or deformed. Swaddling is still practised in some parts of eastern Europe and among some Ameri-can Indians. The Columbia River Indians in America bind the baby's head so that it cannot be moved at all, and it remains permanently flattened for life.

The basic needs of a baby are warmth and comfort, cleanliness, food, love, and safety, the opportunity for exercise and for developing his skills, and training in good habits.

A baby is kept at the right temperature by suitable clothes. In tropical countries babies and small children wear no clothes, or hardly any; but in very cold countries, such as Iceland and the north of Canada, they have to wear very warm clothes. In England, in the hot summer weather, it may be enough for the baby to wear a cotton vest and a thin dress, with no gloves or socks. At night he wears a vest and a nightgown. In the winter he must be warmly clad; he wears one or two wool vests, a wool dress, and socks, and is carried in a wool shawl. Out of doors he wears a thick coat or a sleeping bag, a hat or bonnet, mittens, and bootees. It is difficult to keep his hands and feet warm, for he pulls his

SWADDLING A BABY IN THE 17TH CENTURY
Engraving by Abraham Bosse

mits, shoes, and socks off, or sucks his mits and makes them wet. If the mits are fastened with satin ribbon, the bows come undone because the satin slips. Some mothers sew the mits on to the cuffs of the coat, or on to tape threaded through sleeves, so that the baby cannot take them off. The best way to keep the baby warm at night is to put him into a sleeping bag with sleeves and a zip up to the neck; if he is too warm, however, he will cry because he is uncomfortable.

Toddlers wear pants and vests, with trousers and a shirt or pullover for boys and a dress for girls. Dungarees for both boys and girls when they are playing, especially

Planet News

QUADRUPLETS IN INCUBATORS AT WESTMINSTER HOSPITAL

The babies were so frail that they had to be kept in incubators in which the temperature, humidity, and air were carefully controlled

out of doors, are most suitable because the children can get them thoroughly dirty without being scolded for spoiling good clothes.

All children should spend a lot of time out of doors; even in the coldest weather there is no reason why even a very young baby should not be outside in a pram provided he is properly wrapped up, covered with blankets, and kept out of draughts. Boys and girls of any age should play outside for part of the day, however cold it is, but they must have warm clothes—dungarees, lumber jackets, and thick wool gloves and stockings.

A baby cannot be comfortable if he is not kept clean. Up to the age of about 18 months babies wear nappies in the daytime, and up to about 2 years of age they wear them at night—usually one of smooth muslin or gauze next to the skin, with one of Turkish towelling outside. Disposable nappies are available, made of cellulose wadding to be burnt after use; these recall the absorbent moss which Eskimoes use in place of babies' napkins. Some mothers put rubber pants over the nappies, but these often cause irritation of the skin, and plastic nappie holders are more satisfactory. The nappie must be changed frequently, especially when the baby is young, for young babies wet them many times a day. When a baby has had a motion in his nappie,

the buttocks are cleaned with a soft sponge or wet cotton wool, dried, and powdered with baby powder: sometimes baby cream is gently rubbed in to prevent the skin becoming sore.

A baby is bathed daily in water of blood temperature with a special baby soap which does not irritate his tender skin. The mother, if she has no thermometer, tests the water by dipping in her elbow. The baby enjoys splashing in the water, and then the mother lifts him on to her lap to dry him thoroughly, particularly behind the ears and in the armpits, places which if forgotten soon become sore. She cleans his nose with little wisps of cotton wool, and cuts his finger-nails every few days, for they grow quickly and will become dirty and scratch the skin. She washes his hair every day or every other day while he is tiny, but for older babies about once a week is enough.

Babies often feel lonely when lying in a pram out in the garden, and want to be loved, and it is not good for them to feel unhappy. So a wise mother picks her baby up when he makes a distressed cry, changes his nappie if it is wet, feeds him if he is hungry, and, if he is not wet or hungry nor too hot nor too cold, she just cuddles him for a few minutes before putting him back where he was. After the age of about 3 months babies often dislike being separated from their mothers, and cry if left alone, but are quite happy if they are somewhere where they can watch what their mother is doing.

Babies sleep much more than older children, and they cry when they get tired. A young baby goes to sleep several times in the day, but by the time he is a year old he will probably have only two sleeps a day, and by the time he is 2 he may want only one nap in the middle of the day (*see* SLEEP). Unless it is raining, it is usually better to let him have his daytime sleep outside in the fresh air in his pram, and to bring him in when he begins to cry. When older babies and toddlers become too tired they get very cross and cry a lot. They may refuse to eat their dinners, and often have trouble in getting to sleep. So it is important to put them to bed before they are too tired. Sometimes a baby cries when put to bed and screams unless his mother goes and sits with him or rocks him to sleep. If she does this every day, the baby very soon gets to expect it and will not sleep without it. Some babies cry out frequently in the night just to make their mothers come and talk to them. In these cases, to prevent their developing bad habits, the mother has to leave them to cry so that they will learn that she does not go in and see them every time they wake up. She has to judge whether the cry is one of distress or merely a call for attention. Many young children also get into the habit of waking early in the morning and expecting their mothers to play with them.

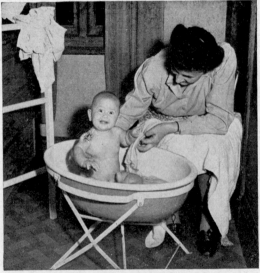

BATHING A BABY

When a baby is a few months old, his nappie is taken off when he gets up in the morning, after every meal, and before he goes to bed, and he is placed on his pottie. He may or may not use it, but it is the beginning of learning a good habit. He does not learn to ask for his pottie until he is about 15 to 18 months old, and then, until he is about 3 years old, he is liable to forget to ask for it and to wet his pants at times when he is absorbed in play. After he has learnt to ask for the pottie, he does without his nappie in the daytime. A child must never be smacked or punished in any way for not using the pottie or for wetting his pants—indeed that would be likely to make him wet his pants all the more. Nothing is said about these mishaps, and he soon learns to keep himself dry.

When, at about 6 months, a baby can roll, and even more when at 9 or 10 months he can crawl, it is very difficult to keep him out of mischief. Babies love to explore the coal bucket, the waste paper basket, and the rubbish bucket, to pull table cloths, to take books out of the book case, to tug at the lamp flex, and to seize flower vases or anything else within reach. Many of these things are dangerous, and it is difficult to watch a baby all the time. When he is about 15 months, if the door is left open, he may make for the stairs and creep up them, and there must be someone to watch him then, for he is likely to lean back half-way up and fall down. When he is little, the playpen is useful for keeping him safe, but an older baby will probably refuse to stay in it. Mothers find children at this age very difficult to look after, because they get into trouble all day long, and particularly in the kitchen, where they are very liable to harm themselves. The mother has to remember to turn all pan handles out of reach, for a baby may get hold of the handle, upset the pan, and scald himself. She must never leave buckets of water on the floor, nor fires unprotected by a fireguard. She must find other harmless things to attract his attention and keep him happy.

As soon as he is old enough, a baby should have every chance to do things for himself. He should be able to feed himself with a biscuit by the age of 6 months, and by the age of a year he will want to help to feed himself with a spoon. He will spill a lot of food, for babies twist the spoon round just before it enters the mouth and so drop the food. When he is about 15 months old he can use a cup without help, and can feed

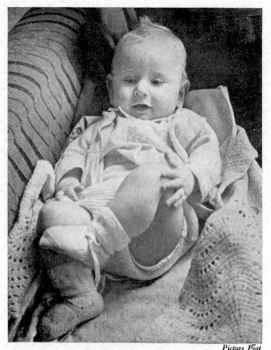

Picture Post

A BABY TAKING EXERCISE

himself as long as the food is cut up. When he is 2, he can begin to become interested in cleaning his teeth thoroughly, and by the age of 3 he should be able to dress himself if help is given over tying shoe laces and fastening buttons; by 5 he can do these things too. Many children could do much more for themselves if they were not constantly helped by their mother, who has to exercise great patience in allowing these daily events to take rather a long time.

See also BIRTH; NURSERY EQUIPMENT; STORY-TELLING; CHILDREN, UPBRINGING OF.

BABIES, FEEDING OF. The natural and best way to feed a young baby is on the breast. Babies feel safe and happy when feeding from their mother's breast and they usually get fewer colds, coughs, and other illnesses than those fed on cow's milk; the mother does not have to mix feeds or to keep bottles and teats clean. The mother's breasts, which have been growing larger while she was carrying the baby, are normally ready to produce milk when the baby is born (*see* BIRTH).

For hundreds of years well-to-do mothers used to employ 'wet nurses' to breast-feed their babies. We know that in India, as early as

1000 B.C., wet nurses were employed, and that they had to be neither too old nor too young, of good health and character, and affectionate. Long before the time of Christ, women of high rank in many east Mediterranean countries handed their babies over to wet nurses (or foster mothers) at birth. In Egypt and Rome women captured in battle were often used in this way. In Paris, 200 years ago, there were agencies for wet nurses, who brought suitable women from all over France. Nowadays, in most civilized countries, if a woman is unable or unwilling to feed her baby on her breast, the baby is fed on cow's milk, but in some Eastern countries wet nurses are still used; in parts of New Guinea and Java, where women go to work in the fields a few days after the baby has been born, the grandmother often feeds the baby on her own breast. Amongst some of the Arabs in Morocco, the mother is not the only one who breast-feeds the baby: the best servant may feed it too, and so may any nursing mother who visits the house.

In England a baby feeds on the breast a few hours after birth; but among many primitive peoples in Africa and North America the mother does not feed the baby herself for about a week, the baby sometimes being put to the breast of another woman during that time, or sometimes being given some other food. In ancient India it was the practice to give babies nothing but honey in the first days of their life.

Many mothers in England give babies only boiled water or sugar water in the first 2 days of their life. In parts of Africa water is thought to be necessary, and it is poured over the baby's face so that he will swallow some of it. Actually it is not necessary to give new-born babies water, except in very hot weather when they may be thirsty.

When a baby is put to the breast he finds the right place to suck by instinct. He lies in his mother's arm in front of her body in a tilted position—for it is difficult to swallow milk when lying flat—and his head rests in the crook of her arm. Some mothers feed their baby at rigidly fixed times—every 3 hours or every 4 hours. The wise mother, however, will not refuse to feed him if he is crying because he is hungry—for young babies cry as soon as they are hungry. She can soon learn to distinguish the cry which means he is hungry from one which means he has a pain or needs some other attention. Young babies need to be fed much more frequently than

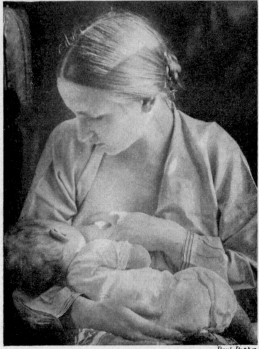

Paul Popper

A MOTHER FEEDING HER BABY

older ones: a 7-day-old baby will want five or even more feeds in the day; when he is a year he will not want more than three or four feeds.

A mother feeds her baby on both breasts at each feed, giving him 5 to 15 minutes on each breast. Some babies suck the milk more quickly than others, the older baby usually taking much less time than the young one.

While a baby is feeding, he swallows some air which would cause him to have wind pain in the stomach if the mother did not help him to bring it up; so, after every feed, she sits him on her knee or holds him up to her shoulder and gently pats his back until he belches the wind up. Then she puts him down in his cot to sleep. The young baby goes to sleep after a good feed, but he occasionally brings a little milk up, and sometimes hiccoughs.

Most babies in the first 10 weeks need a feed in the night. After that age, however, they begin to sleep through the night, though they are likely to awaken early in the morning, about 5 or 6 o'clock, for their feed.

Babies are given no other food but breast milk until they are 4 or 5 months old; then they are given a small amount of cereal food mixed with milk. They often spit it out at first, but with gentle persuasion they learn to take it. As they grow older, they also have soups, puréed vegetables or fruit, gravy, eggs, custard, or other soft foods. This is called 'weaning' the baby. When he learns to chew, at about 6 months, he starts having some solid foods, such as rusks, banana, or apple, and minced meat or fish. He can chew these perfectly well even though he has no teeth. The first tooth usually comes through at about 6 months. He gradually takes less and less breast milk, until at about 9 months he is completely weaned and can live from that time on cow's milk and ordinary foods.

In many countries breast-feeding continues much longer than this, but it is not good for the child. It is common in China and Africa to breast-feed a child till he is 3 or 4 years old, and some North American Indian and Eskimo children are fed on the breast till they are 12 or older.

Some mothers have not enough breast milk to feed their baby. All sorts of strange ideas and superstitions used to exist about a mother's milk. It was believed that powdered earthworms, cooked sea slugs, garden snails, or the flesh of an owl would enable the mother to produce more milk, and in Perugia, in Italy, to this day mothers wear a special pin in their hair in order to increase the milk supply. In parts of eastern Europe a woman who has not enough milk believes that she must catch a fish alive, squirt some of her milk into its mouth, and then let it go. In ancient Greece babies for whom no breast milk was available were put on to a rubbish heap and left to die; and in some primitive countries babies are killed if there is no breast milk for them.

In England, if there is not enough breast milk, the baby is put on to the bottle and fed with cow's milk. In some countries babies have been fed on milk from the ass, goat, water buffalo, reindeer, caribou, sheep, camel, llama, bitch, and mare. Sometimes babies have been fed direct from animals—as Romulus and Remus are said to have been fed by a she-wolf. In quite recent times babies in Malta and India have been fed direct from goats: the goat is tethered by its feet so that it cannot kick, and the baby is held under it so that he can suck. In Paris, towards the end of the 19th century, asses were used in this way.

Other foods besides milk have deen devised for babies who could not be fed on the breast.

In the 17th century babies were given pap (bread cooked in water) or panada (flour, cereal, or bread, cooked in broth and generally combined with butter or milk). In France a 17th-century doctor advised that babies should be fed on bread cooked in beer.

Feeding-bottles were first used many hundreds of years ago. In ancient Greece clay globular bottles were used, but in Roman times glass was introduced. Elsewhere bottles were made of earthenware, pewter, or wood. In the Middle Ages milk was poured direct into the baby's mouth from cows' horns, with a hole bored through the narrow end. Sometimes a calf's teat, the finger of a glove, or a piece of wash-leather was fixed to the narrow end of the horn, and the baby sucked through this. In the 18th century a sort of cup with a spout was used, the end of the spout being perforated with fine holes or open and covered with perforated skin for the baby to suck through. Some feeding-bottles were made of elaborately decorated china. Nowadays all feeding-bottles are made of glass or some similar material, preferably heat-proof.

Cow's milk for a young baby is always boiled and mixed with a little sugar and water. More commonly, various special preparations of dried

Wellcome Historical Medical Museum

EARLY 19TH-CENTURY FEEDING BOTTLE
It was probably for use after weaning

milk are used, the powder being mixed with water, and sometimes sugar, and then given to the baby.

Feeding-bottles and teats have to be boiled before use to prevent any possible infection. The hole in the teat must be big enough to allow the baby to obtain the milk easily—that is, when the bottle is held upside down, the milk should drop out rapidly. If it does not, the easiest way of enlarging the hole is to stick a needle into a cork holder, make the other end of the needle red hot, and then use that to enlarge the hole. The milk should be given to the baby at blood temperature. The mother may test its temperature by dropping some on to her bare arm. The baby takes 10 to 20 minutes for the feed, and then his wind is brought up just as if he were fed on the breast.

Abnormally small babies, before they can suck, are fed by a rubber tube passed down their throat, or by a pipette or spoon.

When a baby is old enough, at 5 or 6 months, he begins to take his milk in a cup and, like breast-fed babies, to eat solid food. By the age of 9 months, he no longer sucks from the bottle but takes all his food by cup or spoon. All babies are given cod-liver oil and orange juice from the age of about 1 month to prevent certain vitamin DEFICIENCY DISEASES (q.v.), such as rickets or scurvy.

See also BIRTH; FOOD VALUES; BABIES, CARE OF; MILK.

BABY TRANSPORT. Babies are moved from place to place in a wide variety of ways in different parts of the world. Women in many countries, such as Java, New Guinea, Africa, and Japan, carry their babies on their backs as they work in the fields. The Eskimoes put them in the hoods of their fur jackets, and North American

Wallace Collection

FEEDING A BABY WITH A SPOON
Painting by N. B. Lépicié (1735–84)

Pitt Rivers Museum Coll.

NORTH AMERICAN INDIAN BABY ON A CRADLE-BOARD

AN EDWARDIAN BASKET PERAMBULATOR

Indians used to carry them on cradle-boards fixed on their backs. The Japanese, Hottentots, and Fijians carry them in a sort of shawl on the back. Bedouin women in the desert carry their babies on their shoulders.

It is difficult to say when perambulators were invented, but the term does not seem to have been used for much over 100 years. Modern

Paul Popper

NORTHERN BURMESE GIRL CARRYING A BABY

prams are of various shapes and sizes. A good pram is well sprung and has wheels running on ball-bearings; some have a sort of strut which pulls down so as to keep the pram steady and prevent it from upsetting when the baby is jumping about in it. The pram has a mattress, a waterproof sheet, pram sheets, and blankets. A waterproof cover made of two layers of mohair, a hairy cotton and wool fabric, with a layer of rubber in between, is fastened to the top of the pram. The baby is kept from climbing out by means of straps which fit over his shoulders and round his waist. These shoulder straps, with reins attached, can also be used as a harness for walking.

For taking the baby by car special seats have been devised made of canvas with a metal frame and a wooden tray; the frame has rounded hooks which fit over the back of the car seat. The baby car seat, which will fold up, can also be used in the house or in the country on a picnic.

See also BABIES, CARE OF; NURSERY EQUIPMENT.

BAKING. Oven-cooking with crusting and browning of the food on the outside, which is called baking, is used especially for bread and cakes, and also for batters, soufflés, starchy vegetables such as potatoes, and fish. The story of baking is largely the history of ovens (*see* COOKING STOVES). Originally, these were massive affairs, built of stone or brick and needing a lot of fuel to keep them going; an oven, therefore, was often shared by a community such as a village, and oven-baking is not as a rule found at all in very poor or in nomadic communities:

for example, raised bread, which must be oven-baked, was hardly found in Scotland before the 19th century, and even today almost all the bread for the West Highlands is baked in Glasgow. In rural Sweden there was hardly any raised bread, nor among the nomadic Arabs nor the Indians and Chinese in those parts where fuel is very scarce. The art of baking dates from the Stone Age, and oven bread was well known in ancient Egypt and is mentioned in Genesis. The Romans had public bakeries and a kind of guild organization of bakers with special rules and privileges. In the Middle Ages, the craft of the baker was strictly regulated. Home baking of bread was practised only in the country and, traditionally, in certain areas—for example, Lancashire, where, as late as 1804, Manchester had no public baker.

Australian damper—a dough cooked under a tin plate in the dying embers of a wood fire—illustrates a primitive kind of baking. The Polynesians invented a delicious way of baking their breadfruit, taro, and fish by wrapping them up in banana leaf parcels and putting them in a pit lined with hot stones, the whole being covered with leaves and earth and left for several hours. This earth oven has the attractive name of *umu*. The Maoris used something very similar but deeper, and they splashed the hot stones with water to make steam. The gypsies bake hedgehogs encased in wet clay in an earth oven, and, when the baked clay is broken open, the spines

Pitt Rivers Museum Coll.
A PUEBLO INDIAN OVEN, NEW MEXICO
A fire is made inside the oven, and when the walls are well heated, the coals are raked out and the dough put in to bake

and skin come away with it. We have most of us baked potatoes in the hot ashes of a bonfire.

Modern Western ovens make it easy and quick to bake at home, but they are relatively expensive, and it is still common in many European countries to find housewives hurrying to the local bakery with their uncooked cakes in their arms and the baking fee of a few pence in their pockets.

See also Cooking Stoves; Breadmaking; Cakes.
See also Vol. VII: Baking Industry.

BALCONIES. The word balcony comes from Italy and means a railed platform projecting from an upper window. It was a common feature in houses of the Italian renaissance, and was adopted in northern Europe when Italian architecture was widely imitated in the 17th and 18th centuries. Italian balconies had stone balustrades and English balconies also had them in the 17th century, but later they were often replaced by iron railings.

Towards the end of the 18th century, when towns in Britain were expanding rapidly, houses were built in great numbers up and down the country to an almost standard pattern (*see* Georgian Architecture, Vol. XII). They were plain in appearance, interest being given by a series of small balconies outside the first-floor windows, which were taller than the others and opened right down to the floor. These balconies were almost wholly decorative in their purpose, neither their size nor their position making them suitable for sitting on. They had wrought-iron railings of geometrical design, of great variety and delicacy. Sometimes all the first-floor windows shared one balcony, which ran right across the front of the house and had a curving roof of copper or lead, supported on slender columns. These long balconies (sometimes called Verandahs (q.v.), though this word is usually used only for ground-level structures) were especially characteristic of Regency Architecture (q.v. Vol. XII) and also of early Victorian houses built at spas and seaside resorts, such as Cheltenham, Brighton, Leamington, and Sidmouth.

The Victorians liked all kinds of ornamental detail in their houses, and this included balconies. They imitated the Regency wrought-iron work in coarser cast iron, and later made balconies in various materials. The Edwardians favoured more spacious balconies with white-painted wooden posts and balustrades. In the

National Buildings Record

REGENCY WROUGHT-IRON BALCONIES IN BEAUMONT STREET,
OXFORD

present century, balconies have become a feature
of blocks of FLATS (q.v.), at first on the Continent
and later in Britain. Nearly every flat has at
least one, either projecting from the wall or
receding into it (*see* Vol. X, p. 416). Sometimes
it is large enough for the family to sit on, sometimes so small as to be little more than decoration, though even a tiny balcony is large enough
to give a baby an airing in his cradle. Small
balconies, too, will allow sitting-room windows
to be opened safely down to the floor.

See also VERANDAHS.

BATHS, *see* PERSONAL HYGIENE, HISTORY OF.

BEARDS AND MOUSTACHES. The amount
of facial hair with which Nature has provided
mankind varies considerably. The Red Indian
has hardly any, the Negro very little. The beard
of the Chinese is very straggly; his moustache,
when he has one, long and thin. The Semitic
peoples had abundant hair on the face and in
general let it grow. The beards of the Assyrian
monarchs, for example, were splendid affairs,
curled and sprinkled with gold dust (*see* Vol. I,
p. 4); and the Jews in ancient times were
a bearded people, as were also the Arabs.
Mohammedans still swear 'by the beard of the
Prophet'. The Egyptians, on the other hand,
were accustomed to shave both the head and
the face. On ceremonial occasions the Pharaohs
wore an artificial beard. The ancient Greeks
were bearded, at least until the 4th century B.C.;
but the Romans, by the time of Julius Caesar,
were almost all clean-shaven. The barbarian
tribes who invaded and finally overcame the
Roman Empire were particularly proud of their
beards. Among the Franks beards were held in
the highest veneration, as they were among the
Danes, but when the Normans (the descendants
of the Norsemen) conquered England in the 11th
century, they were clean-shaven.

The fashion for wearing long beards reappeared in the reign of Henry I, in spite of the
disapproval of the clergy, but Henry II returned
to the old Norman fashion of close-shaving. In
the 14th century Edward I is represented on his
seals as shaven; but the effigy of the effeminate
Edward II shows a beard elaborately curled;
Edward III had a full beard, and Richard II a
forked one.

The beard disappears with Henry V, probably for a practical reason. By the time of
Agincourt the knight in armour wore a helmet
constructed of steel plates with movable vizor.
A beard would easily catch in such a contrivance
and so naturally men preferred to be clean-
shaven (*see* ARMOUR, Vol. X).

The beard reappears with Henry VIII, and
indeed throughout the 16th century beards
were in the height of fashion. Edward VI died
too young to wear one, but Philip of Spain
was bearded and so were all the French kings.
During Elizabeth's reign beards ran riot.
Stubbes, a Puritan satirist of the period, remarks
that the barbers 'have invented such strange
fashions . . . that you would wonder to see. They
have one manner of cut called the French cut,
another the Spanish cut; one the Dutch cut,
another the Italian. . . . Then when they have
done all their feats, it is a work to consider how
their mowchatowes (moustaches) must be preserved or laid out from one cheek to another,
and turned up like two horns towards the forehead.'

In the 17th century beards began to dwindle.
Charles I had what was later to be known as an

BEARDS

Top left, medieval; right, Elizabethan. Bottom left, goatee, *c.* 1860; right, Dundreary weepers, *c.* 1863

'Imperial' (*see* Vol. V, p. 83). By the end of the century beards and moustaches had disappeared and were not worn again until well into the 19th century. Indeed, in the 18th century, if you had a beard you were a curiosity, almost a monstrosity; and if you had a moustache you were almost certainly a Hungarian or a Swede, and certainly not French or English.

It is true that some of the Regency bucks had 'side-burns', but when real beards began to appear again in the 1830s, they were an indication of bohemianism and revolutionary sentiments. How anti-social they were considered is shown by the story of an American, Joseph Palmer, who lived near Harvard, Massachusetts, about 1830. He was persecuted unmercifully for wearing a full beard, and finally ended in prison because he refused to shave it off. Soon after the middle of the century, however, the return of the bearded warriors from the Crimea brought beards back into fashion, and they became increasingly common. There were many varieties: the goatee (less common in England than in America), 'mutton chops' (*see* Vol. V, p. 376), Newgates (a fringe under the chin) (*see*

Vol. V, p. 59), Dundreary 'weepers', and others. Napoleon III revived the pointed Vandyke beard, which is still called an 'Imperial' in his honour.

In the last quarter of the 19th century beards began to disappear again, the younger men wearing moustaches only. Moustaches persisted until the First World War, but they gradually dwindled to the 'eleven-a-side', the tiny under-the-nose moustache made famous by Charlie Chaplin (*see* Vol. IX, p. 130), and infamous by Hitler. Then, after the war, moustaches vanished. In the 1920s beards were persecuted out of existence largely by a game called 'Beaver', which was popular with all young people. By 1930 there was hardly a beard to be seen in Western Europe. The Second World War brought them back again, especially among naval officers in the submarine service and on Arctic convoys. Moustaches also became rather more common. The steady improvement in modern shaving appliances encourages most men to wear no facial hair.

BED COVERINGS. These consist of blankets, quilts, and eiderdowns for warmth, sheets and pillowcases for cleanliness, and a counterpane or coverlet for decorative finish. All such bed

Victoria and Albert Museum

DETAIL OF A 19TH-CENTURY ENGLISH PATCHWORK QUILT

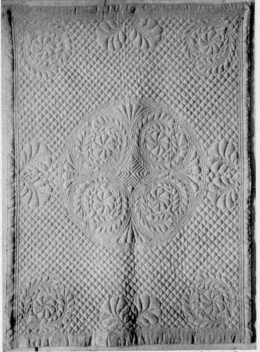

Rural Industries Bureau

COT QUILT IN A TRADITIONAL NORTH COUNTRY DESIGN

coverings have usually been an important part of a bride's trousseau.

From pictures, we know that white sheets and pillowcases were used on state beds in the Middle Ages and early Renaissance; the fine linen for making them came from the Netherlands. Blankets were of woven wool, and rich counterpanes matched the bed hangings. Poorer people had no bed linen until about 1600, but only rough homespun blankets.

In 16th- and 17th-century England, pillows had decorative loose covers of linen or velvet, often embroidered in many-coloured silks and gold and silver threads. Tudor coverlets often consisted of several layers of material stitched together for warmth, and this stitching soon took a decorative form. Jacobean counterpanes were of wool embroidery on linen; those of the later 17th century were of linen or brocade, decorated with coloured braid and tasselled fringes (*see* EMBROIDERY, ENGLISH).

In the 18th century, fine linen was being made in Ireland as well as in Holland (*see* LINEN INDUSTRY, Vol. VII). The counterpane was of printed chintz or linen, embroidered silk, tufted 'candlewick', or patchwork. Quilted counter-

panes padded with wool or feathers began to appear. These had top covers of coloured silk decorated not only by the quilting stitches but by appliqué work in designs of flowers, animals, and birds (*see* NEEDLEWORK). The 18th-century patchwork quilt was a special feature not only in England but also in Connecticut and New England, U.S.A., where a bride might have about fourteen in her trousseau. The women made these at home by sewing patches in local traditional patterns, and later in geometrical designs with motifs connected with happiness and good fortune.

During the 19th century, bed coverings of all sorts were factory produced. The bed linen was often lavishly decorated with white embroidery or 'broderie anglaise', with scalloped hems and borders and insertions of handmade lace or crochetwork. Pillowcases had lace or frilled borders. Patchwork quilts continued in many-coloured pieces; plain quilts were of white silk or homespun, quilted in intricate patterns and padded with cotton wool. In south Wales and northern England, traditional designs signifying plenty were often used. Heavy, white cotton coverlets, embroidered in white and with coarse plain fringes, were common.

In the 20th century, eiderdowns, stuffed with down or flock and covered in silk or chintz, became popular. About 1930 it became fashionable to have coloured sheets and pillowcases, of Irish linen or Egyptian cotton, with plain wide hems. Blankets dyed to match and coloured bath and hand towels also became popular. Shaped covers of velvet, chintz, tweed, or one of the new fabrics in interesting weaves, tailored to fit a divan bed, are now made particularly

Everwear Candlewick Ltd.

CANDLEWICK BEDSPREAD

for use in a bed-sitting-room. Of recent years 'electric blankets' have become very popular with invalids and all people who find it hard to keep warm in bed. The 'blanket', which is placed just above the mattress, is attached by a flex to an electric point, and possesses a device for regulating the heat.

See also HOUSEHOLD LINEN; FURNISHING MATERIALS.

BEDS. The oldest bed in existence, an Egyptian one of about 3000 B.C., is similar in structure to a modern European bed. The Greeks and Romans, who used very little furniture, had beds —the Greek ones very simple wooden couches, the Roman ones sometimes richly decorated with carving and metal inlay. Couches used for reclining at meals were important pieces of furniture in a Roman home.

In medieval Europe only wealthy people slept on beds; the vast majority of people slept on straw palliasses or simply on straw on the floor. The lord's bed was probably the most elaborate and highly regarded piece of furniture in the household, and beds were often specially mentioned in wills. The value of these beds lay, not in the wooden frames, but in the rich draperies and curtains which covered them—sometimes of velvet, satin, or silk, and even occasionally of cloth of gold. Before there were separate bedrooms, the lord's bed stood on the dais at one end of the hall beside his table, and was used during the day, as well as for sleeping in (*see* FURNITURE, HISTORY OF).

Beds came into more general use in England during the 16th century. They retained their hangings to keep the cold out, and the frames of grand beds were elaborately carved, inlaid,

Victoria and Albert Museum
BEDSTEAD OF INLAID WALNUT, 1593

and painted. These were pierced and threaded with cords to support the mattress. From the 17th century slats of wood slotted into the framework replaced the cords. The rich had elaborately carved beds with gorgeous hangings (*see* CURTAINS AND WALL-HANGINGS, Section 3). At the head and foot high panelling with posts protected the sleeper from draughts, while the ceiling of the bed was either entirely of wood or had a wooden framework with a fabric 'tester' or canopy stretched inside. The rich curtains which hung from it often stretched right round the bed to give some privacy.

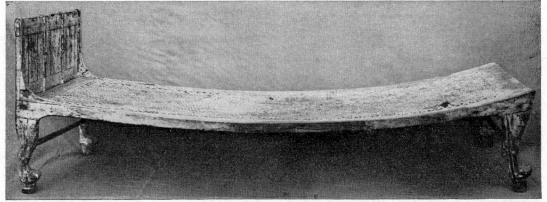

Griffith Institute
EGYPTIAN BED FOUND IN TUTANKHAMEN'S TOMB. 14TH CENTURY B.C.

Victoria and Albert Museum

BEDSTEAD OF PAINTED WOOD FROM DAVID GARRICK'S VILLA
AT HAMPTON, *c*. 1775

The hangings are of Indian printed cotton

The head of the household and favoured visitors slept in elaborate four-poster beds such as these; servants and children slept in small, low, truckle beds—really just boxes on wheels—which were kept under a bigger bed in the day-time.

The design of bedsteads followed the changes in the design of other furniture. New woods were used—oak gave way to walnut, walnut to mahogany, mahogany to satinwood and rosewood. In the late 17th century, state beds were enormously high, often almost touching the ceiling of the room for which they were made. The hangings were heavy and rich, and the tops of the bedposts were often shaped like vases and held ostrich plumes (*see* Vol. XII, p. 100).

In the 18th century four-poster beds were common even in smaller households. During the 19th century, when houses were less draughty and separate bedrooms gave privacy, these curtained beds gradually disappeared. Large, solid bedsteads of mahogany or iron, often with brass knobs on the top and bottom rails, took their place. Coiled wire springs on which rested feather mattresses made beds much more comfortable; firm hair mattresses were not common

until the end of the 19th century. Of recent years mattresses are made with internal springs or of some springy material such as sponge rubber (*see* UPHOLSTERY, Vol. VII).

See also BED COVERINGS; HOUSEHOLD LINEN; FURNITURE, HISTORY OF.

BEER, *see* ALES AND BEERS. *See also* Vol. VII: BEER BREWING.

BEVERAGES, *see* ALES AND BEERS; COLD DRINKS; HOT DRINKS; WINES AND SPIRITS.

BIRTH. The article on the REPRODUCTIVE SYSTEM (q.v.) explains that men and women, like other animals, produce sperms and eggs respectively, and that conception takes place when a male sperm unites with a female egg to form a fertilized human egg. After the woman's egg has been fertilized it passes down the oviduct into her womb (uterus), where it becomes embedded in the innermost layer of its wall. Here it develops into the human child.

The details of its development are very complicated. This is, in effect, what happens. When conception occurs, the lower opening of the womb into the vaginal canal is closed off, and the menstrual flow (*see* LIFE CYCLE) ceases. Quite early in its development the child becomes enclosed in two thin but strong membranes, between which there is fluid, and this very efficient water-bag protects the child from shocks and injuries. The child is nourished during its development inside the womb first by the yolk of the egg (of which compared with a bird's egg there is very little) and later, during most of its life inside the womb, by food contained in the blood of its mother. This blood reaches the developing child through a pad of tissue called the 'placenta', which is embedded in the inside wall of the womb and is connected with the child's navel by the 'umbilical cord', a soft cord containing arteries and veins. In both the placenta and the wall of the womb there are numerous blood-vessels with very thin walls, those of the wall of the womb being close to those in the placenta. Nourishment in the mother's blood, therefore, passes easily from the blood-vessels in the womb into those in the placenta, and then passes in the umbilical artery down the umbilical cord to the child. In the umbilical cord there is also a vein which carries the waste products of the child in the opposite direction, that is, from the child to the placenta. From there they pass into the blood of the mother, who gets rid of them in her urine and other excreta.

When the child is ready to be born, normally 9 months after conception, the muscular walls of the womb contract and squeeze the child out of the womb into the vaginal canal. The mother is then said to be 'in labour', and the pains caused by the contractions of the womb are called 'labour pains'. When labour begins, the narrow lower opening of the womb widens to let the child pass out. Certain of the mother's pelvic joints, having previously become loosened, are able to separate to some extent to let the child pass between them. The expulsion of the child is also helped by the softness of the bones of its head and body. The water-bag round the child bursts, letting out its protective fluid; the placenta is detached from the wall of the womb and, with the umbilical cord, is expelled from the womb after, or sometimes with, the child. At the end of the vaginal canal the child reaches the external opening of the female genital organs, which has to stretch enormously to let it out. Usually the child comes out head first, but sometimes the other way round. After it, or with it, comes the umbilical cord, the empty water-bag, and the placenta, these now useless organs being often called the 'after-birth'.

As soon as the child is born it takes air into its lungs, usually uttering a cry as it does so. If it does not do this, the doctor or the midwife may have to stimulate breathing in various ways. The doctor or midwife also washes it and ties a sterile ligature round the umbilical cord close to its navel. The cord is then cut off and, with the rest of the after-birth, is destroyed. The cut end of the umbilical cord soon shrinks up and heals (its shrunken end being visible inside the navel of every human being). The great majority of births follow this normal course, but occasionally it is necessary for the child to be removed from the womb by a surgeon, who cuts through the wall of the abdomen to release it. This is called the 'Caesarean' operation because Julius Caesar was supposed to have been brought into the world in this way. In other difficult cases the aid of forceps is sufficient to assist the birth by the normal route. In a few cases, the baby is found to suffer from some disease or abnormality of development owing to accidental injury or to

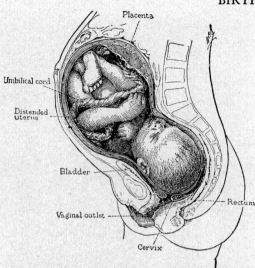

PREGNANCY IN A LATE STAGE JUST AS LABOUR BEGINS
From Logan Clendening, *The Human Body*, Alfred Knopf

disease suffered by the mother during pregnancy (*see* HEREDITARY DISEASES).

After the birth, the womb of the mother undergoes changes which restore it to its normal resting state. The wound left on its inner wall from where the placenta was detached soon heals up; the muscular wall, stretched by the growth of the child, recovers its normal condition; and in due course the menstrual flow begins again—usually after the mother ceases to suckle the child.

The making of eggs is not the only function of the ovaries. They also make 'hormones', just as the male sexual organs (testes) do, and pass these into the blood of the woman. These hormones dominate not only the changes that occur during the development of the child and those that occur during and after its birth, but also all the sexual activities of the woman, whether she is having a child or not (*see* ENDOCRINE GLANDS).

After the human child has been born, it is entirely dependent upon its mother. It cannot feed itself but must get its food from its mother's breasts (mammary glands). For the first 3 days or so, the mother's breasts secrete, not milk, but a fluid called 'colostrum', which contains substances which have an important influence on the child's development and on its resistance to certain diseases. After 3 days or so the mother's breasts make milk, and this is the principal food of the child for the next 6 to 9 months of its life.

The actual making of the mother's milk is started by the hormones made by the ovaries,

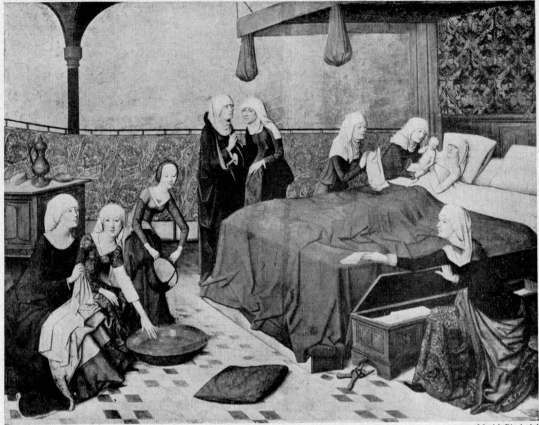

THE BIRTH OF THE VIRGIN
Late 15th-century German painting

Munich Pinakothek

and it has recently been discovered that, when the child sucks at the nipples of its mother's breasts, nervous impulses pass to a gland underneath the brain, called the 'posterior pituitary gland'. This gland secretes and passes into the mother's blood another hormone which not only stimulates the breasts to make the milk but also stimulates the womb to return to its normal resting state after the child has been born. This recent discovery explains scientifically the reason for what many people have for a long time noticed—that when a mother feeds her child on her own milk rather than on cow's milk from a bottle, her womb returns more easily to its normal state. It is one of several reasons why it is much better, both for the mother and the child, for the child to be breast-fed (*see* BABIES, FEEDING OF).

About the end of the 6th month the mother begins to teach her child gradually to do without the milk from her breasts and to feed on cow's milk and other suitable foods. The change from the mother's milk to other foods is called 'weaning' the child, and is an important stage in the child's development. The wise mother will, therefore, give it very careful attention. Some mothers have to resist the temptation to go on feeding their children on their own milk long after it is good for them. At this time the child begins to learn to be less dependent upon its mother not only for food but also in other ways. Often the child vigorously resents being weaned, and some children keep, long after weaning, a desire for the comfort of feeding from their mother's breasts and for her loving care and protection.

See also BABIES, CARE OF; NURSERY, HISTORY OF; CHILDREN, UPBRINGING OF.

BIRTHDAYS, *see* FAMILY FESTIVALS.

BISCUITS AND COOKIES. The word 'biscuit' means twice baked. The Italian *biscotto*, like the French *biscotte*, is a slice of bread returned to the oven to be toasted; the German name for this is *Zwieback* or 'doublebake', but in English it is called a rusk, while a biscuit is a small, thin crisp cake baked once only. Further confusion is added by the Americans who call a SCONE (q.v.) a biscuit, and a biscuit a cooky (from Dutch *koekje*). So what we discuss here are English 'biscuits' or American 'cookies'.

The foundation of home-made biscuits and cookies is a sweet, very short, PASTRY mixture (q.v.), often enriched by eggs. The special quality of biscuits is their crispness, so that any addition which enhances this is desirable—oatmeal, rolled oats, nuts, seeds, cornflakes, chocolate, and crisp icings. To keep this crispness, biscuits must be stored in absolutely clean, airtight tins—never in the same tins as bread, scones, or cake. For plain biscuits the rather dry dough is rolled out thinly, cut into rounds or fancy shapes with biscuit-cutters, or into diamonds or squares with a pastry wheel. These are then pricked to avoid bubbles, and baked in a moderate oven at 350°–375° F., for 10–15 minutes, on greased trays or cooky sheets. Richer, moister mixtures are dropped in spoonfuls on to trays or forced through a piping bag or cooky press (*see* ICINGS AND FILLINGS). Spritz cookies (from German *Spritze*, syringe) are piped in squiggles and whorls. Some mixtures, such as flapjack and shortbread, are spread smoothly in a tin with a spatula and cut into fingers after baking while they are still hot. Any firm mix-

Allen Jobson

MOULDS USED FOR MAKING GINGERBREADS
At one time gingerbreads were decorated with gold leaf.
They used to be sold at fairs

ture (or two mixtures) may be rolled up like Swiss Roll and cut in slices for baking. Such rolls wrapped in greaseproof paper will keep for a week or two in a refrigerator and can be sliced and baked as needed.

Shortbread is a Scottish biscuit pastry with no moisture other than that supplied by the butter, of which there is a larger proportion than in other kinds of pastry and which is patiently kneaded in by hand. It is often shaped into round, fluted cakes about 8 inches across in carved wooden moulds, and is slowly baked to pale gold. Flapjack is a mixture of rolled oats, melted fat, and syrup, spread in a baking tin. Macaroons are large, light biscuits made of ground almonds, sugar, and beaten egg whites. Ratafias are similar, but much smaller and browner and should taste of the cherry-stone-flavoured liqueur, called ratafia, with which they were traditionally eaten. They are used in rich trifles and dessert creams. Wafers are very light, thin biscuits sometimes baked, like waffles, between wafer irons, and now eaten chiefly with ice cream. Brandy-snaps are sticky, ginger wafers rolled and filled with whipped cream. *Petits fours* (*four* is the French for 'oven'), are the tiniest and most fancy of biscuits, which are eaten as dessert at the end of elaborate dinners. They are made from an almond paste or a rich cake batter, piped through a cooky press, glazed, and garnished with angelica, nuts, or crystallized fruits. Gingerbread cookies, in

MAKING BRANDY-SNAPS
The lower tray is being put into the oven and the cooked brandy-snaps taken out. They are rolled up while still hot

such forms as little men, animals, fairies, stars, or hearts, elaborately iced and painted with mottoes, are a feature of an Austrian Christmas. They are often used to decorate the Christmas tree and are even saved from year to year as we might save silver baubles.

See also PASTRY; CAKES; BAKING.
See also Vol. VII: BAKING INDUSTRY.

BLINDNESS, see EYE STRUCTURE. *See also* Vol. X: SPECIAL SCHOOLS, Section 2.

BLOOD. The blood which oozes from a cut finger is a complicated substance which has many and varied functions to perform in the human body. In a healthy adult the blood contributes about 6% to 8% of the body-weight. It consists of microscopic blood-cells suspended in a fluid called 'plasma'. There are three types of cells—red cells, white cells, and blood-platelets. Together, they make up about one-half of the blood-volume.

The red cells, the most numerous, are minute bi-concave disks, stuffed with an iron-containing pigment called 'haemoglobin', which gives the blood its red colour. The white cells, which are somewhat larger as well as fewer, have a pale fringe of cellular material around a central part or nucleus, and some of them have small granules in the outer part. The platelets are not true cells as they have no nucleus, but are, rather, fragments of larger parent cells.

The fluid part of the blood contains many salts in solution, as well as more complex chemical substances, the plasma proteins. The blood-plasma absorbs food substances as it passes through the small vessels in the wall of the stomach and intestines; it delivers them as it passes through the other parts of the body. As it flows through the capillaries (small blood-vessels), the plasma is separated from the tissue fluid bathing the body cells only by a thin membrane, the capillary wall, through which salts and other food substances can pass freely. In this way the body cells receive the nourishment they need, and at the same time the blood-plasma carries the waste products of the living cells to the KIDNEYS (q.v.) from which they are excreted. This work of nourishing the body cells is the most important function of the plasma.

The blood-cells are produced from a division of the parent cells; they are released into the blood-stream, perform their life's work, grow old, die, and are eliminated from the body. The red cells are formed in the bone marrow (*see* BONES AND JOINTS); but as the cell matures, the nucleus is pushed out, and the cell takes up its supply of pigment, becoming a passive carrier of pigment rather than a living cell. This iron-containing pigment or haemoglobin, being able to combine either with oxygen or carbon dioxide, enables the red cells to carry oxygen from the lungs to the body cells and carbon dioxide in the reverse direction. In arterial blood, the pigment is combined with oxygen, and is a bright red colour; in the blood in the veins, the pigment is combined with carbon dioxide, and is dark blue.

In a condition of the blood called anaemia, the red cells are either too few or carry insufficient pigment to do their work properly. The most common form of this condition is caused by too little iron in the diet, and is effectively treated either by giving iron in the form of a medicine or by adding more iron-containing foods, such as spinach or dried apricots, to the diet. In other types of anaemia, there is plenty of iron, but the parent cells lack certain factors needed for cell division and growth. This type of anaemia is treated by giving the patient liver extract, which contains those substances needed for the proper growth of the red cells. In recent years these substances have been made artificially in the laboratory, and liver is no longer necessary. Anaemia is an example of a disease of which the exact cause is unknown and which can yet be treated effectively because much is known about the chemical alterations which have to be put right.

The white cells are also formed in the bone marrow, as well as in the lymph-nodes and in the spleen. The white cells are truly living individuals, able to reproduce by dividing in two. Their function is to defend the body against infection by BACTERIA (q.v. Vol. II), which may enter a wound and spread to other parts of the body. The white cells, however, gather at the site of infection, flow around the invading bacteria, and digest them. If tissue from an infected wound is examined under the microscope it will be seen that the white cells contain dead or dying bacteria. Not only in wounds, but in diseased conditions generally, the number of white cells in the blood is increased so that the body can combat infection.

If the tissues giving rise to the white cells grow too rapidly, and produce cells in numbers far

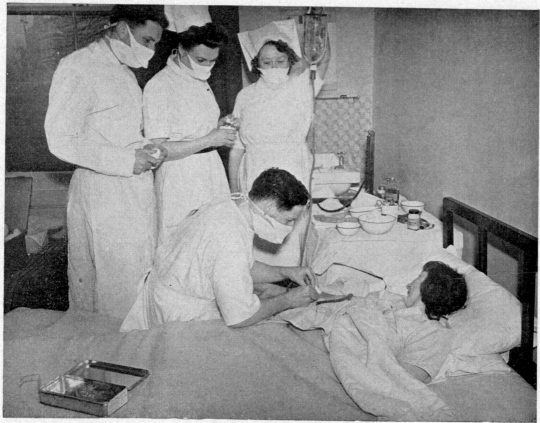

GIVING A BLOOD TRANSFUSION

Nursing Mirror

greater than the body requires, a disease called leukaemia results. This is treated by X-rays or with chemicals which, if overdone, can cause a fatal lack of white cells.

One of the most important ways of finding out what is wrong with sick people is to examine their blood. The blood is diluted so that the number of white and red cells can be counted under the microscope; a dried film of blood, suitably stained, gives information about abnormalities of cells; and the amount of pigment in the blood can be estimated by diluting a sample and comparing it with a standard solution. Chemical analysis of the blood-plasma tells a great deal about the way in which the kidneys, liver, pancreas, and other organs are working; and the presence of many infectious diseases can be shown by suitable tests.

All people do not have the same kind of blood; there are four main groups, depending on the presence or absence of certain substances in the red cells. If a patient has lost a great deal of blood as the result of an injury or operation, or has very severe anaemia, he may be saved by a blood transfusion. Blood from a healthy person, the donor, is run through a hollow needle into the veins of the patient. The doctor must be sure, however, that the donor's blood belongs to the same blood group as the patient's. If the wrong type of blood is given, this may set up serious reactions, and the patient may even die. But blood transfusion is perfectly safe when properly done, and many thousands of lives have been saved by it.

See also HEART; RESPIRATION.

BLOOD, CIRCULATION OF. There are two separate circuits in the circulation of the blood: the 'systemic' circulation, in which blood is supplied to the BRAIN, liver, KIDNEYS, MUSCLES (qq.v.), and other tissues of the body; and the 'pulmonary' circulation, in which blood flows from the HEART (q.v.) to the lungs and back to the heart.

We can trace the flow of blood through both of these circuits by describing the journey from the left ventricle of the heart (Fig. 1). Blood

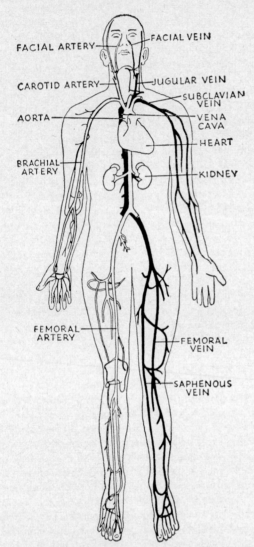

FIG. 1. THE CIRCULATION OF THE BLOOD

Arteries are shown on the left and veins on the right. The smaller veins of the hand are not drawn. From I. M. Burdon and S. MacDonald, *Anatomical Atlas*, Faber and Faber

passes from this main pumping chamber into the aorta, the largest artery in the body. The aorta curves downwards and backwards in the chest, and as it does so it gives off large branch arteries which supply the head and neck, the upper limbs, and the organs in the abdomen and

thorax. At the lower end of the abdomen, the aorta divides into two large arteries which supply the lower limbs. These main branch arteries again give off smaller branches; and this process is repeated till finally very small arteries or arterioles supply a network of tiny blood-vessels or capillaries. It is through the walls of the capillaries that the nutrition of the body tissues takes place.

When the blood passes through the capillaries, it enters the smallest veins or venules; these join one with another, making up larger and larger veins. Larger veins from the upper half of the body flow into the 'superior vena cava', and from the lower half into the 'inferior vena cava'; both of these, the largest veins in the body, empty into the right auricle of the heart. From there the blood passes to the right ventricle.

The blood is pumped by the right ventricle into the pulmonary artery, and in the lungs it passes through the branches of this artery into the pulmonary capillaries; after being oxygenated by oxygen from the air drawn in by the lungs, it passes back to the left auricle of the heart by the pulmonary veins, and so to the left ventricle, having completed its circuit.

Because of the special functions of the stomach and intestines, the drainage of blood from these organs differs from the rest of the body. A system of veins collects the blood, which flows to the liver; from there it passes into a system of capillaries in close relation to the liver cells. From these capillaries the blood is collected by the 'hepatic' veins, which empty into the inferior vena cava. The blood thus passes through two systems of capillaries, one around the gut in which it absorbs foods, and one in the liver in which certain of the food substances are given up.

The blood is kept moving through the arteries by the mechanical pumping action of the heart, with a normal heart-beat of 72 per minute and a normal range of 50 to 90 beats per minute. The blood is, therefore, constantly under pressure, which varies from moment to moment as the heart contracts. In the veins the blood pressure is very low; and the blood flows back to the heart partly as a result of gravity and partly due to the action of the muscles of the legs, abdomen, and body wall.

As with all the other organs of the body, the structure of the various blood-vessels is nicely adapted to the particular part they have to play. The arteries and veins are lined by a smooth, glistening layer of cells, which offer a nearly frictionless passage to the blood. The aorta, which has to receive large amounts of blood from the heart, has elastic tissue in its wall which enables it to expand with each heart-beat; while the heart rests, the elastic tissue relaxes, pressing on the blood within and so helping to keep up the blood-pressure. The smaller the arteries, the smaller is the amount of elastic tissue in their walls and the greater the amount of muscle tissue. This enables the size of the smaller arteries to be changed and the flow of blood varied in accordance with the varying demands of the tissues which it supplies.

Surrounding the capillaries and bathing the cells themselves is a tissue fluid; this passes into small lymphatic vessels, which are quite distinct from the blood-vessels, and which passively drain all the regions of the body. The lymph vessels flow to and around the lymphatic glands, and unite to form larger vessels which eventually empty into the large veins. Substances are able to pass from the blood-stream to the tissue fluid and thus back to the blood by way of the lymphatics.

With advancing age the tissues lose their elasticity ('hardening of the arteries'), and blood-pressure increases above the normal limit, especially after any unusual exertion. This means that old people must to some extent modify both their way of life and their diet for fear that too great a strain may block a blood-vessel or cause it to bleed, resulting in a 'stroke' (see NERVOUS SYSTEM).

See also BLOOD; HEART; KIDNEY; RESPIRATION.
See also Vol. II: BLOOD SYSTEM (Animals).

BOILING. Perhaps the most obviously simple way to prepare food is to cook it in boiling water, or in juices or gravies which boil at the same temperature as water. For certain things such as cereals and green vegetables boiling is ideal, but unless the cook boils them intelligently and with caution she may produce only the watery, tasteless, and tough results for which British cooks are notorious. Successful boiling accomplishes the same three things as all other methods of cooking: it makes food tender, tasty, and nutritious.

MEAT and FISH (qq.v.) consist mainly of connective tissue and protein. The connective tissue is softened by boiling, but the protein is hardened because it coagulates—a process we see when white of egg 'sets'. Some sort of compromise is needed. Most cookery books give advice based on the old theory that by plunging meat into boiling water and boiling it hard for 2 or 3 minutes a protective jacket of hardened protein, or 'pellicle', is formed, which retains flavour and juices. If this fast boiling were continued, however, the whole of the meat would harden and become indigestible, even uneatable. So the heat is reduced to simmering point, a kind of suppressed boiling, and cooking is continued gently for several hours until the connective tissue is softened. There seems to be little scientific evidence that any such pellicle is formed or that it acts in this way, but it is true that prolonged cooking in a well-covered pot, with as little liquid as possible, at just below boiling-point, gives the best results for boiled meat. Meat needs at least 20 minutes for each pound weight, and longer for salted meat. Fish, having much more delicate tissues than meat, needs only from 6 to 10 minutes to the pound. The best cuts of meat and the finer fish, which do not need boiling to make them tender, should, however, be grilled, fried, or roasted.

There are two ways of boiling CEREALS (q.v.), such as rice and macaroni: if the recipe demands a soft, rather gluey result, as for porridge and milk puddings, the cereal is brought slowly to the boil in cold water and then cooked gently; but if a firm, dry result is needed, as for many Oriental rice dishes and for Italian PASTA (q.v.), the cereal should be put into fast-boiling water and boiled as quickly as possible.

VEGETABLES (q.v.) are boiled to soften the woody, cellulose fibres in their tissues, and to burst and gelatinize the starch grains. Sometimes, as in the case of potatoes, parsnips, and beetroot, boiling improves the flavour by subtly changing it. These root and tuber vegetables, not being a main source of vitamins or mineral salts, can be boiled until tender, quickly if flavour is to be retained, slowly if it is to be extracted, without losing any of their quality. On the other hand, the valuable mineral salts and ascorbic acid or vitamin C (see VITAMINS) of green vegetables, such as cabbage, kale, or spinach, are best conserved by putting them into very little boiling water and boiling them quickly—10 minutes is ample—in a closely covered pan. Salt should be added for flavour, but never bicarbonate of soda, which, being alkaline, immediately neutralizes and so destroys the acid vitamin and, furthermore, gives an unearthly green colour and flat, slimy taste to leafy vegetables. The natural green colour of leafy vegetables is destroyed, not so much by the boiling process, as by an enzyme or ferment in them which, in the presence of warmth and moisture, attacks the green colour substance. If the leaves are cut small, plunged into fast-boiling water, and immediately well stirred and tossed, the enzyme is killed before it can destroy the green colour. In spite of every precaution, some of the salts, vitamins, and flavours get into the vegetable water, which, unless it has an unpleasant taste, as with beetroot or cauliflower water, should never be thrown away but used as stock for Soups (q.v.) or gravy, or just as a drink. For this reason vegetable water should be salted only lightly.

Fruit is boiled gently to soften its fibrous cell walls, and to enable the sugar put with it to penetrate. Boiling changes a certain amount of the starch present in some fruits, especially unripe fruits, into simple sugar; thus the cooking has an effect not unlike that of ripening. Hard or unripe fruits should be boiled for long enough to soften them before any sugar is added; ripe fruit keeps its shape better if sugared at the beginning; in both cases there should be enough water to make the syrup pleasant in flavour and consistency—neither watery nor sticky.

See also BAKING; BRAISING; FRYING; GRILLING; ROASTING; STEWING.

BONES AND JOINTS. The bony system of the body, or skeleton, consists of two main parts, the bones which protect and contain the vital organs of the body, and those which are designed to transport the body from place to place, the limbs. In MAMMALS (q.v. Vol. II) the skeleton is built up around the vertebral column which forms its central axis, with forelimbs and hindlimbs attached at each end.

Bone is living tissue, composed of special cells which secrete around themselves material rich in calcium salts and as hard as marble. The formation of bone (ossification) is a complex process which usually begins in cartilage (the gristle of meat and the elastic substance of the ear or nose). In a growing child, the bone starts to form in the middle of the cartilage and spreads towards both ends, turning it all into bone with the exception of the tips. From these points the bone grows in length as the child grows, and when the child has finished growing and becomes an adult, these growing points close by joining the main shaft of bone. This happens in the different bones of the body at various times between the ages of 15 and 25.

Bones vary greatly in their shapes and sizes: the long ones are levers; the flat ones, such as the shoulder blades, are centres for muscle action. No bones are solid; they all possess a cavity in the middle containing a yellow or red fatty substance called bone marrow. The marrow cavity not only makes the bones light without reducing their strength, but also constitutes the blood-making factory of the body. Around it the bony substance is spongy in consistency, and becomes more compact nearer the surface where the calcium is densest. On the surface of the bone is a special layer of fibrous tissue (the periosteum), which is rich in bone-building cells. When a bone is broken, these cells set to work at once to join up the gap by producing a nobbly mass known as 'callus'; this is later absorbed by bone-eating cells, so that the final repaired bone is nearly as smooth as the original.

The basic part of the skeleton is the vertebral column, or spine, composed of thirty-three vertebrae (Fig. 1). This not only has to carry the weight of the body and be able to bend in all directions, but must also contain and protect the delicate spinal cord. To carry out these roles it has many vertebral bones strongly tied together with ligaments, each vertebra being hollow to allow of the safe passage of the spinal cord and separated from the next by intervertebral disks. The upper seven, supporting the skull, are the cervical vertebrae; the next twelve, the thoracic vertebrae, have the twelve ribs of the chest or thorax fixed to them; below these, five large lumbar vertebrae form the back of the belly or abdomen; then come five more, fused into a curve called the sacrum which is wedged in between the two sides of the pelvis; lastly, four diminutive vertebrae form a short rudimentary human tail.

The two upper cervical vertebrae have an especially ingenious mechanism for allowing the head to move. The first consists of a ring, with two hollowed surfaces on its upper side which articulate with corresponding surfaces on the base of the skull, allowing the head to rock backwards and forwards as in nodding. The second vertebra thrusts up a peg which is fixed to the first above it in such a way as to allow of side to side movement, as in shaking the head, when both the skull and the first vertebra rotate on this peg.

The skull consists of two parts, the cranium which shelters the brain, and the face. The cranium is made of bony plates at the sides and

broad sword-shaped sternum down the middle in front.

The arms are attached to the trunk of the body by shoulder girdles which consist of a plate of bone at the back—the shoulder-blade or scapula—and the collar-bone or clavicle in front.

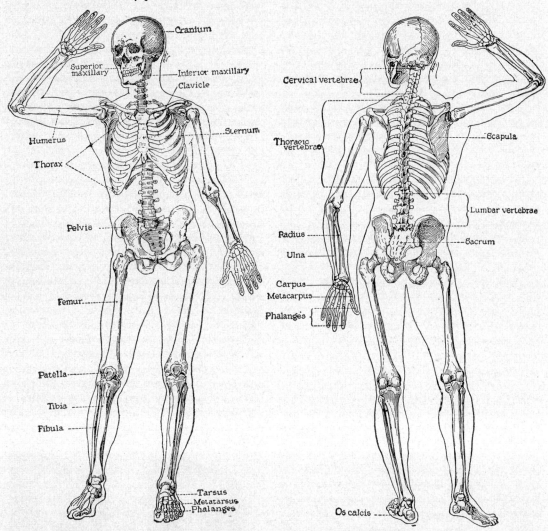

FIG. I. THE BONES OF THE HUMAN BODY, FRONT AND BACK VIEWS
From Logan Clendening, *The Human Body*, Alfred Knopf

top which do not all join up until a year or two after birth. The face is built up of fourteen bones, those of the cheek, the nose, and the upper jaw being fixed. The lower jaw moves on the upper at a joint just in front of the ear.

The ribs, encompassing the heart and lungs on each side like a series of bucket handles, are joined to the thoracic vertebrae behind and to the

The rounded head of the humerus or upper arm-bone fits into the scapula, and articulates with the radius and ulna at the elbow. The wrist is composed of eight small bones packed firmly together to give elastic stability. The palm of the hand owes its firmness to five bones which underlie the flesh, on to the end of which the jointed bones of the fingers are articulated.

The legs are attached to the pelvic or hip girdle by very strong hip-joints into which the head of the femur or thigh-bone fits like a ball into a socket. The knee-joint consists of the lower end of the femur, the tibia, and fibula, encased in front by the mobile patella. The ankle is made up of seven bones in a manner similar to that of the wrist, with the foot joined to it as the hand is to the wrist. The bones forming the human foot (but not that of any other animal) are arranged in the form of an arch. If this were not so, man would walk like the apes, flat-footed.

Many bones are bound together at the ends by strong ligaments to form joints. Inside these is a thin membranous bag which secretes a lubricant to make the joint move smoothly. Joints move in various ways. Some glide on one another, as the lower jaw slides on the upper; some, such as the elbow or knee, hinge on each other; some, such as the hip-joint, make a ball-and-socket articulation.

If the capsule of the joint becomes inflamed, and the joint becomes swollen with excess of fluid, a condition known as arthritis is set up. Osteo-arthritis occurs when the cartilage at the ends of the bones becomes brittle and flakes off, so that the joint creaks and grates when it moves.

Arthritis can be acute or chronic. The acute form can arise from any general infection, such as TUBERCULOSIS (q.v.), if the joint becomes a special focus for the disease; therefore treatment of the general infection usually leads to improvement in the condition of the joint.

Rheumatoid arthritis is a chronic disease— one of the most widespread disabling diseases, which affects more women than men, and the cause of which is still unknown. As the disease progresses, the joints become fixed and the muscles serving them gradually waste away. If it is unchecked, the spine itself may become involved, leading to great destruction and deformity.

The main factor in osteo-arthritis, which attacks men more than women, appears to be mechanical strain or injury, and the joints most commonly affected are the hip and the knee. This is a purely local condition, with little effect on the general health, but it is painful and probably causes some degree of permanent disablement.

These diseases are treated by rest, drugs, and PHYSIOTHERAPY (q.v.). Surgical operations are sometimes necessary to remedy gross deformity. Most cases can be greatly improved, if not cured, provided that they are taken in time, but at present there is a shortage of suitable clinics where patients can receive special treatment under the best conditions.

The bony skeleton can be injured by accidents as well as by disease, for bones may be fractured or joints dislocated by violence.

There are two main types of fracture, open and closed (Fig. 2). In open fractures the broken bone ends have penetrated the skin and are in direct contact with the air. There is a wound, making the gravest danger of infection, which is always serious when bone is involved. A closed fracture is more difficult to detect, and an X-RAY picture (q.v. Vol. VIII) may be needed to discover just what, if anything, has been fractured. This type of fracture can sometimes be complicated by the fact that the broken bone has penetrated and damaged some adjacent organ—a broken rib, for example, can penetrate the lung.

If the break is a clean one, the broken ends of bone are brought together and the limb splinted or encased in plaster of Paris. In some cases the bone has to be held in the correct position by means of a system of weights attached to cords and pulleys. Shattered bones are sometimes repaired by screwing metal plates to the bone itself or by putting in bone grafts. It takes usually about 6 weeks for a broken bone to 'knit together' again.

A joint is dislocated when the two surfaces of bone which normally lie against each other in the joint have come apart (Fig. 3), so that the ends of the bone can be felt to be displaced and a swelling is visible. A dislocated joint is extremely

From 'First Aid Manual,' H.M.S.O.

FIG. 2. CLOSED AND OPEN FRACTURES

painful, especially when any attempt is made to move the joint. A dislocation, like a fracture, is called a simple dislocation if the skin is not broken, and a compound dislocation where the joint is exposed through a wound.

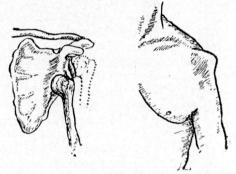

From 'First Aid Manual', H.M.S.O.

FIG. 3. A DISLOCATED SHOULDER

Left: the head of the humerus displaced from its socket. *Right*: as it appears externally

The treatment and healing of dislocations is sometimes complicated by additional injuries. For example, if the blood-supply to the joint is obstructed for any length of time, gangrene may result. Paralysis and loss of feeling may follow the injury to important nerves near the joint. Sometimes it is difficult to replace the parts of the joint because ligaments have been torn. When the bones composing the dislocated joint have been themselves fractured, the injury is known as a fracture dislocation.

Strains and sprains describe different degrees of injury caused to a tendon or ligament by violent muscular exertion, by accidental stretching or rupture of the fibres, or by blows and twists. Sprains are more common in joints which have a limited range of movement, such as the wrist, elbow, knee, or ankle. They are always accompanied by pain and swelling, and the pain increases with particular movements, such as turning the foot in when the ankle is sprained, or with pressure on the soft parts, not the bone. Strains and sprains are treated by applying cold compresses to keep down the swelling and by bandaging firmly to keep the injured part at rest.

See also ANATOMY; MUSCLES; ORTHOPAEDICS; FIRST AID; OSTEOPATHY; PHYSIOTHERAPY.

BONNETS, *see* HEADWEAR.

BOOTS AND SHOES. Prehistoric men wore no shoes, and even today many simple peoples, especially in warm climates, wear them only on ceremonial occasions or not at all. They were probably first used to protect the feet against extreme cold or heat rather than against rough surfaces. The Egyptians, from about 4000 B.C., wore papyrus soles held on by straps (Fig. 1), and from these developed the more elaborate leather sandals worn by Assyrians, Greeks, and Romans (Fig. 2). Shoes were certainly known by 1000 B.C., for contemporary carvings show Hittites wearing shoes with turned-up toes, resembling in shape the later Moorish slippers and Dutch clogs.

For marching, both Assyrian and Roman soldiers wore short boots laced with criss-cross thongs (Fig. 3), and the Norsemen who overran Europe after the fall of Rome wore fur-lined boots and woollen leggings (Fig. 5). In China felt or leather boots were known from remote times, and both men and women wore round-toed slippers of felt or woven rush. Later, from medieval times, the shoes of aristocratic Chinese women were for centuries tiny, to fit the small deformed feet produced by tight bandaging from babyhood and esteemed as a mark of high social standing—a fashion, however, no longer followed. Women's shoes in T'ang figurines (*see* Vol. I, p. 106; Vol. XII, opp. p. 224) all have strange, curled-up toes, designed to take the length of the skirt and prevent tripping. Manchu women's shoes were equally strange, mounted on a pedestal.

In pre-Roman Britain laced or pull-on boots and shoes shaped rather like moccasins were commonly worn, as well as soft slippers which, for the wealthy, were often finely decorated and coloured (Fig. 4).

Early European shoes had no heels, but had pointed, sometimes upturned toes, often extending well beyond the foot. In the later Middle Ages the very long points, called pikes, worn by men, eventually became so exaggerated that their length had to be regulated by law (Fig. 6). Shoes with rounded toes appeared in the 15th century, and in the early 16th century they became very broad and square (Fig. 7). Heels of cork or wood, low at first, gradually rose until fashionable men and women of the 18th century wore them 2 inches or more high (Fig. 10). In the 19th century high heels went out of fashion (Fig. 12); and when they returned in modern times, it was only for women.

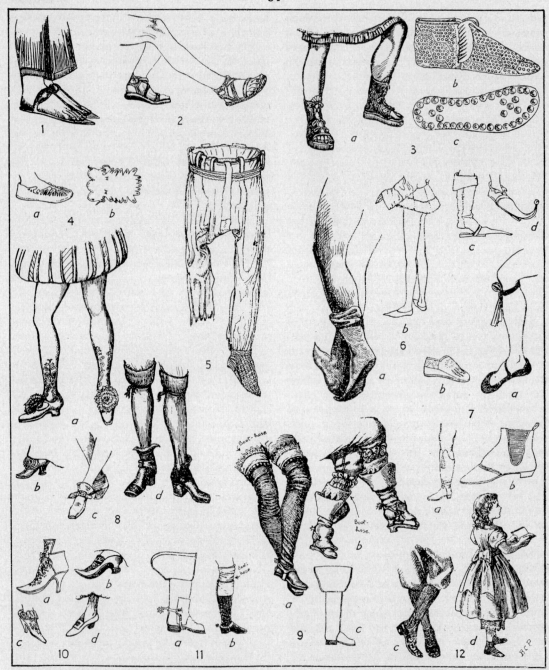

EUROPEAN BOOTS AND SHOES

1. Egyptian papyrus soles. 2. Greek sandal. 3. *a.* Roman marching-boot; *b.* Romano-British shoe; *c.* Romano-British leather sole with hobnails. 4. *a.* Early moccasin; *b.* Pattern for a moccasin. 5. Norse fur-lined boots and woollen leggings. 6. 15th-century pikes: *a.* Piked short boots; *b.* Piked slippers; *c.* Piked boot and patten; *d.* Piked shoe and patten. 7. 16th-century shoes: *a.* Early shoe with flat sole; *b.* Late shoe with cork sole and raised heel. 8. 17th-century shoes: *a.* Early high-heeled man's shoes; *b.* Woman's shoe. *c, d.* Late men's shoes. 9. 17th-century boots: *a.* Long boots, 1616. *b.* Long boots with pattens, 1640. *c.* Long boot, about 1670. 10. 18th-century women's shoes: *a.* about 1736 *b.* about 1742; *c.* about 1775. *d.* 1781. 11. 18th-century long boots. *a.* about 1704; *b.* about 1785. 12. 19th century: *a.* Hessian boot, about 1800. *b.* 'Balmoral' boot, 1862; *c.* Elastic-sided boots, about 1870. *d.* Girl's boots, about 1850.

Men in the 17th century wore elaborate, long boots, sometimes tight and smooth, sometimes loose, turned down, and fringed (Fig. 9*b*). Boots were not generally worn by women until the 19th century, when, for a time, men, women, and children all wore them, both indoors and out, tight leather ankle-boots with cloth or elastic sides being popular (Fig. 12). From the 15th to the 19th centuries, people wore strapped pattens—wooden soles with leather straps—over their shoes for rough walking (Figs. 6*c*, 9*b*). Wooden clogs have been known from at least as early as the 9th century, and were commonly worn by people who worked in damp places. Clogs with wooden, iron-tipped soles and leather tops have continued in use right down to our own time, especially in Holland and Belgium, and amongst certain classes of workers such as dairy-workers and Lancashire cotton-spinners. They have now, however, been largely replaced by rubber Wellingtons and leather boots.

See also Vol. VII: BOOT AND SHOE MAKING.

BOTTLING, *see* FOOD PRESERVING.

BRAIN. This organ comprises that part of the NERVOUS SYSTEM (q.v.) contained in the skull. It is an extension of the spinal cord and is connected with it through a large hole in its base. It consists of three main parts: (*a*) the forebrain, greatly developed into the 'cerebrum' in man; (*b*) the midbrain, largely a junctional stem containing the centres controlling eye movements; and (*c*) the hindbrain, containing vital cells responsible for breathing and blood-pressure, behind which lies the balancing brain or 'cerebellum' (*see* Fig.).

The surface of the soft brain-tissue is protected within the skull by membranes (meninges); between the layers of these there is a space containing a watery fluid, the cerebrospinal fluid, which has a cushioning effect, keeping the brain steady when the skull is moved. As the spinal cord passes into the skull, its small central canal opens into small cavities, called ventricles, one in the hindbrain, and three others lying above it, one in the middle and two within the cerebral part of the brain. Blood-vessels in their roofs make the cerebrospinal fluid.

The large forebrain or cerebrum, which forms nearly nine-tenths of the human brain, is divided into left and right halves (or hemispheres) by a deep fissure, the halves being joined by a bridge.

Deep in its substance are the primitive feeling and responding parts of the brain.

The wrinkled surface or cortex of the two halves of the cerebrum is coated with nerve cells, which appear grey in contrast with the white colour of the deeper nerve fibres. Just over half-way back from the front of the brain, a cleft or fissure runs down towards the tip of the ear. The

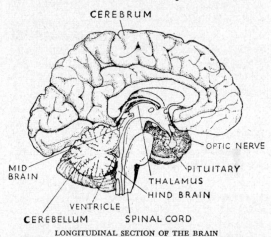

CEREBRUM

OPTIC NERVE

MID BRAIN

PITUITARY
THALAMUS
HIND BRAIN

VENTRICLE

CEREBELLUM   SPINAL CORD

LONGITUDINAL SECTION OF THE BRAIN

From E. B. Jamieson, *Illustrations of Regional Anatomy,* E. and S. Livingstone

grey nerve cells in front of this fissure regulate voluntary movement for the opposite side of the body, the topmost cells controlling the lower limbs, the lower cells the face and head, and so on. Behind the fissure is a similar pattern of quite different nerve-cells which convey sensation. It is a general rule that the left half of the cerebrum controls the right half of the body, and vice versa.

Particular areas of the cortex have been mapped out for the special senses, such as hearing and vision. But the most remarkable feature about the human cerebral cortex, distinguishing it from that of all other animals, is the large area to which no definite function is allotted. These 'silent areas' are centres of MEMORY (q.v.) and association of ideas. They receive rich communication, not only from other areas of the cortex, but from the feeling centre and from the balancing brain or cerebellum. Here, therefore, is made that choice of ideas and actions which, when expressed by our muscles and limbs, reveals the personality.

The thalamus, a mass of grey matter buried in the cerebrum, is the source of instinctive feeling and the emotional urges of love and hate. In man these are to a variable degree controlled by the intellectual activity of the thinking brain or cerebral cortex.

The hindbrain is joined to the forebrain by the thick-stemmed midbrain. The cerebellum, lying in the back part of the skull, also has two halves and a wrinkled surface, and has developed many nerve tracts running between it and the cerebral cortex. The two hemispheres regulate posture and movement on the same side of the body, and are joined together by a bridge of nerve tracts.

Though the brain has many parts with different functions, it is itself only a continuation of the spinal cord. Together they form that supreme nervous organ by which man acquires knowledge and the power to adapt it. In the brain consciousness arises, bringing revolutionary powers of adaptation. And of conscious activities those produced by the union of the intellectual cortex with the creative thalamus are the highest expression.

See also NERVOUS SYSTEM; INTELLIGENCE; MEMORY.
See also Vol. II: BRAIN (Animal); INTELLIGENCE (Animal).

BRAISING, from the French *braise* (hot charcoal), originally meant cooking in a covered pan with fire above and below. Special braising pans were rather shallower than ordinary pans, and had the edges of the lid turned up to hold the glowing embers used to supply the top heat. They were placed over a covered fire. In India, to this day, the usual form of oven is a kind of low brazier, made to hold one large saucepan, with a live charcoal fire on top. The meat to be braised was laced with bacon, embedded in and covered with sliced bacon, onions, and herbs, and moistened with stock. Nowadays, in Europe and in the U.S.A., braising is usually done in the oven and is little different from casseroling (*see* STEWING). 'Braised' onions, celery, chicken, and so on are usually fried first and then finished off in a casserole.

BRASSIÈRES, *see* FOUNDATION GARMENTS.

BREADMAKING. Bread has been the staple food of man in many countries since primitive times (*see* FOOD, HISTORY OF). Although home-made bread is still found, especially in northern England and Ireland and in remote country districts, most people today buy their bread from the baker.

The main ingredient of bread is wheat flour. The best type of WHEAT (q.v. Vol. VI) for bread, such as that from North America, gives a flour containing enough good quality gluten to produce a well-risen loaf. Gluten with water added becomes a sticky mass; this, when kneaded and stretched, increases in elasticity and forms fine strands which, when cooked, set to give the framework of the loaf. YEAST (q.v. Vol. II), the other important ingredient of bread which makes the bread rise, is obtainable in a compressed cake, made from distiller's yeast.

To make bread, yeast blended with sugar and warm water is added to salted flour in the proportion of about ½ pint to 1 lb., and mixed to a soft dough. In order both to distribute the yeast

MAKING BREAD
Left: mixing the sugar and yeast. *Right*: the dough rising

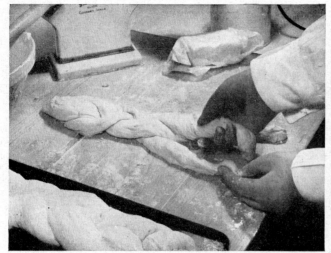 

MAKING BREAD

Left: making a plaited loaf. *Right*: the cooked bread. It is decorated with caraway and poppy seeds

evenly and to produce an elastic dough by developing the gluten in the wheat, the mixture is then kneaded until the dough looks quite smooth. Then it is left for about 2 hours in a covered bowl in a warm place until it has doubled its size—puffed up by the carbon dioxide which the growth of the yeast produces. It is then given a second kneading to redistribute the gas evenly; and after being shaped into a loaf, is put aside a second time to recover or 'prove'. Finally, it is cooked for about 40–60 minutes, according to the size of the loaf, in a very hot oven (500° F.), where the gas expands and blows out the loaf to give a spongy texture, which the 'set' gluten will retain.

Failures in breadmaking generally occur when the yeast has not grown properly, either because it was dry and old or because the temperature conditions were not right. The best temperature for yeast growth is about 80° F.; at lower temperatures the growth becomes slower and finally stops, while at higher temperatures the growth is too great and may make the dough rise so much that it stretches the gluten beyond its limits, breaking the fine strands and so causing the dough to collapse again. Temperatures above 160° F. destroy the yeast.

Different kinds of bread can be made with different kinds of white or brown flour or by the addition of various ingredients, such as milk, fat, malt, fruit, or eggs. Bread can also be made without yeast. In unleavened bread no RAISING AGENT (q.v.) at all is added, and in Ireland soda bread, raised by bicarbonate of soda or baking powder, is quite common. The shape into which bread is formed also varies considerably. Loaves made in tins are now the most common in England, whereas on the Continent round cakes, the long French loaf, and rolls in a variety of shapes are more general.

See also BAKING; SCONES.
See also Vol. II: YEAST.
See also Vol. VII: BAKING INDUSTRY.

BRONCHITIS, *see* RESPIRATION.

BRUSHES, *see* CLEANING EQUIPMENT.

BUSTLES, *see* FOUNDATION GARMENTS.

BUTTONS AND BUTTONHOLES, *see* DRESS FASTENINGS.

C

CABINETS, *see* CHESTS AND CUPBOARDS. *See also* Vol. VII: CABINET-MAKING.

CAKES. 1. HISTORY. Before the arrival of cane sugar in Europe, people ate very few cakes, and those that they did eat were sweetened with honey. Often the word cake referred merely to some kind of unleavened bread, such as Jewish Passover cakes or the oatcakes of Scotland—'the land o' cakes'. After 1400 sugar gradually became more plentiful and cheaper, and cooks began to make cakes more and more with it. The materials and methods of professional cake-makers differed little from those of the housewife until the 19th century, when with cheap labour and the introduction of machinery the flour confectionery business greatly expanded. Because of shortages during the two World Wars and the need to produce cheap cakes, various substitutes for expensive materials such as eggs and butter have been introduced; many confectioners now moisten their sponges with glycerine, use soya bean lecithin instead of eggs, make meringues with skim milk powder and sodium alginate, and fruit flans with agar-agar (*see* JELLIES). Such methods produce cakes which are inferior both in taste and in nutritive value. The housewife, provided she measures accurately from scientifically balanced recipes, and exploits to the full the creaming, foaming, and expanding possibilities of her wholesome materials, can produce far better tasting, more wholesome, and more nutritious results at probably less cost.

2. CAKE-MAKING AND MATERIALS. A typical raw cake batter consists of fat beaten in sugar to emulsify and aerate it, and then mixed with an egg foam and milk and lightly blended with flour and baking powder. During baking the fat melts, and the air dispersed in it expands; the baking powder constituents re-act, producing carbon dioxide gas, and any free moisture is turned into steam, which also expands. These expanding gases extend the protein films of the egg foam and the strands of the flour gluten. The heat coagulates the proteins, which 'set', and thus form the framework in which the rest of the ingredients are supported. The starch swells and is gelatinized. A skin or crust forms on the outside as the cake dries out (loss in weight during baking is 10–15%), and the sugar in the crust concentrates and begins to caramelize, making the crust brown. The drying gluten-and-egg network and the starch films absorb the oiled fats so that the final cake is moist.

(*a*) *Materials*. Soft, low-melting-point fats, such as lard and shortening, make more tender cakes than cooking margarine or butter, though

MAKING A SPONGE MIXTURE

Left: creaming the butter and sugar. *Right*: pouring the mixture into the tin

the latter gives the best flavour. The modern 'super-glycerinated' shortenings are devised to emulsify superbly, and so give the best aeration (*see* FATS AND OILS).

Sugar crystals act as tiny mixing blades during creaming, and so for cakes containing fat a medium-grained sugar is best; but for sponges, a sugar which dissolves easily, such as fine-grained castor sugar, should be used (*see* SWEETENINGS). Sugar lowers surface tension, and so too much sugar disperses and weakens the protein network and results in a sunken cake. The greenish-yellow colour and odd taste of cakes in which too much baking soda has been used are mainly due to the decomposing and caramelizing effect which baking soda has on sugar.

Flour of the special fine 'soft' cake type should be used if possible, as ordinary flour is too coarse for good gelatinization and its gluten is too tough (*see* CEREALS AND PULSES, Section I). As the elasticity of gluten is greatly increased by beating and stirring, the cook must avoid beating the cake mixture after the flour is added or her cakes will be tough and full of tunnels.

The other usual materials in cakes are eggs, which add to the rich flavouring of cakes and, if well beaten, to their lightness, some RAISING AGENT such as baking powder, and whatever FLAVOURINGS (qq.v.) and spices are required.

(*b*) *Methods.* The following are basic recipes for plain and rich home-made cakes made on the sugar-batter or creaming method:

Materials	Plain	Rich
Margarine or shortening	4 oz.	8 oz.
Sugar	4 oz.	8 oz.
Eggs	1–2	4
Flour	8 oz.	8 oz.
Baking Powder . .	2 level tsps.	½ level tsp.
Salt	½ level tsp.	½ level tsp.

Warm milk—about ¼ pint, or as necessary.

Various flavourings can be added: dried fruit (4 oz. to 1½ lb.), ginger, chocolate, and so on.

To make the cake, the fat and sugar are put into a bowl standing in warm water (75° F.) and 'creamed' with a perforated spoon or a clean hand; the eggs, either whole or whipped, are beaten in gradually and then the milk, warmed to 167° F. (Cold liquids break or 'curdle' the mixture.) Next the dry ingredients, having been mixed and sieved, are 'folded' in. The mixture is then gently 'blobbed' into a greased and papered tin—a ring mould gives the most even

MAKING A FRUIT CAKE

Top: the mixture before adding the fruit. *Centre*: the cake ready for the oven. *Bottom*: a finished cake, showing correct texture

DECORATING THE MARZIPAN OF A SIMNEL CAKE WITH A
POTATO PEELER

baking and a shape which slices neatly. The cake is baked in the upper centre of the oven for ¾ hour. A steamy and steady oven is needed, so it is important not to open the oven door once the cake is in.

The flour-batter method, used by bakers to give a better volume to cheap cakes, involves combining two batters, one of creamed fat and flour and the other of beaten sugar and eggs.

The blending method, a trade process introduced into Britain from the U.S.A., is now used by the housewife who possesses an electric mixer. It is very quick, as everything is creamed right away except the eggs which are added last. It requires special, non-toughening, 'high-ratio' flour which can absorb unusually high percentages of liquid, and special high emulsification fats. This method gives very tender, voluminous, low-cost cakes, and is becoming increasingly popular.

True sponge cakes contain no fat; eggs and sugar are whisked together, and the sieved flour is lightly blended in by hand. The best sponges, containing many eggs, are raised entirely by air and steam, but sponges with fewer eggs need baking powder and milk.

	Times for Baking	*Regulo*
Fruit and pound cakes	1½–4 hours at 250°–325° F.	2
Sponge	35–60 minutes at 325°–400° F.	2–5
Fat cakes	30–45　　„　　at 350° F.	3
Thin layer	20–30　　„　　at 375° F.	4
Small cakes	20–25　　„　　at 375° F.	4

3. FESTIVAL CAKES. The rich, dark fruit cakes eaten at Christmas, weddings, and birthdays are peculiarly English; so are the Easter Simnel cakes, which are fruit mixtures with marzipan. The Scots associate black bun with New Year; in northern England, parkin, a kind of oatmeal gingerbread, is eaten on Guy Fawkes Day. The French make huge, flat, sponge *gâteaux* decorated with crystallized fruits at Christmas. In northern Italy the traditional after-dinner Christmas sweet is *panettone*, a light yeast cake containing raisins and candied fruits; *marzipani di Pasqua* are marzipan cakes proper to Easter. In Germany many kinds of ginger, spice, and honey biscuits are prepared for Christmas Eve. *Pfefferkuchen* ('pepper-cakes') of north Germany and *Lebkuchen* ('lively-cakes') of south Germany are well-known spiced gingerbreads.

See also BISCUITS AND COOKIES; ICINGS AND FILLINGS; PASTRY; RAISING AGENTS.
See also Vol. VII: BAKING INDUSTRY.

CANCER. In spite of a vast amount of research, the problem of cancer still remains obscure and difficult. What is cancer? Is it one disease or many? What part, if any, is played by germs such as viruses in causing it? These are great questions which still remain inadequately answered. What we can say about cancer, therefore, at the present time must be accepted as provisional only, and may prove in a few years to have been as mistaken as were people's ideas about rickets or diabetes 50 years ago.

Cancer is a form of 'new growth', as are also non-malignant tumours. In health the growth of the different tissues of the body, such as bone, connective tissue, and mucous membrane, is kept in a delicate balance so that no one exceeds its healthy proportion in relation to the others. All cells receive the correct amount of blood, and with it their food; they also receive regulating chemical substances called 'hormones' which are prepared by the ENDOCRINE GLANDS (q.v.); and they are further controlled by nerves. This controlling mechanism, however, may break down, and a group of cells may suddenly cease to perform its normal duties and instead increase on its own. This reproduction has no relation to the needs of the body and serves no useful purpose at all. In fact, as the mass of cells becomes larger, the body may be harmed by their bulk. This tumour, not being controlled in the normal way, goes on growing according to its own laws. Its vitality appears to be limitless and unrelated to the state of the body that bears it. A tumour of fat cells, for instance, will go on enlarging though the rest of the body is wasting away from starvation, in desperate need of fat.

New growths, then, arise from the abnormal growth of cells of the body tissues. These cells often remain like the tissue from which they have arisen, as, for example, in the fatty tumours (*lipomata*) mentioned above. But sometimes they revert to very primitive cell forms, retaining no other capacity than that of reproduction. This causes reproductive chaos, with the tumour spreading in all directions through the body.

Tumours spread by encroaching on neighbouring organs. Some, called 'innocent', grow in this way only. Unless they happen to occur at a vital spot, they do not threaten life. But should they, for example, be in the brain or block the intestinal tube, they soon cause very serious symptoms. If the doctor can locate such tumours, the surgeon is often able to operate, even on the brain, and to remove the growth. Cancerous tumours, however, are 'malignant', that is, they spread by invading and destroying the tissues around, and they creep into the blood-vessels, particularly into the veins. Once these malignant cells have entered a vein they may be transported in the blood to any part of the body, where seedling growths, called 'secondary deposits', may occur. This most often happens in the lungs and liver, since so much of the blood of the body passes through these organs.

If we knew fully how cancer cells differ from the normal cells of the body, we should have a large part of the answer to the problem as to what causes cancer. We do know, however, certain things about the chemistry of cancer cells: for example, we know that they are much richer in potassium than normal cells and poorer in calcium; and that they are especially rich in the highly complicated kind of protein which is found in the nuclei of cells—nucleo-proteins. It has also been discovered that cancer cells are not only capable of producing their vital energy in the absence of oxygen (which no other cells can), but that they often reject oxygen when it is present. Under the microscope cancer cells differ from normal cells in the appearance of their nuclei: they are always dividing rapidly to produce further cells, and they perform this cell division in an abnormal way, the little nuclear threads called 'chromosomes' being split up quite irregularly inside the nucleus. Some scientists believe that it is in those little beads called the 'genes', which lie along the thread-like chromosomes, that the original change responsible for the perversion of growth underlying cancer is to be found.

Although the cause, or causes, of cancer is still unknown, a great deal is known about its behaviour. For example, cancer is known to affect the elderly much more often than the young. Certain organs of the body, such as the stomach and lungs, seem to be particularly prone to it, whilst others are less prone. People engaged in certain occupations seem liable to get cancer; it was first noted that a type of cancer seemed to have attacked chimney-sweeps, who are continually covered with soot. Workers in aniline dye-works have a tendency to develop cancer of the bladder. Smokers of clay-pipes used to get cancer of the lip so commonly that this was once called 'smoker's cancer'; of more recent years cigarette smoking has been thought to be related to cancer of the lung. All this evidence appeared to indicate that a chronic irritation might be the cause of cancer. Scientists, researching along these lines, discovered that certain chemical substances when painted on to the skins of animals, particularly mice, could produce cancer. These chemical irritants were mostly substances derived from coal-tar. Such experiments threw much light on how cancer is transplanted from one animal to another, and how the body tries to protect itself from the invasion.

Other researchers found that a virus could produce cancerous tumours acting in a rather different manner from the 'irritation' of tar and its derivatives. These researches suggested two factors as necessary for cancer growth—a condition in the cells which rendered them susceptible to attack and a specific factor which made the attack.

For many years the relation between certain forms of cancer and the alteration of balance of the sex hormones has been noticed, and cancer has been produced in mice by giving them sex hormones which stimulated certain glandular cells into activity. Cancer of the breast can be controlled by the use of the synthetic hormone 'stilboestrol', which has the effect of a natural female secretion. It has also been found that by giving the male hormone to women with cancer of the breast the cancer was checked, though not cured. Still the most effective form of treatment is the use of X-RAYS (q.v. Vol. VIII) or radioactive agents such as radium or radio-active cobalt. These have a much more destructive effect on cancer cells than on normal tissue, and so bring about their healing action.

CANDLES, *see* LIGHTING, HISTORY OF.

CANNING, *see* FOOD PRESERVING. *See also* Vol. VII: CANNING INDUSTRY.

CAPS, *see* HEADWEAR.

CARBOHYDRATES, *see* NUTRITION, Section 6.

CARPETS AND FLOOR COVERINGS. Various materials have been used in different times and places for floor coverings, but the woven carpet, with variants in tapestry and needlework, has always had pride of place. Carpets originated in Asia, and were little used in

Europe before the late Middle Ages. They were made in Turkey, Kurdistan, the Caucasus, Persia, India, and China—though it is doubtful whether the Chinese used theirs to cover floors. Tapestry carpets, the earliest known kind (*see* TAPESTRY, Vol. VII), were used in the temples and palaces of the Pharaohs in ancient Egypt. The flat-surface carpet (needlework stitches in coloured threads completely concealing the stout flax or hemp web) appeared later, probably before the cut-pile variety with its velvety texture (*see* CARPET MAKING, Vol. VII).

Greeks in Homer's time thought that men who used floor 'cloths' usurped a privilege suited only to the gods; but from their writers we know of 'purple carpets of finest wool with a pattern on both sides'. In early Christian times also, carpets were symbols of prestige and power. They were used in churches only at special festivals to do honour to God and the saints, and pictures of the time show the Virgin and Child

National Portrait Gallery

A CONFERENCE AT SOMERSET HOUSE, 1604
English, Spanish, and Austrian plenipotentiaries are seated at a table covered with carpet

Lord Willoughby de Broke

LORD WILLOUGHBY DE BROKE AND HIS FAMILY
On the floor is a Turkey carpet. Painting by Zoffany (1734/5–1810)

enthroned with a carpet underfoot. In the Middle Ages the carpet before the royal throne isolated the king from his courtiers.

Carpets, at first used to drape over chests and tables, were imported into England after the Crusades by kings and nobles. As early as 1255 Eleanor of Castile brought several in her dowry when she came to marry Edward I. Both Henry VIII and Wolsey had great collections— Henry VIII's came from Turkey, Wolsey's were imported through Italy. Carpets from the Near East were usually very long rectangles, with small all-over designs symmetrically disposed and set in well-defined borders. As the religion of ISLAM (q.v. Vol. I) forbade the representation of living creatures, artists developed abstract and emblematic patterns; the Persians wrought the most graceful designs, with flowing arabesques and conventionalized motifs of great

antiquity (*see* PERSIAN ART, Vol. XII). Rich and varied colours in wool, or silk for more sumptuous work, were used.

The earliest European carpet that survives is a 16th-century Spanish one. The Moors had long before established carpet-making in Spain, whence it spread to other European countries; consequently the early Spanish carpets had typical Oriental designs and motifs. By the 16th century, however, heraldic emblems were appearing within the medallions, and gradually naturalistic forms were introduced. In France carpet-making began in the early 17th century at the Gobelin works, and soon after at Beauvais, Aubusson, and the Savonnerie works in Paris. Walloon and Flemish immigrants were weaving in England before the end of the 17th century, and the famous Wilton and Axminster industries were well established by the early 18th century.

With the greater luxury of living of the 18th century, carpets came into more general use, and soon began to play an important part in INTERIOR DECORATION (q.v.). Their shapes and designs were freely adapted to the taste of the times: in France, for instance, carpets became a foil for the ceiling decoration, often echoing it in pattern and colour—a fashion seen, too, in the great houses designed by the Adam Brothers in England. In both countries refined taste expressed itself in delicate pastel colours, using forms of classical inspiration; this gave way to the stronger tones and coarser design of the 19th century. Patterned carpets became unfashionable in the 1930s, when plainer styles, close fitting where possible, and in single colours, including the off-whites, were popular.

Special narrow-width, continuous 'runners' for stairs and corridors became common during the later 19th century, when the use of FELT (q.v. Vol. VII) for underlay was established to preserve carpets. Felt or matting is now often used as a cheap substitute for carpet.

Skin hearthrugs of tiger or leopard, the heads realistically worked by the taxidermist, were characteristic of the 19th century. Home-made rugs have included the needlework types made by 18th-century ladies, the 'rag-rugs' of the 19th century, and the hand-tufted ones of today. Mats for specially hard usage include those of coconut fibre and synthetic rubber for entrances, and pressed cork or rubber or synthetic imitations for kitchen and bathroom.

In medieval England the only floor-covering, whether in castle or cottage, consisted of rushes strewn about. Later, as we know from illuminated manuscripts, rushes were plaited together into a kind of matting. Today we have similar mattings of coconut fibre or seagrass—plaited or woven, plain or in coloured stripes or checks—used for stone or brick floors.

Leather covers were used to preserve the fine parquetry flooring in Restoration England. By the 19th century a processed floorcloth and linoleum—both easy to keep clean—were much in use, either for borders or to cover whole floors. These were sometimes designed to imitate wood flooring, particularly parquetry, in all kinds of geometrical patterns, with panels and borders; sometimes they were given more expensive finishes in imitation of marble, mosaic, tilings, and carpets. They were used instead of the material their designs imitated; for example, linoleum with a tiled pattern was considered suitable for a kitchen.

Some modern houses need no floor-coverings, because the builders have used one of the new permanent floor surfaces in a dirt-resisting or easily cleaned material, and because houses with central heating do not need carpets for warmth. But the carpet still has the advantage that it deadens sound, and its decorative value remains unchallenged.

See also INTERIOR DECORATION, HISTORY OF.
See also Vol. VII: CARPET MAKING; WOOL WEAVING; LINOLEUM.

CARPET SWEEPER, see CLEANING EQUIPMENT.

CASTLE. In the Middle Ages land was owned under the FEUDAL SYSTEM (q.v. Vol. X) by princes and nobles who had almost complete power over their domains, and kept an army to enforce that power. From the 10th to the 12th centuries there was more local warfare between these lords in western Europe than perhaps at any time before or since. The castle, a fortified dwelling, was therefore essential for the lord, his family, and his retainers.

In England many castles were built after the Norman Conquest when William the Conqueror developed the feudal system. The typical Nor-

National Buildings Record

THE KEEP OF ROCHESTER CASTLE, BUILT c. 1130

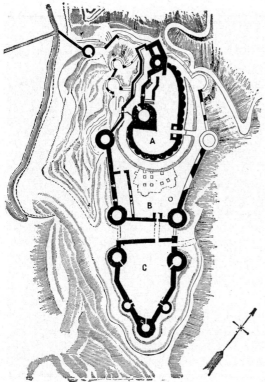

PLAN OF CHÂTEAU GAILLARD

A. Inner bailey and keep. B. Middle bailey. C. Outer bailey

man castle consisted of two parts, a fortified tower or keep, and a walled space, called the bailey, for outhouses and animals. Usually the keep was built on a natural or artificial mound to give it protection from attack. Many of the castles built in the 12th century had wooden keeps with baileys surrounded by wooden palisades, and of these little trace remains today. Many of those with stone keeps are still standing. They were tall, square buildings, with a single room on each floor. The entrance, for greater protection, was sometimes on the first floor with an outside stair leading to it, as at Castle Rising in Norfolk. The lower floors were vaulted, with circular STAIRCASES (q.v.) leading from one to the next. Some of the great keeps, the Tower of London and Rochester Castle, for instance, were large enough to contain halls and chapels and many rooms.

Crusaders who fought in the eastern Mediterranean in the CRUSADES (q.v. Vol. I) learnt new methods of castle-building from the Saracens. These castles did not rely for defence on the keep

alone, but had a 'curtain' wall surrounding both keep and bailey, with round towers placed at intervals along the wall, from which attacks at every point could be kept under fire. Two of the greatest castles of the late 12th century were Krak of the Knights in Syria (*see* Vol. X, p. 164) and Château Gaillard in Normandy. Château Gaillard was built by Richard I in 1197–8 to guard the Duchy of Normandy from French attack along the Seine valley. The King personally supervised its building, using his experience of crusading warfare, and embodying in it the most advanced ideas of the day. At one end the castle was guarded by steep slopes, at the other it was protected by three walled and towered baileys and a moat. The rooms for the defenders were mostly inside the keep, except for a chapel in the middle bailey.

The increasing wealth of the nobles and improved methods of fortification led to the building of very elaborate castles in the 13th century. Often the keep was built on the edge of an unassailable cliff with the curtain wall defending the landward side of it, as at Pembroke Castle. At Beeston Castle, in Cheshire, and others there was no keep at all, and a huge GATEHOUSE (q.v.), with perhaps a drawbridge across a moat, gave

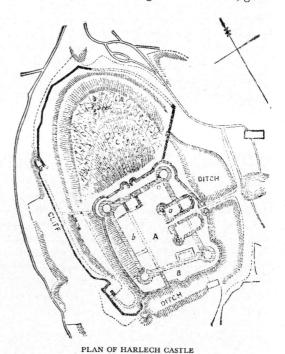

PLAN OF HARLECH CASTLE

A. Inner bailey. *a.* Gatehouse. *b.* Hall. B. Middle bailey. c. Outer bailey

Photoflight Ltd.

KIDWELLY CASTLE, CARMARTHENSHIRE, WALES

Aerofilms

CAERNARVON CASTLE, WALES

access to the bailey. A number of separate buildings, the hall (the main living room), kitchens, and other rooms, sometimes connected by covered passages, were erected within the bailey, and there was a well to supply water.

At the end of the 13th century Edward I built a series of magnificent castles to control the conquered Principality of Wales. The finest of these, such as Beaumaris in Anglesey and Harlech in Merionethshire (see Vol. V, p. 193), which were fortresses and little more, have two concentric rings of towered walls, with living rooms in the towers and gatehouse of the inner ring and no keep at all. Caerphilly, Caernarvon, and other Edwardian castles have a hall and other rooms within the inner bailey.

There was no further development in the building of fortified castles after the time of Edward I. Later castles were built with more elaborate halls and rooms to satisfy a higher standard of living. The hall of John of Gaunt's castle of Kenilworth has delicate tracery in the windows and carving in the wooden roof which contrast with the massive 12th-century keep. The most common types of castle of the 14th and 15th centuries had elaborate buildings behind concentric walls with heavily fortified gatehouses, as at Bodiam and Hurstmonceaux in Sussex, and tower houses, such as Caesar's Tower, which was added to Warwick Castle in the 14th century. Tattershall in Lincolnshire, built in the mid-15th century, has a great tower house with several floors. Each floor has a single large room with small closets opening off it, and a spiral staircase runs up one of the corner turrets. The tower and adjacent hall were surrounded by a moat and fishpond, beyond which stood the village with its church and college of priests which were supported by the owners of the castle.

Many of the English castles were destroyed in the Wars of the Roses, and, after the Tudors had put an end to internal warfare, and gunpowder had made high walls a poor defence, unfortified country houses and PALACES (q.v.) were built instead.

Castles were built in every part of Europe during the Middle Ages. After Crusades in the east Mediterranean had come to an end, the Teutonic Knights (see KNIGHTS, ORDERS OF, Vol. I) built many large castles in Prussia in the course of their long wars against the heathens of eastern Europe. Some of the most beautiful

National Buildings Record
TATTERSHALL CASTLE, LINCOLNSHIRE

castles are those of the Rhineland, Switzerland, and Tyrol. These differ from English castles chiefly because they are built at high points in mountainous country and use the natural cliffs for defence. They are usually small, and have a defended gateway, over which looks a tall, round keep, often with a conical roof. Behind is a small courtyard and the hall, chapel, and kitchen where normal life was lived. These were the castles from which independent robber lords harried the countryside, and continued private warfare long after it had ceased in England.

See also HOUSES, HISTORY OF.
See also Vol. X: FORTIFICATIONS.

CATARACT, see EYE STRUCTURE.

CEILINGS, see FLOORS AND CEILINGS.

CELLS, see ANATOMY; BLOOD. See also Vol. II: ANATOMY (Animal).

CENTRAL HEATING, see HEATING SYSTEMS, DOMESTIC; HEATING, HISTORY OF. See also Vol. VIII: HEATING.

CEREALS AND PULSES. Cereals are the seeds of grain-bearing GRASSES and pulses of pod-bearing LEGUMINOUS CROPS (qq.v. Vol. VI). They are the storehouses of food for the young plant, and consist mainly of starch with some protein, particularly in the pulses, and traces of minerals and vitamins. The main cereals are wheat, oats, barley, maize, rice, and rye, and the main pulses are peas, beans, lentils, peanuts, and soya beans.

1. CEREALS. (a) Some varieties of WHEAT (q.v. Vol. VI) produce a 'strong' flour suitable for BREADMAKING (q.v.), whereas others, notably those grown in England, produce a 'soft' flour with a white, mealy grain, very suitable for BISCUITS (q.v.); for this reason English biscuits have world-wide fame. Various kind of flours and meals can be made from the same wheat, ranging from wholemeal to white flour (see FLOUR MILLING, Vol. VII). Germ meals, such as 'Hovis', have an additional amount of the germ of the wheat seed in them. Self-raising flour is a white flour to which baking powder has been added. Other products made from wheat include semolina, which is crushed but not ground wheat, and macaroni, spaghetti, and vermicelli, which are made from semolina (see PASTA).

(b) OATS (q.v. Vol. VI) can be ground into oatmeals of various grades—coarse, medium, fine, and patent—or treated with heat and made into rolled oats. All these forms can be used for porridge, but not for bread because of the absence of gluten. Oatmeal, however, is a main ingredient of many excellent baked goods, such as parkin, which resembles gingerbread, and the crisp oatcakes in which the Scots excel.

(c) Though BARLEY (q.v. Vol. VI) is grown mainly for malting for BEER BREWING and for WHISKY DISTILLING (qq.v. Vol. VII), the polished grains, called pearl barley, are used for thickening stews and soups, in Scotch broth, for example, or to make a palatable milk pudding by cooking with milk and sugar. Barley grains need very long, slow cooking. Barley ground to a flour, called patent barley, requires much less cooking, and can be used to make a light gruel for invalids and infants or as a thickening.

(d) MAIZE (q.v. Vol. VI) is milled to produce cornflour, which is used as a thickening and as the basis of commercial custard powders. Maize grains heated under pressure make the breakfast cereal, cornflakes. One type of maize is also served as a vegetable, 'corn on the cob', or re-moved from the cob is served as creamed corn (see SWEET CORN, Vol. VI).

(e) RICE (q.v. Vol. VI), the staple food of Asia and an important food generally, can be used to make a great variety of RICE DISHES (q.v.). The grains vary in size and shape according to the country of origin: for example, that from Patna is long and pointed, separates readily when cooked, and is suitable to serve with curry, while that from Carolina is smaller and more suitable for rice puddings. In Japan rice is fermented to make an alcoholic drink called *saké*. Rice is also ground into meal of various grades, the two most commonly used being ground rice and rice flour.

(f) RYE (q.v. Vol. VI), a hardy plant grown in central and northern Europe, is ground into a flour and used to make a dark-coloured and rather sour bread, which in some regions replaces wheaten bread. In Britain rye bread, once widely used, is now rarely served except with strong pickles such as gherkins, or cured meats such as Danish ham (see HORS D'ŒUVRES).

2. PULSES. The PEAS, BEANS, and LENTILS (qq.v. Vol. VI) of the store cupboard are dried vegetables, which must be soaked in soft water for up to 12 hours before being cooked. The fresh varieties are discussed under VEGETABLES (q.v.). There are two types of dried peas—marrowfat and split; the former is served as a vegetable, and the latter is used for soups and pease pudding. The best marrowfat peas are hand picked and should be square and wrinkled. Pea flour serves as a thickening, and, according to the old rhyme 'Pease-pudding hot', used also to be made into a kind of porridge.

There are two types of dried beans—butter and haricot. They are excellent in soups, stews, and casseroles, or as a main dish baked with bacon and tomatoes. Lentils, either red Egyptian or brown German, are combined with herbs and eggs in main dishes, or used in soups and stews. These pulses are valuable as a source of second-class protein, but must be supplemented with animal protein as they are deficient in an essential amino acid (see NUTRITION).

SOYA BEANS (q.v. Vol. VI) are widely used as a food in India, China, and Japan, where they are mainly cultivated. Their chief use in Britain is as a source of oil (see FATS AND OILS), but they are also ground into soya bean flour. GROUND NUTS (q.v. Vol. VI), often called peanuts or monkey-nuts, are another valuable source of oil

THE GRAHAM CHILDREN
Painting by William Hogarth, 1742

and a useful food. They may be eaten raw or roasted, used in curries and for SWEET-MAKING (q.v.), or as a spread for bread called peanut butter.

3. Some other foods, which are not cereals at all, are usually thought of as cereals because they resemble them and are used in the same way. Sago (*see* PALM TREES, Vol. VI) is obtained from the pith of the sago palm, and tapioca and arrow-root from the underground stems of cassava and maranta respectively (*see* TROPICAL ROOT CROPS, Vol. VI). Sago and tapioca are heat-treated during preparation, which facilitates cooking. All three are composed almost entirely of starch, and are used as thickening agents and in the making of milk puddings; arrowroot mixed with flour is used to make arrowroot biscuits.

CHAIRS. The history of the chair dates back several thousand years, though it was not until the 16th century that the chair came into common domestic use. Before that time, from the civilization of ancient Egypt to the Renaissance in Europe, the chair was a symbol of authority, akin to the throne, while the chest, bench, or stool provided the ordinary seats of everyday life (*see* CHESTS AND CUPBOARDS). By the middle of the 18th century chairs had become so numerous that it is possible to make a list of over twenty different kinds, each type designed for some special purpose—reading-chairs, sleeping-chairs, desk chairs, and so forth. The chair has been largely a European development. The civilizations of the East developed CARPETS (q.v.) rather

Ashmolean Museum
A GREEK CHAIR
Detail from a 5th century B.C. vase

than chairs because of the custom of sitting on the ground.

Egyptian chairs, such as those found in TUT-ANKHAMEN'S TOMB (q.v. Vol. XII), dating from about 1350 B.C., were usually made of wood. Most common was a low chair with four square legs and a board or rush seat, the whole being mortised or pegged together without the use of nails. Some chairs had feet shaped like lions' paws or bulls' hooves and solid backs of narrow boards enclosed in a frame, the back perhaps being curved to give better support. The chairs were sometimes of plain wood, sometimes painted, and sometimes richly decorated with ivory, mother-of-pearl, or even gold.

No chairs have survived from early Assyrian or Persian times, though we know from sculptured reliefs that the Assyrians made richly decorated chairs and that Persian chairs were often turned with legs of bulging shape.

In the 6th century B.C. the Greeks made rectangular chairs similar to contemporary Egyptian chairs, but by the 5th century new and more graceful designs were introduced, made of square pieces with elegantly curved legs and backs, like the chairs represented on certain Athenian tombs and on the Parthenon frieze. These were often used with decorative cushions. No wooden furniture, however, has survived. As in Greece, all Roman wooden furniture has perished, but there still exist many bronze pieces, especially those found at POMPEII (q.v. Vol. XII), as well as some furniture made of marble. The chair with curved legs crossed X-wise, a shape which was borrowed from the Greeks, was in common use as a *curulis* or official seat in the senate or law courts.

Throughout medieval times in Europe even large houses and monasteries seldom possessed more than two or three chairs; in the manor there was one for the lord, one for his wife, and one other for honoured guests. As the seat of authority the lord's chair stood at the head of the table in the main hall. It was often similar in design to a church stall, early acquiring a high back, sometimes with a canopy, and always having arms formed by the built-in sides. The lower part was closed in, with panelled or carved front and sides, and the seat was often hinged and fitted with a lock, providing a chest as well as a seat. Some of these chairs were movable, but more commonly they were fixed to a wall. Such chairs were more common in France and

Top row, left to right: 1. ITAL-
IAN RENAISSANCE FOLDING
CHAIR, 16TH CENTURY; 2. ENG-
LISH CHAIR, EARLY 17TH CEN-
TURY; 3. FARTHINGALE CHAIR,
ENGLISH, EARLY 17TH CENTURY.

Second row: 4. WING-BACK
CHAIR, EARLY 18TH CENTURY;
5. QUEEN ANNE CHAIR; 6. LOUIS
XV CHAIR.

Bottom row: 7. CHAIR DE-
SIGNED BY ADAM, LATE 18TH
CENTURY; 8. REGENCY CHAIR,
EARLY 19TH CENTURY.

*All except No. 6 by courtesy of the Victoria
and Albert Museum*

the Netherlands than in England. Cushions of brocade, silk, leather, or needlework, often with tasselled corners, were placed on the hard chairs and also on the benches and chests used by those who did not have chairs.

During the 16th century, when power and wealth had spread to the middle classes, chairs gradually became objects of everyday use, and the customary seats of all who could afford to buy them. Smaller and more movable chairs were made at first in Italy and France and later also in England. The panelled front and sides gave place to arms resting on supports and carved and turned legs (see Vol. VII, p. 243). The back remained solid, and was either panelled or carved. English chairs of the 16th century all had arms, but in Italy chairs which were little more than stools with backs were made without arms.

Early in the 17th century chairs began to be upholstered, the backs, seats, and arms being covered in needlework, velvet, or leather studded with brass-headed nails. Many chairs were now produced without arms, and the 'farthingale chairs' designed for ladies wearing the wide skirts of the period, as the name implied, no longer had solid backs, but upholstered rectangular backs raised above the seats on turned supports. The chairs were for the most part heavy and solid, for they were usually made of oak which was heavy and difficult to work into light designs. It was not until the reign of Louis XIII (1610–43) in France that a lighter and more elegant chair was introduced into Europe, with a high back and a seat filled with canework. This new style of chair, with an elaborately carved frame, was brought to England by the Cavaliers returning from exile in France at the Restoration of Charles II. The arms and legs were scrolled, and the stretchers and supports either turned in barley-sugar twists or exuberantly carved with scrollwork, designs of fruit and flowers, and reclining cupids.

In Queen Anne's reign several new chair designs appeared. Walnut largely replaced oak, and the elegant cabriole leg was introduced from the Continent. Chair backs were filled with plain fiddle-shaped splats, the seats were upholstered, and the decoration more restrained, limited to carving on the tops of the backs and the knees of the legs; at the same time the carved claw-and-ball foot was introduced. In the early years of the 18th century many chairs were entirely upholstered except for the legs; the wing-back arm-chair, covered with needlework, and the armless chair with the solid upholstered back, covered in either needlework, velvet, or leather, being popular.

By the mid-18th century mahogany, a hard wood giving the carver more scope, was replacing walnut, and the backs of chairs were filled with a variety of scroll-work, Gothic tracery, and Chinese lattice-work designs (see CHINOISERIE, Vol. XII). Such richly carved chairs were made by the famous firm of Thomas Chippendale (see FURNITURE, HISTORY OF), and examples were published in his books of furniture designs (see Vol. VII, p. 76). Towards the end of the 18th century the chairs of Adam, Hepplewhite, and Sheraton were all lighter and more delicate in design, with thin, tapering legs and lightly carved backs. The ROCOCO chairs (q.v. Vol. XII) of Louis XV and the oval-backed chairs of Louis XVI are among the finest chairs ever made. Indeed, the 18th century was the greatest age of chair making, both in England and on the Continent.

Most chairs produced throughout Europe in the mid-19th century were heavy and ugly. Mass production and lack of artistic design produced a period of tastelessness and poor craftsmanship, and it was not until the beginning of the 20th century that the artist and the craftsman collaborated again to produce fine work. Furniture design today is still in an experimental stage, seeking new materials and new forms of decoration, but many contemporary chairs,

Heal and Son

MODERN CHAIRS AND STOOL WITH LATEX RUBBER CUSHIONS COVERED WITH TAPESTRY especially those produced in Scandinavia (*see* Vol. VII, p. 199), show a sense of design and an understanding of materials in the best tradition of European chair making.

See also FURNITURE, HISTORY OF; INTERIOR DECORATION, HISTORY OF.

See also Vol. VII: FURNITURE INDUSTRY; CABINET-MAKING; UPHOLSTERY.

CHANDELIERS, *see* LIGHTING, HISTORY OF; INTERIOR DECORATION, HISTORY OF.

CHEESES. Various kinds of cheeses have been made for many centuries; they are mentioned, for example, in the literatures of Greece and Rome. It is suggested that the method of making cheese may have been discovered when the stomach of a calf, which contains rennin, a milk-curdling substance essential in cheese-making, was used as a container for milk.

I. CHEESE-MAKING. The basic method of making cheese is as follows. Rennet is added to milk at 86° F. to produce curds, and these are then separated from the whey, heated gently to 100° F., salted, and pressed to remove further moisture and to make a firm cake. This is then wrapped in cheese cloth and kept at 50° F. while it ripens. During this period FERMENTATION takes place, and the presence of enzymes and BACTERIA (qq.v. Vol. II) causes physical and chemical changes in the cheese which produce its characteristic flavour and texture.

Variations in this general method produce the many different types of cheese, most of them named after their place of origin. The amount of water remaining in the curd after pressing constitutes one of the main differences, giving rise to hard cheeses such as Parmesan and Cheddar, semi-soft such as Roquefort and Gorgonzola, or soft such as Camembert and Brie. The quality and kind of milk used also affect the texture; milk with a high fat content gives a softer cheese than one made from skimmed milk, such as Edam. Although the majority of cheeses are made from cow's milk, ewe's and goat's milk are also used—ewe's for Roquefort, and goat's for the soft brown cheese from Norway. The characteristic texture of the Swiss cheeses Gruyère and Emmenthal is produced by heating the curd to a higher temperature (up to 140° F.); the bacteria during growth produce a gas which makes the familiar holes in the ripened cheese. Yet another variation is produced by MOULDS (q.v. Vol. II) which grow either in or

SOME ENGLISH AND CONTINENTAL CHEESES

1. Parmesan. 2. Stilton. 3. Gruyère. 4. Bondon. 5. Dutch. 6. Camembert. 7. Roquefort. 8. Neufchâtel. 9. Cheshire. 10. Gorgonzola. 11. Cream. 12. Devonshire Toasting Cheese. 13. Cheddar. 14. Single Gloucester. 15. Blue Dorset. From Garrett's *Encyclopaedia of Cooking*, 1891

on the cheese during the ripening process, giving it a characteristic flavour. The blue varieties, such as Roquefort, are the best examples of moulds growing within cheeses, and Camembert is a good example of ripening caused by mould growing on the surface. For blue cheese, a penicillin mould is introduced into the curd before it is pressed, and after pressing, holes are made by inserting needles to let in air, which assists the growth of the mould. In the making of Camembert cheese, yeasts, moulds, and bacteria grow on the surface, and, in the process of ripening, gradually spread down to the middle of the cheese. This method can be used only for small cheeses. For processed cheese, a ripened Cheddar type is heated to prevent its ripening further (pasteurization), and it is then poured into blocks.

2. KINDS OF CHEESE. The best-known British cheese, whether to be served at table or used for cooking, is Cheddar. It originated in Somerset, but is now also made elsewhere, not only in

Britain but abroad, in Canada, the U.S.A., and New Zealand, for example. Cheeses of similar type are Cheshire, Double Gloucester, Wensleydale, Leicester, Caerphilly, and Blue Vinney—many of them rare during the 1940s. The most famous English blue cheese, Stilton, is among the best of this type.

Notable Italian cheeses are the blue Gorgonzola, the hard Parmesan, and Bel Paese. Belgium produces Limburger, a small, soft cheese with a strong flavour; Holland, the round red Edam; and Denmark, the Danish Blue. For its great variety of fine cheeses, however, France has no equal. Many are exported, but others are best enjoyed in the locality where they are made. The best known of the soft types are Camembert, Brie, Livarot, and Pont l'Evêque; and of the semi-soft, Saint Paulin, Pont-du-Salut, and Roquefort. France also produces a variety of fresh, unripened cheeses, of which Petit-Suisse, Pommel, and Neufchâtel are the best known.

3. USE OF CHEESES. Cheese is composed mainly of protein, fat, and water (see FOOD VALUES) in proportions varying from one type of cheese to another. A typical analysis of Cheddar is 24·9% protein and 34·5% fat. It also contains VITAMINS A and D (q.v.) and small quantities of iron and calcium.

The high protein content of cheese makes it a fair substitute for meat. In past centuries, during meat shortages, cheese, milk, and eggs, known as 'the white meats', were the mainstay of the countryman's diet. Cheese is also served as a savoury at the end of a meal to aid digestion by stimulating the digestive juices. It is usually eaten with bread, biscuits, or toast and butter, and goes well with celery, radishes, or pickled onions. The fresh cheeses, such as Petit-Suisse, can be eaten with sugar and cream instead of bread. It is the custom always to scoop a whole Stilton cheese from the middle; in Scandinavia, cheese is always cut in thin slivers with a special cutter provided for this purpose.

Hard cheeses, particularly Cheddar and Parmesan, are most suitable for cooking because they can be grated. Grated cheese can be mixed with PASTRY (q.v.) for cheese straws or pasties, or with white SAUCE (q.v.) to make Sauce Mornay to go with egg, fish, vegetable, or pasta dishes; it can be sprinkled over such dishes and on to certain soups such as minestrone and onion soup. It can be used as a main ingredient in, for example, the two rather similar dishes, Welsh rarebit and the Swiss *fondue*. Welsh rarebit is cheese melted with milk or beer served on toast and grilled, and *fondue* is cheese melted with white wine served in a heated bowl, into which all the diners dip cubes of bread on the end of a fork. It is very important not to overcook cheese dishes or they will become hard and stringy.

Red wine and beer are both suitable drinks to serve with cheese, because in each case the cheese and drink enhance each other's flavour. Cheese is used extensively by professional wine-tasters because it cleans the palate, making it ready for its work.

See also Vol. VII: DAIRY INDUSTRY.

CHESTS AND CUPBOARDS. Chests are among the earliest pieces of furniture, for as soon as people began to lead settled lives and to make homes, they began to feel the need for solid containers in which to keep things. The ancient Egyptians, for example, about 2000 B.C. or earlier made beautiful chests, both with flat and domed lids, and sometimes standing on legs (*see* Vol. XII, p. 461). Some of these have survived because they were put with other personal possessions in the tombs of the Pharaohs. Although no wooden furniture has survived from the days of ancient Greece, Greek vase paintings show that the Greeks also had chests.

In the Middle Ages the chest was an extremely important piece of furniture. The first English chests were made of hollowed-out logs, often with metal bands nailed round to strengthen them and to form hinges at the back. Very soon, however, craftsmen began to make lighter and more economical chests by nailing and pegging six boards together into a box.

These chests were used for all sorts of purposes —storing clothes, tools, armour, and other possessions. Probably nearly every household in Europe in the Middle Ages had at least one chest, and wealthy families would have a great many (*see* Vol. VII, p. 74). They often had locks with large, rough, iron keys. More durable metal chests, often called coffers, were used for storing things of special value, such as documents; for, as there were no banks until the 17th century, everything had to be kept at home. Travellers took chests with them, as they now take suit-cases or trunks, and chests with rounded lids and large square handles at each end were specially designed for being roped on to horses.

They were often strengthened with iron scroll-work fixed on over leather, and sometimes they had rich Genoa velvet coverings embroidered with the owner's coat-of-arms or initials.

Solid oak chests lasted well, but they had one great disadvantage; the planks, being fixed to one another at the ends, tended to split across when the wood shrank, as even well-seasoned timber does to some extent. Many old chests, therefore, have large cracks across the front and top. To overcome this difficulty panelled chests were devised. The front and sides were made of a strong framework, with inner grooves in which panels were set loosely enough to allow for shrinkage of the framework (see WOODWORK, Vol. VII). During the 16th and 17th centuries these panels were often richly carved, the linen-fold pattern being a favourite design (see ORNAMENT, Vol. XII).

For the sake of order people packed things in little boxes inside the chest. Then they began to make fitted boxes that could be drawn out instead of being lifted—and these were called 'drawers'. For a time chests were made with drawers underneath, but later the front of the chest was left out, and several rows of drawers were made. The result was a 'chest-of-drawers'. By the end of the reign of William III, in 1702, these had largely replaced chests for domestic use.

A special kind of chest-of-drawers, very popular at the end of the 17th century, was the tall-boy. This was a high chest, often in two parts, with a great many drawers, but, though most attractive to look at, it was not very practical because the top drawers were too high for convenience.

A cupboard was at first a wooden shelf, fixed against the wall over a chest or a side table, to hold precious pieces of glass and cups or jugs of the new 'china' which was becoming popular in Europe in the 18th century. This shelf against a wall was therefore called a cup-board. Later, more shelves were added, and then a door was put on to the front in order to keep the things inside clean and safe.

A hutch, another kind of early cupboard, was really a broad chest turned on to its end so that the lid served as a door. Sometimes shelves were fitted inside, and sometimes the hutch was divided horizontally into two sections, each with its own small door.

Several kinds of cupboard for displaying valuable table-ware were popular in the 16th and early 17th centuries: cupboards and court-cupboards in wealthy households and dressers in more modest ones. A court-cupboard was a kind of side table with two tiers; a cupboard was a handsome cabinet with display shelves in the middle and cupboards above and below. The doors of the cupboards often had elaborate carving, and the whole had large bulbous supports, also richly carved. A dresser was a much more modest piece of furniture used in country districts and as a kitchen sideboard. It had cupboards below and rows of shelves above. A Welsh dresser had a heavy cornice round the top, projecting above the shelves on which the family plate was 'dressed', or arranged. Sometimes there were drawers in the bottom part and small spice cupboards, as well as shelves above.

A livery cupboard was a small enclosed cupboard for storing a supply of food and lighting materials for the night—a necessary piece of furniture for each member of a household. These cupboards, often elaborately carved, were decorated with a large number of small ventilation holes: the finest 17th-century livery cupboards sometimes had one or two rows of vertical bars, or balusters, for ventilation. Livery cupboards were no longer made when bedrooms were fitted with corner cupboards; but they had a successor in the 'dole' cupboard used in churches and large houses to hold food set aside for the poor.

The beautiful cabinets, which became popular in the 17th century, were made with such skill that the term 'cabinet-maker' came to mean a craftsman who made high-quality furniture of all kinds (see CABINET-MAKING, Vol. VII). Cabinets made in walnut—a new foreign wood brought to England in the 17th century—had either glass doors or solid polished doors which showed the lovely patterns formed by the grain of this wood. The glass-fronted cabinets were often used for displaying specimens of beautiful oriental china. Sometimes there were little pull-out shelves under the glass doors for resting a candlestick on.

As reading and writing became more general among wealthy people, the chest or cupboard was further adapted as a container for books and as a writing desk. These first writing desks, or bureaux or escritoires, usually made of walnut, had tops which opened downwards to make a flat surface for writing, and insides fitted with

Top: EARLY 17TH-CENTURY CHEST WITH DESIGNS INLAID
IN HOLLY AND BOG OAK

Left: EARLY 17TH-CENTURY LIVERY CUPBOARD; LATE
16TH-CENTURY BUFFET OF CARVED AND INLAID WALNUT

Right: EARLY 18TH-CENTURY TALLBOY

All by courtesy of the Victoria and Albert Museum

Country Life

SIDEBOARD, FLANKED BY CUPBOARDS WITH URNS, AND A WINE COOLER
Made by Chippendale for Harewood House, Yorkshire

small drawers or pigeon-holes for writing materials (*see* Vol. VII, p. 75). Later, the larger mahogany bureaux had drawers in the lower part and a bookcase on the top.

Up to the 18th century a wardrobe meant a room where clothes were 'warded' or kept safely (*see* Vol. VII, p. 244). A cupboard fitted with pegs for hanging clothes or with shelves for linen, and mounted on drawers, was called a press. Wardrobe-cupboards with full-length doors did not become common until the end of the 18th century.

The sideboard—which reminds us that a table was once called a 'board'—was at first a small side table with one or two drawers under it. The central table was often flanked by small cupboards, at first separate, later joined on. These had shelves or drawers lined with tin and heated for keeping plates hot, or with lead to hold wine bottles, or with baize to hold silver. Later still, the central part had cupboards and drawers fitted below it and was surmounted with mirrors and shelves fitted into a high back. By the 18th century mahogany sideboards in wealthy houses had become large and imposing pieces of dining-room furniture.

The 19th-century cupboards, which were always heavy, solid, and imposing, and generally very well built, were of all types and sizes to suit the widely varied needs of the times. They were often heavily carved, and were most usually of mahogany or oak.

See also FURNITURE, HISTORY OF; FURNITURE, MODERN.

CHICKEN POX, *see* INFECTIOUS DISEASES, Section 7.

CHILBLAINS, *see* SKIN.

CHILD GUIDANCE CLINICS. These now play an important part in the educational and health services of many countries. Their purpose is to deal with the psychological difficulties of children, whether these are due to some peculiarity of temperament or to faulty upbringing (*see* CHILDREN, UPBRINGING OF). The commonest difficulties are shyness, timidity, frequent crying, bed-wetting, stammering, stealing, wandering from home, and unexplained backwardness at school. Many cases of nervous and mental disorder and of unsocial behaviour in adult life have their origin in childhood, and one of the main tasks of child guidance is to recognize and correct early tendencies towards abnormality. Nearly all children, if given a fair chance and freedom to develop, will make a satisfactory adjustment to life; and the aim of child guidance is to provide the child with these conditions. This means that the clinics must work in close co-operation with the child's parents—and, in some cases it is the parents who need treatment rather than the child.

Child guidance clinics are not concerned with mental deficiency, and they do everything possible to avoid a 'psychiatric' atmosphere, that is, an atmosphere which makes children think they are peculiar. Most children coming to the clinics are involved in difficult family situations, and much of the treatment is carried out through the home and the school by trained social workers attached to the clinic. The staffs of the clinics also include medical and lay psychologists. Talks with the child and its parents are a regular part of treatment. When children are unable, as they usually are, to put their emotional difficulties into words, light is often thrown on the nature of their difficulties by watching their PLAY (q.v.) and their drawings, in which they often give unconscious expression to their fears and desires.

Delinquent children are often referred by the JUVENILE COURTS (q.v. Vol. X) to the clinics for help, but in many of these cases it is necessary to transfer the child to a residential school in order to remove him from a bad home background or harmful companions.

The idea of applying psychological methods to the management of difficult children originated in the United States, where child guidance clinics were established in Chicago (1909) and Boston (1915). In England the Child Guidance department of the Tavistock Clinic was opened in 1920 and the London Child Guidance Clinic in 1928. The acceptance of responsibility for this work by public health and education authorities marks a great advance. The Birmingham Education Committee established a clinic in 1932, and this example was soon followed in nearly all the principal cities of Great Britain.

See also PSYCHOLOGY; MENTAL DISEASES; FAMILY WELFARE SERVICES.
See also Vol. X: SPECIAL SCHOOLS.

CHILDREN'S BOOKS, *see* Vol. XII: CHILDREN'S BOOKS.

CHILDREN'S CLOTHES. For many centuries in Europe all children except infants were dressed in small replicas of their parents' garments, as they still are in many Eastern countries and amongst Lapps, Eskimoes, and other simple peoples. When, however, a clearer understanding of childhood and its needs came into being, separate fashions for the young also appeared (*see* NURSERY, HISTORY OF).

During the first few months of their lives babies used to be tightly swathed in swaddling-bands (*see* BABIES, CARE OF), and, indeed, these finally disappeared from European nurseries only in the 19th century. By the 17th century mothers were beginning to replace them by short linen or silk robes. In the 19th century babies were voluminously clothed in flannel binders, long robes and petticoats extending far below the feet, and wide shawls covering the head and body. The short, loose garments now worn did not appear until after the First World War.

Until the latter part of the 18th century, little children wore ankle-length frocks and petticoats from the time they could crawl until they were 3 or 4 years old, when they assumed clothes similar to those of their parents (*see* Vol. V,

Wallace Collection

DON BALTASAR CARLOS, ELDEST SON OF PHILIP IV OF SPAIN, WHEN ABOUT THREE YEARS OLD

Painting by Velasquez, *c.* 1632

THREE CHILDREN OF CHARLES I
Painting by Van Dyck, 1635

p. 456; opp. p. 224). In the 16th century little girls wore miniature farthingales and ruffs, while their brothers strutted about in slashed doublets and swinging cloaks. Boys in the 17th century shared the feathered hats and high top-boots of their elders and even WIGS (q.v.), when those cumbersome head-coverings were in fashion. Similarly, in the 18th century, they wore wide-skirted coats and tricorne hats, and little girls wore hooped dresses and mob caps (*see* Colour Plate, opp. p. 48). Towards the end of the 18th century, however, more suitable clothes for the young were coming into fashion, and for the first time children ceased to be little models of their parents.

By 1800 distinct styles had emerged. Boys wore long trousers buttoned under the arms on to frilled blouses, with short jackets, peaked caps, and flat heel-less shoes. Girls had long dresses with loose skirts gathered on to a bodice, pelisses (*see* COATS AND CLOAKS), and straw bonnets tied under the chin with ribbons. From about 1805 to 1840 they wore lace-trimmed pantalettes (*see* UNDERCLOTHES) which showed beneath their dresses. In the middle of the century elastic-sided boots for indoor and outdoor wear replaced the flat shoes previously worn by both sexes. Stockings with coloured circular stripes were then popular. Girls wore wide, flounced skirts, with tight-fitting jackets, and straw, silk, or beaver poke bonnets, which were replaced a few years later by small, feathered hats and caps.

CHILDREN PLAYING MARBLES, LATE 18TH CENTURY
Engraving by F. Bartolozzi after W. Hamilton

Older girls, not yet out of the schoolroom, often turned their hair up in a loose chignon confined in a chenille net. Boys wore belted tunics with rather baggy knee-length breeches, or cut-away coats and long trousers, the latter often of plaid or checked material.

In the 1860s fashionable little girls wore crinolines like their mothers, but with skirts extending only halfway down the calf. Over these a top-skirt was sometimes worn, bunched up to give the effect of paniers. Braid was lavishly used in trimming. Pantalettes had by then disappeared, but loose drawers still showed an inch or two below the dress-hem. When the bustle, 20 years later, replaced the crinoline, girls wore small pads under the backs of their frilled skirts, and draped overskirts intended to look like an apron. Boys at this period usually wore either sailor suits with fisher-caps or tam-

o'-shanters, or black velvet jackets and knee-breeches, lace collars, wide sashes, and long curling hair—a style which came to be called the 'Little Lord Fauntleroy' style. The 'Kate Greenaway' style, called after the 19th-century illustrator of child-life, belongs also to the 1880s and 1890s. The girls had long, high-waisted dresses with wide sashes and mob caps, and the boys had trousers well above the ankles, fly-away jackets, and large lace collars (*see* Vol. IX, pp. 449, 469).

Smocked serge or silk frocks came in with the artistic fashions of the 1890s; they were worn with white lace-trimmed pinafores reaching from neck to hem. Party frocks were usually white, often of Swiss embroidered cambric or muslin, with wide coloured silk sashes and hair-ribbons to match. In the early 20th century, coloured accordion-pleated silk or delaine dresses were popular for best occasions. With them silk elbow-length mittens were often worn and, for younger children, white or coloured three-quarter-length silk socks. Pleated serge skirts, with long woollen jerseys or sailor blouses, were usual for everyday wear, and, in the summer, white or coloured muslin and cotton frocks and big Leghorn hats. Gym-tunics (known as drill-dresses) were first worn only for games, but about 1910 they were adopted as uniform by many schools, and became the customary daily wear of schoolgirls. Boys of the same period wore sailor suits or jerseys and short trousers until they were old enough to wear Eton or Norfolk suits.

The amount of underclothing worn decreased considerably after the First World War. Before that time little girls normally wore several petticoats, including one of flannel, a chemise or perhaps combinations, frilly drawers, and a liberty-bodice on to which the drawers were buttoned. The bodice, which was hung from straps over the shoulders, had replaced the corsets worn in the 19th century. Today, when the emphasis is on freedom and comfort, the chemise or combinations have been replaced by a vest, the flannel petticoat and most of its companions

Victoria and Albert Museum

A GENTLEMAN AND TWO CHILDREN, 1799

Water-colour by Henry Edridge

VICTORIAN CHILDREN'S FASHIONS

Picture Post Library

EDWARDIAN CHILDREN

have disappeared, and the frilly drawers have given way to knickers supported by elastic round the waist—fashions which seem healthy and natural to us now, but which our ancestors would have regarded as both improper and dangerous to health.

See also COSTUME, HISTORY OF.

CHILDREN'S HOMES, *see* Vol. X: CHILDREN'S HOMES.

CHILDREN, UPBRINGING OF. It is generally accepted that the experiences of the child in his first years largely determine his character and later personality—as Wordsworth said, 'The Child is father of the Man.' Every experience teaches the child something and the effects are cumulative. The term 'upbringing' refers to the treatment and training of the child within his home. This is closely related to the treatment and training of the child in school, which is referred to as 'EDUCATION' (q.v. Vol. X). In a society such as ours, both parents and teachers are responsible for the opportunities provided for the development of the child, so that upbringing and education are interdependent.

The ideals and practices of child-rearing vary from culture to culture, race to race, class to class, and family to family. In general, it may be said that the more primitive the community the more uniform are the customs of child upbringing (*see* SOCIAL ENVIRONMENT). Again, in more civilized societies, the period of childhood and adolescence tends to be extended over a longer time, and the result of this is more opportunity for education and greater variety in character development. Early upbringing in the home is naturally affected both by the cultural pattern of the community and by the parents' capabilities and their aims for the child in adult life. How far parents are able to achieve their aims depends not only on upbringing and education but also on the innate abilities of the child. Wide differences of innate intelligence and temperament are often to be found even in children of the same family.

Parents are able to judge whether their children are normal in physical, mental, and social growth by referring to books written on the succeeding phases of child development. This body of scientifically obtained knowledge has taken the place of the old generalizations, such as 'Children should be seen and not heard', and 'Spare the rod, spoil the child'. Intelligent parents, however, realize that the particular setting of each family is unique and there can be no rigid general rules. They use such general information only as a guide in making their own decisions and solving their own problems. For example, today it is recognized that a quick slap may be the right thing for one child in a particular situation and completely the wrong thing for another child in very similar circumstances. Problems of upbringing are recognized to be problems of individual family relationships, the one necessity being a secure family background, with parents who are united in their attitude to their children.

Parents are very much influenced in what they are able to achieve by their own personality. As we have seen, this depends largely on the upbringing they have had as children, and so the upbringing of one generation affects the next. In this sense the child 'inherits' an environment. Thus a cultured home may be the inherited environment which enables a child of superior intelligence to develop into an intellectual genius. Similarly, neurosis and delinquency may descend from one generation to the next through the influence of

Nationalmuseum, Stockholm

A LADY DRESSING HER LITTLE GIRL
Painting by J. B. S. Chardin (1699–1779)

the family environment on the child (*see* CHILD GUIDANCE CLINIC).

All parents have to solve the problems of freedom and discipline, which take different forms at different ages. The younger the child, the more readily the mother gives in to his demands and avoids disappointing him. She knows that for his successful upbringing the child's instinctive wishes have to be considered as well as controlled. If he is not given sufficient satisfaction and outlet at every age, his instinctive energy becomes turned in on itself and is not available for the more civilized ends of growing up. An example of this is the need the young child has to make 'mud pies'. Playing with sand and water, or some such materials, is an essential stage in development. Picture books and hard toys are no alternative, but they also can be used and enjoyed to the full if the sand-water stage is satisfied. Similarly, throughout life each stage to some extent depends on the ones before. Where one stage has been left out, the child may have to go back and recapture the experience of it. A good home makes this possible: for example, by providing the child with the oppor-

tunity to play with dolls or a train up to any age, if he still needs to do so. This principle underlies all psychological treatment of children in difficulties, and is a basis of the work in clinics.

The beginnings of discipline are in the nursery. Even the youngest baby is usually taught by gradual stages to wait for food, to sleep and wake at regular intervals, and so on. If the child feels that the world around him is a friendly one, he slowly accepts its rhythm and accustoms himself to conforming to its demands. As he masters the experiences of 'time', he does not need to cry as soon as he is hungry, because he knows the food will be coming. As he becomes confident in the regularity and safety of his surroundings, he is prepared to accept a temporary discomfort. This learning to wait is a very important element in upbringing and is achieved successfully only if too great demands are not made before the child can understand them.

Every parent watches eagerly the child's acquisition of each new skill—the first spoken words, the first independent steps, or the beginning of reading and writing. It is often tempting to hurry the child beyond his natural learning rate, and so to set up a state of anxiety and feeling of failure. This can happen at any stage. A baby may be taught to be clean too early, a young child may be expected to share his toys or to learn to read before he knows the reality of other children he shares with, or the meaning of the words he reads. On the other hand, if a child is left alone too much, or without any learning opportunities, he loses his natural zest for life and his desire to find out new things for himself.

Learning together is a fruitful source of relationship not only between children but also between children and their parents. By playing together, parents learn a lot about their children, and children learn a lot from their parents; for this, toys which the father and child can play with together are useful. PLAY (q.v.) and games are vehicles of learning, as well as the most important beginnings of social experience. Brothers and sisters teach one another relationships with older and younger children, but contemporaries outside the child's own family provide experiences of a more purely social character uncomplicated by the feelings of jealousy which often exist between brothers and sisters. From 3 onwards the child should have children of his own age to play with.

Parents vary greatly in the degree of their strictness or leniency towards their children. Some are strict in one field and lenient in others. Many have special fields in which they enforce their authority. Some may be especially strict over matters of money, insisting that a rigid code over payment and expenditure of pocket-money encourages a responsible attitude to finances in later life. Others are severe over times of coming in at night, punctuality for meals, or cleanliness. The battle for tidiness is usually a fierce one in the family, but there seems to be little connexion between early training and the later character trait of order or disorder.

It is not possible here to discuss in detail the development of morality in the child and its dependence on parental teaching. Consistency of upbringing is very important and 'example is better than precept'. At a very early stage the child is aware of parental standards and adopts them. Similarly he takes over religious beliefs and practices. A consistent background helps him to formulate his position and at the same time may give him something to rebel against in adolescence.

Adolescents accept their new roles as men and women happily or with difficulty according to their upbringing. A straightforward attitude to masculine and feminine characteristics, changes, needs, and responsibilities enables both the boy and the girl to be pleased to be members of their own sex. A strictly fair allocation of duties and privileges, and mutual acceptance of advantages and limitations, is necessary. The choice of a vocation often helps the adolescent to gain sufficient confidence to take on adult responsibilities and status.

See also BABIES, CARE OF; BABIES, FEEDING OF; NURSERY, HISTORY OF.

See also Vol. I: INITIATION CEREMONIES.

CHILD WELFARE CLINICS, see FAMILY WELFARE SERVICES. *See also* Vol. X: CHILD WELFARE.

CHIMNEYS. It is only in cold climates, where warmth is one of the most important things a house has to provide, that chimneys and FIREPLACES (q.v.) have played a prominent part in the design of houses. The first chimneys in British houses date from the 12th century, for before this the fire was built in the middle of the floor. Indeed, for some while after the 12th century, it was only the grander homes—the

P. S. Spokes

CHIMNEYS AT ABINGDON ABBEY
The tall chimney in the centre and the outlet for smoke from another flue, seen to the left, date from the late 13th century

MANORS, PALACES, and CASTLES (qq.v.)—that had fireplaces with flues to carry away the smoke, and the central hearth remained in some large halls even as late as the 14th century, the smoke finding its way out through a 'louver' in the roof.

In the few early stone chimneys which still exist, the flue has its outlet in the face of the wall or is carried up to a chimney pierced with small slits. The earliest flues in ordinary houses were wooden structures covered with clay, which became baked as hard as brick; but in the 15th century these were prohibited in towns because of the risk of fire, and so were gradually superseded, even in houses built of timber, by chimneys of brick and stone. In small houses the whole building was often planned round a central chimney-stack.

In the 15th and 16th centuries tall brick or stone chimney-shafts, growing in groups out of a square brick base rising above the ridge of the roof, gave a picturesque outline to farmhouses and manor-houses. They were often moulded, twisted, and ornamented with diaper patterns and crowned with heavily moulded capitals. In Elizabethan mansions they were less richly decorated, but retained their bold outlines and heavy capitals.

By the end of the 16th century separate chimney-shafts had given way to solid square or rectangular masses of brick or stone, all the flues being taken up inside them. In GEORGIAN ARCHITECTURE (q.v. Vol. XII), especially in larger houses, these chimney-stacks were given a classical character, crowned with cornices, and panelled and moulded on the face. Sometimes they were pierced with arches and linked in various ways to make, as it were, little temples above the roof. They were so large that the most convenient way of sweeping them was by sending small boys up them with brushes—a practice which continued until the passing of the Chimney Sweepers' Act in 1875 (see CHILD WELFARE, Vol. X). Later, when horizontal roof-lines became the fashion, chimneys became simpler and lower, sometimes even being partly hidden by a parapet. They became a more important part of the design in the 19th century, both because the Victorians imitated earlier styles and because they liked picturesque details.

In the 18th century the chimney-pot was introduced; this, embedded in cement on the top of the chimney-stack, allowed a more scientific control of the draught, and consequently the heavily moulded capitals disappeared. The earliest chimney-pots were pyramidal in shape, but later they were made square or, most commonly, circular. Builders in the 19th century made endless experiments with different shaped chimney-pots and various kinds of attachments to improve the draught; consequently a view over the roof tops of most English cities presents an extraordinary array of chimney-pots of different sizes and shapes, in clay and metal, bending, branching, and even revolving.

Modern chimney-stacks are generally plain, rectangular brick structures, with pots projecting only an inch or two above the top. They play far less part in the appearance of the modern house, if only because most houses have only one or two open fireplaces instead of one in every room, as was the custom earlier. Electric fires do not need chimneys, gas fires need only a small flue, which can be built in the thickness of the wall, and central heating requires only one chimney for the whole house.

The height and grouping of chimneys is determined not only by the appearance outside but by the need for a good draught—but not a down-draught—in the fireplace. No chimney should be less than 3 feet above the ridge of the roof; the exact height depends on such local

Central Press

HAMPTON COURT: TUDOR CHIMNEYS

SUDBURY HALL: LATE 17TH-CENTURY CHIMNEYS

conditions as the direction of the prevailing wind and the height of neighbouring trees and hills. The need to conserve heat must also be considered. If the chimney is placed on an out-side wall, much of the heat that goes up it is wasted, but if it rises through the centre of the house, the hot air in it warms several rooms at once; also the fireplaces in adjoining rooms can be built back to back so that their flues can conveniently share the same chimney-stack.

See also FIREPLACES; HEATING, HISTORY OF; HOUSES, HISTORY OF.

CHINA, see JUGS AND VESSELS; TABLE DISHES. *See also* Vol. VII: POTTERY; PORCELAIN.

CHLOROFORM, see ANAESTHETICS.

CHOLERA, see EPIDEMIC DISEASES.

CHRISTMAS DAY, see FAMILY FESTIVALS. *See also* Vol. I: CHRISTIAN YEAR; FATHER CHRISTMAS.

CIDER, see COLD DRINKS, Section 4. *See also* Vol. VII: CIDER-MAKING.

CLEANING EQUIPMENT. The satisfaction that a housewife can gain from keeping house

well is lessened if she finds the work arduous and monotonous. Undoubtedly some of the drudgery of housework disappears if suitable and adequate equipment is bought, and is then well cared for.

Brushes specially designed for different tasks, of different degrees of stiffness and softness, and with different lengths of handle are available. The following are usually necessary: a soft-bristled, long-handled brush for general sweeping; a soft-bristled, short-handled brush for sweeping into a dustpan; a stiff-fibre, short-handled brush for carpet sweeping; a soft, long-handled wall brush; a stiff-bristled, short-handled brush for cleaning the lavatory pan; two stiff brushes without handles for scrubbing floors and tables; and special brushes for cleaning shoes, silver, vegetables, and saucepans.

Suitable cloths for each task should be chosen. A good duster is made of soft material with a surface to which the dust will cling, either because of the special finish given to it in manufacture or because it is impregnated with a small amount of oil. Woollen cloth is most satisfactory for polishing. For 'wet' jobs, such as drying dishes and swabbing floors, which need absorbent and hard-wearing cloth, linen and cotton are suitable. For cleaning windows the material should be non-linty as well as absorbent, and for this purpose a chamois leather is far the best. There are mops on handles to replace dusters, dishcloths, or floorcloths. The long handle of floor-mops saves unnecessary bending and makes it easier to clean under furniture. Modern wet floor-mops have a device for wringing the mop head (or squeezing it, if it is made of sponge); such devices may be attached to the handle or to the bucket.

Among aids to housework invented during recent years, the carpet-sweeper and vacuum-cleaner are perhaps the most important. The

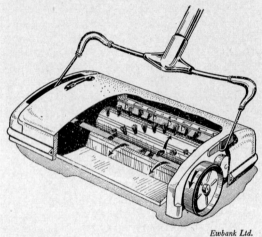

Ewbank Ltd.

DIAGRAM OF A CARPET-SWEEPER

The arrows show the direction of rotation of the wheel and sweeper and how the dust is thrown into the dustpan

carpet-sweeper runs on wheels, and between the wheels is fixed a roller on which there are brushes. When the sweeper is pushed, not only the wheels but also the roller and brushes rotate, and the dust is swept into an encasing dust-pan. There is a contraption for emptying the dust-pan after use. The vacuum-cleaner sucks up dust into a bag, an easy and efficient method which, unlike sweeping, does not raise the dust. In early models the power to produce suction was supplied by bellows operated by hand, so that two people were needed; but now the cleaner is fitted with an electric motor which drives a fan, so that by attaching it to an electric point one person can work it. Modern vacuum-cleaners are of three types—the barrel, the upright sweeper, and the hand or duster model, the latter being especially useful for cleaning small areas, such as stairs, which may be inaccessible to the larger models. The upright model combines suction and sweeping; it has a mechanically

driven roller with brushes attached, which are very useful in removing stubborn threads and fluff. Modern vacuum-cleaners have extra attachments for cleaning upholstered furniture and cushions and getting dust out of cracks and crannies. Another mechanical device, especially useful in houses with large polished floors, is the electric polisher in which two or three circular brushes driven by an electric motor revolve at high speed on a vertical axis. A similar machine can be used for either polishing or scrubbing floors, and one recent model with suitable attachments not only combines the work of all three machines, the suction cleaner, the scrubber, and the polisher, but in addition has a squeegee attachment to suck up dirty water off the floor after scrubbing.

A brush, after use, should be freed from fluff and hung up, and not left standing on its bristles. Frequent and careful washing, followed by thorough drying, also helps to keep the bristles in good condition. Cloths, also, should be washed after use (see LAUNDRY METHODS). The chamois leather should have its last rinse in water containing a little soap, for this keeps it soft. The carpet-sweeper should always have its dust-pan emptied and the roller and bristles freed from dust and threads after use, and at regular intervals its moving parts should be oiled. The care of the vacuum-cleaner entails brushing the inside about once a month and emptying the bag after every use. The bag is made of material which permits the passage of

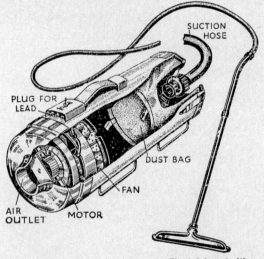

PLUG FOR LEAD

SUCTION HOSE

DUST BAG

FAN

AIR OUTLET

MOTOR

Electrical Assoc. for Women

DIAGRAM OF A CYLINDER-TYPE SUCTION CLEANER

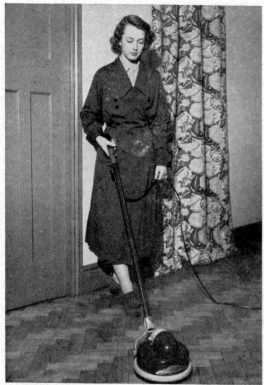

USING AN ELECTRIC POLISHER

air but not dust; if it becomes clogged with dust, the air cannot pass through, suction fails, and the cleaner does not work. Paper liners for these bags, which can be removed and destroyed with the contents, have recently become available in some countries, and are proving satisfactory in use.

See also HOUSEWORK.

CLEANING MATERIALS. These are grouped according to whether their action is detergent, abrasive, protective, or bleaching.

1. DETERGENTS. Articles are more easily washed if a detergent is added to the water. Detergents include soap, soda, synthetic detergents, glue or size solution, Fuller's earth, and infusions made from bran and quassia (a decoction from a South American tree). A detergent makes washing easier in three ways—by increasing the wetting power of water, by emulsifying grease, or by suspending the particles of dirt so that they do not settle again on the articles being washed. Soda (*see* ALKALIS, Section 3, Vol. VII), for example, increases considerably the wetting

power of water, and has good emulsifying properties. Soap has both these properties, particularly at higher temperatures, and in addition it has good suspending powers.

Soap is obtainable in different forms, the main types being bar, flakes, and powder (*see* SOAP MANUFACTURE, Vol. VII). All types contain water in varying amounts, and all, except most flakes, contain additions made for special purposes, such as scent to toilet soap, disinfectants to medicated soaps, and a variety of different substances to powders. Most of these additions, or 'builders', are intended to increase detergent properties; but one of them, a fluorescent powder, makes white clothes look whiter because it glows in the presence of ultra-violet light.

In many homes today synthetic detergents are used both for washing and washing-up because they readily emulsify grease at low temperatures, and because they can be used in hard water without scum forming (*see* WATER, DOMESTIC). These detergents are of different types but are known generally as sulphated fatty alcohols. The commercial preparations on the market usually consist of mixtures of synthetic detergents with the addition of builders, and sometimes also of fluorescent powders and bleaches. The presence of strong alkalis such as soda in the builders may increase the efficiency of the detergent, but may make them very harsh on the hands. Recent cases of dermatitis, associated with using synthetic detergents, may have occurred because the detergent had removed the natural grease from the skin, which was then attacked by the soda. Synthetic detergents are available as powders or as liquids. The unbuilt ones are particularly useful for washing fabrics with delicate dyes which alkalis would affect, and for washing woollens which prefer a neutral or slightly acid medium.

2. ABRASIVES. The abrasive or rubbing action of a number of naturally occurring materials has long been known: the camper, for example, cleans his knife by rubbing it up and down in the ground, and the gardener's spade is shining after a day's digging. Domestic materials vary in hardness, and to avoid scratches suitable abrasives must be used for cleaning them. Silver, being rather soft, needs a fine, soft abrasive, whereas steel is less easily damaged by hard and coarse ones. Glass windows and the enamel and porcelain surfaces of baths, sinks, and wash basins need a moderately fine abrasive.

The substances used as abrasives for domestic cleaning materials are silica in various forms, such as silver sand, china clay, Tripoli powder, pumice, and silica flower; calcium carbonate as whiting, precipitated chalk, and kieselguhr; red iron oxide (rouge); and emery, which is impure aluminium oxide and Fuller's earth. In commercial preparations these substances are mixed with other materials which often perform a further function in cleaning, and are sold as powders, pastes, and liquids. For example, a synthetic detergent is added to some scouring powders, and ammonia is added to some silver polishes to act as a solvent for the tarnish.

3. POLISHES. Leather, wood, and painted surfaces are cleaned by applying polish containing waxes, oils, and suitable solvents. These not only remove the dirt, but at the same time feed the surface with oil and provide a protective film against dust.

Floor, furniture, tile, shoe, and car polishes are similar in composition, in that wax is their most important ingredient. Originally bees' wax was generally used in Britain, but waxes are derived from other sources—from animal sources, for example, including wool, spermaceti, ants, and shellac; waxes such as carnauba are derived from vegetable sources; and montan, paraffin, and some new synthetic substances from mineral sources. A polish is made either by dissolving the wax in a solvent, such as white spirit or turpentine, or by emulsifying it by adding a suitable liquid. The emulsion type, under trade names such as 'Dry bright' or 'No Rub', is becoming very popular today both for floor and car polish because it is labour saving. The liquid is spread over the surface, and when dry leaves a fine film of wax which requires little polishing to give a lustrous effect; hard wax polish, on the other hand, has to be applied with a great deal of 'elbow grease' to get a good shine (*see* FURNITURE, CARE OF).

4. BLEACHES. A commercial preparation, sold under a variety of trade names and consisting of a solution of sodium hypochlorite in water, is much used in the home, not only for whitening cotton fabrics (*see* LAUNDRY METHODS) but also as a disinfectant and for cleaning sinks and lavatory pans.

See also HOUSEWORK.
See also Vol. VII: SOAP MANUFACTURE.

CLOAKS, *see* COATS AND CLOAKS.

CLOTHES. In his natural state, man is an unclothed creature. Our first forefathers went about naked, as some backward peoples still do, and it was only gradually that they adopted the custom of covering themselves with skins, grasses, and, later, woven cloth. We do not know when the change began; all we know is that it was in some very remote period, and that the man who first thought of putting a girdle round his waist or a bracelet on his arm was an inventor who had unknowingly started something which was to have an immense effect upon the history of the human race.

It is usually said that primitive men and women took to clothes for the sake of warmth in cold climates or as a protection from the sun in hot countries. This undoubtedly influenced the development of dress, but it was not the only or, indeed, the oldest reason for its adoption. Early peoples seem to have been better able to withstand heat and cold than their civilized descen-

Dr. T. H. Dalrymple

A PAGAN PRINCESS FROM THE CAMEROONS, WEST AFRICA

dants, and, except in very rigorous climates, protection against wind, rain, and frost was not the urgent necessity for them that it is for us. Some undeveloped races are still as hardy; for instance, AUSTRALIAN ABORIGINES (q.v. Vol. I) go naked in all weathers and suffer no ill-effects; and in Tierra del Fuego, a very cold country, the natives wear only a kind of shield made of skins, which they hang round their necks and shift from one side of their bodies to the other, according to the direction of the wind.

Many people believe that early men took to clothes from a sense of modesty. It is probable, however, that this feeling arose only after clothes were generally adopted, and not before. Modesty is a matter of custom and tradition (*see* SOCIAL ENVIRONMENT). Its demands vary from age to age and from country to country. Where all go naked, no one is ashamed, and it is only when most are covered that it seems indecent to be otherwise. In ancient Egypt the well-to-do customarily wore clothes, but the poor did not, and no one thought any the worse of them because of it. Even slaves in great houses frequently waited naked upon their masters. On the other hand, the Chinese, until quite recently, considered it shocking to expose the feet; and, until ATATÜRK's sweeping social reforms (q.v. Vol. V) after the First World War, no respectable Turkish woman ever went out with her face unveiled. Many Asiatic peoples today are horrified by the low-cut evening dresses of European women; and there was a time in our own history when it would have been unthinkable for women to appear in slacks or breeches. Nevertheless, if modesty was not the primary cause of clothes, it had great influence upon their development, and to a large extent dictated, in any given time or place, which were the necessary garments.

The love of adornment and the fear of evil magic seem to have been amongst the first causes of the wearing of clothes. Naked tribesmen decked themselves with bracelets, necklaces, and head-bands (*see* Vol. I, p. 153), and tattooed or painted their bodies, both as a protection against evil spirits and because they thought such embellishments were beautiful (*see* TATTOOING). In central Australia today, the aborigines paint their skins with elaborate totemic designs on ceremonial occasions, and wear magical ornaments made from kangaroo teeth upon their foreheads (*see* TOTEMISM, Vol. I). These designs and ornaments guard them, as they believe,

R. Gorbold

AN ARAB WOMAN IN OUTDOOR DRESS

against the Evil Eye and the malice of ghosts, and also satisfy their love of colour and display. For the same reason the Choco American Indians of Darien dye their skins blue and wear silver or bead necklaces and head-dresses. Amulets and JEWELLERY (q.v.) almost certainly preceded protective clothing, and some scholars think that even true garments, when they first appeared, were worn more for magical reasons than for comfort (*see* MAGIC, Vol. I).

See also COSTUME, HISTORY OF; PRIMITIVE COSTUME; ORIENTAL COSTUME.

CLOTHES, CARE OF. To prolong the useful life of clothes, it is best not to wear the same clothes day after day but to alternate them in order to rest the fabric. This applies particularly to shoes, trousers, skirts, and roll-on belts, which recover their shape during the rest. Coats, dresses, trousers, skirts, and blouses should always be put on suitable hangers when not in use, and trees should be put in shoes directly they are taken off. Clothes last longer if they are kept well brushed, and shoes if they are cleaned regularly. All garments and footwear should be repaired as soon as they show signs of wear. Skirts can be prevented from 'bagging' at the seat if a back lining of some non-stretching material is stitched in from one side seam to the other. Wet clothes and shoes, especially leather and rubber goods, must be dried slowly, and precautions against moth (*see* HOUSEHOLD PESTS) must be thorough, especially with furs and woollen garments put away for the summer.

All washable fabrics should be washed frequently and the dirt never allowed to get so embedded that hard rubbing is needed to remove it. Nylon stockings, for example, should be washed through daily. Woollens and delicate fabrics must be washed carefully so as not to spoil their texture or pull them out of shape (*see* LAUNDRY METHODS). A suitable and not too harsh detergent (*see* CLEANING MATERIALS) should be chosen, and the garments rinsed thoroughly. Rain water should be used where possible. All garments which cannot be washed should be dry cleaned. This can be done in the home, but in most cases it is better to send them to professional dry cleaners (*see* DRY CLEANING, Vol. VII).

Hats and furs can be cleaned quite satisfactorily at home with warm sawdust, preferably from oak. The sawdust, which absorbs grease and loosens the dirt adhering to it, is rubbed into the article very carefully and then removed by thorough brushing.

Garments made of woollen materials, such as men's and women's suits, need frequent sponging and pressing to keep them looking their best. After the garments have been brushed thoroughly, any dirt marks can be removed by rubbing first with a damp sponge, dipped in warm water containing soap or another detergent, and then with a cloth wrung out in clear water. Any stains or grease marks, especially on the collar and cuffs, which do not come out with sponging, will often respond to carbon tetrachloride, or to a reliable commercial preparation containing this or another suitable spirit. These preparations are invaluable for any fabrics which are not washable. Care must be taken, however, not to leave a dark ring on the fabric round the place that has been cleaned, but to disguise it by careful blending into the rest of the garment. Other stains which are easily removed are grass, which dissolves in

methylated spirits; iron, in oxalic acid; and most paint, in turpentine.

After the garment has been cleaned it must be pressed. Woollen garments should be pressed with a hot iron through a damp cloth spread on the wrong side of the material. In this way pleats can be pressed back into shape and the whole garment given a fresh, smart appearance.

CLOTHES, HISTORY OF, *see* COSTUME, HISTORY OF.

COATS AND CLOAKS. The first outdoor garments were probably unadorned and unsewn lengths of skin or cloth, wrapped shawl-wise round the body as a protection against severe cold or rain. From these developed cloaks and capes, both known from very early times. In its simplest form the cloak was a wide, unshaped piece of material, usually knee- or ankle-length, and secured on the shoulder by a brooch or pin (*see* DRESS FASTENINGS)—a type still to be seen in the Scotch plaid and in the Red Indian blanket. The latter, though now usually a sober-hued product of the blanket-mill, used to be elaborately patterned and woven of mountain-goat's wool mixed with dog's hair or shredded cedar-bark (*see* PRIMITIVE COSTUME). The early European explorers of Virginia found the AMERICAN INDIANS (q.v. Vol. I) wearing well-made deerskin mantles trimmed with polished shells. In Peru, where a high civilization prevailed for centuries before the Spaniards reached South America, the INCAS (q.v. Vol. I) and their predecessors wove cotton, alpaca, vicuna, or llama-wool into brightly coloured capes and mantles, with intricate designs of animals, men, and fish woven into or embroidered upon the stuff. They were not unlike those still worn by South American Indians today (*see* Vol. I, pp. 358, 154).

The ancient Egyptians wore linen shoulder-capes with embroidered yokes over their white kilts and robes. Hesiod tells us that the Greek farmers of the 8th century B.C. had soft cloaks woven with a scant warp and a full woof and, for wet weather, kidskin cloaks stitched with ox-sinew. The usual Greek mantle, worn by men and women alike, was a rectangular piece of cloth, often with embroidered borders, draped sometimes in elaborate folds covering the whole body, but usually drawn away from the right shoulder; sometimes an extra fold was drawn up to form a hood. For riding, knee-length mantles

COATS AND CLOAKS

1. Greek mantles. 2. Medieval: 8th-century shawl; 11th-century bratt; 15th-century huke; 15th-century mantle. 3. 16th-century French cloak. 4. 17th-century: riding coat and cloak; cavalier's short cloak; woman's cloak; woman's riding habit. 5. 18th-century wrap. 6. 19th century: pelisse, 1816; pelisse, 1850; mantle, 1897; mantle, 1899; 'Inverness' with cape, 1892

or flowing short capes were worn, knotted or pinned in front for out-door wear. Roman women had a draped mantle similar to the Greeks, and men wore either an open mantle, fastened by a brooch on the shoulder, or a cloak with a hole for the neck and a hood attached.

In Europe, in the early Middle Ages, noblemen and their wives wore long, full cloaks, while peasants wore capes or short coarse mantles called 'bratts'. People of the highest rank often wore double mantles, which were square cloths with a hole for the head, often lined with a contrasting colour or with fur, and worn without fastenings. Shawls were also worn, wrapped round the waist to form a loose skirt over the tunic, and the free end drawn up over the shoulder. Hooded cloaks were long popular in the Near East, and still survive there in the burnous worn by Arabs. In the 11th and 12th centuries Europeans also adopted them, and they remained a part of feminine attire at least until the early 18th century, when long red 'cardinals' were fashionable, that is, cloaks of the same pattern as those shown in pictures of Red Riding Hood. Brown cardinals, with hoods of different colours denoting party allegiance, were also worn.

In the 15th century the 'huke', formerly worn only by fighting men over armour, became general for civilians. It was shaped like a tabard and put over the head, usually belted, and occasionally sleeved. Sleeved cloaks and capes were fashionable in the 16th century, together with the French cloak, which was long, lavishly trimmed, and worn draped over the left shoulder. In the mid-17th century, when the full-skirted suit-coat finally replaced the doublet (*see* COSTUME, HISTORY OF), it was for a time modish to go about without additional covering. Pepys tells us how he caught cold through following this fashion in 1666. Women in the 17th century often relied for outdoor protection only on light shawls, tippets, or fur pelerines, with MUFFS (q.v.) for their gloved hands. For riding over the muddy and ill-kept roads of the day, they sometimes put on an extra skirt, known as a safe-guard, over the ordinary skirt, and wore loose cloaks or habit-coats above.

In the early 19th century cloaks finally gave way to heavy riding coats and, later, to overcoats for men and to pelisses or shawls for women. The pelisse was a sleeved variety of the short, fur-trimmed mantlets which women had worn in the early 18th century. About the middle of the 19th century cashmere or lace shawls came in and, towards the end of the century, cloth capes, which fitted tightly round the neck. During the crinoline era, short jackets were often worn instead of shawls, and these remained fashionable after the shawl's disappearance.

The modern feminine overcoat evolved slowly from the sleeved mantle worn about 1870, which resembled a loose three-quarter length coat, and from the long velvet coat of about 10 years later. Although cloaks and capes, mantles and pelisses remained fashionable after the introduction of the overcoat, the latter had, by early Edwardian times, almost entirely superseded them. Light linen dust-coats were worn for driving in summer as a protection from the flying dust of the roads, and in winter long coats of heavy cloth, frequently lined with fur, were

Metropolitan Museum of Art

A ROMAN WOMAN IN A CLOAK

Terra-cotta figure

A YOUNG MAN WITH A CAPE OVER HIS SHOULDERS
Victoria and Albert Museum
Miniature by Nicholas Hilliard, *c.* 1547–1619

usual. Between the First and Second World Wars fur collars and cuffs were general, the more expensive coats often having wide bands of fur round the bottom of the coat-skirt. This, with other forms of trimming such as braid or velvet, went out of fashion during the Second World War, when clothes rationing and high prices enforced plain 'utility' styles. Modern feminine styles have still remained simple compared with those of Victorian or Edwardian days.

The masculine overcoat, which developed from the heavy riding or driving coat about the middle of the 19th century, has, with variations in style, continued ever since. The early driving coats, which had three or four capes on the shoulder for greater protection, were usually coloured, but when, about 1850, men's clothes became drab in hue, the greatcoat followed suit. The first overcoats were black or brown, short, double-breasted, capeless, and fastened up to the throat with large buttons. Long, close-fitting overcoats resembling those now worn came in a few years later.

Another 19th-century innovation, the mackintosh or waterproof coat, was only slowly adopted, in spite of its usefulness; but by the end of the century it was usually an item in the wardrobes of both men and women.

See also FURS.

COCOA, *see* HOT DRINKS. *See also* Vol. VI: COCOA.

COFFEE, *see* HOT DRINKS. *See also* Vol. VI: COFFEE.

COLD DRINKS. 1. NATURAL AND SALINE WATERS. In the 18th and early 19th centuries there was a vogue for taking the mineral and saline waters at different SPAS (q.v. Vol. IX), in the belief that they had curative properties for certain ailments. These waters were bottled and distributed more widely, and later still imitations of them were manufactured commercially. To-day, they are used as ordinary table waters rather than as medicinal drinks. The best known of them come from France—Evian, Apollinaris, Perrier, and Vichy.

2. AERATED AND CARBONATED WATERS. Carbon dioxide introduced into a drink makes it 'fizzy', brighter, and more attractive, and it also acts as a preservative and gives flavour. Soda water is a solution of carbon dioxide in water at 40–60 lb. pressure. All other aerated waters have further additions, which always include a sweetening substance. Many of them, such as lemonade and orangeade, are fruit-flavoured; others are flavoured with ginger, such as ginger beer; sarsaparilla is flavoured with herbs; and tonic water and cream soda water with mineral substances. Coca Cola, which is prepared from the kola nut, is very popular in the United States, probably on account of its high caffeine content, higher generally than that of coffee. All aerated waters have to be kept sealed, for if the gas escapes they become 'flat'.

3. FRUIT JUICES AND SQUASHES. Fruit juices,

either canned or bottled, are pure juice of fruit with a small quantity of a suitable preservative. Fruit squashes, on the other hand, often contain synthetic flavourings, and are sweeter and more concentrated and need to be diluted with water. Fruit syrups and cordials are concentrated extracts prepared either commercially or in the home from a wide variety of fruits, among them blackcurrants and pomegranates—the syrup from the latter being known as grenadine.

4. CIDER. In Europe 'cider' means the fermented juice of apples, but in the United States it means the unfermented juice, a drink obtainable in Europe under various trade names, such as Cydrax. The percentage of alcohol in cider varies considerably from one type to another, and is usually higher in the still or draught ciders than in the bottled aerated types, in which it may be only about 2%. The best English cider comes from Devon, Somerset, and Hereford, where special small cider apples are grown. France, particularly in Normandy and Brittany, also produces considerable quantities of cider. A drink similar to cider but made from pears is called perry (*see* CIDER-MAKING, Vol. VII).

5. OTHER DRINKS. Iced coffee is made by mixing together full cream milk and black coffee which have been chilled in a refrigerator. Iced tea is made in the same way, and can be served with sugar, lemon, and ice or used to make a summer punch by the addition of a liqueur. Barley water is a basis for many summer drinks. The barley is boiled in water in the proportion of 2 oz. to a pint for about ½ hour, and is then strained. The liquid thus obtained is sweetened, cooled, and flavoured with lemon or other fruit flavourings. Oatmeal water can be made in the same way and flavoured with fruit juices and perhaps cinnamon or cloves.

See also ALES AND BEERS; WINES AND SPIRITS; HOT DRINKS.

COMMON COLD, *see* INFLUENZA AND COMMON COLD.

CONDIMENTS AND RELISHES. 1. Salt, different kinds of pepper, mustard, oil, and vinegar, when added to food during cooking, are called seasonings; when set at table they are called condiments or 'cruets' (from the bottles or cruets in which they are served). Salt (*see* SALT MANUFACTURE, Vol. VII) is the universal condiment, necessary to human life, and valuable in FOOD PRESERVING (q.v.). The usual varieties are coarse salt for kitchen use and finely powdered salt for the table. The latter is sometimes iodized as a preventive against goitre (*see* ENDOCRINE GLANDS), and occasionally flavoured with onion or celery.

Pepper may be purchased already ground, either black or white, the latter being made from peeled or ripe berries; but a richer flavour is obtained if the whole peppercorns are bought and ground in a little pepper-mill as needed. The mild, red Hungarian paprika used in goulash and the still milder Spanish pimento are made from the dried fruits of local varieties of *Capsicum annuum*. More pungent varieties are ground into the very hot Cayenne or chilli pepper used in pickles and strong sauces (*see* SPICE CROPS, Vol. VI).

MUSTARD (q.v. Vol. VI), made from the seeds of *Brassica nigra*, gets its name from the condiment which the Romans made by mixing this yellow powder with must, that is, unfermented wine. English mustard, which is very pungent, owes part of its yellow colour to the addition of turmeric (*see* TROPICAL ROOT CROPS, Vol. VI); it is mixed at home with milk or water and perhaps a drop of olive oil, and is eaten with ham, bacon, beef, and cheese dishes. The milder and brownish-coloured French mustard contains vinegar, salt, and extract of tarragon (*see* HERBS AND SPICES). German mustard or *senf*, also mild, is prepared with Rhine wine or tarragon vinegar, spices, and salt, and is eaten liberally with frankfurters and other SAUSAGES (q.v.). It is this mustard which correctly accompanies American 'Hot Dogs'.

Oil (*see* OIL-BEARING PLANTS, Vol. VI) as a condiment is used for dressing vegetables and SALADS (q.v.), a high-quality oil being necessary. The best oil is virgin olive-oil—that which runs out first from the oil press; it is pale, of very good flavour, and hardly congeals at all in cold weather. Inferior oils are deep yellow or dark in colour, and they thicken and then solidify as the temperature falls; they also go rancid easily —though even the best oils do not improve with keeping. VINEGAR (q.v.) brewed from malt is best for strong pickles, but red or white wine vinegar tastes more delicate in salad dressings and sauces. Cider vinegar blends best in chutneys and relishes containing apples.

HORSERADISH (q.v. Vol. VI) appears in England only as a condiment with roast beef; but

The Goldsmith's Company

THE VINTNERS' SALT, 1569. SILVER-GILT

The ceremonial salt was used at the high table in the hall
from medieval times to Charles I's reign

in Poland it also goes with fish and stiff cubes of
calves-foot jelly, while the Danes grate it on to
salads. Mint sauce, apparently a peculiarly
British condiment, is made from finely chopped
fresh mint leaves (*see* HERBS, GARDEN, Vol. VI),
infused in boiling water and mixed with sugar
and vinegar; it is traditionally eaten with roast
lamb, especially at Easter.

2. RELISHES. Pickles, catsups (ketchups), and
chutneys are rather strong relishes eaten in such
countries as India, where large parts of the
population need to enliven their rather dull
staple diet of cereals and vegetables. In northern Europe, particularly in Britain where
much cold meat is eaten, relishes seem to serve
the purpose which in Mediterranean countries
is served by vegetables in a bland sauce or by a
salad. The pickles usually eaten with cold meat
are made from raw vegetables shrunk in strong
brine (1 lb. salt: 1 gallon water) and then
preserved in vinegar and spiced. Onions, cauli-
flowerets, small cucumbers, beetroot, and shredded red cabbage are commonly pickled in

Britain; green walnuts, gherkins, marrows, and
nasturtium seeds less frequently. Cucumbers,
pickled in brine only and flavoured with the herb
dill, are on sale in big barrels in most grocers'
shops in Germany and Poland and other cold
northern countries, where in winter they help to
take the place of fresh vegetables. Mushrooms
and other FUNGI (q.v.) pickled in vinegar are
popular in many European countries. Piccalilli
is a mixed pickle, and so is chow chow (of
Chinese origin), often flavoured and yellowed
with mustard and turmeric; in the East chow
chow is a mixed fruit and ginger preserve.

Catsup or ketchup (from Chinese *koe-chiap*,
'brine of pickled fish') is a smooth, concentrated,
sharp sauce made by combining with vinegar
and spices the strained pulp of acid fruits—such
as tomatoes, plums, gooseberries—green walnuts,
or mushrooms; it is eaten with grilled chops,
steak, or sausages.

Chutney (from Hindi *chatni*), eaten in India
with curry, came to Britain at the beginning of
the 19th century. It is a hot, rather sweet relish
made from cooked acid fruits such as mangoes,
tomatoes, damsons, gooseberries, and apricots,
with vinegar added, and flavoured with spices,
chillies, raisins, and onions. A good chutney is
mellow and has about the consistency of jam. It
should be made when fruit is cheap, and served
with cold meats or as a sandwich filling with
cheese.

Americans like rather sweet relishes with their
meat, and their cookery books give recipes for
sweet pickled peaches and pears, brandied peaches
(superb with roast turkey), grape catsup, and
spiced currants and rhubarb. This sweet pickle
habit probably comes from northern Europe,
notably Denmark, where ordinary jam is often
eaten with meat. In England it is the custom to
eat red currant jelly with mutton, venison, and
hare, and apple sauce with pork and goose; in
America cranberry jelly goes with turkey.

Strong sauces include those called 'English
sauces' by foreigners and by gourmets who
usually dislike such overpowering condiments.
One can almost judge how low the standard of
cooking in a restaurant may be by the size of the
battery of commercial sauce bottles on its tables.
English bottled sauces are made by macerating
very strong aromatic seeds and leaves with vinegar, sugar, garlic, and strong catsups. The type
is Worcester Sauce, which certainly originated in
Worcestershire, and the commercial brands

often claim to be made 'from a recipe by a nobleman of the county'. The Chinese and Japanese Soy sauce, pungent, sweetish, almost black, and made from fermented soya beans, is similar in that it is a relish pure and simple and has no food value. The Chinese have a wonderful name for their special sauce, *Mei Jing* sauce, which means 'essence of flavour'. Anchovy essence, another commercial preparation, is used with fish and for flavouring bland sauces and savoury butters. Tobasco sauce, named after a state in Mexico and about the hottest sauce on earth, is made from the Tobasco variety of chilli pepper and is eaten (in minute quantities only) with raw oysters and other sea food.

See also Herbs and Spices.
See also Vol. VI: Spice Crops; Mustard.

CONSERVATORY, *see* Garden Buildings.

CONSUMPTION, *see* Tuberculosis.

CONVERSATION. It takes at least two to make a conversation. The talk of a preacher or a public orator or a teacher is not conversation, partly because it is a solo effort, and partly because its first aim is to instruct or persuade listeners. Although conversation may achieve the same end, its chief aim is the pleasurable exchange of ideas. There are occasions when people exchange ideas by talk which is not conversation—for example, in a debate in the House of Commons. A conversation is a social activity, more personal and less formal than a debate. In theory, any number of people may take part in it, but in practice it is difficult to carry on with more than a few people.

We cannot know the conversation of any past age as accurately as future generations will be able to know ours, for our talk can be recorded and our successors will be able to listen to it on records or tape-recorders exactly as it was spoken. But, in fact, unrehearsed conversation is not often recorded, although occasionally there are broadcast programmes where a theme is discussed by chosen good talkers (for example, in a Brains Trust) or where reminiscences of some well-known man who has died are contributed by a group of his friends.

Although we cannot hear the talk of other centuries, we do know something of it from written records, even though these cannot convey the accent, the tone of voice, the pace, or the hesitancies which go to make conversation. Conversations have been reported in private Letters and Diaries (qq.v. Vol. XII), and also in public records, notably law reports which were often taken down word for word. Literary forms, notably the Drama (q.v. Vol. XII), often give examples of the kind of conversation likely to have taken place at a particular period. Plays, novels, and narrative poems do not, however, by their nature, present spontaneous utterances, but the carefully wrought work of the writer who, though he fashions the conversation in the idiom of his day, does so for his own literary purpose. The writing of conversation is a valuable technique for the novelist, for this is one of his ways of making his characters come alive to the reader. Many of us would agree with Alice in Wonderland's comment: 'What is the use of a book without pictures or conversation?'

The most notable written record of a man's talk is contained in Boswell's *Life of Johnson*. Johnson's excellence in talk (q.v. Vol. V) was matched by his love of it; he said, 'That is the happiest conversation where there is no competition, no vanity, but a calm quiet interchange of sentiments.' What is said is at least as important as how it is said, and so we should expect the best conversationalists to be well-informed and wise, as well as witty and quick with words. The testimony of their contemporaries usually praises the conversation of men whose writings and deeds show us they possessed these qualities. For example, Beaumont in his *Letter to Ben Jonson* recalls the conversation of Shakespeare and his companions:

What things have we seen
Done at the Mermaid! heard words that have been
So nimble, and so full of subtil flame,
As if that every one from whence they came,
Had meant to put his whole wit in a jest,
And had resolv'd to live a fool, the rest
Of his dull life.

The 'Mermaid' was not the only tavern famous for conversation. Drinking and talking have always been closely associated, both at home and in taverns and coffee-houses, pubs and cafés. This is not only because alcohol, coffee, and tea are stimulants, but more simply because talking is a thirsty business. The most celebrated occasions for brilliant conversation were at the taverns, the 18th-century tea- and coffee-houses, and also after dinner, when the ladies withdrew to the drawing-room and left the men over their

The Viscount Rothermere

A PARTY ON THE TERRACE OF SHOTOVER HOUSE
Painting by Philip Mercier, 1689–1760

port. Women kept the conversation at a lower level not because they were less intelligent but because in those days they were usually less well educated (*see* MARRIAGE, HISTORY OF). Conversation demands that those taking part in it, even those who are merely listening, shall have roughly the same standards of ability—like members of an orchestra or a ballet. As a character in *The Dolly Dialogues* of Anthony Hope says, 'Your ignorance cramps my conversation.' Again, it embarrasses the flow of talk if there is one member of the company who is not taking any part—not even the encouraging part of a good listener. Equally, the conversation is spoilt if one person wants to 'hold the floor', and shows himself not so much interested in an exchange of ideas as in a prolonged pronouncement of his own ideas.

Topics of conversation are all-embracing.

When they are confined to the weather and trivial daily happenings, 'small-talk' results. When they are concerned with the actions of people we know, the result is 'gossip'. Notable bores are usually limited, if not obsessional, in their choice of topics. Dr. Johnson once rebuked a man, saying, 'Sir, you have but two topics, yourself and me. I am sick of both.' All fields of human interest and knowledge can provide subjects, but as personal talk which is not informed by ideas can easily become gossip, so talk on specialized subjects without lightness or inconsequence can easily become 'shop'.

Each age and even each group of society has its own style; the laconic phrases of such modern characters as Ernest Hemingway depicts in his novels are utterly different in style from the long polished periods of 18th-century gentlemen, or the sparkling, witty give-and-take, interspersed with lively anecdote, that went on at the dinner table in Patterne Hall in Meredith's *The Egoist*. Different ornamental devices and FIGURES OF SPEECH (q.v. Vol. XII) appear; for example, the 17th century loved metaphor in conversation as in poetry, and used figures of speech which, like puns, depend on the relation between sound and sense—often much more effective in talk than in writing. The anecdote is a favourite feature, but it must be brief and to the point. Some effects depend so much on pace and timing or on tone and expression that their brilliance fades in writing. Good actors can use these aids to such effect that a dull text in their hands becomes lively.

The most effective conversation often moves from one topic to another either logically or with irrelevance, by long leaps or short steps, with deliberation or at whim. Wit is always a favourite ingredient, whether it is used to produce the 'words so nimble and so full of subtil flame' of the 'Mermaid', the paradoxes which Oscar Wilde loved, or the 'wisecracking', the art of making witty rejoinders, of sophisticated Americans of our century. Slang, informal grammar, and unfinished sentences are permissible in talk to a much greater degree than in written prose. Talk is subject to interruption, to quick cutting in and out, exclamation, questioning, unexplained allusion.

Like any other art, conversation has to be cultivated and practised; but good conversation is not self-conscious or stilted. It moves free and fast, giving delight by its themes, its sentiments, its ideas, and its style, so that all who join in the interchange agree with Sydney Smith that 'One of the greatest pleasures of life is conversation.'

See also Vol. IV: LANGUAGE; SPEECH.

COOKERY BOOKS, *see* RECIPES AND COOKERY BOOKS.

COOKING, HISTORY OF. Three quite different themes can be traced in the history of cooking. First, there is the development of the materials of cooking, from the natural products of primitive societies, such as corn and animal flesh, to the varied cooking materials of today (*see* FOOD, HISTORY OF); second, the development of the means of cooking, from the open fire of the first tool-using men to the scientific electric ovens and refrigerators of the 20th century (*see* COOKING STOVES); and third, the story of local styles in cooking, or *cuisines*, particularly of the French and Chinese *cuisines*, usually regarded as the greatest achievements in the art of cooking.

We can only guess about the origins of cooking, but clearly the primitive man who held the rewards of his hunting over the fire, or perhaps dropped them into the ashes, was the first cook. Either by accident or by experiment cookery was born, and GRILLING and ROASTING (qq.v.) were probably the first two methods to be developed.

Greek and Roman kitchens were equipped with a wide range of utensils—cast-iron pots, saucepans, and frying-pans of the same type as we use today; double-bottomed pots for boiling liquids; earthen soup pots, basins, and serving dishes; and large jars for oil and wine. In the great households the cooking staff was highly specialized. In Greece the master-cook was in complete charge of buyers, stokers, cellarmen,

British Museum

BOILING AND MIXING FOOD
Marginal drawing from the Luttrell Psalter, *c.* 1340

A 16TH-CENTURY KITCHEN WITH SPIT

Picture Post Library

waiters, and pastrycooks. In Rome the head chef would have under him a cook, a baker, a server, a carver, a stoker, and last but not least a *praegustator*, a person specially appointed to taste all food. The great Roman banquets of the last days of the Roman Empire were supplied with all sorts of extravagant dishes, skilfully designed from exotic foods to please the sophisticated tastes of the diners.

The medieval kitchen provided for cooking on a large scale. In the large MANOR houses (q.v.) the kitchen was often detached from the main building; the ovens were as much as 20 feet in diameter, and high enough for a tall man to stand upright in them; the grates were big enough for an ox to be roasted whole; and spits were large enough to turn the ox. BOILING, broiling, and BAKING (qq.v.) dominated cookery. The great iron cauldrons for boiling meat or broth, often for hundreds of people, were necessary apparatus in the winter, when only salted meat, unsuitable for roasting, was available, because most of the animals had to be killed off on account of inadequate winter feeding stuff. Diet was a question of economic necessity, not

of choosing among likes and dislikes, and the aim of the cook was usually to disguise the natural and often unpleasant flavour of the food. Some of the HERBS AND SPICES (q.v.) used for this purpose often cost more than the meat itself, because most spices, such as pepper, cinnamon, and ginger, had to be imported from great distances overseas. Standards of hygiene were non-existent: cooks blew their own breath into their pastry to make it rise, and stirred their dishes with their own, by no means clean, hands. There was division of labour among the cooks, who ranged from master-cooks at the top to scullions, under-cooks, and bellows-men, and below them the boys (or sometimes dogs) who turned the spits, and the inferior servants who did the dirty work—'blackguards' as they were called (*see* DOMESTIC SERVICE). The master-cook was an important person in the household. He had a long wooden spoon as his badge of office, which he used alternately to stir the food and to beat his scullions. He would often himself bear into the hall the first dish of a banquet.

By the late Middle Ages elaborate artistry was displayed in the presentation of food. Court

By gracious permission of H.M. the Queen

COOKING AT SANDPIT GATE, WINDSOR

Water-colour by Paul Sandby, 1725–1809

feasts, for example, were often punctuated at the end of each course by the entry of 'soteltes', elaborate confections constructed with great skill out of sugar, jelly, or almond paste, and forming symbolic emblems depicting either a legend or a topical theme which the diners would recognize. Small delicacies of every kind, highly flavoured with sharp and pungent sauces, were prepared, as well as giant dishes.

Specialized cooking utensils were used long before the fork made its way to the dinner-table (see TABLE-WARE). In one of the first English cookery books, written by the master-cook of Richard II, we read of a table for chopping and mincing, a pestle and mortar, a pot-stick, a cauldron, a frying-pan, a vessel for mixing, a pepper-mill, and a contrivance for making bread-crumbs. Some of these utensils would be found even in the homes of the poor, although in the Middle Ages there was as great a gulf between the standards of the rich and the poor as there had been in the Roman Empire. In Tudor England this gulf was even wider. In the 16th century the English as a whole had the reputation of being the world's champion meat-eaters: 'the Spaniard eats, the German drinks, and the English excel in both', as one writer put it. Although English cookery books reflect the influence of Continental fashions, particularly French and Italian styles, they show that there was a distinctive national cookery. Many Tudor dishes are now forgotten; among them, 'a tarte of marygoldes, primroses or cowslips' described in a *Proper Booke of Cokerye*, which Parker, the Archbishop of Canterbury, bequeathed to his Cambridge college. By the 17th century the pudding had established itself as a national dish, even the Christmas pudding or pie, 'a most learned mixture of Neat's-Tongues, Chickens, Eggs, Sugar, Raisins, Lemon, and Orange Peel, various kinds of spicery etc.' Other dishes were essentially local, such as the oyster-loaves or the damson-cheese of the north Midlands. In wealthy houses products imported from the Far East and the Indies were being used more and more. The influence of the Puritans, however, brought in simpler tastes in food, with more emphasis on natural flavours and less on spices.

In the early 18th century eating clubs were the fashion; many cookery books were being published, a cookery school was established in London, recipes were more precise, and cooking processes began to be described in modern terms. Samuel JOHNSON (q.v. Vol. V) was interested in the subject: he claimed that he could write a better cookery book than any existing. 'As you cannot make bad meat good', he told his fellow guests at a dinner party, 'I would tell you what is the best butcher's meat, the best beef, the best pieces: how to choose young fowls; the proper seasons of different vegetables: and then how to roast and boil, and compound.' In spite of Dr. Johnson's opinion that no woman could write a cookery book, it was Mrs. Beeton in the most famous of all English cookery books, *Household Management* (1863), who put Dr. Johnson's ideas into systematic form (see RECIPES AND COOKERY BOOKS).

The history of cooking in 18th-century England is mainly concerned with elaborate materials and often elaborate means of preparation: cooking utensils and cooking processes showed little change. The 19th and 20th centuries have witnessed a technical revolution which has transformed the whole appearance and layout of the kitchen and the apparatus at the cook's disposal (see KITCHEN DESIGN). The gas-ring and later the gas cooker and the REFRIGERATOR (q.v.) appeared in the late 19th century; the electric cooker in the 20th century. New ways of preserving and processing food were worked out during the 19th century, notably canning or tinning. By 1939 every sort of fish, meat, and fruit was being tinned. While tinned food has made for a more varied diet, it has perhaps lowered the general standards of cooking, although traditional methods of Food Preserving (q.v.)—curing, pickling, and preserving with sugar—have by no means disappeared. Freezing has extended both the range of foods available and cooking methods. Deep freezing has made it possible to freeze certain foods in the summer and to eat them the following winter. Another development, of great importance during the Second World War when fresh food was short, was the improvement of dehydration processes, particularly for eggs, milk, and potatoes.

New Kitchen Utensils (q.v.) have been developed, and old ones improved. Aluminium has increasingly taken the place of tin and copper, and fireproof glass and earthenware have made it possible to cook and serve food in the same dish. Such inventions have been adopted only in countries with high standards of living, and their use does not necessarily raise the standards of cooking, though it greatly simplifies the work of both the housewife and the master-cook. The most recent development and perhaps the most revolutionary in its implications, Pressure Cooking (q.v.), enables food to be cooked in a fraction of the time previously needed.

Despite, or perhaps because of, this enormous technical revolution, which has been most influential in the United States, the reputation of French cooking, relatively uninfluenced by new methods, has never stood higher than it does at the present time. First prominent in the 16th century, it was raised to the pinnacle of prestige in the reign of Louis XIV and during the Second Empire of Napoleon III. It became the international hotel *cuisine*, or at least provided the names of dishes consumed throughout the world (*see* Menu Terms) in the same way that the French language became the language of

THE KITCHEN OF THE ROYAL PAVILION, BRIGHTON
Coloured aquatint from Nash's *Views of the Royal Pavilion, Brighton, 1826*

diplomacy. Celebrated French chefs, such as Carême (1784–1833), the creator of modern PASTRIES and SWEETS (qq.v.), Soyer (1809–58), the great cook who lived in England and volunteered to help Florence Nightingale during the Crimean War, and Escoffier (1846–1935), 'the Emperor of Cooks', are remembered long after their sumptuous meals have been forgotten except by collectors of menu-cards.

See also FOOD, HISTORY OF; MEALS.

COOKING STOVES.

In ancient times (and still among some primitive peoples) most cooking was done on the open fire, by boiling and roasting. A pot was hung on a hook over the flames, or the food was rotated on a spit in front of the fire. Sometimes, too, food placed on a metal grid was grilled over the glowing embers or over burning charcoal; or top GRILLING (q.v.) was achieved by using a 'salamander', a ball of metal of about 1 foot diameter attached to the end of a metal pole; this was made red-hot in the fire and then slowly moved over the surface of the food, a few inches above it, thus producing a brown finish. Early ovens were always separate cooking units. Primitive people used to dig a hole in the ground, line it with stones, and later bricks, cover it with turf, and light a fire in it; then they used the heat retained in the walls and embers for slow BAKING (q.v.). Later, ovens were built into the wall or chimney of the house. Wood fires were burnt in them, and then the embers were raked out, and the food to be cooked was put in. The Roman cooking stove, which had an arched recess on the floor, where the fire burnt, and a stone stove above, was similar in shape to a modern gas stove.

Medieval kitchens, which were often in separate buildings, perhaps connected to the main hall by a covered passage, had very large, open FIREPLACES (q.v.). Glastonbury Abbey, for example, had four huge fireplaces for roasting meat in its cook-house, and many CASTLES and large MANOR houses (qq.v.) had fireplaces large enough to roast an ox whole. Oxen, however, were also often roasted in the open—in the courtyard or in a field. In the 17th and 18th centuries the great open fireplace in the stone-flagged or brick-floored farm kitchen was the centre of the farmhouse, not only for the farmer and his family but also for his men who, after their communal meal, would sit round the fireplace on high-backed settles. The kitchen hearth was decorated with beautiful local-made, wrought-iron trivets, on which the saucepans stood in the hot ashes, fine iron fire-backs, cranes to adjust the height at which the pots hung over the log fires, and 'fire-dogs' with hooks to hold the long meat spits which were turned by an ingenious pulley-wheel device. In the great chimney-places hung the hams and sides of bacon to be smoked; and round the fireplace hung or stood pots and pans and pottery jugs and cups.

The Victorian kitchen was often a much less attractive place. It was very frequently in the basement, and there the great uneconomical coal range stood, built of iron with a barred grate and an iron oven on the side. It kept the kitchen warm in the winter, but made it very hot in the summer. Coal had to be hauled for it, and the range had to be black-leaded till it shone like jet. In a Victorian household there was usually a large staff of servants, but in the 20th century, when people could not afford so many servants, these old-fashioned ranges in basement kitchens presented a serious problem.

The first gas cooker appeared as early as 1830, and after about 1860 domestic gas cookers were becoming available (see GAS INDUSTRY, Vol. VII). Electric cookers did not become practical until well into the 20th century. Modern cooking stoves are heated by solid fuel, gas, electricity, or

Meade Collection

A VICTORIAN KITCHEN

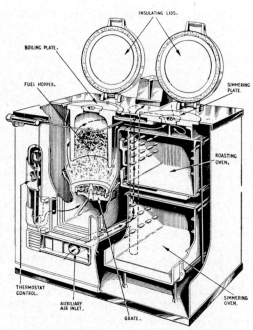

Coal Utilization Council

DIAGRAM OF A SOLID FUEL HEAT STORAGE COOKER

The arrows show the direction of the hot gases

itself (water vapour and carbon dioxide) must also escape, a flue is usually provided at the bottom of the back wall so that these gases can pass out of the oven into the kitchen.

A very important factor in a good oven is evenness of cooking. It is inevitable, since hot air rises, that the temperature at the top of an oven should be higher than at the bottom, even in an electric oven where the variation is much less than in a gas oven. But the temperature should be the same at all points on a horizontal plane, or uneven cooking will result. The control of temperature has been simplified by the introduction of the THERMOSTAT (q.v. Vol. VIII), which, when set to the required temperature, maintains it without attention from the cook. This has done away with the old, somewhat haphazard methods of testing with the hand, or putting in a tray with flour to see how fast it browned.

Convenient height, suitable capacity relative to the size of the household, and a hard-wearing, easily cleaned finish are all important points in a cooker. In Britain the height of the hot-plate is usually 36 inches—a comfortable height for most people. The stove must be placed in the kitchen in such a way that the oven doors open

oil. In the oven heat is transferred to the food in three ways—by radiation from the walls, by conduction along oven bars and baking tins, and by convection currents in the air (*see* HEATING, Vol. VIII). The contribution of each of these varies according to the design of the oven and the type of fuel used for heating, but usually the latter is the most important. In ovens heated by solid fuel, such as coal, the walls are heated as the flue gases pass over them, whereas in electric stoves the heated elements radiate heat within the oven. In domestic gas stoves the jets are usually within the oven and heat the air, but in some gas ovens used for commercial baking the jets are placed between the inner and outer walls of the oven, and heat it in much the same way as the flue gases of the solid fuel stove. The oven of the oil stove is usually of much lighter construction than the other three, and is not usually insulated as they are. It is heated by burners, which can also be used for boiling purposes. In all types of oven ventilation is necessary to allow steam given out during cooking to escape. A ventilation vent is usually placed in the door of the solid fuel, electric, and oil stoves, but in the gas oven, where the need for ventilation is greater because the products of combustion of the gas

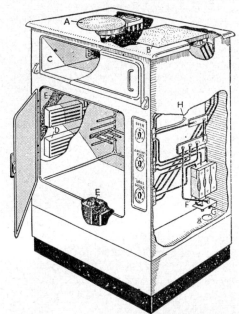

Electrical Assoc. for Women

DIAGRAM OF AN ELECTRIC COOKER SHOWING THE WIRING

A. Boiling plate. B. Grill boiler. C. Warming cupboard. D. Oven heating elements. E. Insulating material. F. Fuses. G. Main cable entry. H. Thermostat

A GAS COOKER

Gas Council

The grill is at eye level, the burners light automatically, and the oven is thermostatically controlled. Plates can be warmed in the drawer beneath the oven

conveniently, and as much natural and artificial light as possible is admitted. It must not be so placed that the cook stands in her own light.

Some modern stoves have special features, such as a glass oven door to allow the cook to examine what she is cooking without opening the door; an electric light over the hot-plate, and another inside the oven, which switch on automatically when the door is opened; an electric clock, which controls cooking by switching off the electric current at a set time; and a griller fitted to a gas stove at eye-level, to make bending unnecessary. In solid fuel cookers the most important recent development is heat storage. The heat-storage cooker, in addition to the heavy insulation which reduces to a minimum heat losses by radiation, has inside, near the fire-box, a large block of cast iron in which heat is stored when the cooker is not in use. Electric cookers based on the same principle are also available, their value lying in the fact that current for them is used during off-peak periods.

See also COOKING, HISTORY OF.

COOKING UTENSILS, *see* KITCHEN UTENSILS.

CORSETS, *see* FOUNDATION GARMENTS.

COSMETICS, HISTORY OF. It is probable that the first primitive effort to paint the face was made for the purpose of frightening the enemy or of propitiating the gods. But, at least as early as 2000 B.C., we find cosmetics used by the ancient Egyptians for the purpose of enhancing personal beauty according to the fashions of the time. The Egyptian lady painted her eyebrows and added a thick dark line under each eye, but this was only the beginning. There were different eye-paints for different seasons of the year. Rouge was used on cheeks and lips, and the finger-nails and toe-nails were stained a reddish yellow with henna.

The Hebrews when they marched out of Egypt took with them many of the practices they had learned in captivity, including the use of cosmetics. The Phoenician Jezebel is said to have painted her face to receive Jehu. The Jews' neighbours, the Assyrians, likewise used Egyptian *kohl* for darkening the eyes, and so did their successors, the Medes. Xenophon tells us that when CYRUS (q.v. Vol. V) was taken as a boy to see Astyages, King of the Medes, he found him with paint on his cheeks and round his eyes.

Although the austere Greeks were at first more surprised than attracted by Persian luxuries,

Metropolitan Museum of Art

A GREEK TOILET BOX

after the conquests of Alexander they gradually became more familiar with them. Certainly some Greek women, such as the celebrated Aspasia (*see* PERICLES, Vol. V), wore cosmetics to increase their charms.

Roman women used cosmetics and face-powders lavishly: Egyptian *kohl* for darkening the eyelids, white lead or chalk for whitening the skin, and a red colouring matter called 'fucus' as rouge for the cheeks. A patrician lady spent many hours over her toilet. The Roman satirists enable us to picture her surrounded by a crowd of young slaves of various nations, who were marshalled by the *ornatrix*, or grand mistress of the toilet, and were punished for the slightest mistake with a slap or a pinch or even pricking with a pin.

The Roman poet OVID (q.v. Vol. V) wrote a book on cosmetics but, unfortunately, only a small fragment of it has survived. He recommends, for what we should now call a face-pack, that a paste made of barley and bean-flour with eggs should be dried and ground, and then mixed with narcissus bulbs pounded in a mortar with honey. The poet claims that the use of this paste on the face 'will render it smoother and more brilliant than a mirror'. He also advises a mixture of roasted lupins, beans, white lead, red nitre, orris, and honey for removing blotches from the skin. Ovid also wrote a treatise on 'glamour'.

The DARK AGES (q.v. Vol. I) did not offer many opportunities for the refinements of the toilet, but the Crusaders reintroduced into Europe the knowledge of Arabian perfumes and cosmetics. They were used by European women from the 13th century onwards and by the beginning of the Renaissance were in general use in Italy, France, and, rather later, in England. By the time of Elizabeth I beauty-specialists had found their way into popular drama. In Marston's *The Malcontent*, one of the characters asks: 'Do you know Dr. Plaster-face? By this curd (face-paste) he is most exquisite in forging of veins, sprighting of eyes, dyeing of hair, sleeking of skins, blushing of cheeks and bleaching of teeth, that ever made an old lady gracious by moonlight.'

In France an even greater use was made of cosmetics, by men as well as women. Henry III, in the 16th century, appeared in the streets outrageously 'made-up'. Make-up remained so much in favour in the French Court that it is

Picture Post Library

A LADY PUTTING PATCHES ON HER FACE
Engraving after a painting by C. H. Coypel (1694–1752)

hardly possible to imagine a fine lady of a century later making her reverence at Versailles without her *maquillage*. In England, after the restoration of Charles II, it became customary for all ladies of fashion to paint their faces and even to wear patches. This latter curious custom lasted for more than a generation. It began as an attempt to hide some disfigurement by means of a small black wafer of what is still called 'Court plaster'—Pepys in his *Diary* describes the Duchess of Newcastle as 'wearing many black patches because of pimples about her mouth'. The craze swept through society, and many women whose complexions were faultless wore black patches, sometimes of the most extraordinary shapes: suns, stars, crescents, and even a silhouette of a coach and horses cut out and affixed to the forehead. It was also the fashion for both sexes to blacken the eyebrows, and all the rouge was certainly not worn by the ladies.

The 18th century was a period when the painting of the female face was taken for granted, but with the French Revolution, the cult for nature restored to favour the natural complexion. In the early 19th century it was men rather than women who persisted in the practice, the Prince Regent being notoriously fond of cosmetics. The new Romantic ideal of women favoured a pale face, as it was almost a convention that all 'nice' women were about to 'go into a decline'—a robust, healthy complexion being considered uninteresting and almost coarse. Until about the end of the century a lady who used make-up would be excluded from polite society. Girls were advised, just before entering the drawing-room or the ball-room, to bite their lips and to slap their cheeks hard. The real cult of make-up belongs especially to the 20th century and, surprisingly, began after the First World War when simplicity in dress was pushed to an extreme. Fashionable girls of the 1920s wore boyish bobs and unfeminine clothes, but they painted their faces with a daring which would have been considered disreputable a generation before. For the first time it was possible to see respectable women and girls making-up in public.

There has been a considerable improvement in the chemical constituents of beauty preparations, in which America has played a large part. The use of harmful white lead has been abandoned and a talcum powder base (powdered magnesium silicate) is now universal. The comparative cheapness of cosmetics has made them available to women of all income groups.

See also Make-up; Manicure and Pedicure.
See also Vol. VII: Cosmetics Industry.

COSTUME, EUROPEAN, see European Peasant Costume.

COSTUME, HISTORY OF. The first clothes, apart from the simple girdle, were made of skins by people living in cold climates (see Primitive Costume). A great advance in the evolution of costume took place when the arts of spinning and weaving were discovered at some unknown date in Neolithic times (see Prehistoric Man, Vol. I). By the beginning of the Bronze Age, which happened at different times in different places, woven cloth was already in common use.

White linen kilts, plain or pleated, with long linen coats or robes, were worn in ancient Egypt (Fig. 1). Men of the Minoan Civilization (q.v. Vol. I) wore coloured bands tightly bound round waist and thighs, with fringed ends hanging down on one side, and their women had long flounced skirts and tight-fitting jackets made of fine patterned stuffs. Minoan clothes, as depicted in wall-paintings at Knossos (q.v. Vol. XII), had a surprisingly modern appearance, perhaps because, unlike most garments in the Ancient World, they fitted the wearer and were very skilfully cut.

Greeks in the classical period wore tunics of varying lengths, cloaks or capes, and sandals or short boots. Older men frequently wore long, straight robes ornamented at neck and hem with coloured borders. Greek women had graceful

Victoria and Albert Museum

A ROMAN WOMAN OF THE END OF THE 4TH CENTURY A.D.
Leaf of an ivory diptych probably made to celebrate a marriage

dresses falling in folds from shoulder to ankle and secured by brooches and a girdle (*see* Vol. I, p. 209). Saffron-yellow, red, and white were the favourite colours, the most usual materials were wool or linen and, for the wealthy, silks imported from the East. Over the dress a mantle, which might be of any length, was worn. Both these garments were often embroidered with a formal key-pattern, or with more elaborate designs borrowed from the Trojans and Persians.

Trousers were known at an early period in western Asia, Russia, and the Balkan countries. The peoples of these lands loved colour and display, and commonly wore vividly hued kirtles, heavily embroidered, and adorned with carved ornaments of gold, silver, or bronze. In ancient Rome trousers were considered fit only for barbarians, and were never worn by aristocrats. Men working in field or vineyard, however, sometimes wore loose breeches. The distinctive Roman garment was the toga, a wide piece of cloth cut in a semicircle and fastened round the body with the straight side uppermost (*see* Vol. I, p. 409). In the last years of the Roman Empire it was gradually abandoned, except on ceremonial occasions, in favour of the more convenient tunic, a change which many regarded as a sign of decadence.

The tunic, or kirtle, remained usual in Europe until it was superseded by the doublet about 1335. In the early medieval period men's dress consisted of a loose tunic, with a super-tunic over it, knee-length drawers or, occasionally, trousers, spiral leg-bandages, and heel-less boots or shoes. Women also wore super-tunics over their long full dresses, with veils covering their heads and shoulders (Fig. 2). By the 13th century the earlier legwear had been replaced by long, tight hose, and the super-tunic by the cote-hardie, a short, tight-fitting jacket worn by either sex (Fig. 3). About 1500, men adopted the jerkin, worn over the doublet, in place of the cote-hardie. Medieval clothes were usually brightly coloured and, amongst rich people, ornamented with embroidery, fur, and jewels. In the 14th and 15th centuries very elaborate styles were fashionable, especially in sleeves, shoes, and HEADWEAR (q.v.).

The new and lively ideas which swept over Western Europe in the 16th century influenced costume as well as more serious matters. Men then presented a swaggering and top-heavy appearance in full, swinging capes, lined and

Musée Condé, Chantilly

LORDS AND LADIES OF THE EARLY 15TH CENTURY
Illumination for the month of May in the calendar of the *Très Riches Heures du Duc de Berry*

faced with fur, wide-skirted jerkins worn over doublets and tight hose, and very full sleeves, often slashed to show a contrasting colour beneath (Fig. 4). Alternatively, they wore long gowns with wide, hanging sleeves and rich fur trimmings. Breeches, either skin-tight or extremely full, became fashionable in the second half of the century. Neck-ruffs of linen or cambric appeared about the same time. Breeches and ruffs developed together; as the former swelled out widely, so the ruff became larger, to maintain the necessary balance (*see* p. 73). By 1580 the enormous 'cartwheel' ruff was general. It was starched, usually with white but occasionally with blue, red, or yellow starch, and was sometimes lined with pasteboard and supported by a framework called an underpropper. Women also had spreading clothes during this period. They wore low-cut bodices narrowing

1. EGYPTIAN COSTUME. *a.* Man's kilt. *b.* Woman's cloak. *c.* Woman's cloak or dress. 2. MEDIEVAL TUNIC AND SUPER-TUNIC (about 1100). *a.* Man's. *b.* Woman's. 3. MEDIEVAL COTE HARDIE. *a.* Early type of man's, 14th century. *b.* Later type of man's, with tippets hanging from sleeves and cape, and liripipe, 14th century. *c.* Woman's, 15th century. 4. ELIZABETHAN HALBERDIER. 5. 17TH CENTURY. *a.* Woman, 1643. *b.* Man, about 1660. 6. 18TH CENTURY. *a.* English, about 1770. *b.* French, 1790. 7. 19TH-CENTURY CRINOLINE, 1852. 8. HOBBLE SKIRT, 1910. 9. SHORT SKIRT AND CLOCHE HAT, 1928

to a point at the waist and stiffened by whalebone or steel busks, with full sleeves padded at the shoulder, and wide skirts, supported at first by numerous petticoats and after 1550 by farthingales (*see* FOUNDATION GARMENTS). They, too, wore ruffs or, after 1580, wired collars standing high at the back to form a frame for the face (*see* p. 186). High cork heels were worn by both sexes, with cloth or silk stockings, richly ornamented gauntlet gloves, and embroidered, fringed, or tasselled handkerchiefs, intended for display rather than for use.

In the early 17th century clothes became freer and less formal than they had been in Elizabeth I's reign, but they were still both ornate and colourful. Ruffs and farthingales went out before 1630. Breeches became loose and baggy, rather like 20th-century plus-fours, and to preserve due proportion, the

National Gallery

THE AMBASSADORS

The figure on the left is wearing the dress of a fashionable nobleman; the one on the right is a bishop. Painting by Holbein, 1533

tassets of the doublet were elongated into small flaring skirts. Men wore wide feathered hats over long hair curling to the shoulders, falling lace collars and lace-trimmed cuffs, ribbon garters at the knee, and enormous boots or rosetted shoes (Fig. 5*b*). Women's dresses had charming tabbed bodices with full sleeves, and skirts looped up in front to show a second skirt beneath (Fig. 5*a*). Feminine hats were rare during this century, except for a brief period during the Commonwealth, when they were regarded as a sign of modesty. Occasionally they were worn for riding, but more often hoods were worn. When travelling, women often wore face-masks as a protection against the weather. Indoors it was customary to go bareheaded until towards the end of the century, when elaborate caps became fashionable. Both men and women wore gay colours, embroidered stuffs, and lavish trimmings of ribbons, lace, and rosettes. In the troubled years before and during the Civil War dress assumed a political significance, the Royalists

stressing their allegiance by elaborate garments, and their Puritan opponents affecting a severe style with sober colours and an almost total absence of adornment.

The second half of the 17th century saw a radical change in men's costume, and the very first beginnings of the modern tradition of masculine dress. The doublet finally disappeared and was replaced by a knee-length coat worn over a waistcoat called a vest. This coat was straight at first, but by 1700 it had developed a waist and wide flaring skirts stiffened with buckram. Breeches were close-fitting, and remained so throughout the following century. Full-bottomed WIGS (q.v.) became general about 1663, the first of a long series of wigs.

In the 18th century wealthy gentlemen wore coats and waistcoats of fine coloured cloth, velvet, or embroidered or brocaded satin, with silk or buckskin breeches, silk stockings, and buckled shoes. Coats at one period were so tight that extremely fashionable gentlemen wore stays to

Ashmolean Museum

MID-18TH-CENTURY WOMAN IN A SACQUE DRESS
Drawing by Gravelot (1699–1773)

with fantastic ornaments (*see* HAIRDRESSING, HIS-TORY OF).

The popularity of India muslins and light China silks at the end of the century effected a revolution in women's dress. As these materials were relatively cheap and washable, women of moderate means were able to own many more dresses than had been possible when only heavy satins, cloths, and velvets were available. Their appearance coincided with a general simplification of styles which was one of the more unexpected fruits of the French Revolution. Men began to affect a more 'manly' fashion, with less adornment and darker colours. The plain coats, top boots, and stout breeches, once seen only in the country, were now worn in the town also. Women's frocks became narrower, high-waisted, and girdled (*see* p. 464, Fig. 7). Greek styles were much admired, and simplicity was the keynote of feminine dress until frills and furbelows appeared again about 1820.

In the 19th century masculine costume became decidedly plainer and gradually assumed

ensure a close fit. The freer cutaway coat came in about 1750. Much attention was paid to neckwear, which included lace cravats, neckcloths, and solitaires, or black ribbon bands fastened in front by jewelled pins. If a wig was not worn, the hair was powdered and tied behind with a black ribbon (Fig. 6). About 1790 the fashion for wearing the hair cut shorter began to come in, and a powder tax imposed in 1795 finally brought the fashion of powdered hair to an end.

Women wore hooped dresses in the early part of the 18th century, with low-cut bodices and softly-draped fichus, and skirts looped above a satin petticoat (*see* p. 465). About 1740 loose sacque dresses with straight folds of material falling down the back from shoulder to hem became fashionable for a short period. About 1770 extremely elaborate head-dresses became fashionable. The hair was piled high on the top of the head, stretched over a wire frame, augmented when necessary by pads and false hair, greased, pomaded, powdered, and decorated

National Trust

LATE 18TH-CENTURY COSTUME; THE EARL AND COUNTESS OF ELY

Painting by Sir Joshua Reynolds. From the Collection at Upton House, Oxon.

CRINOLINES: A FASHION PLATE, 1859

Picture Post Library

its modern form. Coloured coats were still worn in the early years, but after 1855 black became the predominant shade. The reign of the frock coat and the top hat then began (*see* Vol. V, p. 235). Broadcloth was the most popular material, though tweeds were worn in the country. Trousers, checked or strongly patterned, and always of material differing from that of the coat, superseded breeches about 1812, and remained supreme until knickerbockers became popular for sports-suits at the end of the century. Formality was the prevailing note until about 1870, when the sack coat, ancestor of the modern lounge suit, first appeared, to be followed 20 years later by the loose and comfortable Norfolk jacket.

Women's fashions during this period were more attractive, in spite of their addiction to crude tartans and violent colours, especially purple, which became popular after W. H. Perkin accidentally discovered aniline dyes in 1856. Dresses supported by crinolines, and later by bustles, were the distinctive garments of the time until 1890 (*see* p. 142), when the bustle was replaced by the bell-skirt. In 1851 Mrs. Bloomer, an American, attempted to introduce 'rational dress' (*see* Vol. IV, p. 46), consisting of ordinary jackets and bodices, but with loose trousers tied at the ankle instead of skirts. This style was so hideous and so shocking to most people that it

had little chance of success, though a few devoted women adopted it.

In 1910 the bell-skirt was replaced by the 'hobble-skirt', so tight and so narrow that it was impossible to hurry in it, and mincing steps were necessary (Fig. 8). The outbreak of war in 1914 swept away this inconvenient fashion; and from the freer styles necessitated by women's work in that war developed the more informal feminine fashions prevalent today. The most remarkable change has been the fashion for short skirts for women which came in after the First World War. For a short period in the 1920s women's skirts were worn up to or above their knees, and at the same time waists were worn very low (Fig. 9). Later, the most usual custom was to wear long skirts for evening dresses and shorter ones for day dresses.

See also CHILDREN'S CLOTHES; COATS AND CLOAKS; HEADWEAR; BOOTS AND SHOES; UNDERCLOTHES; FOUNDATION GARMENTS; DRESS DESIGN; COSMETICS, HISTORY OF; JEWELLERY, HISTORY OF.

COSTUME, ORIENTAL, *see* ORIENTAL COSTUME.

COSTUME, PRIMITIVE, *see* PRIMITIVE COSTUME.

CRINOLINES, *see* FOUNDATION GARMENTS; COSTUME, HISTORY OF.

CROCHET. Crochet work, though its origin is unknown, is probably a very ancient craft. Early knitting needles were hooked, and it is probable that crochet, using only one hooked needle, was invented before, or as early as, KNITTING (q.v.). A lady's hair net of the Bronze Age which seems to have been made by crochet has been found in Denmark. The earliest exact record of crochet work is in 1672, when, at an exhibition in Dublin, there was a special class for crocheted articles. Crochet does not, however, seem to have become very popular in Ireland at this time.

Crochet work is more suited for making openwork fabrics and for decoration than for making solid wool fabrics, for which knitting is more suitable. With the introduction into Europe of fine cotton threads, crochet work became an important occupation of nuns, who made altar fronts and other religious trappings; it was then known as 'nun's work'. In the 19th century

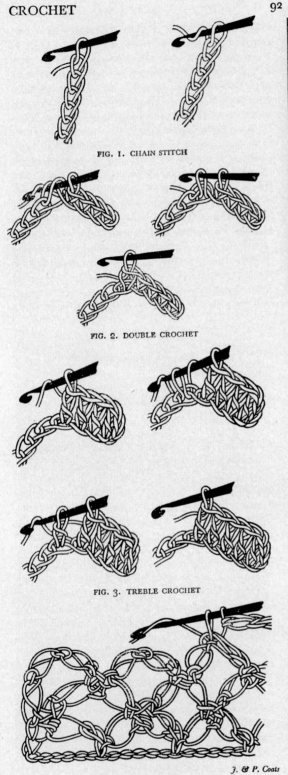

FIG. I. CHAIN STITCH

FIG. 2. DOUBLE CROCHET

FIG. 3. TREBLE CROCHET

FIG. 4. SOLOMON'S KNOT

J. & P. Coats

J. & P. Coats

FIG. 5.   IRISH CROCHET.   ROSE, SHAMROCK, LEAF, AND
WHEEL MOTIFS

crochet was reintroduced into Ireland, probably from French convents (*crochet* is a French word). At the time of the great Irish famine of 1845 an enterprising abbess taught the Irish nuns to crochet lace, and they sold their work to make money to help those in need. Crochet lace had previously been mainly an imitation of filet lace, which was woven, but in Ireland there developed a crochet lace which has a special character of its own, being built up from motifs representing natural objects, such as roses, leaves, shamrock, and wheels. By the end of the 19th century crochet work had become very fashionable in England and was a major occupation of the ladies of the house, who made tea cloths and doilies as well as antimacassars to protect chairbacks from the stain of the fashionable macassar hair-oil.

Crochet consists of making, with a hook, a chain of loops, to which are added other chains by cross links. The chain is formed as shown in Fig. 1, and the second chain can be joined, as it is made, to the first chain by various methods. Double crochet (Fig. 2) gives a solid fabric; treble is more open (Fig. 3). From variations on these simple actions can be built lacey stitches such as Solomon's knot (Fig. 4) and the beautiful Irish crochet (Fig. 5). Tunisian, or tricot, crochet is worked with a long hook. In one row all the stitches are on the hook together, and in the next row they are worked off, one at a time, until only one remains. The repetition of these two rows gives a fabric suitable for blankets and rugs.

Ordinary crochet hooks, usually made of bone, steel, or plastic material, are generally only a few inches long and of varying thicknesses. For lace-work a fine needle and fine cottons are used. Both silk and wool can be crocheted in lace patterns, but fabrics crocheted in wool tend to lose their shape more easily with washing than do knitted fabrics. The crochet GLOVES (q.v.) of Brittany have long been famous, and today very fine French crochet gloves of dainty, lace-like design in silks and cottons are popular.

See also KNITTING; TATTING.
See also Vol. VII: LACE-MAKING.

CUPBOARDS, *see* CHESTS AND CUPBOARDS.

CURING (Meat), *see* FOOD PRESERVING.

CURTAINS AND WALL-HANGINGS. Draperies for walls and openings have ranged in character from the carpets hung in the tents of Asiatic nomads to the delicate lace curtains of 19th-century England. Sometimes curtains have actually taken the place of walls or doors, and they have been considerably used in draping beds and other furniture.

1. WALL-HANGINGS. In ancient Egypt and classical Greece and Rome these took the form of pictorial TAPESTRIES (q.v. Vol. VII). In Europe, in the Middle Ages, tapestries, together with cloths painted in imitation, usually hung flat. Later, in Spain, wall-coverings of embossed leather, painted and gilt and in various patterns, were popular. Both on the Continent and later in England, patterned fabrics were mounted on light wood frames and attached to the walls. The favourite materials were cut-pile Italian velvets of bold design and silk damask in plain

LATE 17TH-CENTURY HANGINGS IN THE VENETIAN BEDROOM, KNOLE, KENT
The walls are hung with tapestries, and the bed curtains and upholstery of the chairs are Italian cut velvet

colours or in panels with contrasting borders. These were very popular in large houses throughout the 18th century. The Prince Regent's saloons at Carlton House, for instance, were hung with rich damask draped in folds, an effect reproduced elsewhere by realistic wall-painting. During the 18th century, however, WALLPAPER (q.v.) was beginning to replace the damasks and velvets.

2. DOOR AND WINDOW CURTAINS. In medieval times doors and windows were usually

FIG. I. 17TH-CENTURY WINDOW CURTAINS

covered by continuous wall-hangings; but from the 17th century onwards WINDOWS (q.v.) had separate curtains. Shaped pelmets of fabric, copiously ornamented with braids and fringes which were often made by the ladies of the house, were hung from elaborate wood cornices. The curtains, usually of damask, were drawn up in festoons by means of tasselled cords and pulleys

FIG. 2. 19TH-CENTURY DOUBLE WINDOW CURTAINS

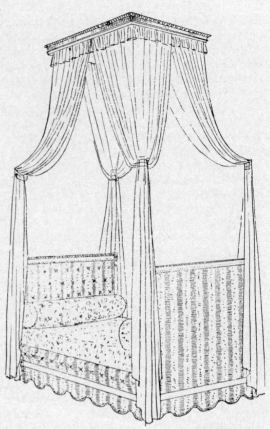

FIG. 3. LATE 18TH-CENTURY FRENCH BED HANGINGS

(Fig. 1). Towards the end of the 18th century draping, either fixed or adjustable, became increasingly elaborate, using silk, damask, brocade, or rich needlework; printed chintz or linen was a favourite for bedrooms. During the 19th century, archways, recesses, and windows were very heavily draped. Windows often had two sets of curtains and valances, the chief set being of velvet, serge, or some heavy silk fabric, braided and fringed. They were hung by brass rings from great brass poles with knobbed ends, and were looped, low down at the sides, into hooks or metal holders (Fig. 2). Inside these hung a set of richly patterned lace curtains, similarly draped. Blinds of glazed linen, with bottom edgings of heavy lace, were drawn against sunlight, and at night. Heavy curtains ('portières') hung on doors, and small flat pelmets in embroidered velvet or serge with bobble fringes were fixed along mantelshelves. Curtains of coloured beads or canework across archways were fashionable for a short time in Edwardian England. Simpler styles prevailed as the 20th century advanced. Window curtains, with no braids, fringes, or loops, usually hung straight, and were surmounted either by plain, shaped pelmets of painted wood or stiffened material, or by frilled, gathered valances in chintz, cotton, or cretonne. In place of blinds the curtains were lined and made to draw. Town windows were screened with net or ninon, either hanging straight or fully draped with ruffled edgings. Plastic materials, which are easily wiped clear of steam, became popular for bathrooms and kitchens. The traditional method of hanging curtains from rods, by means of rings sewn to the fabric, is today largely superseded by the 'tramline' device.

3. BED DRAPERIES. The great state BEDS (q.v.) of the Middle Ages and early Renaissance were entirely enclosed with fixed bedheads and with curtains at sides and feet. These were either drawn sideways on rings or bunched up in festoons at the corners. From the huge wood cornices of Renaissance beds hung shaped pelmets, often matching the window pelmets. In 18th-century beds, where the bed-curtains were drawn aside by day, extra narrow panels were fixed each side of the bedposts, and gathered valances, braided or embroidered, concealed the framework of the mattress (Fig. 3). Bed drap-

ings varied from the richest fabric to plain linen, and braids, tassels, ball fringes, and ruchings in matching or contrasting colours were very popular (*see* p. 22). In the 19th century bed draperies were reduced to curtains at the bedhead in some coloured fabric, valances being usually in white; today draperies have disappeared altogether.

4. OTHER DRAPERIES. In the 18th century muslins and chintzes were lavishly used on ladies' dressing-tables—a fashion which has returned in recent years. Regency cabinets sometimes had, instead of glass doors, a brass wire trellis, lined with pleated or gathered silk, usually green, and the brass rail on the back of Georgian sideboards often had similar little curtains.

In modern houses curtains are often used instead of fixed partitions; for many people, especially with central heating, like to be able to transform their living space into one large room, or to divide it up, to suit their needs, by drawing curtains.

See also FURNISHING MATERIALS; INTERIOR DECORATION, HISTORY OF.

CUSTARDS, *see* SAUCES; EGG DISHES.

CUTLERY, *see* TABLE-WARE.

D

DAMP. The appearance of damp patches inside a house may be caused by a variety of defects, some much more easily remedied than others. Except in new houses, which need time to dry out, it is unsafe to ignore dampness, for unless the cause of the damp is removed, walls and ceilings may become discoloured, paint and paper peel off, plaster sag, and eventually dry rot may attack the woodwork.

A proper damp-proof course, that is, a strip of water-proof material, such as tiles or slates, inserted horizontally in the wall 6 inches above the ground-level, prevents moisture from the ground from seeping upwards into the walls (see BRICK-WORK, Vol. VIII). Cavity WALLS (q.v.) help to prevent the damp from penetrating through the fabric of a building; and 'air bricks', that is, bricks with holes in them, ventilate the space between the walls and help to dry them out in good weather.

The outside of the house should be examined at intervals to guard against such faults as defective tiles at the base of chimney stacks; brickwork in need of repointing (that is, replacement of cement which is crumbling); broken or blocked-up rain-water gutters and pipes; blocked air bricks; earth or coal piled against the house above the level of the damp-proof course. Treatment for such faults usually involves repairs to the outside of the house first—repointing or replacing faulty pipes, for example.

Some bricks absorb moisture, and these can be weather-proofed by being treated with a liquid material which penetrates and makes them water-proof for at least a period of several years. Walls can also be made damp-proof by lining them inside with pudlo cement before painting or distempering them.

After damage has been done by damp, interior surfaces must be thoroughly dried out before redecorating. Penetrating damp can be hidden, but not cured, by treating the inside walls, after they have dried out, with a water-proofing liquid, or by lining them with an under-layer of pitch paper. There are also bituminous preparations which make a rubbery, watertight skin, over which paper or distemper but not paint can be put.

Damp patches appearing at skirting level on the ground floor usually mean that the damp-proof course has been damaged and is failing to work. Solid ground floors laid direct on the earth must have a horizontal damp-proof course meeting and overlapping those in the walls. A gap between these will be a source of trouble. There should also be a damp-proof course below stone and cement window-sills to prevent rain soaking into the walls. The only certain remedy for old buildings with no damp-proof course is to build in an impervious layer through the thickness of the wall—a skilled job which should be undertaken only by a competent builder.

If walls remain damp when there is no rain, the cause is likely to be condensation—that is, moisture in the air which condenses in contact with cold wall surfaces. If the house is well aired and the air temperature raised by adequate heating so that the walls get warm, the moisture usually disappears quickly. For bathrooms and kitchens, decorating with anti-condensation paint, or plastic emulsion paint which absorbs moisture, helps to stop condensation.

See also INTERIOR DECORATION; HOUSEHOLD REPAIRS. See also Vol. VIII: BRICKWORK.

DARNING, see MENDING.

DEAFNESS, see EAR STRUCTURE. *See also* Vol. IV: DEAF LANGUAGES. *See also* Vol. X: SPECIAL SCHOOLS.

DEATH, see LIFE CYCLE. *See also* Vol. I: DEATH CEREMONIES.

DECORATION, see INTERIOR DECORATION, HISTORY OF; ORNAMENTS, HOUSEHOLD; FLOWER DECORATION. *See also* Vol. XII: ORNAMENT.

DEFICIENCY DISEASES. The name 'deficiency disease' is given to a number of conditions which are caused by the absence or shortage of certain elements in our food. The commonest of these elements, and the most important from the point of view of deficiency diseases, are the VITA-

1, 2

3, 4, 5

6, 7

DOLLS

1. Child's doll from the north-west of Pakistan. 2. Pueblo Indian doll from Arizona, representing a masked dancer. Carved wooden dolls are given to children to teach them the myths of their tribal gods. 3. Doll sold at the New Year, from Mukden, Manchuria. 4. Doll from the Bolivian Highlands. 5. Pottery doll from New Mexico. 6. Japanese costume figure. 7. North-American Plains Indian doll

MINS (q.v.), chemical substances which play an essential part in the nutrition of the body. Unlike the carbohydrates, fats, and proteins which make up the bulk of the normal diet, only minute amounts of them are required; but they are, nevertheless, essential for the repair and maintenance of the body tissues and for building up resistance to infection. Apart from deficiency diseases due to lack of vitamins, such as beri-beri, scurvy, and rickets, other diseases may be caused by the lack of certain acids and minerals or of the complex substances called proteins. Iron deficiency prevents the red blood-cells from growing and functioning properly and causes a condition of anaemia, very prevalent among girls in past generations, and sometimes called 'green sickness' because it caused a greenish pallor of the complexion (see BLOOD). All deficiency diseases are preventable by making good the deficiency.

Deficiency diseases range from sheer starvation through obvious cases of malnutrition to cases in which the symptoms may easily be overlooked. Many people who, though not actually ill, are easily tired and complain of feeling 'below par' are suffering from a dietetic deficiency of some kind. Nutritional deficiencies may occur singly, but are often combined. The most serious deficiency diseases are usually found among the people of poor and undeveloped countries, where there is an overall shortage of food or where the staple diet consists of a food not very rich in protein and fats, such as maize or rice. In these countries the ever-present problem of deficiency diseases is economic rather than medical. Deficiency diseases can occur in any community when there is a disturbance of the food supply; they are, therefore, common in time of war and used to be prevalent in prisons and among sailors and arctic explorers. The greatly improved standard of living has almost eliminated them in Britain.

There is little risk of deficiency diseases so long as a reasonably balanced and varied diet is taken (see NUTRITION). It is possible, however, to have too much of certain vitamins. Excess consumption of vitamin pills and extracts (especially of vitamin D) may lead to a condition quite as serious as that which they were designed to cure.

See also VITAMINS; NUTRITION.

DENTISTRY. Primitive peoples look upon teeth with special veneration, and, indeed, teeth have been the subject of many superstitions even among civilized races. This may be due to the belief that they are endowed with some special 'life-force', a belief which has arisen because the teeth are the most indestructible part of the human body.

There is ample evidence that dental disease was recognized very early in historical times. Babylonian texts dating from about 3000 B.C. contain references to 'worms' in the teeth, and if for 'worms' we substitute 'bacteria' the ancient observers were not so far out in their ideas about the cause of dental sepsis and decay.

There were specialists for diseases of the teeth in ancient Egypt, and a famous medical text of about 1500 B.C., the *Ebers Papyrus*, contains

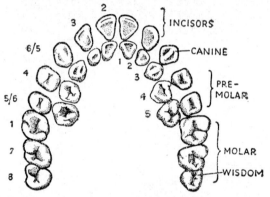

DIAGRAM OF TEETH

The inner ones are the milk teeth. The numbers give the order in which they are cut, the milk teeth between the ages of 6 months and 2½ years, and the second teeth between 5 and 22 years

a great many prescriptions for diseases of the teeth and gums. But although the jaws of Egyptian mummies provide much evidence of disease, there is no instance of any preventive or restorative work having been performed. The Etruscans, on the other hand, had reached a high level in dental surgery by the 9th century B.C., and several examples of their work have survived. One of these consists of six lower teeth bound together with gold wire, and in another specimen a calf's tooth has been used as a substitute for a human one.

Dentistry was highly developed in ancient India. The Hindu writings show considerable knowledge of the anatomy of the teeth and jaws, many dental instruments are illustrated, and there are descriptions of the operations of extraction, scaling, and filling, and also of the fitting of artificial teeth. There are not many references to dental surgery in China, but the famous traveller, MARCO POLO (q.v. Vol. V), who visited the land of Cathay about 1280, mentions that it was customary for men and women to cover their teeth with thin plates of gold.

Dental disease was prevalent in Greece and Rome, and there are many references to it in classical writings. Aristotle made some valuable contributions to dental anatomy, but he made strange errors, as when he stated that men have more teeth than women. Celsus in the 1st century A.D. describes the wiring of loose teeth. The Arab surgeons of the Middle Ages devised a number of dental instruments; Ablucasis, in the 10th century, describes the making of artificial teeth from the bones of an ox. But after his time little progress was made for centuries.

In early medieval times barbers and barber-surgeons were usually the dentists, though a good deal of practice fell into the hands of wandering tooth-drawers, blacksmiths, and even executioners. People were very superstitious about their teeth and seem to have been extraordinarily reluctant to have them extracted, however bad they may have been. John Arderne, a celebrated surgeon of the 14th century, recommended rubbing an aching tooth with the gum of ivy or with the fat of a green frog. One of the earliest references to dentistry as a profession is in 1400 when Henry IV made a grant of sixpence a day to Matthew Flint, 'tooth-drawer in our city of London', on the condition that he would attend the poor without further charge. Some advance was made in the 16th century, especially by French surgeons who devoted much attention to the making of artificial teeth of ivory and of white wax. Artificial teeth were well known by Shakespeare's time.

From 1530 onwards textbooks of dentistry had been published. One of the earliest of these, the work of Francisco Martinez of Valladolid, printed in 1557, contains a woodcut picture of St. Apollonia, the patron saint of sufferers from toothache. The first English book on dentistry was Charles Allen's *Operator for the Teeth*, published at York in 1685; but a more important work is the *Surgeon Dentist* (1728) of Pierre Fauchard, who is regarded as the father of modern dentistry. *The Natural History of the Teeth* (1771), by John HUNTER (q.v. Vol. V), is an important scientific landmark. Hunter was mainly responsible for the foundation of dental education in Britain, and in 1782 he persuaded William Rae, an Edinburgh surgeon, to give lectures at his house in Leicester Square. The teaching of dental students at Guy's Hospital began in 1803, but the first separate school of dental surgery was started at Baltimore, U.S.A., in 1839.

Some dental instruments, notably the forceps, are of great antiquity, but many of them date from early in the 19th century. One of the most important of these was the dental drill, invented in 1829 by James Nasmyth, the Scottish engineer who invented the steam hammer. The discovery of ANAESTHETICS (q.v.) was of the greatest importance in the progress of dental surgery; it was two American dentists, Horace Wells and W. T. G. Morton, who first introduced nitrous oxide and ether respectively in 1844–6. Local anaesthesia by cocaine, first used in eye surgery by Karl Koller of Berlin in 1884, soon found a great field of application in dentistry.

Throughout the 19th century experiments were made in manufacturing artificial teeth of porcelain, tortoise-shell, and vulcanized rubber. From about 1880 onwards, much was discovered about the causes of dental decay and the effects of diet on the teeth, and it became increasingly understood how important a factor oral sepsis is in many general diseases (*see* ANTISEPSIS AND ASEPSIS). Röntgen's discovery of X-RAYS (q.v. Vol. VIII) in 1895 proved of immense value in dentistry.

The first British dental hospital was established in 1859; in 1878 the Dentists Act was passed and an official Dental Register was instituted; and in 1880 the British Dental Association was founded. At the present time there are more than 15,000 registered dentists in Great Britain.

Dental surgery has now been brought to an extremely high state of efficiency. The rapid developments of recent years have led to a certain amount of specialization. For example, orthodontics is the branch of dentistry concerned with the study and correction of irregularities of the teeth and jaws, and prosthetic dentistry includes the provision of artificial substitutes for teeth or for their supporting structures when these have been lost. In these two branches the dentist often works in close collaboration with the plastic surgeon (*see* SURGERY, MODERN). The modern tendency is towards the preservation of the natural teeth for as long as possible, and this aim can more easily be achieved now that modern methods of anaesthesia and analgesia have robbed the dentist's chair of its former terrors.

A 17TH-CENTURY DENTIST
Engraving after the Dutch painter David Teniers (1582-1649)

Patients, however, must co-operate by making regular visits to the dentist. In no department of medicine is there greater force in the maxim 'Prevention is better than cure'.

See also Vol. II: TEETH AND TUSKS.
See also Vol. X: NATIONAL HEALTH SERVICE.

DETERGENTS, *see* CLEANING MATERIALS.

DIABETES. One of the earliest known diseases, diabetes was described by a Greek physician, Aretaeus, about A.D. 200, as 'a melting down of the flesh and limbs to urine'. That the large quantity of urine passed contained sugar was noted by a great Arab physician, Avicenna, about A.D. 1000. Together these two observations make a good definition of diabetes mellitus.

The cause of this disease, in which the body wastes, and sugar is passed in the urine, is a failure of the tissues to use sugar normally. The cells cannot use sugar because of a lack of insulin, a hormone prepared in little groups of cells called the 'islets of Langerhans', scattered about the substance of the pancreas (or sweetbread) which lies behind the stomach in the abdomen (*see* p. 101).

In a healthy body, sugars and starchy foods, such as bread and pastry, are broken down in the stomach and intestines to glucose or 'grape-sugar', in which form they can pass the barrier of the gut wall and enter the blood. The glucose in the blood, therefore, increases after a meal, and the blood carries it round to all the tissues that need it. The muscles of the body usually take by far the largest part, but only with the aid of a sufficient supply of insulin secreted by the cells in the pancreas. In this way a great deal of the glucose in the blood is used up; but in order that the glucose should not be too much used up, hormones from two other ENDOCRINE GLANDS (q.v.), the pituitary and the adrenal cortex, oppose the action of the insulin. In a healthy person these actions are all balanced. But in a diabetic person there is not sufficient insulin, either because the disease affects the insulin-producing cells in the pancreas, or because the pituitary or adrenal glands are producing an excess of hormones to oppose the action of the insulin. In either case the unused sugar in the blood is carried to the kidneys which excrete it, dissolved in large amounts of water in the urine. The muscles and tissues, not receiving their normal supply of glucose, tend to waste away, and since the body is starved and is losing a lot of water in excess urine, the sufferer from diabetes gets very hungry and thirsty. If untreated, he becomes exhausted and finally dies, probably in a comatose state.

Since the body cannot get glucose it uses a second source of energy, fats, a supply being drawn from under the skin, brought to the liver, and there broken down into molecules about the same size as glucose. These breakdown products of fat accumulate in the blood faster than they can be used and so poison the body, particularly the brain, and finally produce 'diabetic coma', a condition of physical collapse.

Insulin restores to normal this chain of misfortunes. But insulin, being a protein, is destroyed by the digestive ferments if taken by mouth; it therefore has to be injected, enough being given to balance the amount of food the patient is allowed. Both food and insulin injections can be so adjusted that the patient can lead a normal life, have a normal blood-sugar and urine free of the poisonous fatty acids. But insulin injections do not cure diabetes; they only control its effects. We still do not know why the insulin production in the pancreas has gone wrong, or how to put it right.

See also DIGESTIVE SYSTEM; ENDOCRINE GLANDS.

DIET, see NUTRITION; FOOD VALUES; VITAMINS.

DIGESTIVE SYSTEM. The food which we eat is destined for a long journey before it ends in the tissues of the body. The first stage of this journey is in the alimentary or digestive system. The process of digestion consists of breaking down the large and complex molecules of food into simple substances which are able to pass into the BLOOD (q.v.) through the wall of the intestine. This is brought about by the powerful acids, alkalis, and ferments or 'enzymes' contained in the digestive juices.

The digestive system consists of all those organs which are concerned with this compli-cated process, starting at the mouth and finishing at the rectum. It includes the liver and the pancreas or sweetbread, as well as the long tube, the different regions of which are known as gullet (oesophagus), stomach, duodenum, small intestine, large intestine (colon), and rectum. This alimentary tube is muscular throughout; it is lined by a layer of cells, the mucous membrane, which secrete a slimy substance called mucus, and it contains microscopic glands which pour out special digestive juices. It is also supplied with nerves—the vagus nerve, so named because it starts up in the brain and wanders through the chest and belly, and the sympathetic nerve. The vagus increases the activity of the intestine both in its secretion of juices and its muscular action; the sympathetic diminishes these two activities; the state of the intestine at any moment is the result of the balanced action of the two.

This digestive apparatus begins work even before the food enters the mouth; the sight of appetizing food is itself enough to excite the flow of what is called 'psychic juice' or saliva in the mouth and gastric juice in the stomach. When the food is put into the mouth it finds there already the salivary juices from glands beneath the tongue and from the parotid glands in front of the ear, which lubricate the food. The parotid gland in particular secretes saliva containing an enzyme or ferment which helps to split up starchy foods. For this chemical action to be effective, the saliva must be well mixed with the food, as it is when the food is crushed with the teeth and stirred with the tongue.

The crushed and pulped food is pushed by the tongue and cheeks into the back of the throat or pharynx and swallowed; after this it goes out of conscious control, and the rest of digestion is an unconscious process. The act of swallowing is a good example of how complex is the mechanism in many so-called simple reflexes: the soft palate is raised to separate off the nasal cavity; the larynx or voice box rises and closes its entrance; the tongue moves backwards and upwards forcing the food into the opening of the gullet, which relaxes to receive it. All these nicely adjusted movements are necessary because at the back of the throat the food canal crosses the respiratory tract, and the food might easily enter the respiratory tract, either through the back of the nose, or down the wind-pipe, inducing a fit of choking. Indeed, a faulty swallow often produces these results.

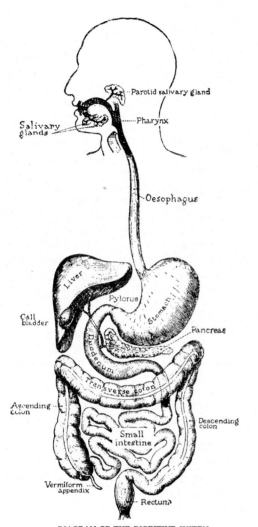

DIAGRAM OF THE DIGESTIVE SYSTEM

From Logan Clendening, *The Human Body*, Alfred Knopf

The action of swallowing sets off a wave of contraction which pushes the food down the gullet, through the chest, and into the midriff or muscular diaphragm. There it may be delayed a while until another wave of contraction of the muscle behind it pushes it through the diaphragm into the stomach.

In the stomach the gastric phase of digestion takes place by a combination of chemical and mechanical actions. Gastric juice is a mixture of hydrochloric acid and a ferment called pepsin; the former starts the breaking-down process on sugars and starches, the latter on protein foods. These processes are assisted by the churning of the food in the stomach, especially in that part of the stomach which opens into the intestine, the pylorus or antrum. Round this is a ring of muscle which opens only from time to time. When this ring is closed, the pylorus continuously pushes the food against it, thus breaking it up and mixing it.

After some time—varying from about 3 hours for starchy foods to 6 hours or more for fatty foods—the stomach is empty, all its contents having been pushed through into the duodenum, the first part of the small intestine. Sometimes, even when empty, the stomach continues to contract strongly; it then produces 'hunger pains', which are rapidly relieved by taking more food.

If the lining of the stomach is strongly stimulated by bad food, or even by the thought of it, a reflex is set up, and the diaphragm and muscles of the belly wall contract down on the stomach squeezing its contents up the gullet into the mouth; this is the mechanism of a vomit. If a person has taken poison, this reflex can save his life by enabling him to eject the poison. It is, on such an occasion, deliberately stimulated by drugs called 'emetics'.

Food leaves the stomach in the form of an acidified liquid, and enters the first part of the small intestine, the duodenum (named over 2,000 years ago from the Latin word for 'twelve' because it was noted to be 12 inches long). There it is mixed with bile from the gall-bladder and liver and with the juices of the nearby pancreas. Bile is stored in the gall-bladder which contracts and empties itself quickly after food, particularly after fatty food, has been eaten. Later, the bile flows straight from the liver. Bile consists of a mixture of orange and green bile pigments, bile salts, a fatty substance called 'cholesterol', mucin, and water. Orange bile pigment, which is formed from destroyed red blood-cells, is excreted by the liver; on its way to the duodenum it is oxidized to green bile, and is further changed as it passes down the gut into a brown pigment which colours the excrement from the bowels. The function of the bile salts is to split up the fat globules in the food, so that they can be more easily absorbed into the blood.

If the bile duct becomes blocked, for example, by gall-stones, the bile pigments accumulate in the blood and then seep into the tissues, causing jaundice. This is particularly easy to detect in the skin and the whites of the eyes, and may vary from a daffodil yellow to a deep green if green bile has been forced back into the blood.

The pancreas secretes an alkaline juice which contains three powerful enzymes, one for the digestion of each of the three main types of food, proteins, fats, and carbohydrates (starches and sugars). The pancreas is also the source of the important substance 'insulin', which it secretes not into the intestine but into the blood, where it is essential in the breaking up of sugar into glucose. When the pancreas, through disease or injury, is unable to supply sufficient insulin for the purpose, the resulting condition is known as DIABETES (q.v.).

When food passes from the duodenum to the small intestine it is very nearly fit for absorption into the body tissues. The final stage of mixing takes place in the small intestine, where another group of enzymes completes the process of digestion. The products are then absorbed from several feet of coiling gut. These coils are continually writhing and contracting so as to continue that mechanical mixing process which is so important a part of each stage of digestion and must accompany the chemical action of the enzymes. In the meantime the liquefied food mass is steadily pushed on until, about 6 hours after a meal, it flows through the valve at the end of the gut into the large intestine.

The large intestine or colon consists of three main parts, an ascending part running up on the right side of the abdomen, a transverse part crossing from right to left under the liver and spleen, and a descending part running down the left side of the abdomen and making a loose loop before it joins the rectum. This connects directly with the anus, the opening by which waste food is passed out of the body. In the large intestine colonies of BACTERIA (q.v. Vol. II) act on the food residues which pass from the small intestine. They split up tough vegetable fibres called cellulose, producing quantities of gas; this is usually absorbed by the gut walls, but if the gas is excessive it causes unpleasant flatulence and 'wind'. The bacteria also act on protein material, breaking it down into rather foul-smelling matter which passes out of the body as excrement. They also play another useful part in enabling the body to form essential VITAMINS (q.v.), for example, vitamin K.

See also FOOD VALUES; NUTRITION.

DIPHTHERIA, *see* INFECTIOUS DISEASES.

DISEASE, *see* MEDICINE.

DISHES, *see* TABLE DISHES.

DISINFECTANTS, *see* ANTISEPSIS AND ASEPSIS.

DISTEMPERING. This finish for ceilings and walls is inexpensive and easy to apply. It is particularly suitable for new walls during the very slow stage while the plaster is drying out and while a satisfactory finish cannot be obtained with paint or paper.

Distemper consists of whiting tinted with colour and mixed with glue size. The size binds the distemper so that the finish does not rub off. The distemper is mixed to the consistency of thick cream with either water or petrifying liquid. The mixture is then applied with a brush, spray, or roller, tools which can now often be hired by the amateur decorator.

As with any decorating material, success depends on the correct treatment of the surface before applying the distemper. The surface should be first scraped clean of loose distemper, washed down thoroughly, and then allowed to dry. Distemper can be applied to a papered surface provided the paper is in good condition; but if there is a danger that the paper may come away with the weight of another coat of distemper, then the wall should be stripped and repapered if necessary.

Badly stained patches due to burst pipes or leaking roofs can be treated effectively only by giving the whole area an undercoat of flat paint before distempering.

Cracks in plaster walls and ceilings must be

LOADING THE ROLLER WITH DISTEMPER

DISTEMPERING A WALL WITH A ROLLER

filled in. After the old plaster has been scraped away gently and the edges of the crack cut back underneath to hold the new plaster, the hole is thoroughly wetted, and the plaster well pressed in with some flat tool, such as an old knife. The plaster should be mixed as wet as possible, and a little at a time because it hardens rapidly. After being levelled off it is left to dry, and then rubbed down with glass paper before decorating. Keen's cement, which is pale pink, is often used; but equal quantities of plaster of Paris and Keen's cement give a whiter finish, though it is more difficult to use as it sets faster. There are, however, various proprietary plasters of the slow-setting kind.

A preliminary coat of weak size, applied and then allowed to dry completely before distempering, often makes the surface absorb the distemper more evenly. As distemper appears several shades darker when wet than after it has dried, touching up should be avoided until the surface is quite dry, when the effect can be properly judged. If a second coat is necessary, this can be applied 24 hours after the first, using a slightly thinner mixture.

The distemper should be applied quickly, with long strokes in all directions, keeping a 'flowing edge' and so preventing a streaky finish. It is best to distemper walls from left to right, covering strips about two brush-widths across from ceiling to floor. This should make it possible to reach the next strip while the strip before is still wet.

Ceilings dry more rapidly than walls because the warmer air rises. It is best to start from the far end of a room and work towards the light rather than in a 'side to side' direction, because small ridges are less easily seen when the light shines along them rather than across them. Doors and windows should be closed during the work so that the distemper does not dry too quickly, but when the job is completed a current of air helps to dry it.

Plastic emulsion paint has a similar finish to distemper, but is easier to apply, dries quickly, and covers a larger area for a given quantity. It has a good covering power, although for the best effect two coats are nearly always necessary.

See also INTERIOR DECORATION; PAINTING AND ENAMELLING; PLASTERING; WALLPAPERS, HISTORY OF.

DOCTOR, see MEDICINE; SURGERY.

DOLLS are small models of human beings, used in children's PLAY (q.v.). The word is sometimes also applied to pagan figurines (see Vol. I, p. 308),

Pitt Rivers Museum

ANCIENT DOLLS

Above, Peruvian. *Below*: *left*, Greek; *right*, Cypriot. It is not known whether these were children's playthings or whether they had some other purpose

Pitt Rivers Museum

PRIMITIVE DOLLS

From left to right: Eskimo doll in woman's dress; leather doll from South Africa; doll from Africa made of sticks and black wax and dressed in cloth and beads

Anthony Panting

A DUTCH DOLL

marionettes and PUPPETS (q.v. Vol. IX), or to souvenirs dressed in national costume. Sometimes the significance of dolls is made clear in ceremonies at national festivities. A good example is in present-day Japan at the traditional annual Girls' Festival on 3 March, when womanly character is portrayed through children's care of dolls, or at the Boys' Festival in May, when the dolls represent famous warriors (*see* JAPANESE Vol. I).

Some play dolls have come down to us in shapes which once were those of semi-religious objects or totems. The 'dolls' found in Egyptian tombs buried together with small children may have been religious objects, not playthings. But ancient Greeks and Romans had play dolls, some of which can still be seen in museums. The oldest known 'dolls'—and most prized by collectors—are baked clay figures of some 3,000 years B.C., such as those unearthed at Mohenjodaro in north-west India (*see* INDIAN CIVILIZATIONS, Vol. I).

Dolls have varied greatly in appearance, design, material, and process of manufacture according to the cultures and the climates which have produced them. The oldest surviving examples have remained intact largely because they are made from very durable substances, such as beads, terracotta, glazed clay, or seasoned wood. Most of those made from hair, straw, papyrus, linen, or other fabrics decomposed when they were buried. Among primitive societies, dolls are usually made of various kinds of wood, but also of cured skins, corn-husks, pine-bark, feathers, and of some straws, reeds, and cane. These are sometimes crude effigies, fashioned in a single piece, often ugly to a European eye (*see* Colour Plate, opp. p. 96).

In Europe, in the last two centuries, a great variety of dolls have been made in many different materials. The rag dolls or painted wooden dolls made from soft woods of the Thuringian forests in Germany had the advantage that they were able to endure much hard treatment, and were often far more beloved by their owners than the elaborate, life-like china dolls of a later period, with opening and closing eyes and various devices for moving limbs and making sounds.

There have been many books on doll history with accounts of famous dolls now preserved in private or public collections throughout the world. Doll collections are very popular, and particular makes of dolls, such as those from the

Victoria and Albert Museum

ENGLISH PAINTED WOODEN DOLL, EARLY 18TH CENTURY

Anthony Panting

FRENCH DOLL MADE IN THE JUMEAU FACTORY, EARLY
19TH CENTURY

Anthony Panting

ENGLISH DOLL DRESSED AS A DUCHESS, EARLY 20TH CENTURY

London Museum

DOLL IN A VELVET JACKET OVER A BUSTLE
DRESS, 1880

Jumeau factory in France of the 18th and 19th centuries, have special value. A very important doll collection is at the Wenham Museum, Massachusetts, U.S.A.

See also Vol. IX: Toys, History of.

DOLLS' HOUSES. Examples of dolls' houses were extremely rare before 1700, and until the 19th century they were not children's toys, but elaborate pieces of cabinet-making with glass fronts, used to house ornamental figurines. Many carved and turned pieces of so-called 'doll's furniture' were probably designed as travellers' samples and were carried by merchants, notably from Holland; and the miniature and superbly wrought 'silver toys' of the 17th, 18th, and 19th centuries were replicas of household effects, never intended for children's play.

During the reign of Queen Victoria, many German ideas were introduced into England, among them the accepted idea that little girls should learn housecraft and mothercraft from dolls'-house play. Such play naturally led to the invention of all kinds of games dramatizing the grown-up world, and these games created a great demand for dolls' houses, doll accessories, clothes, furniture, utensils, vehicles, and even miniature picture-books. Examples of Queen Victoria's own remarkable doll-dressing may be seen in the Royal Room of the London Museum.

A later importation to Britain from Germany was a doll's house of a much less expensive kind, known as a 'Nuremberg kitchen'. It was at first just a single room with pots and pans designed to encourage cooking games. Later, new elaborate equipment was added; and soon there came on the market realistic models of glassware, crockery, cutlery, silverware, ornaments, period

Victoria and Albert Museum

AN 18TH-CENTURY DOLL'S HOUSE

furniture, nursery items, baby carriages, bassinets— every conceivable imitation of domestic objects. These produced a demand for dolls' houses in which the rooms were differentiated. A doll's house, usually of a box shape, with doors which opened to reveal four or six rooms furnished as kitchens, living-rooms, and bedrooms was a regular piece of equipment of a Victorian or Edwardian NURSERY (q.v.).

Victoria and Albert Museum

A NUREMBERG KITCHEN IN A DOLL'S HOUSE MADE IN 1673

English dolls' houses are interesting not only as playthings but also as reflections of changing architectural styles in dwellings. There are examples of dolls' houses of the Queen Anne, Georgian, Regency, Victorian, and Edwardian periods on view at such museums as the Victoria and Albert, Bethnal Green, and Gunnersbury Park Museums, London; the Castle Museum, York; and the Alton Museum, Hampshire. Some of these houses, completely furnished, have been bequeathed by families of the neighbourhood. A famous doll's house is that designed by Sir Edwin Lutyens, and presented in 1924 to the late Queen Mary (herself a devoted collector) as a token of national goodwill. This is now at Windsor Castle.

See also Vol. IX: TOYS, HISTORY OF.

DOMESTIC SCIENCE TRAINING. 1. In

Britain all instruction in the domestic arts took place in the home until about 80 years ago. Then, as the result of cookery lectures and demonstrations given at the Third International Exhibition, the National Training School of Cookery was established. Soon more colleges began to appear throughout the country, at first providing only a few months' course in cookery, but soon also including laundrywork, housewifery, and needlework. Later, the course was extended to 2 years. The early courses were designed mainly for teachers, but very soon short courses were also available for housewives. Most of these colleges were founded by individuals or voluntary societies but have now become part of the national system of education and, like State schools, are controlled by the local authority.

Today, training ranges from scientific courses in universities to the more vocational ones in training colleges and TECHNICAL COLLEGES (q.v. Vol. X). Instruction may be whole time and residential, or part-time including evening classes (see ADULT EDUCATION, Vol. X). A student who has taken any one of the recognized courses is certain of a wide choice of employment.

2. UNIVERSITY DEGREE COURSES. The degrees in the United Kingdom are the B.Sc. (Household Science) and the B.Sc. (Nutrition) of London University, and the B.Sc. (Domestic Science) of Bristol University. Students must comply with the normal entry requirements prescribed by those universities. The courses, which cover a period of 3 years, include chemistry, physiology, nutrition, physics, and biology, in addition to practical and experimental work in cookery, laundrywork, and housewifery.

Degree courses in domestic science are also available in many colleges in the United States and in Canada, and also in the University of Otago, New Zealand. In Australia, and in several countries in Europe, there is a move towards creating degree courses.

Degree courses may lead to research and experimental work for industrial concerns and government departments, advisory and research work on the problems of NUTRITION (q.v.), or posts in catering and institutional management as managers, organizers, and inspectors. A degree is a valuable qualification for teaching, but needs to be supplemented by a year's training for the Diploma in Education (*see* TEACHERS, Section 2, Vol. X). Most students who wish to take up teaching, however, go to a special Teachers' Training College where they take a 3 years' course not only in their craft but also in English and the principles of teaching.

3. VOCATIONAL TRAINING. Courses designed to prepare students for a definite career may place emphasis on the craft side, as in the courses for cooks, the administrative side, as in the training for catering and institutional management (*see* CATERING INDUSTRY, Vol. VII), or the application of science to maintaining health, as in the diplomas for dietetics. These courses are held mainly in technical colleges, but other bodies, including universities and training colleges, also arrange courses for some parts of the work.

(*a*) *Catering and Institutional Management.* In both technical and training colleges students who have a General Certificate of Education may prepare for the certificate of the Institutional Management Association. For 2 years they study cookery, catering, and nutrition, book-keeping, business affairs, laundry-work, household management, needlework, upholstery, physiology, hygiene, first aid, home nursing, and English; then they must do a year's practical work in an approved establishment before they can receive their certificate. A similar course, but including more science, is available at Queen Elizabeth College, University of London. Other catering courses, usually available at technical colleges, prepare students for the examinations of the City and Guilds of London Institute.

Students who have completed any of these courses are qualified to undertake catering in industrial and school canteens, or in residential institutions such as colleges, hospitals, boarding schools, and hostels. As domestic bursars or housekeepers, they probably have responsibility not only for catering but for all the domestic arrangements of the institution.

(*b*) *Dietetics.* Dietitians are trained to apply the principles of NUTRITION (q.v.) to diets suitable either for the healthy or for the sick. All courses in dietetics demand as entry qualifications a suitable university degree, or a teacher's certificate in domestic science, or a certificate of the Institutional Management Association, or State Registration in Nursing. The courses take from a year to 18 months, one half of the time being spent in gaining practical experience in a therapeutic department of a hospital. Students who qualify may practise as therapeutic dietitians in hospitals, as caterers in large institutions, as organizers of school canteens, or as inspectors or advisers in various government departments.

(*c*) *Other Short Courses.* Part-time courses, usually intended for housewives, in cookery, needlework, upholstery, and other crafts are held in some technical colleges and technical institutes, and these sometimes lead to an examination and award of a certificate. Lectures and demonstrations to adults in many domestic subjects are given by domestic science advisers, who may be employed by local education authorities, by gas and electricity supply authorities, or by manufacturers of domestic equipment and food products. The lecturers have usually taken a 2- or 3-years' course in the theory and practice of cookery, laundrywork, and homecraft at any technical or training college which runs such a course.

DOMESTIC SERVICE, HISTORY OF. There have always been 'hewers of wood and drawers of water'. The number of domestic servants, their status, and their distribution have not been constant, however, but have varied according to the social and economic conditions of different countries and different generations. In those countries where there is a large contrast in fortune and way of life between rich and poor, the very wealthy family tends to employ an army of servants, whose number often reflects the power and prestige of the master. In more highly developed countries, the domestic servants are distributed among a larger number of families, with fewer to a family. In the Britain of 1851, with its large staffs in prosperous middle-class homes, one in nine of all females over 10 years old was employed in domestic service. Since then, especially in the present century, there has been a steady decline in the number of servants for many reasons: families have grown smaller; taxation and higher servants' wages have made it economically impossible for many families to pay for the servants they would previously have employed; the opening up of many other careers for young women in industry and commerce has reduced the numbers wishing to enter domestic service. On the other hand, simpler houses and an increasing number of labour-saving household gadgets have made servants less necessary. In new countries, such as the United States and Australia, the full-time resident domestic servant has almost disappeared.

In the Middle Ages the domestic work of the MANOR (q.v.) was done by serfs, who did the cooking, scullery work, cleaning, laundry, and valeting. Men of gentle birth were often among the upper servants in the houses of the nobility, and even the simplest menial tasks were not considered degrading when they were carried out for kings or nobles. It was considered an important part of a boy's education to be employed in a noble house as a page (*see* EDUCATION, HISTORY OF, Vol. X). A medieval household was a large and complicated community, and its chief officials held positions of great trust.

In the large country and town houses of the 16th century many servants were employed—both men and women. The Earl of Derby had three officers who supervised the household—a steward, a comptroller, and a receiver general. Each had three servants at his disposal, and the head of the household had seven gentlemen-in-waiting and a page. Household tasks were laid down for each servant, such as looking after 'the seller that the wynnes be carefullie kepte and the plate belonge to the same well looked into', supervising the buttery and pantry, and making sure that 'in the scullerie . . . the vessell be well and cleanlie kepte'. In the town houses of merchants the servants were mainly women, but there were also some menservants to run errands and to attend to the master of the house.

During the course of the 17th and 18th centuries methods of HOUSEKEEPING (q.v.) gradually took the form which they retained until the First World War. In the biggest houses the steward was the head of the household. The housekeeper, the butler, the footman, and the housemaid replaced the older clerk of the kitchen, gentleman usher, yeoman of the hall, and 'chamber'. The staff of smaller houses consisted of a cook, a chambermaid or housemaid, a manservant, and an odd-job boy. The chef or cook was perhaps the key figure: he or she was expected to be 'skilful in dressing all sorts of Flesh, Fowl, and Fish, to make varieties of sauces for each of them, to raise all manner of Pasts and Kitchshaws, to be curious in garnishing your dishes, and in making all manner of Pickles, &c.' (*see* COOKING, HISTORY OF). In smaller households, the cook might be expected to help with the housework as well.

The conditions with which servants were expected to be content were often very bad. They worked long hours for a wage of perhaps £3 to £6 a year. In the large households the men might be expected to sleep in the cellars and the women in the attics, often in a single dormitory; in the smaller households they might be cramped into miserably small rooms; the odd-job boy probably slept in the kitchen. This did not prevent employers from claiming that the servants were usually trying to live 'above their station', particularly in the 18th-century town houses of London. As one writer in 1756 put it, 'the valet-de-chambre cannot be distinguished from his master but by being better dressed, and Joan, who used to be but as good as her lady in the dark, is now by no means her inferior in the daylight'.

In the 19th century, when the organization of a large house was at its most elaborate, the

SERFS PREPARING AND SERVING A MEAL
Marginal drawing from the Luttrell Psalter, *c.* 1340

British Museum

Tate Gallery

THE STRODE FAMILY
A manservant is pouring tea. Painting by William Hogarth, 1697–1764

servants formed a self-contained community. The male staff would consist of a steward, a groom of the chambers, a butler with an assistant, two or three valets, several footmen, an usher, a small boy, and several lamp-men; the female staff would include a housekeeper, a cook with a bevy of assistants, a still-room maid who made the jams, pickles, home-made wines, and various preserves, one or two laundry maids and dairy maids, several ladies' maids and housemaids, governesses, nurserymaids, and so on. There was as well a large outdoor staff of coachmen and grooms, gardeners, and gamekeepers. 'The premises constituted a settlement as large as a small village', one economist wrote. 'Carrying coals, making up fires, and attending to the vast number of candles and lamps required in such houses necessitated the employment of several footmen. Every department was under the general supervision, as regards the men, of the house steward, and the women, of the housekeeper.'

The butler and housekeeper had great power and prestige among the lower servants. The housekeeper, severely dressed in black with the store-cupboard keys jangling at her waist, engaged the staff, bought the stores, and kept accounts; the butler was responsible for the wine cellar. Both had their own rooms, and were waited on by other servants; the housekeeper might allow some of the higher servants, the lady's maid, the butler, and the valet, to have meals in her sitting-room, but no one else. The cook held sway in the kitchen. Rigid rules of precedence were enforced, and the duties of each servant were clearly defined. Every morning the whole staff assembled for prayers, entering and leaving the room in strict order of precedence. Every Sunday they attended Morning Service. A girl would start in domestic service when she was about 12. She would begin on the lowest rung of the ladder, in a small household in what was often called a 'petty place', or in a large household either as scullery-maid or under-housemaid. From scullery-maid after 2 or 3 years' service she would become kitchen-maid, and so on, if she did not marry, up the ladder of promotion. The under-housemaid would rise from fourth or third housemaid to first house-maid, serving under the direct orders of the mistress of the house herself.

In middle-class houses three female servants were regarded as almost indispensable, although the man-servant in the house was beginning to be considered 'an expensive luxury, adding at least £50 or £60 to the kitchen expenses, and leading to various kinds of annoyance in addition'. It would not have seemed possible in those days for gentle people to do their own work, however hard up they might have been.

Domestic work in the 19th century had both its attractive and its unattractive side. 'Housemaids were then not overburdened with work', one writer put it, 'so that they could assist their mistresses at the toilet, a hairdresser being employed either by the quarter for daily dressing, or on special occasions. The spare time of the domestics was generally occupied in needlework.' Houses, however, were inconvenient and the demands of employers often inconsiderate and unending. Heavy scuttles of coal and cans of water had to be carried up long staircases, and bells answered at all times of the day. Brass and silver had to be cleaned and fireplaces black-leaded. There was very little free time, and holidays were almost non-existent. £15 a year was a high wage. The lower servants, especially, often had a hard life. In small households with a cook, a parlourmaid, and a housemaid there was often a young girl, the 'tweeny', who was at the beck and call of all, dividing her time between the kitchen and the house. She was at the mercy of the tyranny of the senior servants and was often hard at work from early morning, when she rose at 5 a.m. on winter mornings to clean the grates and light the fires, till late at night when she would creep, tired out, to her cold attic.

On the other hand, the big Victorian house-hold provided its domestic staff with some valuable assets. There was plenty of company, not only from fellow-servants of both sexes, but from servants who accompanied their masters or mistresses on visits. At Christmas time there would be great festivities in the servants' hall, including

Paul Popper

A GROUP OF SERVANTS IN 1886

A PARLOURMAID AND HER MISTRESS
Drawing by G. du Maurier from *Punch*, 1893

a servants' ball opened by the master of the house with the housekeeper and the mistress with the butler. Servants usually stayed for long periods, perhaps all their lives, in one household and identified themselves with the fortunes and interests of the family. The mistress of the house more often than not had a feeling of responsibility for her servants, and the young girls learnt household skills which were valuable to them when they married.

In Victorian times the duties and relations of mistress and maid were formalized and standardized by Mrs. Beeton's *Household Management* and by books on etiquette. Maids' dress was standardized in 1877, as livery for male servants in great houses had long been. One book described the appropriate clothes for housemaids and parlourmaids as 'scrupulously neat clean light print dresses, white thick muslin aprons, neat caps without ribbons . . . and though large ones are not worn now, they should be caps and not rosettes of lace and ribbon, which give a fast look to a servant and an air of vulgarity to the house where such inappropriate costume is permitted'.

Mrs. Beeton wrote, 'A general servant's duties are so multifarious that unless she be quick and active she will not be able to accomplish this. To discharge these various duties properly is a difficult task and sometimes thankless office.' In the 20th century, as alternative occupations, particularly for girls, increased, 'the thankless office' has become less and less popular. Open criticism has been expressed about the bad conditions, and consequently conditions have been enormously improved. Wages are now good compared with other employment, and proper times off and annual holidays are arranged. It still remains, however, that few girls wish to take up domestic work, and most households now, instead of having servants living in, depend on daily help, largely from married women who work by the hour. A new form of casual service is provided by 'baby-sitters' (a term which originated in the U.S.A.) who look after children while their parents are out. The most common form of resident domestic help now is the working 'housekeeper', who runs the house for elderly people or for single professional men.

Class-distinction between master and servant, or between different grades of servants, has been more noticeable in England than in some continental countries where, after the end of feudalism, such inequalities were seldom stressed. In Asiatic countries, however, domestic service is often associated directly with social inferiority and low CASTE (q.v. Vol. I), just as formerly— for example, in the south of the United States before the Civil War—it was associated with SLAVERY (q.v. Vol. X).

See also HOUSEKEEPING, HISTORY OF.

DOORS. These are generally of wood or glass set in a wooden frame. In ancient times the wood surface was sometimes covered with bronze. Egyptian and Roman doors were pivoted at top and bottom instead of being hinged (Fig. 1). A common form of hinged wooden door, much used in the Middle Ages and still to be found in some country houses and outbuildings, consists of vertical boards fixed on to a frame or simply to cross-pieces at top and bottom and half-way up. This is called a 'ledged and battened door'; if it also has diagonal pieces joining the cross-pieces to make it more rigid, it is a 'ledged, braced, and battened door' (Fig. 2). The side showing the flat, boarded surface faces into the room if it is a partition door, or to the outside of

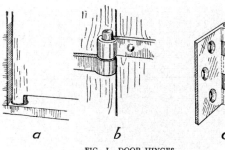

FIG. I. DOOR HINGES

a. Roman pivot hinge. *b*. Socket hinge. *c*. Internal hinge

the house if it is a main door, the cross-pieces being exposed on the other side. Medieval doors were often elaborately panelled in oak, carved with tracery or linenfold pattern, or embellished with ornamental wrought-iron strap hinges. They were set in moulded archways, following the styles of ROMANESQUE ART (with rounded arches) and GOTHIC ART (with pointed arches). In the 15th century and the Tudor period door heads were in the form of the four-centred ARCH (qq.v. Vol. XII), and the corners above the angles were sometimes filled in with carving. Outside doors had a projecting dripstone above them to protect the door from the rain running down the wall (Fig. 3).

From the 17th century onwards doors were usually rectangular, though the front door was often given a more elaborate frame. In Geor-

National Buildings Record

FIG. 3. 15TH-CENTURY DOORWAY WITH DRIPSTONE AT LICHBOROUGH, NORTHANTS

gian houses this might have a semicircular head, the space between it and the door being filled with a glass 'fanlight' admitting light to the hall, the panes of glass being sometimes arranged in a fan-shaped pattern (Fig. 4). Often the door was flanked by columns or pilasters and surmounted by an entablature and pediment. Dignity as well as protection from the weather was often given by a PORCH (q.v.).

Since the 17th century doors have been panelled. The two vertical pieces forming either edge of the door are called the 'stiles', the cross-pieces are called 'rails', and the shorter vertical pieces dividing the panels are called 'muntins' (Fig. 5). A panelled door looks the same on both sides, and the stile is thick enough to take a mortice LOCK (q.v.), that is, one let into the thickness of the wood, which is neater and safer than a lock screwed to the inside. The door can either be of polished hardwood or of painted softwood. It is opened by a handle, and doors to rooms often have a metal or glass finger-plate to protect the surface from finger-marks. The most usual Georgian door has six panels, the pair at the top being square or nearly so and the other two pairs rectangular. The panels are arranged so

FIG. 2. LEDGED, BRACED, AND BATTENED DOOR

National Buildings Record

FIG. 4. 18TH-CENTURY DOOR WITH FANLIGHT
AT SHREWSBURY

FIG. 5. 18TH-CENTURY PANELLED DOOR
AT HOUGHTON HALL, NORFOLK

that the rail dividing the lower from the central pair is the right height for the lock and handle.

In the 1920s flush doors were introduced; these have flat sheets of plywood or laminated wood forming both the inside and outside faces. Lever handles are sometimes fitted instead of the older knob-shaped handles.

The moulding round a door, against which the plaster of the wall stops, is called the 'architrave'. Nowadays metal door-frames are often built into the structure of the wall, and the door-surround reduced to the minimum necessary to give a neat finish to the junction between wood, metal, and plaster.

A house door opens inwards, and the door of a room usually opens into the room; otherwise it might get in the way in the passage or hall. It is customary for the handle to be on the left-hand side as you face it from within the room, so that when you pull it towards you with your right hand you find yourself at the opening. But, as opening the door should neither cause an obstruction nor direct a draught into the room, doors are sometimes made to open left-handed to fulfil these conditions.

In Georgian and Victorian town houses there was a fashion for placing double doors between the front and back rooms on the ground or first floor so that when necessary they could be thrown into one large reception room. In modern houses the rooms are sometimes separated by sliding and folding screens, which make it possible to arrange the interior in different ways.

See also HOUSES, HISTORY OF.

DRAINS, *see* HOUSEHOLD PLUMBING; SANITATION, HISTORY OF. *See also* Vol. X: DRAINAGE.

DREAMS. The fascination of dreams has been felt by all people at every stage of human history. In primitive societies it is sometimes believed that the soul takes leave of the body during sleep and actually visits the scenes of the dream. In general, however, the view that dreams are illusory experiences is universally accepted. To the psychologist (*see* PSYCHOLOGY), the dream is a simple form of natural expression which occurs only when the activity of the brain is depressed by sleep or by the influence of anaesthetics or drugs. It has much in common with the phantasies and day-dreams of waking life, and differs from them mainly in being expressed in a dramatic form in which the dreamer himself appears to play a part. When dreaming, moreover, one tends to believe fully in the 'reality' of the dream-world, however inconsistent, illogical, and bizarre it may be. It is only when one awakes that the happenings of the dream dissolve into a half-forgotten tissue of phantasy.

Although most dreams appear to arise spontaneously, there is no doubt that dream-activity may be provoked by external influences. 'Suffocation' dreams, for instance, can usually be traced to partial interference with breathing, and a dream of racing fire-engines may be set off by the ringing of an alarm-clock. Internal influences, too, provoke vivid dreams, as so many sufferers from indigestion will testify. Experiments have been carried out in which a sleeper is pricked by a pin and asked on awakening to relate any dream which he experienced. In such cases it is commonly found that the painful sensation has provoked a vivid dream. Thus a mild prick may induce the dream of fighting a duel and receiving a severe wound. It will be apparent that although the dream is provoked by the external stimulus (that is, the prick), its content (that is, the duel) is largely determined by the associations to which it gives rise in the mind of the sleeper (*see* MEMORY).

The sense of time is often said to be greatly altered in dreams. There is some evidence that dream happenings which seem to occupy a very considerable time occur, in fact, within the space of a few seconds. Thus a dreamer who is awakened by the striking of a clock may report quite elaborate dreams which appear to have been provoked by the first stroke. Similar distortions in time-sense may also be induced in the waking state by certain drugs, such as hashish or opium; and they are probably due to chemical changes in the activity of the brain.

People differ very much in the frequency of their dreams. Some claim to dream every night, others but very occasionally. Although it is probable that there exist real individual differences in the capacity to dream, it must be borne in mind that some people appear to forget their dreams much more rapidly than others and are therefore apt to claim that they seldom dream.

Many superstitions and occult practices have been built round the supposed power of dreams to foretell the future (*see* DIVINATION, Vol. I). Instances of dreams which have later turned out to be 'prophetic' have often been recorded, some by men of the highest intellectual integrity. Further, a few scientists and philosophers have argued that some dim knowledge of future happenings may occasionally be conveyed by dreams. Although it is well to keep an open mind in the matter, it is certainly true that the alleged power of dreams to predict future events still remains unproven.

Do animals dream? Unfortunately, we cannot be sure of the answer. Everyone knows that a sleeping dog often behaves as though he were dreaming, but it is impossible to tell whether his whines and twitches really mean that he is dreaming. By analogy with human experience, however, it is reasonable to suppose that at least the higher animals are capable of dreaming.

Theories of dreams are many and various but none is completely accepted by all scientists. The best-known theory we owe to FREUD (q.v. Vol. V), the founder of the science of psychoanalysis. According to Freud, we revert in our dreams to modes of thought which are characteristic of our early childhood. Not only does our thinking become concrete, pictorial, and non-logical, but it is apt to express ideas and wishes which we have long outgrown, and which are no longer in our conscious minds. In particular, the unfulfilled wishes of early childhood may sometimes be fulfilled directly in the dream. For example, a child who wished to go up a mountain with his parents, but who was not allowed to do so, later dreamed that he had climbed the mountain alone and planted a flag on the summit! These subconscious wishes, however, are not usually presented in the dream in so simple a form, and many appear in elaborate disguises that successfully conceal their true nature. In Freud's view, the mysterious and absurd qualities of dreams are directly due to the need for disguising wishes which our conscious minds will not acknowledge. Although some of Freud's interpretations of dreams appear extremely fanciful, there is almost certainly some truth in his view that dreams express the thinking of the unconscious mind.

See also SLEEP; PSYCHOLOGY.

DRESS, *see* CLOTHES; COSTUME, HISTORY OF.

DRESS DESIGN. Whether a dress is made to individual measurements or is bought from a store selling mass-produced goods, it is the final product of many hands and minds. There are various branches of the CLOTHING INDUSTRY (q.v. Vol. VII), each with its own clientele—the *haute couture*, the wholesale couture, and the wholesale firms which make mass-produced clothes.

The *haute couture* model dress houses make and exhibit original designs each season. It is these designs which determine fashion. The term '*haute couture*' has no explicit explanation but originated during the mid-19th century, when the now famous Worth started making gowns for the Empress Eugénie. This enterprise led to other clients wishing to have gowns made for them individually, and eventually the House of Worth was established in Paris, the forerunner of all the famous dress houses.

In London the Incorporated Society of London Fashion Designers consists of ten or eleven of the foremost designers who are elected on merit to the society. They hold two large 'collections' each year, in February and July, and sometimes mid-seasonal collections in between these dates. The Paris houses show their collections at about the same time and often clash with those in London, so that buyers may have to choose which one they shall see. Italy has also started several dress houses and is vying with Paris to attract customers.

There is a very rigid copyright attached to these 'dress shows', and no newspaper is allowed to reproduce any designs before a pre-arranged date, usually a month later, when the monthly magazines are printed. At the dress shows individual customers may buy exclusive models, or wholesale houses may buy models from which to make cheaper modified copies for sale to retail shops.

The designer in one of the *haute couture* houses sometimes sketches his or her ideas for an original model, but often drapes the material straight on to the mannequin (or dress-stand padded to the required measurements), pinning in pleats, darts, folds, and fitting lines in the correct places, and cutting away the surplus material as the work proceeds. A very complicated design may be modelled in mull, a kind of muslin. The mull pattern for the model, which is called a 'toile' in the trade, is taken off the stand, unpinned, and the pieces used as a pattern for cutting out the garment in the correct material. The cut-out model is tacked and fitted and, under the direction of the designer, is made up by a gown hand, with little or no machine stitching. When finished, it is ready either for exhibition or for a private customer.

A medium-priced dress of good design and workmanship may have originated in a wholesale *couture* house, which makes models based on *haute couture* designs, but modified to suit a wider public. These models are probably exclusive to one firm, and are not mass-produced but cut singly by the designer or cutter. They may be copied in any size and fitting, in different colours, and with variations in detail to suit individual customers. The designer may create the design, or he may adapt a gown bought from a *couture* collection, but his design will be less extravagant · in style than an original *haute couture* model. He drapes and cuts the design in mull on a stand of stock size and average proportions (these stock sizes are worked out with proportionate measurements in relation to those of the bust and hips). After the mull has been unpinned and a garment with proper material cut from it, the garment is made up, mostly by machine but with hand finishing, under the supervision of the designer or designer-cutter. The completed gown is shown in a wholesale *couture* collection for retail buyers, who may order a number of models in different fittings and colours for their shops.

If a dress is bought ready made 'off the peg', it may be one of a thousand or more garments similar in size, colour, and fabric; and it will have been through a number of departments in the wholesale factory before reaching the store. The designer of such garments must work within certain limitations of cost, using the minimum amount of material, simplifying considerably the current styles, but at the same time producing a smartly cut dress which will have a ready sale. A pattern is cut in mull from the design and used for the sample dress, which is assembled entirely by machine from a working drawing, showing seams, darts, fastenings, and all incidental details. The finished dress is shown to a buyer from a large multiple store, who may order as many as a thousand copies of it in various stock sizes and colours.

The original mull is used as a master pattern.

Picture Post Library

A MANNEQUIN SHOWING A DRESS FROM SCHIAPARELLI'S COLLECTION IN PARIS

From it a pattern grader, working to a given formula, cuts patterns in thin card in larger and smaller fittings, ready for the cutting-rooms. The materials, trimmings, bindings, and sewing threads for the garments are selected from the stock room, where 'job' cards giving details of each order are kept. These are bundled together with the pattern card and are sent to the cutting room. There a 'marker' is prepared, that is, a length of fabric on which the patterns are placed on the correct weave as economically as possible, with all designs, such as checks and stripes, matching up. One or more sets of patterns may be laid on one marker, which is placed on top of the 'lay' or pile of about fifty thicknesses of material. If the lay contains many sets of patterns, it may be divided into blocks for easier manipulation. Each block is then cut, an electric knife or band-saw cutting through all the thicknesses in one action (*see* Vol. VII, p. 109).

A sorter separates all the cut pieces either into sets for individual garments or, in some factories, into sets of so many sleeves, bodices, skirts, and so on. These are given, in bundles, to machinists, who either machine 'through' a whole garment or work on sets only. A conveyor belt between two rows of machines may carry the bundles from one girl to the next, then to the assemblers, and then to a passer at the end of the belt who examines the finished garments. Seams are pressed as the work proceeds, and all trimmings and fastenings are machine-stitched by machines specially designed for the purpose.

The firms specializing in the designing and distribution of paper patterns may employ a designer of their own, who may cut the first pattern. This is made up by an assistant into a toile so that any alterations or adjustments may be made in the final paper pattern before it is graded. On the other hand, many firms employ freelance designers who sell drawings to them, and from these drawings the pattern cutter cuts the pattern. It is made into a toile, adjusted, and then graded into many sizes and fittings.

Those patterns which have printed instructions on them are rolled off in large numbers on the printing machine, while those without are cut in piles of about 500, in a manner similar to the cutting of mass-produced garments in the wholesale trade.

See also DRESSMAKING; TAILORING.

DRESS FASTENINGS. 1. HISTORY. Woven cloth made its first appearance in Europe during the New Stone Age (*see* PREHISTORIC MAN, Section 4, Vol. I), and although no remains of actual clothes have been found, hoards of pins suggest that the garments worn were in the nature of cloaks (*see* COATS AND CLOAKS), fastened at the shoulder or elsewhere to keep them in position. Buttons have also been found, implying perhaps a type of coat or waistcoat, fitting more closely to the body. We are able to trace where pin-users and where button-users dwelt in the Bronze Age; for example, in early Bronze Age graves in Yorkshire and Scotland, rows of buttons have been found down the front of the skeleton. People living in Germany, central Europe, and Scandinavia, however, wore pins to fasten their cloaks, and buttons seem not to have been widely used until the Middle Ages.

The Greeks and Romans used pins and brooches (the brooch being a pin with a guard, generally circular, a kind of primitive safety-pin). The Anglo-Saxons practically never used buttons, and in Ireland and Scotland brooches, sometimes very elaborately worked, were worn by all the Celtic tribes for the purpose of fastening the mantle on the breast, or for closing the tunic at the throat (*see* CELTIC ART, Vol. XII). Chaucer speaks of the elaborate brooches worn in his day, and the brooch long survived as an ornament when it had ceased to serve any useful purpose. Simple pins, which were also often marvels of craftsmanship, were much used in the early Middle Ages, and were valued enough to be given as presents in the 13th and 14th centuries.

Meanwhile, buttons were being increasingly used. The introduction of tighter fitting garments in the reign of Edward I made them almost a necessity and, as they became more decorative, they were soon worn in far larger numbers than need dictated. Effigies of the period show rows of buttons thickly set on the sleeve from wrist to elbow. They were closely set down the front of gowns and coats during the reign of Edward III, but seem to have been later replaced by laces and 'points' (string or ribbon tags which could be tied together). They reappeared in the 16th century, both for use and decoration, but did not really come into their own again until the end of the 17th century, when men began to wear coats and waistcoats instead of doublets. Throughout the 18th century buttons went through many changes. They were worn particularly large by those affecting continental styles in the 1770s and were sometimes extremely costly, being set with diamonds and other precious stones. They were very little worn, however, on female costume until the end of the century. The semi-masculine clothes affected by women at the time of the French Revolution were often adorned with buttons, but there was no place for them on the flimsy garments of the early 1800s. The early Victorian bodice was frequently buttoned down the front, and from time to time there has been a positive orgy of buttons on female dress, notably in the years immediately before the First World War.

Meanwhile, men's buttons had ceased to be decorative, although they were (and are) still worn in greater numbers than necessary, as, for example, on the sleeve of the modern coat. Buttons can be made of metal, bone, and even porcelain and glass. Pearl buttons (that is, buttons stamped out of shells) began to be manufactured in large numbers about 1850. Button collecting, particularly of the beautiful enamelled or painted specimens which have survived, has recently become a popular hobby, especially in America.

Hooks and eyes of silver were used by 16th-century nobles; by the 17th century very cheap ones were in common use. They are now largely superseded by press-studs or 'poppers', and since 1925 by the 'zip', a lightning-fastener device by which the opening in a garment is closed by the interlocking of metal strips placed on adjacent edges. At first appearing only on women's clothes, within recent years this invention has been used for men's garments also, especially for sports clothes.

2. PRACTICAL APPLICATION. (*a*) *Buttons and Buttonholes.* A buttonhole must be a little longer

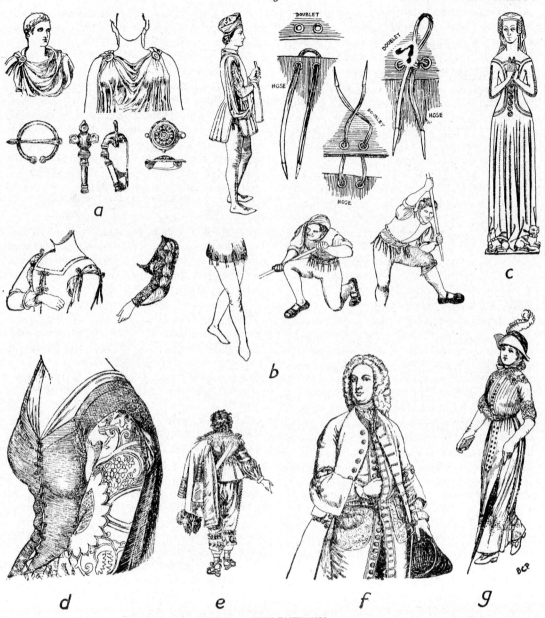

FIG. I. DRESS FASTENINGS

a. Roman penannular, trumpet, and disk brooches and positions at which they were worn. *b.* Medieval points showing how they were tied. Workmen sometimes wore them unfastened. *c.* Medieval buttons. *d.* Medieval lacing and pin used to fasten sleeve to bodice. *e.* 17th-century ribbon points round waist and knees and ornamental buttons on cloak and breeches. *f.* 18th-century buttons. *g.* Early 20th-century buttons

than the width of the button it is to fit. A stitched buttonhole placed horizontally has a round end on the outer side, into which the button fits, and a square end on the inner side to keep the hole closed. Vertical buttonholes are square or round at both ends. After the exact line of the hole has been marked, the material is machine-stitched or backstitched about $\frac{1}{8}$ inch from the line on each side to prevent the material fraying during the work. If the hole is to be worked in a single thickness of material, it may be better to back it with tape or fabric. The slit for the hole is then cut with sharp, pointed scissors and worked in tailor's buttonhole stitch with a thread long enough to complete the job. (A 1-inch button-hole takes about 1 yard of thread.) The round end is overcast, and the square end worked with a buttonhole-stitch bar (Fig. 2).

A bound buttonhole is used only on garments

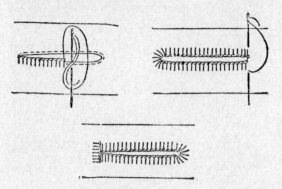

FIG. 2. STITCHED BUTTONHOLE

where the edge is faced with another thickness of material. The facing must be detached, and a strip, about 2 inches wide and twice the diameter of the button, cut for binding. This strip is tacked over the line of the hole, its right side facing the right side of the garment, and then stitched down about $\frac{1}{8}$ inch from the centre, making a rectangle with firm corners. The slit for the hole is then cut, and the corners snipped up diagonally to the line of stitching (Fig. 3a). The edges of the binding are then folded over and taken through the hole, small inverted pleats being made at the corners (Fig. 3b). On

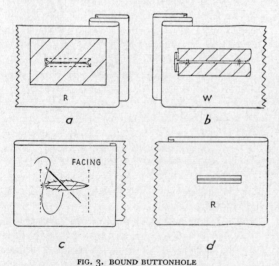

FIG. 3. BOUND BUTTONHOLE
R. Right side. W. Wrong side

the wrong side, a slit is cut in the facing, and the edges are turned in over the binding and hemmed to it (Fig. 3c). On the right side, the binding should meet neatly on the opening with an equal width on each side (Fig. 3d).

The exact place for the button must be marked carefully, and if the material to which the button is to be attached is single, a piece of tape or fabric should be fixed at the back to reinforce it. The button must be sewn on with a shank (threads between the button and the material), long or short according to the thickness of the material. When enough threads between the button and the material have been sewn, the cotton should be wound several times round the shank to strengthen it and make it compact. On heavy fabrics buttons are some-times held in place by small buttons on the wrong side. Eyelet holes, made with a stiletto and overcast or buttonholed over a running stitch, are often used for buttons with their own shanks or for belts.

(b) *Hooks and Eyes.* Loop eyes are used on meeting edges such as petersham belts, and bar eyes on overlapping edges. The loops of both hooks and eyes are attached to the garment by blanket stitching, and a neat finish can be ob-tained by covering the loops of the hooks with bias tape. Press fasteners are blanket stitched or overcast into position, the part with the pro-jection being fixed to the overlap of the garment and that with the hole to the underlap.

(c) *Zip fasteners.* These can be sewn into the garment so that they are concealed or allowed to show for decoration. The zip, which should be slightly longer than the opening, should be tacked into place in the closed position, and a large enough turning made in the material to give a firm edge. After it has been stitched, the ends of the zip at the back should be neatened with a piece of tape and the edges oversewn together.

(d) *Other fastenings.* Cords, made of any num-ber of threads twisted together and perhaps finished with tassels, can be used for fastenings. Loops, made out of several strands of thread loop-stitched together or a narrow strip of fabric cut on the cross, are sometimes used at or under the edge of an opening instead of buttonholes. Tapes attached to the wrong side of the garment used to be common forms of fastening on under-garments, but are much less used now.

See also COSTUME, HISTORY OF; SEWING.

DRESSMAKING. **1.** *Fabrics.* Materials are made in different widths, from 18 inches to 54 inches for woollens and tweeds, and up to 72 inches for worsteds; silks, cottons, and linens are usually 36 inches wide. Stiff fabrics will not drape; pile fabrics should not be cut on the cross, and all the pieces must be cut with the pile in the same direction; pleats will not stay in crease-resisting fabrics or springy ones; jersey is more difficult to sew than woven cloth; and one-way patterns, stripes, tartans, and material with pile are uneconomic in cutting. Some materials, especially woollens, require shrinking before using; a good method is to fold the fabric in a damp sheet for a day, and then hang it out to finish drying slowly. All these facts should be taken into consideration when choosing fabrics and dress designs.

2. *Patterns and cutting out.* A foundation block can be drafted to the measurements of a particular figure, and used as the basis of a variety of styles. But most people use instead paper patterns, which can be bought in stock sizes for average figures, with bust measurements from 34 inches to 40 inches and the other measurements to correspond; smaller or larger sizes are also made. If an in-between size is needed, it is easier to adapt a size larger than a size smaller.

Instructions for cutting out the fabric and making up the garment are given with each pattern. On most patterns the fitting lines, along which the seams are sewn, are indicated by small circles, and the straight weave of the fabric by large circles on each piece of pattern; there are also small Vs for balance marks to show how the seams fit together, and special marks for darts, pleats, pockets, and so on.

Before cutting the material, the main parts of the pattern should be pinned together and fitted on the right side of the figure to see whether any alterations are necessary. These must be made before cutting out. The alterations do not change the basic shapes of the patterns but are made by slashing and inserting paper to increase lengths or widths, or by pleating or darting to decrease them (Fig. 1).

After the creases have been pressed out, the fabric is laid flat on a table, and the main parts of the pattern are pinned on top. The straight pieces must be exactly in line with the selvage, and the crosswise pieces on the exact cross. With a fraying material, more turnings should be allowed than the pattern shows. A material

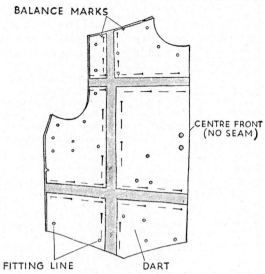

BALANCE MARKS

CENTRE FRONT (NO SEAM)

FITTING LINE   DART

FIG. 1. PAPER PATTERN OF A BODICE SHOWING WHERE ALTERATIONS SHOULD BE MADE TO ENLARGE IT

without either pile or pattern raises no difficulties, but with a patterned material, especially if it is cut on the cross, it is wiser to cut each piece separately to ensure, for example, that stripes or checks match. The cutting out must be very accurate if the garment is to fit well. Before the patterns are removed, balance marks, fitting lines, darts, and other details are marked on the material in chalk, and then tailor tacked.

3. *Fitting and assembling.* First, all darts and pleats are tacked and gathers run in; then the side seams are tacked and the bodice attached to the skirt. At this point the garment is tried on, the right-hand half of the figure being carefully fitted, and any alterations pinned. The alterations are then tacked in a different coloured thread, those for the left side being copied exactly from the right-hand ones, and the garment is fitted again. Then the main part of the garment is stitched, and any facings for buttons and buttonholes are attached. The neckline is finished next, as it is inclined to stretch. Pockets are made, and the sleeves are finished and set in. (Raglan sleeves are sewn before the side seams.) The DRESS FASTENINGS (q.v.) are then attached, and the garment is fitted for the last time, and the hem measured.

Raw edges are neatened by oversewing or binding, and seams are pressed on the wrong side of the garment as work proceeds. A heat-controlled iron may be regulated for dry-pressing different fabrics; but for damp-pressing, it is wise to test an odd piece before pressing the garment itself (*see* LAUNDRY METHODS). To shrink any fullness, the garment is first pressed on the wrong side with a damp cloth, and then on the right side with a less damp cloth.

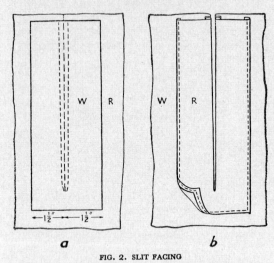

FIG. 2. SLIT FACING

a. The facing tacked to the right side (R) of garment. *b.* The completed facing on the wrong side (W)

4. *Facings* are used to neaten openings, and are shaped to fit them. A slit facing may be used for a neck or sleeve opening (Fig. 2). The facing is 1 inch longer than the slit, and 1½ inches wider on each side. It is stitched to the garment ⅛ inch on either side of a line marked for the slit, tapering to a point. The slit is then cut, and the facing folded over the edges of the slit to the wrong side.

5. *Necklines.* A rounded or V-neckline can be finished off with binding (*see* SEWING, Section 5), the V-point being 'mitred' to avoid bulk. A shaped neckline is faced with fabric 2 or 3 inches wide, cut to the shape of the neckline. After the shoulder seams have been stitched, the facing is slightly stretched on to the neckline, right sides facing, shoulder seams matching, and the centre front and back corresponding (Fig. 3). It is stitched and then turned to the inside of the garment and hemmed in place.

Collars, if they are to fit properly without sagging or poking, should be cut slightly smaller than the neckline and stretched to fit it. There are several basic styles: the flat collar, the semi-⟩ roll or roll collar, and the stand-up collar; they may be of single or double thickness, attached or detachable. The flat double collar (Fig. 4) has

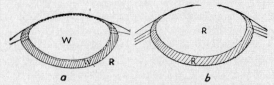

FIG. 3. FACING A NECKLINE

a. Stitching the facing on to the right side (R) of the garment. *b.* The completed facing on the wrong side (W)

two similar pieces, stitched together on the outside edge with right sides facing. It is then turned right side out and, if detachable, the neck edge is bound with bias binding. If the collar is to be attached, the centre back of the collar and garment are matched, the edges are tacked and stitched all round, including the facings, which are then turned right side out, and the remaining raw edge is finished with binding. When there are no facings the whole neckline is bound.

A roll collar (Fig. 5) can be cut in one with the bodice front, the two sides being joined at the back to make the under collar. The upper collar is cut in one with the front facings, joined at the back, and stitched to the under collar round the outside edge, right sides together.

A straight collar (Fig. 6) is sewn on the out-

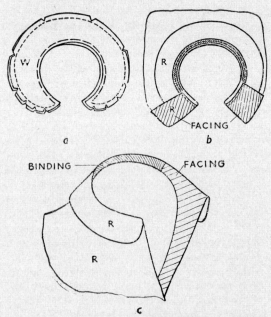

FIG. 4. A FLAT DOUBLE COLLAR

a. The two pieces of the collar stitched together. *b.* Attaching the collar with bias binding. *c.* The finished collar. R. Right side. W. Wrong side

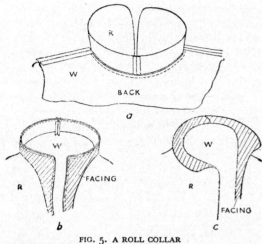

FIG. 5. A ROLL COLLAR

a. The collar stitched to the back of the garment. *b.* The facing stitched to the collar. *c.* The finished collar. R. Right side. W. Wrong side

side of the garment, and the facing hemmed over the raw edge inside; a single collar is bound, scalloped, or shell-edged, and attached with a crossway binding.

6. *Waistlines.* Openings on skirts and waists of garments are called plackets. The 'continuous opening' (Fig. 7*a*) is often used for lingerie or dresses. It is made with a straight strip twice the length of the slit plus turnings, and about 2 inches wide plus turnings. It is stitched to both

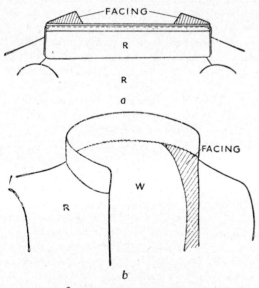

FIG. 6. A STRAIGHT STAND·UP COLLAR

a. The collar attached to the garment. *b.* The finished collar. R. Right side. W. Wrong side

sides of the opening, the front side being turned back against the garment, and the back extending to underlap beneath the front. This placket can also be used on a sleeve opening, but the strip is then cut on the cross. A 'dressmaker's placket' (Fig. 7*b*) is made at waist openings on skirts and dresses; it has a facing on the front seam 1 inch wide, with a folded piece on the back seam 2 inches wide, both being at

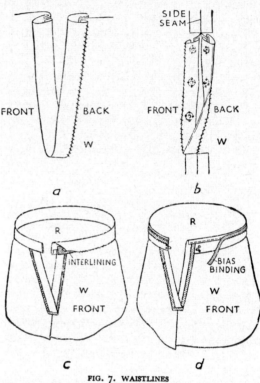

FIG. 7. WAISTLINES

a. Continuous opening. *b.* Dressmaker's placket. *c.* Belt of same material as skirt with interlining. *d.* Petersham belt

least 1 inch longer than the opening. The base of the two pieces is neatened with straight binding.

The waist of a skirt is often finished with a belt of the same fabric, stiffened with interlining cut to the depth of the belt without turnings (Fig. 7*c*). The belt is cut to twice the depth plus turnings and to the length of the waist measurement plus overlap. Petersham belting in various widths, boned or unboned, is used for the waist of a fitted skirt. A 1-inch petersham needs no shaping, but a wider one needs shrinking or darting to fit. The belt is made with turnings at each end, and the bottom hook and loop are attached; the top ones are sewn on after the peter-sham is stitched to the skirt. It is then fastened round the waist, and the skirt fitted on to it with pins. The petersham is attached on the inside waist on the fitting lines, the raw edge being turned over and bound with straight or bias binding (Fig. 7d).

7. *Pockets* should have a backing of muslin or canvas across the top edge for strength. The 'patch pocket' is simple to make; if unlined, the edges may be hemmed or bound; if lined, all the outside edges are turned in and tacked; the lining is turned in and tacked to fit; and the two edges are slip-stitched all round. A 'bound pocket' is similar to a bound buttonhole (*see* Dress Fastenings, Section 2). The lining is cut to twice the depth of the pocket plus turnings, and is stitched round and neatened after being pulled through the slit opening.

8. *Sleeves.* Magyar, kimono, and cap sleeves are cut in one with the bodice, and any seams

they have are extensions of the side and shoulder seams. The one-piece and two-piece tailored sleeves are set in on the shoulder line; the dolman is deeply set; and the raglan is extended to the neckline (Fig. 8a–g). They may be bound, finished with cuffs of various types, or faced. Tight-fitting long sleeves have easing on the elbow points, and placket openings at the wrists.

A sleeve which is set into a fitting armhole must hang with the grain straight from the shoulder point. The point should be marked in thread on the head of the sleeve, and the sleeve armhole, which should be about 1 inch bigger than that of the bodice, is eased in. Shoulder pads can be added if required.

A straight cuff for a full sleeve on a blouse is cut double, with an under wrap; the strip is folded inside out, the ends stitched, and the cuff turned right side out (Fig. 8h). A faced or continuous placket is made for the sleeve opening. The bottom edge of the sleeve is gathered and fitted into the cuff from the right side, and the facing is hemmed over the gathers on the wrong side. Buttonholes and buttons are applied afterwards. A long tight sleeve has a slightly curved cuff.

9. *Hemlines.* Skirts cut on the cross should be hung up for several days before the hemlines are fixed so that the uneven dropping may be adjusted. Facings should be sewn over the turned-up hem. The depth of the hem varies for different fabrics. The correct length of the hem can be marked with a hem-marker, but it is easier if the hem is measured with a yard-stick during the last fitting.

See also Sewing; Tailoring; Dress Design.

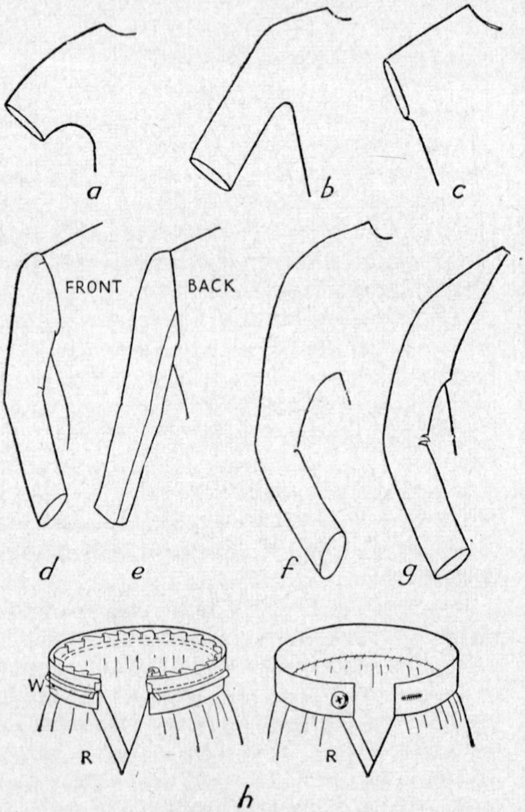

FIG. 8. SLEEVES

a. Magyar. *b.* Kimono. *c.* Cap. *d* One-piece straight. *e.* Two-piece tailored. *f.* Dolman. *g.* Raglan. *h.* Method of attaching cuff

DRUGS. A drug is any substance or mixture of substances used as a medicine. The word is also often now used to mean a narcotic to relieve pain or procure sleep, but this is not its primary meaning.

Drugs may be of animal, vegetable, or mineral origin, and are classified chemically as either inorganic or organic. Inorganic substances include the metals and their salts and elements, such as iodine and sulphur; among the most important inorganic remedies are iron, mercury, bismuth, bromides, magnesium sulphate (Epsom salts), boracic acid, hydrogen peroxide, and calomel (a salt of mercury). The organic remedies are all composed of the three elements, carbon, hydrogen, and oxygen (*see* Matter,

A MEDIEVAL APOTHECARY
Assistants are gathering herbs and preparing medicine with a pestle and mortar

Bibliothèque Nationale

Vol. III), in different combinations. By far the larger proportion of all drugs used in medicine belongs to this group. In addition to the organic substances which occur in nature, synthetic compounds are made artificially in the chemical laboratory, and these often contain nitrogen as well as carbon, hydrogen, and oxygen. The organic group of drugs includes the sulphonamides, general and local ANAESTHETICS, and ANTISEPTICS (qq.v). Some of the most valuable drugs, including aspirin and phenacetin, are obtained from coal tar, a by-product of the coal-gas industry.

Many of the best-known drugs come from plants. Herbal remedies were among the earliest medicines to be used, and almost everything that grows has been used in medicine at some time or other. Sometimes the whole plant is used, sometimes the leaves, roots, bark, seeds, juices, resins, or gums. In earlier times the plant was eaten or a crude infusion was made by boiling. Now the chemist isolates the active principle of the plant and produces such powerful drugs as strychnine, derived from nux vomica, the seed of an East Indian tree; morphine from the opium poppy; atropine, from the plant belladonna (deadly nightshade); cocaine, from the South American coca plant; and quinine from the cinchona tree.

Important remedies from the animal world include cod and halibut liver oil; hormones such as insulin, thyroxine, and the corticoids; and a wide range of antitoxins and vaccines (*see* INOCULATION AND VACCINATION). Minerals are the source of iron, mercury, and the other inorganic chemical remedies. Some VITAMINS (q.v.) are obtained from plants and some from animals, but as prescribed by the doctor they are usually in synthetic form.

The history of many common drugs can be traced back to the ancient civilizations. The *Ebers Papyrus*, an Egyptian medical work of about the year 1500 B.C., contains 900 recipes or prescriptions and mentions a number of drugs which are in use today, including the familiar castor oil. Opium, rhubarb, aconite, iron, arsenic, and sulphur were used by Chinese physicians at an equally remote period.

Many ancient remedies, especially those taken from animal sources, were of a rather revolting nature. There is frequent mention in old medical books of such strange things as crabs' eyes and claws, spiders' webs, moss from a dead man's skull, cast-off snake skin, viper's flesh, cow dung, oil of puppies, and earth-worms. Some drugs were extremely costly. Bezoar stones, found in the stomach or intestines of goats, were at one

A MODERN DRUG-MAKING PLANT

many new drugs were produced, resulting in modern chemotherapy or treatment by drugs. In 1909 Paul Ehrlich made an important advance when he introduced the drug salvarsan. Salvarsan was first known as 606 because it was the 606th arsenic compound prepared and tested by Ehrlich in his search for a drug which would be effective in the treatment of all infections. The drug did not quite realize this hope, but the use of Ehrlich's methods has resulted in the discovery of many chemical agents of great power and efficacy in medical treatment. In 1935 the chemist Domagk discovered the curative properties of the red dye prontosil, and other observers showed that sulphanilamide was the active principle in prontosil. This substance was the first of the sulphonamides—drugs such as 'M. and B.'— which have saved thousands of lives and shortened innumerable illnesses. In 1929 Sir Alexander Fleming discovered that penicillin, a substance obtained from a mould or fungus called *Penicillium notatum,* had powerful properties of destroying bacteria. This discovery was developed 10 years later by Sir Howard Florey and E. B. Chain at Oxford, and has since led to the finding of a number of other 'antibiotics' (substances which kill or inhibit bacteria). Drugs such as streptomycin, aureomycin, chloromycetin, and terramycin have been described as 'the most potent weapons yet known to man in the war of science against disease'.

The isolation of the 'hormones', or internal secretions of the human body, has also been of profound significance for medicine. Various preparations or extracts made from the thyroid, the pituitary, and other ENDOCRINE GLANDS (q.v.) are among the most powerful drugs known, and they have made possible successful treatment of a number of diseases which were formerly regarded as incurable. The discovery of the powerful remedial properties of some of the corti-

time sold for ten times their weight in gold. There was also a great demand for the fabulous unicorn's horn; for mithridate, a cure-all which contained about a hundred ingredients; and for theriac, or Venice treacle, which consisted of a mixture of vipers, red coral, pearls, emeralds, and other costly and out of the way substances. In the Middle Ages the Arabs introduced a number of new drugs such as benzoin, camphor, saffron, myrrh, musk, and senna. The discovery of America opened up a great new source of medicinal plants, among the most valuable of which were cinchona, ipecacuanha, and coca.

In former times most drugs were given in the form of crude extracts, and their exact chemical composition was not known. Although enormous doses were given, they had far less effect than the pure drugs and the active principles used today. When as many as a hundred substances were combined together in one remedy they probably cancelled one another out, and any effect on the patient must have been due to faith. In the early part of the 19th century chemists succeeded in isolating the alkaloids (*see* ALKALIS, Vol. VII) which are the active element in most medicinal plants. In the 20th century

coid substances isolated from the suprarenal glands has recently opened up new fields of medical research.

Drugs have been considered so important that even from early times public control has been exercised over their preparation and distribution. Public pharmacies were set up in Italy in the 13th century, and in 1498 the first pharmacopoeia, or official list of approved drugs, was published at Florence. The Society of Apothecaries of London was granted a new charter in 1617, and the first English pharmacopoeia appeared in the following year. The Pharmaceutical Society of Great Britain was founded in 1842, and in 1868 an Act of Parliament was passed requiring all future chemists and druggists to pass examinations and to be registered. In the old days many doctors used to make up their own prescriptions, but this work is now almost entirely in the hands of the retail chemists. One of the most striking features of present-day prescribing is the great use made of proprietary medicines, drugs evolved in the research laboratories of the great pharmaceutical firms.

See also MEDICINE; NURSING.
See also Vol. VII: CHEMISTRY, HISTORY OF; MEDICAL SUPPLIES.

DRYING (Food), see FOOD PRESERVING.

DRY ROT, see FURNITURE, CARE OF.

DWELLINGS, PRIMITIVE, see PRIMITIVE DWELLINGS.

DYEING. The housewife occasionally practises home-dyeing to freshen up faded fabrics or to change the colour of an article. She usually buys synthetic dyes, sold in convenient packets with explicit directions. But today, when dyeing is done efficiently and at a reasonable cost by commercial firms, home-dyeing is done less and less.

Wherever home-spun wool and home-woven tweeds are produced, in Skye, Orkney, and the Shetland and Western Islands, for example, and in Norway, Sweden, and Iceland, lichens are still used, as they have been for centuries, to produce a variety of different colours. It is

claimed that natural dyes have more beauty than synthetic dyes because they seem to give life and lustre to the fabric and an underglow of rich colour. They also have a delicious aromatic smell: the characteristic smell of Harris, Donegal, and Shetland tweeds comes from the lichens with which they have been boiled. Those who practise the crafts of weaving, knitting, and embroidery, therefore, often do their own dyeing with natural traditional dyes.

Natural dyes are of three types: animal, such as cochineal, obtained from the dried bodies of beetles; mineral, such as iron rust, still used to dye the sails of fishing boats in the Mediterranean; and vegetable, such as lichens, indigo, and logwood.

The vegetable dyes are most commonly used in craft work, and a great variety of colours can be produced. Lichens, for instance, of which there are between forty and fifty varieties, can be used to obtain many of the colours used in Highland TARTANS (q.v.), the scarlets, reds, yellows, purples, crimsons, and browns. Lichens growing on stones rather than trees are preferable, and produce the best results when used with a weak acid such as acetic (see VINEGAR). Many British plants will give excellent dyes if they are used with a mordant or dye-fixer (see DYES, Vol. VII). One type of broom, which gives a bright yellow, is called Dyers' Greenwood because it was once used with woad to give green. The bark of oak gives a brown dye, that of birch a deep gold, walnuts (both husk and shells) a dark brown, and ling an olive yellow, which can be turned to moss green if gall apples are added and an iron mordant used.

The nature of the material on which the dye is used affects the final colour: for example, some of the new synthetic materials will not take dyes which produce satisfactory results with natural fabrics. Wool is the fabric with which the amateur has most success, mainly because the fibre is porous and takes up the dye and the mordant most easily.

See also Vol. VII: DYES.

DYSENTERY, see TROPICAL DISEASES, Section 6.

E

EAR STRUCTURE. The ear consists of three distinct parts: the external, middle, and internal ears. The external ear comprises the shell of skin and cartilage (the auricle) which projects from the side of the head and a short canal which leads to the middle ear. The inner end of this canal is closed by a thin membrane known as the ear-drum. The middle ear, which lies on the inner side of the drum, is a small cavity hollowed out of the skull bone. Three small bones or 'ossicles' reach from the ear-drum to the inner wall of the middle ear, and are called respectively the 'malleus' (hammer), the 'incus' (anvil), and the 'stapes' (stirrup), because of their resemblance to those objects. A small tube—called the 'Eustachian tube' after a famous anatomist named Eustachius—runs from the middle ear to the back of the nose, allowing air to pass into and out of the middle ear. The inner ear or 'labyrinth', called the 'cochlea' because its spiral chamber resembles a snail's shell, is filled with fluid, and also contains the fine nerve endings of the auditory or acoustic nerve which enters the central body column of

this inner ear and breaks up into many fine branches. The inner ear also contains the semicircular canals which are the structures concerned in the maintenance of balance and the sense of position during movement.

Every sound that is heard is due to waves of air beating upon the ears. As the waves vary in frequency, size, and form, the sounds which the ear distinguishes vary in pitch, quality or timbre, and loudness.

A sound is first caught by the shell of the ear and is then directed down the canal to the ear-drum, causing the latter to vibrate. These vibrations are carried across the middle ear by the small chain of bones to an opening known as the 'oval window', set in the bony partition which separates the middle and inner ears. They are thus transmitted via the fluid of the cochlea to the auditory nerve endings, and so to the brain. The three bones or ossicles of the middle ear are joined together in such a way that they act as a lever and magnify the movements of the ear-drum, thus increasing the force exerted upon the oval window. The function of the Eustachian tube is to regulate the pressure of air in the middle ear so that it is the same as the pressure of the atmosphere, for if the ear-drum did not have equal pressures on both sides, it would be permanently pushed in and would not be able to vibrate. Rapid changes of atmospheric pressure, as in flying and diving, have such a temporary effect. The slight deafness which sometimes accompanies a cold in the head is caused by a temporary blockage of the Eustachian tube.

Impaired hearing—which may be of any degree from slight 'hardness of hearing' to complete deafness—may be due to causes affecting any part of the ear: accumulated wax in the external ear, infections, injury to the drum, degenerative diseases of the bony parts of the ear or diseases of the auditory nerve. In cases where the actual cause of the deafness cannot be removed, hearing may be greatly improved by the use of ear trumpets or electrical aids which amplify sounds, or by the provision of an artificial ear-drum. The external ear is subject to inflammatory diseases, particularly boils, skin diseases, and injuries such as the boxers' 'cauliflower' ear. Wax is deposited in the ear by special glands, its function being to prevent dust and similar foreign material from entering. If allowed to accumulate it may interfere with hearing, in which case it must be

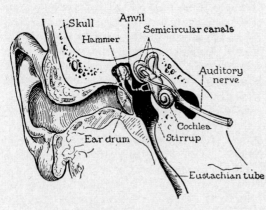

DIAGRAM OF THE EAR

From Logan Clendening, *The Human Body*, Alfred Knopf

removed with a syringe by a doctor. The ear-drum may be injured by the introduction of foreign bodies or by gunfire or blast. 'Otitis media'—inflammation of the lining membrane of the middle ear—is very common in children; it is usually due to the spread of infection from the nose and throat, though it is sometimes brought on by excessive nose-blowing or by swimming and diving. Acute otitis may result in a burst ear-drum, and to prevent this the drum is sometimes deliberately pierced. Chronic otitis may lead to infection of the mastoid bone which lies behind the ear. Mastoid disease, if neglected, may have serious results, though if treated in the early stages with a sulphonamide drug, an operation can often be avoided.

See also Vol. II: SENSES, Section 3.
See also Vol III: SOUND.

ECZEMA, *see* ALLERGIC DISEASES.

EGG DISHES. The egg has been a symbol of fertility from the time of the ancient Persians to the Easter Egg of today (*see* CHRISTIAN YEAR, Vol. I). To the cook, 'egg' now usually means hen's egg, but the eggs of ducks, geese, turkeys, guinea fowl, plovers, turtles, gulls, and even song birds and penguins have all been used as food at various times.

In Britain the common ways of cooking eggs are to boil, poach, fry, or scramble them. On the Continent the favourite egg dish is the omelette, and in New York there is a shop devoted entirely to the preparation and sale of dozens of different kinds of omelettes. A French omelette is made in a heavy frying pan, preferably with rounded sides, which is heated and coated well with butter or oil. For one person, two eggs are beaten slightly with seasoning and a tablespoonful of cold water or milk. This is poured into the sizzling fat, and, as soon as it has set a little, the edges are lifted with a spatula, and the pan tilted to allow the liquid parts to run underneath. When there is no runny egg left but the top is still wet, the omelette is folded over and slipped on to a hot plate. Chopped parsley, thyme, and sage, or tarragon and chives (*see* HERBS AND SPICES), added with the pepper and salt, make omelette *aux fines herbes*. Chopped ham, kidney, tomatoes, mushrooms, grated cheese, and other savoury fillings may be spread on the omelette just before it is folded. For sweet omelettes a teaspoonful of sugar is used

AN OMELETTE WITH MUSHROOMS

instead of pepper and salt, and the filling is warmed jam or cooked fruit.

Baked eggs are cooked in little fireproof pots, each holding an egg with butter, crumbs, and sauce or milk. Eggs mornay are baked eggs with a cheese sauce, and Florentine eggs are served with spinach. Hard boiled eggs, stuffed, coated with sauces, curried, sliced, or chopped, are a mainstay of entrées, HORS D'ŒUVRES, and SALADS (qq.v.). Raw eggs are very digestible. A prairie oyster is a raw egg swallowed whole with vinegar and a dash of Worcestershire Sauce. An egg flip is a raw egg beaten to froth with sugar and hot milk; if beaten with wine or spirits it is called an egg nog.

Eggs improve the texture and flavour of many less interesting materials. The yolk, consisting of fat and protein (mainly phospho-proteins), has the properties of emulsifying, thickening, and binding. It is used for emulsifying in making mayonnaise (*see* SALADS), and for thickening in SAUCES (q.v.), such as hollandaise and mornay, and in custards, which are egg and milk mixtures baked, steamed, or cooked in a double saucepan. Crème caramel and Crême brulée are baked custards flavoured with burnt sugar. Egg yolks and sugar, beaten in a bowl over steam, gently coagulate and hold the air bubbles; flavoured with Marsala wine, this mixture is the Italian sweet, *Zabaglione*; with white wine or cider, it is the French sauce, *Chaudeau*. The binding properties of yolks or whole eggs are important in batters for pancakes, Yorkshire pudding, and fritters, and in the egg-and-crumb coating for fried fish and escalopes. The best

SCOTCH EGGS

thickening temperature for eggs is about 177° F. —above that, they curdle.

Egg whites consist of water and protein (albumen and some globulin). When whipped, they increase their own volume 6 times. The point of greatest 'stability' is reached when the foam forms peaks and the surface looks shiny; after that, further beating tends to shrink the foam and it becomes what cooks call 'dry'. The beating causes the egg proteins to coagulate, forming a thin film or gel round each tiny air bubble (a similar process causes the 'scum' of jam), and these relatively strong, white foams make possible fluffy omelettes, soufflés, meringues, and angel-food cake. Fluffy omelette, or *omelette mousseuse*, is more of a British and American dish than a Continental one. Soufflés (French *souffler*, 'to inflate') are made from a base of double or treble thick white sauce, containing egg yolks and flavourings and made very light with beaten whites (three whites to two yolks). Soufflés can be flavoured in various ways: savoury soufflés with cheese, fish, spinach, or chicken, for example, and sweet ones with lemon, chocolate, coffee, and other things, and perhaps also with liqueurs. The mixture is baked in a deep fireproof dish for about 20–25 minutes in a hot oven (450° F., gas 8 or G), and is supported during the expansion and setting process by a paper band tied round the dish. A soufflé must not be asked to wait, as even a perfectly set soufflé deflates when it begins to cool. Cold soufflés, more accurately called mousses, Spanish cream, or snow pudding, are combinations of gelatine with beaten egg whites and whipped cream or custard with some kind of flavouring. Meringues are egg whites, beaten to a stiff consistency with

sugar and baked for a long time in a cool oven. Angel-food cake, very popular in the U.S.A., relies entirely on whipped egg white for its aeration—8 to 10 whites to a cup of flour. Egg white as a binding agent, especially raw, is important in sugar confectionery—for example, for centres of chocolates, marzipan, and Royal ICINGS (q.v.).

In making CAKES (q.v.), eggs serve other purposes besides being emulsifiers. They make the rubbery protein of flour (gluten) more elastic so that the dough or sponge can hold more air, steam, or gas without bursting (*see* RAISING AGENTS), and so become light and open in texture. The more or less stable foams of whipped egg lighten cakes by incorporating extra air. The egg proteins which, with the gluten of the flour, form the thin, elastic walls of the sponge network, harden by coagulation during baking and help to strengthen and set the sponge so that it will not fall down and 'go sad' on cooling.

Eggs can be preserved when plentiful for use when they are scarce. Chinese Ancient Eggs, sometimes called '100-year-old eggs' or *Pay Dahn*, are preserved by thickly smearing fresh duck eggs with a clay made from wood ashes, lime, and salt, moistened with strong tea; they are then buried in the earth for at least 3 months. Domestic preservation methods, such as immersion in water glass (sodium silicate), pickling in brine, and packing in sawdust, are very old. Modern commercial methods of egg preserving include dehydration and freezing. These methods have made eggs accessible to cooks at reasonable prices all the year round. In 1954 the number of eggs eaten in Britain averaged 216 per person.

See also Vol. VI: POULTRY.
See also Vol VII: EGG TRADE.

ELECTRICITY, DOMESTIC. There are not many houses in Britain today without electric lamps and fires; and electric power, which is cheap, clean, and easy to control, is frequently used for heating water and cooking and many other domestic purposes.

1. MAINS. Electric power is generated in POWER STATIONS and brought to houses by electric CABLES (qq.v. Vol. VIII) buried in the ground beneath the streets and pavements. These cables, which enclose a pair of thick copper wires, are usually called 'mains'. When an electric lamp is switched on, an ELECTRIC CURRENT (q.v. Vol. VIII) flows from the power station through one of the wires in the mains cable, through the lamp, and back again to the power station through the other wire of the pair in the cable. In the country, overhead wires are often used instead of underground cables.

In most parts of Britain the mains supply ALTERNATING CURRENT (q.v. Vol. VIII), or A.C., which surges continually to and fro 50 times a second. In a few places, direct current, or D.C., which flows smoothly one way, is supplied by the mains. Some domestic appliances are only suitable for A.C., and this should be checked before they are used. It is also necessary to make certain that the appliance is suitable for the particular electrical pressure or voltage of the mains' supply, as this varies between about 200 volts and 250 volts in different districts.

ELECTRIC CURRENT (q.v. Vol. VIII) flows only when there is a complete circuit from the power station and back. If two wires carrying current touch each other, a 'short circuit' is caused. A very powerful current rushes through the contact and may make the wires hot enough to start a fire. Short circuits are prevented by 'insulating' the wires from each other by a coating of some insulating material, which does not allow elec-

tric current to pass. As a further precaution, a small piece of thin wire, called a fuse, is introduced into the wiring system. As the fuse is so thin, it quickly melts when there is a short circuit and interrupts the current before the other wiring is damaged.

2. WIRING. The wiring used to carry electric power to different rooms in a house must be protected from damage, and there must be no risk of fire or electric shock. As electric shocks often happen when someone touches a 'live' electric wire, causing the current to flow through his body into the ground, the live wires are insulated. They should also be 'earthed', that is, enclosed in a metal sheath which is joined to a wire buried in the ground. This prevents the sheath from becoming alive, even if the insulation should become damaged and the live wire touch the metal sheath.

With one method of wiring, separate stranded copper wires with VIR insulation are used, the wires being placed inside black enamelled steel pipes, called 'conduits'. The conduits are screwed together and joined to cast iron boxes containing the switches and connexions between the wires; the whole conduit system is then joined to earth. Though sometimes rather conspicuous and clumsy, this system is both fireproof and shockproof and difficult to damage. A second method is to use lead-covered cable, with two rubber-covered copper wires inside a thin lead sheath. A bare copper wire is used for earthing the sheath, and steel boxes for the switches and connexions. This system is cheaper and less conspicuous than a conduit system, but as some kinds of plaster corrode lead, the cables must be spaced away from plaster and brickwork. A third, and perhaps the most common, method is to use 'cab-tyre' cable, in which two rubber-covered copper wires are moulded with a bare copper earthing wire inside a tough rubber sheath. The switch- and connexion-boxes consist of plastic mouldings which act as insulators. This method is cheap and efficient, but the cable has to be protected from direct sunlight which makes the sheath brittle.

The general arrangement of the wiring of a small 'all-electric' house is shown in Fig. 1. The power is brought from the mains by a short length of armoured cable, and is connected to the house wiring through two main fuses and the electricity meter. From the meter the wiring goes to a main distribution fuse-box, which has

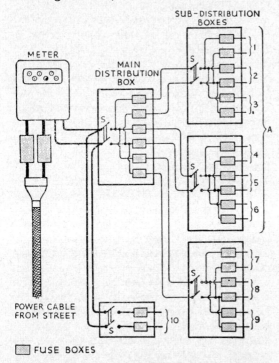

FIG. 1. ELECTRIC WIRING ARRANGEMENT FOR A SMALL HOUSE
A. To power points. 1, 2, 3. Bedrooms. 4, 5, 6. Downstairs rooms. 7, 8, 9. To upstairs, downstairs, and garage lights. 10. To electric cooker. s. Switches

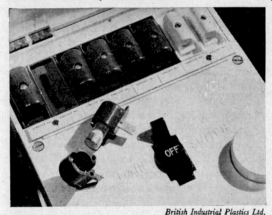

A FUSE-BOX WITH A FUSE-HOLDER OPENED TO SHOW THE
CARTRIDGE FUSE

a safety-switch and three pairs of fuses. This box feeds three similar sub-distribution boxes. Two of these boxes are connected to power points in each of the main rooms for electric fires, vacuum-cleaner, and so on. The third box is connected to the electric lighting. A separate fuse-box, joined directly to the meter, is used for the wiring of the electric cooker as this has to carry a much heavier current. The separate sub-distribution fuse-boxes are very useful when a fuse blows, for the short-circuit can be traced and removed, and the broken fuse-wire replaced, without having to switch off the whole supply.

Fuse-wires are usually fitted in porcelain holders, which plug in to sockets in closed cast-iron fuse-boxes. The fuse-boxes cannot be opened until a safety-switch has disconnected the main supply. To replace a blown fuse, the terminal screws holding the wire must be loosened and the old wire removed (Fig. 2); a short length of new fuse-wire of the correct

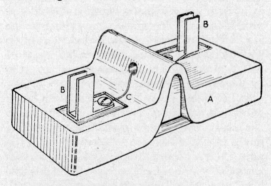

FIG. 2. A FUSE

A. Porcelain body. B. Springy copper contact blades.
C. Fuse wire

rating is fixed between the terminal screws, passing under their heads; the screws are then tightened and the holder replaced. In another type of fuse-box cartridge fuses are used; these are made with the fuse-wire fixed inside a cardboard tube with metal ends. When a cartridge fuse blows, a new one is fixed.

3. PORTABLE EQUIPMENT, SWITCHES, AND PLUGS. Particular care must be taken with the wiring of portable equipment, such as an electric fire, because in time the wires inside the flexible leads fray and break. If the broken wires touch the metal frame of the fire, the frame becomes 'live' and can give a severe shock. As a precaution, the frame is connected to a third wire in the lead, which is joined to earth through the plug and socket, often by connecting

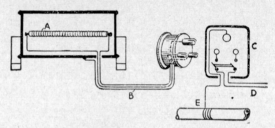

FIG. 3. THE WIRING OF AN ELECTRIC FIRE

A. Element of fire. B. Three-wire lead. C. Three-pin socket and switch. D. Wires from fuse in distribution box. E. Earth connexion to water pipe

it to a water-pipe (Fig. 3). If one of the live wires breaks and touches the frame, the wire automatically becomes connected to earth, which short-circuits the supply and harmlessly blows the fuse. It is most important that a 3-pin plug and socket and a 3-wire lead should be used for all portable equipment, and that the earth connexion should be well made. Very great care with wiring and earthing is especially necessary in kitchens and bathrooms, where there are exposed water and gas pipes and where people have wet hands. In bathrooms, electrical equipment should never be within reach of someone in the bath.

The supply of electricity to a lamp is usually controlled by a simple switch, as in Fig. 4a; the switch has a movable brass link that can be used to break the circuit and stop the flow of current. For lights on staircases and in bedrooms, two switches are often used, so that the lamp can be turned on or off from either switch. The electric wiring of a staircase light is shown in Fig. 4b; two two-way switches are connected by a pair of wires A and B, so that whichever way the switches are left, one of the wires must be 'alive' and the other 'dead'.

The sockets provided for plugging-in portable electrical equipment are of different sizes, and are usually marked with the strength of the most powerful current that they are intended to supply. Electric current is measured in amps, and 2-amp., 5-amp., and 15-amp. sockets are common sizes. A

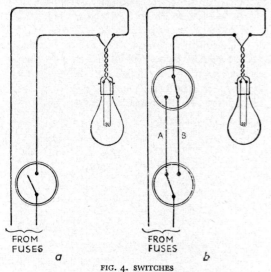

FROM FUSES

FROM FUSES

a　　　　　　　*b*

FIG. 4. SWITCHES

a. Simple switch. *b.* Two-way switch

2-amp. socket is joined to a fuse that blows when the current is more than 2 amps. The current that can be taken by an electrical appliance can be worked out by dividing its power consumption in watts by the voltage of the mains. For example, a 1,000-watt electric fire from 250-volt mains would take 1,000 watts ÷ 250 volts = 4 amps; it would clearly blow the fuse if it were plugged into a 2-amp. socket.

See also HEATING SYSTEMS, DOMESTIC; LIGHTING, HISTORY OF.

See also Vol. VIII: ELECTRIC CURRENT; ALTERNATING CURRENT; POWER STATION.

EMBROIDERY, ENGLISH. From the 10th century onwards England has produced a fine and varied collection of embroidery. In the Middle Ages it was used chiefly for ecclesiastical work, such as priests' vestments, altar frontals, and palls. Even the 11th-century BAYEUX TAPESTRY (q.v. Vol. XII), though its subject, the conquest of England by William the Conqueror, is secular, was made to adorn a church.

Embroidery was an important craft, often practised by men, and so fine in technique and design that it became famous throughout Europe as *Opus Anglicanum* or *façon d'Angleterre* (English work).

The designs were worked in silk and metal threads on linen in split and satin stitch and couched and laid work. The whole of the ground was covered with designs often consisting of geometric shapes or scrolls of leaves and stems, forming roundels containing figure subjects. The faces of the figures were worked in the tiniest stitches. One of the finest examples of this type is the 13th-century Syon Cope (*see* Vol. XII, p. 47). In the 15th century the work became coarser; ground materials, such as velvet, were used which were not wholly covered. A favourite design was of angels, worked in colours and gold on velvet.

Tudor embroidery bears no relationship to earlier work. It was no longer used only for religious purposes but for women's bodices, caps and gloves for both sexes, bed covers and hangings, cushions and curtains, mats and towels. Chain, buttonhole, cross, stem, long and short, and back stitches and plaited braid stitches were used (*see* p. 320). The designs were mostly all-over scroll patterns, frequently worked in gold, silver, or silver-gilt plaited braid stitch, with honeysuckle, roses, pansies, carnations, and strawberries in the circles formed by the coiling stems of the scrolls. They were worked in costly silks, imported from the Levant, on a ground of linen or twill fabric. Table CARPETS (q.v.) were worked in tent stitch, in geometric patterns or showing hunting or mythological scenes.

Towards the end of the 16th century 'Black Work' was fashionable; this was worked on linen in black silk, sometimes relieved with gold and silver thread. The designs were similar to the floral scroll patterns of the period, the spaces within the scrolls being filled in with a wide variety of lace stitches and darned patterns made by the counted threads.

In the 17th century, 'stump work' was used to decorate work-boxes or trinket-boxes or to border a mirror; sometimes it was framed as a picture. It was a form of raised work on white satin, with a design of figures, often biblical or allegorical. The figures were worked in buttonhole stitch, resembling needle-point LACE (q.v. Vol. VII), on separate pieces of linen, cut out, and applied to the main fabric, from which they

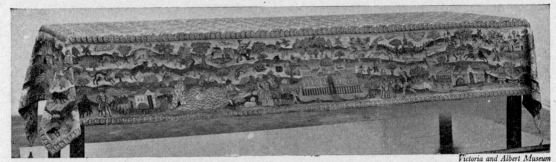

Victoria and Albert Museum

TABLE CARPET EMBROIDERED IN TENT STITCH IN SILK ON CANVAS; LATE 16TH CENTURY

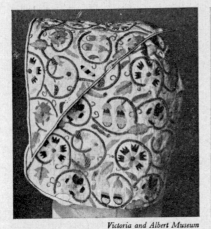

Victoria and Albert Museum

COIF EMBROIDERED IN BLACK SILK AND
SILVER-GILT THREAD; LATE 16TH CENTURY

Victoria and Albert Museum

LONG PILLOW COVER WITH THE STORY OF NOAH EMBROIDERED IN CRIMSON
AND BLUE SILK AND SILVER-GILT ON LINEN; EARLY 17TH CENTURY

Needlework Development Scheme

SATIN EMBROIDERED WAISTCOAT; 18TH CENTURY

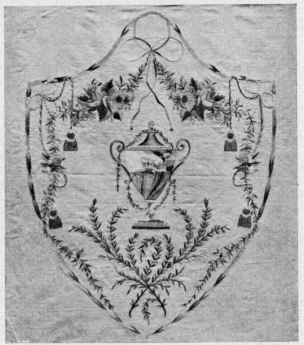

Victoria and Albert Museum

EMBROIDERED SATIN PANEL FOR A POLE SCREEN; c. 1800

were raised by a padding of tow. The faces were made of small, rounded pieces of boxwood covered with painted silk. Sometimes figures were placed under a raised canopy with free-hanging curtains; in other examples, figures were placed in a country landscape, and the foreground and sides filled in with animals, birds, and flowers symmetrically arranged with a curious disregard for scale or perspective. As in most Jacobean decoration all the details were crowded together (see Colour Plate, opp. p. 304).

Larger designs for hangings or cushions were made in 'crewel-work'. A favourite design was the 'Tree of Life', derived from the cotton prints imported from India. The tree had large curled branches with leaves and exotic fruits, and grew out of a base of small curved hillocks on which were animals of many kinds. The work was done on twill in bright coloured wools with gradual shading in long and short stitch. The leaves and flowers were filled in with varied fillings in chain, buttonhole, herring-bone, stem, and satin stitches.

At the beginning of the 18th century silk embroidery thread superseded wool, and as a result designs were more delicate and refined. Gay birds, peonies, chrysanthemums, and oriental figures under a Chinese ceremonial umbrella show the current vogue for CHINOISERIE (q.v. Vol. XII). Petticoats were decorated with quilting, which was often combined with embroidery; men's coats and waistcoats and women's and children's dresses and aprons were elaborately embroidered.

Embroidered pictures were made at the end of the 18th century, with figures worked in bright coloured silks on a satin ground and faces painted in water-colours; fire screens were panelled with copies of famous paintings laboriously stitched in coloured wools. This marked the beginning of a decline in the quality and design of embroidery which led to the Berlin wool-work of the 19th century—coarse embroidery in highly coloured thick wools in densely overcrowded geometrical designs, which were worked out on squared paper and mechanically copied square by square.

Many kinds of embroidery are done today, including appliqué for curtains and pictures, canvas work for chair seats and stool tops, broderie anglaise and cut and drawn work for household linen, and quilting for bed-covers and skirts (see NEEDLEWORK, DECORATIVE). Patterns can be bought which can be transferred on to the material by tracing over carbon paper with a hard pencil, but for rough fabrics 'pouncing' is necessary: the outline of the design is pricked, and powdered charcoal (for light materials) or powdered chalk or baking powder (for dark ones) is lightly rubbed through the holes and on to the material beneath. The marks are fixed with not-too-wet water-colour. Transparent materials may be pinned on to the drawing, and the lines traced with water-colour or pencil. Designs may be traced on to canvas in the same way if the drawing has a very black outline.

Many of the stitches mentioned in this article are illustrated on p. 320.

See also EMBROIDERY, WORLD; NEEDLEWORK; SEWING; SEWING MACHINE.

EMBROIDERY, WORLD. Most countries have a traditional style of embroidery, which depends on the materials, threads, and stitches (see p. 320) that are used, and the character of the designs. Both fabrics and patterns have a direct relationship to the raw materials produced in the country and the way of life of the people. Oriental countries most frequently use rich silks or cotton, and European countries are very fond of linen, woven from the flax that grows in cool moist climates, though they also use silk and wool. Some primitive people, especially the North American Indians and the Eskimoes, who wear leather and fur because of the cold climate, have a fine tradition of decorating these materials with leather thonging and beads (see PRIMITIVE COSTUME). The patterns, determined by the nature of the thread used, are simple geometrical ones.

China, producing one-quarter of all the silk in the world, has long been famous for silk embroidery on silk fabric. Chinese robes—long, voluminous garments with wide, capacious sleeves—were usually covered with fine, meticulous stitchery, depicting dragons, fabulous animals, and birds, and a variety of flowers, among which the chrysanthemum and the peony appear most often. All the objects and even the colours in these designs were symbolic —perhaps of virtues or of desirable attributes, such as long life or friendship. The designs were very conventional and stylized, and were worked in rich colours. The methods of depicting wave, water, and cloud forms were peculiarly Chinese and unlike the work of any other nation (*see* CHINESE ART, Vol. XII).

Indian and Persian embroidery have many features of design and technique in common. Both frequently use the 'Persian Pine' motif, from which the designs of Paisley shawls are derived. Both countries have used embroidery extensively, and India still does, for clothing and for many household articles; and they both use cotton and silk as their background fabric. In some Indian embroideries unusual and ingenious materials are incorporated in the decoration, notably seeds, gleaming blue beetles' wings, and small mirror disks. These bright, glinting objects on, for example, the gauze skirt of a dancing girl are extremely effective. Exquisite embroidery, on fairly loosely hand-woven white muslin for flounces, skirts, and blouses, was done in India in the 17th and 18th centuries. It was stitched in white, in a pleasant contrast of solid and open stitches. Colourful hand-woven and richly embroidered woollen materials are worn in northern India, but the more famous Indian embroideries are the rich and elegant designs on fine silk *saris* worn by women throughout the country (*see* ORIENTAL COSTUME).

India also produces in large quantities very pleasant embroidered rugs and CARPETS (q.v.), made of a natural coloured felt-like woollen fabric, embroidered in chain stitch in coloured wools.

Needlework Development Scheme

BULGARIAN WOMAN'S ROBE EMBROIDERED IN COLOURS, PRINCIPALLY RED ON WHITE SILK

Museum of Eastern Art, Oxford

EARLY 19TH-CENTURY CHINESE EMBROIDERY IN COLOURED SILKS AND GOLD THREAD

All European countries have a long tradition of embroidery. Peasants in Mediterranean countries and in eastern Europe embroider clothes and household articles. The fabrics, frequently hand-spun and hand-woven, are usually of linen or wool, and are decorated with home-dyed threads. The costumes of Roumania, Turkey, Greece, Bulgaria, and Hungary are embroidered with elaborate designs (*see* EUROPEAN PEASANT COSTUME). White linen blouses are embroidered round the neck and sleeves; woollen skirts in bright colours or black may be decorated all over with woollen or silk stitchery; embroidered kerchiefs are worn on the head; and the aprons, which are an important feature of these costumes, are often elaborately decorated, being for show rather than use. The men's costume also gives great scope for embroidery. The homespun shirts worn outside the trousers are decorated at the neck, sleeve, and hem, and are confined round the waist by a heavy leather belt, also stitched with slender thongs of coloured leather. In some countries sheepskin waistcoats

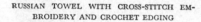

Needlework Development Scheme

RUSSIAN TOWEL WITH CROSS-STITCH EM-
BROIDERY AND CROCHET EDGING

PANEL FROM CRETE EMBROIDERED IN BLUE SILK, MOSTLY IN CRETAN STITCH,
ON LINEN

Needlework Development Scheme

Above: SWEDISH CUSHION EMBROIDERED IN THIN WOOL ON
BLACK WOOLLEN MATERIAL

Needlework Development Scheme

Right: SPANISH ALTAR CLOTH EMBROIDERED IN BROWN WOOL

are worn over the shirt, with the skin side gaily trimmed with flowers and foliage in bright wools. Scarves, mats, cushions, and towels are decorated with fine stitchery; the design is frequently geometrical, particularly in those countries influenced by ISLAMIC ART (q.v. Vol. XII), with repeat patterns worked by the counted thread.

French embroidery has very largely followed the same pattern of development as English work (*see* EMBROIDERY, ENGLISH). It has been a cultivated art, used by the leisured classes for the decoration of their clothes and homes, rather than, as in eastern Europe, a peasant art found nearly everywhere. Very refined designs and methods have followed the cultured taste of each period, in contrast to the traditional peasant designs which have not changed for generations. In the 17th and 18th centuries elegant CHAIRS (q.v.) and settees were covered with the finest needlework in either petit or gros point (tent or cross stitch) or a combination of both, usually on a light coloured background with flowers, foliage, and scroll work. Sometimes a figure subject filled the centre panel. Costumes at this time, both men's and women's, were also elaborately decorated with stitchery; silk dresses and petticoats, coats and waistcoats, scarves, and gloves were all embroidered.

Scandinavia has a strong tradition of linen embroidery, both coloured and white, used mainly for household linens, curtains, and cushions. Its greatest charm lies in its clear freshness of design and colour.

The embroidery of Spain and Portugal has a strong, bold design, frequently in bright colours; but there are also handsome pieces entirely in white. The Portuguese island of Madeira exports quantities of brightly coloured, wool-embroidered articles, and also table linen decorated in self-coloured thread. Though these are not of very fine work, they are gay and attractive.

See also EMBROIDERY, ENGLISH; NEEDLEWORK; SEWING.

EMOTION, see PSYCHOLOGY; MIND AND BODY.

ENDOCRINE GLANDS. Every cell of the body, in order to live, continually undergoes complex chemical changes, some for growth or preservation, some for active function. Within the cell these reactions are harmonized by organic substances called 'enzymes'. But cells are built up by growth into tissues and organs, and the separate activities of these, too, need to be regulated. This is achieved to a great extent by special chemical substances known as 'hormones', which the endocrine glands manufacture. Whereas the central NERVOUS SYSTEM (q.v.) co-ordinates activities that take but a short time to complete, such as the action of muscles, the endocrine glands are concerned with changes occupying weeks or months, such as menstruation and growth (see LIFE CYCLE), though of course the two do overlap to some extent.

The endocrine glands are situated in various parts of the body. The 'pituitary' gland, the regulator of all the others, lies like a large pea

enclosed in a bony cage in the middle of the base of the skull, embedded in the BRAIN (q.v.). The 'thyroid' gland is folded round the windpipe just below the thyroid cartilage or 'Adam's apple'. The 'parathyroid' glands, four in number, are often concealed in the substance of the thyroid and were not distinguished from it until a century ago. The 'thymus', lying behind the breastbone in the upper chest, is one of the largest endocrine glands in the infant but dwindles and disappears with adolescence. On top of the kidneys lie the 'adrenal', or 'suprarenal', glands which have attracted a great deal of attention in recent medical research. The 'pancreas' or sweetbread, near the stomach, pours its external digestive secretions into the gut, whilst its internal secretion flows into the blood in the form of insulin (see DIGESTIVE SYSTEM). Finally the sex glands consist of the ovaries close to the womb in females, and the testes of the male (see REPRODUCTIVE SYSTEM). All these glands have the important feature in common that they are ductless, that is, they send their secretion, or hormone, into the blood-stream, in which it circulates until it reaches the tissues on which it acts, stimulating or controlling them.

The pituitary gland consists of a front and a back lobe. From its front lobe it produces hormones which act on the other endocrine glands, stimulating them to action or controlling them (as in the case of the insulin-producing pancreas). The pituitary also produces a growth hormone of its own which, if secreted in excess during childhood, causes excessive growth in the child. If the growth hormone continues to be poured out, it may in time exhaust the special insulin-producing cells in the pancreas, in which case the individual will not only have grown very large but will suffer from DIABETES (q.v.) and not be as strong as he looks. Just as too much growth hormone produces a giant, so too little during childhood produces a dwarf, or sometimes more tragically still, a rapid premature ageing, so that a child of 8 may look like an old person of 80. In addition to these changes insufficient pituitary means that all the other endocrine glands lack stimulation, and all their deficiencies, particularly the thyroid's, produce a variety of results.

The back lobe of the pituitary gland makes quite different hormones. One, acting on the KIDNEY (q.v.), stimulates that organ to reabsorb water so that the volume of urine passed is diminished; it may also act on smooth muscle

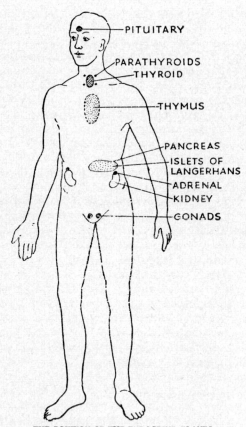

THE POSITION OF THE ENDOCRINE GLANDS

After Logan Clendening, *The Human Body*, Alfred Knopf

tissue, particularly that of the blood-vessels. The other makes the womb or uterus contract at the end of pregnancy so that the child is expelled (*see* BIRTH), and assists in the expulsion of milk from the breast.

The thyroid gland in the neck secretes and stores a hormone called 'thyroxin', rich in iodine, which stimulates the tissues all over the body to consume more oxygen. If there is insufficient iodine in the diet, the thyroid over-grows and enlarges into a goitre, which disappears as soon as the shortage of iodine is made good. Such goitres are particularly common in mountainous districts far from the sea, such as the Alps and the Himalayas. In England 'Derbyshire neck' is a form of them. An infant born of a mother suffering from goitre may lack thyroxin and be born a 'cretin', with an inactive mind and body, a protruding tongue, a dry, coarse skin, a swollen belly, and a condition of mental deficiency. This pathetic state may be changed to normal by early treatment with a few grains of thyroid extract—a treatment which must be kept up for life. The cretinous condition may begin to reappear, however, in adult life if the thyroid becomes exhausted, but thyroid treatment will again effect the cure. An excess of thyroid may also enlarge the gland into a goitre. A patient suffering from this type of goitre is nervous and over-excitable, with protruding eyes. This condition was usually cured by an operation, but drugs can now also be used. A substance called 'thiouracil', for example, checks the production of thyroxin by the gland. Nowadays patients may be given a remarkable treatment—a drink containing radioactive iodine, which, becoming concentrated in the thyroid, gives the gland a measured dose of gamma-rays, thus diminishing its excessive activity (*see* RADIOTHERAPY).

The parathyroid glands, buried in the thyroid, produce a hormone called 'parathormone' which raises the calcium in the blood. Too much parathormone draws the calcium out of the bones, leaving them so soft that they bend and twist. Parathyroids have been on occasions inadvertently removed with the thyroid in operations for goitre. In such an event the calcium in the blood drops, and the muscles of the body go into spasms called 'tetany'.

The thymus, so large in infancy, is still a gland of mystery, and no hormone has yet been found to come from it. Since it disappears at the time the sex glands develop, it may be that its function is in some way antagonistic to them.

The adrenal glands, lying one on top of each kidney, are composed of two parts, the cortex outside and the medulla within, each producing different hormones. The adrenal cortex produces hormones called 'corticoids', one of which has far-reaching effects on the water and salts of the body, particularly acting on the kidneys. Another affects the fate of the protein, fat, and carbohydrate in the body, and also enables the body to deal with all harmful stimuli which disturb its healthy balance of function. The corticoids play a part, for example, in the response of the body to injury, infection, and even fright—though exactly how we still do not know. The adrenal cortex is closely related to the sex glands, and too much activity or overgrowth of this gland, for example, produces premature sex development in boys, with early appearance of hair on the face.

The medulla, lying beneath the cortex of the

adrenal, secretes adrenalin, which flows through the blood-stream to act on the tissues supplied by the 'sympathetic nerves'. The gland is itself brought into action by the sympathetic nervous system, a system mainly concerned with the regulation of blood-pressure and therefore with the emotions of anger or fear and with the corresponding activities of fight and flight. These emotions cause adrenalin to be liberated, the blood-pressure to be raised, and the blood-supply to the muscles to be increased.

The sex glands are the ovaries of the female and the male testes (gonads). Besides making the ovum or egg, the ovary produces two hormones —one concerned with sexual characteristics and the preparation of the body for fertilization of the ovum, the other concerned with the nourishment and growth of the embryo in the womb. The sex glands of man not only manufacture spermatozoa but secrete a hormone which brings about the sexual changes of puberty, rendering the body capable of sexual activity. In man the breaking of the voice, the growth of the beard and of hair on the body, and the distinctive mental outlook of the male, all depend on the hormones provided by the glands, which in their turn depend, as has already been emphasized, on the presence of the stimulating hormones from the pituitary gland.

See also DIGESTIVE SYSTEM; REPRODUCTIVE SYSTEM; LIFE CYCLE.

ENTERTAINING. The way in which we entertain friends and strangers today is a matter of choice, influenced by our own tastes, by a desire to satisfy our guests, and by what amusements happen to be fashionable. This has always been true of settled, peaceful societies that have reached some degree of civilization.

In early societies, however, entertaining, and in particular the entertainment of strangers, was a solemn business, subject to certain rules which often had a religious background. Thus among the Greeks of Homeric times, a stranger was welcomed, bathed, clothed, and fed before he was asked who he was or why he had come; and among several primitive peoples, a host's generosity has extended to sharing his wife, as well as his food and shelter, with strangers. A stranger was a mysterious figure, and possibly a dangerous one. He had to be placated and, as it were, bribed by acts of kindness to be friendly. There was also the desire to show off one's own wealth and importance by lavish entertainment —and this motive still exists today. There was, too, the desire to receive and exchange news which might, indeed, be of crucial importance. But as society became more peaceful and more settled, as roads extended and commerce flourished, hospitality became less solemn and more flexible. Yet even today there remains a feeling that special obligations are due to a guest because he is a guest, and not just because he is a friend, or a relation, or a stranger.

In the history of entertaining there are certain constant features. The most important of these is MEALS (q.v.). We flatter a distinguished guest by planning a meal that is carefully different from others, or we endear ourselves to familiar friends by inviting them to take pot-luck at a meal that is not specially planned at all. From the giant carousals of the Anglo-Saxons to the formal dinner party of today, the meal has remained the most convenient form of entertaining. Second only to eating together is talking, fostered by the desire to exchange news in times when communications were bad, and encouraged when LIGHTING (q.v.) was inefficient and costly: some of our earliest literary fragments record riddles and stories told by the fire. And in some societies CONVERSATION (q.v.) became an art, as in the Courts of Renaissance Italy, where both men and women talked not merely to exchange news but to display their wit and learning. Victorian books on good manners show an attempt to revive conversation as a fine art and as a means of providing entertainment.

Music is another constant feature. Great houses maintained MINSTRELS (q.v. Vol. IX) throughout medieval times, and some continued to support private orchestras into the 18th century. Moreover, most families of any standing were able to provide music for themselves (see CHAMBER MUSIC, Vol. XII), and this tradition lasted well into the 19th century. The well-educated Victorian girl could play the piano and perhaps also the harp and the guitar, and her brothers might be expected to sing reasonably well on sight. Dancing, a natural accompaniment to music, was enjoyed not only at formal balls but at private dances, got up perhaps impromptu, with the family's musical resources eked out by the village fiddler (see DANCING, HISTORY OF, Vol. IX).

From the 18th century it was common to combine dancing with cards, and during this and

Capt. E. G. Spencer-Churchill

A MUSICAL PARTY IN THE 18TH CENTURY
Painting by J. Nollekens, 1737–1823

the next century, at routs, crushes, drums, assemblies, and soirées, while the young people danced, their elders played—and possibly gambled—at cards. As there were fashions in dances, so there were in CARD GAMES (q.v. Vol. IX). The Ruff and Honours, French Ruff, Gleek, Ombre, Lanterloo, Bankafelet, and Beast of the Restoration gave way to rivals. Lady Mary Wortley Montagu wrote in 1749, 'Your new fashioned game of brag was the genteel amusement when I was a girl: crimp succeeded to that, and basset and hazard employed the town when I left it to go to Constantinople. At my return, I found them all at commerce, which gave place to quadrille, and that to whist; but the rage of play has been ever the same, and will be so among the idle of both sexes.' The point of this last prophetic sentence is proved by the bridge and canasta parties of the 20th century.

Dramatic performances were yet another way of entertaining one's guests. By the 15th century no great banquet would be considered complete without an entertainment of the kind that developed into the MASQUE (q.v. Vol. IX). Such amusements continued to be a feature of domestic entertainment even when the theatres of London supported flourishing professional companies, in much the same way as CHARADES (q.v. Vol. IX) and amateur theatricals continued into an age when the cinema had taken its place beside the theatre.

Another popular form of entertainment was the picnic. This owed its popularity partly to its association with hunting, and has been used not only for small parties but for great and formal ones, sometimes enlivened with music.

The occasions for entertaining often varied with the time of year. The London Season, FAMILY FESTIVALS (q.v.), and harvest-time and shearing-time in the country were popular times

Guildhall Art Gallery

'TOO EARLY'. PAINTING BY JAMES TISSOT, 1836–1902
Guests are beginning to arrive at a ball

to invite guests. House-parties were organized for sporting events, such as HORSE-RACING, and for sporting pursuits such as GAME SHOOTING, DEER STALKING, and ANGLING, which continued from the 16th century onwards as a means of entertainment. A game more nearly related to the home was ARCHERY, which was revived, much to the advantage of the ladies, at the end of the 18th century, and remained a popular form of entertainment until the 1850s, when it was supplanted by CROQUET and, later, LAWN TENNIS (qq.v. Vol. IX). Just as entertaining took place in the well-to-do family's London house during the Season, and in the country house during the sporting seasons, so, when SPAS (q.v. Vol. IX), such as Bath, and coastal resorts, such as Brighton, became centres of fashionable life, people dispensed hospitality during the spa season from a house taken for this purpose. Jane AUSTEN's novels give lively accounts of the season at Bath (q.v. Vol. V).

When roads were bad, friends and relatives made visits for weeks or months at a time. But as roads improved, and as the hours of business of well-to-do people increased through the 19th century, visits gradually became shorter, until entertaining was so concentrated into 'the week-end' that this phrase now has a special association with entertaining. As married women have developed wider interests, even taking jobs, they have devoted less time to acting as hostess in their homes, and so the pattern of entertaining has changed. The cocktail party has now taken the place generally of elaborate dinners, for it provides the opportunity to entertain many guests at a time with the minimum of work in cooking and service. Also, now that there are means of entertainment—music, plays, dances, as well as meals—available outside the home, a host may take his friends to a restaurant or place of entertainment instead of to his home.

See also ETIQUETTE; MEALS; CONVERSATION.

ENVIRONMENT, *see* SOCIAL ENVIRONMENT.

ENZYMES, *see* ENDOCRINE GLANDS. *See also* Vol. II: FERMENTATION.

EPIDEMIC DISEASES. 1. These are diseases, such as smallpox, typhus fever, poliomyelitis, or influenza, which show, or used to show, a tendency to attack large numbers of people at once. Modern methods of scientific control have greatly reduced the risk of epidemics, though we still have outbreaks of INFLUENZA and POLIOMYELITIS (qq.v.). The pestilences, however, of plague, cholera, smallpox, and typhus fever, which for so long ravaged mankind and often changed the course of history, have almost ceased to be a danger in most parts of the world.

2. PLAGUE. This disease is transmitted to man by fleas from rats, and is almost invariably fatal. It devastated European populations in the Middle Ages: in a period of 2 years, 1348–50, this so-called 'black death' killed off perhaps half of the population of Europe, and played a considerable part in bringing about the final break up of the medieval system of LAND OWNERSHIP (q.v. Vol. VI) and control of labour.

For more than 300 years outbreaks of plague occurred at frequent intervals in different parts of Europe. The worst since the 'black death' itself occurred in London in 1665. The horrors of this epidemic are painted vividly in the pages of Pepys's *Diary* and in Defoe's *Journal of the Plague Year*. The Great FIRE OF LONDON (q.v. Vol. X) which followed the epidemic seems to have helped by destroying a regular breeding ground of plague, for after that date it rapidly receded.

3. SMALLPOX. The great devastating disease of the late 17th and 18th centuries was smallpox. In addition to causing profound constitutional disturbance, smallpox attacks the skin, producing eruptions of small septic spots about the size of a pea. These spots, at first solid, liquefy and become small blebs or blisters known as 'pocks'. As the disease progresses the blebs dry up and become crusts which are eventually shed, leaving permanent disfiguring scars in the form of pitting of the skin.

The virus of smallpox is contained in the blebs, and the infection is mainly spread by the scurf shed by the patient during convalescence and by contaminated bedding and clothing. When blebs occur in the mouth, the virus may be spread by talking or coughing.

It had been known for centuries in countries where smallpox was habitually prevalent that it seldom attacked the same person more than once, and it had been the practice deliberately

to infect healthy people with a mild form of the disease in order to confer upon them immunity from a more dangerous form.

In 1796 Edward JENNER (q.v. Vol. V) observed that a very mild disease known as cowpox produced an immunity from smallpox, and so he established the practice of 'vaccination' (*see* INOCULATION AND VACCINATION). In those countries where vaccination was carried out on a large scale smallpox was practically abolished.

Vaccination protects against smallpox for about 7 years, after which time its protection diminishes. Children, therefore, who have been vaccinated as babies need to be revaccinated at 7 and again at 14 years in order to be properly immunized. A recently vaccinated person probably escapes catching smallpox at all; at the worst the severity of the disease is greatly reduced.

Magdalene College, Cambridge

SCENES OF THE PLAGUE OF LONDON, 1665

The upper scenes show people fleeing from London; beneath is a man with a warning bell preceding a coffin, and a burial scene

'A COURT FOR KING CHOLERA'

Drawing by John Leech in *Punch*, 1864, showing the conditions which encouraged epidemics of cholera

4. CHOLERA. Only a generation after Jenner had devised the method of abolishing one epidemic disease, a new and dangerous disease came to Europe from the East. This was cholera, which spread from its traditional home in the valley of the Ganges throughout Asia and eastern Europe, following the ancient trade routes and moving at about the same speed as the caravans traversing them.

With the great increase of international trade and commerce in the 19th century the disease found its way for the first time to western Europe, the first large epidemic being in 1831-2. The low standard of public and personal hygiene at that time (*see* SANITATION, HISTORY OF) gave the disease every chance of spreading, and it was not until 1848, when a second epidemic occurred in London, that the connexion between lack of sanitation and the spread of the cholera was

guessed at, and the first Public Health Act was passed (*see* PUBLIC HEALTH, Vol. X).

Cholera is an acute and often fatal disease caused by the presence in the alimentary canal of a small curved bacterium known as the *cholera vibrio*. Myriads of these bacteria so irritate the stomach and intestines that vomiting and intense diarrhoea result, thus rapidly draining from the body essential fluids and salts. This may cause the patient to die in a few hours either from the derangement of the working of vital organs or from acute exhaustion.

Dr. John Snow, after studying the London outbreak of 1848, reasoned that cholera was contracted by drinking contaminated water, and the accuracy of his reasoning was confirmed by studies of subsequent epidemics in Europe and elsewhere. Cholera is the classical example of a mainly water-borne disease. When this was realized, large cities and towns took steps to have the domestic water supply purified, and wherever this has been done cholera epidemics have nearly always ceased.

Cholera is still prevalent in the Ganges basin, and threatens neighbouring countries where the sanitary resources are poor. The crowds who attend religious pilgrimages and festivals in the East still create a risk of an epidemic, though precautions are now taken to minimize it.

5. TYPHOID FEVER. This disease, which can also be spread by contaminated water, affects principally the small intestine and causes diarrhoea. The patient's excretions contain myriads of the typhoid bacilli, and infection may be passed on by contaminated dressings and bedding and by flies, as well as by water supplies contaminated through inadequate sanitation. It was this disease which caused the death of Albert, the Prince Consort, very likely because of the then poor sanitary arrangements at Windsor Castle. Typhoid fever was formerly a scourge of armies, and in the Boer War it was responsible for more British casualties than was enemy action.

6. TYPHUS FEVER. Until 1849 typhoid and typhus fevers were often confused, although they are two quite different diseases. Typhus fever, formerly known as jail fever, ship fever, putrid fever, or camp fever, was always associated with conditions of misery and overcrowding. It is spread by lice and, so far as we know, only by lice; people who do not harbour lice do not usually contract it. In 18th- and 19th-century Europe an astonishingly large proportion of people carried lice on their bodies or in their hair—and the disease was, consequently, prevalent. It became rare when people became more fastidious.

These great epidemic diseases are not, unfortunately, mere historical curiosities. The wars of the present century, as well as natural disasters such as serious earthquakes, have in various parts of the world produced conditions where plague, cholera, and typhus have broken out with all their former virulence. Large areas of the Middle and Far East, where millions of people live in what we should regard as medieval conditions, have been brought, as the consequence of air transport, much closer to western Europe. Public health authorities, therefore, have to take steps to ensure that epidemic diseases carried by air passengers do not spread. There are strict regulations at airports, and passengers are directed that should they sicken they must report immediately (*see* QUARANTINE REGULATIONS, Vol. X). Indeed, all these diseases, as well as certain other highly INFECTIOUS DISEASES (q.v.), are notifiable to the health authorities.

See also MEDICINE; INFECTIOUS DISEASES; TROPICAL DISEASES.
See also Vol. X: PUBLIC HEALTH.

EPILEPSY. This is a chronic disorder of the NERVOUS SYSTEM (q.v.), and its most striking feature is a complete or partial loss of consciousness, with or without convulsions.

In major epilepsy the patient suddenly loses consciousness and falls to the ground, often injuring himself. After a period of about half a minute the muscles go into spasm, and the whole body is thrown into convulsive movements. The patient's eyes roll, his teeth are gnashed together, his breathing is noisy and laborious, and foam issues from his mouth. This stage lasts from a few seconds to several minutes or even hours, and then the patient gradually relaxes and comes to himself. He may recover completely or he may remain drowsy and stuporous for some time. One of the most peculiar features of epilepsy is the 'aura' which immediately precedes the fit in certain cases. The aura, when it occurs, may take many different forms, such as pain in the limbs or stomach, strange sensations of smell, or visual hallucinations.

An epileptic fit is extremely distressing to witness, but it is very important to prevent the patient from doing himself injury during an attack. Tight clothing should be loosened, and, as epileptics very often bite their own tongues during a fit, a pad should be inserted between the teeth. When the fit is over the patient should be allowed to sleep, his head and shoulders having been well raised. Epileptics should avoid car driving, cycling, mountaineering, swimming, and any occupation where the sudden occurrence of an attack would make them a danger to themselves or other people.

Nothing is definitely known about the cause of epilepsy; the fits are, however, always accompanied by a disturbance of the electrical activity of the BRAIN (q.v.). Epilepsy usually begins in childhood, and is more frequent in females than in males. It can be to some extent controlled by drugs, but normally epilepsy cannot be completely cured.

In early times an epileptic fit was considered as a temporary departure of the soul from the body. Even today in some parts of China a garment of the sufferer is waved from the house top, gongs are sounded, and his name is called in order to attract the soul back. The Greeks regarded epilepsy as a special affliction sent by the gods, and it was therefore known as the Sacred Disease. In Biblical times and throughout the Middle Ages it was thought that epileptics were possessed by demons or evil spirits, and sufferers were subjected to barbarous methods of treatment in an effort to expel the invading demon. In England the disease was long known as the Falling Sickness. Epilepsy does not usually affect the intellect, indeed, it is a striking fact that some of the most famous men in history are reputed to have been epileptics, including Julius Caesar, St. Paul, Mohammed, Peter the Great, and Napoleon.

See also NERVOUS SYSTEM; BRAIN.

ETIQUETTE. The origins of 'the conventional rules of behaviour and ceremonies observed in polite society' are complex. One of them is a respect for authority. From the most primitive times subjects showed their respect for their ruler by bowing, prostrating themselves on the ground, not speaking until they were spoken to, and never turning their backs to the throne. Sometimes monarchs developed these rules in order to stress the respect due to them. The emperors of Byzantium used to make their subjects kiss their feet. When an ambassador from abroad was introduced, he had first to touch the ground before the throne with his forehead. During this obeisance, in order to impress the foreigner, the throne itself was raised in the air, so that on looking up the ambassador saw the Emperor far above him, even more haughty and remote than before.

Absolute rulers have, as a rule, made etiquette more complicated rather than simpler. The purpose is not only to make the ruler seem a different order of being, almost god-like, but also to protect him from familiarity, since, without some such protection, his life, lived inevitably so much in the public eye, would be intolerable. The Court of LOUIS XIV (q.v. Vol. V) is an excellent example of how the rules of etiquette worked and how necessary they were. Because the King and his family were considered to 'belong' to France, they were almost continually on show. They woke, prayed, washed, and dressed before crowds of courtiers; even larger crowds watched them eat their meals; and access to their palaces was free to all their subjects. Yet this public life was organized so minutely, with such a refinement of ceremonial, that the authority of the King, and the respect in which he was held, grew throughout his reign. A crowd watched him dress, but only the Duke who was his first *valet de chambre* might hold out the right-hand sleeve of his shirt, only the Prince who was his Great Chamberlain might relieve him of his dressing-gown, only the Master of the Wardrobe might help him pull up his breeches. These were not familiarities, nor even mere duties, but highly coveted privileges. By the end of the 18th century the value of ceremony to a ruler was so established that NAPOLEON (q.v. Vol. V), when he became emperor, discarded the Revolutionary custom of calling everyone 'citizen', as though all were of equal rank, and restored much of the Court ceremonial which the Revolution had destroyed. He recalled members of the nobility to instruct his new Court in the old formal manners.

Rules of etiquette have also proved necessary on occasions which without them might lead, not merely to embarrassment, but to serious disputes. A complicated and precise order of SOCIAL PRECEDENCE (q.v.) now decides the order in which those concerned sit at a lord mayor's banquet, for example, or ride in a coronation procession. But before the rules of diplomatic precedence were worked out in the early 16th century, there were often brawls between rival ambassadors fighting for the most honourable position at an important function. Before the principle was established that ambassadors of various countries should sign treaties in order of seniority, great difficulty often arose as to which nation's representative should sign first. The establishment of rules for such matters prevented uncertainty and discord, as do rules for lesser occasions—for example, that at a wedding the mother of the bridegroom should sit in the first pew on the right. The result is dignity and order.

The ceremonious etiquette of royalty had its effect on all polite society, though etiquette outside the palace was concerned with harmonizing the behaviour of equals rather than sustaining the eminence of an individual. Etiquette can be used as a weapon against intruders by a class as well as by an individual. As a king can use

A DINNER PARTY, 1890

Picture Post Library

formality to repel familiarity, a class can refine its manners in order to mark itself off from a lower class. In 16th-century Italy and in 18th-century France waning prosperity and increasing social unrest led the ruling families to try to preserve their superiority by withdrawing into their own special world behind barriers of etiquette. On the other hand, when a community is prosperous, polite society readily absorbs social climbers who, having won their riches, wish also to learn the manners which should go with their new way of life. At such periods, the 15th century in Italy and the 19th century in England and in the U.S.A., the market was flooded with books on etiquette, instructing people how to behave in the class to which they were rising.

Every code of etiquette has contained three elements: basic moral duties, practical rules which promote efficiency, and artificial, optional 'gallantries'. In the first category are consideration for the weak and respect for age. Among the ancient Egyptians the young stood in the presence of the old; among tribes such as the Mponguwe of Tanganyika the young men bow as they pass the huts of the elders; in England, it is only within the last 100 years that children have dared to sit in their parents' presence without asking leave. Practical rules deal with the ordinary occurrences of life: helping a lady into a vehicle, making an introduction, or listening to CONVERSATION (q.v.). As new customs are introduced, new rules arise. Before the invention of the fork, etiquette directed that the fingers should be kept at least as clean as possible; before the common use of the handkerchief, etiquette suggested that, after spitting, the phlegm should be rubbed inconspicuously under foot. Besides practices based on moral duty or convenience, there are a number of small observances which give polite society its particular tone—refinement for the sake of refinement, behaviour cultivated as an art. These belong only to societies where there is wealth and leisure, and where women are admitted as the social equals of men.

After the fall of Rome the first European

THE JAPANESE TEA CEREMONY

A very strict etiquette is observed in the ceremonial drinking of tea. From Jiro Harada, *The Lesson of Japanese Architecture*, Studio Ltd.

of polite society in other countries. The *salons* of great French hostesses of the early 17th century, in particular those of the Marquise de Rambouillet, were moulded on the Italian pattern, and at these men and women of wealth and leisure discussed fashionable literary topics.

The rules of behaviour of fashionable society for a long time little affected the behaviour of other people, even of the wealthier class. The manners of the provincial nobility of 17th-century France, for example, were very different from those of *salon* and Court society; and the English 18th-century country squire had a crude code of behaviour which had nothing in common with that of fashionable London society. Improved communications in the 19th century gradually brought about a common code of behaviour among educated people in town and country; and the publication of many books on etiquette to instruct those who were trying to acquire the manners of the aristocracy helped to standardize the rules of correct behaviour.

See also TABLE MANNERS; SOCIAL CLASSES; SOCIAL PRECEDENCE.

society which regulated behaviour in private life in accordance with a complicated code of etiquette was that of 12th-century Provence. Provence had grown wealthy; the lords had returned to their castles from the crusades; CHIVALRY (q.v. Vol. X) had exalted the position of women; and the conventions of ROMANCE LITERATURE (q.v. Vol. XII) demanded that a knight should profess a highly artificial love for a lady. And as marriage was based on convenience and seldom, if ever, on affection, his love was commonly for a married woman, which according to the rules of etiquette was perfectly correct.

In 15th-century Italy, too, a wealthy and leisured society evolved a courtly etiquette. It was fashionable to spend the summer months in a villa in the country, discussing favourite topics, such as the rival merits of arms and learning or the nature of love. This led to the elaboration of little private rules of behaviour by this small and exclusive society, rules which had nothing to do with the ordinary code of good behaviour affecting everyone. Books were written about the etiquette of Italian wealthy society, such as *The Courtier* by Baldassore Castiglione, which describes the sort of society that helped elaborate the etiquette, and the *Galateo* of Giovanni della Casa, which is a guide to the etiquette itself. Both these and other books were widely translated and so influenced the manners

EUROPEAN PEASANT COSTUME. Distinctive peasant costumes survive in the rural areas of most European countries. In some they are still the customary daily wear of the people; in others, where ordinary modern clothes are gaining ground, they are reserved for holidays, weddings, and festivals. Although such costumes, particularly those best known to tourists, are often called 'national dress', peasant styles are regional rather than national. They are rarely the same throughout any one country, but vary considerably from district to district, particularly in mountainous areas where every rather isolated valley has its own.

The so-called 'Spanish costume', for instance, which consists for women of a long, full dress, brightly coloured and trimmed with pompons, and a lace mantilla worn over a high comb, and for men of tight, high-waisted trousers, coloured sash, short jacket, and hard black hat, is found only in southern Spain. The full red skirt, laced bodice, and flat white head-kerchief, popularly supposed to be the national dress of Italy, belongs to the area around Rome, and is not worn elsewhere. Similarly, many people think that all Dutch peasant women wear or used to wear wide checked skirts and many petticoats, and the men baggy breeches and loose shirts, with sabots. These garments are indeed seen in Holland, but only in the Volendam region. In other regions a quite different but equally distinctive costume is worn (*see* Vol. I, p. 147). In all these countries, as in others, there is a great variety of traditional styles, many of which themselves differ in detail according to the age, married or single state, and communal standing of the wearer.

Peasant costume is the product of native art and tradition, and is naturally related to the climate, character, and history of the region. Most local styles are lively and vigorous; often they are beautiful, with vivid colourings, distinctive embroidery patterns, and intricate feminine head-dresses. The festival dresses of many regions are lovely creations of silk, velvet, or handwoven cloth, trimmed with flying ribbons, fine laces and silver ornaments, and lavishly embroidered with wool, silk, or beads. Vivid reds, greens, blues, and coloured stripes are common in many countries; in others, black or sober hues are preferred, but colour is supplied by bright kerchiefs, shawls, embroidered aprons, and head-scarves (*see* EMBROIDERY, WORLD).

In some parts of Brittany the holiday dress is black, with a brightly coloured apron and a falling white lace coif resembling a hood. At Pont Aven, in the same province, the black or dark blue dress is heavily embroidered in colours and surmounted by a pale blue apron. The cap is a beautiful, winged erection of white lace or linen trimmed with blue ribbon. In Alsace an enormous butterfly bow of stiff red or black ribbon is worn over a little cap. In Valencia, Spain, delicate pastel shades and pale-flowered fabrics are usual at festivals; even the men sport pale-hued satins, in contrast to the masculine greys, blacks, and dark shades common in other parts of Spain. Sometimes the colours chosen have a symbolical meaning, as in the Black Forest region of Germany, where Protestant villagers wear blue, green, or purple, and Catholics red or yellow.

Similarly, in Alsace, Protestant women wear long green skirts, Jews wear mauve, and Roman Catholics red.

Although peasant costume is traditional and changes slowly, it is incorrect to suppose that it never alters, or is uninfluenced by outside fashions. Some Swedish and Finnish styles have a distinctly 18th-century flavour, derived from the national costume introduced by Gustavus III. Many of the beautiful embroidered Norwegian dresses date from the Renaissance period, and were later influenced by the Baroque styles. Some Jutland costumes date from 1840, the women wearing long red, braided skirts and stiffened bodices, and the men white breeches, with knee-buckles, navy-blue jackets, and high upstanding collars. In Fanö Island, off the Jutland coast, a distinctive touch is added by the black masks often worn as a protection against wind-blown sand. Some Swiss styles are of late 19th-century in tone, though with a subtle difference which sets them apart from anything worn elsewhere in that period. In Canton Valais the men have light-coloured trousers and jackets, lined and collared in contrasting colours, and

Paul Popper

BRETON WOMEN IN TALL LACE CAPS
Each district has its special cap

soft hats with coloured bands; the women have full black skirts, gaily striped aprons, tight black bodices with white sleeves, and curious flat hats surmounted by ribbon bows.

In Greece the influence of the long Turkish domination can be seen in the red felt fez (*see* Vol. I, p. 30), the turban-like black scarf often worn by men, and in the fez-like head-dress worn by women with the Amalia costume. This consists of an ankle-length coloured skirt, a white blouse, and a heavily embroidered short bolero. Epirote women wear gauze scarves on their heads, embroidered jackets, waistcoats, and aprons; those of Macedonia have peaked felt caps with a fringed veil floating from the peak.

In Bulgaria women wear a kind of kirtle, with or without sleeves, over long skirts, the variety known as a *saya* being open all the way down and surmounted by a long narrow apron. They normally go bareheaded, but on high days they wear kerchiefs, loose or tied behind. Men have two main styles, the 'black' and the 'white'. The former is made from the wool of black sheep, with trousers tight to the knee and bulky above, black leggings, coloured waistcoats, and fur caps. The latter includes tight white trousers, an embroidered shirt, and a sleeveless white coat

Picture Post Library

PEASANTS IN NATIONAL DRESS IN SOUTHERN CZECHOSLOVAKIA

trimmed with black braid (*see* Vol. I, p. 84). Roumanian dress is often white also, with black embroideries and, for men, black hats or fur caps. Women wear a *maramă*, or head-kerchief, which, after marriage, is tied under the chin, so that no hair shows.

In Hungary high boots are worn by both sexes. Women have vividly coloured pleated skirts, ornamented aprons, and bodices either embroidered or covered by white kerchiefs fastened behind (*see* Vol. I, p. 233). The most characteristic masculine garments are the felt *szur*, or overcoat, and the sleeveless sheepskin *suba*, worn with tight-fitting trousers or wide skirt-like breeches. High boots also appear in Czechoslovakia where, as in Hungary, the native styles are very varied, richly colourful, and splendid with barbaric embroidery and ornament (*see* Vol. I, p. 136).

See also COSTUME, HISTORY OF; PRIMITIVE COSTUME; ORIENTAL COSTUME.

EYE STRUCTURE. Normal sight requires a functioning eye and also intact nerves to conduct

Paul Popper

SWISS HERDSMAN WITH COW BELLS

the visual impulses from the eye to those parts of the brain which are concerned with their reception and interpretation. MEMORY (q.v.), experience, and education play an important part in the function of the eyes in recognizing objects by their shapes (*see* INTELLIGENCE).

The eyeball, which contains the sense organ of sight, is globe-shaped. The front part, the 'cornea', is more curved than the rest, and is transparent, forming a window which transmits the rays of light into the interior of the eye.

The ball of the eyeball is formed of three coats (Fig. 1). The outermost coat, which reaches in front up to the cornea and is seen as the 'white of the eye', is tough and elastic and forms the main support of the eyeball. Immediately beneath this lies the middle coat, which carries blood-vessels and contains black pigment to prevent the 'scatter' of light—thus serving the same purpose as the matt black paint inside a CAMERA (q.v. Vol. VIII). This coat continues behind the cornea in the form of a circular curtain, the iris, which is the coloured part of the eye. The colour of a person's iris depends on the amount of pigment present. The muscle in the iris enables its central opening, the pupil, to contract in bright light, preventing the entrance of too strong a light, or to dilate in dim light so as to allow the greatest amount of light into the eye.

The innermost coat of the eyeball is composed of nervous tissue, and is called the retina. Specific sense elements in the retina are responsible for the forming of images. The colour of the retina is purplish, due to the presence of a pigment—the visual purple—which to some extent corresponds to the emulsion on a photographic film. When the eyes are exposed to bright light, the purplish colour fades, because the visual purple is transformed into a colourless substance; but it usually rapidly re-forms, and the retina becomes responsive again. For this process vitamin A seems to be essential, and without it the ability to adapt one's eyes to the dark is impaired, and other damage may result (*see* VITAMINS).

The nerve fibres of the retina come together to form the optic nerve at a point called the 'optic disk', the so-called blind spot of the eye. The optic nerve is a part of the BRAIN (q.v.), in fact, the only part of the brain accessible to observation. Its function is to convey impulses from the retina which the brain interprets, thus completing the process of 'seeing'.

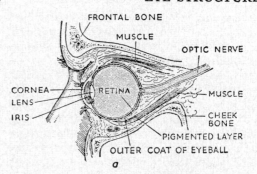

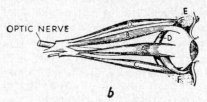

FIG. 1. DIAGRAMS OF THE EYE

a. Section. *b*. Muscles controlling movement. A and a corresponding muscle on the other side move the eye from side to side. B and C move it up and down. D, which passes round E, and F swivel it.

In the interior of the eyeball the most important structure is the lens, which resembles in shape an ordinary magnifying glass. It is enclosed in a transparent capsule which is attached by its margin to a muscle in the middle coat, the contraction of which alters the curvature of the lens, and hence its focal length. The space between the cornea in front and the lens behind is divided by the iris into the front and back chamber of the eye, which communicate with each other through the pupil. Both chambers are filled with a fluid which is secreted by the blood-vessels and is reabsorbed by a circular vein in the angle between the cornea and the iris. Interference with the absorption of this fluid leads to an increase of tension within the eye, a condition known as glaucoma. If this pressure is not relieved it results in the destruction of the eye nerves and in blindness. The space between the lens in front and the retina behind is filled with a jelly-like transparent substance.

The human eye responds to three different kinds of stimuli, namely light, form, and colour. Rays of light coming from a distance of 20 feet or more from the eye must be regarded as parallel from a practical point of view. To be focused on the retina these rays must, therefore, be bent, and this is effected as they pass through the cornea and the lens. The two eyes normally

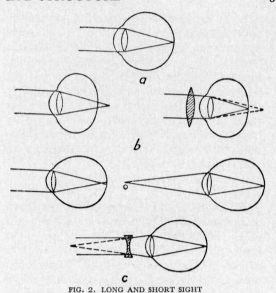

FIG. 2. LONG AND SHORT SIGHT

a. A perfect eye in which parallel rays of light from distant objects are focused by the lens on to the retina. *b.* A long-sighted eye in which parallel rays of light are focused behind the retina. Spectacles with convex lenses bend the rays to meet on the retina. *c.* A short-sighted eye in which parallel rays of light are focused in front of the retina. When the eye is looking at a near object o, the divergent rays are focused on the retina. A similar divergence is given to parallel rays by concave spectacle lenses. From Sir Stewart Duke-Elder, *The Practice of Refraction*, J. and A. Churchill Ltd.

work together, and this depends on the accurate co-operation of the muscles moving them. If these muscles are wrongly balanced, a squint is the result. When both eyes work harmoniously together, we are able to direct them towards the object we are looking at and at the same time to focus them so that sharp images will be produced on the retinae. Focusing is attained by altering the curvature of the lens itself, not, as with most optical instruments, by moving the LENS (q.v. Vol. VIII) back and forth.

The function of tears is to moisten the cornea and to wash dust and other impurities from it. Tears are secreted by the tear gland which lies in the roof of the bony cavity containing the eyeball. Normally, the tears are got rid of by evaporation, but if a person weeps very profusely, the fluid may pass to the inner angle of the eye and from there into the nose.

There is plenty of opportunity for things to go wrong at any stage of the process of seeing. In any case focusing becomes less efficient as age progresses and the lens becomes less elastic, so that the majority of people over 40 years old need glasses for near work.

In some people the eyes are shorter than normal, and light therefore focuses in them behind the retina. This condition is called far- or long-sightedness and is corrected by the use of glasses with convex lenses which bring together parallel rays. When the eye is longer than normal, the light comes to focus in front of the retina, and the person is near-sighted. This can be corrected by the use of concave glasses which spread rays of light passing through them. When the rays of light do not fall on the retina in a point but on a line, the resulting abnormality is known as astigmatism.

For normal vision it is essential that the cornea and the lens should be completely transparent. An opacity in one of them will interfere with vision. Opacities in the cornea are usually due to scars following injury or inflammation, and they can sometimes be improved by removing the scar tissue and replacing it with a piece of cornea taken from another human eye (corneal grafting). Opacities in the lens are called cataracts. They occur most commonly in old age but may also be caused by injury. They, also, can often be removed by an operation.

A person with normal colour vision recognizes six or seven distinct colours in the solar spectrum and is able to appreciate hundreds of varieties of COLOUR (q.v. Vol. III) produced by mixtures of them. In defects of colour vision there may be an inability to recognize all colours of the spectrum. People suffering from the more common type of colour blindness are able to see only three colours in varying shades of black and white, or can distinguish only two colours. In this case their spectrum is made up of yellow and blue, the one passing gradually into the other. They see red, orange, and green as one colour, and blue and violet as the other. Scarlet and green, therefore, appear the same to them. Defects of the colour sense are usually hereditary and cannot be corrected.

See also Vol. II: SENSES, Section 2.
See also Vol. III: LIGHT; COLOUR.
See also Vol. VIII: CAMERA; LENS.

F

FAIRY-STORIES, *see* STORY-TELLING. *See also* Vol. I: FAIRY-TALES AND TRADITIONAL TALES; FAIRIES.

FAITH HEALING. Faith was, and still is, a powerful factor in the cure of some bodily and mental ills. Primitive peoples and some civilized peoples, too, have believed that all happenings, good or ill, reflected the will of the gods, and those who were in the habit of invoking the aid and protection of the gods naturally did so in time of sickness, since the god or the demon who sent the disease could also remove it (*see* MAGIC, Vol. I). People have also believed in the power of SPELLS AND CHARMS (q.v. Vol. I) to cure them of their ills. A famous Anglo-Saxon charm to remove pain runs, 'Out, little spear, if therein thou be.' Healing power has also been attributed to water, wells, springs, stones, and mascots of many kinds. Some men have been thought to have special healing powers, and usually this belief has been closely associated with religious belief—for example, the sovereigns of England from Edward I to Queen Anne were thought to possess the power of healing scrofula or 'King's Evil' by their touch, and this belief was closely related to the belief that kings ruled by virtue of being chosen by God—the theory of 'the divine right of kings'. Similarly, many saints who led dedicated lives were believed to have the power of curing ills, and their relics and dwelling-places often became places of PILGRIMAGE (q.v. Vol. I).

The belief that one will get well can assist healing, particularly in cases where the main cause of the disease is psychological, for many ailments of the body arise from mental or nervous disorders (*see* MIND AND BODY). In cases which cannot be cured except by surgical or medical treatment, faith helps the morale of the patient. But some people, and notably CHRISTIAN SCIENTISTS (q.v. Vol. I), reject most medical or surgical aid, and rely completely on faith healing. Moreover there are many individual itinerant 'healers' who belong to no sect and whose claims of curing diseases are rejected by informed medical men. When such men dissuade sufferers from seeking medical aid for diseases which need it, they undo the good they do in cases which they can help, where suggestion is an aid to recovery.

See also Vol. I: MAGIC; PILGRIMAGES.

FAMILY BUDGET. Every year in the House of Commons the Chancellor of the Exchequer presents the national Budget (*see* NATIONAL FINANCE, Vol. X). In it he says how much he expects the national income to be, and what proportion of it he is going to spend on defence, the civil service, pensions, and so on. Each family, too, has some money income—from wages, salaries, dividends, pensions, or allowances—and also certain expenses that it must meet, and it must balance income against expenditure.

A family has to pay in money or in work for its house. Rent and rates, it is generally agreed, should not take up more than one fifth of the total income of a household, though a couple buying their own house may pay a higher proportion than this. More and more of the families in this country are living in local authority or council houses (*see* HOUSING, MUNICIPAL, Vol. X); and for them rents are often subsidized so that they will not exceed or even reach this proportion of an average wage. Since local authorities own about five houses out of every twelve, their policy on rents is most important: if they are guided by the Government, they will charge between 10% and 15% of the family's weekly income for rent, rates, and water charges.

A family must be not only sheltered but fed: food purchases usually take about 30% of the income. In 1900, when the weekly wage of a labourer was a little over £1, 60% of this sum had to be spent on food and 18% on rent; that is, three-quarters of the income had to go on the minimum necessities, eating and shelter.

As wages and salaries go up, people spend a smaller proportion of their income on food, and at the same time tend to buy higher quality food which costs more. From 1910 to 1938 the average housewife bought much the same amounts of bread, flour, potatoes, and other cereal foods.

In pre-war budgets cereals, fats, sugar, and jam accounted for 27% of expenditure. By 1951 29% of the weekly family expenditure on food was being spent on these items. Compared with a pre-war household everybody in 1950 ate less meat and less fish; for instance, housewives in 1935 bought 45 oz. of meat per person per week, whereas in 1950 they bought only 29 oz., of which 12 oz. was unrationed meat. At the same time, however, housewives were buying almost twice as much fruit and vegetables as they were before the war. The cost of these items had risen until in 1951 they accounted for 20% of family expenditure. Consumption of milk had also risen from 3½ pints per person per week to just over 5 pints; and by 1951, 11% of the weekly budget, almost as much as the rent, was being spent on milk. In 1951 the average housewife's expenditure was as follows: 16% on dairy products, 28% on meat and fish, 20% on fruit and vegetables, 28% on fats and cereals, and 8% on other foods. In terms of money, the average English housewife spent 18s. 9d. to feed one member of the family for a week. When we look at budgets where the total family income is £1,000 per year or more, the quantity and variety of more costly foods form one of the ways in which they differ from budgets for the rest of the population; no doubt, given enough money to make choice easy, we should all add salmon or chicken to our food bill on occasions.

The housewife usually spends about 10% of the income on clothes for herself and her family. Fuel and light absorb a further 10%, and soap, polishes, and miscellaneous purchases for the good running of the house account for 4%. These groups of expenses, together with the rent and rates, absorb some 60% of the family income at the present time, but in 1914, as the table shows, they would have absorbed 96% of the income.

Comparative expenditure by wage-earning families in 1914 and 1950 is shown in this table:

Percentage of Income spent in:

	1914	1950
Food	60	29
Rent and rates	16	11
Fuel and light	8	10
Clothing	12	10
Drink and tobacco	—	17
Household	—	7
Other goods and services . .	4	16
Total	100	100

Apart from the 1950 expenditure on drink and tobacco, which represents tax for the government more than payment for the goods, the figures can be compared fairly enough, even though the 1914 figure is for an 'ideal' rather than an actual budget. Reasons for this change are that most wages in Britain have increased more quickly than prices, that rents have been held almost constant by Acts of Parliament, and that few people are now unemployed for long periods.

So it has happened that, as the century progressed, families have had more to spend on items formerly considered luxuries. Entertainment, travel, and holidays, unheard of for the average working-class family before 1914, now appear as a normal item, included in the table under the heading 'Other goods and services'. At the same time, some middle-class families, who have to pay more in direct taxation, have had to remodel their expenditure, spending a higher proportion on education and less on drink and holidays, for example. In general, we may say that there are fewer differences in the family budget between SOCIAL CLASSES (q.v.) now than there ever have been. Indeed, a standard budget common to all the nation may be coming into existence as taxation evens out the amount of 'taking-home money' and as education increases the ability of people to choose wisely and to plan their expenditure.

FAMILY FESTIVALS. The family is both the smallest community and the unit from which larger communities are formed. Normally everyone is born in a family, with a father and mother to take care of him (*see* FAMILY, HISTORY OF). As the members of a nation or a religion keep yearly FESTIVALS (q.v. Vol. I) to express and deepen what they have in common, so families keep festivals at home. These aim at preserving and strengthening the family unity.

Family life in Western Europe springs from Roman civilization and some of its customs have their origin in ancient Rome. Chief of these are the Christmas customs. Christmas celebrates the birth of Jesus Christ. But in ancient Rome there was a festival, the Saturnalia, lasting from 17 December to 24 December. This was largely a festival of the home; and when in the 4th century the Church began to keep the religious festival of Christmas openly, persecution having ceased, many Saturnalian customs of innocent domestic mirth were allowed to continue, to

Wallace Collection

THE CHRISTENING FEAST
Painting by Jan Steen, 1664

make Christmas 'merry'. These included the giving of presents, lighting of candles, and parlour games with teasing and mockery. While the festival lasted, slaves were treated as their masters' equals and could wear the pointed hat, then the head-dress of free men only (*see* HEAD-WEAR). This hat later on degenerated into the dunce's cap, but it still remains, with the rest of the revelry, as part of our family Christmas.

The Yule log, or Christmas block, comes not from Italy but from Teutonic lands of the colder north. It was burnt on Christmas Eve, when the sun begins to regain strength. No doubt the log was once supposed to have a magical effect, helping the sun to shine more brightly; but its cheerful warmth in the dark evenings will account for its survival when the superstition was no longer believed. At Yuletide houses and churches were decked with evergreens, especially mistletoe. Much feasting took place, favourite foods being boar's head, plum pudding, and mince pies. Then, as now, the home customs formed a natural counterpart to the Church festival. As the latter centres round the Holy Family, that is, Jesus, Mary, and Joseph, it can easily be adapted to the home, where it provides an occasion for family reunions and for innocent gaiety, as well as emphasizing the sacred character of family relationships.

The birth of a child is the most important event in family life. Among primitive peoples, a child is an asset, making the tribe stronger for work and survival. In civilized lands the stress is of a more personal kind; the child demands love and care, and in a few years will be able to return this love. Thus the family is spiritually

Harrogate Corporation

'MANY HAPPY RETURNS OF THE DAY'
Painting by W. P. Frith, 1856

enriched. But the BIRTH CEREMONIES (q.v. Vol. I) must follow shortly after the birth. In primitive communities the child is presented to the tribal god, or formally acknowledged by the father. Mohammedans baptize their children 40 days after birth, and friends of the family assemble for this rite of dedication and for the feast which follows it. Christians also dedicate their children by baptism (*see* SACRAMENT, Vol. I) or, as it is popularly called, christening, and the religious service is followed by a home feast, with a christening cake.

The keeping of birthdays is ancient and almost universal. It began as soon as men had learned to reckon time by the changes of the moon; for only then could the exact day be calculated. The birthday was thought of as a kind of repetition of the birth; and the feasting and giving of presents was meant to increase the vitality of the person concerned. Our greeting 'many happy returns' has the same meaning, and behind it lies the same latent hope.

Among Christians generally the child is given a name at baptism, or, if he is not baptized, he is named at the legal registration (*see* VITAL STATISTICS, Section 2, Vol. X). Names are of great antiquity, for without a name it is impossible to treat either child or adult as a personality with rights and duties. The birthday generally commemorates the name as well as the birth; but in Roman Catholic countries, where it is customary to name children after Christian SAINTS (q.v. Vol. I), the name-day is kept on the saint's festival. In primitive times the name was felt to be more than a mere distinguishing mark; it was a part of the personality. Indeed, even today, when a child receives the name of a parent or an ancestor, there is a hope that it will influence him to preserve all that is best in the family's history. In the same way a saint's name may set before its bearer an example of courage and goodness. The family festival, therefore, not only repeats the joy of a birth by presents and feasting; it also celebrates the naming of the child, and thus reaffirms the ideals of individual and family life.

Within recent years an old family custom has been revived and extended in the keeping of Mothering Sunday on the Fourth Sunday in Lent. In the Epistle for that day in the Book of Common Prayer, the 'Jerusalem which is above' is called 'our mother'. This Jerusalem was understood to be the Church, in contrast to the earthly Jerusalem of the Jews. On that day pilgrimages were made to the cathedral, the mother church of a diocese, or else to the parish church. To the thought of the Church as the Mother of all her children was naturally joined the thought of each family and the mother who ministered to her own children. So it became customary for sons and daughters who had left home through work or marriage to visit their mother and bring her a present, either of money or flowers—violets being considered the most appropriate—or of a special cake called a Simnel cake. There are many varying local traditions about the composition of this cake, but they all aim at making it the best possible. The name 'Simnel' comes from a Latin word meaning 'the best flour'. A dish called furmety (or frumenty), from the Latin *frumentum*, 'corn', also traditionally associated with Mothering Sunday, consists of grains of wheat boiled in milk and well flavoured. The Mothering Sunday observances, like those of the other family festivals, express the belief of the common man that the family is a sacred society whose permanence and well-being is essential to the prosperity of the world.

See also Vol. I: ANCESTOR WORSHIP; BIRTH CEREMONIES; FESTIVALS; MARRIAGE CEREMONIES.

FAMILY, HISTORY OF. From primitive times the family has been the basic unit of social organization. A man and woman had to combine to provide for the rearing of children, and men needed the domestic crafts of women while women required the protection and labour of men. When ARISTOTLE (q.v. Vol. V) traced the way in which civilization had developed, he took the family as his starting-point; a basic Roman unit of land was the *terra unius familiae*, the amount of land needed to support one family. The family has so strong a tradition of solidarity that the State has often hesitated to interfere with what happened inside it. The Roman father could kill an unwanted baby, and his wife might crucify a slave (*see* SLAVERY, Vol. X), without referring to any higher body than a council of members of the family. In England

it is only within the last 100 years that the State has insisted on interfering when families were failing to educate their children properly, or treating them with cruelty (*see* CHILD WELFARE, Vol. X).

This feeling of independence, symbolized by such phrases as 'The Englishman's home is his castle', has naturally affected man's ideas of his relation to the State, and of his own personal liberty. In places where loyalty to the family is a religious cult, as in China, there can be little idea of liberty at all: man exists for the family, not for the development of his own personality. At the other extreme, some cultures have deliberately attacked family solidarity. The ancient Greeks believed that children should be educated primarily by the State for its own ends. Some primitive tribes, the MASAI (q.v. Vol. I), for

The Yorkshire Museum

MONUMENT ERECTED TO A ROMANO-BRITISH WOMAN, JULIA VELVA

She is reclining on a couch with her family beside her

Sir Kenneth Clark

THE SALTONSTALL FAMILY

Painting by David des
Granges, 1611–*c.* 1675

National Gallery

A DUTCH FAMILY IN THE
17TH CENTURY

Painting by Michael
Sweertz

example, achieve the same effect by taking all boys from the family at an early age and educating them in the male club house in the traditions of the tribe as a whole, not in those of a family. In the 15th and 16th centuries Turkish sultans acquired a devoted body of men by removing likely children from their families and educating them in absolute obedience to the head of the State. Generally, however, the family has had the first claim on man's conscious loyalties, and has the greatest influence over his unconscious mind, as PSYCHOLOGY (q.v.) has shown.

The basic composition of the family is father, mother, and children. But this has been varied in many ways. We often find several generations all living together, particularly among poor families in the Mediterranean countries, where there is difficulty in providing new homes on marriage. As the father has to work outside the home all day, and the mother is occupied with domestic work within it, the children are largely brought up by the grandparents. Their first notions, therefore, are those of two generations previous to their own. Again, until women were freely able to earn their own living, the unmarried woman was a regular feature of the household.

On the other hand, there was a general tendency among well-to-do families, especially in the Middle Ages, to get rid of children as soon as possible, or at least to keep them on the fringe of family life. Babies were given to foster-parents who often took them to their own homes and kept them for several years. Complaints against this custom were made in ancient Rome, and repeated at intervals in Italy, France, and England from at least the 14th century until the 18th. An 18th-century child, Susan Sibbald, was put out to nurse with the wife of a smuggler, and when she finally returned to her family, she felt so different from them that she was convinced that a mistake had been made, and that she was in reality the child of the smuggler. When children returned from the foster-parent, they commonly lived isolated from the family in the NURSERY (q.v.), and were as soon as possible married off. Foreigners commented on the tendency of English parents of the 16th century to get rid of their children by sending them to be pages in some great house at the age of 7 or 8 (*see* DOMESTIC SERVICE), or apprenticing them to some trade, or arranging marriages for them at

the age of 12 or 13. This lack of sympathy towards childhood made relations between parent and child very formal.

Another factor that determines the atmosphere of family life is, of course, the respective positions in it of the father and the mother. Authority has generally been vested in the father, but not always. Some tribes, as widely scattered as North America, South America, Africa, India, and Arabia, have not only admitted the family authority of women but have given the children the mother's family name rather than the father's. Among civilized societies, however, the position of women until recent times has been everywhere inferior to that of men. The tendency was clearly shown in Greece. In Homeric times, women were greatly respected, but gradually their prestige declined, partly owing to influence from the East, where women lived as virtual prisoners in harems. At the height of Greek civilization the married woman was kept at home, her education neglected, her interests entirely domestic, and she was not even allowed to eat with her husband when he had guests. All progress lay outside the family; intellectually, the mother was a stranger to her husband and sons.

In Rome her position was stronger. Wives could attend banquets and walk freely in public, and they had control over their own possessions at law. But there were still separate moral codes for men and for women: while a man could publicly acknowledge his concubines, a wife's infidelity might be punished with death.

The belief in the sanctity of every individual soul introduced by Christianity gradually eliminated the custom of infanticide, which had been widespread in antiquity; but, though Catholicism glorified woman in the form of the Blessed Virgin Mary, and its CANON LAW (q.v. Vol. X) forbade a man to have a mistress and made it difficult for him to divorce his wife, woman's inferiority to man was taken for granted. Every woman was bound to serve her husband. English medieval law expressed this view very clearly. A woman by marriage lost all her legal standing including control of her property. Women had no legal power over their children, and their evidence was not accepted in a court of law.

A few wealthy or unusually energetic women achieved a freedom in practice that they were denied in theory. Whereas in countries where

Tate Gallery

AN ENGLISH FAMILY IN THE 18TH CENTURY
Painting by Johann Zoffany

polygamy (the marriage by one man of many wives) was practised, it was impossible for the married woman to take any active part in affairs, in the West, in the monogamous family, there was always a chance for the individual to make herself felt. Thus in 15th-century England there were women merchants trading professionally, for example, in fish, fruit, and cloth; there were women members of CRAFT GUILDS (q.v. Vol. VII); and widows frequently continued to run their husbands' businesses. Women could have an important voice in the running of parish affairs as churchwardens, and although a woman could not sit in Parliament, she could govern a castle and take part in certain administrative duties, such as the collection of loans. This admission that women could play an active part in the world caused foreigners to envy the Englishwoman of Queen Elizabeth's day. 'England in general', reported a traveller, 'is said to be the Hell of Horses, the Purgatory of Servants, and the Paradise of Women.' By this time, too, many women were highly educated. In the next century Milton was to claim that they should have a right to divorce husbands who mercilessly ill-treated them, and yet, in *Paradise Lost*, the older view was clearly still uppermost in his mind, when he described how God created Adam and Eve, 'He for God only, she for God in him.' A wife was still her husband's servant, and at his mercy; her legal identity was sunk in his. Unless he committed adultery and she could prove it, she could never get her freedom by divorce.

Towards the end of the 18th century, the so-called Age of Reason, the 'rights of man' were being claimed eagerly in France, England, and America, but the rights of women were not considered. The French National Assembly in the revolutionary year 1789 refused to consider any improvement in their status. But women in the West, though legally almost the chattels of their husbands and constitutionally powerless since they had no vote, could nevertheless make themselves heard in print and at public meetings, and were not kept in ignorance of what was going on about them by the gratings, locks, and veils of the harem which submerged Eastern women. Thus in 1792 Mary Wollstonecraft was able to publish *A Vindication of the Rights of Women*; in 1845 the United States woman's rights programme was publicly organized at the Seneca Falls Convention; in 1903 Mrs. Pankhurst was able to found the Woman's Social and Poli-

tical Union in England. When women finally achieved full legal and constitutional equality with men, and some approach to economic equality, it was to a considerable extent the result of their own actions (*see* WOMEN'S SUFFRAGE, Vol. X). In Britain by the Married Women's Property Acts of 1882 and 1893 they gained control of their own property and could not be liable for their husbands' debts. Women were given equal voting rights with men in 1928; and their claim for educational equality, too, has gradually been receiving recognition.

These changes in women's status affected the family in many ways. Better education and wider experience made women more fully companions for their husbands and children. But,

Rheinisches Museum, Cologne

A GERMAN FAMILY IN THE 19TH CENTURY
Painting by Karl Begas

as these growing interests and abilities took them more and more into the general life of the community, the family, to a greater or less degree, suffered the loss of its domestic centre. Poor families were affected first when, at the INDUSTRIAL REVOLUTION (q.v. Vol. VII), the mother left her domestic craft to work in a factory. The Industrial Revolution affected family life in other ways. When the main pattern of life was a peasant one, the children joined in their parents' work at an early age; the father was the foreman of the family, and shared work was a bond. This pattern has vanished except in remote rural places. Moreover, changing social conditions have imposed great changes on the relation between family and State. The State has accepted many responsibilities that were formerly the parents', such as housing, health, and education, and this shifting of responsibility has to some extent weakened the family bonds. The Victorian family, frequently consisting of ten or twelve children, formed a self-sufficient community in a way that the modern families of one or two children cannot. Consequently there is an increasing tendency for children to find their recreation outside the family, and with others of their own age, in youth clubs and in such pursuits as hiking and dancing. The different interests of each age group are emphasized in magazines and children's books, and by manufacturers who point out profitably that each age group has its own type of clothes, amusements, and way of life. The result has been that in place of family unity, which brought the generations together, there is now a horizontal division between them. There is a feeling of solidarity among children, particularly those in their 'teens; children tend almost to form a separate class. So great is the cleavage that, whereas children 100 years ago were often virtually ignored by their parents, parents today often have to make desperate efforts to learn the interests and thus enlist the sympathy of their children.

See also SOCIAL ENVIRONMENT; MARRIAGE, HISTORY OF; NURSERY, HISTORY OF.

FAMILY WELFARE SERVICES. 1. Services to the FAMILY (q.v.) have increased steadily, particularly during this century, for a number of reasons. During the 19th century a sense of general responsibility for social conditions gradually developed, and, of recent years, an understanding, too, of how many social problems have their roots in an unsatisfactory family life. A high divorce rate, a low birth-rate, delinquency among children, and many problems of health are problems which closely affect the family. The modern emphasis on prevention rather than cure has led to increased efforts of social service and to the establishment of a variety of organizations to give skilled guidance to meet the various problems of family life. Since the area of the State's interest has widened so greatly, the State has in recent years taken over some voluntarily established social services and encouraged the continuance of others.

Voluntary societies for family welfare are of three kinds. First, certain societies, often religious bodies, now include family welfare work within their closely drawn charitable purposes. Secondly, some organizations have changed the nature of their work to cope with the new demands: for example, the Society for the Organization of Charitable Relief, now the Family Welfare Association, not only supports the activities of other groups, such as marriage guidance clinics, but also includes among its own work Family Discussion Bureaux, set up in association with the Tavistock Institute of Human Relations, for research, case work, group discussion, and training. Thirdly, special new organizations, such as the Family Service Units, have sprung up specifically to do family welfare work. The Family Service Units, which were started during the Second World War, seek to help 'problem' families by working for them, living among them, and offering friendship as well as advice.

The voluntary services available to families are thus both numerous and varied. The National Council of Social Service plays the important part of linking these various voluntary services to avoid wasting effort and to ensure that they are both widely known and widely used. There is room for still more co-ordination, for it sometimes happens that the members of a problem family are being 'treated' by several voluntary or statutory services not in touch with each other. This is not necessarily all duplicated effort, but there is clearly need for closer co-operation than sometimes exists.

2. MARRIAGE GUIDANCE. Since the two World Wars there has been an enormous increase in the number of marriages which have ended in separation or divorce (*see* MARRIAGE, HISTORY

Tate Gallery

THE BLIND FIDDLER. A POOR SCOTTISH FAMILY IN THE 19TH CENTURY
Painting by David Wilkie

OF). This is partly because after the Matrimonial Causes Act (1937) it became much easier to obtain a divorce (*see* DIVORCE LAWS, Vol. X). The social effects of two long wars, bad housing and social conditions, and changes in moral standards have all probably played their part in bringing about so many broken marriages. This high divorce rate is a serious social problem, and a Royal Commission has been appointed to consider it and associated matters.

The present high divorce rate is causing anxiety both because marriage is considered an essential part of a stable civilization and because investigations show that much unhappiness, juvenile delinquency, and serious crime follow the breaking up of marriages. From 1938 local Marriage Guidance Councils were started in different parts of Britain, and in 1947 the National Marriage Guidance Council united all these local councils. About the same time Roman Catholics formed the Catholic Marriage Advisory Council. These two organizations are partly State-supported. A marriage guidance council is normally staffed by one or a few trained advisers, and these call on the services of specialist advisers, such as doctors, priests, or solicitors, to help with special problems. The council is always ready to help a couple who seek help because their marriage is likely to break up. No official figures are available, but the National Marriage Guidance Council probably handles more than 8,000 cases a year.

The Council soon found that their main difficulty was that they did not hear of distressed marriages until it was too late; so now they are concentrating on preventive work by giving lectures and courses on marriage, particularly for engaged couples. As well as the two advisory councils, other organizations, particularly religious bodies, arrange such courses, which vary, therefore, according to the view of marriage held by the organizers. A typical course might consist of talks by an experienced married social worker on practical problems, by a solicitor on legal responsibilities, by a doctor on the physical side of marriage, and by a priest on the spiritual meaning of marriage.

3. FAMILY PLANNING. The first British birth control clinic was started in 1921 by Marie Stopes. In 1930 the National Birth Control Association, which later became the Family Planning Association, was formed. The change of name was intended to mark an enlargement in activity, for the Family Planning Association now may give advice and treatment to those who fail to produce the number of children they want. In practice birth control remains the largest part of its work partly because those couples who fail to produce sufficient children, or even a child at all, now receive help through the National Health Service. The Association derives its income partly from the sale of literature and contraceptives (see REPRODUCTION) and partly from subscriptions and donations. It has about 170 clinics and gives training to doctors, students, and nurses on how to help people to practise birth control satisfactorily.

Some local authorities run their own birth control clinics, but most of these now work jointly with the Family Planning Association or have asked the Association to run a clinic on their behalf.

4. MATERNITY CLINICS. These provide medical care for women before and just after their baby's BIRTH (q.v.). The first clinic was started in Woolwich in 1915; later, six other clinics were opened by the National League for Maternity and Child Welfare. In 1918 the powers of local authorities to provide ante-natal clinics were extended by Act of Parliament, and the Act also gave to expectant mothers the right to dental treatment, home visiting, educational classes, and free or cheap milk and other foods. Now the maternity clinics are a part of the NATIONAL HEALTH SERVICE (q.v. Vol. X). They may be run by local authorities or occasionally by voluntary institutions, or be attached to hospitals. In most instances ante- and post-natal clinics are run together; in 1952 there were 1,828 ante-natal clinics, of which 29 were run by voluntary institutions. There were 248 post-natal clinics run by local health authorities and 10 voluntary ones.

An expectant mother visits the ante-natal clinic for the first time about her 10th week of pregnancy; she returns once a month until the 7th month, fortnightly during the 8th month,

and weekly during the 9th, and on each occasion is examined by a doctor. At an early visit the expectant mother's BLOOD group (q.v.) is discovered and her pelvic measurement taken to determine whether it is wide enough for a normal birth, and she is given an internal examination. At each visit tests are made of her urine, weight, and blood-pressure, and she is directed how to do exercises to relax the abdominal muscles. Some hospital clinics also give diets. The aim of the clinic is to ensure that everything is done to make for a normal delivery and to enable the mother, if possible, to breast-feed the baby (see BABIES, FEEDING OF).

At the clinic the expectant mother also meets the hospital almoner or local authority health visitor, who sees that she has all she needs in clothing and furniture for herself and the baby and, if the baby is to be born at home, helps with her arrangements, particularly with the provision of home-helps to do domestic work. Some clinics provide classes for teaching mothercraft.

About 6 weeks after the baby is born, the mother attends a post-natal clinic, where again she is given an internal examination. Normally only one visit is necessary, and the mother is then passed on to the ordinary health service and the baby to the child welfare clinics. During pregnancy and until the child is a year old, the mother is given dental treatment free of charge.

5. CHILD WELFARE. The first clinics in England for infants and young children were started by voluntary societies at the beginning of the century. At Liverpool, in 1901, centres were opened at which health visitors weighed the babies at regular intervals and gave advice to their mothers on their care and feeding. During 1906 and 1907 centres were opened at Glasgow, St. Pancras, and Marylebone at which mothers could learn how to look after their babies. In 1907 the Notification of Births Act forced parents to notify their local authority immediately after the birth of a baby. This enabled the local authorities to give medical supervision, and they began from that time to set up clinics for infants. Now there are infant and child welfare clinics run by the local authorities all over the country. There are also some child welfare clinics attached to hospitals.

Now that the National Health Service is in operation, the child welfare clinics have the task of looking after infants between the time they leave the maternity clinics and the time they come under the care of the school medical services at the age of 5. A doctor attends the clinic, and the health visitor follows up each case, visiting the mother in her home to give advice on home conditions.

Any mother may take her baby to the clinic and, especially if it is her first baby, she will be encouraged to attend weekly while the baby is very young. On the first visit the baby is undressed and weighed and thoroughly checked by the doctor. Later, if the baby is healthy, he is seen normally by the health visitor and less regularly by the doctor. The mother receives advice on feeding, clothing, and training the baby, and his teething and weight are checked. In addition, she can obtain orange juice, vitamin tablets, dried milk, and cod liver oil and buy certain foods at cheap rates. At some clinics she can buy and sell NURSERY EQUIPMENT (q.v.). She can, too, often have her child immunized against diphtheria and inoculated against whooping cough, although these services are also provided by local doctors. The job of the clinic is to help the mother to rear healthy babies but, although illnesses are often first detected at the clinics, the babies must go to their normal doctors or hospitals for treatment.

See also CHILD GUIDANCE CLINICS.

FARTHINGALES, *see* FOUNDATION-GARMENTS.

FASHIONS, *see* DRESS DESIGN; COSTUME, HISTORY OF.

FATS AND OILS. These are similar in composition, the main difference being that fats are solid at normal temperatures and oils are liquid. A fat which is very soft at normal temperatures, such as goose fat, is called a grease. The naturally occurring fats, such as butter, lard, and suet, are of animal origin. The majority of edible oils (*see* OILS, VEGETABLE, Section 3, Vol. VII) are of vegetable origin, olive, cotton seed, and soya bean being typical examples; but fish oils also form an important group, including whale oil, cod liver oil, and halibut liver oil. MARGARINE (q.v. Vol. VII) and cooking fat, which are in common use today, are made from whale oil or oil of vegetable origin, such as soya bean or cotton seed.

In cooking an important use of fats is as shortening agents in cakes, pastry, and such foods. The fat is thoroughly mixed with the flour, either by being rubbed or grated into it, as in making PASTRY, or by being creamed (beaten up) with sugar before the flour is added, as in making most CAKES (qq.v.). Some fats are better for one purpose, and some for another. Thus, though lard (the fat from pork) and dripping (the fat from beef) can be used to produce an excellent pastry, they are unsuitable for creaming. Both margarine and butter are good for creaming, and some of the proprietary brands of white fat are even better.

Both fats and oils are used for frying, and here the important factor to determine is the smoking temperature of the fat. If it is 400° F. or higher, cooking can be carried out more successfully than if the fat has a lower smoking-point, for then it starts to decompose before a high enough temperature for satisfactory cooking has been reached.

Oil, particularly olive oil, is used for making mayonnaise and French dressing (*see* SALADS). Much of the national character of the cooking in different countries depends on the basic oil or fat most easily available and therefore most usually employed. A country's recipes are devised to suit the commodities available, and it is no accident that the most characteristic cooking of Spain needs olive oil, that French omelettes must be cooked in butter, and Yorkshire pudding in beef dripping.

See also OIL-BEARING PLANTS, Vol. VI.

FIREPLACES. In cold climates the fireplace is the natural centre of interest in a room, and it has usually been given emphasis by decoration. The first fireplaces in Britain were built in the 12th century; they often had a projecting hood resting on corbels or columns; the fire was made on the ground, or logs were supported on metal bars called 'dogs'. During the Middle Ages fireplaces in the large halls of CASTLES and MANORS (qq.v.) were very wide, for only wood was burnt and a great deal was needed to warm the draughty stone-walled rooms. The hood was replaced at first by an arch, and in the 15th century by a broad slab of stone, often carved with floral, geometric, or heraldic designs, or by a stout beam of wood. Such beams of both stone and wood, known as chimney 'breasts', continued in use in cottages for hundreds of years. These fireplaces often had seats and small cupboards to hold kindling wood on either side of

National Buildings Record

12TH-CENTURY HOODED FIREPLACE AT BOOTHBY PAGNELL
MANOR, LINCOLNSHIRE

the fire. There was sometimes a bread oven in the wall at the back or side of the chimney, which was heated by being filled with burning faggots; when these were burnt and the ashes removed, the bread was put in (*see* COOKING STOVES).

Elizabethan houses had very elaborate fireplaces, with carved stone or wooden overmantels reaching to the ceiling. Sometimes there were columns on either side of the fire and of the panel above it, or sometimes there were little figures which supported the breasts. 'Fire-dogs' were larger, and their uprights were richly decorated; a metal fireback embossed with heraldic designs protected the back of the grate. In the 17th century the fireplace was usually surrounded by a simple projecting moulding, but carved overmantels, which sometimes framed a painting, remained popular (*see* Vol. V, p. 189).

Fireplaces in the 18th century followed the refined and elegant styles of GEORGIAN ARCHITECTURE (q.v. Vol. XII). The overmantel was supported on columns or pilasters, and above was a simple panel with a picture or mirror let

National Buildings Record

16TH-CENTURY CARVED STONE FIREPLACE WITH FIRE BASKET AND FIRE BACK, AT RED LODGE, BRISTOL

National Buildings Record

LATE 18TH-CENTURY FIREPLACE WITH HOB GRATE IN A HOUSE IN ROYAL CRESCENT, BATH

into it. At the end of the 18th century Robert ADAM (q.v. Vol. V) designed marble fireplaces to suit the decoration of his rooms, with delicate carving or designs inlaid in coloured marbles.

When coal fires became common, smaller grates were built, and instead of dogs a fire basket was provided to keep the coal off the hearth and so allow a draught through the fire. In the 19th century the grate was of cast iron and was fixed permanently into the opening. At first it was high and sometimes had hobs on either side for standing a kettle on; later, it was placed lower and usually in a semicircular frame. The Victorian love of elaborate ornament brought a return of the overmantel, in carved or painted wood or bamboo, on which ornaments were displayed or above which might be a large gilt-framed mirror.

In other countries central heating or enclosed stoves which give an even heat throughout the room have been preferred to open fires, and the fireplace has not been the focal point of the room as it has been in Britain (*see* HEATING, HISTORY OF). Now that gas and electric fires are often used the fireplace is losing its importance. It is often simply a heatproof panel with no strongly marked surround. The mantelshelf may be retained because, as well as being convenient, it prevents the wall above the fire from being stained by dirt carried upwards by rising currents of warm air.

See also CHIMNEYS; HEATING, HISTORY OF; HEATING SYSTEMS, DOMESTIC; HOUSES, HISTORY OF.

FIRST AID. 1. Anyone may be called upon at some time to render first aid before a doctor can be obtained. The right action on such an occasion may be the means of saving a life. In the first place it is essential to be able to recognize a situation when the death of a patient may be caused by a delay of minutes or even seconds in starting treatment. For instance, in cases of severe bleeding (haemorrhage) or suffocation (asphyxia), immediate action must be taken to stop the bleeding or to enable the asphyxiated patient to breathe. For most other conditions, an attempt should be made to find out the nature of the injury or illness before trying to apply any treatment. Quiet, warmth, and reassurance are, however, three essentials which can be given before the doctor arrives, and in many cases, where the nature of the injury is not obvious, it is better to attempt no more. The wrong action may well make the condition worse—for example, choking an unconscious patient by pouring fluids into his mouth, or giving hot drinks to somebody with an internal haemorrhage.

2. SHOCK. This is a common cause of death after any injury, and the condition is not difficult to recognize. The patient's face goes a grey, earthy colour, his skin cold and clammy, his pulse rapid and weak, and his breathing shallow. If there is no obvious or suspected haemorrhage the best treatment is to lay the patient down with his head slightly lower than his feet so as to increase the supply of blood to the brain, to keep him warm and absolutely quiet, and to give him a hot drink such as strong, sweet tea. A doctor will often treat a serious case of shock by administering a blood transfusion. A patient who has fainted, if laid down with his head low, usually recovers rapidly.

3. HAEMORRHAGE. The bleeding may be external or internal; if external, an attempt should be made to stop it. Bleeding from an artery (a not very common occurrence) must be treated instantly by one of two methods: firm pressure over the bleeding point to seal the gap in the wall of the artery, or pressure on a pressure point between the wound and the heart.

These pressure points exist for each part of the body, and it is much better to use them than to exert direct pressure in the wound. They are found wherever the main arteries run close to a bone, against which the artery can be pressed, in the groin, in the arm above the elbow, above the collar-bone, and at the temples. A less tiring method of applying pressure is to use a tourniquet which encircles and compresses the limb; but this can be very dangerous, especially if it is left too long. Only in the gravest emergency should this be tried by the inexperienced, and the handkerchief or whatever is used should be tied only tight enough to stop the bleeding. It should always be relaxed for a short time after 15 minutes. The patient should never be moved, for example, by ambulance men, without their being informed that a tourniquet has been applied.

The commonest type of bleeding from a vein, apart from actual wounds, is caused by the bursting of a varicose vein in the leg. In this case the patient should be laid flat, the affected leg held up to reduce the blood flow (a measure also useful in minor arterial bleeding), and pressure should be applied with a clean pad placed over the bleeding point. Bleeding from a vein is stopped much more easily than arterial bleeding because the pressure within the vein is less.

Sometimes bleeding occurs from a tooth socket after a tooth has been extracted, and this can be stopped by simple pressure. A plug of clean cotton wool soaked in hydrogen peroxide solution should be inserted in the socket and pressed firmly home for a few minutes by holding a cork between the teeth at the bleeding point.

The existence of internal gastric haemorrhage is made obvious because the patient spits up or vomits blood and shows signs of shock. This is a serious matter, and a doctor should be called immediately. In the meantime the patient should be treated as for shock, except that he should on no account be given food or drink.

4. ASPHYXIA (suffocation). Unless relieved the patient will die quickly because of insufficient oxygen in his blood. Asphyxia is caused in several ways—by drowning, for example, where the patient's lungs are filled with water instead of air; by the accidental inhalation (swallowing the wrong way) of food or other objects; by breathing carbon monoxide from a car engine

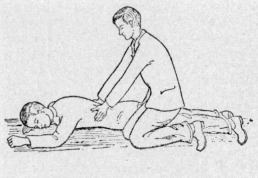

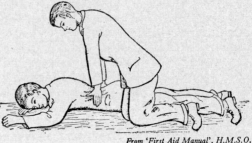

From 'First Aid Manual', H.M.S.O.

FIG. I. SCHAFER'S METHOD OF ARTIFICIAL RESPIRATION

running in a closed garage or from coal-gas; or by breathing smoke fumes which contain practically no oxygen. Again, the breathing muscles of the chest may have been made unable to act either because of severe pressure from a crowd or because the patient has been buried under a fall of earth or sand; or they may have been paralysed by an electric shock, possibly from a stroke of lightning.

In all these conditions, two things must be done at once: the airway to the lungs must be cleared, and the process of breathing must be carried on for the patient until he can do it again for himself.

The first thing is to remove any obstruction to breathing. This may be done by thumping the victim on the back if he has, for example, swallowed a coin; by hooking out the obstruction, perhaps a piece of food, with the fingers from the back of the throat; by removing false teeth; by hanging a drowning person's head down lower than his body to let the water run out of the lungs; or by pulling an unconscious patient's tongue forward if it has fallen back and is blocking his throat. When the airway is cleared, it is best to keep the patient with his head turned to one side to prevent further trouble.

Artificial respiration, which is a skill everyone

should possess, is best taught by demonstration and practice. By Schafer's method, the simplest (Fig. 1), the patient is laid on his stomach with his head to one side, his mouth unobstructed, and his arms above his head. The operator kneels beside the patient's hips facing the head, places his hands on the lower ribs in the small of the back, one on each side of the midline, with the thumbs almost touching. He then swings his body forward from the knees so as to apply steady pressure to the body and force air out of the lungs, and then swings gently back to release pressure and let air enter the lungs. The whole movement, which takes about 5 seconds, is repeated again and again until the patient is breathing well without assistance and his face is no longer blue. Unless it is absolutely certain that the patient is dead, it is usual to persevere with artificial respiration even for 2 hours—a tiring process but often attended with miraculous results.

5. CUTS AND WOUNDS. The main aims of first aid treatment are to stop bleeding and to prevent infection. Slight bleeding is harmless, indeed, may even do good, for the flow of blood

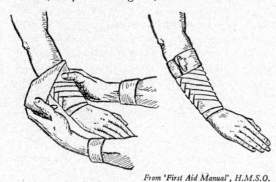

From 'First Aid Manual', H.M.S.O.

FIG. 2. BANDAGING AN ARM WOUND

washes out harmful germs which may have entered the wound. Dressings should be simple and clean. It is not usual in an emergency to be able to obtain asepsis, but the inner folds of a clean towel or handkerchief are usually fairly germ-free and can be applied to a wound without fear, provided that the material is handled with clean hands and by its ends only so that the fingers are kept away from the wound. The wound should not be smeared with ointment or other 'remedies'.

6. FRACTURES, DISLOCATIONS, AND SPRAINS. These are best left for the arrival of the doctor, though the patient should be given the usual treatment for shock. An inexperienced person cannot usually distinguish one injury from another, and clumsy handling and attempts at splinting can do more harm than good, as well as often causing the patient unnecessary pain. The injured limb should be kept quite still, and the patient covered with a blanket or coat.

7. BURNS AND SCALDS. These should be covered lightly from the air, preferably by a clean, soft, linen cloth. On no account should oils or other 'dressings' be applied, but treatment should be left for the doctor. The patient should be treated for shock.

8. POISONING. Accidental poisoning is usually recognized. The patient may still be conscious and so able to tell what has happened. If not, the container may reveal what poison has been taken, or the patient's vomit may make this clear. The patient should be rushed to the nearest hospital with all possible speed, accompanied by somebody who knows the circumstances and by any evidence such as a container and a specimen of the vomit, which will help to identify the poison quickly. For some poisons an emetic is the right treatment; for others it is the worst possible treatment; so professional knowledge is necessary. If, however, a child has swallowed poisonous tablets, such as a number of sleeping pills, an emetic administered immediately, before taking him to hospital, may save his life.

Poisoning is such a sudden and dangerous event that prevention is of first importance. All poisonous substances used in the home should be kept in containers clearly marked 'POISON' and in a place by themselves. Poisons for use in the garden should be kept locked up. All such things should be kept well away from the reach of children.

FISH. **1.** *Choice of Fish.* The British national dish is said to be 'the roast beef of Old England'; but in reality it is fish and chips from the fish and chips shop. It suits many of the conditions of modern life for it is cheap, standardized, takes no time to prepare, and even very little time to eat. Fish is a digestible and relatively cheap source of first-class protein. It also contains calcium and phosphorus and nicotinic acid which is one of the B VITAMINS (q.v.). White fish has fat in the liver only and is useful in INVALID COOKERY (q.v.); oily fish, such as herring, is suffused with fat rich in vitamin D,

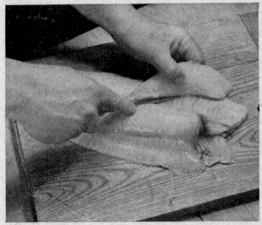

FILLETING FISH

128 recipes for it. Plaice, flounders, and dabs, of which lemon or Torbay sole is a variety, are not quite so good.

The white, round fish which swim actively have a firmer texture and muscle bundles which form big flakes. JOHN DORY, grey and red mullet (the *rouget* of the Mediterranean), bass, and conger EELS are not as well known as they deserve to be; the most common fish of this type in the shops are haddock, COD (qq.v. Vol. II), and whiting, which are in general either coarser or less tasty. Ling, hake, and coalfish (Scottish, *saithe*), all members of the cod family, are moderately good fish.

Only two kinds of cartilaginous fish (*see* SHARKS AND RAYS, Vol. II) appear in shops— dog fish and skates. Dog fish, which is coarse, is sold as 'flake'. The prickly skinned variety of skates taste better than the smooth; only the 'wings', that is the pectoral fins, are used. 'Rock salmon' is a trade name used for several varieties of rather coarse white fish.

Oily fish, mostly fast-swimming and surface-feeding, and therefore heavily muscled, are MACKEREL, HERRINGS (qq.v. Vol. II), pilchards, sprats, sardines, tunny or tuna (a giant mackerel), and whitebait (the fry of herring or sprat). All of these fish are canned very successfully in oil for HORS D'ŒUVRES (q.v.). Scandinavian tinned sild is herring; Danish *gaffel bitte* (fork snacks) are very slightly decomposed herring fillets; while roll-mops are rolled herring fillets pickled in vinegar. Brisling are sprats tinned in oil. Other oily fishes are SALMON, quinnat or Pacific salmon, sea trout, and EELS (qq.v. Vol. II).

Dried and salted herrings are known as bloaters. Dried and salted cod is the *bacalao* of Spain. Kippers, from herrings, and two of the famous smoked haddocks of Aberdeenshire, Arbroath smokies and Finnan haddies, are salted and dried over oak sawdust, peat, or sea-weed smoke. Smoked eels are a Danish delicacy.

3. *Freshwater fish.* The best freshwater fish are trout—brown and rainbow (*see* SALMON, Section 2, Vol. II). CARP is not eaten in Britain except by Jewish people, but is much used in Europe, especially in land-locked countries, such as Austria, where it is cultivated in ponds; it is associated with Christmas. Other river and lake fish, such as PIKE, PERCH (qq.v. Vol. II), tench, roach, char, and chub, are eaten mainly by enthusiastic anglers, for their flesh is rather savourless. With careful cooking, however, and

and it should appear on the menu at least once a week (*see* FOOD VALUES).

In the choice and preparation of fish these basic rules should be followed: the fish must be absolutely fresh, it should be cooked at once, and it should be properly seasoned and garnished and often served with a good SAUCE (q.v.). Fresh fish is firm but elastic, the scales sparkling, the eyes and gills bright, and the smell entirely wholesome. Big fish are often coarse, and little ones too bony to be economical; so the medium-sized ones are the best buy. Fish is best and cheapest when it is in season and just before spawning (a well-developed roe is a good sign). Prime cuts, though dearer, are often more economical than the cheaper tail ends because every bit can be used, but the dearer kinds of fish are not necessarily the best. John Dory, a cheap fish, is much superior in texture and flavour to cod, a medium-priced fish; and fresh mackerel at 1s. per lb., well stuffed and braised, is preferable to indifferently boiled salmon at 10s. per lb. Plaice is an uninteresting fish and more expensive than sea bream which, when it is available, is a good buy. A generous allowance for a main meal is ½ lb. of undressed fish or ⅓ lb. of filleted fish per person. Frozen fish must be thawed out slowly and all fish inspected for cleanliness.

2. *Sea Fish.* The white FLAT-FISHES (q.v. Vol. II) are lazy swimmers and hence tender and fine fleshed; turbot (up to 40–50 lb.), brill, and halibut are the largest of them. Of the smaller flat-fish, Dover sole is supreme; Madame Prunier, of the famous fish-cooking family, gives

the help of herbs and sauces, they can be quite worth eating.

4. Fish of Southern Oceans. Magnificent fish, different species from those of northern waters, abound in southern seas. There are hardly any flat-fish except soles and flounders; instead there are a variety of tender-muscled, kelp-feeding rock fish: in New Zealand the green bone and blue and red cod; in South Africa, the rock cod. The groper and the barracuda are big edible Australasian fish. The big South African fish are the steenbras (stone bream), the geelbek (yellow snout), and the snoek, the Africaans name for barracouta. The snapper and hapuka are common to New Zealand and Australian waters; leatherjacket and flathead are caught in Australia. There are no herrings in the south, but pilchards and sardines are fished in South Africa. New Zealand whitebait, very much smaller than the English kind and a superb delicacy, is netted in the estuaries of Southland rivers. Though it does reach Britain in tins, much of its quality is then lost.

5. Fish Cookery. Fish may be cooked by FRYING, BAKING, BOILING, GRILLING, or STEAMING (qq.v.). Large fish can be gently simmered, preferably in a fish kettle with a strainer, in *court-bouillon*, a liquid made from water, vinegar, carrot, onions, and herbs, boiled, cooled, and strained. About 10 minutes is needed for 2 lb. of fish, 15 minutes for 4 lb. Smaller or cut fish should be steamed rather than boiled. Fillets can be steamed with butter between two plates. Dory, codling, or haddock can be baked or braised in milk and butter for 10–15 minutes at 375° F.—Reg. 4, and then flavoured with a rub of garlic, thinly sliced onion, tomato, or grated cheese. Whole mackerel, herring, haddock, or whiting are delicious stuffed and braised (*see* STUFFING). A good way of cooking flaked kipper or New Zealand whitebait is to bake them in Yorkshire pudding batter or egg custard. Almost all kinds of fillets, or small fish such as smelts and whitebait, are suitable for frying, preferably in oil. They should be dipped first in egg-and-crumb or batter and then dropped into boiling oil or fat. Cod steaks, haddocks, or herrings, dusted with seasoned flour or oatmeal, can be fried in shallow fat; when done with browned butter and garnished with lemon this is called *à la meunière*. Whole herrings, mullet, sole, cuts of salmon, cod, halibut, and other fish can be grilled on a well-oiled griller.

Poached or steamed fish should be served either with a hot SAUCE (q.v.), such as parsley, caper, cheese, tomato, mornay, anchovy, shrimp, egg, or hollandaise, or with a cold dressing, such as mayonnaise or tartare sauce. Accompaniments which go well with grilled fish are savoury butters, tartare, mornay, or mustard sauce, and asparagus, fried apples, or bananas. Fried fish should be served with lemon slices, tomato salad, or orange and lettuce salad—the latter is especially good with herrings.

See also SHELLFISH.
See also Vol. VII: FISHING INDUSTRY.

FLATS. A flat is a suite of rooms on one floor; in the U.S.A. and other countries it is generally called an 'apartment'. The primary and original purpose of building flats, or of converting existing buildings into such dwellings, was to save ground space. Today, when there are few domestic servants and many women go out to work, there is the added advantage that flats are in many ways easier to run than houses.

Flats are not a modern invention. In the Roman port of Ostia ruins of apartment houses of four storeys, dating from the 1st century A.D., are still standing to the first floor level. In Rome

RECONSTRUCTION OF ROMAN FLATS AT OSTIA

The third doorway on the left leads to a passage through the block. The door to the right has a staircase leading to an upper floor, and the next one leads into the ground floor flat

JAMES COURT, EDINBURGH. TENEMENTS BUILT IN 1725

S.N.B.R.

expand freely, there has been a traditional distaste for flat dwelling, in contrast to its almost universal acceptance abroad.

In Scotland, especially in Edinburgh, where the need for security led to building within the town fortifications, flats have been built since the 16th century. The town houses of the Scottish nobles were 'lands', tall blocks of flats built round a courtyard, which Defoe describes as 'thronged buildings from seven to ten or twelve storey high'. Large-scale flat development in Scotland began in the 18th century, when Glasgow was expanding from a market town of 12,500 inhabitants in 1707 to an industrial port of 80,000 by 1800. The bulk of this new population was housed in blocks of unbelievably insanitary, unhealthy, and overcrowded flats, with no drains and perhaps only one pump to supply water to a whole block.

As a result of industrial development, tenements were built in London in the 19th century to house the growing number of poorly paid workers. To keep rents low in parts where the value of the land was high, and to house people as near as possible to their work so as to save time and fares in travelling, tall, dingy, cliff-like blocks were built, in which as many families as possible were crowded. Tenement blocks were also built to rehouse the inhabitants of the SLUMS (q.v. Vol. X), and though many of them seem depressing today, they were an advance on the insanitary houses they replaced.

As early as 1851 blocks of flats were built for wealthier people, or large houses were converted into small groups of luxury flats. At first the

itself there is evidence of tenement blocks comparable to some built in London in the 19th century.

For many centuries flats have been built in Europe in towns whose size was limited by defensive walls; as their populations increased, the people had to be crowded into a small space. In England, where towns have been able to

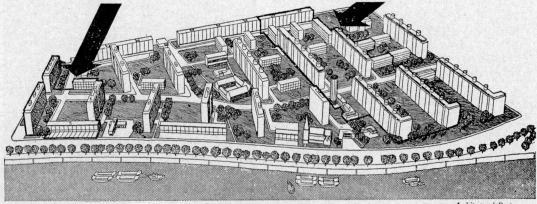

Architectural Review

DRAWING OF CHURCHILL GARDENS, PIMLICO, LONDON

The scheme includes flats and maisonettes, shops, schools, public houses, a church, and halls and playgrounds. The arrows and the black outlines indicate the parts built by 1955

wealthy lived on the lower floors and the poorer tenants above. But with the development of LIFTS (q.v. Vol. IV) in the second half of the 19th century, tall blocks became possible. Since the First World War particularly, flat dwelling has increased, and many large blocks have been built, and town houses, now too big for most people, have been converted into flats. In some cases each floor has been made into a flat; in others two floors form a 'maisonette'. Another type of conversion, possible in small terrace houses with one or two rooms on each floor, is for two or three houses to be joined, so that each floor contains a flat of several rooms on one level, thus saving staircase space.

During the period between the two World Wars great advances were made in flat design and layout on the Continent, especially in Germany, Holland, Switzerland, and Scandinavia. The general standard of design, workmanship, finish, and the layout of the blocks was much higher on the Continent than in England, though as a rule the rooms in each flat were fewer in number and smaller. In England flats were often built round an internal courtyard which made them overshadowed and noisy; they were crowded together; and their plans were restricted by existing roads and buildings. In northern European countries, on the other hand, sites on the edge of towns were used, and flats could, therefore, have a more open layout; most of them have internal bathrooms and w.c.s, so that there is more outside wall space available for windows and balconies in the other rooms. The essence of their design is simplicity and the proper use of available materials; there is no attempt to disguise a 20th-century building as an inflated Grecian temple or Georgian house.

The principles of planning and design of Continental flats were followed in a few instances in Britain in the 1930s. Two interesting experiments were carried out in the Quarry Hills Estate in Leeds: PREFABRICATION (q.v. Vol. VIII) was used in the structure; and the flats are provided with a special system of refuse disposal, garbage being emptied down an enlarged kitchen sink waste and carried to a central furnace, where it serves as fuel to provide heat for central heating and hot water.

About 1920 the French architect Le Corbusier began to make designs for blocks of flats of up to sixty storeys high, which would make possible, even in the heart of a city, buildings with large

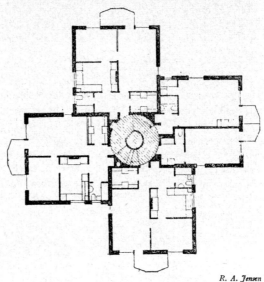

R. A. Jensen

POINT BLOCK FLATS IN STOCKHOLM
Below is the plan of one floor. Four flats are built round a central stair

areas of open space around them. 'Unité d'Habitation' at Marseilles is an eighteen-storey block containing 337 apartments. A shopping centre, restaurant, and hotel occupy the seventh and eighth floors; there are also a laundry, a crèche, a kindergarten, a swimming-bath and open-air gymnasium, a running track, and a sun roof. The whole block stands on reinforced concrete legs so that the ground floor is open.

Many experiments in the design of flats have been carried out in Britain since the Second World War. In some, restaurants, nurseries, laundries, and gardens are provided for the use of the tenants, and flats are made of different sizes, suitable for families, single people, and old people. The problems of noise and the overshadowing of lower buildings, the need for privacy, and the orientation (so that all the flats in a block get sunlight) are being studied. Flats are more expensive to build than houses, and consequently higher rents have to be charged for them; but they take up less land, and services, such as roads, electricity, gas, and drains, do not have to be carried such long distances.

See also Houses, History of.
See also Vol. X: Town and Country Planning.

FLAVOURINGS. The best and often the cheapest flavourings are those from natural sources; essential oils (*see* Oil-Bearing Plants, Vol. VI) extracted from the natural product are generally the next best; and synthetically produced imitations are much less good. Flavours at first-hand include vanilla pods (*see* Spice Crops, Vol. VI), orange and lemon rind, coffee, chocolate, and cocoa, home-made caramel (burnt sugar), Nuts (q.v. Vol. VI) such as pistachio and almond, liqueurs, wines and spirits, fruit juices, and praline, that is, almonds browned in sugar. Essential oils usually available as 'essences' are vanilla, orange, lemon, almond, ratafia (from cherry and peach kernels), peppermint, rosewater, aniseed, sassafras (extract from dried tree bark), sarsaparilla (root extract), and wintergreen oil (from the leaves of an American creeping plant). The flavours synthetically made from chemicals include banana, pineapple, strawberry, raspberry, rum, and vanilla.

Colourings from natural sources include saffron yellow from the dried stigmas of the autumn crocus, spinach green from leaves, 'browning' from sugar, and cochineal red from the dried bodies of the cactus beetle. Synthetic colourings are just as good and provide a much wider range. The colouring serves no purpose apart from decoration.

FLOORS AND CEILINGS. The simplest and most primitive floors are of beaten earth. Stone or brick floors have been used for centuries and are still in use in the kitchens of old houses, especially in the country. Quarry tiles—square red tiles of clay—have also been much used for ground-floor rooms, especially kitchens. In the Middle Ages tiles were often decorated with a design in cream-coloured clay on the red ground (*see* Tiles, Ornamental, Vol. VII); and in Victorian houses patterned tiles were popular for the floors of halls. Marble, often patterned in black and white, was used in the halls of large houses in the 18th century. In warm climates marble, stone, or tiles are used for rooms on upper floors as well as on the ground-floor, because they are cool. A particular type of floor used by the Romans was Mosaic (q.v. Vol. XII), which consisted of patterns made with small pieces of coloured marble set in cement.

The boards of wooden floors are supported and nailed on to wooden joists, which are beams on edge placed at intervals and at right angles to the floor boards (Fig. 1). On the ground-level the joists are supported on 'sleeper walls', which raise them above the concrete surface covering the ground. Ventilation in the house walls allows air to circulate between the boards and

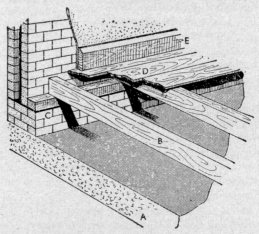

FIG. I. DIAGRAM OF A WOODEN FLOOR AT GROUND LEVEL
A. Concrete foundations. B. Joist. C. Sleeper wall.
D. Floorboard. E. Skirting.

the ground, thus preventing Damp (q.v.) which would cause dry rot in the wood. In some houses the surface concrete itself forms the floor; it is finished with a layer of smoother concrete, called screeding, on which cork, linoleum, or tiles can be laid direct. There are patent tiles of varying composition which are less cold than quarry tiles. Parquet consists of small strips of polished hardwood, laid in patterns.

The floors of upper storeys are usually similar in construction to the wooden floors on ground-level, except that the joists are supported by the house wall instead of on sleeper walls. Until pine was imported into Britain in the 18th century it was not easy to make joists long enough to span a large room, and massive oak beams were laid from wall to wall to support the smaller joists which were laid across them.

The ceiling is simply the underside of the floor, though before the 16th century the word was also used to mean the lining of the walls with boards, panelling, or tapestry. In cottages both joists and beams were often exposed, but in most houses the joists were usually plastered, and sometimes the

National Buildings Record

A CEILING WITH EXPOSED BEAMS AND JOISTS IN A COTTAGE AT HAFOD-Y-LLAN, CAERNARVONSHIRE

beams too. When they were left uncovered the edges of the beams were bevelled, or they were carved and sometimes painted. In the 16th and 17th centuries the ceilings of important rooms were plastered in elaborate patterns of strap work in deep relief, sometimes falling in points in imitation of the fan tracery of Vaults (*see* p. 166). In the 17th century heavy beams often ran in both directions across the ceiling, forming rectangular spaces which were decorated with moulded and painted plaster.

In the 18th century beams were concealed above a flat plaster surface, which might be decorated in low relief (*see* Vol. V, p. 3). Later, the decoration was concentrated in the centre of the ceiling where the chandelier or 'gasolier' was suspended (*see* LIGHTING, HISTORY OF). In the 20th century ceilings are made of plain plaster, sometimes papered and white- or colour-washed, like the walls.

A separate ceiling beneath the joists not only looks

better but is warmer and prevents noise from penetrating from one room to the other. The need for insulating floors against noise has long been understood, and in old houses the space between the floor boards and ceiling was sometimes packed with some dense but not too heavy substance, such as cockle shells. Nowadays

National Buildings Record

A 17TH-CENTURY CEILING WITH MOULDED PLASTER DECORATION AT EYE MANOR, HEREFORDSHIRE

glass-wool or mineral and vegetable fibres are used to make floors soundproof (*see* SOUND INSULATION, Vol. VIII).

See also HOUSES, HISTORY OF; ROOMS; CARPETS AND FLOOR COVERINGS.
See also Vol. VIII: BUILDING CONSTRUCTION.

FLOWER DECORATION. 1. Flowers have been used for decoration in most civilized countries for many centuries. The tradition of Japanese flower arrangement, for example, is said to go back to the 6th century, and then to have been influenced by the Chinese. Oriental countries had traditional schools of flower arrangement which raised it to the level of a great art. They devised characteristic settings for their floral arrangements, and often special alcoves were reserved for them. A minimum of ornament, simple austerity, and a clear light allowed every detail to make its intended effect. The kind of flower decoration which is suitable for our own homes, however, owes its inspiration more to a study of the flower pictures of the great painters of the 17th and 18th centuries (*see* STILL-LIFE PAINTING, Vol. XII). If we think of flowers, leaves, and fruits as material with which to make living pictures, the art of flower decoration can become highly satisfying.

2. *The picking and preparation of flowers for decoration.* The giving off of water vapour, called TRANSPIRATION (q.v. Vol. II), hastens the death of cut flowers, so every effort has to be made to minimize this. Picked flowers must not be left lying about exposed to the air but must be put into deep water as soon as possible. Wild flowers, when they are being carried home, should be wrapped up in newspaper, for example, to protect them from the air. Flowers which show signs of wilting after a journey can best be revived by having their stems cut and being plunged into warm water and left in a cool dark place overnight, before being arranged. Woody stems with no leaves respond best to hot water; others respond to water warm enough to be borne comfortably with the hand.

The tips of woody stems, those of flowering shrubs, roses, or large chrysanthemums, for example, should be bruised before being put in water and those of soft-stemmed flowers should be split or cut off. Any superfluous leaves and broken bits should be removed, for this reduces the area of transpiration. Leaves should not be allowed beneath the surface of the water or they

J. M. Dent and Sons

WHITE SWAN POPPIES AND GODETIA ARRANGED IN A WHITE VASE

will decompose. Some blossoms carry so much foliage that they will not last well when cut unless a good deal of it is taken away. Garden lilac, for example, with its heavy foliage, lasts much less well in water than forced lilac with long leafless stems. If all the leaves of garden lilac are picked off, however, and separate pieces of foliage arranged with the leafless flower stems, the whole will last much better. Other flowers that benefit from having at least some foliage removed are wallflowers, rosebay or willow herb, certain of the syringas (mock orange), and lime blossom.

It is important when picking flowers to cut them and not tear them, not to pick too many from one plant, not to pick shoots or shrubs which are needed for next year's growth, and not to pick all the leaves off plants such as lilies and tulips so that the plants cannot form food substances (*see* PHOTOSYNTHESIS, Vol. II).

3. *The arranging of flowers.* Many vases need some kind of holder to fix the flowers in the best position. A very practical holder is a tangle of 2-inch-mesh wire netting, crumpled in such a way that each stem must pass through three or four layers of wire. A tangle such as this can be pushed down the neck of a vase, and then a piece of it pulled up to form a dome above the rim. In a shallow bowl the netting may be tied in place by passing string over both vase and netting, and, when the flowers are in place, removing the string.

A successful arrangement has a good balance and outline and good flowing lines within the

THE PICNIC

Painting by James Tissot (1836–1902)

outline. In arranging a bowl of flowers the best effect is generally obtained by making all the flowers proceed from the centre. But it is possible to adhere too rigidly to an over-formal pattern, and so to force flowers to a shape which fails to show their natural qualities. Handsome flowers cut to pieces to make them conform to a pattern unsuited to them give an unpleasant effect.

The size of an arrangement must be related to the position it has to occupy in a room, and the height of the flowers to the size of the vase. A rough guide, though not to be taken too literally, is that the tallest flower may be one and a half times the height of the container, and the side flowers in proportion.

Colour combinations must always be a matter of personal taste, but everyone should be ready to experiment with varieties of colour combinations. The effect of green is to cool down strong colour effects, so that when intense colour is wanted, green must to some degree be suppressed. On the other hand, the effect of varying tones of green can be most pleasing. White flowers in a room, or a single pale flower in a mixed vase, may be like a high-light in a picture.

French, Dutch, and Flemish still-life painters of the 17th and 18th centuries frequently associated fruit with flowers to get rich effects. We are accustomed to use berries in flower decorations, but seldom other fruits or even vegetables. A spray of ripe redcurrants or damsons can produce a most exciting effect in a mixed vase, and the clear fresh green of garden peas, the purple decorative kale (used for generations by the Japanese), globe artichokes, ears of corn, and the vivid colours of autumn carrot leaves are all worthy of experiment. Very good effects can also be obtained with the gone-to-seed heads of some flowers—wild parsnip and willow herbs, wild clematis and sorrel. Some of these, with ferns dried and pressed under the carpet and beech leaves preserved in a 50% solution of water and glycerine, can make winter as well as summer decoration possible.

See also INTERIOR DECORATION, HISTORY OF.
See also Vol. XII: STILL-LIFE PAINTING.

FOOD, HISTORY OF. Some historians divide the whole history of mankind into four phases in this order—the phases of hunting and fishing, of sheep and cattle tending, of agriculture, and of industry. For modern man, of course, all four phases of activity exist side by side; but PREHISTORIC MAN (q.v. Vol. I) hunted or collected all his food, and did not think of keeping flocks or growing grain. AGRICULTURAL HISTORY (q.v. Vol. VI) is the story of how man gradually moved from the first to the last phase, and these four phases can be seen as four stages in improving food supplies. The latest industrial phase (see INDUSTRIAL REVOLUTION, Vol. VII) has brought about both the greatest increase in the production of food and also the most effective system for distributing it. Despite the enormous increase in world POPULATION (q.v. Vol. I) during this phase, and the fears held by certain writers that there would be more mouths to feed than the world could supply, food production has so far kept pace with population, and nourishment is in general better, not worse.

It is impossible to study the history of food without also taking account of the history of cooking, which makes raw food materials

Pitt Rivers Museum

PRIMITIVE FOOD BOWLS

From left to right: above, South African wooden bowl; Solomon Islands carved wooden bowl inlaid with shell, in the form of a frigate bird; Andaman Island shell plate. Below, American-Indian wooden bowl carved in the form of a seal; Russian pottery plate with cup for butter in the centre; basket-work plate from Madagascar

Berlin Museum

AN OPEN-AIR MEAL IN THE 17TH CENTURY
In the centre of the table is a dressed peacock. Painting by A. Palamedesz

palatable and attractive (*see* COOKING, HISTORY OF). It is necessary also to pay attention to basic facts of geography. The types of food available differ considerably from one part of the world to another. In the Arctic regions, for example, starch and sugar are almost unobtainable, while in the tropics it is difficult to produce edible meat. The development of international trade in foodstuffs, and improved methods of FOOD STORAGE and FOOD PRESERVING (qq.v.), have helped to make good local deficiencies and to produce much greater variety throughout the year.

International trade in food was practised in the Ancient World (*see* TRADE, HISTORY OF, Vol. VII), and the quest for cereal-growing lands influenced MIGRATION and settlement (q.v. Vol. I). In the Middle Ages the trade in salt and wine survived the breakdown of many of the traditional TRADE ROUTES (q.v. Vol. IV). Trade with the Far East—for SPICE CROPS (q.v. Vol. VI) such as cinnamon and pepper, and later for tea

—was the most important trade of the 16th and 17th centuries. In the last 70 years the quest for cocoa, and for vegetable oils with which to make margarine, has been of equal importance. England has become so densely populated that she is dependent upon imports of foreign foods, not only those which would not grow at home, but also those, such as wheat or meat, which cannot be produced at home in large enough quantities to meet domestic demand. It is difficult now to realize that, as late as the middle of the 18th century, England was a wheat-exporting country.

Despite the growth of international trade in food, local and national differences still persist, both in the types of food and in styles of cookery. England and Germany have bread and potatoes as their staple food and fat as their distinctive cooking base. Italy relies chiefly upon farinaceous foods (foods from corn), such as macaroni, and oil is its distinctive cooking base. France consumes less potatoes per person than England,

and still uses butter as its distinctive cooking base. For China and most of the Far East, rice is the staple food and oil the cooking base. Even within the same region there are considerable differences: for instance, different districts in Germany have developed different types of SAUSAGES (q.v.), and in Britain there are Cornish pasties, Yorkshire pudding, Scotch broth, Irish stew, and so on.

Improved methods of storing and of preserving have revolutionized food in the last century. In the Middle Ages it was difficult even to store corn. As late as 1641 a writer warns, 'It is a folly to sende more corn to the mill then one hath present use for.' Better warehousing was the first essential: but it was not until about 1850 that the principle of refrigeration was discovered (*see* REFRIGERATOR, Vol. VIII). In the next 30 years its application was worked out in new food-producing countries, particularly Australia and New Zealand, which had surpluses of meat (*see* COLD STORAGE, Vol. VII). In 1878 the first cargo of frozen lamb and mutton arrived in London, and was tasted and commended by Queen Victoria and the Prince of Wales. The recent development of deep-freezing now makes it possible to store perishable foods for very long periods of time (*see* REFRIGERATOR).

In the Middle Ages the methods of curing, pickling, preserving with sugar, extracting oil, and fermenting were all in use, but canning or tinning food was unknown. There were experiments with canning in France during the Napoleonic Wars, and in the early 19th century canned foodstuffs were prepared for explorers and sailors; but canned food was not general until the 20th century, when the U.S.A. perfected the method both for meat and fruit, and expanded its CANNING INDUSTRY (q.v. Vol. VII). At the same time there was a great increase in the number and consumption of synthetic foods (for example, margarine sales first exceeded butter sales in England in 1916). The number of branded foods, that is, foods marketed under trade names, also increased. Down to 1870 most goods, such as tea or sugar, were sold by the grocer out of large casks or boxes; after 1870 they were to an increasing extent weighed out, packeted, and labelled by the manufacturer (*see* GROCERY AND PROVISIONS, Vol. VII).

Modern food and food products are on the whole better in quality, variety, and nutritional value than they have ever been. The lower a

Paul Popper

A CHINESE BOY EATING WITH CHOPSTICKS

community's standard of living, the more it is dependent upon CEREALS (q.v.)—for example, wheat, rye, or rice—as its basic food; as the standard rises, other foods making a more balanced diet enter the shopping bag and the oven.

New foods are not always given an immediate welcome. For example, the potato, though introduced to England in the 17th century, did not become a national staple food until the 19th century. The Royal Society had recommended it in the middle of the 17th century; but when the poor began to eat it in large quantities at the end of the 18th century, William Cobbett condemned it as 'the root of wretchedness', and claimed that it 'resulted in slovenliness, filth, misery and slavery'. The tomato, which began to be consumed in very large quantities in England only from about 1880, was not given such a rough reception, though it took several years to establish itself.

Certain peoples have certain food taboos, that is, foods which are not eaten usually because of religious law. Many American-Indian and South African tribes do not eat pork, nor do the Jews; the origins of the Jewish food laws are described in the Old Testament. Hindus do not eat beef,

Paul Popper

A FEAST IN THE TONGA ISLANDS, PACIFIC OCEAN
The main dishes are sucking pig, chicken, and roast vegetables

for to them the cow is a sacred animal. Different prejudices against particular foods are rooted in the histories of peoples: the Chinese, by tradition, have not been milk-drinkers, and their recipes for cooking have remained unchanged for thousands of years. One French writer has claimed that a people's food preferences affect its history, that 'the destiny of nations depends upon the manner in which they eat'.

The biggest recent changes in diet are due to the knowledge of FOOD VALUES (q.v.), a knowledge which can be applied universally. The science of NUTRITION (q.v.), which has made remarkable advances since 1900, has thrown new light on necessary minimum standards of consumption and on food deficiencies which occur even in highly developed countries. The food standards of the well-to-do and of the poorer people are not so different in most countries as they used to be, largely because the average standard of living is much higher. Rationing during the two World Wars reduced everyone, whether rich or poor, to much the same level,

and accustomed the well-to-do to simpler MEALS (q.v.).

See also COOKING, HISTORY OF; MEALS; FOOD VALUES.

FOOD POISONING. Taken in its widest sense food poisoning would include many diseases caused by micro-organisms taken into the body with food—diseases such as typhoid fever, cholera, dysentery (*see* EPIDEMIC DISEASES), and some forms of TUBERCULOSIS (q.v.); and it would also include cases of the deliberate addition of toxic substances such as arsenic. But this is not what is usually meant by the term. Food poisoning in its usual sense arises from the accidental consumption of something which is of itself normally poisonous or which has been rendered poisonous by contamination from outside sources.

One of the commonest forms of accidental poisoning is by noxious FUNGI (q.v. Vol. II) which are mistaken for mushrooms. Other cases are due to certain tropical fish, or to parts of plants eaten in mistake for foods (for example, aconite root for horse radish or deadly night-shade berries).

The second and commonest type of food poisoning is due to contamination by BACTERIA (q.v. Vol. II), by fungi, or by certain chemical substances. For example, microbes of the Salmonella group (so called after Salmon, the bacteriologist) can contaminate any kind of food, but most usually attack meat, fish (especially shellfish), or milk. Occasionally potatoes, which belong to the same genus as nightshade, become infected by bacteria during storage and can cause Solanine poisoning. Lack of care in the preparation and storage of foods obviously increases the danger of food poisoning; steps, therefore, have been taken recently to improve the conditions under which foods are prepared and sold and to ensure that food is stored, when possible, in refrigerators (*see* FOOD HYGIENE, Vol. X).

A common cause of contamination is the handling of food by 'carriers', people who harbour in their bodies the germs of some disease without showing any of the symptoms of the disease themselves. Food poisoning may also be caused by eating meat or milk derived from a diseased animal, or food contaminated by metallic poisons. Modern methods of sterilization have made canned foods particularly safe—safer, in fact, than many so-called 'fresh' foods (*see* CANNING INDUSTRY, Vol. VII). But canned food can be contaminated if left in the open tin, and some pots and pans can contaminate food during cooking. It used to be thought that poisoning was caused by substances called ptomaines produced during the decomposition of foods, but it is now known that poisoning from this cause rarely, if ever, occurs. Botulism (from the Latin, *botulus*, 'sausage') is a special and very deadly form of bacterial food poisoning which is, fortunately, extremely rare.

Symptoms of food poisoning usually appear within a few hours of eating the contaminated food, and they commonly consist of a sick headache followed by diarrhoea and acute abdominal pain. Skin rashes often occur, especially in people who are allergic to certain kinds of food (*see* ALLERGIC DISEASES). In all but the mildest cases medical aid should be sought at once.

FOOD PRESERVING. 1. Drying, salting, curing, smoking, bottling, and canning are all methods of preserving food. They prevent decay due to organisms such as BACTERIA and FUNGI (q.v. Vol. II), either by destroying these organisms and preventing their re-entry, or by inhibiting their growth. As bacteria need moisture for their development, they cannot grow if foods are dried. Salting, like drying, reduces the moisture content of food, and, in addition, salt destroys certain organisms. Curing, whether with salt or some other curing substance, both destroys some of the organisms and renders others more liable to destruction by heat. Smoking, usually carried out as a final process after food has been salted or dried, removes further moisture and ensures the death of any remaining bacteria by substances absorbed from the smoke. In canning and bottling the moisture content of the food is not altered, but all spoilage organisms are destroyed by heat and prevented from re-entering by airtight sealing.

2. DRYING AND SALTING. These two methods have been practised for many centuries; they were particularly important when meat had to be kept throughout the winter—when there were no feeding stuffs to keep animals alive. Drying is still used commercially for preserving fish, meat (pemmican and biltong), fruit (prunes, sultanas, raisins, apple rings, and so on), milk, eggs, and soups. In some countries fruit, herbs, and mushrooms are dried at home. An even, slow heat is needed, so that the moisture is drawn out of the food, which is otherwise unchanged.

Sliced runner beans and *sauerkraut* are often salted at home, and two preservatives—salt and vinegar—are combined in making pickles (*see* CONDIMENTS AND RELISHES). Salted beans, if the salt is thoroughly rinsed out of them before they are cooked, are not dissimilar to the fresh vegetable. The sliced cabbage used for *sauerkraut*, on the other hand, undergoes a considerable change: the micro-organisms which the salt does not destroy feed on the sugar in the cabbage, producing lactic acid and carbon dioxide, giving as a result the appearance and flavour of fermentation. Meat and fish are preserved either in brine or with dry salt. In salting food with brine the food is either placed in the brine which soaks into it slowly, or, as is often done in salting meat, the brine is forced into the flesh by pumping. Saltpetre (sodium nitrate) and sugar are added to the salt to help to make the meat tender and to give flavour and

Metal Box Co. Ltd.
A DOMESTIC CAN SEALER
As the handle is turned, the lid is drawn tightly over the edge of the can and gripped to seal it

COOKING STOVES (q.v.) with the smoke of the log fires.

4. BOTTLING AND CANNING. These are used commercially for preserving meat, fish, fruit, and vegetables (*see* CANNING INDUSTRY, Vol. VII). The housewife is concerned almost exclusively with fruit and vegetables, and in this way she provides variety during the winter months by preserving the food when it is plentiful and cheap. In both bottling and canning the food is heated to destroy spoilage organisms, and the containers are then sealed so that they are air-tight and no organisms can enter. In canning the container is sealed before it is heated; in bottling, it is sealed afterwards. Bottling is cheaper because the bottles can be used again and again; but canned goods are more convenient for storage, and canning is more suitable for foods such as vegetables which have to be brought to a high temperature to sterilize them completely.

Fruit can be bottled in jam jars with lids specially made to effect a seal on heating, but special preserving bottles are better. These are made in sizes ranging from 1 lb. to 7 lb., and have rubber bands which fit under glass lids, and metal tops to screw or clip down the lids to produce a seal after the heating. The fruit, which must be in good condition, is carefully packed into the bottles and covered either with water or with a syrup (made by boiling sugar and water together). Then the bottles are fastened up and immersed in water in a vessel which is gradually heated to a temperature of about 160–180° F. During this slow heating the fruit is cooked, the harmful organisms destroyed, and the air driven out. The jars are then removed and allowed to cool. The liquid contracts as it cools, thus creating a partial vacuum which ensures that the specially designed cover adheres firmly. If the oven method is used, the bottles, not screwed up tightly, are put into a cool oven for 3 to 4 hours according to the number of bottles in the oven; when taken out, they are screwed up, and a seal is made in the same way.

For canning fruit it is necessary to have a machine which seals the lids on to the cans. (Lacquered cans should be used for red fruit.) The process is as follows. After the fruit has been packed into the can, water or syrup is poured in to within ⅜ inch of the top and then the cover is sealed on with the machine. The

colour. The sugar is converted by bacterial action to lactic acid which helps in tenderizing, and the saltpetre produces the red colour in the meat.

3. CURING AND SMOKING. These are generally used together. They are applied to pork to produce bacon and ham, to herrings to produce kippers, red herrings, bloaters, and bucklings, and to other fish, including salmon, trout, eels, and haddock. The food is cured by salting, as already described. To cure pork, either dry salt alone or salt mixed with saltpetre and sugar is rubbed into the piece, usually a whole 'side', that is, half a pig, which is then left for several weeks. Fish, on the other hand, is usually steeped in strong brine for a short time. The food is then smoked both to increase its keeping qualities and to improve its flavour. It is hung in a specially constructed room which is filled with smoke from a smouldering wood fire of hardwoods, such as oak, ash, and elm, or the sawdust of those woods, at a temperature of 80–150° F. Formaldehyde, and other volatile substances present in the smoke, give flavour to the food and assist the preservative action of the salt and the drying. In old days smoking, especially of sides of bacon, used to be done in the big chimney places of the

cans are immersed in boiling water and kept there for times varying from 10 to 30 minutes, according to the type of fruit being canned. At the end of this time the cans are removed, cooled in running cold water, and then labelled.

Vegetables can be canned in the home, but because of the difficulty of destroying the bacteria except at high temperatures, PRESSURE COOKING (q.v.) is essential, and this must be at 240° F. (10 lb. pressure). Cans with a sulphur-resisting lacquer lining are packed with vegetables which have been previously blanched. Boiling brine (1 oz. to a quart of water) is then poured on to within ⅜ inch from the top, the lids are placed on and the cans are exhausted of air by being stood in water at simmering point for 5 minutes. The lids are then sealed to the cans, which are sterilized at 240° F. for about 25–30 minutes, and then cooled and labelled. Although vegetables can be bottled, it is often unsatisfactory because of the inevitable loss of liquid from the jar at 10 lb. pressure, and also because of the danger of the bottle exploding.

See also FOOD, HISTORY OF; COOKING, HISTORY OF; JAM. See also Vol. VII: CANNING INDUSTRY.

FOOD STORAGE. The accommodation needed for food storage in the home is now much less than it used to be because supplies are easier to obtain. Formerly, when adequate supplies of meat, vegetables, and other foods had to be stored for the winter months, houses had a number of different storage rooms: the larder, originally used for bacon, but later for meat and provisions; the pantry, used for bread and other provisions, and for the plate and linen used by the butler or housemaid; the stillroom, originally used for the distillation of perfumes and cordials, and later for the preparation of tea and coffee; the storeroom for keeping groceries and other dry goods; and the cellar, an underground room, for storing beer, wines, and spirits in barrels, casks, and bottles.

Today, though houses in the country, particularly farmhouses, still need fairly extensive storage space in separate rooms, the average town house has a store cupboard, a larder, and a REFRIGERATOR (q.v.), and possibly a cellar.

Storage accommodation must be so planned that the food is not only kept in good condition and clean, but is also easily accessible. Perfect storage conditions vary according to the kind of food, temperature and humidity being the main factors concerned. Perishable foods, such as milk, meat, and eggs, need temperatures in the region of 40–50° F., such as are found in refrigerators. But in Britain, for 8 or 9 months of the year, a reasonably low temperature can be found in an unheated and ventilated room with a northern or eastern aspect; and such a room makes an ideal larder. Because cold and damp tend to go together, it is better for dry goods to be kept at a slightly higher temperature (about 60° F.) to avoid mould growth and rusting of tins. It is best, therefore, to place the storeroom or store cupboard where it will share the general heating of the house. Fruit and vegetables need cool, humid conditions with good ventilation; a warm dry atmosphere wilts and dries them, and frost causes them to decay. The

KITCHEN UNIT FOR A SMALL FLAT
The narrow shelves provide single-row storage. The back of the right-hand shelves lets down to make a dining table on the other side of the unit

best temperature for satisfactory storage of wines is 56° F., the correct temperature for the maturing process—for wines go on maturing while in the bottle. Underground rooms maintain this temperature naturally, and, as they also fulfil another essential condition, namely freedom from vibration, the cellar is the ideal place for wine storage. Apart from temperature and humidity, freedom from contamination by flies and rodents is essential (*see* HOUSEHOLD PESTS). All food should, therefore, be kept covered, holes and cracks in walls and floors stopped up, larder windows covered with wire-mesh sheeting, and rustless fittings chosen with no crevices to harbour insects, and with easily cleaned surfaces.

For ready access, a well-designed room or cupboard should be placed as near as possible to the point in the kitchen where the foods will be used (*see* KITCHEN DESIGN). Badly designed cupboards have shelves so deep that goods must be stored behind each other, and those at the back cannot be seen or removed without disturbing those at the front. Shelves just wide enough to take one layer of goods, and placed fairly close together, are easier to keep tidy and waste no space. This method, known as single-row storage, is now being adopted by makers of kitchen cupboards. It is convenient if the shelves are movable, so that the distance between them may be adjusted.

As the majority of foods are best used fresh, stocks should be kept as low as possible without risk of running out, and old stocks should be used up before the fresh supplies are broached.

Easily cleaned containers with airtight covers are needed. They should be of adequate size to hold the total amount usually purchased at one time, and should be clearly labelled. Glass jars with covers or tins with lids are the usual kinds of container, but recently Scandinavia has been producing new types made of plastic. Supplies can be taken from these in less time and with considerably fewer movements than from a tin kept in a cupboard.

See also KITCHEN DESIGN.

FOOD VALUES. The food we eat has to supply us with energy, with body-building material, with mineral salts, and with vitamins (*see* NUTRITION). Some foods are good in one respect but poor in another. In the accompanying table the foods most usually consumed are

arranged to show how they best supply these needs. Everybody should eat something from each of the eight groups every day. In each group the foods are listed approximately in order of merit. However, those that we eat in large quantities, bread, for example, may make an appreciable contribution even though they are towards the end of the list; and conversely those that head the list, but are eaten only in small quantities, may contribute less to the particular need which they satisfy.

1. ENERGY FOODS. All foods supply us with some energy, those shown in the first column of the table on p. 185 being the most important. The energy is measured in Calories according to the amount of heat it produces: one Calorie produces enough heat to raise one kilogram of water 1° C. The following list shows how enormously the calorific value of some of the more common foods varies:

Food	Approx. Calories per oz.	Food	Approx. Calories per oz.
Butter	215	Baked beans	25
Chocolate	150	Potatoes	20
Bacon	130	Milk	17
Sugar	110	Apples (fresh)	12
Mutton	95	Tomatoes	4
Bread (National)	70	Lettuce	3
Eggs	45		

Carbohydrate food is the cheapest source of energy available to man. One ounce of carbohydrate in the form of sugar or starch produces on an average 116 Calories in the body. Starch is present in all CEREALS AND PULSES and in POTATOES (qq.v.).

2. BODY-BUILDING FOODS. Such foods contain the chemical substances called 'proteins', of which 70 grams a day is generally accepted to be the body's requirement. Proteins derived from animal foods are generally better for building new body tissues than those derived from plant sources. They are said to have a higher biological value, and for this reason are called 'first-class' protein, whereas vegetables are called 'second-class' protein. The problem of the vegetarian, therefore, is entirely a problem of how to get enough protein into the diet, since he is cut off from most first-class protein. He can get plenty of carbohydrates, for these are in any case derived almost entirely from vegetable sources.

Proteins are built up from approximately twenty 'amino acids'. In the process of digestion,

TABLE OF FOOD VALUES

ENERGY FOODS	BODY-BUILDING FOODS	FOODS THAT GIVE CALCIUM	FOODS THAT GIVE IRON
Butter	Cheese	Fat fish, including:	Kidney
Margarine	Lean beef and mutton	Herrings	Liver
Cooking fat	Other meat: rabbit, liver,	Mackerel	Meat
Bacon	kidney, and so on	Sprats	Oatmeal
Biscuits	Fish and fish roe	Sardines	Egg yolk
Sugar	Eggs	Salmon	Dried fruits
Breakfast cereals	Milk (including dried and	Pilchards	Spinach
Honey	condensed)	Cheese	Black treacle
Oatmeal	Soya beans	Milk (including dried	National bread
Bread	Lentils	and condensed)	Wholemeal bread
Jam	Peas	Green vegetables	
Potatoes	Haricot and butter beans	Black treacle	
Haricot and butter beans	Nuts (especially almonds		
Dried peas	and peanuts)		
	National bread		

FOODS WHICH SUPPLY VITAMINS

VITAMIN A	VITAMIN B	VITAMIN C	VITAMIN D
Halibut and cod liver oil	Liver	Blackcurrants	Halibut liver oil
Liver	Yeast	Rose hip preparations	Cod liver oil
Butter	Yeast extracts (Marmite,	Oranges and lemons	Butter
Carrots	Betox, and others)	Green vegetables*	Margarine
Margarine	Oatmeal	Cauliflower	Eggs
Green vegetables (especially	National and wholemeal	Gooseberries	Milk (including dried and
spinach)	bread	Watercress	condensed)
Egg yolk	Milk	Tomatoes	
Milk	Cheese	Swedes	
		Potatoes	
		Lettuce	

* See details of cooking under VEGETABLES.

the proteins, both animal and vegetable, are broken down into their constituent amino acids, which subsequently re-form as new body-building material. These amino acids are found more abundantly in animal protein than in vegetable protein. When vegetable protein is converted into body-building material, some waste may result, since a great deal more vegetable than animal food has to be broken down in order to supply enough of these particular amino acids. From the physiological point of view, therefore, there is not much to be said in favour of vegetarianism. The economic side of the question, however, must also be considered. Vegetable food is, in general, much cheaper than animal food; for example, a shilling will buy more fuel for the body in the form of bread or potatoes than in the form of meat or eggs, and more vegetable protein than animal protein can be bought for the same money. Since only a small proportion of the vegetable protein is useful for body-building purposes, a consistent vegetarian, if he is to gain his 70 grams of protein, has to consume a greater bulk of food than

his digestive organs can comfortably deal with. Vegetarians, however, claim that the body needs far less. Whether or not vegetarianism should be advocated for adults, it is unsatisfactory for growing children, who need more protein than they can get from vegetable sources. A 'lacto-vegetarian' diet, which includes milk and milk products such as cheese, can, however, be satisfactory so long as enough milk and milk products are consumed.

Meat and cheese are the best sources of animal protein. Milk, fish, and eggs are, however, also valuable. Soya beans are the richest source of vegetable protein, and they, and the flour made from them, should be more often used. Nuts contain a high proportion of protein, but it is generally not of any great biological value nor is it easily digested.

The nutritive value of foods is influenced by their preparation and cooking. Good cooking improves the appearance and flavour of food, and these factors, in their turn, stimulate the secretion of the digestive juices within the body, and so improve digestion. It is usually true to say that those methods of preparing and cooking food which retain or improve the flavour also retain the maximum nutritional value. In INVALID COOKERY (q.v.) it is particularly important to produce attractive and palatable food. In the case of MEAT (q.v.), cooking increases tenderness, aids mastication, and assists in the subsequent breaking down of its protein material. When preparing and cooking VEGETABLES (q.v.), it is important to take care that their vitamins, particularly the water-soluble vitamin C, are not lost. In the case of fruit, losses in cooking are negligible because the water used for stewing is normally consumed, and the acids present in the fruit have a stabilizing effect on the vitamin-C content.

3. FOODS CONTAINING VITAMINS. Half-a-pound of carrots per week will ensure adequate vitamin A, but butter, margarine, and green vegetables are also good sources of this vitamin (*see* VITAMINS). In recent years margarine has been fortified during the process of manufacture by the addition of vitamins A and D. A number of foods contain the B-vitamins, the best of them being shown in the table. National bread, which uses a larger proportion of wheat grain, is far richer in these vitamins than white bread.

Vitamin-C requirements are mainly supplied by fresh vegetables and fruit. The vitamin-C content, however, is considerably reduced in stale vegetables, and can be easily destroyed by cooking the vegetables for too long in too much water (*see* BOILING).

As the appropriate list in the table shows, not many foods contain vitamin D. Halibut and cod liver oils are rich sources of this vitamin (and of vitamin A), and are given to babies as soon as they are a month old. Margarine, as we have said, is fortified with this vitamin, and butter and milk contain it naturally. Vitamin E is contained in green leaves and in the embryo of seeds, particularly the wheat germ, and it is also present in some vegetable oils. Vitamin K is present in lettuce, kale, spinach, tomatoes, and pig liver.

4. FOODS CONTAINING MINERALS AND IODINE. Calcium, needed for bone-building, is obtained from green vegetables, cheese, and fresh or dried milk; and considerable amounts of it are present in canned fish, especially fish such as sardines where the backbone of the fish is also consumed. In districts where the WATER (q.v.) is hard, appreciable amounts of calcium are supplied through drinking; where the water is abnormally soft, calcium sometimes has to be added. Phosphorus is contained in milk and eggs, and in smaller amounts in meat, fish, and cereals. Iron is found in kidney, liver, and other meat products and in egg yolk. Although spinach contains appreciable amounts of iron, only a small part of its iron content is available for nutrition.

Foods which contain iodine are sea fish, the edible seaweeds, and watercress. Onions also contain a fair amount when grown in soil which is rich in iodine. Table salt is often 'iodized' by the addition of potassium iodide in very small amounts—about 1 part in 200,000. One European country where goitre was prevalent used to add iodine to chocolates and sweets, and made the eating of these sweets by school children compulsory. Potassium iodide is also added to the vitamin tablets which are issued to expectant mothers.

Tate Gallery

A 16TH-CENTURY CART-WHEEL FARTHINGALE
Portrait of Anne Vavasour by an unknown painter

5. WELFARE FOODS. Some sections of the community require abnormally large amounts of certain essential food factors. As expectant mothers, babies, and young children need extra vitamins, they are issued with concentrated orange juice to supply vitamin C, and with cod liver oil to supply vitamins A and D. Expectant mothers are sometimes given tablets which supply these vitamins together with iodine and calcium. Invalids also need extra amounts of vitamin C, and this can be obtained from blackcurrant purée or rose hip preparations.

See also NUTRITION; VITAMINS.

FOUNDATION-GARMENTS.

The earliest foundation-garment of which we have certain knowledge is the underbodice, stiffened with wood or whalebone busks, which women wore in the 15th century. Probably some sort of supporting undergarment was known before this, for medieval dresses were often so tight-fitting that something of the kind must have been used. Women in the 16th century wore dresses with boned bodices and skirts standing out over farthingales, which were petticoats distended by whalebone hoops (Fig. 1*a*, *b*). In a later form of farthingale, known as the 'cart-wheel', a roll of cloth stuffed with wool or rags was tied round the waist, so that the top skirt was forced outwards in a wide circle; the whole effect was rather like a round table with a long cloth falling over the sides (Fig. 1*c*, *d*). While this ungainly fashion lasted, ordinary corsets were hardly needed; but these reappeared when a looser style of dress came in about 1620.

In the 17th century corsets were low-cut, heavily boned, and tightly laced before and behind. Unlike modern corsets, they had no suspenders, the stockings being kept up by garters. In Georgian times they were made of coarse, strong fabrics, with steel busks, and were cumbersome and unyielding (Fig. 2*a*). Lighter stays of silk or velvet were sometimes worn as a top bodice. Hooped petticoats, with bentwood or whalebone hoops, were worn at this period (Fig. 2*b*). Very fashionable young men occasionally wore corsets also, and, when knee-breeches were usual, they sometimes fitted artificial calves under their silk stockings if their own legs were not sufficiently well-rounded.

Crinolines were introduced in the mid-19th century, when dresses were very full and needed some framework to support them. They were

FOUNDATION GARMENTS

1. *a*. Dress with farthingale, 1570. *b*. French farthingale, 1570–80. *c*. Cart-wheel farthingale, 1610. *d*. Lady being fitted with cart-wheel farthingale, 1610. 2. *a*. Corset and side panniers, 1783. *b*. Dress with side panniers, 1783. 3. *a*. Crinoline, 1861. *b*. Walking dress with crinoline looped up over petticoat, 1861. 4. *a*. Dress with bustle, 1873. *b*. Bustle, 1872. *c*. Bustle, 1888. *d*. Dress with small bustle, 1888

enormous cages of whalebone or steel, over which the many-flounced skirts spread like over-blown roses (Fig. 3). Like farthingales, they took up a great deal of room and were rather awkward to manage. They were replaced about 1870 by the bustle, a small steel frame fixed to the petticoat, which raised the skirt behind at the waist and made it flow gracefully downwards like a waterfall (Fig. 4). Bustles went out of fashion about 1890, when flat, bell-shaped skirts began to be worn.

Tight-lacing was common in Victorian times when every girl desired the fashionable but very unhealthy 18-inch waist; if she did not possess one she relied upon her corsets to provide it. Bust-bodices, made of strong material reinforced by wire, came in about 1889, when dress bodices were very tight. These ugly though effective garments were generally hidden under camisoles. Their direct descendants are the modern brassières, which came into fashion in 1916. Modern corsets are much lighter garments than their predecessors, with far fewer bones, and with metal clips, hooks, or zip fasteners instead of laces. Most young women, however, now prefer to wear the yielding elastic belts which came into fashion after the First World War.

See also UNDERCLOTHES; COSTUME, HISTORY OF.

FRACTURES, *see* BONES AND JOINTS; ORTHO-PAEDICS; FIRST AID.

FRYING. This means boiling in fat, butter, or oil, which may be shallow or deep. Shallow frying, called dry-frying in Britain and pan-broiling in America, needs a hot pan and enough clear fat to keep food from sticking. The French word for shallow-fried is *sauté* (*sauter*, 'to jump') because the pan is shaken constantly to keep the food from sticking and from absorbing too much fat. The food should be turned frequently at first to sear the surface, and then cooked until done. Shallow frying can be a bad substitute for deep frying, merely resulting in greasy, carbon-specked food. Pancakes, bacon, kidneys, sausages, onions, and tomatoes all need shallow frying, though fried eggs need enough fat for basting unless they are going to be turned. Cut up, preboiled potatoes can be given a brown and tasty finish in the frying pan. Deep or French frying is used for all kinds of food encased in batter or in egg-and-crumb. Cutlets, scallops, fish fillets, fritters, potato chips, and doughnuts need deep frying. A thick, deep pan is needed, with plenty of clean fat—oil is best for fish—and if possible a frying basket which fits the pan. The fat must be hot enough to be still and to emit blue smoke before any food goes in: 370° F. is best for uncooked foods and 390° F. for precooked foods. If wet or ice-cold food is put in, or an overloaded basket, the temperature will be so much lowered that the outside layer will not seal quickly enough, and the food will be greasy. When taken from the pan, the food should be drained well on soft paper or on a hot sieve, and the fat carefully strained ready for the next using. The time taken for deep frying depends on surface area rather than weight, and varies from 3 to 5 minutes for fritters to 8 to 10 minutes for cutlets and potatoes.

See also FATS AND OILS.

FUNGI. These were eaten throughout the Ancient World, and throughout Europe and Asia, as they are to this day. At various times many attempts have been made to frame simple rules for distinguishing edible from poisonous fungi (for example, that a dish containing poisonous fungi would turn a silver spoon black; that edible fungi could be peeled, poisonous ones not), but none of these stand up to scientific investigation. The only certain way is to learn the individual characteristics of the different species, and it is wise to take no risks (*see* FOOD POISONING). Fortunately, Britain has only one deadly fungus, the Death Cap, though there are about a dozen dangerous ones (*see* FUNGI, Vol. II).

In countries with large forests, such as Russia, Austria, Germany, or Poland, great quantities of fungi are collected every year and sold fresh or dried. In England, in early Victorian times, blewits were still sold, but nowadays only the common MUSHROOMS (q.v. Vol. VI) are usually on sale, and most of these are cultivated.

The best-known European edible fungi are the field, horse, and St. George's mushrooms, blewit, beefsteak fungus, giant and common puff-ball, shaggy inky-cap, chanterelle, fairy-ring mushroom, *Boletus edulis* (French, *cèpe*), rough-legged boletus, orange-milk mushroom, oyster mushroom, and parasol mushroom. Only sound specimens, free from maggots, should be picked, and the younger the better. After being cleaned they may either be cooked fresh, or prepared for storage by being sliced and air- or oven-dried, preserved in bottles or tins, or pickled. There are many ways of serving fungi: grilled, fried, as fillings in omelettes, as savouries and canapés, and as enriching additions to pastries and pies, especially steak pie. Excellent stew can be made by frying slices of fungi and bacon in oil or butter, adding salt, black pepper, a clove of garlic, one large red or one small sliced green pepper, nutmeg, some chopped parsley, and a wine-glassful of sherry; and then stewing the whole slowly for $\frac{3}{4}$ hour. The juice of half a lemon is added before serving. A simpler stew, which can be used as a filling or on toast, is made by frying the fungi in butter, adding milk or cream, and thickening before serving with a little flour or cornflour. If more milk or stock is added, cream of mushroom soup results.

Truffles and morels are the gourmet's fungi. Neither is much used in England, but France has a flourishing truffle industry, especially in Périgord. Forests of holly, oak, and hazel are specially planted by the French government to encourage their growth. Black, round, and knobbly, they grow underground and have an aromatic odour which enables trained dogs and pigs to find them. Truffles are mostly used with other foods, such as *pâté de foie gras*, stuffings, and aspic, to which their velvety texture, black colour, and interesting flavour make them an excellent addition. Italian truffles (*Tartufi bianchi*) are white.

Fungi add variety and interest to other foods but have in themselves no great nutritional value. In sufficient quantities, however, they add some protein to a diet. Their spongy, fungal-cellulose tissue absorbs butter and oils very readily, and so they provide a vehicle for extra fat; this is probably why some people find fungi too 'rich' to be easily digested.

See also Vol. II: FUNGI.
See also Vol. VI: MUSHROOMS.

FURNISHING MATERIALS. These include materials used to make CURTAINS AND WALL-HANGINGS, coverings for FURNITURE (qq.v.) and cushions, and panels for screens. They have varied in design, colour, and style from one period to another. Furnishing materials, whether hung, draped, or stretched, have included skins, hide, leather, and fabrics woven from fibres of animal, vegetable, or mineral origin. In this century synthetic materials and plastics have provided further variety.

The earliest furnishing materials were used as

Victoria and Albert Museum

16TH-CENTURY ITALIAN CUT VELVET ON A SILK AND SILVER GROUND

hangings, either for decoration or for protection against heat or cold. These early TAPESTRIES (q.v. Vol. VII) were woven of linen and wool threads until, about the beginning of the Christian era, silk was introduced into Europe. Tapestries, sometimes with quite complicated patterns, were used in ancient Egypt, in the Near East (Babylonian tapestries, for example, adorned the Temple at Jerusalem), and in ancient Greece. They were often used as substitutes for doors and walls, and as covers. The designs were mainly pictorial, those of Rome in the 4th century A.D. closely resembling contemporary frescoes and mosaics.

In the Middle Ages the wealthy had tapestries, such as those of Arras, painted cloths, and woven fabrics of rich design, such as damask—a figured silk stuff from Damascus. These displayed the owner's wealth, and were easy to pack away in times of danger. New kinds of costly stuffs were brought to England by those returning from wars or in the trains of foreign princesses making marriage alliances in England. The hangings, especially for great state beds, were sometimes specially designed for high occasions and festivals. They were made of velvet, silk, patterned damask, brocade (baude-kin), a twilled cotton cloth (fustian), or a fine wool (camlet) in rich and gay colours. For very great occasions, cloth of gold, or silver thread, or tissue (silk threads interwoven with gold or silver) was used for hangings and cano-pies of state. Such rich materials also garnished lavish outdoor spectacles, PAGEANTS, and TOUR-NAMENTS (qq.v. Vol. IX)—as at the Field of the Cloth of Gold in 1520, when Henry VIII of England met Francis I in France. Such costly fabrics, which had been known as far back as the time of Darius of Persia, were not imported into England until the 13th century, when they were already being manufactured in Spain and Italy. Edward IV restricted their use by law to royalty and great nobles.

The more settled way of life which developed during the early Renaissance, and the rise of a wealthy middle class in the towns, meant that the comfort and refinement of domestic life increased greatly. Improved domestic heating and lighting and comfortable furniture for sitting and reclining encouraged indoor leisure occupa-tions. CHAIRS (q.v.) and settees were at first covered simply with leather or pieces of carpet-work stretched flat over the seat and back; later however, they covered the arms as well and pad-ded stuffing or horsehair mixed with wool filled the wood framework of seat and back.

Victoria and Albert Museum
ITALIAN SILK DAMASK FROM HAMPTON COURT, 1699

In the 17th century softer fabrics soon became popular for furniture and loose cushions, and this move towards the use of more luxuries, especially fine fabrics, increased with the Restoration. Taffety (a glossy silk) and its linen imitation were used for cushions and hangings, and bro-cades, damasks, or Italian velvets were used for walls, upholstery, and bed and window curtains, one material often being used throughout a room.

In the 18th century tapestry and needlework (the latter often the work of the ladies of the household) were used to hang on walls and beds, to cover stools, chairs, settees, and cushions, and to make panels for firescreens. As well as the silk fabrics already mentioned, satin, sarcenet, and lutestring (a glossy stuff with a ribbed pattern) came into use. Silk velvet, which had been made in Italy from the 13th century, was produced in the Low Countries from the 16th century, and at Spitalfields in London after 1685. By the mid-18th century silk velvet was being replaced by an imitation made of worsted or mohair and by plush with its longer pile made of cotton, silk, wool, or hair; later in the cen-tury painted silk, originally a French fashion, was used for ornamenting walls. In France rich silks, brocades, cotton printed with scenic sub-jects, and the tapestries from Gobelin, Aubus-son, and Beauvais were used for hangings and upholstery. Some Beauvais tapestries were im-ported by very wealthy English people.

A wide variety of materials was used for upholstery and hangings in England during the 17th and 18th centuries, including linens, mohair, and mixtures of wool and cotton. Morocco leathers, green or red, with arabesque borders in plain or gilt tooling, were used for desks and library tables, and plain leather for seats; green baize was a favourite for card tables.

Cotton fabrics, which Eastern peoples had made for many centuries, became very popular in Europe from the late 17th century onwards. Calicoes were imported by the East India Com-pany, and chintzes painted or printed in colours or fast dyes, and patterned with scenes and figures of the Far East. Such imported fabrics, however, were heavily taxed in an attempt to protect the home woollen industry. Later, English imitations were manufactured.

During the 19th century, as well as the tradi-tional materials, Nottingham lace became

FURNITURE, CARE OF.

The first essential in looking after furniture is to keep it thoroughly clean and well polished. A good-quality furniture polish or cream, both of which are basically beeswax or some substitute, mixed with turpentine, not only brings out the colour and figure of the wood, but helps to keep the timber in good condition. The decorative effect of many pieces of furniture depends on the polished surface of the wood, and this is lost if the piece is covered in dust. The furniture polish should always be applied sparingly, for if too much is used, the result is almost always smeary.

Anything spilt on a polished surface, even water, should be wiped off immediately, for if a mark, such as the ring made by the bottom of a wet glass, is left, the whole surface may have to be stripped and repolished to remove it.

Sudden changes of temperature and humidity in a room can easily damage furniture, causing it to warp; veneer, inlay, and marquetry work may come away from its ground, and lacquered furniture may blister and peel. Furniture should, ideally, be kept in rooms where the humidity remains fairly constant and the temperature is not too hot. Central heating is not good for furniture, and pieces should not be put too near a radiator.

Woodworm should be treated immediately, and if possible professional advice should be taken. A piece of furniture that has worm in it can infect every other piece in the same room within 6 months or less. Worm can be detected by the presence of a number of tiny round punctures in the wood—the tracks made by the furniture-beetle, boring its way to the surface to escape. The beetle larva, or worm, casts out a very fine dust, which is another sign of its presence. Furniture stored away in a cellar or an attic should be inspected from time to time to see that it is free of worm. There are two ways of treating worm. An infected piece can be fumigated, but this requires a gas chamber and is a professional job; or it can be treated with one of the well-known worm-killing chemical solutions that are on the market. The solution should be applied twice or more until the worm has been completely destroyed. The surest, if most tedious, way of killing worm, apart from fumigation, is to inject each hole with the solution. Dry-rot, a fungus which can be a deadly plague in the timbered roofs of old houses and churches, does

Victoria and Albert Museum

FRENCH SILK BROCADE, 18TH CENTURY

exceedingly popular for window curtains. In the 20th century factories began to produce many cheaper imitations—such as rayon for silk and leatherette for leather—to meet the increasing demands of a larger but less well-to-do public. Printed chintzes, sometimes glazed, are much used for loose covers for settees and armchairs, for draping small dressing tables, and for summer curtains. Furnishing ninon, net, and terrylene have replaced lace to screen the windows of town houses and flats. Plastic materials, transparent, plain, or patterned, are often preferred to bright cotton for bathroom and kitchen curtains, and nylon often replaces rayon.

Machine-made, mass-produced materials are today available in great variety, and schemes for INTERIOR DECORATION (q.v.) are no longer exclusively the concern of the wealthy. In the 17th and 18th centuries one material, in the same design and colouring, was likely to be used for walls, hangings, and upholstery. Today wall-hangings have been almost entirely superseded by paper, paint, or distemper; and for curtains and upholstery a contrast—pattern against plain, or light against dark—is often chosen. Traditional patterns and textures remain, influencing even the newest synthetic materials. But abstract designs are also used for printed and woven textiles.

See also INTERIOR DECORATION, HISTORY OF; FURNITURE, HISTORY OF.

not normally occur in movable furniture (*see* HOUSEHOLD PESTS).

No one should attempt to repair furniture, especially if it is of value or historical interest, unless he is certain that he has sufficient skill and knowledge. Old furniture is often extremely fragile, and the well-meaning amateur, even attempting the simplest repair, may double or treble the damage at the first tap of his hammer. Often what appears to be only the smallest defect is really the symptom of something more serious, and is almost certainly the job for a professional cabinet-maker or carpenter.

See also HOUSEHOLD REPAIRS; HOUSEWORK.
See also Vol. II: DEATH-WATCH BEETLE.

FURNITURE, HISTORY OF. The furnishing of the houses of ancient Egypt and Greece was extremely simple. Furniture was limited to a few types such as chairs, tables, beds, and chests, and these for the most part were plainly designed and constructed. The interior of a Greek house would have looked bare to the modern eye. But even in the simpler Greek homes what furniture there was was well designed, and brightly coloured rugs and cushions made the rooms homely and colourful. The Romans were the first to appreciate fully that furniture could be used not only for a practical purpose, but also to decorate a room. For example, the Egyptians and Greeks always removed the table from the room when the meal was over, but the Romans began to keep their tables and other furniture permanently in place, decorating them with fine and elaborate carving and making them important features in the decorative scheme. This idea of making each piece of furniture play its part in the decoration of a room has affected the design and decoration of furniture ever since.

During the DARK AGES (q.v. Vol. I), after the fall of the Roman Empire, many of the refinements which Rome had introduced into the countries of her Empire disappeared. It was many centuries before Europe again attained a standard of domestic comfort and furnishing equal to that developed by the Romans. During the Middle Ages only a few types of furniture were made, and the majority of these were crude both in design and craftsmanship. Even in the most wealthy households there was little fur-

Lord De L'Isle and Dudley

THE MEDIEVAL HALL AT PENSHURST PLACE, KENT
There was little furniture in medieval halls except long tables and benches

17TH-CENTURY FURNITURE IN A ROOM FROM CLIFFORD'S INN, LONDON
In the centre is a marquetry table, and in the left-hand corner is a spinet

niture, and a nobleman who owned more than one house or castle had only one set of furniture, which he took with him from house to house. Life centred in the great hall, and until comparatively late in medieval times, this room was used by the whole household for eating, sleeping, and living in (*see* ROOMS). A hall of this kind, such as the one at Penshurst Place in Kent, was furnished in the simplest manner. A raised platform at one end was the domain of the lord, his family, and their guests. Here were the only CHAIRS (q.v.), often joined to the wall like church stalls; and set in front of these was a trestle table, which was dismantled and the top leant against the wall when not in use (*see* TABLES). Before the introduction of separate rooms for sleeping, the owner's bed was also placed on the dais, alongside the table. The bed, a simple wooden frame covered with hangings of tapestry, silk, or velvet, provided not only a place for sleeping, but in the winter a welcome refuge from the cold draughts of the hall during the day: it was not unusual to receive visitors while lying in bed (*see* BEDS). The lower part of the hall, below the dais, was furnished with trestle tables, stools, and perhaps a few CHESTS (q.v.),

and the retainers slept on the floor on palliasses (straw mattresses) around the central fireplace. In the wealthier households the walls were hung with tapestries or painted CURTAINS (q.v.), and brightly coloured cushions and draperies were often set on chairs and sideboards. A great deal of medieval furniture was originally painted in bright colours, and the plain oak of the few surviving pieces of early furniture, the paint now worn off, gives a false impression of the medieval interior, which though not comfortable by modern standards, was much more colourful than is often imagined.

The spread of the RENAISSANCE (q.v. Vol. I) from Italy to other parts of Europe during the 15th and 16th centuries brought about many changes in the furnishing and decoration of people's homes. Power and wealth spread to the middle classes, and consequently more large houses were built and the demand for furniture increased. The design and construction of furniture improved, and new types were developed. New motifs of decoration, inspired by classical models, spread from Italy throughout Europe, reaching England in the first quarter of the 16th century. In Tudor times Renaissance forms

Victoria and Albert Museum

18TH-CENTURY DINING-ROOM FURNITURE DESIGNED BY ADAM. OSTERLEY PARK, MIDDLESEX

of decoration were employed on furniture of basically Gothic design; but by the end of the 16th century and the beginning of the 17th new types of furniture were being widely introduced. For example, chairs without arms were made in sets, smaller tables were introduced, and also upholstered chairs and settees. All furniture tended to become lighter in design and construction and to show a new appreciation of domestic comfort and convenience.

When Charles II and his Court returned from exile in 1660, they brought back with them from Europe fresh ideas of furnishing and interior decoration—particularly from France and Holland. The last 40 years of the 17th century saw the introduction of bookcases, bureaux, cabinets, and a variety of small tables, some of these pieces being decorated with INLAY AND MARQUETRY (q.v. Vol. VII). Pictures and MIRRORS

(q.v.) in elaborately carved frames decorated the walls, and fine clocks and vases imported from the East stood on overmantels and on side-tables.

The reign of Queen Anne produced furniture which was lighter and more elegant in design than that of previous periods. The introduction of the graceful cabriole leg and the use of walnut veneers, often on oak, gave furniture a simple but dignified beauty, relying for its decorative effect on the colour and figure of the wood and the carefully calculated proportions (*see* Vol. VII, p. 75). Chairs, stools, and settees were usually simple in design, but had brightly coloured needlework upholstery. In Queen Anne's period, however, marquetry and japanning were still frequently used for decorating bureaux, cabinets, and other kinds of furniture.

During the early Georgian period a quantity

of elaborately carved and gilt furniture was made for the spacious rooms of the Palladian houses that were built at this time (*see* AUGUSTAN AGE, Vol. XII). Chairs, settees, mirror frames, and other furniture were carved with swags of flowers, large shells, eagle heads, lion masks, and other elaborate motifs, all richly gilt, while side and console tables were fitted with marble tops imported from Italy.

The designs in such pattern books as Chippendale's *The Gentleman and Cabinet Maker's Director* (1752) show the variety of domestic furniture that was being made in England by the middle of the 18th century. The Rococo style of decoration introduced from France, and its two offshoots, CHINOISERIE and the GOTHIC REVIVAL (qq.v. Vol. XII), demanded elaborate carving on many of these pieces of furniture; and mahogany, which had largely replaced walnut by 1740, was a good medium for the carver's skill. The furniture of this period provided pieces for every function of the day, with its

breakfast and tea-tables, library writing-tables, shaving stands, and so forth. Not all of it was profusely carved with rococo decoration; there are less elaborate designs in the *Director* which show that those with simpler tastes or less money to spend were also provided for.

Throughout Europe in the 18th century taste and fashion in furnishing was largely influenced by France. The rococo furniture of Louis XV's reign and the severer style of Louis XVI's were copied and adapted in Italy, Spain, Germany, and other European countries. By 1770 the straighter and more severe lines of the neo-classic style were being introduced into England by the architect Robert ADAM (q.v. Vol. V). But though the style of decoration changed, the variety of types, as illustrated in the designs of Hepplewhite and Sheraton, remained as numerous as before. Satinwood, sometimes inlaid with other woods, was generally used in place of mahogany, and furniture was decorated with painting and gilt brass mounts. In the early

Castle Museum, York

FURNITURE IN A VICTORIAN PARLOUR
The room is filled with over-decorated furniture and ornaments

19th century English Regency furniture drew its inspiration not only from Greek and Roman models but also from the furniture of ancient Egypt, which prompted such motifs as winged sphinxes and even crocodile legs.

After about 1830, both in England and on the Continent the introduction of machinery and mass production led to a rapid deterioration both in the design and the construction of furniture. Throughout Victorian times people crowded their rooms with hideous and often shoddily made furniture. It is only in comparatively recent times that artists and craftsmen have again combined their skills in an attempt to produce a style of furniture which is in accord with contemporary life. Once again, as in the 18th century in the work of Kent and Adam, furniture is being designed by architects to relate to the rooms which it is meant to furnish. One of the conspicuous developments of modern times has been built-in furniture, especially cupboards and bookcases, which forms part of the wall of the room.

The eastern countries of the world have produced less furniture than those of the west. Their culture and way of life is such that it does not demand a large variety of furniture. In China there are a few such basic types as chairs and tables, but the Japanese have hardly any furniture at all. Much of the furniture produced in the east during the past 4 centuries was not intended to be used by the people of those countries, but was made either for export to western markets or for people from the west who came to live there.

See also INTERIOR DECORATION, HISTORY OF.
See also Vol. VII: CABINET-MAKING.

FURNITURE, MODERN. By the middle of the 19th century the furniture industry was producing large quantities of cheap cabinet-work and upholstery, much of it, as can be seen from the contemporary pattern books, inaccurate and tasteless copies of medieval or French 18th-century models (*see* FURNITURE, HISTORY OF). While the widespread use of the machine in the furniture-making trade lowered the general standard of workmanship, a strong tradition of craftsmanship survived in certain quarters, and throughout this period there existed pioneers, both in Europe and the United States of America, who experimented with such new materials as bentwood and metal, producing furniture that was the true ancestor of modern furniture today. But although some of this work was shown at the Great Exhibition of 1851, it was for the most part neglected by the furniture-makers of the time.

William MORRIS (q.v. Vol. V), inspired by the arts and crafts of the Middle Ages, attempted to revive in England a love of craftsmanship and to give to his contemporaries a new sense of beauty. He founded the furnishing and decorating firm of 'Morris and Company', and with the aid of such artists and designers as Philip Webb, Ford Madox Brown, and D. G. Rosetti produced a large quantity not only of furniture, but of finely printed books, textiles, wallpapers, and other objects of decorative art, all examples of Morris's own high principles of design and craftsmanship. But in spite of this large output, Morris's influence was limited, for he turned away from new materials and new industrial techniques, attempting to deny the possibilities of the machine in an age where the machine had already become an essential part of the structure of society. If only Morris had applied the principles of medieval craftsmanship to the use of the machine, his influence on modern design would have been far greater.

However, a few of his followers, designer-craftsmen such as Ernest Gimson and Ernest and Sidney Barnsley, made fine furniture which was ultimately to influence the furniture-making industry. Such cabinet-makers, working with a few assistants, could have only a limited influence, for they could make only a small amount of expensive, handmade furniture. But they did re-establish high standards of design and craftsmanship which had been lost in the mass-produced furniture of the large commercial firms, and they did attempt to produce furniture in a contemporary idiom, and not mere slavish imitations of the furniture of other times. The work of these men was taken more seriously on the Continent than in England, and there its influence became so widespread that many people now imagine that contemporary furniture design originated in France, Germany, Austria, and Scandinavia.

Until the beginning of this century the work of those designers and cabinet-makers who were to play so important a part in the history of modern furniture had all been produced in small workshops on a small scale. Ambrose Heal was the first to produce on a large commercial scale

Heal and Son

MODERN UNIT FURNITURE WHICH CAN BE ARRANGED IN A VARIETY OF WAYS
It is made of teak veneers with rosewood-coloured handles and legs. Designed by Christopher Heal

good, simple furniture of modern design, relying for its decorative effect on its good lines and the beautiful surface of the woods of which it was made. As he was the head of a well-established furniture-making and retailing firm, Heal was able to put on the market for a wide public a large selection of modern furniture designed by himself and other contemporary British designers.

In Germany designers were strongly influenced by the work of Morris and Gimson, though unlike them they did not ignore the potentialities of the machine. Exhibitions were organized in Germany and France which influenced modern furniture design throughout Europe and America. The exhibition held at Cologne in 1914, for example, led to the formation in Britain of the 'Design and Industries Association', a body that aimed to bring the artist and the manufacturer together in a collaboration which would exploit the full possibilities of machine-made goods.

After the First World War, though people were ready for changes and new ideas, furniture designers were handicapped by the persistent fashion for reproduction furniture. Some designers, such as Heal and Gordon Russell, persisted, and during the 1930s an interest in the new designs was beginning to awaken; but it was not until after the Second World War that a wide public interest in and taste for contemporary furniture was aroused.

Today a large quantity of modern furniture, using both traditional and new, experimental materials, is being produced in many countries, in particular in England, America, Italy, and Scandinavia. Metal in many forms, moulded plywood, leather, glass, and other materials are being tried out, some in designs that are inspired by furniture of the past, others in designs completely modern and revolutionary. The modern designer no longer tries to ignore the machine, but exploits it to the fullest extent, trying all the time to produce furniture that is not only excellent in workmanship and design, but cheap enough to be within everyone's reach.

Modern furniture design is still in an experimental stage. The designers have concentrated on line rather than on decoration, with the result that many pieces seem stark and over functional. A satisfactory solution to the problem of finding a modern idiom of decoration for furniture of simple lines seems so far to have eluded the designers, though some successful effects have been produced with the natural surfaces of woods, many of them grown in the Empire. Designers, however, have not yet found a satisfactory substitute for the decorative carving, inlay, and other forms of decoration that enriched the furniture of the past. Simplicity is the keynote of modern furnishing, but a simplicity that is in place in the furnishing of offices, waiting-rooms, and other public places may leave the home looking cold and impersonal. This is but one of the many problems which face the designer of contemporary furniture; problems which are attacked daily by workers who are alive to new and experimental ideas.

See also INTERIOR DECORATION, HISTORY OF.
See also Vol. VII: FURNITURE INDUSTRY.

FURS. After primitive man had given up dressing in skins (see PRIMITIVE COSTUME) it was many centuries before fur was used again in European dress. The Chinese, however, used fur as an ornament on clothing as early as 2000 B.C. In the Middle Ages it was a mark of rank. Strict sumptuary laws, that is, laws laying down what garments were permitted to the different ranks of society, forbade the use of fur trimmings to all but nobles and the higher ecclesiastics. They were worn chiefly by men, and were regarded as a mark of dignity. This usage persists today in a judge's ermine and in the robes of peers and peeresses on such ceremonial occasions as a coronation. A duke is allowed more bands of miniver than a marquis, and so on down the scale (see SOCIAL PRECEDENCE). The fur-trimmed garments of mayors and other civic dignitaries resemble those worn by the courtiers of Henry VIII.

Comparatively little fur was worn on garments during the 17th century, although it was a common practice to carry MUFFS (q.v.). It was not until the 19th century that fur became important in fashionable attire, chiefly for women. When men wear fur coats, the fur, except sometimes for the collar and cuffs, is nearly always worn inside. At first, fur served chiefly as a trimming and the skins used were not usually valuable. Tippets of sable are, however, mentioned in the fashion magazines of the 1820s. It was not until towards the end of the century that whole garments were made of fur. Among the most popular skins were astrakhan, which is not, properly speaking, a fur but the curly fleece of a sheep, and sealskin. Short

1. FUR BOA, 1804. 2. FUR TIPPET, 1871. 3. SEALSKIN JACKET WITH TRIMMING AND CAPE OF LONG FUR, 1880. 4. THREE-QUARTER LENGTH COAT IN BROADTAIL TRIMMED WITH CHINCHILLA, 1898. 5. SEALSKIN CLOAK TRIMMED WITH SABLE AND LINED WITH ERMINE, 1898

jackets, long coats, capes, and boas were made of the soft, warm seal fur, and the demand for it became so great that to prevent the extinction of the seal international laws were passed to regulate its killing (*see* Fur Hunting, Vol. VI).

Towards 1900 a much greater variety of furs appeared. Sealskin coats were trimmed with sable, and there was a revival of ermine for evening cloaks. An advertisement of the period mentions 'a luxurious model cloak of mink with a yoke of rose-pink velvet, . . . a dainty sac coatee of Russian sable, . . . an elegant three-quarter-length coat in broadtail, . . . collar, front and cuffs are either sable or chinchilla, . . . a smart full-length coat of seal, with collar of Russian sable and wide edging of the same fur. The lining is composed of ermine.' It need hardly be said that such garments were only for the wealthy.

Fur became so popular in the early 20th century that it was used even for such absurd purposes as sealskin blouses and fur-trimmed underwear. Fur toques with matching muffs were the rage, and fur was used for trimming the larger hats. Chinchilla was becoming as popular as sealskin, and by about 1903 such furs as musquash were appearing. A little later moleskins were extremely popular; they were arranged in patterns, especially in a chessboard pattern. Mink was still comparatively cheap, because it was at that time regarded as an inferior substitute for sable.

An advertisement for 1911 shows a still widening choice. The furs offered include 'a very pretty bear stole'; 'a very elegant squirrel set (that is, stole and muff to match) containing forty-eight skins, trimmed tails and paws'; and a 'coney seal cravat, two yards long lined with squirrel, flat muff to match'. The use of 'coney' (rabbit skin) was just beginning, and by 1914 the very greatly improved methods of fur-dressing and fur-dyeing made it possible for furriers to turn out cheap furs, such as rabbit, marmot, and musquash, looking like expensive furs such as ermine, mink, or sealskin.

As a result of the Russian alliance in the First World War new furs such as Russian pony were introduced, and there was a revival of the fashion for astrakhan. After the war fox, especially silver fox, became the fashion, and in 1925 a new source of supply became available when the silver fox was successfully bred in captivity (*see* Fur Farming, Vol. VI). White fox dyed to various shades of beige, or in its natural colour for an evening wrap, was much used, and a silver fox tie formed of a single skin became a regular item in many women's wardrobes.

In the late '20s Persian lamb (a kind of astrakhan with a smaller, silkier curl, obtained by killing lambs as soon as they were born) became increasingly popular. At that period almost every fur that exists was used, some in their natural state, others dressed and dyed to resemble something else. A catalogue of this time, besides listing a short coat of Canadian sable at 235 guineas, mentions kolinsky (a kind of rat), grey squirrel, skunk, stone marten, blue-dyed white fox, sheared beaver, nutria, musquash, Russian ermine, broadtail, sealskin, civet, opossum, and ocelot. Mink was no longer looked down on and, with the possible exception of sable, had become the most expensive fur of all. It was possible, even before the imposition of purchase tax on furs, to pay anything up to 2,000 guineas for a full-length mink coat.

The high price of natural furs has led to experiments in producing synthetic fabrics which have the warmth and appearance of real fur. Nylon furs have already made their appearance and may become popular. Indeed, as the wild regions of the world are increasingly encroached upon by civilization, and as only a few fur-bearing animals can breed successfully in captivity, the 'fur coat' of the future may be a synthetic product.

See also Vol. VI: Fur Farming; Fur Hunting.
See also Vol. VII: Fur Trade.

G

GAMES, *see* Vol. IX: Board Games; Card Games; Hiding Games; Paper Games; Party Games; Singing Games.

GARDEN BUILDINGS. Architecture has at most periods played an important part in the design of Gardens (q.v. Vol. VI). Stables were essential to large houses until the 20th century, as garages are today, and they were often elaborate buildings, designed to fit into the general plan of the house and garden.

In the 17th century many people, including Charles II, took an interest in growing exotic plants, and in building orangeries for their protection. The orangery designed by Wren (q.v.

National Building Record

18TH-CENTURY GAZEBO IN A GARDEN AT OUNDLE

Vol. V) at Kensington Palace is built of brick with windows along one side and at the ends. Orangeries were used for the display of plants, as well as for growing them, in which they resemble the Victorian conservatory. The greenhouse, on the other hand, is more utilitarian; it is used by the gardener for rearing both Greenhouse Plants (q.v. Vol. VI), until they are ready to be taken indoors, and seedlings for bedding-out (*see* Bedding Plants, Vol. VI). Greenhouses are not usually designed as decorative features in a garden, but Regency and early Victorian ones are often elegantly proportioned. Few exist from before the 19th century.

The Victorian conservatory usually adjoined the house, opening off one of the sitting rooms, and was used as an extra reception room. Ornamental plants, such as exotic ferns, were ranged tier upon tier—an example of the Victorian love of fussy and overcrowded decoration. The structure was often elaborate, with transepts and vaulted roofs crowned with iron crestings. The whole of the sides and roof were of glass, with panes of ruby and amber glass arranged in patterns here and there.

Before the days of refrigerators an ice-house was often built in the gardens of country houses in which ice, gathered in the winter from a neighbouring lake, was stored for use in the summer. It was a cave-like structure, usually built partly underground to keep it cool.

Summer houses have been a feature of gardens since the 16th century. Elizabethan gardens were designed as a series of more or less enclosed

B. T. Batsford

A GARDEN HOUSE, MONTACUTE HOUSE, SOMERSET, 1580

THE ORANGERY AT KENSINGTON PALACE, 1704

National Buildings Record

Country Life

A PAVILION AT STOWE, BUCKINGHAMSHIRE

The grounds were laid out in the 18th century with vistas between the trees leading to temples and pavilions

spaces, and one or more of these might have a garden house as its focal point. At Montacute House in Somerset, two square garden houses stand at the corners of the wall enclosing the 'parterre' in front of the house. Each has two tiny rooms, one above the other. Garden houses were gay and playful in intent; the most elaborate was probably the Petit Trianon, built in the middle of the 18th century in the park at VERSAILLES (q.v. Vol. XII), where Marie Antoinette played at being a shepherdess.

In England, in the 18th century, the garden and surrounding park were laid out as a single unit (*see* LANDSCAPE ART, Vol. XII), and little buildings, often resembling classical temples, were erected to give interest to the view. Sometimes a 'gazebo' or 'belvedere' was placed on top of a park or garden wall where a good view of the road could be obtained. It had a little room reached by a flight of steps inside, and this often had decorative features such as a dome or bay window. The same names were sometimes used for turrets or cupolas on the roof of a house, with windows from which to admire the view.

The ROMANTIC MOVEMENT (q.v. Vol. XII) of the late 18th and early 19th centuries led to a fashion for fantastic summer houses and grottoes in Gothic or Eastern styles, some designed as rustic arbours, some made gruesome with encrustations of strange-shaped rocks and shells. Even imitation ruins were built to give a romantic impression.

Nowadays, summer houses are generally small buildings designed primarily to catch the sun; revolving summer houses can be turned to face

GATEHOUSE AT BURTON AGNES HALL, YORKSHIRE

By the 16th century gatehouses were designed to make impressive entrances rather than for defence

the sun at different times of the day. More often, houses have BALCONIES or VERANDAHS (qq.v.) on which people can sit in the sun.

GARDENS, *see* Vol. VI: GARDENING, HISTORY OF.

GAS (heating), *see* HEATING SYSTEMS, DOMESTIC; (lighting), *see* LIGHTING, HISTORY OF; (cooking), *see* COOKING STOVES. See also Vol. VIII: GAS MANUFACTURE.

GATEHOUSES. The entrance to medieval CASTLES and MANORS (qq.v.) was guarded by a strongly fortified gatehouse (*see* Vol. V, p. 193). It had a heavy wooden door in an archway flanked by battlemented turrets, and there were usually rooms in the turrets and above the arch.

National Buildings Record

GATEWAY AND LODGES AT EASTON NESTON, NORTHAMPTONSHIRE, BUILT IN 1824

When the need for FORTIFICATION (q.v. Vol. X) had passed, the gatehouse was retained for decoration and display. Gatehouses in the 16th century were elaborately ornamented with cupolas, oriel WINDOWS (q.v.), and richly carved arches; this gave an impressive formal entrance to what was still an informally planned house (*see* HOUSES, HISTORY OF).

In 17th-century houses the gatehouse was usually replaced by a gateway placed on the axis of the symmetrically planned house or at the entrance to its park. It had stone arches or piers, surmounted by urns or heraldic figures, which framed ornamental iron gates.

In the 18th and 19th centuries gate lodges were built on either side of the park gates of country houses. They were designed to make an impressive entrance, and often had ornamental details in keeping with the grandeur of the estate, but out of proportion to the tiny dwellings they provided for a gardener, gamekeeper, or forester.

GERMAN MEASLES, *see* INFECTIOUS DISEASES, Section 3.

GERMS, *see* ANTISEPSIS AND ASEPSIS. See also Vol. II: BACTERIA.

GLANDS, *see* ENDOCRINE GLANDS.

GLASS, *see* TABLE GLASS. See also Vol. VII: GLASS-MAKING.

GLOVES. The first hand-covering was probably a simple piece of fur or material wrapped over the hand and tied at the wrist as a protection against thorns or cold. From this the sewn glove developed very early. Gloves were found in Tutankhamen's tomb (Fig. 1), and Homer in his *Odyssey* describes a pair worn by Laertes. The ancient Persians and Romans also had them, but not the Chinese, probably because their long loose sleeves made them unnecessary (*see* ORIENTAL COSTUME). In northern Europe they were adopted only towards the 8th century by kings and nobles. The gloves that Englishmen then wore were imported from the Continent, but by the 12th century they were manufactured in England also, and they came into general use about the first half of the 14th century. Jointed metal gauntlets were a necessary part of ARMOUR (q.v. Vol. X); from them derives the stitching down the back of modern gloves.

Griffith Institute

FIG. 1. GLOVE MADE OF WOVEN MATERIAL FROM TUTANKHAMEN'S TOMB, 14TH CENTURY B.C.

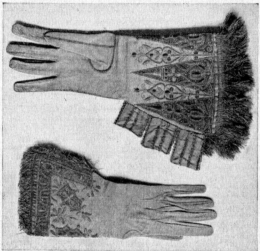

Victoria and Albert Museum

FIG. 2. MAN'S AND WOMAN'S LEATHER GLOVES, 17TH CENTURY
Embroidered in silk and silver gilt with silk appliqué

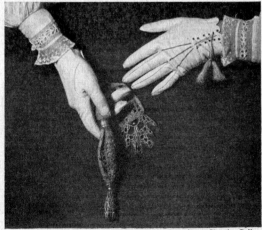

Manchester City Art Gallery

FIG. 3. LADIES' GLOVES, 1860-70

Medieval gloves were loose and gauntleted, sometimes fingered, and sometimes with only a thumb-compartment. Those worn by medieval noblemen were splendidly jewelled and embroidered, with gauntlets often reaching almost to the elbow. Aristocratic ladies wore linen gloves to protect their hands from sunburn, and labourers had thick mittens with two compartments for the thumb and first finger, and another for the remaining three fingers. In the 17th century very elaborate gloves were generally worn, white or coloured, made of fine skins or lace, with heavily embroidered gauntlets trimmed with fringe, lace, or ribbons (Fig. 2). The tight-fitting glove (Fig. 3) did not appear until the early 18th century, when kid mittens and knitted gloves of silk or wool also came into fashion. Evening gloves are now less worn than they used to be, but for ceremonial occasions ladies wear long kid gloves coming well above the elbow, and men wear short white kid gloves for dancing.

Gloves have had many symbolic uses. Oriental merchants often sealed a bargain by giving the buyer a glove. Medieval lands were sometimes held under condition of rendering gloves to the king on particular occasions, and fairs were opened and closed by the hoisting and taking down of a glove. Throwing down a gauntlet during a quarrel constituted a challenge, and picking it up indicated that the challenge was accepted. White gloves symbolized innocence: it is still customary in England to present a pair of white gloves to the ASSIZE judge (q.v. Vol. X) when there are no criminal cases for him to try. At Abbotts Ann, in Hampshire, a funeral custom, which was once general, is still observed: at the funeral of an unmarried girl a maiden-garland, with a white glove in the middle, is carried in the funeral procession.

See also COSTUME, HISTORY OF.

GOITRE, *see* ENDOCRINE GLANDS.

GRILLING. This form of cooking, known in the U.S.A. as 'broiling', is suitable for protein foods containing some fat, such as meat, poultry, or fish. They are exposed, usually on greased bars or *grilles*, to a clear fire, gas flame, or bare electric element, and turned with a spatula. Grilling has the advantages that it is quick, it seals in juices and develops flavour, and, because it requires no extra fat, results in more digestible food than does frying. However, as it affords no time for softening of connective tissue, it is suitable only for tender, expensive cuts such as fillet steak, lamb chops, salmon steaks, fillets of sole, and whole trout. Grilled steaks and whole fish are sometimes 'planked', that is, laid on a buttered oaken board, surrounded by piped, mashed potato, and finished off in a hot oven. A barbecue, of Spanish-American origin, is a huge, outdoor iron frame on which whole carcases can be grilled.

Gas or electric grillers are also useful for making toast, for browning custards and dishes topped with grated cheese or crumbs, and for caramelizing sugar, in place of the old-fashioned salamander. The temperature and the time taken for grilling depend on what is being grilled and what result is required.

H

HAEMORRHAGE, *see* First Aid.

HAEMORRHOIDS, *see* Varicose Veins and Haemorrhoids.

HAIR, CARE OF. The hair of the head, like the Skin (q.v.) and the nails, is made up of groups of cells which are no longer alive in the true sense of the word. The live part of the hair is just below the surface of the skin, where it springs from follicles congregated very closely together over the whole surface of the head. A blood-vessel at the root of each hair feeds it, and a gland at the side of the follicle oils it (*see* Vol. II, p. 193).

To keep in good condition, the hair needs daily treatment. Brushing and combing help to give a gloss and shine to the hair, and also stimulate the circulation of the blood in the head, which encourages fresh growth. The best kind of brush to use is one of strong, natural bristle. The hair should be brushed forwards as well as backwards from different partings for 3 or 4 minutes, then the correct parting should be re-established and the waves pressed into place. An occasional change of parting is, incidentally, quite helpful in preventing the hair from getting thin in any one place.

It is very good for the skin of the scalp to be stimulated by massage, and to be pressed and squeezed with firm fingers. Since both sweat and grease are released from the scalp and dust settles on the head from the outside, it is most important to cleanse the hair with daily brushing and with regular shampoos.

Everyone, even those with dry hair, should shampoo their hair very frequently, and if there is any tendency to dandruff, the hair should be washed at least once a week with shampoo containing pine tar derivatives. Dandruff shows its presence by flaky, dusty particles of skin working off the scalp, accompanied usually by some head irritation. It is not easy to get rid of it because, unless great care is taken, the head becomes re-infected before the first infection has cleared up. People suffering from dandruff or, indeed, any skin infection in the scalp should, therefore, wash their combs and brushes daily. In an advanced case of dandruff, large and very irritating pimples form on the head; for difficulties of this kind a skin specialist should be consulted.

Ordinary shampooing consists of two sets of lather, followed by two thorough rinsings, perhaps under the warm tap, so as to remove every

Victoria and Albert Museum

QUEEN ELIZABETH OF BOHEMIA BEING DRESSED BY HER MAIDS
Painting by the Queen's daughter, Princess Louise Hollandina, 1622–1709

British Museum

GREEK AND ROMAN TOILET IMPLEMENTS
Combs, brush, mirror, pins, and rouge pot and lid

particle of lather. Soft water brings out the grease and soap much more easily than hard. Afterwards, the scalp should be given a brisk rubbing on a towel, working from the back to the front of the head; then the waves and curls can be set in place with pins and combs before the hair is dried thoroughly in a warm room. Brilliantine or hair oil can be applied when the hair is being dressed; but too heavy an application will give the hair a fixed, greasy look.

See also HAIRDRESSING METHODS; SKIN, CARE OF.

HAIRDRESSING, HISTORY OF.

The most elaborate hairdressing of the Ancient World was practised among the Assyrians. They did not, like the Egyptians, shave off their natural hair and put on WIGS (q.v.), but wore a mass of luxuriant curls falling over their shoulders, over which the kings wore a kind of conical helmet, the women a simple head-band. The Hebrew peoples were equally proud of their hair. The women wore it confined in a net or caul and ornamented with 'round tires like the moon' (presumably semicircular fillets of metal). The men also wore their hair long and loose on the shoulders. Absalom, whose hair is said to have weighed about 30 ounces, was caught and killed by his enemies when his long locks became entangled in the bough of a tree.

In ancient Greece both sexes wore their hair knotted on the crown of the head, and many varieties of adornment for women were devised, including a network caul, a bag of silk or wool, and a long band of cloth bound in various ways round the head. It was the custom for boys to cut their hair when they attained manhood and to dedicate it to Apollo or some other god. The Romans were experts in dyeing the hair. The admired blonde locks being somewhat rare among them, they bleached their hair by various means, using, for instance, soap made from goats' fat and ashes. Their methods of dressing the hair were largely borrowed from the Greeks.

After the collapse of the Roman Empire there followed a period of nearly 1,000 years during which the women of western Europe almost entirely concealed their hair by means of veils (*see* HEADWEAR), for to show any hair at all was deemed a sign of immodesty. It was not until the middle of the 14th century that, as part of a new fashion, hair became visible again, at first in small knobs confined in a decorated mesh and worn over the ears. The top of the head remained veiled until the 16th century. The Tudor lady looked through a frame like an arch until Mary Queen of Scots introduced the fashion of wearing the arch farther back to reveal the hair, at least in part. Once revealed, it could be dressed and even powdered. The practice of powdering the hair—sometimes with gold dust— which had been known to antiquity, became fashionable again in the 16th century. Marguerite de Valois, for example, softened the black colour of her hair with powder, and the courtiers of her brother, Henry III of France, powdered their hair silver.

Philip Stubbes, the Puritan satirist, in his *Anatomie of Abuses* (1583), violently attacked all the extravagances of fashion, such as the custom of Elizabethan women not only to reveal their hair but, after the Queen's example, even to dye it. 'There followeth', he says, 'the trimming and tricking of their heads, in laying out their hair to the shew, which of force must be curled, fristed (frizzed) and crisped, laid out (a world to

HAIRDRESSING STYLES

1. Greek. 2. Medieval. 3. 15th-century Italian. 4. Elizabethan. 5. 18th-century 'high head'. 6. Victorian chignon.
7. Edwardian 'crown of hair'. 8. Eton crop, 1920s

see) on wreaths and borders from one ear to the other. And lest it shall fall down, it is under-propped with forks, wire, and I cannot tell what like grim stern monsters, rather than chaste Christian matrons.'

In the 17th century it is men's hairdressing that excites interest. The Elizabethan courtiers had worn their hair short, but in the reign of Charles I the typical 'Cavalier' long locks began to appear. In contrast, more austere hair-styles distinguished the Parliamentary party, and gave them the name 'Roundheads'. Shortly after the restoration of Charles II the Cavalier locks were replaced by elaborate full-bottomed WIGS (q.v.). Women often wore their own hair but dressed in imitation of the masculine wig, curled at the temples, and powdered. An old ballad proclaims women's right to do so:

If Pride be a sin and a folly, why then
    Han't we a far better example from Men?
If Gaudy Apparel those Gallants do wear,
    We will have our Topnots and Powdered Hair.

Fashionable men and women, and even children, wore their hair powdered for nearly 100 years.

In the late 1760s the women's coiffures again took the lead. The hair began literally to rise from the head, draped over a foundation of wire or basket-work and crowned with anything that took the fancy: clusters of feathers, bunches of flowers, baskets of fruit, and even miniature ships in full sail.

The satirists of the day made much of the preposterous head-dresses of the ladies of the 1770s and 1780s, pointing out their great discomfort and the danger of their catching fire from candles. A lady visiting the Court of Versailles explains that she has had attached to her head little curved water-bottles from which appeared real flowers among the curls. The effect, she says, though charming, was extremely inconvenient, as we may well believe. Another inconvenience was the insanitary and verminous nature of these towering head-dresses built up on wire foundations with pomades and flour.

The great lady was often constrained by the intolerable itching to scratch her head, which she did by inserting into the complicated structure a little ivory hand on a slender ivory stick. Such sticks are usually sold by the antique dealers as 'back-scratchers', but their primary purpose is only too plain.

After the French Revolution these elaborate fashions ceased: men no longer wore wigs and cut their hair reasonably short; women wore their hair in a fashion closely resembling the 'Eton crop' of more than a century later. But side-curls began to creep back by the year of Waterloo, and these curls, smoothed out, became the typical early Victorian coiffure with flat pads over the ears.

So fashion remained until the 1870s when there prevailed a new mode of wearing the hair rather high on the head with an immense bunch of curls behind. Men's hair styles remained almost unchanged except that they tended to be a little shorter as the century progressed. Women wore their hair very close to the head in the 1880s, but began wearing it higher again by the end of the century, and in Edwardian times they wore large crowns to support the big hats which were the fashion until the First World War. The war brought drastic changes,

and by the middle 1920s most women wore bobbed hair or Eton crops. In the 1930s a small roll began to appear at the back of the neck and in general a somewhat softer effect was aimed at. The ideal of the small neat head, however, still remained.

See also COSTUME, HISTORY OF; HEADWEAR.

HAIRDRESSING METHODS. The services of expert hairdressers, with all their modern equipment of electric dryers and permanent waving machines, have now largely replaced the services of the lady's maid.

The modern fashion of short hair depends very much on skilful cutting. It is most usual to taper the hair, which is thinned underneath and the ends tapered to encourage any natural tendency to wave or curl. In this way thick, bunchy hair can be made to shape neatly to the head, and even fine hair, normally difficult to handle, is given a sense of direction. Another method of cutting, known as 'clubbing', is used sometimes to make thin hair look thicker.

If hair has a natural tendency to curl or wave, then water waving is best. The hair, having been cut and shampooed, and while still very wet, is set in place in waves and curls with the fingers and pinned or clipped. It is important to

Vasco

Left, HAIR STYLE FOR A LONG FACE; *right*, FOR A ROUND FACE

Vasco

Left, HAIR STYLE FOR AN OVAL OR HEART-SHAPED FACE; *right,* FOR A SQUARE FACE

follow the natural inclination of the hair, and the hairdresser must judge how tightly or loosely to set the waves so as to give the best long-lasting effect. After about half an hour under an electric dryer, when the hair is completely dry, it is freed of pins, combed out, and dressed.

Hair which has not enough natural wave for water waving is generally given a permanent waving, a method which entirely superseded the old Marcel waving done with hot curling tongs. Permanent waving is of two main types—hot and cold. In both, the hair is divided into small locks, each of which is saturated with a lotion and then wound round a curler. In the hot method, heat is then applied, either by means of a machine to which each curler is attached (the older method), or by means of a heating element inside each of the curlers (the more modern method). After the heat process, which has to be timed exactly to suit different types of hair, the curlers and clips are removed, and the hair is shampooed and set. Cold permanent waving, which has gained much popularity in recent years because it can be done at home, requires no heat, for the lotion with which the curls are saturated sets up a chemical action which makes the hair pliable. Some of the best results are obtained by 'cool' waving, a com-

promise between the hot and cold techniques, which uses some heat combined with a not too strong chemical lotion. Whichever method is followed, the wave or curl is permanently fixed and lasts until the hair grows out. The skilled hairdresser can judge which treatment will suit each type of hair best.

Tinting and dyeing are not very widely practised, for the charm of grey and white hair is now accepted, and the emphasis is therefore rather on brightening ageing hair with rinses than on changing its colour. Some rinses now in fashion give a golden or auburn tone or a metallic glint which lasts until the hair is shampooed. But such fashions, more suitable to the theatrical world than to ordinary life, are not usually long-lived.

Hair styles should be chosen not only to suit the fashion but also to suit the individual face. A round face can be balanced by a dressing of curls high on the head, a square face can lose its angularity by soft upswept waves, a little heart-shaped face can gain piquancy by a short, boyish cut with a curled fringe, and a long face can gain breadth by a low-placed side parting and curls bunched over the ears. The style should be one that the wearer can manage easily, for, however well-dressed in the first instance, hair which does not remain neat in all circumstances loses its charm. The emphasis in modern hairdressing is on simplicity, but with plenty of variety.

See also HAIR, CARE OF; HAIRDRESSING, HISTORY OF.

HANDBAGS AND PERSONAL LUGGAGE.

The bag must be one of the most primitive of human inventions. Even before he had begun to wear clothes, man must have found that he needed a bag, and a girdle to hang it from, for holding the stones which were his weapons and the provisions for a journey. Later he must have discovered the use of a hollow tree-trunk and gradually transformed it into what is still known as a 'trunk'. All the containers discussed in this article are alike in being either bags or boxes; they differ down the ages in material, skill of manufacture, size, and shape.

The Egyptians had bags made of leather or cotton and coffers or caskets made of such materials as sandalwood. Travelling chests, as well as leather bags, were in use among the ancient Assyrians. Similar luggage was used by the Greeks and Romans, and they had certainly arrived at the idea of a small leather bag for keeping money in—that is, a purse. But even as late as the Middle Ages the term 'purse' obviously had a wider meaning: for example, the leather purse, worn by Chaucer's Wife of Bath, was clearly too large to be used merely for carrying money but was a general kind of handbag. Throughout the 15th and 16th centuries both men and women wore such pouches attached to the belt, sometimes ornamented with gold and silver and sometimes containing a smaller purse.

These universally worn pouches were usually in the form of a flat bag, with the mouth drawn together by tasselled strings. An inventory of 1510 speaks of a 'tawny bag with tassels of gold and strings of green silk'. Similar objects can be seen in Holbein's portraits of the courtiers of Henry VIII. Towards the end of the century women began to wear underneath the skirt a purse called a little poke, or pocket. Men, too, had a little pocket sewn into their trunk hose, and after about 1570 into their breeches. There were also pockets in the sleeve in this century. About 1610, when the doublet was displaced by the long-skirted coat and waistcoat, it was possible to have pockets in these also (*see* COSTUME, HISTORY OF). Henceforward the male pouch dis-

1. MEDIEVAL PURSES. *a, b.* 12th-century aumonière. *c, d.* 14th-century pouch. *e.* Purse, worn at back, 1515.
2. 16TH-CENTURY WOMAN'S PURSE. *a.* Manner of wearing. *b, c.* Back and front of purse.
3. REGENCY RETICULE, 1809.
4. EDWARDIAN HANDBAGS. *a.* 1910. *b.* 1911.
5. GLADSTONE BAG.
6. SARATOGA TRUNK *a.* Open. *b.* Shut. *c.* Tray.

appears from history, except for the Scottish 'sporran' (*see* CLOTHES).

The flimsy female dresses in fashion in the post-French Revolution period made the 'little poke' underneath the skirt no longer practical, and it was replaced by a handbag or 'reticule'. Though still in use at the time of Queen Victoria's accession, these became less common as skirts became more ample and were made of stiffer materials. They do not seem to have come back into common use until about 1910, when the extremely narrow hobble skirt made pockets impossible. Handbags were then used instead, sometimes immensely large and carried by absurdly long chains. As women wanted to carry more about with them—not only money, but lipstick, face-powder, and cigarettes—handbags became even more of a necessity and are now an inevitable accessory of female attire.

Strong wooden chests barred with iron were part of the furniture of all large medieval houses, and when the king or nobleman went on a journey he would take his possessions and household belongings packed in these and loaded on to heavy carts. But most people in the Middle Ages travelled on horseback because of the bad state of the roads, and so they carried their possessions in rolls on the shoulder or bundles slung over a pack-horse. People travelling by stage-coach took with them as little as they could; but by the 19th century, when roads were better and the carriages were sprung, most coaches had special places, either on the roof or in the boot, for travellers' trunks.

The early 19th-century traveller provided himself with a small box, or trunk, and the ladies had 'band-boxes' for their hats. As the trunk was sometimes covered with leather, there evolved by the 1880s the 'Gladstone' bag, which might be called a box at the bottom and a bag at the top. From America came the Saratoga trunk, a large trunk with a rounded top used by ladies. In the 20th century the expanding suitcase, which could be made large or small according to need, became popular. Modern luggage has been much influenced by air travel, where lightness is of first importance. The greater simplicity of life has made it possible for most people to travel usually only with hand luggage so that they can be their own porters.

See also COSTUME, HISTORY OF.

HATS, *see* HEADWEAR.

A HAY-BOX

HAY-BOX. If a sealed vessel containing food at boiling-point is surrounded by non-conducting material such as tightly packed hay, the food will continue to cook, since hardly any heat can escape. The hay-box method is, in fact, very little used in England, but much more in Denmark. It is a very economical way of cooking dishes, such as porridge and stews, that need slow cooking for a long time.

A box or old trunk with a well-fitting lid is lined thickly with newspapers; pans of the size to be used in the hay-box are then put in and tightly packed round with hay or old woollies, with at least 5 inches' thickness of packing round each pan. The pans are then lifted out leaving nests ready to receive the hot saucepans. The saucepan is brought to the boil on the stove, and, tightly lidded, is put in its nest, covered with a cushion of hay, and tucked in with an old blanket. The box is closed firmly. The food cannot be overcooked and so may be left overnight, but it may need re-heating when taken out. Porridge, for example, put in overnight, is ready for breakfast the next morning.

Timetable

	Stove (minutes)	Hay-box (hours)
Salt beef and salt ham	40	6
Stews	20–30	4
Milk puddings	5–10	3–4
Porridge	5	all night

A modern substitute for the hay-box is the vacuum bucket, a variation of the vacuum flask.

HAY FEVER, *see* ALLERGIC DISEASES.

HEADWEAR. Originally headwear was symbolic rather than utilitarian. Except in very cold or very hot climates, ordinary men normally went bareheaded, but kings, priests, and chieftains wore crowns or fillets as a sign of rank. Distinctive headgear indicating position survives today in the king's crown, the bishop's mitre, the cardinal's scarlet hat, and the coronets worn by peers on ceremonial occasions. Rank or occupation is similarly denoted by caps or helmets worn with service uniform, the priest's biretta, and the scholar's mortarboard. The ancient symbolic importance of headgear persists in the modern custom of raising the hat in greeting. This is now a mere gesture of politeness, but formerly it was an act of homage to a superior. This idea still underlies the removal of hats in church and in the presence of the sovereign.

The cap and the sun-hat seem to have been the earliest utilitarian head-coverings. Woollen caps have been found in northern European graves of the Bronze Age, and Greek and Roman vase-figures and carvings show husbandmen wearing wide-brimmed hats to protect them from the sun. In Eastern countries turbans, broad scarves twisted round the head and frequently worn over a cap, were, and still are, common. Helmets for protection in battle developed in very early times; they were first made of basketwork or leather, and later of metal. When they covered the face they were surmounted by elaborate crests by which the wearers could be recognized (see HERALDRY, Vol. IV).

In ancient Rome only free men covered their heads. The first action of a slave on receiving his freedom was to assume the Phrygian cap, or 'cap of liberty'. A modification of this cap, known as the Phrygian bonnet, was worn by Europeans in the early Middle Ages (Fig. 1). Cloth hoods, sometimes surmounted by caps or hats, were commonly worn until the end of the 15th century (Figs. 2–7). In the 14th century these hoods developed a long tail, called a liripipe, which either hung down behind or was twisted up to form an ornament rather like a bunch of cock's feathers (Figs. 8–9). The wealthy wore plumed and decorated hats which in the following century became very elaborate and variously shaped (Figs. 10–11).

Flat caps, or tall-crowned, small-brimmed hats, often jewelled or feathered, were fashionable during the 16th century (Figs. 12–14).

A hundred years later the wide, feathered hat came to its full glory, to match the splendid, colourful garments then worn by men (Fig. 15). When periwigs (see WIGS) became common towards the end of the 17th century, hat-brims were symmetrically cocked and looped on each side, and from this developed the tricorne hat worn during most of the 18th century (Figs. 17–18).

After the French Revolution, when masculine clothes became simpler and the embroidered satin coat was replaced by one of plain cloth, high-crowned beaver hats without adornment (Fig. 23) came into fashion. These slowly developed through the 'chimney pot' into the black silk top-hat which was in general use in the early 1900s, and is still used for formal occasions (Figs. 22, 24). In the 19th century, the hard, round 'bowler' and also the cloth cap appeared, later followed by the straw 'boater', the 'panama', and the soft felt 'trilby' (Figs. 25–27). Masculine head-gear had become plain and sober-hued.

The oldest feminine head-covering, the veil, survives today in Europe in the bridal veil and in the beautiful lace mantillas worn by Spanish women. Throughout the East it is still widespread, and until quite recently was considered essential as a face-covering for modest women when they went out (see Vol. I, p. 29). The medieval European veil, a long, broad scarf arranged to cover the hair completely, was in general use until the 15th century. From the 13th century it was usually accompanied by a neckcloth, called a wimple, which was drawn up to make a frame for the face (Fig. 28). This form of covering can still be seen in some nuns' habits. Beneath the veil a brightly coloured crespine, or net, confined the hair, and over it a barbette, or goffered linen fillet, was sometimes worn. Unmarried girls, who, unlike their married sisters, were allowed to show their hair, often wore wreaths of flowers of goldsmiths' work instead of veils.

In the 15th century the veil declined in importance and was partly replaced by tall head-dresses, tilted backwards off the face. Among these were horned head-dresses; the beautiful butterfly head-dress made of stiffened, transparent gauze; turbans; high-crowned bonnets; and the fashionable French 'hennin', shaped like a steeple and having a small veil floating from the point (Figs. 29–33). By all these head-dresses the hair was hidden, and if it

1 c. 1154
2 c. 1220
3 c. 1338
4 c. 1250
5 c. 1300
28 c. 1300
29 1416
6 c. 1400
7 c. 1400
8 c. 1330
9 c. 1484
10 c. 1534
11 c. 1534
30 1449
31 c. 1490
32 c. 1504

MEDIEVAL

12 c. 1502
13 c. 1539
14 1588
15 1629
33 c. 1504
34 1578
36 1693
16 1649
17 1693
18 1744
19 c. 1793
37 1790
35 c. 1620
38 1784

16TH, 17TH, AND 18TH CENTURIES

20 1806
21 c. 1813
39 1807
40 1823
41 1837
42 1857
43 1860
22 1842
23 1828
24 1880
25 1911
26 1907
27 1928
44 c. 1873
45 1880
46 1896
47 1908

19TH AND 20TH CENTURIES

Louvre

AN EARLY TOP-HAT
Drawing of M. Leblanc by Ingres, 1780–1867

grew too low on the forehead for the backward-tilting headgear, it was frequently shaved to give the fashionable 'bald' appearance.

These 15th-century extravagances, the ancestors of the feminine hat, were, unlike the latter, worn indoors as well as out. High-crowned feathered hats (*see* Vol. V, p. 395) were popular in the 16th century, as well as small bonnets, and hoods with side-lappets (*see* Vol. V, p. 321). Hoods were usual throughout the 17th century when hats were commonly reserved for riding, but in the 18th century hats came into general use (Figs. 37, 38). They were large and elaborately trimmed to match the large wigs and piled-up masses of powdered hair (*see* Vol. V, opp. p. 176). In the 19th century, when, as with men's costume, simpler styles prevailed, hats were soon superseded by bonnets, and later by small hats trimmed with flower-posies or little feathers (Figs. 39–43). When outdoor games, cycling, and other sports became popular with women towards the end of the century, hard straw hats, like men's 'boaters', and a feminine version of the trilby were often worn (Fig. 46). Large, heavily trimmed hats appeared in the early 20th century (Fig. 47), and were followed after the First World

War by the cloche hat, shaped like a pudding basin and pulled well down over cropped and shingled heads. Since the Second World War many young women go bareheaded, except on formal or ceremonial occasions.

Caps made of linen, silk, or velvet, and later of lace and ribbons, were worn indoors from the 16th century onwards. In the 17th and 18th centuries they were elaborate confections, trimmed with flowers or feathers and stiffened with wires (Fig. 36). Caps were also worn at night (*see* NIGHTCLOTHES). As this long-lived fashion slowly declined, caps became a sign of advancing years, and by the end of the 19th century they were worn only by old ladies. Indoor head-coverings are now rarely seen, except in the form of tiaras, wreaths, or flower-ornaments sometimes worn with full evening dress.

See also COSTUME, HISTORY OF; HAIRDRESSING, HISTORY OF; WIGS.

HEART. The human heart is a double-barrelled muscular pump, whose task it is to drive arterial blood through the body and venous blood through the lungs (*see* BLOOD CIRCULATION). The two sides of the heart are quite separate, so that the arterial and the venous blood do not mix. Each side consists of a receiving chamber or 'auricle' and a pumping chamber or 'ventricle'. Venous blood from the body, laden with carbon dioxide, flows into the right auricle; it is pumped into the right ventricle and is forcibly ejected by each contraction or beat of the ventricle into the pulmonary artery, and so to the lungs. Oxygenated blood from the lungs flows into the left auricle, then passes to the left ventricle, and is pumped into the great artery, the 'aorta', and so to all the arteries of the body (*see* Fig. 1).

The heart, which in an adult weighs just over half a pound, rests in the lower left chest or thorax. It lies loosely in a fibrous, glistening pocket containing a small amount of watery fluid which serves as a lubricant. Its four chambers are lined by a smooth, continuous layer of tissue, called the 'endocardium', which is like that lining the arteries and veins. Another layer of tissue, the 'pericardium', forms the outer surface of the heart; and between the two lies the muscle layer. The heart muscles of the auricles, though strong and tough, are quite thin; in the ventricles, however, the muscle layer is thick and strong. As the left ventricle has a good deal more work to do than the right, its muscle is much thicker.

When the body is at rest, the heart muscle contracts or beats some 72 times per minute, and each time it does so about 4 ounces of blood are pumped by each ventricle. When the body, however, is taking violent exercise, or suffering from a fever as a result of sickness, the body tissues need much more fresh blood. The heart meets this need by beating faster and so pumping more blood. The pulse at the wrist, which corresponds with the heart-beat, tells the doctor how fast the heart is beating. Although the heart continues to beat throughout the lifetime of the body, it rests after each contraction. Like other muscles of the body, it is strengthened by exercise; therefore the heart of an athlete in training, so long as it is not overstrained, is capable of doing a great deal more work, and doing it more efficiently, than that of a person who seldom undertakes physical effort.

The heart is under the control of two sets of nerves which are able to make it beat faster or slower. The beat starts in a small group of special cells in the muscle of the auricle. An impulse like a small electric current is given off and travels down the conducting cells to the

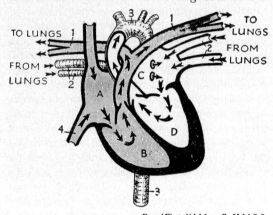

From 'First Aid Manual', H.M.S.O.

FIG. I. DIAGRAM OF THE HEART

A. Right auricle. B. Right ventricle. C. Left auricle. D. Left ventricle. I. Pulmonary arteries. 2. Pulmonary veins. 3. Aorta. 4. Vena Cava

muscle cells. When the impulse reaches the muscle cells, they contract in an orderly fashion, causing the heart-beat to take place. The electrical changes which occur can be picked up, magnified, and recorded by means of an electrocardiograph. These records are of great value in studying and treating heart disease.

After the ventricles contract, valves at the opening of the aorta and pulmonary artery close to prevent the backward flow of blood; other valves prevent a reverse flow from ventricle to auricle. Each beat of the healthy heart makes two sounds, most clearly heard through a stethoscope, which are caused by the contraction of the heart muscle and by the closing of the valves. Heart disease may cause the sounds to change, and in some cases the nature of the disease can be found out by listening carefully to the changed sounds.

As the heart is a muscular organ it must have its own blood-supply, apart from that which it pumps through to the rest of the body. This blood-supply is derived from the coronary arteries which lie buried in the heart muscle and bring oxygenated blood from the aorta to it. The most common forms of heart disease in older people are due to changes in these arteries, for, like other blood-vessels, the tubes of the coronary arteries tend to become smaller with age, and consequently the amount of blood which can be delivered to the heart muscle is reduced. This is one of the main reasons why older people are unable to take as vigorous exercise as younger people can. Usually the heart can still do quite enough work to supply the normal needs of the body, but sometimes the blood-supply becomes so reduced that the heart cannot carry on except when the body is at rest. Even a small amount of exercise causes pain in the chest due to the work of the heart exceeding its blood-supply.

A more serious happening is the formation of a blood clot in one of the coronary arteries, that is, coronary thrombosis; when this happens a part of the heart muscle is deprived of its blood-supply, and the cells soon die. In many cases, however, the dead muscle cells are replaced by fibrous tissue which requires less oxygen, and the unharmed muscle cells which remain are able to carry on quite well.

This type of heart disease can now be treated with a variety of drugs. Some of them (the nitrites) are able to cause the coronary arteries to relax and become wider; others are used to prevent the blood from clotting, and others again to put the patient at complete rest for a period so that the demands upon the heart are reduced as much as possible and it has a chance to recover. Angina pectoris ('constriction of the chest') is not a disease but may be a symptom of several forms of heart disease, or even of other diseases, when the heart and blood-vessels are sound.

In the last few years surgical treatment, as well as drugs, has been used for heart disease. Babies are occasionally born with malformations of the heart and great vessels, and in many such cases, venous and arterial blood are able to mix. Consequently the body receives blood which is partly lacking in oxygen, and the skin has a blue tinge. It is now sometimes possible to operate on the heart itself, and so to restore the child's normal colour and good expectation of life. Some infectious diseases may attack valves as well as the heart muscle, making them become thick and stiff. The surgeon can now often help by cutting and repairing them. Indeed, it may soon be possible to use an artificial heart during these operations, so that the surgeon can take as much time over the operation as he wishes whilst a machine pumps the blood to keep the body alive. This has already been done successfully with animals.

See also BLOOD CIRCULATION; RESPIRATION.
See also Vol. II: HEART (animal).

HEATING, HISTORY OF. The need for a regular system of domestic heating varies from country to country according to the climate. In

G. Roper

A HYPOCAUST IN THE ROMANO-BRITISH VILLA AT CHEDWORTH, GLOUCESTERSHIRE

Part of the mosaic floor which was supported by brick piles is still in position. Hot air came through the opening on the right and circulated beneath the floor

tropical countries domestic heating is obviously not necessary except for cooking or heating water. In temperate countries, however, such as Britain, the indoor temperature, especially in winter, has to be raised by some form of local heating. The position, too, of the house in relation to sun and wind, the size of ROOMS, the position and size of WINDOWS (qq.v.), and the prevention of draughts all play a part in warming the house.

For many hundreds of years, right down to the middle of the 19th century, the only form of domestic heating in general use was the open fire, burning wood, peat, and, from the 17th century, coal. The one remarkable exception was in ancient Rome, where elaborate systems of central heating were devised. Flues carried hot air and combustion gases under the paved floors and upwards behind the walls. This method of heating is still used in some countries, including parts of Russia.

In early times great importance was attached to the open domestic fire. The Greeks and Romans considered the 'hearth' a sacred place, rather like an altar with which it was often associated. To Norsemen, the fire was so important that their homes were often described in their poems as 'hearth ships' or 'fire ships'. In the course of time, the open fire was improved in three main ways: the FIREPLACE itself was improved, CHIMNEYS were built (qq.v.), and coal was more widely used, until, by the 18th century, it was burnt as the normal fuel in town houses, though wood was still used in the country. One of the worst consequences of the enormous increase in coal consumption, from the 19th century onwards, has been the problem of smoke pollution which causes damage to health, vegetation, and buildings. Attempts to deal with the problem were discussed in England as early as the 1780s; in Birmingham, in 1785, James WATT (q.v. Vol. V) took out a patent for a furnace which made less smoke, and in Manchester, an attempt was made to control smoke by legislation. Today, Manchester and some other cities have established special smokeless zones in an effort to improve conditions.

At the beginning of the 19th century closed stoves came into general use in Europe and the United States, one of the first having been invented by the American Benjamin FRANKLIN (q.v. Vol. V). The great advantage of such stoves is that they will burn any kind of fuel, for

Berlin Museum

A POLISH FAMILY IN THE 18TH CENTURY

The elaborate stove behind the cradle is typical of the kind used to heat rooms in Eastern Europe from the 18th century onwards. Painting by D. Chodowiecki, 1726–1801

example, wood, peat, coal, and coke. They are more efficient, too, in terms of fuel consumption, although they deliver all their heat by radiation and are consequently not as comfortable as some other forms of heating. In England the disadvantages were held to outweigh the advantages, and, despite the growing shortage of coal and its great rise in price, the open grate still survives. As early as 1850, new smoke-reducing grates were widely advertized, but not until recently have improvements in fireplace design, such as 'convector jackets' and 'all-night burners', produced real fuel economies (*see* HEATING SYSTEMS, DOMESTIC). Dirty and wasteful as coal fires are, more than one-quarter of the coal produced in England in 1939 was burnt in open fires—a much higher proportion than anywhere else in Europe; in the same year in Denmark, for example, the average amount of coal used per head was not quite half that used in England.

Though the age of the coal fire is certainly not over, many alternative methods of domestic heating have been introduced since the 1870s. There have been three main lines of development: first, the use of new fuels or sources of power—gas, electricity, and oil; second, the development of fuel-saving economies; and third, the development of central and district HEATING (q.v. Vol. VIII).

Gas was the first of the new fuels to appear. It was first used for street LIGHTING (q.v.) in 1813, and for domestic heating some 70 years later. This introduced a new system of fuel supply; for the first time houses were linked together direct to a centralized supply point—in this case the gasometer. Fuel-transmitting systems of this kind, more than any other factor, distinguish modern domestic heating from that of a century ago. Gas systems were followed by electricity systems, and in 1926 the national

GRID SYSTEM (q.v. Vol. VIII) brought ELEC-TRICITY (q.v.) to innumerable homes which had previously been heated only by coal fires.

Since the late 19th and early 20th centuries, with greatly improved methods of heating water and air, and, more recently, with the refinement of automatic controls such as the THERMOSTAT (q.v. Vol. VIII), systems of central and district heating have been widely used. Most big blocks of flats and many private houses are now heated or partly heated by hot-water or hot-air pipes running all over the building from a boiler in the basement or kitchen. The first experiments in district heating, that is, supplying heat from a central boiler-house to groups of houses, took place in the United States as early as 1877, and the system has since been adopted in parts of the U.S.S.R., Germany, Switzerland, and Denmark. A small district in Pimlico is heated from the power station by pipes under the river. Since 1920 many experiments have been made with methods of radiant heating, through the ceiling, floors, or panels in walls, for example (see HEATING, Vol. VIII). Radiant heating produces a feeling of equal warmth in all parts of the room, and today, especially in the United States, is accepted as the ideal method.

In many parts of the world where the more important fuels are scarce, the main material used in heating is refuse or dung, supplemented where possible by timber and charcoal. Methods of heating remain simple. In some parts of eastern and northern Europe, for example, stoves are constructed with a large flat upper surface under which pass flue gases, and upon which the whole family can sleep in comfort. Farther East, in parts of Persia, a charcoal brazier is placed in a shallow hole in the ground. In China and Japan charcoal heating is still common, and braziers are in regular use. Such charcoal burning is well suited to countries where only moderate heating is necessary.

See also HEATING SYSTEMS, DOMESTIC; FIREPLACES; CHIMNEYS.
See also Vol. VIII: HEATING.

HEATING SYSTEMS, DOMESTIC. About 80% of British homes are heated by coal fires (see HEATING, HISTORY OF). Though cheerful in appearance, they have many disadvantages. Not only do they cause much extra work and dust, but many of the older grates are so inefficient that only about one-fifth of the heat is used to warm the room. The rest escapes up the chimney, partly as smoke (which is unburned fuel and amounts to about $\frac{1}{2}$ cwt. for 1 ton of coal) and partly as hot chimney gases. The principal heating effect of open fires is by radiation (see HEATING, Vol. VIII). Radiant energy from the burning fuel passes through the air until it strikes an opaque object, such as a wall or furniture, when it is transformed into heat. This warms the object, which in turn warms the air, but an hour or more elapses after a fire is lit before the room is comfortably warm.

Coal is likely to provide the main source of heat in British homes for many more years, since other fuels are not available in sufficient quantities for general use. Other fuels include wood,

A JAPANESE ROOM WITH A BRAZIER FOR HEATING

peat, and oil, which are often burned in country districts; anthracite, coke, and various manufactured smokeless fuels, which are much used for stoves and boilers; and the 'refined fuels'—gas and electricity (*see* FUELS, Vol. VIII).

Many improvements have recently been made in fireplace design in order to cut down the very great wastage of fuel. For example, to reduce the amount of heat that escapes with the air up the chimney, fires are now often fitted with 'convector jackets' (Fig. 1). With these, the air is warmed by contact with the back of the fire casing, and is then passed out into the room or through ducts to other rooms. Other improvements include systems of accurate draught control, and 'closure plates', which can keep a fire alight without attention for 10 hours or more. A 'back boiler' can also often be fitted to the back of the fire to provide hot water, or a fire in the living-room may be used to heat the cooker in the kitchen. With these improvements the total efficiency of a fire can be raised to about 50%, about one-third of the heat being used to warm the room by convection, that is, by heating the air directly.

An alternative to the open fireplace is the closed heating stove, which has an efficiency of about 70%. The whole of the stove surface becomes hot, and warms the air by convection. 'Semi-closed' stoves, in which the doors can be opened, are more popular in Britain than in other countries, but they have an efficiency of only about 55%, or a little more if a small boiler is incorporated.

Gas fires have an advantage over solid-fuel fires because they can be carefully regulated to avoid overheating. They involve no labour, and are very suitable for bedrooms and sick-rooms. The temperature of the 'radiants' is about 1,500° F., or about the same as a bright coal or coke fire. As with solid-fuel fires, convector patterns are now made, increasing the efficiency from 50% up to 70%. With high efficiencies, however, the temperature of the gases escaping up the chimney is relatively low, and, as 1 lb. of gas in burning produces about $1\frac{1}{2}$ lb. of water vapour, there is some risk of condensation in the chimney.

With electric fires, the heating is nearly all by radiation, with an efficiency of practically 100%, though the high cost of electricity makes them expensive to use. The temperature of the elements is about 1,000° F. Electric convectors,

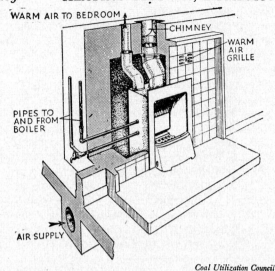

Coal Utilization Council

FIG. 1. DIAGRAM OF A CONVECTOR OPEN FIRE WITH BOILER

which are mainly air heaters, are made in many types. Tubular heaters, consisting of steel tubes, 2 inches in diameter, have a surface temperature of about 200° F. Another pattern contains an electric heater and a small fan which distributes the warmed air (Fig. 2). Another resembles a central-heating radiator, but is filled with oil heated by an electric element.

Central heating, on the low-pressure hot-water system (*see* HEATING, Vol. VIII), is often installed in large houses, but in small homes one or two radiators can be heated from a boiler supplying domestic hot water. The provision of

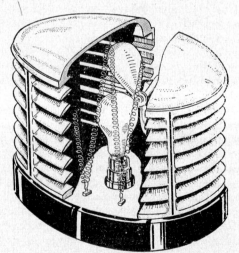

H.M.V. Household Appliances

FIG. 2. DIAGRAM OF A HEATER WITH A FAN WHICH DRIVES THE WARMED AIR THROUGH THE LOUVERS

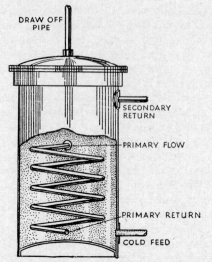

FIG. 3. DIAGRAM OF AN INDIRECT HOT WATER CYLINDER

adequate hot water is very important, and an average family of two adults and two children requires from 250 to 350 gallons a week at a temperature of 140° F. Back boilers in fires and stoves can heat from 3 to 12 gallons an hour, and the smallest independent boilers heat about 20 gallons an hour.

In a typical domestic hot-water system, hot water from the boiler rises to the upper part of a storage tank or cylinder, usually placed in a linen cupboard, through a 'primary flow' pipe. The 'primary return' takes the cooler water from the bottom of the cylinder back to the boiler. From the top of the cylinder the 'draw-off pipe' runs to the hot-water taps. A 'vent pipe' releases the air which is driven out of the water when it is heated, the outlet being turned down over the cold water 'supply tank', usually in the roof. From this tank, cold water flows into the bottom of the cylinder to replace hot water as it is drawn off (see p. 231).

In districts where the water is scale-forming (see WATER, DOMESTIC), a continuous change of water passing through the boiler would clog both the boiler and pipes. In such cases an 'indirect' cylinder is often used, the primary flow pipes forming a continuous coil so that the water in the boiler is unchanged. The water in the cylinder is heated by contact with the hot coil (Fig. 3). Though unnecessary in a small house, a 'secondary return' connexion is also usually fitted in blocks of flats so that the water is continually circulating. With a single draw-off pipe (often called a 'dead-leg'), the water

cools between periods of use, and this cold water must be drawn off before hot water appears at the taps. With a complete secondary circulation, however, hot water can be drawn off at once.

If an electric immersion heater is fitted in the cylinder, no boiler or fire is necessary; this is a great advantage in summer. An immersion heater has an electric element sealed inside a metal tube. When the heater is switched on, the water in contact with the tube is heated, and rises to the top of the cylinder. A 3-kilowatt immersion heater heats about 10 gallons an hour; it is usually provided with a THERMOSTAT (q.v. Vol. VIII), which automatically switches it off when the water has reached a set temperature.

Many hot-water systems depend on gas. Some gas-heaters are 'instantaneous': when a water tap is turned on, the change in water

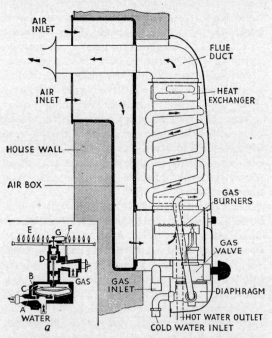

Ascot Gas Water Heaters Ltd.

FIG. 4. DIAGRAM OF A GAS WATER HEATER

a. Section of diaphragm and gas valve. When the hot water tap is turned on, water flows from the cold main through the constriction A. This reduces the pressure in the tube B leading to the top of the diaphragm C, making it rise. It pushes up the gas valve D from its seating and allows the gas to flow into the burners E, where it is ignited from the pilot jet F. Hot gases rise and heat the water in the pipes which run through the heat exchanger. If the pilot goes out, the bimetallic strip G straightens and closes the safety valve, so that gas cannot reach the burners

pressure operates a gas valve, and a cluster of gas jets is lighted by a small pilot flame (Fig. 4). An alternative is the 'storage' heater, in which water in an insulated container is continuously heated by a small gas flame. Another type is the 'circulator', which consists of a small gas boiler connected to the hot-water cylinder in the same way as a solid-fuel boiler.

See also HEATING, HISTORY OF; HOUSEHOLD PLUMBING. See also Vol. VIII: HEATING; FUELS.

HERBS AND SPICES. Fragrant leaves and spices have been used in cooking for a very long time. The Romans were especially fond of them and, in the Dark and Middle Ages, before the rediscovery and development of VEGETABLES (q.v.), they were used to vary monotonous meals and to disguise unwelcome flavours (*see* COOKING, HISTORY OF).

1. HERBS. The ONION family (alliums) (q.v. Vol. VI) includes chives and spring onions which are chopped and put into SALADS, EGG DISHES, SANDWICH fillings, and SOUPS. Garlic flavours salads and mutton and, used sparingly, it improves most STEWS (qq.v.). It is used more liberally in many Mediterranean and Indian dishes. In ancient Greece those who had eaten garlic were forbidden to enter the temple.

The mint family (labiates)—balm, basil, marjoram, mint, rosemary, sage, savory, and thyme—have fragrant leaves which are used in STUFFINGS and SAVOURY dishes (qq.v.). Basil traditionally flavours turtle soup, and is a favourite Italian pot herb. Marjoram, one of the chief ingredients of Queen Elizabeth I's perfume, is good with rabbit and in Italian tomato sauce. Rosemary, which used to be a wedding and funeral emblem, garnishes stews and fish. Thyme, parsley, and bayleaf are the three herbs tied together to make a *bouquet garni*, which is immersed in stews and casseroles, and removed before serving.

The leaf of only one member of the parsley family (umbellifers) is used in cooking, and that one, common parsley, is used more than any other herb. It is the seeds of other umbellifers that are used: aniseed and caraway, in liqueurs, on bread and cakes, and in the poorer cheeses; celery, on apple salad and in stuffing; coriander, in curry; dill, in pickles; and fennel, the *erbe precyous* of the 14th century, in fish sauces and in apple pie. Fennel and celery are also served as vegetables.

Other fairly common herbs are chervil, for cucumber and green salad; tarragon, chopped with chives and parsley, for *omelette aux fines herbes*; bayleaf, a very pungent, eucalyptus-like laurel, used in pickling vinegar, in making a *bouquet garni*, and in certain sauces; and *fenugreek* or 'Greek hay', now scarcely heard of in Britain, but popular in ancient times and still an ingredient of curry.

2. SPICES. Most of the sweet spices are described in SPICE CROPS (q.v. Vol. VI), and the hot ones in CONDIMENTS (q.v.). Allspice, ground from the dried berries of the all-spice tree (Jamaica pepper or pimento tree), combines the flavourings of cinnamon, nutmeg, and cloves. With the exception of turmeric, all the sweet spices are used in cakes and biscuits or to flavour sweet dishes. Almost all are used in chutneys and curries, and a few in Western savoury dishes, for example, a clove in onion sauce and nutmeg gratings in German red cabbage. Poppy seed is sprinkled on bread, and, when ground, is used as a filling in Hungarian cakes.

See also CONDIMENTS AND RELISHES. See also Vol. VI: HERBS, GARDEN; SPICE CROPS.

HEREDITARY DISEASES. In man, constitution, stature, and certain physical and mental characteristics are mainly determined by HEREDITY (q.v. Vol. II), but favourable environment and proper care will protect a weak constitution, while neglect or disregard of the laws of health may limit growth or ruin a good constitution.

Some diseases are definitely inherited, while in others heredity plays no part at all. Between the two extremes lie a number of conditions in which heredity and environment play more or less equal roles. Apart from the inheritance of a definite disease, some people inherit a morbid tendency which makes them susceptible to certain diseases; others are endowed with a 'constitution' or condition of the body which makes them react to certain stimuli in a special way.

It is important to distinguish between congenital, familial, and hereditary diseases. Congenital diseases are those which are apparent in the infant at birth. They may be of hereditary origin, but they are often due to the transmission of infection from the mother to the child during pregnancy, or to accidents, poisoning, malnutrition, or overwork from which the mother has suffered during this time. Some are the result of injuries suffered by the infant during the actual process of BIRTH (q.v.). Abnormalities of development occur in certain organs; for example, there is a congenital heart defect which makes it difficult for the BLOOD (q.v.) to receive sufficient oxygen, so that the child's skin has a blue tinge (a 'blue baby'). This can often be remedied by an operation. Other abnormalities may occur in nerve cells so that the brain and spinal cord are affected, as with 'spastics'. Among the infections which are responsible for faulty development is German measles contracted by the mother during her early pregnancy (see INFECTIOUS DISEASES). Sometimes a mother has a certain rare blood condition which causes her child to be born with a blood disease of which the signs are severe jaundice, anaemia, or dropsy. It is now possible to drain off the child's abnormal blood, at the same time completely replacing it by fresh normal blood.

Familial diseases are those which occur with abnormal frequency in members of the same family. They may be due to heredity, but they are sometimes brought about by contagion or by a common environment, occupation, or mode of life shared by all the family.

True hereditary diseases are transmitted by lineage, through the generations. They may appear at birth, in early childhood, at adolescence, or in adult life. In the course of successive generations they may become less severe or even disappear, or they may become more frequent and more severe. The disease may be latent for long periods, skipping whole generations, and then reappear. Knowledge of heredity helps in the diagnosis and prevention of disease provided that a full pedigree, with all the relevant medical histories, is available—which, in fact, is seldom the case.

There are perhaps 200 or more hereditary diseases, the majority of them, however, affecting only a small proportion of the population. Many are very rare and constitute medical curiosities rather than practical problems. Among the most important are various forms of MENTAL DISEASE, deaf-mutism, a number of EYE conditions (notably myopia or short-sightedness and colour-blindness), many SKIN diseases, dental deformities, abnormalities such as supernumerary fingers and toes, dwarfism, some ALLERGIC DISEASES (qq.v.) such as asthma and migraine, and various muscular disorders. Heredity plays an important part in causing EPILEPSY and DIABETES (qq.v.). The role of heredity in TUBERCULOSIS (q.v.) is problematic; it is most likely a susceptibility to the disease that is inborn rather than the disease itself, for, in fact, almost everyone is infected with the tubercle bacillus, and whether the disease develops or not is largely determined by such factors as environment, nutrition, and occupation. CANCER (q.v.) does not ordinarily appear until a relatively late period of life, which makes it difficult, usually, to get accurate information regarding family history: few people know what caused the death of their grandparents and whether they ever had tumours. Indeed, little is yet known about the actual cause of the various kinds of cancer, and all that can be said at present is that there is evidence that a tendency towards the development of cancer is inherited in certain families. Some hereditary diseases, such as haemophilia (liability to uncontrollable bleeding), affect almost exclusively the male sex, but are transmitted only by the female. Some varieties of anaemia are inherited, as are the 'blood groups' (see BLOOD), a fact which has important applications in legal medicine.

See also Vol. II: HEREDITY.

HERNIA. This means the escape of any organ of the body from its containing cavity. Cerebral hernia, for example, is the protrusion of part of the brain following injury to the skull. The most frequent form of hernia, known to the layman as 'rupture', is the escape of a portion of gut through a weak spot in the abdominal wall—most commonly in the groin; this is caused by strain, as in lifting heavy objects, or by excessive coughing. A swelling appears at the navel or the groin, usually disappears when the patient lies down, but returns when he stands. It is often possible to 'reduce' a hernia by manipulation or by standing the patient on his head, and to keep it from recurring by giving him a truss to wear, an appliance which should be fitted by an expert. In the case of young patients and those leading an active life it is often better to operate, and, indeed, in cases where reduction by manipulation is impossible, an operation is nearly always essential. Strangulated hernia, the most serious consequence of neglect, means that the hernia is constricted or twisted, so that the blood-supply is interfered with. There is danger of gangrene unless the condition is relieved by operation.

HIRE-PURCHASE. This system of buying has three features. First, the buyer pays a proportion of the price at the beginning and afterwards makes regular small payments until the full price, which includes an INTEREST charge (q.v. Vol. VII), has been paid. Secondly, the buyer obtains possession of his goods at the time of the first payment. Thirdly, the title or legal ownership of the goods stays with the seller until payment is completed; in this last respect it differs from mortgage (*see* PROPERTY LAW, Section 4, Vol. X). Big firms run their own hire-purchase organizations, and special finance companies arrange hire-purchase for smaller firms. The Hire-Purchase Act (1938) gives some legal protection to buyers who are unable to fulfil their payments.

The system began in the 19th century with the buying of clothing and other necessities through thrift and mutuality clubs (*see* FRIENDLY SOCIETIES, Vol. X), but it is now used by householders chiefly for buying what are called 'consumer durables'—radios, washing machines, furniture, motor-cars, and so on; and in the world of commerce for acquiring trawlers, aircraft, railway engines, and machinery, which can be put to work to earn the money to pay for themselves. In America, hire-purchase is much more widespread than it is in England, and at the end of 1953 the American people were spending nearly 11% of their income on hire-purchase payments.

Hire-purchase has many advantages. It enables people with small incomes to buy goods which they could not afford to buy outright; this, in turn, increases the demand for such goods and helps trade and employment. But there are difficulties. When trade is good, people are tempted to buy more and more by hire-purchase; when trade is bad, hire-purchase buying falls off rapidly because it is most commonly used for 'luxury' goods which people can, if need be, do without. Thus, hire-purchase tends to make good business into a boom and bad business into a slump, which is just what the Chancellor of the Exchequer wishes to avoid. In 1951, therefore, at the time of a severe economic crisis, the Government restricted hire-purchase in Britain by making buyers of certain goods pay big first instalments and pay off the remainder more quickly than before; the banks also were asked not to lend money to help firms to run hire-purchase schemes. These restrictions

were meant to be only temporary, but they show the economic importance of hire-purchase. Unfortunately, there is no means of knowing what is the right amount of hire-purchase for a country to have at any one time.

HOME NURSING. Although hospital treatment is necessary for many types of disease and is widely available at the present day, the best place for the management of minor illnesses is still the home. Most households meet with sickness or accidents at some time or other, and beds are not always immediately available in hospital even for those who need them. A knowledge of nursing and of FIRST AID (q.v.) is, therefore, highly desirable, especially for mothers. NURSING (q.v.) is a highly specialized profession, and the home nurse cannot aim at a knowledge of more than the basic principles; but the more she knows about the common illnesses the more intelligently and efficiently will she be able to carry out her duties. Much depends, however, on the use of common sense and on strict compliance with the doctor's directions.

Since nursing the sick is a trying and arduous occupation, the nurse should herself be fit in mind and body. She must obey rules of strict personal hygiene, and she must have regular meals and sufficient sleep and fresh air. She

Nursing Mirror

PENICILLIN INJECTION BEING GIVEN BY A DISTRICT NURSE TO A PATIENT IN HIS HOME should get away from the atmosphere of the sick room for part of every day and should take some exercise in the open air. She should wear comfortable clothing, and since she will have to spend long periods on her feet she should have well-fitting, good shoes. She should take care of her hands and be sure to wash them both before and after attention to the patient.

A correct attitude towards the patient calls for certain personal qualities, the most important being sympathy, tact, and cheerfulness. Sympathy does not mean sentimentality, and it is vitally important that the nurse should not allow herself to be unduly upset or influenced by the reactions of the patient. She should go about her work quietly and efficiently, without hurry or fuss, not over nursing her patient. For example, she often has to allow her patient to refuse food even when a great deal of time and trouble has gone to its preparation. But even though she must to some extent bear with the whims of the sick, the nurse must be very firm in carrying out the doctor's instructions, especially where the taking of medicines is concerned. She must keep calm in every emergency and must never lose her temper. In nursing children an ability to divert the child's attention away from his ills and keep him entertained and happy is of the greatest importance.

The nurse's first duties towards the doctor are loyalty and obedience. Responsibility for the management of the case and the line of treatment to be followed rests with him; he will outline the general plan of campaign, and it is the nurse's job to carry out his instructions precisely. It is also her duty to observe the course of the illness, taking note of any changes that may occur and keeping records of temperature, bowel action, appetite, and sleep. She should report to the doctor any untoward happening, such as any occurrence of vomiting or complaints of pain or discomfort made by the patient. She should prepare for the doctor's visit beforehand so that his time is not wasted. She should have ready hot water, soap, and towels, and if she knows that the doctor will need to carry out certain examinations or to use instruments, she should make the necessary arrangements beforehand and be ready to assist if called upon.

The nurse's relations with the other members of the household are most important. Anxious and fussy relatives are sometimes more trying than the patient, and the nurse often has to use considerable tact in dealing with them. Her first duty is towards the patient, and even though sickness in the house is apt to cause frayed nerves, she must not allow these to upset her patient. She may often have to regulate visits to the patient strictly, and watch vigilantly that visitors do not rouse the patient's anxiety by discussing his condition in his presence, or bring him food or tobacco which the doctor has forbidden. Many foolish people believe that a little of the 'medicine that did grannie so much good a year ago' will cure this patient too and so bring him the remains of the bottle.

The choice of the sickroom has to be governed by many considerations, but it should be as quiet as possible. An upper room close to the bathroom and lavatory is usually the most suitable, and ideally it should face south in order to ensure the maximum amount of sun. It is best to remove all superfluous articles of furniture. A proper supply of fresh air without draughts is essential, and a coal fire is probably the best form of heating. If a gas or electric heater is used, a bowl of water should be placed nearby. Lights must be placed so that they do not shine into the patient's eyes, and if they are to be left on at night they must be carefully shaded.

See also FIRST AID; NURSING.

HOMEOPATHY. Derived from Greek words meaning 'similar suffering', homeopathy is a system of medical practice and treatment based on the theory that 'likes may be cured by likes' (*similia similibus curantur*)—an idea summed up in the familiar saying 'A hair of the dog that bit you'. The idea is old, being not unknown to the Greeks as well as the Romans, but it was first given definite expression by Samuel Hahnemann (1755–1843), a German physician and chemist who, having become dissatisfied with orthodox medical teaching, set out to discover sounder principles upon which to base his practice.

At this period the researches of great scientists such as PRIESTLEY and LAVOISIER (qq.v. Vol. V) were revolutionizing the study of CHEMISTRY (q.v. Vol. VII). New elements were being isolated, the laws of chemical combination were being worked out, and new facts were constantly being discovered. Hahnemann investigated the action of many drugs by taking them himself, but for years he made little progress. Eventually he found that doses of cinchona (the plant from

JEWELLERY OF THE 16TH AND 17TH CENTURIES

1. Italian necklace of gold and coral beads strung with pearls. 2. Spanish pendant of enamelled gold set with rubies and hung with pearls. 3. The Canning jewel (Italian) composed of a baroque pearl mounted in enamelled gold set with pearls, rubies, and diamonds. 4, 5. Spanish pendants of enamelled gold hung with pearls. 6. The Barber jewel (English); enamelled gold set with rubies and diamonds enclosing an onyx cameo of Queen Elizabeth I. 7. French necklace and pendant of enamelled gold set with diamonds, hung with a pearl and a pale sapphire

which comes the drug quinine) could produce fever in a healthy person, and this convinced him that he had found the vital clue. He extended his experiments to 'prove' a large number of drugs. If he found that doses of, for example, a substance such as arsenic would produce symptoms of stomach ache, vomiting, and diarrhoea, he would give very small doses of the same substance to patients having such symptoms; and in this way he claimed many cures. In 1796 he published *An Essay on a new Principle for Ascertaining the Curative Powers of Drugs*, and in 1810 he followed this up by his famous *Organon of the Rational Art of Healing*. The underlying idea was that the drug used induced a condition which substituted for the actual disease, and that the body could more easily get rid of the substitute. Hahnemann directed that the drugs were to be given in single doses and in the minutest possible quantities.

Homeopathy made converts throughout Europe in the early years of the 19th century. In 1825 it was introduced into America; the London Homeopathic Hospital was founded in 1849. Like most systems, homeopathy contains some truth, and Hahnemann undoubtedly did good by simplifying medical treatment; but he really knew very little about the nature of disease, and much of his teaching was not scientific. With modern advances in pathology and bacteriology homeopathists have had to modify their doctrine, and in practice they exercise the right possessed by every doctor to use any method of treatment which may help the individual patient.

See also DRUGS.

HOMES, *see* HOUSES, HISTORY OF; HOUSES, TYPES OF; PRIMITIVE DWELLINGS.

HORMONES, *see* ENDOCRINE GLANDS; DRUGS.

HORS D'ŒUVRES. These are extra dishes served at the beginning of a meal as a relish, and, as their name indicates, 'outside' the main courses. In France this course is most usually served before luncheon, especially in a private house; it may be quite simple: a few olives, a sardine, and some sliced tomatoes, served with a crisp roll and butter, or perhaps some pâté (*see* OFFAL), such as *foie gras*, with thin toast and butter. In hotels and restaurants trolleys packed with little dishes containing dozens of dif-

HORS D'ŒUVRES CONSISTING OF TOMATO, SALAMI, MIXED VEGETABLES, SAUSAGE AND BEETROOT, AND OLIVES

ferent kinds of dressed vegetables, salted and pickled fish, egg mayonnaise, cold meats, or sliced sausage are wheeled about, and the customers can choose half a dozen or more of these *hors d'œuvres variés*. This type of French hors d'œuvres is now to be found in fashionable restaurants all over the world, and is used increasingly in English and American homes as a main course for luncheon or supper. In Italy the appetizer course, already well established by the 16th century, is called *antipasto* because it precedes the 'repast'. Usually it is thin slices of smoked ham, either raw or cooked, and *salami* or *mortadella* (*see* SAUSAGES). In summer the ham may be accompanied by a slice of melon or some fresh figs. Less frequently there are anchovies, tunny fish, shellfish, or tiny globe artichokes prepared in olive oil. In Chile and Argentina cold meats are served before lunch.

Enormous quantities of appetizers and open sandwiches are consumed before a meal in Russia, helped down by vodka. In the 18th century the excellence of this Russian *zakuska* inspired the French to improve their own hors d'œuvres. To the Russians we owe *caviare*, the tiny black eggs from the female STURGEON (q.v. Vol. II), which are regarded as the supreme appetizing delicacy. Red caviare, the larger and not so expensive roe of the hen pike, is a Roumanian appetizer. Other eastern European countries, as well as Scandinavia and Germany, have their characteristic buffet spreads, which are entertaining to the British visitor but sometimes too much for his digestion before the real meal. In Sweden this cold table is called *Smörgåsbord*, in Finland *Violeipapoyta*, in Norway *Koldtbord*, in Denmark *Smørrebrød*, in Poland *Kanapka* (from *canapé*) (*see* SAVOURIES), in Czechoslovakia *Obložený Chlebíček* (spread bread), and in Germany *belegte Butterbrot* (*see* SAND-WICHES). The basis of most of these 'laden' breads is a thin, square slice of dark rye bread, thickly buttered. On this is piled cured and salted fish, eggs, meats, cheeses, and salads, either separately or in imaginative combination, and always beautifully garnished. A well-known restaurant in Copenhagen supplies 200 kinds of sandwiches on five different kinds of bread, and they are freshly made while one waits. An example from Germany illustrates how different these are from British sandwiches: it is called *tartaren Bröte* and consists of finely minced raw steak and onion on a platform of buttered rye bread; a raw egg yolk is slipped into a hollow in the meat, and the whole sprinkled with grated horseradish. It sounds peculiar but is, in fact, delicious, nourishing, and digestible. Obviously, many of these laden breads must be eaten with knife and fork.

Oriental hors d'œuvres are lighter in character: Chinese appetizers include melon seeds, candied ginger, salted nuts, ancient eggs (*see* EGG DISHES), and sliced oranges. Bombay duck (a dried and salted herring-type fish, looking like chips of wood), *puppadums* (thin savoury wafers), and chutneys and pickles are appetizers accompanying Indian dishes; but the true Indian hors d'œuvres are called *sambals*, and consist of fish, fruits, and vegetables, highly peppered and pickled.

As the U.S.A. has been able to draw upon the cookery lore of many peoples, almost all these hors d'œuvres can be met with there, sometimes changed or modified but usually quite recognizable.

In Britain the hors d'œuvres habit is not a native one, but melon, grapefruit, tomato juice, smoked salmon, or *hors d'œuvres variés* are steadily ousting soup from British menus, especially at luncheon. The practice of serving little SAVOURIES (q.v.) as appetizers with sherry or cocktails, and at evening coffee-parties, is probably a modest British adaptation of the more robust eating habits of the Continent.

HOSPITALS, *see* NURSING. *See also* Vol. X: HOSPITALS, HISTORY OF; HOSPITALS, MODERN.

HOT DRINKS. Tea, coffee, and cocoa were first introduced into Britain about the middle of the 17th century. Tea was brought to Europe by the Dutch from China, where it had been used as a beverage as long ago as the 2nd century B.C. (*see* TEA TRADE, Vol. VII). COFFEE (q.v. Vol. VI) probably originated in Ethiopia and subsequently spread to Arabia, where it has been cultivated for many centuries. It was used first as a food, ground up and mixed with fat, then as a medicine, and later as a drink. It came to Britain from the Levant. COCOA (q.v. Vol. VI) was introduced to Europe by the Spaniards, who brought it from Mexico and Peru. These drinks quickly became popular and soon replaced beer at some meals, particularly breakfast.

In 1652 the first London coffee house was opened by a Turkish merchant in St. Michael's Alley. This was quickly followed by other coffee houses and chocolate houses, which in the 18th century gained world-wide fame as the meeting places of literary, artistic, and commercial circles (*see* CLUBS, HISTORY OF, Vol. IX). Towards the end of the 18th century, however, tea was becoming more popular because it was cheaper, and many of the coffee houses disappeared. Coffee and the coffee houses have been celebrated by writers, painters, and musicians. Pope in *The Rape of the Lock* says:

> Coffee which makes the politician wise
> And see thro' all things with his half-shut eyes.

J. S. Bach composed a Coffee Cantata, and many painters, including Hogarth and Rowlandson, have left us pictures showing aspects of the social life of their times as reflected in the coffee houses.

TEA (q.v. Vol. VI), as we buy it, consists of dried leaves which have been withered, rolled, and fermented. China tea and Indian tea owe their difference in taste to different degrees of fermentation. In the kitchen they are made in the same way, by pouring freshly boiled water on to the leaves (1 teaspoon per person) in a heated teapot, and allowing them to infuse for a few minutes. If the liquid is then poured off into another heated teapot, there will be only the minimum extraction of tannin, for this increases as the water stands on the leaves. But, in fact, most people send the tea to the table with the leaves still present in the pot. Tannin is the part of the tea which is bad for the digestion, and consequently very strong 'stewed' tea is not a healthy

FIG. I. A VACUUM COFFEE MACHINE

apparatus is needed (*see* Fig. I), the water in the lower container is boiled and bubbles up through a filter into the upper vessel holding the coffee. When the lower container cools, a partial vacuum is created, and the liquid above is sucked back. Turkish coffee is made in yet a different way. The powdered coffee berries are mixed with boiling water and sugar, boiled to a froth three times in a long-handled copper container, and then poured into small cups. Turkish coffee is always served black. Coffee for breakfast is served with hot milk. After-dinner coffee, usually served in small cups, is taken black, or with cream or hot milk, and sugar crystals are served with it.

The beans of CACAO (q.v. Vol. VI) are always sold in powder form. A teaspoonful per cup of cocoa or chocolate is made into a paste with cold milk, and then boiling water or milk is poured on to it and stirred well. The best results are obtained by boiling it for a few minutes and whisking it thoroughly.

Tea, coffee, and cocoa have certain stimulating properties which are due to the presence of small quantities of caffeine in tea and coffee, and of theobromine, a similar substance, in cocoa. Coffee as well as tea contains tannin.

Substitutes for tea are tisanes, which are infusions of various leaves or flowers such as lime flowers, mint, sage, orange flowers, camomile, and black currant leaves; and yerba maté, produced in Brazil, Paraguay, and Argentina from the treated leaves of *Ilex paraguayensis*.

Various hot drinks can be made with fruit juices or WINES AND SPIRITS (q.v.), mixed, for instance, with hot lemon water and herbs and spices. Examples are mulled claret and rum punch.

See also COLD DRINKS.

drink and, in particular, should not be given to young children. The tea is served according to taste with various additions such as milk, sugar, or lemon.

In Britain coffee beans are usually roasted and ground in the coffee shop; but in most other countries people prefer to do this at home, since the flavour of coffee is much better if the beans are roasted and ground just before making the coffee. Coffee merchants often add chicory root, roasted and ground, to coffee because it is cheap and increases the colour and flavour; but connoisseurs in coffee prefer pure coffee. Liquid or powdered coffee extracts are also available in shops, but these produce inferior results. Coffee can be made, just as tea is made, by pouring boiling water on to the coffee in a jug, but it should be poured out through a strainer to eliminate the grounds. Various methods have been devised for straining the coffee as it is made, the two main systems being the 'drip' and the 'vacuum'. In the former the ground coffee (I dessert-spoon per cup) is placed in a container above a filter paper or gauze. Boiling water is poured on to the coffee and slowly filters through into the pot below, which is kept warm. In the vacuum method, for which special

HOUSEHOLD LINEN. We use the name 'linen' as a collective term for household textile articles, whether they are, in fact, made of coarse-woven linen, fine damask, cotton, rayon, or mixtures of these materials.

Household linen has been traditionally an important part of a bride's dowry in most countries. Before the Industrial Revolution girls made sheets, pillowcases, towels, and table linen for their bridal chests or 'bottom drawers', and good housewives spun, wove, sewed, mended, and laundered to keep their linen dresses full and fair and to build up linen chests

Victoria and Albert Museum

BORDER OF A LINEN DAMASK TABLECLOTH, WITH MOTIFS OF THE ORDER OF THE GARTER, 1831

for their daughters. Often the weaving was done by a visiting weaver. George Eliot's Silas Marner, for example, went round to the big houses of the neighbourhood perhaps once a year to weave all that they needed.

The LINEN INDUSTRY (q.v. Vol. VII) is very ancient indeed, linen being used, for instance, in ancient Egypt and in Greece and Rome. Illuminated manuscripts of the Middle Ages show white sheets and pillowcases (*see* BED COVERINGS) and white cloths with diaper patterns on dining-tables and sideboards. The

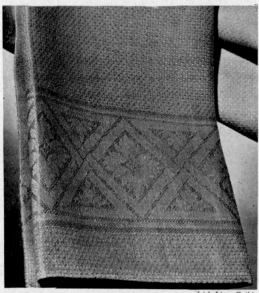

Irish Linen Guild

LINEN HUCKABACK TOWEL

material appears to have a simple woven trellis pattern, sometimes with a fringed border. Gradually more elaborate ornament was introduced into the weave, including special motifs such as crowns or coronets, initials or ciphers, or mottoes from a family coat-of-arms. Sometimes embroidery or lace insertions or edges were added for decoration.

From early Renaissance times until the 20th century white damask tablecloths, woven in designs of flowers or fruits, were generally used. Dinner-napkins were in use by the 17th century; we read, for example, that one well-to-do family used 26 yards of 'huggabag' for two dozen table-napkins. In wealthy houses tablenapkins were often of fine damask, woven in designs of flowers, fruit, or birds. In the 19th century the table linen became more elaborate, including cloths for side-boards and serving tables and very elaborate tray-cloths and tea-cloths. Lace-edged 'doyleys' appeared on plates and silver cakebaskets, with matching teanapkins. The 20th-century need to simplify life and reduce labour has led to the abandonment of this elaborate table linen. Table cloths are now often replaced by separate table mats, usually of embroidered linen, but sometimes of plaited rush or raffia, canework, or some plastic material. Coloured prints (of birds, old London views, and so on) form an attractive decoration on mats with a cellulose finish. Paper napkins and doyleys usually imitate those of linen or lace.

During the 19th century kitchen equipment increased considerably, and included bordered hand roller-towels of linen or huckaback, and various washing-up cloths in linen, cotton, or a mixture. In the great variety of towels now used, the 19th-century fringed or crocheted lace borders have generally been superseded by plain hems, perhaps emphasized by a different colour or texture.

In 17th-century England the finest linen was imported from Holland, then a great centre of the industry. In the poorer homes the linen was usually 'unbleached', that is, it retained its natural pale brown, but the technique of BLEACHING (q.v. Vol. VII) is old. Today Irish linen from Belfast is the most esteemed. Table linen should be laundered with starch, and for the best linen a final rinse in milk gives a firm, but not too stiff, finish, especially to articles with lace decoration (*see* LAUNDRY METHODS). Linen, after being aired in artificially heated cupboards, should be stored in a cool temperature.

See also BED COVERINGS; TABLE SETTING.
See also Vol. VII: LINEN INDUSTRY.

HOUSEHOLD PESTS. 1. There are certain creatures which are a serious nuisance if they invade and breed in a house. Some, such as flies, rats, mice, and cockroaches, carry BACTERIA (q.v. Vol. II) with which they may infect food. Some, such as moths and beetles of various types, silverfish, and mites, may damage clothes, carpets, furniture, and certain foods. Some, such as bugs, fleas, and lice, may attach themselves as parasites to people, causing personal discomfort and probably skin disease. Some may consume food or spoil it for human consumption, as do ants and mice. It is important to know something of the life history and habits of these pests and the best methods of controlling them.

2. VERMIN. RATS (q.v. Vol. II) and mice are the VERMIN (q.v. Vol. VI) which cause trouble in the house, mice being more troublesome inside and rats outside the house. Both can convey diseases to men, and both are very destructive to all types of food, to woodwork, and to fabrics which mice will use to make soft nests.

Mice gain entrance through any small opening, such as those made for pipes or resulting from ill-fitting doors. They make a home in a convenient quiet place—a cupboard, a sack, or the space behind skirting boards—and they breed and increase at a tremendous rate. To be free from mice all means of entry should be blocked up, all foods kept out of reach, and any mice already in the house destroyed. Householders may keep a good hunting cat or use the spring break-back type of trap baited with cereal, or put down poison bait if there is no danger of other animals picking it up. Poison bait is made by mixing a small quantity of zinc phosphide or arsenic with milled oats, or with 'sausage rusk', or with a mixture of one part of flour to nine of sugar.

Similar precautions and methods are used for exterminating rats, but rats are more suspicious and more difficult to poison or trap. Their suspicions may be lulled by accustoming them to unpoisoned food for several nights and then adding the poison. In the country the Ministry of Agriculture rodent officers will give advice and help, and in towns, the Ministry of Health sanitary officers.

3. INSECT PESTS. Two types of MOTHS (q.v. Vol. II) are serious household pests, one destroying fabrics such as furs, feathers, and woollens, and the other flour and some of its products such as biscuits. In both cases it is the grublike larva that causes the damage; it eats voraciously during the growing period, then builds a cocoon (or pupa) from which the adult emerges and lays more eggs to hatch into more larvae.

The clothes moth, of which there are three species—the case-making moth, the webbing clothes moth, and the tapestry moth—is greyish yellow in colour with a wing span of $\frac{1}{2}$ inch. These moths occur in most parts of the world. Under natural conditions they hibernate during the winter, but in centrally heated houses they may be active all the year round. There is now a method of moth-proofing yarn before it is made up, and this gives complete protection. The yarn is treated during processing with one of various chemical substances which render it either poisonous or indigestible to the larvae. Cleanliness—brushing, washing, dry cleaning, ironing, and airing—helps to prevent moths from attacking materials, and the use of sealed bags and zipped plastic containers prevents their gaining access to garments. Where moths are already breeding, fumigation with preparations containing paradichlorobenzine and naphthalene is effective; the infested material is either placed in a sealed compartment with crystals which vaporize, or sprayed with the vacuum-cleaner attachment designed for this purpose.

The presence of the flour moth is revealed by the net which the larva spins as it passes through

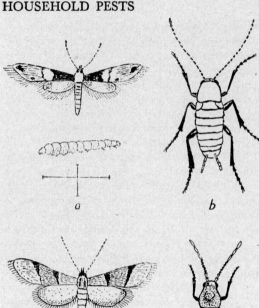

SOME HOUSEHOLD PESTS

a. Clothes moth and larva. *b*. Cockroach. *c*. Flour moth and larva. *d*. Furniture beetle

the meal. Infected goods should be burned, and the containers thoroughly washed.

There are a number of BEETLES (q.v. Vol. II) which cause damage to certain foods, carpets, and furniture, the most harmful being those which attack wood—the furniture beetle and the DEATH-WATCH BEETLE (q.v. Vol. II). The adult beetle lays its eggs in crevices in wood, and when the larvae emerge, they burrow into the material and eat it. The grubs can be destroyed within the wood either by heat (about 130° F. is effective) or by fumigation with such substances as carbon tetrachloride and benzene, which can be washed over the surface or sprayed into the holes (*see* FURNITURE, CARE OF).

The HOUSE-FLY, the BLUEBOTTLE, and the BLOWFLY (qq.v. Vol. II) have become a less serious nuisance now that there is less horse manure, which is their favourite breeding ground. During the summer months, however, they are still a danger. The best way of controlling them is to eliminate their breeding places—

for example, to keep refuse bins covered and regularly disinfected, to keep all food, especially meat, covered, and to spray regularly with insecticide. Any bluebottle should be destroyed on sight with a fly-swat. Some factories, hospitals, restaurants, and even clubs, especially in the U.S.A., are now installing electrocuting fly screens and traps, and these may become more generally used.

ANTS (q.v. Vol. II), though not a serious danger to health, are tiresome in a kitchen. They like warmth and food, particularly sweet food. But if no crumbs are left about and sweet foods are out of their reach, they may disappear. A firmly established infestation may be attacked with D.D.T. or Gammexane sprays and powders, repeated at intervals of 2–3 weeks; or by setting poisoned bait made of honey, sugar, water, and thallium powder, which is carried back to the nest by the foragers.

SILVERFISH (q.v. Vol. II) are slender wingless insects which feed on the sizing in paper, rugs, and bookbindings, or on starch in clothing and food. They like warm, damp conditions, such as are often found in basements near to chimneys, or in new buildings where the walls are still damp. Frequent use of an insecticidal spray containing pyrethrum and D.D.T. or Gammexane will soon clear them.

The COCKROACH (q.v. Vol. II), commonly but erroneously called a black-beetle, likes centrally heated blocks of flats and warm bakeries where scraps of food are left about. The two species most commonly found in houses are the common cockroach or black-beetle, and the German cockroach or steam bug. Both species are nocturnal in their habits, occupying crevices in walls and floors in the daytime. They are destroyed by the use of insecticides—sprays or powders—applied to the floors and repeated at frequent intervals. The CRICKET (q.v. Vol. II), another hearth-dweller, can also be destroyed by sprays in the same way.

The BOOKLOUSE (q.v. Vol. II) is a tiny creature, which may damage books and papers in old libraries. It can be destroyed by fumigation with rock-sulphur, after which the walls and shelves should be washed down with a disinfectant.

4. PARASITES. The BED-BUG, LOUSE, and FLEA (qq.v. Vol. II) live by sucking the blood of human beings and other mammals. Fleas, and lice which attach their eggs (nits) to hair,

live on their host; bed-bugs come out at night to attack human beings and then return to cracks and crevices in floors, walls, and furniture. These insects are found in dwellings where standards of cleanliness are not high, and they cause an unpleasant smell. The best defence is absolute cleanliness of person and clothing and the use of insecticidal powders. If an old house is badly infested, a thorough fumigation by the sanitary officer is essential.

See also Vol. VI: ANIMAL PESTS.

HOUSEHOLD PLUMBING.

Local authorities are required by law to provide houses with a pure and wholesome WATER SUPPLY and an efficient system of SANITATION (qq.v.) and drainage. The purpose of plumbing is to ensure that fresh water for drinking, cooking, and washing is properly distributed about the house, and soiled water removed quickly and efficiently to the public sewer. All plumbing installations are regulated by local BY-LAWS (q.v. Vol. X).

Fresh water is brought to a house by a 'service pipe', usually ½ inch in diameter, which is connected to an underground distribution main. To avoid damage by frost, the service pipe should be laid at least 2¼ feet under the ground and should enter the house on an inside wall. The pipe rises vertically inside the house until it reaches the cold supply tank of the hot-water system (see HEATING SYSTEMS, DOMESTIC) near the roof, other pipes branching off it on the way to feed the cold-water taps in various rooms and the w.c. cistern (Fig. 1).

So that the water supply can be cut off in an emergency, two 'stop taps' are fixed to the service pipe, one outside, but close to, the boundary wall of the property, and a second at ground-level where the pipe enters the house. Immediately above this second stop tap is a 'drain tap'. All water pipes in the house must slope back to this drainage point so that the system can be completely emptied either for repair or as a precaution against frost damage if the house is left empty during the winter.

All taps must be of a valve type (Fig. 2a) so that they can be closed gradually. If a moving body of water is suddenly stopped, pressure surges are caused, leading to 'hammering' and possibly to burst pipes. Ball-valves (Fig. 2b) are used to regulate the amount of cold water entering a cistern, and these shut off the water automatically when a set level is reached.

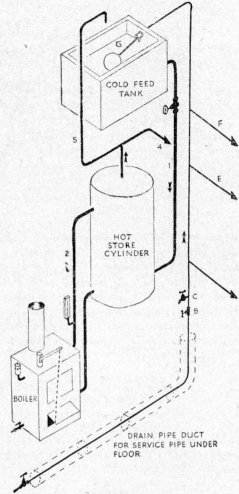

FIG. 1. DIAGRAM OF THE WATER SUPPLY FOR A SMALL HOUSE

Cold water supply. A, B. Stop taps in service pipe. C. Drain tap. D, E, F. Supplies to sink, bath, and basin, and w.c. cistern. G. Ball-valve

Hot water supply. 1. Cold feed pipe with control valve. 2. Flow pipe from boiler with thermometer. 3. Return pipe. 4. Supply to hot taps. 5. Vent pipe. 6. Safety valve. 7. Emptying cock

Siphonic flushing cisterns automatically regulate the amount discharged in flushing the w.c. pan —usually 2½ gallons. Overflow pipes, discharging water where it can be easily seen or heard, must, however, always be used with ball-valve fittings so that defects can be detected and repaired quickly.

The minimum sanitary arrangements of an average house should include a sink, basin, bath, and w.c. pan, each with its own waste-pipe and 'trap'. A trap is a U-shaped pipe

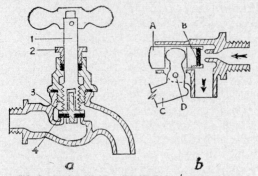

FIG. 2. DIAGRAMS OF *a*. VALVE TAP; *b*. BALL-VALVE

1. Spindle. 2. Nut to prevent water leaking. 3. Valve.
4. Washer. A. Piston. B. Washer. C. Lever arm with ball
on end. D. Fulcrum

carried below ground by the main house drains. Above ground, wastes flow into the drain by one of three pipework arrangements. In the 'two-pipe' system (Fig. 3*a*), which is the most common, the soil pipe, a vertical extension of the underground drain, receives waste from the w.c. only. The bath, basin, and sink wastes discharge into the drain, but are disconnected from it by a gully-trap. A serious objection to this system is the insanitary condition likely to arise from decomposing soap and other fats in the gully-trap and at the 'hopper-head' which collects the bath and basin wastes. In the 'one-pipe' system (Fig. 3*b*), all waste-pipes are connected to the soil pipe and therefore directly to the drain. As no gully-trap is ever fixed at the bottom of a soil pipe, ventilating pipes must be provided for all wastes so that only fresh air is in contact with the trap seals of the w.c. and other appliances. The third system is the 'single-pipe' (Fig. 3*c*), which is a modern simplification of the 'one-pipe'. Rain-water is led from gutters round the roof to separate drainage systems.

which retains sufficient water to form a seal and thus prevents waste-pipe air entering the house; it is fitted as close as possible to the bath, basin, sink, or w.c. The waste-pipes from bath, basin, and sink are usually $1\frac{1}{4}$ inches in diameter, but the w.c. pan, with a $3\frac{1}{2}$-inch diameter outflow, discharges into a 'soil pipe' which is usually $3\frac{1}{2}$ or 4 inches in diameter. All waste is

All pipes and their fittings must be easily

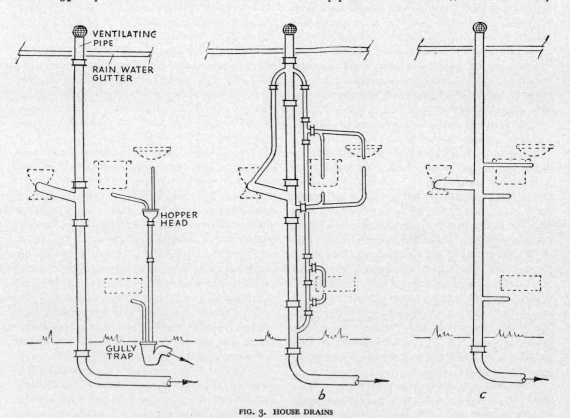

FIG. 3. HOUSE DRAINS

a. Two-pipe system. *b*. One-pipe system. *c*. Single-pipe system

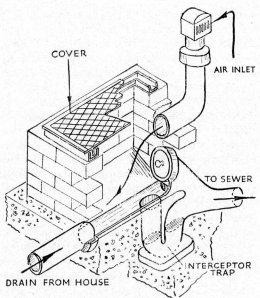

COVER

AIR INLET

TO SEWER

INTERCEPTOR TRAP

DRAIN FROM HOUSE

FIG. 4. DIAGRAM OF A MAN-HOLE TO PREVENT SEWER AIR
ENTERING DRAIN FROM HOUSE

accessible for inspection, cleaning, and repair. Where they pass through walls, pipes should be wrapped in bituminous felt as a protection against corrosion from cement and plaster, and should be fixed at least $\frac{3}{4}$ inch from the wall. To prevent damage by frost in cold weather, they must be installed as far as possible from the coldest parts of the house; where this is impossible, they must be properly insulated.

Underground house drains, usually about 4 inches in diameter, can be inspected and cleaned through brick manholes, fitted with airtight, cast-iron covers. With old sewers, an 'interceptor trap' (Fig. 4), fitted at the outlet end of the last manhole within the house boundary, is used to prevent sewer gases passing back into the house drain. In such cases the house drain is ventilated by providing a fresh-air inlet to the interceptor manhole; fresh air passes through the inlet, along the drain, and up and out of the house soil pipe which is extended above the roof. Interceptors, however, tend to slow up the flow of sewage and restrict ventilation inside the sewer itself; and so, since tests show that the air in modern sewers is less polluted than in the open street, interceptors are now often omitted.

All fittings used in plumbing must be able to resist corrosion from water and from atmospheric or soil conditions. In soft-water districts (see WATER, DOMESTIC), where the water contains excess carbon dioxide making it mildly acidic, all pipes, tanks, and cylinders should be of copper, which is highly resistant to corrosion. Lead pipes in such districts may result in 'plumbo solvency', causing lead poisoning, whilst iron pipes would quickly rust through. Generally, however, cold water and waste pipes may be of lead with soldered joints, or of copper with joints soldered or compressed together by special fittings. Soil pipes are usually of cast-iron, lead, or copper. Hot water pipes may be of copper, though mild steel tubes with screwed fittings are often used.

See also WATER SUPPLY, HISTORY OF; SANITATION, HISTORY OF; WATER, DOMESTIC.
See also Vol. VIII: WATER SUPPLY; SEWAGE DISPOSAL.
See also Vol. X: DRAINAGE.

HOUSEHOLD REPAIRS. 1. TOOLS AND EQUIPMENT. If small faults in the house can be remedied promptly, it often saves time and money and avoids inconvenience. Every household, therefore, should possess a toolbox properly stocked with the basic necessities. The tools must be kept in good condition, and cleaned and put away in the proper place after use. Distemper brushes, for example, should be washed in warm, soapy water, rinsed, and hung up by the handles to dry; paint brushes should be cleaned in turpentine and then washed. Both should then be stored lying flat. Knives and scrapers should be wiped with an oily rag and left with a smear of vaseline on the metal.

Every household toolbox should contain hammers of at least two sizes, nails and screws of various sizes, a screwdriver and bradawl, a pair of pliers, a chisel, a file, a ruler and tape measure, an oil can, linseed oil, turpentine, and some sandpaper and glass paper. Further repairs may need a brace and bit, a plane, a saw, and a spirit level. If a small vice can be fitted up somewhere, it is likely to prove very useful. Materials such as pieces of timber, plastic wood, putty, and whiting are sure to be useful, though these can be bought as they are needed. A supply of washers, fuse wires, insulating tape, sash-cord, and other such household necessities ought also to be available.

2. REPAIRS TO FLOORS. The gaps between shrunk floor boards can be filled in with narrow strips of wood cut to the right size and pinned to the joists below. Spaces between the floor

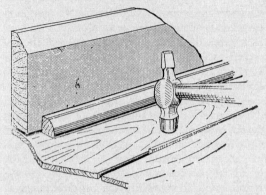

FIG. I. GAP BETWEEN FLOOR BOARDS FILLED WITH NARROW STRIP OF WOOD, AND AT SKIRTING COVERED WITH BEADING

and the skirting can be closed by nailing lengths of quarter-round one-inch beading to the floor close to the skirting. This not only makes a neat finish when decorated to match either the floor or the skirting but also stops draughts (Fig. 1).

Holes where nails have been removed or punched below the surface should be filled in with putty mixed with linseed oil, or plaster, or plastic wood. It should be remembered that the latter shrinks slightly when it sets. Any of these, when hard, should be rubbed down with glasspaper or fine steel wool, working with the grain of the wood; both plaster and plastic wood can be stained to match the floor.

Loose tiles, those round the fireplace, for example, should be fixed at once to prevent their loosening others. The tile is taken out and soaked in cold water for an hour. Meanwhile the bed is cleaned of all loose cement and dust, leaving $\frac{1}{8}$ inch clearance for the fixing cement, and is well damped with water. A stiff paste of equal proportions of Portland cement and fine sand mixed with water is spread on the back of the tile, which is replaced and tapped into line with the surrounding tiles. The mixture takes a few hours to set, and any excess cement should be wiped off first. It is safer not to subject the tile to the heat of a fire for 2 or 3 days.

Worn parts of linoleum can be neatly patched with new pieces. After the worn part has been cut out, a new piece which matches the pattern, if any, is slid underneath, and the edge of the hole is marked on it. When it has been cut out, the patch should fit exactly, and can then be tacked down firmly with headless brads.

3. Repairs to Doors and Windows. Stiff locks are usually due to dirt, or to corrosion,

often by rusting; and if an application of oil is not sufficient, the lock should be removed, taken to pieces, cleaned with paraffin on an old tooth brush or rag, and then oiled with lubricating oil. After the key has been cleaned and turned in the lock several times, the lock can be replaced.

Squeaking doors can usually be cured by oiling the hinges; but doors that do not shut properly are probably working on loose hinges. It may be enough to tighten up the screws, but if these turn in the holes, a larger size screw should be tried or the countersinking enlarged.

If the door swings freely but has to be forced to make it shut it is probably suffering from too many coats of paint on the hinged edge and the door frame. Rubbing down with glasspaper may put this right, or it may be necessary to unscrew the hinges and remove the paint with a plane. If the wood has warped, the door must be unhinged and the hinged edge planed down until it fits properly. Doors tend to drop in course of time and the lower edge may scrape the floor. The door must then be taken off its hinges and the bottom planed.

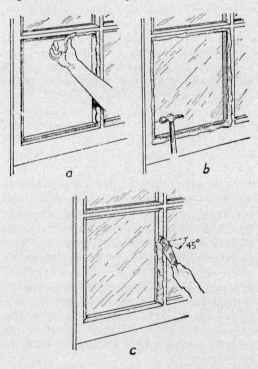

FIG. 2. REPLACING A PANE OF GLASS IN A WINDOW

a. Pressing the bed of putty into the frame. *b.* Securing the pane with brads. *c.* Smoothing off the facing putty

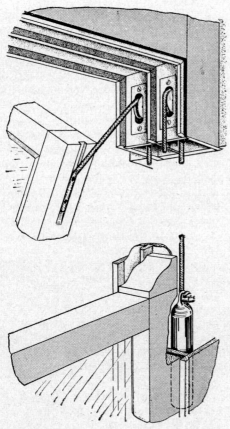

FIG. 3. HOW A SASH WINDOW WORKS

The cord, attached at one end to the window, runs over the pulley and behind the window frame, where the other end is attached to a weight. This balances the window so that it will stay in any position. To mend a broken sash cord, the beading holding the window in position must be removed, the window taken out, and the old cord replaced by a new one

When replacing a broken pane all the old putty and broken glass must be carefully chipped out with a stout knife, so as not to cut the frame. The bare wood must be painted before the new bed of putty is pressed in. Then the new glass, which must allow a little room for expansion, is placed and secured with small brads driven in to within $\frac{1}{4}$ inch. The facing putty is pressed on with thumb and finger, smoothed off with a putty knife, the blade being held at an angle of 45°, and the surplus trimmed off. New putty must be painted after a few days to preserve it (Fig. 2).

A badly fitting window sash is usually due to shrinkage of the wood. It can be temporarily wedged to prevent rattling, and can be properly corrected by removing the beading of the lower sash and fixing it farther in to make the channel narrower. The top sash is more difficult to deal with; the window may have to be removed and some thin strips of wood glued on to adjust the frame to the proper thickness.

A broken sash-cord is easily mended so long as the mender understands clearly how a sash works (Fig. 3). A sash sometimes gets jammed by paint which has glued it to the frame, and can often be released merely by a blow with the hand. A tight sash often only needs oil on the working parts, especially the pulley wheels, to make it move smoothly.

4. STRIPPING WOODWORK. Old furniture and woodwork are often so loaded with paint and varnish that the natural wood and the clean lines of the mouldings and carving have disappeared. This old paint or varnish can be 'stripped' in various ways.

Small articles, provided they are not deeply carved and the old polish or paint is brittle enough, can be very cheaply stripped by using a sharp pull-scraper for the plain surfaces and scraping the carved pieces with suitably shaped pieces of broken picture glass. A small blowlamp is also suitable for plain painted surfaces, but it is no good for varnish, and cannot be used for ornamental work without much skill and experience.

The many chemical strippers available, mostly containing chloroform or carbon tetrachloride, are satisfactory for varnish or soft paint, but they are expensive, quickly evaporate, and are hard on hands and skin; a further disadvantage is their strong, obnoxious smell. Hot washing soda or sugar soap are adequate for poor quality paint or thin varnish; for old enamels and french polishes caustic soda should be used. These wet methods have an excellent effect on stained or dirty wood, and help to smooth out chips and kick marks, but are no good for veneer or other glued parts, as the glue is soon dissolved and the veneer fetched right off.

After stripping, the colour of the wood, which greys and darkens, is restored by dabbing on a solution of a few ounces of oxalic acid crystals in hot water. As the wood dries, a white, sharp-smelling powder, a deposit of sodium oxalate, appears; this is dissolved with a 50% solution of vinegar in water.

Whichever stripping method is used, the wood must afterwards be smoothed down with medium and fine sandpaper, and then polished with white wax polish.

5. GAS REPAIRS. Serious faults are not jobs for the amateur. Temporary repairs, however, can be made to a leaking gas pipe so that the supply can be used until a professional can deal with it. After the leak has been found and the gas turned off at the main, a thick layer of grease or soap is put in and around the crack, and the pipe bound with insulating tape or sticking plaster.

6. OUTSIDE REPAIRS. Most of these, especially repairs to the roof, need the attention of a builder. The amateur can get into great difficulties in trying to replace slates or tiles at any distance from the eaves. Repairs to outhouses, however, can often be done. A leak in a greenhouse may be cured by reputtying or replacing the glass. A leaking toolshed roof may be made water-tight by putting on a felt covering. The felt should be nailed down with galvanized (rustless) large-headed nails, and then the whole should be given a good coat of one of the water-proof bituminous preparations sold for the purpose.

Other repairs, such as those connected with HOUSEHOLD PLUMBING, FURNITURE, and ELECTRICITY (qq.v.), are dealt with in the appropriate articles.

HOUSEKEEPING, HISTORY OF. The

business of running a house was the first of all businesses, and our word 'economics', derived from the Greek words for 'house' and 'law', suggests that the examination of the problems of housekeeping was the first financial study.

Large Greek and Roman households were managed on the basis of slave labour (*see* SLAVERY, Vol. X). 'First a house, then a wife, then an ox for the plough, then the slave', as a Greek poet put it. Wives and slaves were expected to obey: 'Domestic government is a monarchy', wrote Aristotle, 'for that is what prevails in every house.' It was the master of the house who laid down the essential rules of good housekeeping and determined what specialization of labour there should be among the servants; and most masters realized that slaves gave better work when well treated—and, no doubt, wives also.

Slavery persisted in the Middle Ages in the form of 'serfdom'—a hereditary form of service, for the serf could not normally move from one household to another. The lord was still unmistakably the head of the manorial household, although he might have a steward to arrange the detailed routines of its daily management. In the smaller households of the medieval towns, where the serf system did not prevail, housekeeping was left to the care of the merchant's wife, daughters, and apprentices.

After the medieval period methods of housekeeping were modified by three notable changes. Serfdom was replaced by free labour; bartering of goods and services gave way to the general use of money; and the internal development and arrangement of the house were altered. The rising standard of cleanliness and comfort led to an increased demand for domestic servants

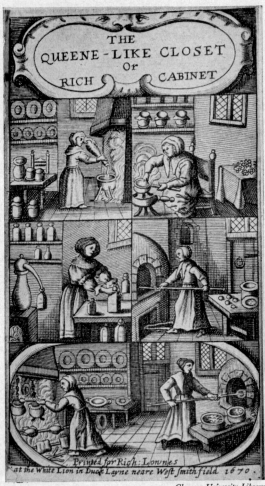

Glasgow University Library

A 17TH-CENTURY HOUSEKEEPER

Title-page of Hannah Wolley, *The Queene-like Closet . . . of Rare Receipts*, 1670 and to new notions of housekeeping. In the 16th century the great nobility took pride in the lavish style of their housekeeping and in the number of their servants. For example, in one year alone the household expenses of the Earl of Derby amounted to nearly £3,000 (equivalent to about £90,000 today). Open house was kept, and it was not unusual for forty strangers to dine with the family.

In the 18th century domestic government was still largely under male control. Indeed, because Cabinet ministers usually belonged to the class of great landed proprietors and were familiar with the organization and control of a large and highly specialized staff, the public administration of the country was to a considerable extent modelled on the administration of a great house and estate. Economics, in consequence, was still, as in Greece, influenced by rules of housekeeping.

In the largest houses the details of housekeeping were in the charge of the housekeeper, and the under servants were ruled by her and had no contact with the mistress of the house (see DOMESTIC SERVICE, HISTORY OF). In smaller houses the mistress and her daughters took part in the work and supervised the immense variety of household occupations. All food was prepared at home, and each season had its special activities. The still room was an important place where jam and pickles were made, as well as wine; the dairy adjoined the house, and there was often a separate laundry where all the household washing was done, either by laundry maids, or by washerwomen who came in regularly (see LAUNDRY (History)). Candles and soap were often made at home, and even medicines, as well as all the linen. Grates had to be cleaned and coal carried to all the rooms, including bedrooms. Lamps and candles had to be kept in order and replenished. Water had to be heated in the kitchen and carried upstairs; and warming pans filled with red hot coals had to be taken round to warm the beds at night. Labour was cheap and goods expensive; there was, therefore, little occasion for reducing the work of the servants by inventing labour-saving devices, but rather a need to avoid buying new things, however much work was involved in preserving the old.

There were important changes in the 19th century. In the first place the growth of industry and business took the master of the house away

Institutional Management Assoc.

A HOUSEKEEPER IN CHARGE OF THE STORE-ROOM
Title-page of Anne Cobbett, *The English Housekeeper*, 1851

from home far more, and the mistress gradually assumed command. During Queen Victoria's reign, the many books published on 'domestic economy' were intended for the mistress, not the master, and were designed not so much for great households as for the homes of the rising middle classes. At the same time there was a far greater range of goods and services to be bought with the money available. 'In small houses', one writer observed in 1851, 'we now see, not carpets merely, but many articles of furniture which were formerly in use only among the nobility and gentry.' Good housekeeping began to be considered as much a science as an art, and the conspicuous display, which had been a feature of Tudor and later noble households, gave way to a more careful study of making ends meet and of securing good value for money.

The decoration and management of the home began to serve as subjects for innumerable books, magazines, and articles, with titles such

A MISTRESS GIVING THE DAILY ORDERS TO THE COOK
Drawing by G. du Maurier from *Punch*, 1893

as *Hints on Household Taste*, the *Housewife's Treasury*, or even *High Living with Low Means*. The most famous of all such studies were those of Mrs. Beeton (*see* RECIPES AND COOKERY BOOKS): prudent and fortunate possessors of her *Housewife's Treasury* and her *Book of Household Management* were promised that they would have at their side 'a library by whose aid everything will go well, and family life be happier and more prosperous every day'. But Mrs. Beeton's methods of sound housekeeping depended upon a plentiful supply of domestic servants, just as Greek housekeeping depended upon slaves. The middle-class housewife could not conceive of managing the home without servants. An inquiry made in the middle years of the 19th century revealed that there were 175,000 men and women employed in domestic service in London alone.

Victorian systems of housekeeping, which differed according to social class, continued into the 20th century, but not without great strains and stresses. As early as 1849, one far-sighted writer foresaw the day when the daughters of the working classes would cease to work for the upper and middle classes, and claimed that the only remedy would be to increase the number of mechanical aids and labour-saving devices in housekeeping so that the middle classes would 'make themselves self-dependent as fast as their domestic servants become independent'. The distant prospect of this social revolution moved significantly nearer between 1870 and 1914. In the first 30 years of this period female domestic servants' wage rates rose by 30% to 37% as compared with only 19% for women's wages generally. At the same time, compulsory education and the changed position of women in society were further complicating the picture (*see* MARRIAGE, HISTORY OF).

In the early 20th century the work of the house was lessened by many factors: the size of families fell from its mid-Victorian level; houses were designed to be more convenient; retail agencies provided domestic services outside the home, such as baking and washing; and labour-saving devices, such as lifts and fitted basins, were introduced. The growth of the CANNING INDUSTRY (q.v. Vol. VII) made it possible to buy many foods that previously had been made or preserved at home. Yet, in spite of this general simplification, the middle-class family still conceived of housekeeping in terms of resident servants and of two standards of living going on within one house. It was still expected that there would be a maid in uniform to open the front door, to answer bells, to serve meals, and to 'turn down' the beds at night.

Modern housekeeping has had to dispense with such notions and to adopt methods of simplifying the management of the home against the background of a more equal society. Housekeeping is now taught at school as part of DOMESTIC SCIENCE (q.v.), and is discussed in even more magazines and books than in the Victorian era. The layout of the house or flat and its furnishing are arranged for efficiency and convenience (*see* ROOMS). 'The ideal home' is discussed freely both by experts and by the general public. But all this discussion and planning assumes today that people are doing the work of their own houses, and is therefore principally concerned with the practice of the household arts without the expenditure of too much time and labour. Nor is the discussion addressed principally to men, for the master of the house has abdicated; domestic government has become a republic, or even, some would argue, a female monarchy.

See also DOMESTIC SERVICE, HISTORY OF; COOKING, HISTORY OF; LIGHTING, HISTORY OF; KITCHEN DESIGN AND ARRANGEMENT; HEATING, HISTORY OF; LAUNDRY (History); ROOMS; FAMILY BUDGET.

HOUSES, HISTORY OF. The earliest houses of which we have any knowledge were built between 3000 and 2000 B.C. in Mesopotamia by the SUMERIANS, and in the Punjab by people of the ancient INDIAN CIVILIZATION (qq.v. Vol. I). In both these places large cities have been excavated which reveal the ruins of elaborately planned houses built of bricks.

There are few remains of ancient Greek houses. It is probable that most of the care and skill of the Greek architects was lavished on public buildings, such as temples, rather than on private houses. In ancient Rome a characteristic plan was developed from the Greek type. The house was built round courts with a columned passage giving access to the rooms, which were thus cool and shady (*see* ROMAN ART, Vol. XII). The walls were of sun-dried brick, the roofs of tiles, and floors commonly of earth, though in important rooms they might be of patterned MOSAICS (q.v. Vol. XII). Under the later Roman Empire houses became very luxurious, and it was the fashion to live in a villa in the country. These villas were elaborate groups of buildings consisting not only of the house but also of quarters for slaves and farm buildings. Instead of the enclosed courts of town houses, villas often had wings flanking the main rooms, which were entered by an outside corridor.

The Romans and wealthy Romanized Britons built villas in Britain of the corridor type. The main rooms of the house were in the centre, with baths and a furnace room to heat the hypocausts (*see* HEATING, HISTORY OF) on one side and slaves' quarters on the other. An open corridor with pillars supporting the roof gave access to the rooms, and there was probably an upper storey built of wood, the ground floor being of stone. The villas were self-contained units in which many people lived and worked, so besides the house there were usually farm buildings and craftsmen's workshops; at the Roman villa at Chedworth in Gloucestershire there was also a dyehouse, and gardens surrounded the house.

In the Roman town of Silchester, in Hamp-

shire, there were some houses of the Roman type, but others, probably shops, were rectangular with gables facing the street, a shape perhaps derived from the wooden huts in which the British lived before the Roman Conquest.

After the Romans had left Britain and Saxon invaders overran the country, the Roman houses fell into ruin. Occasionally the Saxons used them, but as they did not know how to make use of their amenities, for the most part they

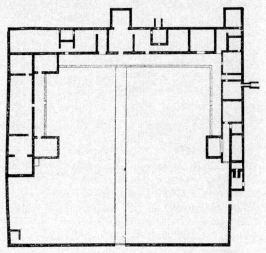

PLAN OF A ROMAN VILLA IN SPOONLEY WOOD, GLOUCESTERSHIRE

A verandah running round the inner walls gave access to the rooms. The living rooms were in the centre, the right-hand wing contained bathrooms, and the left-hand wing was probably slaves' quarters

avoided them. They brought from their forest country a tradition of building in wood. A Saxon house consisted of a single room—a large hall for a chieftain and a tiny wattle-and-daub hut for an ordinary family. The hall was the home not only of the chieftain and his family but of his men and animals. It was a long building with a roof supported by two rows of wooden uprights, which divided the space into 'bays'.

The hall remained the basis of the medieval house—there are still some country houses called 'The Hall'—even when it was built of stone after the Norman Conquest. Gradually other rooms were added at either end and then above, or separate buildings nearby were connected to the hall by covered passages. The living quarters in CASTLES and MANORS (qq.v.) were built on the same plan; indeed, early manors were like castles in many ways, for they also had to be fortified against attack. Sometimes the hall was built on the first floor, reached by an outside stair, with store-rooms below, an arrangement which lasted in Scotland for centuries; sometimes it was on one side of a walled court, with a strong GATEHOUSE (q.v.) on the opposite side. At first the WALLS were very thick and the WINDOWS (qq.v.) small, both for protection and because without glass they made the rooms cold. The peasants continued to live in one-roomed huts with a hearth in the centre, the smoke finding its way out as best it could.

Wooden houses were usual in parts of the country where there was no stone. In towns they were common, in spite of the risk of fire which led to many unsuccessful attempts throughout the Middle Ages to compel Londoners to build in stone. The upper storeys of the houses overhung the narrow streets, supported on beams which were often richly carved. In Holland, Belgium, and Germany the houses were tall with steeply sloping roofs. In Holland the gables were stepped or curved, shapes that can be seen in some East Anglian districts where Dutch emigrants settled, and in South Africa which was colonized by the Dutch in the 17th century. In Scotland the gable with 'crow steps' is common (see Vol. I, p. 432).

Since the medieval house grew by the addition of rooms to the central hall, its external shape was more or less haphazard, with windows at various levels and roof gables at all angles. In the 16th century, though the basic plan remained the same, the wings at either side were made symmetrical which, with the protruding PORCH (q.v.) in the centre, gave the characteristic E shape. Renaissance ornament was added in the form of little columns and niches; windows were enlarged and arranged in an orderly fashion; a profusion of chimneys made an exciting skyline.

In the warm Mediterranean countries houses retained the Roman characteristic of being built round a central courtyard; but in the 16th century the architect PALLADIO (q.v. Vol. V) built country villas for the Venetian nobility which broke with tradition. The central rooms, usually set back behind deep BALCONIES (q.v.), might be square, circular, or rectangular, and were covered by domes or low-pitched roofs. Such houses had a great influence on northern architects for centuries.

When Inigo JONES (q.v. Vol. V) visited Italy he studied Palladio's villas with great care. The Queen's House at Greenwich—the first Renaissance house to be built in England—has a deep balcony and many of the features of the Italian villa. Inigo Jones did not simply use Italian details, as architects before him had done, to decorate houses which were essentially medieval

COMPTON WYNYATES, WARWICKSHIRE, EARLY 16TH CENTURY

The house, built round a court, has no important façade; walls jut out or recede and roofs and windows are at different levels

H. Felton

TINTINHULL HOUSE, SOMERSET, LATE 17TH OR EARLY 18TH CENTURY
The symmetrical façade is decorated with Renaissance pilasters and pediment

in plan; the plan of the Queen's House is entirely different. It is a compact, almost square building with the details, such as windows, carefully related in size and position to the walls. Henceforth, for 300 years, houses were planned with formal elevations, the rooms being fitted into the four walls as into a shell. Only in this century has there been a return to plans which grow in whatever direction the rooms dictate.

The revolutionary plan which Inigo Jones introduced was not at all universally adopted, and houses in the old style were built, especially in the country, throughout the 17th century. Smaller houses and cottages continued even longer to follow traditional designs, and consequently it is often difficult to tell to which century they belong. But, by the end of the 17th century, many fine houses had been built on the new plan, and the early 18th-century houses, Mereworth and Chiswick Villa, for example, were built in imitation of Palladio's Villa Rotonda (see Vol. V, p. 346). Brick, which was first used extensively in England in the 17th century, became the most usual material for town

J. H. Stone

HALF-TIMBER HOUSES IN LAVENHAM, SUFFOLK
Houses were built in this style from the 15th to the 17th centuries in districts where there was no local stone

National Buildings Record

A GOTHIC-REVIVAL HOUSE AT CHELTENHAM

houses. In the 18th century towns grew rapidly (*see* TOWNS, HISTORY OF), the houses being built in the modest, neat style of GEORGIAN ARCHITECTURE (q.v. Vol. XII) which evolved in Britain from the Palladian style. The Georgian house was symmetrically designed, with rows of rectangular paned windows and an ornamental porch. The walls were crowned by a moulded cornice underneath the eaves, or the cornice was surmounted by a parapet which partly hid the roof. Inside there were elegant staircases, and for the first time corridors were built so that the rooms no longer opened into each other. The top floor, called the attic, had small windows beneath the cornice, or dormer windows in the roof behind the parapet.

In the late 18th century new streets, squares, and crescents were built which gave an opportunity for large-scale TOWN PLANNING (q.v.). A terrace of houses would be planned as a single unit, and its unity emphasized by the repetition of identical doorways and windows, and perhaps by a central pediment. Externally the design was restrained, but, inside, the larger terraced houses were planned with great ingenuity and variety. Each was tall and narrow, usually the width of a single room. The dining-room was on the ground floor, the drawing-room on the first floor, and the kitchens were in the basement. The rooms were high and well proportioned, with tall windows. REGENCY ARCHITECTURE (q.v. Vol. XII), a style belonging to the beginning of the 19th century, though lighter and

gayer, retained many of the features of the Georgian house.

In the 19th century classical and Gothic styles were used indiscriminately and with little understanding; architects were prepared to design a house which could be dressed up in whichever style their client favoured. Little thought was given to practical planning; the rooms were ill proportioned, long dark corridors wasted space, and the inconvenient arrangement of the rooms made extra work for the numerous servants. These features were typical of the villas set in spacious gardens, which grew up around the towns as the townspeople became rich and wanted to display their wealth. At the same time, rows and rows of houses were built for factory workers; they were crowded together, sometimes built back to back, and soon became appalling SLUMS (q.v. Vol. X).

At the end of the 19th century English architects began to study the traditional Jacobean and Georgian country houses, and to build houses designed for comfort and simplicity and made of local materials, so that they fitted into the landscape. These houses had a great influence on the Continent at the beginning of the 20th century, and it became the fashion to build in the 'English style'. In Britain, however, suburban villas were built in imitation of, but without an understanding of, period styles; and traditional materials, such as 'half-timbering', were applied as ornament without playing any part in the structure.

The revival of styles, especially the Georgian, has continued during this century, and an interest in old houses has led people to recondition and modernize them rather than to build new ones. Nowadays families are smaller, and there are fewer domestic servants than in the 19th century. Houses, in consequence, are smaller, and the rooms are designed for the convenience of their occupants; the aspect of the house is carefully considered so that, for example, sitting-rooms should be sunny and larders cool; space-wasting corridors have disappeared; kitchens are planned for convenience (*see* KITCHEN DESIGN). In contrast to the tall rectangular Georgian house, modern houses are unsymmetrical, with the emphasis on horizontal rather than vertical lines. Steel frames and reinforced concrete make possible a more flexible arrangement of rooms since, if the walls do not bear the weight of the floors and roof, they need not be above each

HOUSE AT FROGNAL, HAMPSTEAD, BUILT IN 1938 BY CONNELL, WARD, AND LUCAS
The circular columns are part of the reinforced frame construction which supports the whole building. The walls can,
therefore, be treated freely, and on this side, which faces the sun, they are almost entirely of glass

other (*see* BUILDING, PRINCIPLES OF, Vol. VIII).
The growing size of towns has led to the building of large blocks of FLATS (q.v.).

In America Frank Lloyd Wright, and many
architects since, have designed houses of an
informal kind, based on the nature of the materials used and the requirements of the interior.
Many such houses bring the rooms into close
contact with the garden. Open spaces within
the house create a feeling of airiness, and
rooms and terraces are linked by walls of
plate glass. These houses are especially well
suited to warm climates such as that of California, but are possible in Britain only if elaborate systems of heating are installed to keep
them warm. There are few houses in Britain
which carry the principles of modern architecture so far, but many have been built since the
Second World War which show the influence of
new techniques and styles.

See also HOUSES, TYPES OF; ROOMS; INTERIOR DECORA-
TION, HISTORY OF; TOWN PLANNING, HISTORY OF.
See also Vol. VIII: BUILDING, PRINCIPLES OF; BUILDING
CONSTRUCTION.
See also Vol. X: HOUSING, MUNICIPAL.

HOUSES, TYPES OF. The PRIMITIVE DWEL-
LINGS (q.v.) of many native tribes are often little
more than shelters of mud, skin, or wood, hardly
deserving the name of 'house'. It is only in
settled civilizations that permanently constructed
houses have developed. Their forms differ
widely according to the kind of life people live,
the climate, the materials available for building,
and the skill with which these are used. In
modern times houses differ less from country to
country because people do not depend solely
on local materials and because ready-made
building components are widely used. Nevertheless, many local characteristics persist.

The shape of the house is strongly influenced
by the climate. Where it is warm, as in the
Mediterranean and Arab countries, the plan of
the house is open, with the rooms often arranged
round a courtyard which admits air but not too
much sun. In the north houses are more compact so that they can be more easily kept warm
in winter; where there is much rain, they have
steep ROOFS (q.v.) to throw it off; but where there
is much snow and frost, as in Switzerland, they
generally have flatter roofs where the snow will

K.L.M

A MANY-STORIED BRICK HOUSE IN AMSTERDAM, WITH STEEPLY
PITCHED ROOF

Paul Popper

TALL HOUSES IN SIENA, ITALY, WITH LOW-PITCHED TILED
ROOFS

lie, making a warm blanket over the house. Tiled roofs in the south of France and in Italy have a still flatter pitch than those of the north. In hot countries flat roofs are common because no slope is needed to throw off rainwater and because a flat roof is useful for sleeping on in the hottest weather.

The shape of WINDOWS (q.v.) is also dependent on the climate. They are large in the north to admit sunlight, though not so large as to make the rooms too cold; in the south, windows are small so as to keep the house as cool as possible inside, and are often shaded from the direct glare of the sun by BALCONIES or VERANDAHS (qq.v.) which provide a cool sitting place in the open air (*see* Vol. XII, p. 23). Shutters outside the windows also provide protection from the sun. Windows are placed facing away from the sun in hot countries and, where possible, towards the sun in cold climates to let in as much light and warmth as possible. CHIMNEYS (q.v.) are a prominent feature of the exterior of the northern houses.

The materials of which houses are built play a large part in giving character to the scenery of different countries. In England, before modern transport made it possible to carry cheap bricks all over the country, and before standardized building materials were made in factories, every region had its characteristic building material. In the Cotswolds and other stone-bearing districts walls and roofs were of stone, with gables and stone-mullioned windows; in Shropshire, Herefordshire, and Cheshire half-timbered houses were usual (*see* Vol. XII, p. 23); in Essex the timber was covered all over with plaster. A mixture of timber, brick, and tile was used in Kent; and the Norfolk brick houses were given roofs of pantiles or reed-thatch. In Wales, Cornwall, and the Lake District the houses had roofs of slate from the local quarries. Because old houses are built of local materials they fit into the landscape, and their colour and texture harmonize with it. Efforts are still made, therefore, to build as far as possible in local materials, especially in country districts.

Other countries, especially those less highly industrialized than Britain, likewise retain many traditional materials and building methods. In Mediterranean countries the prevailing building materials are white-washed brick and plaster, with roofs of half-round Roman tiles. In many parts of central Europe the prevailing

FLAT-ROOFED HOUSES IN ADEN

Paul Popper

material is timber, though nowadays in towns timber is used less because of the danger of fire. In Holland and Denmark red or yellow brick is used, with roofs of red pantiles or plain tiles.

In Oriental countries houses are most commonly built of local sun-dried brick or of timber. Japan is probably the country where the houses have retained their characteristic structure and appearance with fewest changes. The traditional house has a timber frame and the walls and partitions are light screens of paper, bamboo, or similar material. Such a light construction is suited to the climate and is less dangerous in earthquakes than heavy materials would be (*see* Vol. I, p. 270).

The shape and size of the Rooms (q.v.), and therefore of the house as a whole, depend on the way people live. In the Middle Ages, when people spent most of their time out of doors, rooms were few and barely furnished. But as indoor activities increased, there was more emphasis on indoor comfort, and rooms were set apart for different purposes. Nowadays, in the West, the desire for privacy has led to small houses or flats with small rooms, so that each family can have a separate living place and each person a separate room. But not all people want privacy; in the Arab lands of the eastern Mediterranean, and in Mexico, China, and elsewhere, parents, children, grandchildren, and other relatives all prefer to live together in the same house,

forming one large household. In warm countries people live much more out of doors than in the north, and, consequently, the houses are simpler and more barely furnished. In Japanese houses the dimensions of all the rooms are based on those of the mats with which all the floors are covered. The mat is always of the same size, so that each room is so many mats wide and so many long, thus making all houses consistent in scale and proportion. A similar standardization is beginning to appear in Western buildings with the increasing use of factory-made building components—walls, windows, doors, and so on —of standard sizes and shapes.

In the United States of America houses have changed as social customs changed. At first, American houses followed the patterns brought from Europe by the early immigrants, but, since timber was the most easily obtainable material, boarded walls and shingle roofs largely replaced bricks and tiles (*see* Vol. XII, p. 10). Lately, different regions have evolved their own methods of house building to suit local conditions; for instance, a low, rambling house with widely spreading eaves, extending into loggias and terraces, is typical of the Pacific coast. In addition, the plan of the house has begun to change as the American way of life has diverged more and more from the European. Houses are less formal, and rooms merge one into the other, providing more space for general family life and fewer rooms for special purposes.

Paul Popper

A SMALL MODERN JAPANESE HOUSE
The large windows and rooms running into each other are typical of Japanese houses

In the last few generations industrial populations have increased so greatly that immense numbers of new houses have been built. New materials and methods of BUILDING CONSTRUCTION (q.v. Vol. VIII) have made it possible to build large blocks of FLATS (q.v.) which are suited to the habits of town dwellers, and which are necessary to prevent towns from spreading over too large an area (see TOWN PLANNING, HISTORY OF).

See also HOUSES, HISTORY OF; ROOMS.

HOUSEWORK. There are three distinct divisions of housework: daily work, weekly work, and periodical work such as chimney sweeping and curtain washing. Some housewives prefer to do such special tasks during spring cleaning, which usually involves putting a room out of action for one or more days. Others, however, consider that if daily and weekly cleaning are carried out properly, and the special tasks at regular intervals, intensive spring cleaning is unnecessary.

There should be a routine for cleaning, depending on the size of the house, the amount of help available, and the time the housewife can afford. In houses of small or moderate size, a practical plan is for one morning to be given to the weekly cleaning of upstairs rooms, one to downstairs rooms, and one to the kitchen; this leaves three mornings for washing, shopping, and ironing, and a free Sunday morning.

1. *Daily Cleaning.* If a house is to be well kept, every room in use demands some work daily, varying according to how much the room has been used. This consists mainly of tidying, bedmaking, beating up cushions, emptying waste-paper baskets, ash-trays, and so on, and of removing dust from floors, furniture, and fittings by sweeping (or using a vacuum cleaner or carpet sweeper), dusting, and scrubbing. Fireplaces, baths, wash-basins, lavatory pans, and sinks have to be cleaned daily. The order in which these jobs are done is important; for example, jobs that stir up dust, such as cleaning fireplaces or sweeping carpets, should be done before dusting.

2. *Weekly Cleaning.* This includes polishing floors and furniture, cleaning windows, washing paintwork and all china and glass articles, sweeping down walls and ceilings, cleaning curtains and pelmets with a vacuum-cleaner attachment, and brushing, shaking, beating, or vacuum-cleaning carpets and rugs thoroughly. Some of these tasks, such as cleaning windows and paintwork, need not be done every week in districts where the air is clean; the routine should be so arranged that some part of this periodic work is undertaken each week, together with the unvarying daily tasks.

Beds need special weekly attention; they should be stripped, thoroughly aired, have their mattresses turned, and should have clean linen every week. In the bathroom, baths and wash-basins should be washed, debris cleared from the grids, and drains (and drain-traps also, occasionally) flushed with boiling water. Each week the lavatory pan should be cleaned with a special cleaner, either a hypochlorite bleach (*see* CLEANING MATERIALS) or one containing nitre cake (sodium bisulphate and sodium acid sulphate).

In the kitchen, the larder and store-cupboard should be cleaned, preferably the day before the bulk of the weekly shopping is done. The REFRIGERATOR (q.v.) needs to be defrosted, the cooker cleaned, windows and walls washed, and drain traps, overflow wastes, and outside gulleys thoroughly cleaned with boiling water and soda. Table silver and articles of silver, copper, and brass need a thorough cleaning once a week.

3. *Seasonal Cleaning.* Curtains, loose covers, cushion covers, blankets, and mattress covers ought to be laundered at regular intervals, more often in a dirty industrial area than in the country. Rugs and carpets benefit by being shampooed once a year, or more frequently if necessary. Drawers and cupboards should be emptied and cleaned, and their contents sorted out and reviewed. This can be done conveniently at the change of season, for example, when winter garments are being put away and summer ones taken out. Beds should be taken to pieces about four times a year, the frames thoroughly dusted and polished, the mattresses and covered springs brushed or cleaned with a vacuum-cleaner attachment, and uncovered springs brushed, dusted, and wiped over with oil.

Chimneys must be cleaned at least once a year to prevent soot collecting in them and blocking them. Dirty chimneys do not draw well, often driving smoke into the room; they drop soot into the fireplace, and they sometimes catch fire. A hundred years ago small boys used to be sent up chimneys to remove the soot with hand brushes (*see* CHILD WELFARE, Vol. X). Now a chimney-sweep cleans them with a circular brush on the end of rods which fit together to give the necessary length. In England the brush is pushed up the chimney, but in Scotland the chimney-sweep pushes it down the chimney from the roof. Chimneys can now be suction-cleaned with a vacuum cleaner—a process which deposits no soot over the room, as the old method of brush-sweeping used to do. Modern non-vacuum sweepers, however, can now also seal fireplaces against falling soot, and some people consider that good brush-sweeping is more effective than suction-cleaning.

I

ICES. The first ices were probably made in Italy in the early 17th century. From there they spread to France, and from France to England. It was not, however, until Victorian times that ices became popular in England. Then they were made in the home for luncheons and dinners and were served at banquets. An Italian, Carlo Gatti, started the practice of selling them to the general public from barrows in London.

The term 'ices' includes both water-ices, made from sweetened water with various FLAVOURINGS (q.v.) added, and ice cream, made with milk, fat (preferably butter fat in the form of cream), sugar, a flavouring, and one or more of the following—cooked starch, eggs, and gelatine. The ice-cream mixture is then frozen, and during this process is beaten in order to keep the ice crystals small and the cream smooth, to incorporate air, and to ensure even freezing.

Commercially, ice cream is made at about 20° F. and then stored in hard blocks at 0° F. Before freezing, the mixture is pasteurized as a precaution against subsequent infection. Commercial ice cream does not usually contain eggs and starch but gelatine and gum tragacanth instead. All these substances, added in small amounts, help to prevent the formation of large crystals, and for this purpose gelatine and gums are better for ices which are to be stored for some time at low temperatures.

In the home ice cream is usually made from an egg custard to which cream or evaporated milk is added. It can be satisfactorily frozen in the ice box of a REFRIGERATOR (q.v.), provided that it is removed at intervals and well beaten. It can also be made by hand in a wooden ice bucket, a double vessel in which the inner metal canister containing the ice-cream mixture sits in the outer wooden bucket containing broken ice and salt. Inside the canister is a hand-operated paddle which must be kept turning until the mixture has thickened. This method was always used before the invention of refrigeration.

Various flavourings may be added, such as vanilla, chocolate, fruit, peppermint, and ginger, but in larger amounts than for food at normal temperatures because low temperatures tend to paralyse the taste buds (*see* SENSES, Section 5, Vol. II).

Water-ices are easily made at home by making a mixture of water, sugar, and fruit juice or fruit squash, and freezing it in the ice box of the refrigerator, in the same way as for ice cream.

ICINGS AND FILLINGS. These should be made only with genuine materials in perfect condition, and decorated with real fruits and nuts rather than with fancy piping.

1. FILLINGS. Any thick, boiled custard (*see* SAUCES), flavoured with, for example, vanilla, coffee, chocolate, crushed macaroons (*frangipane*), or caramel syrup, can be used as a filling. For a butter cream type of filling, icing sugar is creamed with an equal amount of butter or margarine, and flavoured, for example, with lemon or orange juice and rind; it is sometimes blended with eggs, gelatine, or custard to give a lighter cream. Fruit and nut fillings may be made with chopped figs, raisins, prunes, ginger, or nuts, mixed with lemon juice or cream; mashed strawberries or bananas with sugar; chestnuts with sugar and rum; and lemon curd, apple sauce, jelly, or jam.

2. ICINGS. (*a*) *Uncooked.* Water icing, made with icing sugar (4 oz.) and water or fruit juice (1½ tablespoons), can be spread thinly on Danish

SPREADING FONDANT ICING

ICING A CAKE

Left: the icing is poured on to the cake. A palette knife is kept in hot water. Right: smoothing the surface with the palette knife

pastries or thin biscuits or over cakes already covered with, for example, split roasted nuts or sliced ginger. To make glacé icings, the water icing is warmed in a saucepan until the sugar crystals just dissolve, and is then poured gently over the cakes. On cooling, the surface recrystallizes in a continuous glaze. Butter icings are like butter cream fillings but sweeter, with three parts sugar to two parts butter. They can be spread roughly or made into rosettes and swirls with an icing pipe. Royal icing is the professional's joy; with it he constructs those elaborate pipe edifices on wedding cakes, which look so remarkable but which often taste more like sweet plaster of paris than food. It consists of dry icing sugar worked into raw, whipped egg whites. Blue colouring is added to intensify the whiteness and a little weak acid to strengthen the egg foam. The rock-like hardness of the resulting icing can be modified by adding a little glycerine to the mixture. Almond icing (*see* SWEET-MAKING, Section 2*b*), either cooked or uncooked, is patted on to fruit cakes with a broad-bladed instrument dipped in hot water.

(*b*) *Cooked icings* are made with ordinary sugar and are, on the whole, more interesting than the icing sugar type. Fudge icings are described in the article SWEET-MAKING. Chocolate fudge on chocolate cake, and milk fudge spread thickly on dark fruit cake, are delicious. American boiled frostings, or fluffy icings, are made by whipping egg whites and sugar over boiling water until the mixture stiffens. It is then poured on to the cake very quickly as it soon sets to a crisp, delicate meringue. For 'White Mountain Cream', 1 egg white is beaten with 2 tablespoons of cold water, $\frac{1}{4}$ teaspoon of cream of tartar, and $\frac{2}{3}$ cup of sugar over fast boiling water for 10 minutes or until the mixture stands up in peaks by itself. It is used plain on spiced cakes, or flavoured with peppermint on chocolate cakes. Brown sugar can be used instead of white sugar and chopped raisins added. Fondant is a very sticky icing much favoured by the cake trade for 'Fondant Dipped Fancies' and other sickly confections. It is made from sugar and corn syrup (commercial glucose) boiled together, sometimes with saccharin.

See also CAKES; SWEET-MAKING.

INFANTILE PARALYSIS, *see* POLIOMYELITIS.

INFECTIOUS DISEASES. Many diseases are infectious, but the phrase is commonly applied to a group of diseases, sometimes called 'fevers', to which children are particularly susceptible. The reason for this selective attack is that children have not had time to establish the immunity which most adults have acquired. The human body gradually creates its own defences against the invading organism, and these defences remain to ward off a second attack. Doctors take advantage of this fact to forestall the disease and to give an immunity to their patients by inoculating them with the disease in some harmless form. The body reacts to this INOCULATION (q.v.) by creating the defensive bodies in the blood which will protect it against the disease in its natural form. Before this method of protection was discovered, most children caught these diseases at some time or other, and so had to endure a serious illness in order to acquire the immunity. With all these diseases there is a period of incubation—that is, the symptoms do not show until some days after contact with the infection.

1. DIPHTHERIA. This is the most dangerous of the infectious diseases. It is caused by the diphtheria bacillus, which usually lodges in the nose and throat, and emits an extremely poisonous substance known as diphtheria toxin into the material upon which it is living. The period of incubation is 2 to 6 days. There may or may not be fever, but the throat is usually sore and reddened. The most characteristic symptom is a greyish membrane which appears over a tonsil or at the back of the throat. Some days after the appearance of this membrane paralysis may occur owing to the action of the toxin on the nervous system. Sometimes the paralysis affects the heart or the respiratory organs and proves fatal; or the membrane may block the windpipe and choke the patient. When the latter danger is threatened, a tube is inserted through an incision in the throat and the patient is able to breathe through this tube until the windpipe is cleared.

A German doctor named Behring has saved many lives by discovering that patients who had recovered from diphtheria had in their blood a substance which neutralized the diphtheria toxin. He showed how this substance, known as 'anti-toxin', could be supplied in quantity in the blood serum of immunized horses. Later research proved that diphtheria toxin could be made harmless in several ways—for example, by storing it for a period of time, by treating it with formalin, or by heating it. This harmless toxin, known as 'toxoid', could still induce the production of anti-toxin in the blood and so give protection against the disease.

Since 1941 many thousands of children in Britain have been given injections of diphtheria toxoid. The success of the immunization campaign is proved by the figures. In 1935 there were 64,084 cases of diphtheria with 3,408 deaths; in 1953 there were only 266 cases and 23 deaths.

The immunity resulting from these injections, however, lasts only a few years, and it is advisable to have a small maintenance dose at some time during school life, especially if there are any outbreaks of diphtheria in the neighbourhood.

2. MEASLES. This important infectious disease is caused by a VIRUS (q.v. Vol. II). The virus breeds in most countries of the world and is most active in winter and spring.

The first obvious symptoms of measles appear 10 or 11 days after exposure to infection. It begins with sneezing, running at the eyes and nose, fever, and cough. About 2 days later tiny bluish-white specks may be seen in the reddened lining of the cheek inside the mouth. These are called 'Koplik's spots' after the New York physician who first pointed out their significance, since they occur only in measles. A day or two later still, a rash appears behind the ears and on the forehead, and this rapidly spreads to other parts of the body. The rash lasts for 4 or 5 days and then begins to fade, leaving a brownish discoloration of the skin which may remain for several weeks. When the rash has faded, the outer layer of skin peels off in a fine white scaly powder.

Newly born infants still share the mother's immunity from measles, but this immunity disappears after about 2 months. For children under 5 years of age measles is a dangerous disease; but it can be fatal to people of all ages, especially when introduced into a community where it has been previously unknown, and, consequently, no immunity has been built up against it. Its greatest danger lies in the complications which may arise with it, such as broncho-pneumonia, ulceration of the mouth or eye, inflammation of the middle ear, and sometimes diarrhoea. Early confinement to bed reduces the risk of these complications, and careful nursing and dieting usually bring about a good recovery.

Protection may be given to children by inoculating them with serum obtained from the blood of convalescent patients. Even if it does not prevent the attack, it may greatly lessen its severity if given early enough. On account of its scarcity, however, immune serum is generally reserved for young children for whom the risk of death is greatest.

THE NEW LONDON FEVER HOSPITAL, ISLINGTON, *c.* 1848
This was one of the first hospitals in which patients with infectious diseases were isolated

3. GERMAN MEASLES (Rubella). This disease, which has no connexion with measles, is a mild infectious disease caused by a virus. The main signs appear about a fortnight after contact with the infection. They are a slight catarrh, enlargement of certain glands in the neck, and a distinctive rash similar to but more pink than that of measles. It is uncommon in children under five, but adults are more liable to contract German measles than measles. It has recently been discovered that when it attacks a woman in the early stages of pregnancy it may have a harmful effect on the development of the unborn child so that he is born with certain defects.

German measles can be distinguished from measles by the absence of Koplik's spots. The patient is infectious only so long as he shows the rash, and isolation for a week is sufficient to stop the spread of the infection. If the patient is kept in bed on a light diet with plenty of fruit juice until the temperature is normal, and he is given a laxative to make the bowels move, it is very unlikely that there will be any complications.

4. WHOOPING COUGH. This is a much more troublesome disease, with an incubation period of 7 to 14 days. It is an acute disease of the air passages, mainly affecting children under 5. It is thought to be caused by a bacillus which is passed on in droplets from the child's throat and by contact with contaminated articles.

Whooping cough begins as a catarrhal cold, and is at this stage highly infectious. After a few days a hard cough develops and returns in increasing paroxysms. During paroxysms of coughing, breathing is difficult, and the face becomes red or blue. As the fit of coughing ends, a long breath is drawn in through the glottis at the upper end of the wind-pipe, which is narrowed by a spasm so that the victim tends to make a high pitched 'whoop'. During or at the end of the paroxysm of coughing, the patient may vomit, though between paroxysms he may sleep or appear quite well. Complications, of which broncho-pneumonia is the commonest, may be dangerous.

The patient should be isolated for at least 4 weeks, nursed in a light, well-ventilated room, and given a light and non-irritating kind of diet, avoiding toast and other such dry foods. Meals should be small and frequent. In bad cases where the patient cannot keep down what he has eaten, feeding is a matter for the doctor. No entirely satisfactory vaccine has yet been produced, but several exist which very considerably modify the severity of an attack.

5. SCARLET FEVER (Scarlatina). This is a much less dangerous disease than it was 50 years ago. BACTERIA (q.v. Vol. II) known as 'streptococci' cause inflammation of the throat and produce a poison which causes the fever, rash, and other constitutional disturbances characteristic of the disease. Within 2 or 3 days after receiving the infection the patient's temperature rises rapidly, sometimes to as high as 104°, and he suffers from shivering, increased pulse rate, vomiting, sore throat, and headache. Within a few hours a red rash appears, first on the neck and upper part of the chest, and then over the rest of the body. Within a week the rash fades, the patient becomes convalescent, and the skin peels in the form of a fine scaly powder like bran.

Unless properly nursed scarlet fever may produce dangerous complications, including inflammations of the glands of the neck, of the middle ear, of the kidneys, any of the joints or the heart, of which may cause a life-long disability. Today, however, with the use of antibiotic DRUGS (q.v.) and anti-scarlatinal serum, scarlet fever is no longer a disease to be so greatly feared, and with reasonable care the patient should make a complete recovery.

6. MUMPS (Parotitis). Although more common among children than adults, mumps may attack people of any age. It is a virus disease which causes inflammation and swelling of the parotid glands at the back of the lower jaw 14 to 21 days after infection. It is not generally a serious illness, and the swelling, though it looks alarming, soon subsides. It does, however, occasionally cause dangerous inflammation of the testicles or ovaries.

7. CHICKEN POX (Varicella) AND SHINGLES (Herpes Zoster). Chicken pox is so called from the Latin word *cicer*, the chick pea, because of the supposed resemblance of the pocks to this seed. It is caused by a virus and most often attacks children under 10. On the rare occasions when it attacks adults, it may make them very ill, with fever, headache, backache, and vomiting. Its symptoms appear 12 to 24 days after infection.

Its most distinctive feature is the rash which appears about a fortnight after contact with the infection. It first appears on the chest and back in the form of small, raised pocks, which rapidly fill with a clear fluid and become little blisters, known as vesicles. It then spreads quickly to the face, hands, and feet, fresh crops of vesicles appearing during the next 2 or 3 days. The pocks then dry to small scabs, which drop off, leaving brownish spots which gradually fade. The skin is usually clear within 10 days or a fortnight. If the patient is kept warm and quiet, and persuaded not to scratch the irritating pocks, the disease clears away, leaving no after effects; but permanent scars may result if he ignores this advice.

Chicken pox is important because of its resemblance to the milder forms of the much more serious smallpox (*see* EPIDEMIC DISEASES, Section 3), cases of which may be mistaken for chicken pox with serious results.

It has recently been observed that there appears to be a connexion between chicken pox and shingles, an inflammation of the nerve tracts which may be caused by an allied virus. The name is a corruption of the Latin word *cingulus*, a girdle, and the most easily recognized sign of this disease is a line of vesicles appearing round the body below the ribs. The eruption is accompanied by severe pain, and nearby muscles may be temporarily or permanently paralysed. Other parts of the body, such as the face, are sometimes but less commonly attacked.

Treatment is chiefly directed towards alleviating the intense pain and protecting the areas of the skin where the vesicles have broken from picking up any other infection.

In spite of the probable connexion between the two diseases, chicken pox gives no protection against a subsequent attack of shingles. On the other hand, contact with chicken pox may possibly result in an attack of shingles—which makes it all the more important to isolate properly patients with chicken pox.

See also EPIDEMIC DISEASES; TROPICAL DISEASES; HOME NURSING.

See also Vol. II: BACTERIA; VIRUS.

INFLUENZA AND COMMON COLD.

Influenza is an acute infectious disease caused by a virus. Many great outbreaks have been recorded during the last 500 years, the most terrible being the epidemic of 1918–19, which caused more deaths than the First World War which preceded it. In 1933 Drs. Smith, Andrewes, and Laidlow succeeded, by experiments on ferrets, in isolating a VIRUS (q.v. Vol. II) which is now recognized as the infective agent or 'cause' of influenza. Viruses are very much smaller than ordinary bacteria, so small that they pass through the pores of the finest porcelain filters; but it is now possible to see them through the recently invented ELECTRON MICROSCOPE (q.v. Vol. VIII). It is not known for certain, however, whether they are living organisms, though they appear to be endowed with the power of reproduction. In 1940 a second type of influenza virus was isolated, and these two types are known as Virus A and Virus B. But some cases of the disease are believed to be due to a third type of virus, which has not yet been isolated, but has been provisionally named 'Influenza Y'.

Virus infection is spread by droplet discharges —mainly through coughing and sneezing—and entry is through the mouth and nose. The first symptoms of an attack are a general feeling of wretchedness, headache which is often very severe behind the eyes, and pains in the back and limbs. Cold and other conditions adverse to general health make people more likely to catch influenza, and good ventilation and the avoidance of crowds are important means of prevention. At the first sign of attack the victim should go to bed and stay there until the temperature has been normal for 48 hours. Penicillin and other antibiotics (*see* DRUGS) are ineffective against the virus but deal with the lung complications which are the most dangerous feature of the disease. It is hoped before long to perfect vaccines for preventive inoculation, but those now in use give protection for 14 days only. A World Influenza Centre was set up in London in 1947 under the auspices of the World Health Organization.

The common cold, the symptoms of which are familiar to everyone, still presents many mysterious features, in spite of the most intense research. The work carried out on human volunteers by the Common Cold Research Unit at the Harvard Hospital, Salisbury, since 1946 has confirmed that the infection can be transmitted by nasal discharges which are free from ordinary bacteria; and this makes it probable that colds are caused by virus infection. It is important to distinguish between 'catching cold' and 'catching a cold'. Although exposure to damp and cold predisposes towards 'colds', it is unlikely that the exposure by itself can cause a cold in the absence of the infective factor. It has long been known that visits of ships to isolated communities often give rise to outbreaks of colds among the inhabitants, and it is also a striking fact that Arctic explorers never catch colds despite the severe climatic conditions to which they are exposed. The symptoms of an ordinary cold usually subside within 48 hours, but complete recovery may take a week or more. The best preventatives are adequate food, particularly protective foods rich in VITAMINS (q.v.), suitable clothing, the avoidance of stuffy atmospheres, and keeping the hands and feet warm.

Handkerchiefs are a great source of infection and reinfection both of influenza and colds, and there is much to be said for the use of paper handkerchiefs which can be burnt after use. It is important to remember that the initial symptoms of many of the common INFECTIOUS DISEASES (q.v.) may be identical with those of a cold.

See also RESPIRATION; INFECTIOUS DISEASES.

INOCULATION AND VACCINATION.

When a person is inoculated against a disease he is given a mild attack of the disease which will confer protection against a subsequent normal attack. Inoculation against smallpox was first carried out in the East; matter was taken from the 'pocks' of a mild case of smallpox and inserted into the scarified arm of the person to be protected. This usually brought about a very mild attack of smallpox, and when the patient had recovered, his blood would contain protective substances called antibodies which would make him more or less immune from further attacks. Inoculation was introduced into England in 1721 by Lady Mary Wortley Montagu, wife of the British ambassador to Turkey, who had had her own children inoculated during her stay in Constantinople. This method of inoculation was practised with considerable success, but it had the danger that it sometimes resulted in a severe or even fatal attack of smallpox.

The next step was taken by Dr. Edward JENNER (q.v. Vol. V), of Berkeley in Gloucestershire. He decided to test the widely held belief that dairy-maids who contracted cowpox (a mild disease closely allied to smallpox) were immune from smallpox. After carrying out many experiments, in 1796 Jenner inoculated a boy named James Phipps with matter from the arm of Sarah Nelmes, a dairy-maid who was suffering from

Wellcome Historical Medical Museum

BRONZE STATUE OF JENNER VACCINATING A CHILD

cowpox. Some weeks later he inoculated Phipps with matter from a case of true smallpox, but the boy did not get the disease. In 1798 Jenner published a book on his experiences. The efficiency of vaccination was soon confirmed, and the practice spread all over the world. Jenner did far more than discover a method of controlling one dreadful disease; he laid the foundations for the whole science of immunity, which discovers what natural safeguards the body possesses and how these can be called into operation.

Vaccines are of various types. Some contain living bacteria, some dead bacteria, and others consist of the toxins or poisons produced by bacteria. In all cases vaccines are suitably treated in order to lessen their virulence. They are used both for the treatment and the prevention of disease. In active immunization the vaccine is given to stimulate the formation in the patient's own blood of antibodies able to combat the disease. In passive immunization the patient is injected with a serum already containing the appropriate antibodies, and obtained either from the blood of a patient who is convalescing from the disease in question, or from

an animal that has been artificially immunized against the disease. Vaccines and sera are now available for protection against such dangerous diseases as typhoid fever, tetanus, typhus, cholera, plague, smallpox, diphtheria, yellow fever, rabies, and whooping cough. Compulsory vaccination against smallpox was repealed by the National Health Service Act of 1946.

See also INFECTIOUS DISEASES; EPIDEMIC DISEASES.

INSANITY, *see* MENTAL DISEASES.

INSTINCT, *see* PSYCHOLOGY. *See also* Vol. II: INTELLIGENCE.

INSULIN, *see* DIABETES.

INSURANCE. 1. In early times people guarded against the risk of personal injury, loss of life, or damage to property by joining together and agreeing to contribute towards the losses suffered by any one of them. In the Middle Ages this was one of the important functions of the CRAFT GUILDS (q.v. Vol. VII); later, FRIENDLY SOCIETIES (q.v. Vol. X), which from the 17th to the 19th century were to be found in nearly every town and village in England, were developed for this purpose. In some early associations outside the Friendly Societies, each member, according to his means, had to contribute towards replacing property destroyed or damaged by fire. Later, traders would band together to make good the damage that any of them incurred by fire or shipwreck. In effect, these traders were paying premiums for insurance; but not in the modern sense, since they paid after the loss and not before it.

It was realized 200–300 years ago that an average risk could be calculated; but not till the 19th century had sufficiently accurate statistics been collected to enable premiums to be properly assessed (*see* INSURANCE, Vol. VII). Today, insurance may be obtained through a commercial company, or through LLOYD'S of London (q.v. Vol. IV), against almost any known risk. Insurance of this kind, however, should not be confused with SOCIAL INSURANCE (q.v. Vol. X), which is a national concern and covers the death, sickness, old age, and unemployment from most citizens.

2. FIRE AND ALL RISKS INSURANCE. The present practice in Britain dates, in effect, from the Great FIRE OF LONDON (q.v. Vol. X). At first the practice of fire insurance was experimental and uncertain, but by about 1800 the various companies had enough shared experience to give a reasonably accurate basis for premiums. Fire insurance is so planned that, after a fire, the insured person shall be neither better nor worse off financially. But, if he is under-insured, he will be worse off, for his compensation will be less than his loss. It is therefore important to be sufficiently insured.

People owning and living in their own houses are afforded protection under a comprehensive policy for householders. The policy is usually divided into two parts—one covering the building and the other the contents. The building policy usually insures against loss by fire, riots, damage by aircraft, explosion, earthquake, burst pipes and tanks, impact by road vehicles, damage by burglars, and injury to third parties caused by defects in the building, such as a tile falling off the roof and injuring a passer-by.

The contents policy usually covers the perils mentioned above and, in addition, breakage of mirrors, burglary, larceny, and an employer's liability towards servants. Some perils not included, such as breaking of windows, may be added at an extra charge. Landlords and tenants may insure buildings and their contents separately. In all cases policy-holders should discover exactly against what risks they have covered themselves.

'All risks' insurance covers loss by any cause of jewellery, fur coats, or other valuable articles. Though usually limited to loss in the United Kingdom, such insurance may be extended, by paying a higher premium, to cover loss when travelling abroad. Damage due to wear and tear, moth, vermin, and war is normally excluded.

3. SICKNESS AND ACCIDENT INSURANCE. This varies considerably, both in scope and cost. Accident insurance may cover only death by accident, or it may include injury, such as loss of one or both limbs or eyes. Sickness policies may give cover against all illness or only against certain specified diseases. Premiums vary according to the insured person's occupation.

Compensation for sickness usually includes weekly payments of a fixed sum for a maximum of 100 weeks, as well as medical fees. Compensation for accidents is usually an outright sum of money.

4. LIFE ASSURANCE. In the early days of life assurance, contracts were usually for a term of not more than 1 year. In 1705 the Amicable Society began the practice of accepting annual contributions from its members, and distributing each year's total among the estates of members who had died during that year. However, this was not altogether satisfactory as it meant that an uncertain and varying sum was assured. In 1762 the Equitable Society first successfully applied scientific principles to methods of life assurance. They offered whole life assurances with premiums appropriate to the age of the policy-holder but constant throughout the duration of the assurance.

Industrial Life Assurance is concerned with small policies, the premiums for which are paid to collectors every month or less. In Ordinary Life Assurance the policies are larger, and premiums are payable through a bank or direct to the company annually or by half-yearly, quarterly, or monthly instalments.

Life assurance can also help a person to borrow money for buying a house, and ensures that his family owns the house even if he should die before the loan is repaid. If he borrows from a life assurance company, the borrower has to take out an endowment assurance on his life for the amount of the loan. This will repay the loan at the end of a term of years or at his death if that should occur first. If he borrows from one of the BUILDING SOCIETIES (q.v. Vol. VII), he may take out a life assurance policy which will enable the amount of loan still outstanding at his death to be paid off. To obtain such a policy, he can pay either one single premium, which the Building Society will usually advance, or a small annual premium.

5. EDUCATION. Life assurance policies payable at school age or at a parent's earlier death encourage saving for the cost of education and ensure that plans for education can be carried out. The payment is usually spread over 4 or 5 years. Some policies provide for annual payments to start if the parent dies, and to continue until the end of the period at school.

Deferred Assurance policies may be taken out for young children. A usual type of policy is one which gives the child, at the age of 21, the choice of an outright cash payment or of a whole life or endowment assurance policy. Some policies may be given up earlier than 21 to make money available for education. Some provide that, if the person who is paying the premiums dies, no more premiums need be paid, but the benefits will be exactly the same.

6. AVERAGE INSURANCE BUDGET. A tax relief, amounting to two-fifths of the premium is allowed on life assurances, unless the premium exceeds one-sixth of income. The need for life assurance varies considerably with individual circumstances. An indication of the premiums that might be paid by a married man with two children, with an income of £800 a year, is given below:

General fire and burglary cover for house and furniture (house £2,000; furniture £800) .	£4. 10s.
Personal accident insurance . . .	£3
Life assurance cover for Building Society mortgage of £1,000	£6
Pension contribution (5% of salary) . .	£40
Short-term endowment assurances to help with children's education	£30

See also Vol. VII: INSURANCE.
See also Vol. X: SOCIAL INSURANCE; FRIENDLY SOCIETIES.

INTELLIGENCE. What is an intelligent being? The simplest answer is 'a being who can think'. This answer is not altogether adequate, because intelligence can be displayed in our actions, as well as in our thinking. A skilful bicyclist shows intelligence in avoiding collisions and in worming his way through traffic-blocks, but he does not have to think out each movement of the handlebars or the pedals or the brake-levers before he makes it. Nevertheless, thinking is the most important manifestation of intelligence, and all forms of intelligence have something in common, for they all depend on the possession of concepts or abstract ideas. To think about motor-cars, or to act intelligently with regard to them, as the bicyclist does, one must possess the concept or idea of a motor-car; to put it more colloquially, one must know what a motor-car is, or what motor-cars are like. We shall have gone some way towards understanding what intelligence is if we can understand how our concepts are acquired, and how we use them when we have acquired them.

Our basic concepts, without which we could not think at all, are acquired by repeated experience of the things or events which are examples of them. We learn what a cat is (acquire the concept or idea of a cat) by repeatedly seeing and touching actual cats. We acquire the concept of movement by repeatedly seeing things which move. We acquire the concepts of softness and hardness by touching soft things and hard things. It is a process of gradual familiarization. We gradually become aware of some feature which a number of objects have in common, some way in which they are alike. As the philosopher John LOCKE (q.v. Vol. V) said, our concepts are 'founded on the similitudes of things'. In a world of perpetual novelty, where nothing was ever like anything else, no concepts could be acquired at all, and neither thinking nor intelligent action would be possible. The concepts so far mentioned are acquired by observing the things around us. But there are others which we acquire by noticing what goes on in our own minds, for example the concepts of fear, of surprise, of pleasure, of doubt. We know what fear is like (have the concept or idea of fear) because we have sometimes felt afraid ourselves. And there is no other way in which this concept can be acquired. It is said that NELSON (q.v. Vol. V) had no idea of fear because he had never felt afraid himself. In this respect, if the story is true, he was like a blind man who has no idea of red or green, because he has never seen red things or green things.

Many of our concepts, however, are not acquired by experience of actual instances. A person who has never seen a volcano can know what a volcano is like. He may have acquired this concept by hearing other people talk about volcanoes, or by reading what has been written; or, if he is a very original person, he may even have 'made it up' for himself. Most of us have the idea or concept of a dragon, though we have never seen a dragon, and as far as we know there are no dragons in the world at all. When James WATT (q.v. Vol. V) invented the steam-engine, the idea or concept of a steam-engine existed in his mind before there was any actual instance of it, though of course there have been many instances of this concept since. The same thing happens in any kind of 'creative' or 'constructive' thinking. But such concepts as these, although they were not acquired by experience of actual instances and perhaps even have no actual instances, at all, can be analysed into simpler concepts which do have experienced instances. They have therefore been called 'complex ideas'. The idea of a dragon, for example, is the idea of a large winged fire-breathing animal, and we cannot have this idea unless we have experienced

A MODERN LIVING-ROOM AND DINING-ROOM

The walls are papered, the floor is covered with a seamless fitted carpet, with a hand-woven hearth rug. The curtains are printed linen, and the chairs and sofa are covered with furnishing cotton. The tables have lacquered tops and metal supports. The fireplace is on the right, outside the picture; central heating beneath the windows prevents the large expanse of glass from making the room too cold

large things, winged things, fires, breathing, and animals. Such complex ideas, then, are still derived indirectly from experience. The simpler ideas, out of which they are built up, are acquired by experience of actual instances.

When we have acquired a concept, the concept of 'cat', for example, there are two things we can do which we could not do before. We can recognize something as a cat when it is present, and we can think about cats when they are absent. Thinking, unlike sense-perception (*see* SENSES, Vol. II), is not dependent on the physical presence of the thing thought about. We can think about things which are very remote from us in time or space, and even about mere possibilities—what there might be, or might have been, as well as what there actually is. This is what the possession of concepts does for us. It frees us, in some degree, from the narrow limits of our immediate physical surroundings. But though anyone who possesses concepts can think of what is absent, there must be something actually present by means of which he thinks of it. In the most highly developed forms of thinking this 'something present', by means of which we think, is a symbol of some kind, or a series of symbols: a word or a series of words which we say to ourselves under our breath, a mental image representing the absent object, a picture or diagram which we draw on paper, or perhaps an imitative action, a piece of 'dumb show' (as when a man on dry land thinks of swimming, and causes others to think of it, by making the motions of swimming with his arms).

The importance of thinking is that it enables us to trace out the connexions between one fact and another. To do this, we have to make generalizations, 'whenever *A*, then *B*' or 'when *A*, then usually *B*': for example, 'whenever it is very cold, water freezes', or 'lightning is usually followed by thunder'. We cannot make generalizations until we possess concepts. By means of concepts, we are able to classify the things and events we observe into kinds or sorts. Then, but not before, we are able to discover that things or events of sort *A* are regularly accompanied by things or events of sort *B*, and can make the generalization 'whenever *A*, then *B*'.

By means of generalizations we are able to make inferences, to draw conclusions from what we observe. If *A* is always (or usually) accompanied by *B*, then on observing *A* we can infer the existence of *B* (or the probable existence

of *B*). In this way, we are able to anticipate what is going to happen and to draw conclusions about what has happened in our absence, and we can plan our own future actions and choose intelligently between one action and another, because we know what consequences each of them is likely to have. If someone's mind is well stocked with generalizations, he can make a little observation go a long way, because he knows what can be inferred from it. His eyes may be no better than other people's (they may even be worse), but he can tell at a glance that this footmark was made by a deer, or that there must have been a glacier in this valley thousands of years ago. But the power of inference which generalization gives us is important for another reason as well. It enables us to understand the world, and also, of course, to understand ourselves, if the generalizations are about ourselves. We understand something when it appears to us not as a chaotic jumble, but as an ordered whole, in which our minds can 'find their way about', by noticing that one part or feature can be inferred from other parts or features, and could have been expected to be there even if we had not happened to observe it. This understanding, this comprehending or 'making sense of' what we observe, either in the world around us or in ourselves, is the highest achievement of intelligence.

See also BRAIN; MEMORY.
See also Vol. II: INTELLIGENCE (animal).

INTERIOR DECORATION. The modern trend in decoration is towards simplicity. It aims at something which is pleasant to look at and has character, but is also suitable for the purposes of the room. The great variety of materials now available gives scope for original and interesting effects on quite simple lines.

A scheme of decoration has to be carefully thought out as a whole in relation to the purpose of the room, its proportions, the amount of natural light in it, its fixtures, the character of the furniture available, the carpet, pictures, ornaments, and so on, and also the amount of money that can be spent.

If possible, colours of paint and distemper should be tried out on an inconspicuous part and allowed to dry before judging, as paint or distemper often looks lighter when it is dry. It is important to remember that a colour looks darker when used on a large area than when used in a small quantity, and that a colour on a shade card or sample of material appears brighter when seen in bulk.

Walls, ceilings, floor, or carpet are often made to provide a background for the dominant colours of the scheme, which appear in the curtains, covers, and furnishings of the rooms. Texture as well as colour can be used with effect here; for instance, damask and satin finishes give a lighter impression than velvet or woollen materials, and furnishing tweeds and chintzes will look well with oak furniture, whereas silks, satins, or velvets are more suitable with mahogany or walnut. Lastly, accessories such as cushions or pieces of china or glass may be chosen to link the colour scheme together.

Although personal taste is often the best guide to a satisfying colour scheme, experts have suggested as being warm, shades of yellow, red, and purple, and as cool those of blue and green. By adding grey or white to these, pale tints are produced which still retain the character of the original colour.

There are a limited number of colours and colour contrasts, and success depends on how these are used and combined. An understanding of Colour (q.v. Vol. III) and the relationship of one colour to another is helpful in planning colour schemes. There is a limited number of pigments whose colours are pure, and all colour combinations are based on them. If the twelve main colours are arranged in a circle so that their tones vary from light to dark and back again to light, the colours opposite each other, when mixed together, produce a neutral grey (Fig. 1). These are called contrasting or complementary colours. If a bright, clear colour is chosen as the principal one in a scheme, and used for either carpet or curtains, the other parts of the room can be treated with colours adjoining it in the circle or with paler shades of the same or the contrasting colour. Small amounts of a neighbouring colour can be used, or large amounts of this colour mixed with white, grey, or black, so that it does not compete with the dominant colour. Contrast gives interest and variety, but unless the balance is kept, the effect is restless.

Strong colours and large patterns should be kept for small areas or for large rooms; for instance, a bold patterned wallpaper may be used for one wall with good effect, but would be too overpowering if used for the entire room.

The aspect of a room influences the choice of colour: rooms that face north or north-east need warm colours to give an illusion of sunshine, whereas rooms facing south are best decorated in cool shades. An impression of space can be created in a small room by treating the walls and ceiling in the same shade of a cool colour.

Quiet, restful colours are most suitable for bedrooms, while brighter, more stimulating colours can be used in a kitchen or study. Rooms used only for short periods at a time can stand bolder colour schemes and designs.

There has been recently a great revival in the popularity of Wallpapers (q.v.). Papers and fabrics designed to complement each other, patterned papers alternating with matching plain ones, and papers simulating fabrics or panelling can all produce attractive results.

Several plastic emulsion paints have good covering power and are very opaque. Some can be applied successfully to new plasterwork because the surface is porous and moisture can dry through it. They are useful, therefore, in kitchens and bathrooms where the moisture-absorbing properties help to limit condensation. The mat surface can be washed down most successfully.

Enamel paint gives a varnished finish and is also ideal for kitchens and bathrooms because it can be washed (see Painting and Enamelling).

Other aspects of interior decoration are considered in articles such as Curtains and Wall-hangings, Ornaments, Flower Decoration, and Furniture.

See also Distempering; Painting and Enamelling; Wallpapers, History of.

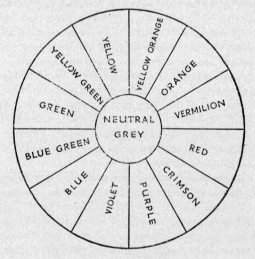

FIG. 1. THE COLOUR CIRCLE

Sommer

PAINTED WALL DECORATION IN THE HOUSE OF THE VETTII, POMPEII

INTERIOR DECORATION, HISTORY OF.

1. Throughout history, as soon as people began to make settled homes, they wished to make their homes beautiful as well as comfortable. When, in more civilized times, houses became more elaborate, the decoration was thought of as a structural feature of the house, wrought in lasting materials, such as stone, marble, wood, glass, stucco, moulded plaster, paint, and metal-work. Details of ornament have been expressed in carving and modelling, inlay and tracery, colouring and gilding, and the total effect often enhanced by mirrors and artificial lighting. The finest and most elaborate forms of interior decoration have usually been carried out by great designers and highly skilled artists and craftsmen for people of wealth and taste. In many countries, however, peasants and farmers have themselves decorated their homes with beautiful carved and painted woodwork and with woven rugs and gay hangings of their own making.

2. ANCIENT WORLD. In Europe, as long ago as 2000 B.C., the walls of Cretan palaces were decorated with beautiful frescoes (*see* Vol. I, p. 318, and Vol. XII, p. 230). In Greece, by about 350 B.C., the finest rooms had painted walls, a fashion adopted, too, by the wealthy Romans of the 1st century B.C., as we can see at POMPEII (q.v. Vol. XII). The walls were sometimes lined with marble, and often painted with realistic pictures of gardens or scenes from legends or with abstract arabesques and other designs. The floors were covered with marble MOSAICS (q.v. Vol. XII) in full colour, with black and white geometric borders. The word *salve* (greeting) or a picture of a dog with *cave canem* (beware the dog) often appeared on the floor near the entrance (*see* Vol. IX, p. 188). The curved ceilings were ornamented with white or coloured stucco designs, small and delicate, and framed in panels with fine mouldings.

3. MIDDLE AGES. After the downfall of Rome in the 5th century there followed in western Europe the period of the DARK AGES (q.v. Vol. I) when domestic life was on a lower level of

N.D. Phot.

CATHERINE DE MEDICI'S ROOM IN THE CHÂTEAU DE BLOIS, FRANCE
The walls and ceiling beams are painted, and the floor is tiled

civilization. Even in eastern Europe the great achievements of BYZANTINE ART (q.v. Vol. XII) were directed towards the glorification of religion rather than of domestic life. In the later Middle Ages, however, decoration again began to appear. The exposed beams in ceilings were painted in bright patterns, and the great stone fireplaces in the halls were carved with devices from HERALDRY (q.v. Vol. IV) and often painted and gilded. In the colder countries of northern Europe the walls were sometimes partly lined with small wood panels, carved with the linen-fold design (*see* Vol. XII, p. 320); sometimes the plain plaster was painted with decorative patterns.

4. RENAISSANCE ITALY. In the 15th and 16th centuries Italian palaces were richly decorated with paintings of mythological subjects inspired by classical Rome and intended to glorify the owners. Walls and vaulted ceilings were painted, or cream walls were hung with Flemish tapestries or lined with decorative woodwork, richly carved or inlaid with ornamental designs in contrasting woods, like a mosaic ('intarsia'). Cool floors were made of marble or tiles, suitable for a hot Mediterranean climate. Italian ideas spread through Europe generally, especially to Spain and Sicily. Some of the later Renaissance palaces had stately marble columns, coloured marble panelling, and wooden ceilings with various shaped panels, sunk in carved borders and painted and gilded. The doors had inlaid panels with marble mouldings round the openings. In many 17th-century palaces, instead of marble columns, panels, balustrades, and great draperies, mural paintings produced these effects (*see* Vol. XII, p. 466). Moulded white and gilded stucco decoration was used for walls and ceilings, with light painted woodwork (*see* BAROQUE ART, Vol. XII). Elaborate chandeliers of gaily coloured Venetian glass hung from the ceilings, and archways leading to courtyards and gardens were filled with decorative wrought ironwork, in graceful designs painted black and picked out with gilding here and there. Increasingly magnificent variations in this manner continued during the 18th century.

5. 17TH- AND 18TH-CENTURY FRANCE. In the 16th century French kings and great nobles began to adopt Italian fashions. The French châteaux of Louis XIV's reign have magnificently painted ceilings, richly panelled and painted walls, often decorated with columns, and floors of marble or parquetry (fine woods in geometric patterns). Huge MIRRORS (q.v.) in carved and gilded frames were placed either between the high windows or opposite them. Large central chandeliers, often Venetian, and carrying hundreds of candles, were supplemented by carved and gilded candle 'branches' arranged on the walls. In the 18th century fine TAPESTRIES (q.v. Vol. VII) from Beauvais and Aubusson, or large paintings, were hung on the walls, and small pictures were fixed in panels over the doors. Low mantelpieces of white, rose, or grey marble were surmounted by large decorative gilt mirrors.

Paul Popper

THE MUSIC ROOM AT SANS-SOUCI PALACE, POTSDAM, GERMANY
The palace was built for Frederick the Great in 1745 in the French Rococo style

In Louis XV's reign fashionable houses were decorated in the fantastic Rococo style (q.v. Vol. XII). Lavish gold ornament on pale backgrounds was used freely and playfully, mostly taking the form of sprays of leaves, garlands of flowers, shells, and flowing ribbons. These decorated the curved tops of doors and windows, ceiling mouldings, and mirror frames. This style was followed towards the end of the 18th century by a more severe style with straight lines everywhere. The simple symmetrical panelling might be painted in delicate, cool colours with arabesques and small figures in classical dress. Rich fabrics were used throughout the century to drape windows at the top and sides. Under Napoleon, many motifs of Egyptian origin, such as sphinxes, were used as ornament following Napoleon's Egyptian campaign. Later in the 19th century, colours tended to become stronger and cruder.

6. THE NETHERLANDS. The early 17th-century houses of Holland and Flanders had tiled floors of black and white marble, dark beamed ceilings which were sometimes painted, and light walls (*see* Vol. XII, p. 117). Brass chandeliers hung from the centre of the ceiling. Later, both in the Netherlands and Germany, people began to copy and adapt French ideas in interior decoration with splendid effects.

7. ENGLAND. Renaissance ideas were gradually introduced into Elizabethan and Jacobean England, pattern books of ornament from the Netherlands often being the source of inspiration. The medieval hall screen, still a common feature in 16th- and early 17th-century houses, was elaborately carved with Renaissance ornament. The walls were lined, almost to the ceiling, with small oak panels, often inlaid (*see* Vol. VII, p. 476) and often with a simple plaster frieze above. Intricate strapwork patterns, sometimes coloured and gilded, decorated the ceilings, and the lead-paned casement windows sometimes had roundels of stained glass, usually coats-of-arms. The balustrade of the main staircase was elaborately carved, the newel posts being crowned with a carved heraldic beast or basket of fruit and flowers. The general effect, however, was much less grand than in Continental houses. In the late 17th century, after the Restoration, rooms were often lined either with figured fabrics or with large oak panels. The very high ceilings in great houses were often decorated with mural painting in the Italian manner, and over the

Victoria and Albert Museum

A MID-18TH-CENTURY ROOM IN NORFOLK HOUSE, ST. JAMES'S SQUARE, LONDON, NOW PULLED DOWN

The walls and ceiling were decorated with moulded plasterwork

mantel an oil painting might be fixed into a framework elaborately carved by Grinling Gibbons or his followers, with realistic fruit and flowers (*see* Vol. V, p. 189). Brass chandeliers were used for candles. Architects, such as William Kent (1684–1748), often designed not only the rooms but also the furniture and decoration. The large, light rooms of the 18th century were sometimes divided up by columns of wood or marble, with fixed mirrors between the tall sash windows, and niches with round carved tops and shaped open shelves to hold fine china, recessed into the panelling on either side of the fireplace.

Robert ADAM (q.v. Vol. V) designed large mirrors to fix above his white or light-coloured marble fireplaces in rooms of coloured plaster, with wood mouldings, also painted white, round the doors and windows. Adam ceilings for grand rooms had a great central oval or circle, with an outline defined by a border in low relief, ornamented with classical motifs such as vases and medallions, with fan shapes filling the corners (*see* Vol. V, p. 3). These were delicately painted, sometimes with dark panels for contrast, and the

carpets often matched the ceilings in design and colour. Wooden floors and CARPETS (q.v.) were more used in England than on the Continent because they are warmer than marble. Although in the houses of the wealthy tapestries might still be hung, wallpaper was coming into use in England, especially in bedrooms, to cover the wall from the dado to the picture rail or cornice. Rooms were lighted by fixed wall-brackets and, in reception rooms, by carved and gilded wood chandeliers of many 'branches' or by 'lustres' of English or Irish cut glass (*see* LIGHTING, HISTORY OF).

Throughout Europe, by the mid-19th century, the classical influence in the interior decoration of houses was fading, whilst the GOTHIC REVIVAL (q.v. Vol. XII) in architecture chiefly affected the exterior of buildings. Indoors there was much less wood panelling, and the walls of rooms were papered from floor to picture rail in large, colourful designs. The white, plain ceilings were edged with small moulded cornices and had central designs, usually of foliage, from which hung the new 'gasoliers' with their white glass globes. The dining-room was usually sombre, with a low, black marble fireplace. In the drawing-room, the fireplace, often tiled, was set in a wood frame, and surmounted by a mirror overmantel with many little shelves on small carved brackets. Simple parquet flooring was used, or linoleum as a cheap substitute. In the later part of the 19th century William MORRIS (q.v. Vol. V) and his followers produced a style of their own, with light and graceful woodwork, daintily patterned WALLPAPERS and FURNISHING MATERIALS (qq.v.), and sometimes a little coloured glass of floral designs in windows.

The extreme simplicity of MODERN ARCHITECTURE (q.v. Vol. XII) was echoed in very simple interiors of the 1920s and 1930s, with hardly any decoration. Fireplaces were plain, low, and flat, often without a mantelshelf. Doors of laminated wood had flush surfaces and were fitted with glass fingerplates and chromium-plated bar handles. The total effect, with painted or distempered walls and concealed electric lighting behind glass-shaded wall or ceiling fittings, was almost severe, and was further enhanced by the fashionable 'off-white' colouring in furnishing fabrics.

Since the Second World War new ideas in decoration have been spreading, chiefly from Scandinavia. These include patterned wallpapers in gay, light colours, with colour applied also to the woodwork. Kitchens and bathrooms are gay, with white or coloured enamelled tiling or washable paint and special types of rubber or synthetic flooring, plain or patterned. Individual electric lamps about the room tend to replace the central pendant, and large sheets of mirror glass are sometimes used to increase the apparent size of very small rooms or corridors.

The old idea of incorporating permanent decoration in the building of the house has given way to the new fashion of transforming plain walls by applying wallpaper or paint, and relying to a much greater degree on colour alone for effect (see Colour Plate, opp. p. 256).

See also HOUSES, HISTORY OF; FURNITURE, HISTORY OF. See also Vol. XII: DESIGN; INDUSTRIAL ART; ORNAMENT.

INTESTINES, see DIGESTIVE SYSTEM.

INVALID COOKERY. In planning and cooking meals for invalids it should be remembered that careful feeding can hasten recovery by helping to restore wasted tissues, that the patient's appetite needs to be stimulated, particularly by serving attractive food with the greatest possible variety, and that, as the patient's digestion is frequently impaired, food must be chosen which is easily digested. It is best to choose fresh food of a kind which does not place a heavy load on the DIGESTIVE SYSTEM (q.v.), and to cook it by a method which helps digestion; frying is not suitable. The protective and the protein foods are best for rebuilding tissues, and the patient needs more of these than of the energy-giving fats and carbohydrates (see FOOD VALUES). Foods, such as beef tea, which stimulate the digestive juices are useful. Meals should be served on an attractive tray with fresh linen, pretty china, and shining glass; the patient should not be given too big helpings; and the tray should be removed as soon as the meal is finished.

The kind of food to be served depends on the stage of the patient's illness. When the patient is at the acute stage, possibly with a high temperature, the diet is either entirely fluid, consisting of milk, fruit drinks, soups, light broths, and gruel; or mainly fluid but including, perhaps, egg custards and thin bread and butter. When the acute stage is over, all the cook's skill is needed to serve temptingly what is known as a light diet. The following foods are suitable: white fish, such as plaice, sole, and whiting (but not oily fish such as herrings); chicken; tripe if the patient likes it; eggs, either by themselves or incorporated with other ingredients as in custards, sponges, and ice cream; fruit; milk puddings; creams; and young vegetables, particularly cauliflower and spinach because they have less coarse fibre. Meat, if served at all, is suitable only when short fibred, as in lamb chop, and is cooked by steaming. Pastry and puddings are not suitable, nor are coffee and cocoa. China tea rather than Indian should be served, as it contains less tannin. When the patient becomes convalescent, but with a digestion and appetite not yet normal, it is necessary to ensure that he derives full value from his food by giving him what he enjoys, by avoiding the heavier indigestible foods containing a great deal of fat, and by making his progress towards a normal diet a gradual one.

See also HOME NURSING.

J

JAM. Any kind of fruit squashed, or 'jammed', and preserved by boiling with sugar is jam. The term 'conserve' implies that the fruit is kept whole and not squashed. Marmalade, usually sliced, is made from citrus fruits; but *marmellata* in Italy and *marmelade* in Germany mean any kind of jam, as do the French *confiture* and the Spanish *conserva*.

The principles underlying successful jam-making are few and simple but important. As many old-fashioned recipes give mistaken advice, only up-to-date books, such as the Bulletin on Food Preservation issued by the Ministry of Agriculture and Fisheries, should be followed. The jellying substance, called 'pectin', is present in small quantities in almost all fruits but more abundantly in acid and under-ripe ones. Lemons and sour apples make the stiffest jam, ripe strawberries the runniest. Fruits which are over-ripe or naturally deficient in pectin can be jelled by adding apple, red currant, or lemon juice, or commercially prepared pectin. To jell effectively, the pectin must be in a sufficiently acid solution and must have the help of sufficient sugar. It tends to lose its powers if the initial boiling is too long. The cellulose fibres of the fruit cell walls must be thoroughly softened by preliminary boiling in water without sugar, so that the fruit is tender and the sugar, when added, can penetrate easily. Only very soft fruits, conserves, and the sticky kinds of marmalade should be boiled with sugar straightaway; hard fruits treated in this way end up as tough, shrunken pieces in treacly syrup.

After the sugar goes in, the jam sets better, is brighter in colour, and tastes more fruity if it is boiled rapidly. The proportion of sugar to fruit varies between $\frac{1}{2}$ lb.: 1 lb. for a sweet fruit, and 1 lb.: 1 lb: for sour fruit; less sugar will do if the jam is to be eaten up quickly. Scum is not 'impurities'; it is merely a jam and air foam. It often disappears at the end of cooking, and if any remains it can either be left on or skimmed off and given to children, who generally clamour to eat it. A nut of butter will discourage it from forming.

A proper preserving pan, a big, thick pot, or a pressure saucepan should be used for making jam. For storage, 1-lb. glass jars are best for the small family; they should be scrupulously clean, dry, and warm so that they do not crack when the boiling jam is poured in. Cellophane circles, sterilized in water and snapped on with rubber rings, are the handiest seals, and have the advantage that one can see through to tell whether the jam is keeping properly. Waxed circles on the surface of the jam are not really necessary. The fruit for jam should be picked over and washed if necessary. Cored fruits should be peeled and cut up; the stones in the plum type of fruit can be left until the boiling stage when they are lifted out with a perforated spoon, and the kernels are extracted and put into the jam to add to its flavour. The prepared fruit should be weighed, and as much water added as the recipe directs. It is then simmered gently until quite tender—from 5 minutes for raspberries to 1 hour or more for hard pears. The sugar is then added and the mixture boiled rapidly to setting-point. Setting-point can be tested by putting a little on a saucer and tilting it; when it wrinkles it is ready. After the jam has been cooled slightly to ensure an even distribution of the fruit, the warm jars are filled, wiped, and covered up at once.

Combinations of soft and hard fruits, such as elderberry, rowan, or blackberry with apple, or rhubarb with fig and lemon, are often cheaper and better than plain kinds. A combination of sloes, the fruit of blackthorn, and blackberries—1 lb. sloes to 4 lb. blackberries—is very successful.

To make marmalade, the fruit is weighed, scrubbed, skinned in sections, and the flesh cut up The pips, which are rich in pectin, are reserved and soaked separately. The skin is sliced or minced, and then soaked with the flesh in water for 36 to 48 hours. After the whole mixture has been simmered gently until very tender, the sugar is added—usually about 1 lb.: 1 lb.—and the marmalade made in the same way as jam. Orange marmalade, which is Scottish in origin, is traditionally brown, bitter, and thick made from Seville and Poorman oranges, which are available in the early spring. Out-of-season marmalade is made preferably with lemons, but sweet oranges and grapefruit can be used.

Jelly can be made only from fruits rich in both pectin and acid, and as both decrease with ripening, slightly under-ripe fruit should be used. Sour apples, red currants, green gooseberries, crab apples, black currants, plums, quinces, sour blackberries, sour guavas, rowanberries, loganberries, and citrus fruits make good jelly. The fruit is picked over and washed; soft berries are crushed in a big pan, and other fruits cut in pieces, leaving out imperfect bits but including skin and cores, as these are full of pectin. A cup of water is added to each 5 lb. of soft fruit; other kinds are barely covered with water. The fruit is boiled rapidly in a covered pan until soft, and then put to strain through a jelly bag or linen cheese cloth hung by tapes from hooks or two chair backs, and left to drip all night. The juice is boiled up, the sugar is added (1 lb. of sugar to 1 pint of juice), and the mixture boiled to setting point. A second extraction may be made by transferring the pulp to the pan without squeezing it, barely covering it with cold water, and boiling it for about 10–15 minutes. This is then strained and either added to the first extraction or used separately.

The boiled pulp, especially that of quinces, pears, or damsons, may be sieved instead of strained in order to make an opaque 'cheese'. Apple butter is sieved apple, sweetened rather more than for a pudding, flavoured with butter and lemon rind or spices, and served lukewarm.

JAUNDICE, *see* DIGESTIVE SYSTEM.

JELLIES AND ASPICS. The shine of meat glazes, the lustrous glassiness of moulded jellies, and the soft foaminess of mousses and some ice creams owe their attractive appearance to the variety of textures imparted by gel-forming substances. The most familiar of these is gelatine, a protein similar to glue, extracted from animal skin, tendons, and ligaments by long boiling. The bones of many fish, too (eels, for example), are rich in gelatine. The best quality gelatine is made in France as a by-product of the kid glove industry; it is sold in thin, transparent sheets and is almost tasteless. Gelatine is also available in powdered form, which is easier to measure. Inferior kinds often have a nasty

FISH IN ASPIC

gluey taste, difficult to disguise. The good cook can make her own gelatine from calves' and pigs' feet and bones, and she will use this, for example, for glazing a tongue. But she cannot purify this jelly sufficiently at home to make it palatable in sweet dishes, so its use is confined to savoury jellies or aspics. Aspics (from the French *espic*, 'spikenard', one of the old herbs used to flavour savoury jellies) may enclose chicken, lobster, shrimps, or prawns, hard-boiled eggs, salmon, truffles, and diced vegetables.

The best sweet jellies are made at home from gelatine and sugar dissolved in fresh fruit juice, wine, cider, or milk, the proportion varying according to the quality of the gelatine, but usually about 1 ounce of gelatine to 1 quart of liquid. Packet jellies are labour-saving and reasonably satisfactory, but the artificial flavour-

FRUIT AND SPONGE JELLY

ings and colours are less pleasing than those of home-made products and the jelly has a lower food value. Jelly is not without nutritional value, as is often said; made from good materials it is comparable with soup. The gelatine lacks the essential body-building elements, but it gives a small amount of very digestible second class protein (*see* FOOD VALUES, Section 2), while the fruit juice is protective (*see* VITAMINS). Perhaps its chief value is as a stimulating vehicle for other foods.

Isinglass (from the German *Hausenblase*, 'sturgeon's bladder') is a very pure form of gelatine obtained from the swim bladder of certain fish: Russian isinglass from the sturgeon and sterlet, Brazilian isinglass from the catfish. Formerly, isinglass was widely used for making moulded jellies; nowadays its principal use is for clearing wines and beer.

Gel-forming substances from plants include the mucilage (gummy fluid) of the seaweed carrageen or Irish moss which, when sunbleached and boiled in milk, yields a delicate blancmange rich in iodine and potassium salts. Agar agar, which also comes from seaweed, is used in the food industry as a cheap substitute for gelatine (1 ounce jells a gallon of water).

Starch, which swells in water and forms a gel, is suitable for making rigid jellies as well as for thickening purposes. Potato starch, cornflour, and arrowroot form very stiff starch gels used for blancmange-type sweets and for the Continental sweet made with red currant and raspberry juices, known in Germany as *Rote Grütze*, or red gruel. Pectin, the gel-forming substance in fruit, is discussed in the article JAM.

See also Vol. VII: SUGAR CONFECTIONERY.

JEWELLERY, HISTORY OF.

Primitive man had the same delight in bright and shining objects as a child has, and long before history began he must have treasured natural 'precious stones' found in the bed of a river, or have taken back with him to his cave a piece of quartz brightly gleaming with gold (*see* Vol. III, Colour Plate, opp. p. 288). To his mind jewels, however crude, were magical things, protectors against disease and the 'evil eye'. Whether he first wore jewels as charms and then grew to like them as ornaments, or whether he wore them first for decoration and then bestowed magical significance on them is still debated by anthropologists. Perhaps the two aspects cannot

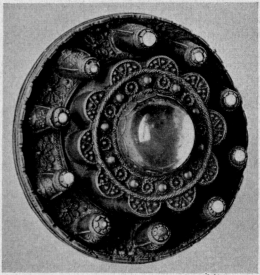

British Museum

THE LOCH BUY BROOCH, 16TH CENTURY
Made of silver, set with rock crystal and pearls

be entirely divided. We still, today, speak of mascots and of 'lucky' (or even 'unlucky') precious stones.

In any case we find jewellery as soon as we find civilization. Fine ornaments of gold, and sometimes of jewels, have been found at Ur of the Chaldees, the Biblical home of Abraham (*see* Vol. XII, p. 444), in Crete, in ancient Egypt (*see* Vol. XII, p. 126), and, indeed, wherever any degree of culture existed. Ear-rings, bracelets, and gold chains of 2900 B.C. or earlier have been found in excavations on the site of Troy. The Greeks were not much addicted to personal adornment; the Romans, under oriental influence, made more use of precious or semiprecious stones (*see* ANCIENT CIVILIZATIONS, Vol. I).

After the fall of the Roman Empire the outlying provinces developed their own styles founded on Roman models. The Franks, the Scandinavians, and the Celts have each their characteristic types.

To come nearer to our own time and our own country: visitors to the Ashmolean Museum at Oxford can see King Alfred's Jewel, found near the Isle of Athelney which he defended so stoutly from the Danes. It is a beautiful piece of cloisonné enamel in a gold fret with the words: *Aelfred Mec Heht Gewyrcan*, which means 'Alfred had me made' (*see* Vol. V, p. 11).

It is fortunate that by the time the custom of

burying jewels with the dead, and so preserving them for posterity, began to fall out of use, sculpture and paintings were being produced in increasing numbers, and these give us some notion of what grand people wore in the Middle Ages. One of the most characteristic medieval jewels is the ring brooch, which now survives only in Highland dress. The splendid Loch Buy brooch of silver, set with rock crystal and pearls, with a large central crystal filling the hole in the ring, is a typical example dating from the 16th century. Pearls used then to be found in Scottish rivers in sufficient quantities to export, and the statutes of the Parisian goldsmiths (1355) ordain that 'no goldsmith shall set in gold or silver Scottish pearls with Eastern ones, except in great jewellery work for the churches'.

It was, of course, chiefly in royal courts that the medieval jeweller found employment. There still survives, in the museum at Munich, the beautiful jewelled crown worn by Blanche, daughter of Henry IV of England, at her marriage in 1402 to the Elector Ludwig III. It is formed of twelve medallions of delicate tracery, from which greater and lesser pinnacles rise alternately. Equally elaborate was the crowned head-dress worn in 1476 by Margaret of Denmark, Queen of Scotland. Her picture by van der Goes is at Holyrood, but the actual jewelled head-dress has not survived.

The Burgundian treasure of Charles the Bold of Burgundy included some famous gems, one of the most remarkable of which was a jewel set with three great rubies called 'The Three Brothers'. Charles the Bold lost it when he was killed in battle in 1477, and it later came into the possession of Henry VIII. At the same battle Charles the Bold lost another stone, now known as the Sancy diamond because it was picked up on the battlefield by a Swiss soldier, who sold it to a French nobleman named Sancy. Henry III of France subsequently borrowed it to help pay his debts, and 100 years later it came into the possession of James II of England, who had it in his pocket when he fled from London into exile: that is why it became part of the French instead of the English crown jewels. It was lost during the French Revolution and turned up in the possession of a Russian Grand Duke. It now belongs to an Indian prince. So extraordinary can be the history of a single jewel.

The Renaissance brought in a different kind of jewellery altogether, based on classical motifs

National Bavarian Museum

BRIDAL CROWN WORN BY BLANCHE, DAUGHTER OF HENRY IV, AT HER MARRIAGE TO LUDWIG III IN 1402

By gracious permission of H.M. the Queen

CROWNED HEAD-DRESS OF MARGARET OF DENMARK, QUEEN OF SCOTLAND

Detail of a painting by Hugo van der Goes, 1476

National Portrait Gallery

ELIZABETH OF BOHEMIA, 1596–1662

She wears pearls given her by James I. Painting by
M. J. Van Miereveldt

Versailles Museum

THE EMPRESS JOSEPHINE

Painting by F. Gérard, 1770–1837

and more personal to the wearer. Sometimes the initials of a name were wrought of gold encrusted with diamonds. Henry VIII had such a jewel with the initials H and K for himself and Katharine of Aragon.

The 16th century delighted in pearls, especially in the large mis-shapen ones known as 'baroque pearls'. In a splendid example, the 'Canning Jewel' (*see* Colour Plate, opp. p. 224), the baroque pearl forms the body of a merman, and the rest of the design is carried out in enamelled gold. Queen Elizabeth I bought for £3,000 (an enormous sum in those days) the wonderful collection of pearls which Mary Queen of Scots had acquired in France. James I, who inherited them, bestowed them on his daughter when she married the Elector Palatine of the Rhine; they can be seen in a great cable across her bosom in Van Miereveldt's picture in the National Portrait Gallery, London.

In the 17th century jewellery became more delicate but less interesting. Jewellers were increasingly skilful in cutting stones, especially diamonds, and they used much smaller settings, often a mere claw to hold the stone in place. The marvellous blends of gold and enamel familiar to a previous age were no longer valued, and people became less reluctant to break up an old setting. Indeed, it is only by an old engraving that we can form an idea of the most famous necklace in history, that of Marie Antoinette, which consisted of a double strand of diamonds. One strand formed a tight necklace of seventeen large brilliants from which hung three festoons and four pendants of diamonds; from the larger strand hung four tassels of the same stones.

Napoleon's wife, the Empress Josephine, was as fond of jewels as Marie Antoinette. In Gérard's portrait painted in 1803, now in the museum at Versailles, she is shown wearing a crown set with diamonds and pearls of prodigious size, equally large pearl pendants in her ears, and round her neck a splendid necklace of pearls, diamonds, and sapphires. The décolleté fashion of the day sets off this superb set of gems to perfection.

The styles of the Napoleonic era did not admit of much jewellery being worn on the dress itself, but with the craze for imitating the dress of the Ancient World went a new fashion for cameos. Antique cameos were successfully imitated and were worn as brooches or on bracelets. A curious fashion for cast-iron jewellery originated in Berlin in the early years of the century, a movement which was encouraged by the demand made on German ladies to sacrifice their gold ornaments in order to finance the campaign against Napoleon. In the 1820s and 1830s amethysts, topazes, aquamarines, and such gems became popular, especially in England, where they were worn rather large in settings which were beginning to be stamped out by machinery. After 1820 there was a passion for naturalistic imitations of flowers and fruits, reaching its climax in the early '50s. The Court of the Second Empire, under Napoleon III and the Empress Eugénie, made a deliberate attempt to revive the glories and the fashions of the 18th century. About this time less exalted persons began to make increasing use of what is known as 'costume jewellery', that is, pieces of no intrinsic value in themselves, using the paste diamond and the imitation pearl, which form part of the general effectiveness of the costume. The styles were derived from earlier modes, especially those of the Renaissance and Gothic periods. In the Great Exhibition of 1851 there was even a bracelet 'in imitation of the Sculptures of Nineveh'.

Towards the end of the 19th century, especially after the opening of the South African diamond mines, the precious stone became increasingly important and the setting of less account. Diamonds, for example, were valued for themselves, quite apart from any beauty of setting. Often they were considered merely as investments to be kept in the bank, while imitations were worn in their place. Today most jewellery is 'costume jewellery' of little intrinsic value, a mere part of the dress it adorns, and unlikely to survive the fashion of the dress.

See also COSTUME, HISTORY OF.
See also Vol. III: PRECIOUS STONES.
See also Vol. VI: PEARL FISHING.
See also Vol. VII: JEWELLERY TRADE; GOLD AND SILVER WORK; DIAMOND INDUSTRY; ENAMEL.

JUGS AND VESSELS. For drinking, primitive peoples have generally used natural objects, such as gourds (with a straw or pipe), and coconuts, horns, or shells. More civilized peoples have often copied these natural shapes, for example, the Frankish glass drinking-horns, or have enriched the objects themselves, for example, the early Renaissance silver-mounted

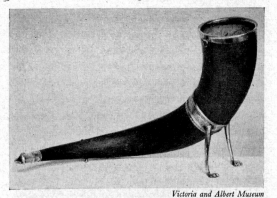

Victoria and Albert Museum
THE PUSEY HORN, MOUNTED IN SILVER GILT
English, early 15th century

coconuts and shells. Prehistoric potters developed various shapes for their earthenware drinking-vessels, and since then a great variety of materials have been used—metal, glass, wood, leather, porcelain, plastic, and others. Jugs, with a handle on one side and a pouring lip opposite, have usually been either the tall-necked 'ewer', or the rounder 'pitcher'. Storage jars for wine and oil were known in the Bronze Age; jars used for fetching and storing water often had movable top handles for use when dipping at the well. 'Crocks' for storing eggs preserved in waterglass are still used, especially in country places.

The ancient Egyptians had beautiful cups and bowls of carved granite or alabaster and enamelled pottery; and the Chinese were making fine porcelain bowls and handleless cups from A.D. 600 onwards. In Crete and the eastern Mediterranean countries, as early as 2000 B.C., cups with one graceful handle were used; these were usually of cream-coloured pottery, decorated in red ochre and black (see Vol. XII, p. 229). Others were of gold or bronze (see Vol. I, p. 329), and so, too, were the beakers (tallish cups without handles). Huge pottery jars with short, wide necks were used for storage, and these 'amphorae' had two loop handles on the body through which ropes for carrying them were passed. The Greeks used these and also various pottery or metal cups or bowls for wine. Both the Greeks and the Romans served the wine from tall-necked ewers.

In the early Middle Ages the peoples of northern Europe, who drank mead and ale, used metal or glass cups, or cow-horns sometimes 2 feet long and mounted in silver. In medieval

British Museum

Victoria and Albert Museum

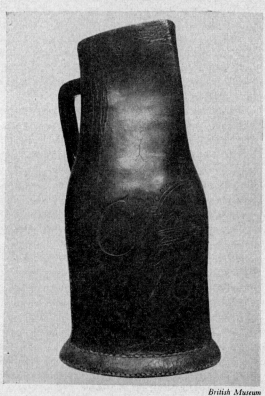

British Museum

Victoria and Albert Museum

Above, left: THE ROYAL GOLD CUP
English 'hanap' of enamelled gold, made about 1380

Above, right: THE CROMWELL MAZER
Made in England of maple wood mounted in silver-gilt,
15th century

Below, left: RHENISH TIGER-WARE JUG, WITH ENGLISH
SILVER-GILT MOUNTS, 16TH CENTURY

Below, right: ENGLISH LEATHER BLACK JACK, WITH INITIALS
OF CHARLES II AND DATE 1646

Europe grape, damson, or currant wine was drunk from wood bowls ('mazers') and cups, and beer, ale, and cider from tall horn or pewter tankards, which were cylindrical mugs with a hinged lid and handle, often with pegs inside to mark the measures. Another kind of drinking-vessel was the ceremonial loving cup, used at feasts; it had two or more handles by which it was easily passed round. The covered standing cup ('hanap'), which was offered to the distinguished guest in princely households, was made of precious metal, often enriched with enamelling or gems. Other standing cups were of wood, and sometimes had spice-boxes fitted into the domed cover or decorative flat roundels in the base for holding fruit and sweetmeats. In most houses there were also simple pottery cups and jugs, in plain grey, green, buff, or yellow, usually decorated with ornaments such as tiny clay rosettes or stars. The more elaborate 'tiger-ware' jugs and others came from the Rhineland. The Germans made 'greybeard' pottery beer-mugs and also silver mugs shaped like heraldic animals with a detachable head as a cup. In the 16th and 17th centuries glass from Venetian and other factories began to be used more generally and some of its shapes copied in other materials. In the late 17th century two-handled silver cups, or 'porringers', perhaps with lids and standing on little trays, were used for caudle and posset (thin gruel or milk mixed with spice or wine). The huge leather 'black-jack' ale-jugs, with incised initials and date, were made only in England.

In the late 17th century, when the new HOT DRINKS (q.v.), tea, coffee, and chocolate, became fashionable, Chinese porcelain dishes were imported in large quantities. The cups in early tea services were made without handles, and people spoke of having a 'dish' of tea—not a 'cup'. By the early 18th century complete tea and coffee services were being made in Europe, and special cups for chocolate, with two handles and a cover, set in grooved saucers (see Vol. XII,

Royal Scottish Museum

SILVER QUAICH MADE IN EDINBURGH, 1685

p. 101). Silver or pottery stirrup-cups, used for drinking on horse-back, were made in the shape of a dog's or fox's head, while handleless cups of wood or silver were made in sets to accompany wassail and punch bowls. The Staffordshire 'Toby' jug, in the form of an old man with a three-cornered hat, was another traditional shape. Glass water 'carafes' and wine decanters were used at table; wine bottles were placed in tubs ('wine-coolers') of decorative pottery or inlaid wood lined with lead. In Scotland the 'quaich' (a shallow silver-mounted bowl with two ear-shaped handles) was used for drinking whisky; and in the Victorian period, pottery 'barrels' with taps and labelled for brandy, whisky, and so on, were often to be seen on side-boards. Most Victorians also possessed a traveller's flask for spirits, a small, flat, glass bottle in a tight case, part leather, part metal, the latter part forming a removable cup.

In the 20th century 'vacuum' flasks were invented for keeping hot or iced liquids at an even temperature until required. Now there are stoppered vacuum jugs of bright-coloured plastic lined with glass, and accompanied by a set of matching plastic beakers. The modern metal cocktail 'shaker' is often a composite article, containing in its tall, round body three glass bottles for the mixing of wines and spirits, and fitted with a hollow screw top making space for a lemon and a nest of beakers.

See also TABLE GLASS; TABLE DISHES.
See also Vol. VII: PORCELAIN; POTTERY.

K

KIDNEYS. The two kidneys are arranged one each side of the backbone in the lumbar region (*see* p. 6). Their main function is to preserve the normal composition of the BLOOD (q.v.). They do this by removing from the blood the waste products of the living cells which it has collected on its way, and any surplus water and acid.

The blood passes through the kidneys, entering by the renal artery, which comes straight off the main artery of the body, the aorta. After the kidney has done its work the blood leaves it by the renal vein (*see* BLOOD CIRCULATION). The water and waste products (including urea and uric acid) are collected in the central cavity of the kidney and passed as urine down the 'ureter',

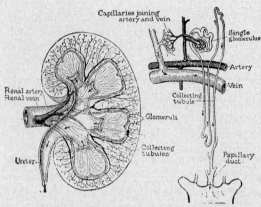

FIG. 2. SECTION OF THE KIDNEY AND DIAGRAM OF A SINGLE TUBULE

Figs. 1 and 2 from Logan Clendening, *The Human Body*, Alfred Knopf

a duct which leads them on to the bladder. From there they are at intervals excreted from the body.

When the renal artery enters the kidney, it fans out into finer and finer branches, called 'arterioles', which are visible only under a microscope. These arterioles break up into the smallest blood-vessels of all, the capillaries. Tufts of capillaries form glomeruli in the thick outer rind or 'cortex' of the kidney. Each glomerulus pushes into the cup-shaped ending of a renal 'tubule' (microscopic tube) which runs a twisting course through the kidney, finally reaching the central cavity, or 'pelvis'. A glomerulus and tubule together form a 'nephron', and there are normally some 2 million nephrons in each kidney.

When the blood is brought to the kidney, it flows into the glomerulus, where some of it filters through the membrane into the tubule. This filtration holds back only the proteins of the blood; otherwise the fluid which passes through is still the same as blood plasma. In the tubule the fluid is concentrated some ninety times by the re-absorption of water, mineral salts, and glucose, so that these are maintained at a normal level in the blood.

See also BLOOD.

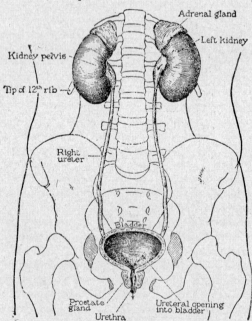

FIG. I. THE POSITION OF THE KIDNEYS, URETERS, AND BLADDER IN THE MALE

KITCHEN DESIGN AND ARRANGEMENT. The kitchen, where meals are prepared, cooked, and served, must be equipped to carry out these three tasks as efficiently as possible. In early kitchens there was an open fire for cooking (*see* COOKING STOVES), a table for preparation work, and a dresser for storing utensils. In time, the range replaced the open fire, and as MEALS (q.v.) became more complicated, more utensils were used and stored in the kitchen. In many small houses the kitchen was, and still is, the centre of the home, being used as a living-room and dining-room as well. In larger houses, particularly in Victorian England, the kitchen, often in the basement, was the domain of the servants, which was separated from the rest of the house by green baize doors. Little thought was given to making it convenient or labour-saving, for DOMESTIC SERVICE (q.v.) was cheap and easy to obtain. It was generally a large room equipped with a large cooking range, table, dresser, cupboards, and larder; and a sink with cold water was in a separate scullery. It was often situated far from the dining-room, so that serving-maids had to carry food a long way; though sometimes basement kitchens were provided with a hand-operated lift. Many houses with these basement kitchens are still in use today, but in most cases the basements are now used for storage, and a room on the ground floor has been converted into a modern kitchen.

Apart from the preparation, cooking, and washing up of meals, the modern kitchen is often used for washing and ironing clothes, and for other household tasks such as cleaning silver. In many homes, too, meals, especially breakfast, are eaten in the kitchen because it is warm and convenient. Today, when most housewives run their homes with little or no domestic help, kitchens are planned carefully with all these points in mind. Indeed, in such countries as Canada, U.S.A., Australia, New Zealand, and Sweden, where domestic labour has never been as plentiful, kitchens have, for long, been more efficiently planned than in Britain.

(a) *Size and Shape.* If the kitchen is too large, the cook has to cover an unnecessary amount of ground in doing much of her work; if it is too small, it will become congested. It should be large enough to allow all the equipment to be conveniently installed and operated, and still provide an adequate working area. The shape is also important, a rectangular kitchen being more convenient than a square one, provided that it is wide enough to allow two persons to pass comfortably. In Britain 100 square feet is considered to be a satisfactory overall area for a working-kitchen for a household of 4–6 persons, and 150 square feet for a dining-kitchen. The

Council of Industrial Design

A MODERN KITCHEN

The working surface is under the window between the cooker and sink. A refrigerator is built in on the right

kitchen should not be a main traffic route of the house. At the most there should be only two doors, one leading to the rest of the house and the other to the back yard, and the route from one to the other should not cross through the working area.

(b) *Arrangement.* Equipment should be so arranged in the kitchen that there is a natural sequence from one operation to the next, with no unnecessary steps. There should be three main work centres for (i) preparation and cooking, (ii) washing-up, and (iii) the preparation of pastry and other baked goods. These three should be arranged near to each other, preferably with the washing-up unit between the cooking centre and the baking centre and easily accessible from either. The linking of these centres by the working-bench in a continuous unbroken line makes not only for efficiency but for easy cleaning. The ideal arrangement for meal preparation and cooking is to have a working-bench on either side of the cooker for preparation and dishing-up, with cupboards and shelves in the walls above and under the bench, so planned that they hold ready to hand the ingredients and utensils needed in cooking operations. The washing-up unit should consist of one, or preferably two, sinks, with a draining-board on one side, and a bench to take the crockery before washing on the other. As the washing-up centre is also used for vegetable preparation, convenient arrangements for the disposal of refuse and for the storage of vegetables are necessary. The centre used for preparing baked food must contain the working-bench, with adjoining cupboards and shelves for storing all utensils and commodities needed in baking.

The only way to obtain a continuous unbroken line between the three work centres is to place the equipment and working-benches along the wall. Consequently, the centre table is disappearing from the modern kitchen, though it is still useful in homes where children eat or play in the kitchen.

Meals served at a table conveniently placed in the kitchen not only simplify the work of serving and clearing away but also make for economy in heating. Even where kitchen-dining-rooms are used, however, it is usual to serve meals in the dining-room on formal occasions; therefore it is important to consider the relation of the kitchen to the dining-room. A hatch connecting them is convenient, with drawers and cupboards for glass, china, cutlery, and linen set in the walls above, below, and at the sides of the hatch, and opening into both rooms. The ideal position for the hatch is between the cooking and washing-up centres, when it is useful both for serving meals and clearing them away. Indeed, unless the hatch is conveniently placed so that it is not necessary to use a tray, its usefulness is much reduced. Again, the shelves and drawers for the china and cutlery should be near enough to the draining-board to dispense with a tray. A trolley is frequently used today, both for serving and clearing away meals; but in small kitchens a convenient parking place for the trolley is not easy to find.

(c) *Lighting and Ventilation.* Good natural lighting and well-placed artificial lighting points are important at all working-benches, at the cooker (both in the oven and on top), and also at the sink. Two points about ventilation must be remembered: firstly, steam, smells, and heat from cooking must be able to escape from the kitchen, preferably through windows, but if this is impossible by an extractor fan at a key point; secondly, the smells of cooking must not escape to other parts of the house, which will happen if the cooker is placed in such a relation to the exit doors that a natural current of air carries the smells through the communicating door.

If the kitchen is used for washing and ironing, or for storage of cleaning equipment, the cupboards to hold the necessary apparatus can usually be placed so as not to interfere with the main work centres. If a washing-machine is used, and there is no separate washing-room with drying facilities, a place must be allotted to it near to the sink.

KITCHEN UTENSILS. As new methods of cooking and intricate recipes have developed, utensils have been invented to carry them out. Also, much small kitchen equipment has been devised to lessen as far as possible the work of the cook. It is a false economy to buy inferior utensils, for not only do those of good quality last much longer, but they prove much more satisfactory in use.

1. CUTLERY. A kitchen needs tea, dessert, and table spoons of standard size and also one or two wooden spoons. There should be vegetable and palette knives, and cutting knives of various lengths with good edges which can be easily sharpened and handles which are comfortable to hold. A palette knife is blunt, with a flexible blade which will spring back to its original shape when released from pressure. Forks, scissors, a flexible fish slice of a suitable shape, and a rubber scraper mounted on a wooden handle are also needed.

2. PANS. When choosing pans, it is wise to

London-Aluminium Co. Ltd.

ALUMINIUM PANS WITH THICK MACHINE-TURNED BOTTOMS FOR USE ON ELECTRIC COOKERS

The group includes saucepans, a double saucepan, kettle, deep fish fryer, frying pan, and egg poacher

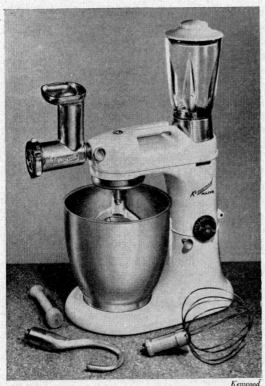

AN ELECTRIC MIXING MACHINE

Different attachments are used to mix, beat, or blend mixtures of varying consistencies in the bowl. Above is a mincer on the left and a pulverizer on the right. The black switch controls the speed

Kenwood

select those with well-designed handles which are comfortable to hold and do not get over-heated during use. Pans with sharp corners inside where the sides and bottom meet are difficult to clean. A lip for pouring is a convenience. Today, aluminium pans are widely used because they are hardwearing, strong, and resistant to moisture, acids, and alkalis. They are not, however, as easy to clean as enamel or stainless steel pans, for they blacken readily when hard water is boiled in them, and have a tendency to become pitted in use. For use on electric stoves with solid hot plates, ground base pans are essential. Stainless steel pans, with copper-clad bases which make them better conductors, are satisfactory but expensive. Other satisfactory materials for pans are iron, lined with tin, enamel, or a silicate; copper with a tin lining; monel metal (a copper nickel alloy); or heat-proofed glass.

3. Tins and Fireproof Dishes. Baking sheets, cake tins, flan rings, and pastry cutters are usually made of tin-plate, though an increasing number today are being made of aluminium. Stainless steel is also used, but it is very expensive. Baking sheets should be heavy enough not to buckle in use. The best cake tins, flan rings, and cutters have wired edges for strength, and the cutters should have smooth joins so that they will cut clean. Dishes to be used in the oven must be heat-resisting, and are therefore made of fireproof pottery or glass ovenware.

4. Mechanical Devices for beating, kneading, grating, and sieving save the housewife's time and energy. They may be hand operated, as are the mincer, the egg whisk, the coffee grinder, and the Continental *moulin* which will grate, shred, and sieve; or they may be driven by an electric motor, as is the mixing machine. The latter is designed primarily for mixing, creaming, and whisking, but models can be bought with attachments which make them able to perform any of the following operations: mincing, grating, shredding, slicing, chipping, coffee-grinding, sieving; making sausages, purées, or ice creams; extracting juice; or peeling potatoes. The mixing operation is performed in one of two ways: either the mixing attachment rotates in a planetary fashion in a stationary bowl, or the bowl rotates, and the mixing action is performed by interaction between the wooden dolly and scraper and the moving sides of the bowl.

5. Other Utensils. Bowls, basins, measures, and lemon-squeezers are easy to choose, but graters, whisks, and tin-openers need more careful choice to ensure that they are easy to clean and to operate. Sieves, strainers, colanders, and salad baskets should be of rust-proof material. Measuring-cups and weighing-scales are also needed, spring balances being more satisfactory than those using weights.

See also Cleaning Equipment.

KNITTING. In the small Arab state of Yemen it is said that knitting has been known for ever, and that the pattern on the serpent's back was knitted by Eve. The craft of knitting spread from Arabia along the trade routes to Tibet and through the Mediterranean to Europe in the early centuries A.D. It does not seem to have been known in China or India until later, when it reached those countries, and also Africa and America, from Europe. A beautiful piece of Arabian knitting in red and gold silk of about the 8th century, and a pair of Egyptian sandal

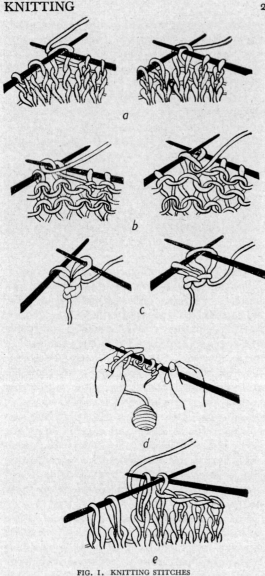

FIG. 1. KNITTING STITCHES

a. Plain. *b*. Purl. *c*. Casting on with two needles. *d*. Casting on with one needle. *e*. Casting off

socks from the 4th or 5th century, may be seen in the Victoria and Albert Museum, London.

In Europe, in the 15th and 16th centuries, Knitting and Hosiery Guilds were formed (*see* CRAFT GUILDS, Vol. VII). Apprentices served for 6 years, after which they submitted for examination a beret, a woollen shirt, a pair of hose with Spanish clocks, and a carpet with a design which had to contain flowers, foliage, birds, and animals in natural colours. In the early days of knitting, the wool fabric was made to look as much like woven material as possible by the process of felting (*see* FELT, Vol. VII). The knitted piece was soaked in dye for 4 or 5 days, blocked, dried, cut into the required shape, and brushed with a teazle brush. The fez and the French beret are still made in this way. Knitting was not confined to the guild craftsmen, however, but was a well-known occupation of women and of shepherds who gathered wool from the bushes. Mistress Lee knitted garments for sale, and it was probably to ease her work that William Lee invented the first stocking machine in 1589 (*see* HOSIERY AND KNITWEAR, Vol. VII). In the 18th century the import of cottons led to the making of knitted lace and fine stockings, whilst garments were knitted in silk from an early time for Court wear.

The tasselled caps of the French revolutionaries were knitted on circular wood frames fitted with pegs, over which the stitches were lifted with the fingers or a bent nail. The cotton bobbin and nails on which children today make tubular reins is just such a frame. Modern machine knitting is based on the same principle, although the pegs are replaced by hooked needles. With the industrialization of knitting in the 19th century, hand knitting as a livelihood died out in England, except in isolated communities. Wales, Ireland, Scotland, and the Yorkshire dales, however, continue to be famous for their hand knitting. A new type of knitting machine which produces a flat fabric is becoming popular for use in the home.

Knitting consists of forming a fabric of successive, joined loops from a single thread with needles or wires. Any long continuous thread can be knitted with the aid of two or more needles. Needles have been made from a variety of materials—wood, bone, ivory, amber, tortoiseshell, steel, and plastic. Early needles were hooked like crochet hooks, and five made up a set. Such needles are still used by shepherds in the south of France. By 1590 straight needles were known in Europe. The earliest examples of knitted fabric are in stocking stitch, and it seems likely that early knitting consisted of plain knitting in rounds on a set of three, four, or five needles always worked from the left-hand needle on to the right. Purl, which appears at the back of a plain stitch, came later. These two basic stitches, plain or knit (Fig. 1*a*) and purl (Fig. 1*b*), retain the same form whether the wool is held in the right hand (English knitting) or in the left hand (Continental and probably the earliest knitting). When plain or knit stitches are knitted in rounds, a continuous spiral of fabric is formed which is smooth on the outside and knobbly on the inside. To produce the same fabric (stocking stitch) with only two needles, the direction of knitting is reversed at the end of each row, and alternate rows have to be plain and purl. From these two basic stitches many patterns can be built up, such as ribbing, where knit stitches alternate with purl, and the purl always lies above the knit stitch of the preceding row; or moss stitch, in which the knit stitch lies above the purl back of the knit stitch in the preceding row, giving a rough surface.

Stitches are cast on by being knitted in the ordinary way except that the loop is not slipped off the needle and the new stitch is hooked on to the left-hand needle (Fig. 1c). Stitches can also be cast on by using only one needle and the thumb of the left hand (Fig. 1d). When the garment is finished, stitches are cast off by pulling each stitch in turn over its neighbour as the row is knitted, to form a chain along the top (Fig. 1e). The fabric can be made narrower by knitting two stitches together or by casting off stitches at the required places; it can be made wider by knitting twice into one stitch, or by wrapping the wool round the needle without knitting a stitch (this makes a hole), or by casting on extra

FAIR ISLE 'TREE OF LIFE' AND 'CROWN OF GLORY' PATTERNS

stitches. The suitable combination of these manœuvres makes it possible to construct elaborately patterned and shaped fabrics. The delicate Shetland shawl uses only these actions, but is peculiar in that it is knitted diagonally from opposite corners so that there are no cast on or cast off edges. This, together with the fineness of the native wool, gives it its elasticity and softness. Many peasant garments are knitted on a single circular needle or set of needles, the sleeves being picked up and also knitted as tubes. These garments are frequently knitted in two colours in designs which very often have a national or religious significance. The well-known Fair Isle patterns in many colours are modern interpretations of these national designs.

Shetland and Scandinavian knitters use a knitting belt: a leather pad stuffed with horse hair and perforated by small holes gives support to the right-hand needle, leaving the hand free to manipulate the wool. String threaded through the base of the fabric and tied to the belt, or to a safety-pin on the left hip, gives a 'pull' to the work which increases the speed of knitting. A bunch of feathers or trusses of straw serve the same purpose in other parts of the country, and the old elaborately carved and decorated knitting sticks were also used in this way. The right needle was put into the bore of the stick, and the stick tucked into the belt on the right hip. With the help of one or other of these devices, an expert can knit 200 stitches a minute.

See also CROCHET; TATTING.
See also Vol. VII: HOSIERY AND KNITWEAR.

A JACKET KNITTED IN TRADITIONAL NORWEGIAN PATTERNS

L

LAMPS, *see* LIGHTING, HISTORY OF. *See also* Vol. VIII: ILLUMINATION.

LAUNDRY (History). As soon as men and women took to wearing woven cloth they were faced with the necessity of washing it when it became soiled, and then restoring its original appearance by smoothing its surface. The launderer's craft was therefore evolved in remote

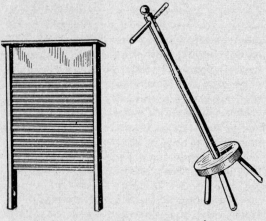

A SCRUBBING BOARD AND 'DOLLY'

antiquity, and by 2000 B.C. was already highly developed in some countries. Its basic principles have remained the same ever since, though naturally the tools and methods used have changed very considerably during the course of centuries.

In early times the clothes and household linen were taken in baskets to a convenient stream, and there soaked, pounded with stones to loosen the dirt, washed, rinsed, and spread upon bushes to dry. Some launderers, instead of using stones, stamped upon the wet linen with their bare feet—a method still used in many African and Asiatic countries today. In the later Middle Ages European housewives commonly beat the clothes vigorously upon a table with bats, or 'beetles', which were small pieces of wood with handles, rather like battledores in shape. A further development was the dolly, or posser, a long pole with a handle at the top and a wooden disk with three prongs at the bottom, used in a tub deep enough to prevent too much splashing. The laundress pulled on the handle, driving the pole up and down, so as to move the clothes against the side of the tub and beat them; the length of the pole gave force to her strokes. Today, the work is made still easier by electrically driven washing machines (*see* LAUNDRY EQUIPMENT).

In time, European housewives took to doing the washing in their own kitchens or yards, though peasant women often continued to go to a stream, and do so even now. By the 16th century it was usual for large houses to contain a special stone-floored room for laundrywork,

Picture Post Library

LAUNDRY WORKERS WASHING, DRYING, AND BLEACHING LINEN

Illumination from a German manuscript, 1582

furnished with tables, one or two boilers for heating water, a variety of wooden tubs with 'ears' for convenience in carrying, bats, irons, barrels, and other vessels. Until the end of the 18th century (and much later in Germany and some other countries), it was customary for household washing to be done in large quantities at intervals of 2 or 3 months. Such an immense amount of dirty linen was thus accumulated by the time washing-day came round that it was often necessary to begin work as early as 4 a.m. in order to get it finished by dusk. For checking, tallies were sometimes used, especially if the laundry-maid could not write. These were oblong blocks of wood, bound with brass and faced with transparent horn, inscribed with the names of the various articles. Under each word was a small disk which could be turned to show the number of articles of each kind.

By gracious permission of H.M. the Queen

WASHING DAY IN THE 18TH CENTURY
Water-colour by Paul Sandby

Soap was in general use for household laundry by the 17th century, but before then many housewives preferred 'lye' because it was cheaper and easy to make. To make lye, wood or vegetable ashes were put into a tub with a perforated bottom; this tub stood upon a second tub, known as a 'lye-letch', and water was then poured over the ashes. The water washed the potash salts from the ashes, and carried them through the holes into the tub beneath. A concentrated solution could be made by steeping wheat, barley, or oat straw in lye already prepared, drying and burning it, and making new lye from the ashes. As lye softened hard water, it could be used for washing, with or without soap; and it could also be made into soap by combining it with fats (*see* SOAP MANUFACTURE, Vol. VII).

A considerable advance in fine laundry-craft was made when starch was introduced. It seems likely that some way of stiffening gauze or linen was known earlier, since the exaggerated winged head-dresses of the 15th century (*see* p. 87) could hardly have been supported by wires alone; possibly a solution of thin glue or size was used. True starch, however, was unknown before the 16th century, and first appeared in Holland. It was made of bran wheat flour or other grains, and it was coloured, the most popular shades being first yellow and then blue. In 1564 a Dutch woman, Madame Dingham Van der Plasse, came to England to give lessons in its preparation and use (for which she charged £5), and thus made possible the spreading ruffs fashionable in Elizabethan times (*see* p. 73). In the 17th century English housewives often made starch at home from cuckoo-pint roots.

The earliest 'ironing' was done with smooth, waterworn stones, which were heated in the embers, and then wrapped in wool to protect the hand. Such smoothing-stones were still in use in the Orkney Islands as recently as 1880. Another early form of 'iron' was a rounded lump of glass, used without heating. True irons seem to have been known in the Middle Ages, and

County Museum, Taunton

A BOX MANGLE

The box above the rollers was weighted with stones

included goffering-tongs for fluting and crimping the edges of frills. In the 17th century heavy box-irons were sometimes used. These stood upon three-legged stands, and were heated by a piece of hot metal thrust into one end.

Mangles, in which clothes were smoothed after washing, were at first made in the form of presses which worked by weight. The rollers of the old-fashioned box-mangle pressed the linen upon a flat surface. They were weighted by a box full of stones, which was moved backwards and forwards by a rack and pinion. In a later and more convenient type, wooden rollers, held close together by weighted levers, pressed the clothes between them. Mangles were the fore-runners of wringers and rotary ironers.

See also LAUNDRY EQUIPMENT; LAUNDRY (Methods).

LAUNDRY (Methods). Two distinct processes are involved in laundrywork: removing soiling matter from fabric by washing, and, later, restoring the appearance of the fabric, usually by ironing. The soiling matter varies with the article. In garments, it consists mainly of grease from the skin and perspiration; in table linen, of different sorts of food; and in town curtains, of dust mixed with soot and grease.

1. WASHING. There are three stages in wash-ing. First, the dirt is loosened by soaking the fabric in cold water, perhaps with a detergent which acts as a 'wetting agent' (*see* CLEANING MATERIALS). The dirt is then separated from the fabric by friction in water to which a detergent such as soap has been added; and finally the

article is rinsed to remove the detergent. After each stage the soiled water is wrung out.

Some fabrics have to be washed with special care. Cotton and linen fabrics can withstand the rougher treatment of scrubbing and rubbing which would damage others. Woollen fabrics, for example, thicken or 'felt' if rubbed, and then shrink and lose elasticity. RAYON fabrics (q.v. Vol. VII), when washed, absorb a great deal of moisture, and swell; this weakens their fibres, which may, perhaps, break if they are at all roughly rubbed. Both woollen and rayon fabrics should, therefore, be squeezed and kneaded rather than rubbed, as should silk because of its very fine-gauge fibre. NYLON fibres (q.v. Vol. VII), while also very slender, are relatively strong and can be subjected to a certain amount of rubbing.

The action of detergents, particularly soap, increases considerably with rising temperature, and so washing is most efficient when done in water as hot as the fabric will stand. This depends on the fibre and dye of the material, and on any special process it has undergone. Temperatures up to 212° F. will not damage white or fast-dyed cotton and linen fabrics, but such high tempera-tures tend to turn other white fabrics yellow, and fade coloured ones. Water for these should be a little above blood heat, that is 110° F. to 120° F. Nylon fabrics will not stand high temperatures, and woollens tend to shrink in very hot water.

Sometimes, though less frequently today than in former times, white articles, such as handker-chiefs, after being washed are boiled in soapy water for 10–15 minutes. This further whitens the articles, mainly because of the increased detergent action of soap at boiling-point. Boiling is more necessary for clothes washed by hand than by washing-machines, because the machine washes very efficiently and at very high tem-peratures.

Washing-water containing soap is slightly alkaline (*see* ALKALIS, Vol. VII). If soda is used, it becomes still more alkaline, with the result that woollens become slippery and 'felt' more readily. They should, therefore, be washed with an unbuilt synthetic detergent (*see* CLEANING MATERIALS). Some dyes are more stable in washing water to which acetic acid has been added (1 tablespoon of vinegar per gallon), but as soap does not lather easily in such water, it is better to use a synthetic detergent with it.

Care must be taken when using bleaches to

avoid serious damage to fabrics. For instance, a chemical bleach to whiten fabrics should be used only for cottons and linens and only in cold water; garments must not be left in it too long, and must be thoroughly rinsed out before drying. Even with these precautions this bleach gradually weakens the fabric. Hydrogen peroxide is suitable for bleaching silks and woollens, and is particularly useful for removing stains in these fabrics.

The starch used in laundrywork, which is prepared from rice, serves as a stiffening agent. It is used in either the cooked or the uncooked state; cooked for a semi-stiff finish, as for table linen, uncooked for a very stiff finish, as for men's collars and evening shirts. The first type is made by pouring boiling water on to a paste of starch and water, which is then diluted according to the stiffness required, and the articles dipped into it. To get a very stiff finish, the fabric is rubbed in a mixture of starch in cold water. The embedded starch grains are then 'cooked' in the fabric by ironing with a hot heavy iron to produce a stiff shining surface.

2. IRONING. Fabrics are ironed to produce a smooth, even surface by flattening the fibres under heat and pressure, to give such stiffness as suits a particular fabric, and to restore a garment's shape by pressing in the right creases and pleats. The moisture present in the material is vaporized by the heat of the iron, and this also assists the process. Some of the most recent fabrics, such as nylon, can be washed and worn again without ironing, because their fibres absorb very little water during washing and are therefore relatively unchanged when dry again. Some of them are woven in a special way so as to disguise any slight cockling of the surface which may occur during drying. Cotton materials, such as cotton seersucker, which need little or no ironing, were given this special surface finish long before the new synthetic materials were developed.

Precise temperatures for ironing cannot be given, because fabrics, apart from their own special nature and the type of finish given to them during manufacture, are affected by such factors as the degree of moisture in them, the speed at which the iron moves over the surface, and the amount of pressure applied. Too hot an iron melts nylon and some rayons, and scorches other fibres. With too cool an iron, however, satisfactory results cannot be obtained.

The lowest temperatures are used for rayons, a little higher for silk and wool, higher still for cotton, and highest of all for linen. Thermostatic irons are usually adjustable at different temperatures to suit different fabrics.

Materials ironed on the right side have a slightly shiny surface. Where a dull surface is required, as for woollens, some silks and rayons, and fabrics with very dark dyes, ironing is done on the wrong side. Woollen fabrics are first dried completely and then pressed on the wrong side with a damp cloth. Velvet is also treated on the wrong side; but, as ironing would flatten the pile, the fabric is steamed, either by playing on it a jet of steam from a kettle, or by stretching it above a damp cloth covering the plate of a hot iron.

See also LAUNDRY EQUIPMENT; LAUNDRY (History); CLEANING MATERIALS.

LAUNDRY EQUIPMENT.

The four processes, washing, wringing, drying, and ironing, are made easier by the use of special equipment. An important development is the use of electricity, through the electric motor and heating element, in the washing-machine, the electric iron, and the mechanical ironers.

1. WASHING. Fabrics are washed in a vessel made of material which will not mark them (as would rust from iron), and which is easy to keep clean. Glazed finishes or stainless steel are suitable for fixed bowls, and galvanized iron or pulp for movable ones. Enamel bowls are satisfactory so long as the enamel has not been chipped. There are many different methods for removing dirt. This is the hardest physical part of the work, and many mechanical aids have been invented, from the wooden dolly peg (*see* LAUNDRY (History)) to the latest electric washing-machine. A hand-operated device still in use is the vacuum washer or posser, which consists of an inverted perforated dome with a perforated plate inside attached to a pole; when the pole is pressed up and down on the clothes the water is sucked through the perforations. Other types of hand-operated washing-machines still exist, though electrically driven ones are now more usual. There are several main types of electric washing-machines (Fig. 1). In one, the water is driven round the tub by an impeller in the side, and removes dirt from the clothes as it rushes through them. In another, the clothes are swished backwards and forwards through the

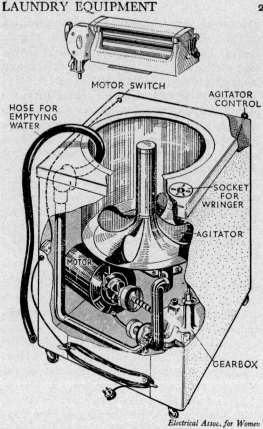

MOTOR SWITCH

AGITATOR CONTROL

HOSE FOR EMPTYING WATER

SOCKET FOR WRINGER

AGITATOR

MOTOR

GEARBOX

Electrical Assoc. for Women

FIG. 1. DIAGRAM OF AN ELECTRIC WASHER AND WRINGER
It is filled by a hose from the tap

water by an agitator, which consists of a vertical post with fins rotating clockwise and anticlockwise alternately. In the third type, a perforated drum, containing the clothes, rotates on a horizontal axis inside a water-filled container. In yet another method, not so far in general use, machines, known by such names as 'super-sonic' and 'vibro-sonic', shake the dirt out of the clothes by very high-frequency waves transmitted through the water. Some machines also have a heating device to enable clothes to be boiled. Boiling (*see* LAUNDRY (Methods)) is not as usual today as in the last century, when a large galvanized copper with brick surround and firebox underneath was to be found in most households; the copper has been replaced today by the wash boiler, which usually holds 10 gallons and is heated either by gas or electricity.

2. WRINGING. Wringing by hand is not only laborious but also injurious to such fabrics as wool, silk, and rayon. There are two mechanical devices for expelling water. The wringer,

whether operated by hand or by electricity, has two rotating rubber rollers, which press the water out as clothes pass between them; their pressure is controlled by an adjustable spring. The electrically driven hydro-extractor consists of a covered perforated drum, which rotates at high speed on a vertical spindle, thus throwing out the water (Fig. 2). Some washing-machines spin the clothes 'damp-dry' in this way.

3. DRYING. After efficient wringing, silk and rayon articles are ready for ironing, but most fabrics need further drying by evaporation. Drying out of doors is best. Spring clothes-pegs attach clothes firmly to the clothes-line. The long stretch of a single clothes-line may be conveniently replaced by a system of lines—rather like a spider's web—depending on a central pole. Where clothes have to be dried indoors, racks which can be raised or lowered by pulleys, clothes-horses, and wall arm-dryers are useful. Best of all is a cabinet heated by either gas or electricity.

4. IRONING. Until quite recently the flat iron, heated on the coal fire or range, was generally used. An iron heated by gas appeared early in the 20th century, but with the development of domestic electricity the electric iron has come into general use. As the heating element is inside, the iron can be used continuously with-

English Electric

FIG. 2. A TUMBLER DRIER
The clothes are spun round while warm air is blown through

Oprun

FIG. 3. A ROTARY ELECTRIC IRON

out waiting for reheating. In the most recent models, which incorporate a THERMOSTAT (q.v. Vol. VIII), a steady and predetermined temperature is maintained. The dial on the cover of the iron can be set at the temperature needed for ironing any given fabric. Such irons are connected to the electricity supply by flex. A new model has been made with no flex; instead, the ironing-board has sockets connected by flex with the electricity supply. The iron has plugs which are slipped into these sockets whenever it is not smoothing the garments, and this intermittent heating maintains the temperature. Another type of iron contains water in a container in the base to supply steam for pressing. Most irons are about 6 inches long, but smaller ones are available.

A table covered with a blanket and a cotton sheet is suitable for ironing flat things, but most garments need a skirt-board over which they can be arranged, and a sleeve-board. The height should be comfortable for the worker if she is to avoid backache and unnecessary fatigue. Equipment for ironing in a sitting position is beginning to appear.

The rotary ironer is useful for all types of work (Fig. 3). The garments are pressed as they pass between a plate, which is electrically heated, and a roller, which is rotated by an electric motor. The rotary ironer can be bought either separately or as an attachment to one type of washing-machine. The press ironer is really satisfactory only for flat work, particularly for such processes as pressing pleats or creases into thick materials. The articles are placed on a base plate, and then an upper heated plate is lowered and kept down for a short time at high pressure, to produce a good finish on the fabric.

See also LAUNDRY (History); LAUNDRY (Methods).

LAVATORY, *see* SANITATION, HISTORY OF; HOUSEHOLD PLUMBING.

LEPROSY, *see* TROPICAL DISEASES.

LIFE CYCLE. The human being, like other animals and also plants, starts from a germ or egg, develops into the adult state, and eventually declines and dies. The article entitled BIRTH (q.v.) describes the life of a human being from the beginning until the time he is weaned and takes the first steps in the process which we call growing up.

The influences which affect a child while he is growing up come both from inside his body and from his surroundings. 'Surroundings' include not only his home in town or country, his toys and pets, and so on, but also the people with whom he comes into contact. The most important of these people are his father and mother and the other members of his family. The mother is naturally far the most important for the little child because, from the moment of his birth, she has fed and protected him with loving care. The gradual withdrawal of the mother's protection and the necessity of learning to feed and look after himself are events which have the greatest influences on the young child when he is weaned (*see* CHILDREN, UPBRINGING OF).

The process of growth involves the enlargement of the baby of about 7 pounds to the young man or woman of, say, 10 stones, that is to say, an enormous increase in size of all the body tissues, bones, muscles, and glands. The skin, too, enlarges enormously; but the brain enlarges least of all, because the baby starts with a much larger head in proportion to his body than the adult has. The bones of the limbs grow in length by means of little caps on the ends, separated from the bone shafts by pads of cartilage. The cartilage gradually builds up layers of bone until, about the age of 17, the caps unite with the main shaft, and growth ceases. Physical growth occurs through the action of various glands in the body, such as the pituitary at the base of the brain, and the reproductive glands, ovaries in the girl and testes in the boy (*see* ENDOCRINE GLANDS). The mental growth is largely a matter of experience and education. The number of brain cells, which is fixed at birth and varies from one person to another, cannot be added to; but our capacity to use our brains and our bodies can grow, and can be helped by education.

The development of the young child starts with speech, crawling, then walking and running, all of which give him a widening experience of the world and more opportunities for learning. During the first 2 years of life, the first set of teeth (milk teeth) appear, and these make it possible for the child to eat adult food. From the 6th year or so onwards the second and stronger set of teeth (permanent teeth) begins to replace the milk teeth. The part of growth and development related to the reproductive glands causes the boy to develop into a man and the girl into a woman.

The change from childhood to adulthood is called puberty. It is then that the boy becomes more muscular, begins to grow a beard, and has a deepening of the voice—people say that the boy's voice has broken. The girl develops breasts, and has a broadening of the pelvis to form a capacious bowl in which a child may grow comfortably inside her womb. About this time the womb also begins to get ready for having children. It changes its lining once a month, and the old lining is passed out, together with some blood, through the external genital opening, the discharge being called the menstrual or monthly flow. About 10 to 14 days after this renewal of the lining of the womb, a single egg ripens in the ovary and is passed along into the funnel-like upper end of the oviduct which leads down into the womb. All through the reproductive life of a woman, one egg ripens each month, but it cannot develop into a child unless it has been fertilized by the sperm of a man.

Boys and girls as they develop change their interests. Dolls give place to books, and toy trains to cricket. By the time they are about 15, boys and girls are physically adult, but they still have much to learn before they are adult in other ways. They have to learn, for instance, how to use in a responsible way their new physical powers and to control the emotions that go with them. This period we call 'adolescence' from a Latin word meaning 'growing up'. With adult life come many other interests, and one important one may be attraction to the opposite sex, which gives rise to the relationship known as love, leading to marriage, and to the physical act by which new members of the human race are born. It is natural for children to be interested in these matters. Some will learn from their parents; some may prefer to read the articles on REPRODUCTIVE SYSTEM and BIRTH in this volume.

The reproductive period of life lasts from about the ages of 15 to 50, but in Western civilizations it is not usual for marriage to occur much before the age of 18, and usually rather later. After about 50 (with women sometimes earlier and with men often considerably later) the ability to have children declines. Elderly men and women, however, develop other interests, to which they can often bring a mellowed wisdom and experience. As at puberty, so at this stage, there are changes in the body due to the decline of the sexual glands. A woman enters upon what is called her 'change of life' or 'menopause', when her ovaries no longer make eggs and her monthly flow ceases. The testes of a man no longer make sperms.

The process of ageing involves a gradual general decline of the tissues, the skin develops wrinkles, the bones become brittle, the teeth and hair begin to fall out, and a majority of elderly persons have to wear spectacles for reading because the lens of the eye becomes less elastic. As the mind and body decline, the old depend more and more on other people, and need to be protected, helped, and fed. Finally even the loving care of younger people cannot keep them alive. The breathing and action of the heart, upon both of which life depends, become weaker and finally cease altogether. When this happens the body is dead. The life, which began with the union of a sperm with an egg, has reached the end which comes to all living things.

LIGHTING, HISTORY OF. In prehistoric times artificial light was provided by small chalk or stone lamps, burning animal fat. Today

Eskimoes (q.v. Vol. I) often use similar flat saucer-like vessels with blubber as the oil and moss as the wick. Although there were enormous improvements in the artistry and craftsmanship of such lamps, there was no fundamental change in the character of domestic lighting throughout the Ancient World and Middle Ages. As a result, houses in cold climates were very dark—places of shelter rather than of light. Improvement in WINDOWS (q.v.) was the first condition of better light, but until the 16th century glass windows were regarded as luxuries, and in England, between 1696 and 1851, they were taxed as such by the government.

In England, until the beginning of the 19th century, artificial lighting depended wholly upon the simple oil-lamp or lantern, the rush or torch dipped in resin, or candles made of beeswax or tallow. From the 15th century the only method of lighting streets was by tallow candles, enclosed in lanterns and hung from individual houses (see STREET SERVICES, Section 2, Vol. X). At the end of the 17th century candles were replaced by oil-lamps in London, and in 1784,

Pitt Rivers Museum

1. ROMAN LAMP FOR TWO WICKS. 2. SCOTTISH CRUISIE.
3. ARGAND OIL-LAMP

with the invention of the Argand oil-lamp, the ILLUMINATION (q.v. Vol. VIII) of large areas first became possible. For domestic use, long rushes (a rush of 2 feet 4 inches burned for exactly an hour) were far cheaper than candles, which were taxed in England until 1832. Gilbert White, the 18th-century writer, claimed that rushes gave 'a good clear light'. Candles, however, particularly when massed in great chandeliers, were far more impressive. They had long been used for religious as well as for domestic purposes; for example, there were ten golden candlesticks in Solomon's temple in the 10th century B.C.

The placing of lights in relation to the internal decoration and furnishing of rooms was raised to an art during the 18th century. At first, in the age of Chippendale, wall-brackets were most frequently used for the display of candles, and candelabra were placed on the tops of tables and writing desks. Later in the century, however, in the elegant houses designed by Robert ADAM (q.v. Vol. V), large chandeliers were suspended from the plaster ceilings. The wall-brackets or sconces, with their reflecting mirrors, had often

Pitt Rivers Museum

1. RUSHLIGHT HOLDER. 2. TAPER STAND. 3. CANDLE
SNUFFERS. 4. IRON CANDLESTICK

Lord De L'Isle and Dudley
17TH-CENTURY CRYSTAL CHANDELIER AT PENSHURST PLACE

A GASELIER
From the catalogue of the Great Exhibition, 1851

made rooms uncomfortably hot, and the chandelier was preferable for reasons of utility as well as beauty.

By the early 19th century, when the INDUSTRIAL REVOLUTION (q.v. Vol. VII) was transforming manufacturing techniques for all kinds of goods and opening up new world markets, the materials from which candles were made came from many different countries. Paraffin might come from Germany, mineral wax from central Europe, and spermaceti, an oil derived from the sperm whale, from the southern seas. It was at this time that the French chemist Chevreul realized that animal and natural fats contained both inflammable material (fatty acids) and non-inflammable material (glycerine). Profiting from his discovery, other French inventors began to produce candles made from the fatty acids alone. These new 'star candles' made their appearance in 1831 just as genuine substitute materials, particularly gas, were beginning to be popular.

In the age of candlelight both rushes and candles had to be lit either direct from the fire or from a tinder box which produced a spark from a piece of steel and a flint. The first matches, invented by a Frenchman in 1805, were made from a mixture of chemicals containing a great deal of oxygen, and cost one penny each. In 1837 the first practicable 'friction' matches, which could be lit by striking on a rough surface, were made by a druggist at Stockton-on-Tees. By 1880 Sweden, with forty-three factories, was the greatest match-making country.

By the time that matches were being manufactured on a large scale, gas lighting had taken the place of oil-lamps or rushes in most English town houses. As early as 1780 William Murdoch had used gas to light a cave near his home, but he was not able to develop the invention because of the difficulties of GAS MANUFACTURE (q.v. Vol. VIII) and gas purification, the poor quality of gas pipes, and the lack of a suitable burner. Large industrial concerns, however, such as the Gas Light and Coke Company of London, founded in 1812, whose engineer, Samuel Clegg, solved most of these difficulties, made commercial use of Murdoch's invention; and by 1829 there were over 200 gas companies in England (*see* GAS INDUSTRY, Vol. VII). Gas was first used for lighting streets in 1813, but the early lamps, which had no reliable burner, were so poor that 'link-boys' with blazing torches were needed until the 1830s to guide people walking about at night.

In 1820 J. B. Neilson of Glasgow invented a new gas burner, the Union jet burner, which produced a 'fish-tail flame', created by two streams of gas impinging at an angle. But the lights were naked and still far from steady, and it was not until 1885 that a German chemist, Von Welsbach, made a satisfactory incandescent gas mantle. It had been discovered many years before that blotting paper, soaked in a solution of calcium chloride and burnt in the flame of a spirit lamp, left a white residue of ashes, which when heated in the feeblest flame emitted a brilliant light. Von Welsbach made his patent upright gas mantle from cotton wool: the fragile and flimsy mantle—a lace-like tube fixed round the gas jet—glowed with heat, which provided a bright and steady light. Inverted incandescent mantles, however, were not perfected for another 20 years, when they were made of the fine, strong, ramic fibre; Germany led the way both in invention and use. In 1900 90% of German gas lighting was provided by incandescent mantles, compared with 30% in England.

Just as candles began to improve when gas was coming in, so before gas had been perfected electricity challenged its hold. The first demonstrations of the use of electricity for lighting had been made as early as 1812 by Sir Humphry DAVY (q.v. Vol. V), who constructed the first arc lamp (see ILLUMINATION, Vol. VIII). Such lamps, however, were much too powerful and unwieldy for domestic use, and it was not until the 1870s that a convenient electric bulb was devised.

Modern electric lamps depend on the principle that if an ELECTRIC CURRENT (q.v. Vol. VIII) is passed through a fine metal wire, the wire becomes hot. Some metal wires, those made of iron, for example, which is a bad electricity conductor, glow and finally melt away; others, such as platinum and carbon, continue to glow and emit considerable light. In 1878 Joseph Swan sealed a thin carbon rod in a glass bulb, evacuated the air from the bulb, and heated the rod to incandescence; a year later, Thomas EDISON (q.v. Vol. V) also used carbon instead of the expensive platinum as a 'filament', and his invention was quickly put to commercial use. The United States led the way, but after 1926, when the national GRID SYSTEM (q.v. Vol. VIII) was

Heal and Son
ELECTRIC WALL BRACKET MADE OF WIRE AND COLOURED BAKELITE

set up, electricity began to supplant gas in most British homes also.

Edison's filament bulb has since been improved in countless ways. The metal tungsten, for example, which has a melting-point of well over 3,000° C., compared with 1,700° C. for carbon, is now used to produce higher filament temperatures and therefore much brighter lighting. The use of an inert gas, such as argon, in the bulb enables this temperature to be raised still higher. In 1932 the 'discharge lamp', in which an electric current is passed through a rarefied gas, was invented to produce fluorescent light (see ILLUMINATION, Vol. VIII). The 'daylight' colours given by fluorescent lamps, and the long life of their elongated tubes, have revolutionized domestic lighting. Just as in the 18th century domestic lighting became an art adapted to the drawing-rooms of the Adam brothers, so in the 20th century it is now possible, by the use of reading lamps, reflectors, and concealed lighting, to produce entirely new lighting effects in the home. Specialists in domestic lighting can determine the most effective placing of lights— in relation to the ceiling, the ground, and each other—for the diffusion of light for various purposes. Reflectors can produce a more even light which will penetrate into the dark corners of a room, while concealed lighting, as well as doing away with obtrusive fittings, can be used to create subtle effects of light and shade or to secure even diffusion.

See also ELECTRICITY, DOMESTIC.
See also Vol. VIII: ILLUMINATION; ELECTRIC CURRENT; GAS MANUFACTURE.
See also Vol. X: STREET SERVICES.

LINEN, *see* HOUSEHOLD LINEN; BED COVERINGS. *See also* Vol. VII: LINEN INDUSTRY.

LIVER, *see* DIGESTIVE SYSTEM.

LOCKS AND BOLTS. The earliest kind of lock seems to have come from the East about 2000 B.C. and was used in ancient Egypt (Fig. 1). The bolt (B) has three or more vertical holes in it, and when it is shot, a corresponding number of pegs (P) fall down from the body (A) of the lock into these holes, thus fixing the bolt. The

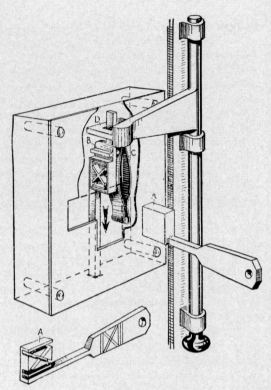

FIG. 3. A ROMAN LOCK

The wards of the key (A) engage with wards on a sliding bolt (B). The key pushes back the spring (c) and pulls the bolt down to clear the eye of the hoop (D), which is part of a bar stapled to the house wall

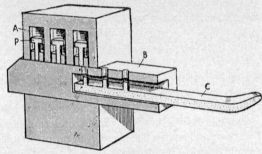

FIG. 1. AN EGYPTIAN FALLING-PEG LOCK
A. Body of lock. B. Bolt. C. Key. P. Peg.

key (C), with similar pegs on it, is inserted through the large hole in the bolt and raised so that the locking pegs are lifted, and the bolt is free to move.

The early Greek keys were simpler, merely pushing back the bolt through a hole in the door. They were often very large (Fig. 2), although by the 6th century B.C. the Egyptian type with smaller keys was also in use.

Locks and keys of iron and bronze have been found at POMPEII (q.v. Vol. XII) and other Roman sites,

FIG. 2. A MAN HOLDING A GREEK KEY

sometimes of the 'falling-peg' Egyptian type, but more often similar to those in use today, in which a key with 'wards' of an early type acts against a spring holding the bolt in position (Fig. 3). For the first time keys were small enough to put on a key ring. Roman keys often had handles of steel so that they could be used to strike a light, and sometimes they were made to wear on a finger.

During the Middle Ages and later, very ingenious and complicated iron locks were made,

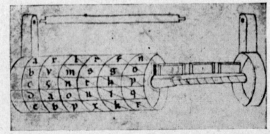

FIG. 4. A PADLOCK WITH COMBINATION LOCK, c. 1420

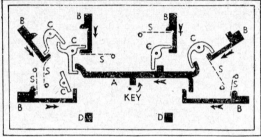

Castle Museum, York

FIG. 5. A CHEST WITH A 6-BOLT LOCK

The drawing shows how the lock works. When the key is turned, the main lever A moves the pivoted cranks C, which in turn move the bolts B. S. Springs.

especially in Germany. Fig. 4 shows a padlock of about 1420 which, with its six movable alphabetical barrels, is an early type of combination lock. CHESTS (q.v.) were often made with very elaborate locks which filled the inside of the lid and fastened at a number of points (Fig. 5).

Until the end of the 18th century, the security of a lock depended on its having 'wards' and perhaps one 'tumbler' (Fig. 6). Wards are small ridges, sometimes arranged in a circle, fixed inside the lock so that only a key with notches the same shape and size (also called wards) can enter them.

A tumbler (a lever is much the same) is a strip of metal pivoted inside the lock, with teeth on it and a spring to keep the teeth pressed into notches cut in the bolt. When the proper key is used, the working edge of the key lifts the tumbler or lever so that its teeth come out of the notches on the bolt, making it free to move.

This common spring lock was hardly any improvement on the old Roman lock of 1,800 years earlier, because it was always possible to find the shape of the wards by simply putting in

a blank key covered with wax and pressing it against them, while a single tumbler could be lifted quite easily with a piece of wire.

In 1778 Robert Barron, and in 1818 Jeremiah Chubb, made improvements in the spring lock. The working edge of the key is no longer straight but notched, so that each projection lifts a different lever. Instead of only one lever there are now six or more, arranged side by side in the lock, and the bolt will draw only if all are raised together to just the right height. In 1784 the famous Bramah lock was invented. It is in the form of two barrels, one turning inside the other. The inner one comprises a number of plates of doubled steel called 'sliders', which are notched so that only a key with corresponding notches will flatten them and make a smooth cylinder, enabling the barrel and key to be turned and the lock opened. Developments of and improvements on this type are the modern Yale, Chubb, and other latch locks (Fig. 7). A really large bolt cannot be shot with a small latch key, so in this case the bolt is shot by hand and secured with a small lock and key.

Modern kinds of lock include time and combination locks, both of which are opened without keys. These are the sort used by banks for their strong rooms and safes. The time lock does not have tumblers or levers moved by a key, but instead has the works of two or more clocks inside it; if there were only one clock it might stop or go wrong. When locking a safe with a time-lock mechanism, the clocks are wound until

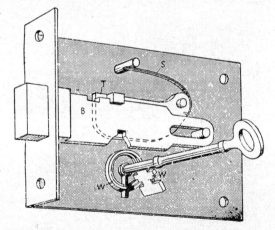

FIG. 6. A LOCK WITH WARDS AND TUMBLER

When the key raises the tumbler (T), the tooth on the tumbler disengages from the bolt (B) and allows the bolt to be moved. w. Wards on key and lock. s. Spring.

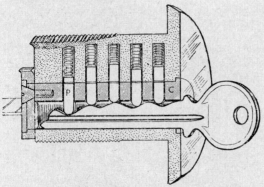

FIG. 7. A CYLINDER LOCK

The key turns the lock when the pins P are pushed upwards, so that the split in each corresponds with the edge of the cylinder c

the dials on the lock show the time when it is to be opened—most likely the time that the bank opens next morning. Until then, a bar will prevent the bolts from being withdrawn, and nobody can open the safe. When the right time comes round, the clockwork turns wheels allowing the bar to fall and the safe to be opened with a key as usual.

A combination lock is a certain arrangement, different for each lock, of numbers or letters or both, and is the secret of the owner of the lock. An ancient example is shown in Fig. 4. The combination lock has a number of disks or levers which all have to be moved into one position, and one only, before the lock will open. There is no key; instead, the person using the lock turns a knob on a numbered and lettered dial to spell out the right numbers or letters of the 'combination'. During this operation, the knob moves the disks or levers inside the lock to the opening position.

LUGGAGE, *see* HANDBAGS AND PERSONAL LUGGAGE.

LULLABIES. The songs which are sung to win a babe to sleep are perhaps the most natural of all songs; and possibly the first music which was heard in the world was that of a mother lulling her infant. Rocking and crooning really help small children to go to sleep; and in the past, when their pains and ailments were understood less than they are today, and babies were more liable to be fretful, cradles were made so that they could be rocked easily and continuously. Some could be rocked with the foot so that a

mother or nurse might knit or spin at the same time, 'singing as her wheel she turneth'. In 1779, in the establishment of the Royal Nursery, there were not only numerous nurses, governesses, and washerwomen, but two women known as 'rockers', whose sole duty was to rock the cradles.

Elizabethan and Stuart poets often seem to have been worried by babies, and wearied by their crying:

Care is heavy, therefore sleep you;
You are care, and care must keep you.
Sleep, pretty wantons, do not cry,
And I will sing a lullaby,

wrote Thomas Dekker, about 1600; and long before this, in Edward II's time, one can hear the exasperation in the voice of an unknown poet:

Lollai, lollai, litil child,
  Why wepistou so sore?
Nedis mostou wepe,
  Hit was iyarkid (ordained) the yore.

Often, the early poets addressed their cradle songs to the Infant Jesus, or consoled their own children by telling them how fortunate they were compared with the Saviour who lay in a manger. They remind their children, as did Isaac Watts in 1720:

How much better thou'rt attended
  Than the Son of God could be,
When from heaven He descended
  And became a child like thee!

Soft and easy is thy cradle:
  Coarse and hard thy Saviour lay,
When His birthplace was a stable
  And His softest bed was hay.

In traditional lullabies the child is frequently

'LIE A-BED
SLEEPY HEAD'
Illustration from Christina Rossetti's *Sing Song*

promised a reward. The Norwegian child is told:

> If thou wilt but sleep and mind me
> Then a sweet cake I will find thee.

In America, 'papa' is going to buy a mocking bird; in Scotland, the stoorie wean is offered 'a tartan bonnet and feather to put upon it'; and in England, baby bunting will get a rabbit skin to wrap him in.

Flattery is another expedient, and the child may be informed of his substance, as in Sir Walter Scott's 'Lullaby of an Infant Chief':

O hush thee, my babie, thy sire was a knight;
Thy mother a lady, both lovely and bright;
The woods and the glens, from the towers which we
   see,
They all are belonging, dear baby, to thee.

Or, if all else failed, the small one was scared into somnolence:

> Baby, baby, naughty baby,
> Hush, you squalling thing, I say.
> Peace this moment, peace, or maybe
> Bonaparte will pass this way.
>
> Baby, baby, he's a giant,
> Tall and black as Rouen steeple,
> And he breakfasts, dines, rely on't,
> Every day on naughty people.

At different times the spectres of various historical figures, Oliver Cromwell, Judge Jeffreys,

'LULLABY, OH, LULLABY'
Illustration from Christina Rossetti's *Sing Song*

and the late Kaiser, have been summoned to the aid of maternal authority in the English nursery.

See also BABIES, CARE OF; STORY-TELLING.

LUNGS, *see* RESPIRATION.

M

MAKE-UP. It is said that at least 80% of women in Britain now use make-up in one form or another, for a carefully chosen make-up is considered an essential factor in a smart woman's appearance. Within recent years make-up has improved greatly, and cosmetic manufacturers now employ all the resources of science to create fine cosmetics, so that none of the undesirable effects on the skin which were alleged to result from the use of old-fashioned cosmetics need be feared. Indeed, make-up correctly selected to suit the type of skin can improve its texture and act as a protection against the extreme effects of climate, hot or cold.

Home House

A WOMAN POWDERING HERSELF
Painting by Seurat, 1859–91

It is best to use a 'foundation' as a base for make-up, a foundation cream, either white or tinted, being probably the most popular and satisfactory. There are also foundation liquids and stick or block make-ups. The foundation should be put on as smoothly and evenly as possible. If rouge is used it should be applied over the foundation towards the top of the cheeks, the edges of the patch of colour being smoothed in to give a soft effect and to improve the contours of the face. Face powder is then pressed quite firmly into the foundation, any surplus powder being dusted off. Eye make-up, which for day use should be light and delicate, needs careful application. The upper lids can be lightly shaded with a blue or green-tinted shadow, the eyebrows given balance with an eyebrow pencil and finally the lashes, with emphasis on the upper ones, touched-up with mascara on a tiny brush. Lipstick, which completes the make-up, should be applied by first outlining the lips and then filling in the centre with light strokes.

The selection of colours for make-up must depend on the wearer's natural colouring, and also on the particular clothes with which the cosmetics will be worn. Colours which are too bright or which clash with a hat or dress can produce a most unhappy effect. The various items of make-up should harmonize with each other, rouge and lipstick being of the same tone, and also foundation cream and face powder. Trained assistants in large stores and in beauty saloons will assist with advice, and colour charts can be consulted. Natural colouring is not the only thing to be considered in the choice of make-up. Personality also affects the matter, for, as with dress, people should wear what is natural to them. Some women with vivid personalities can wear more dramatic cosmetics than others for whom quiet, restful effects are more attractive.

See also COSMETICS, HISTORY OF.

MALARIA, *see* TROPICAL DISEASES, Section 3.

MANICURE AND PEDICURE. The peoples of many earlier civilizations, in particular the Egyptians, took great pains to care for and to decorate the nails of both hands and feet. Today attention to the health and appearance of the nails is an important part of toilet. Dirty, unkempt hands and feet are not only unsightly but are the cause of a considerable amount of infection.

National Buildings Record

THE MANOR HOUSE, BOOTHBY PAGNELL, LINCOLNSHIRE, *c.* 1180
The hall is on the upper floor so that it could be defended from attack

1. *Manicure.* Finger-nails should be filed with a triple cut steel file or an emery board, not cut with scissors. The file should be drawn with smooth, even strokes from the side of the nail to the centre, and not rubbed back and forth, for this produces a rough edge. The best shape for finger nails follows a rounded, slightly almond-shaped outline, the length extending a little beyond the finger tip.

The cuticle, that is, the skin which folds round the base of the nail, should be kept pressed back to prevent its creeping up the nail or becoming ragged or cracked. The cuticles should be pressed back with the towel gently but firmly every time the hands are washed; during the weekly manicure, after the fingers have been soaked in warm soapy water, an orange-stick with a little cotton wool wrapped round the end can be used to push back the softened cuticles. The pressure must not be so heavy as to dent the formative part of the nail which lies under the cuticle. It may be necessary to cut the cuticle if it has been torn or has grown very thick, but this should be avoided as much as possible. Softening cream applied round the cuticles and the quicks keeps them pliable and in good condition.

Women often give their nails a finishing coat of varnish, which should be of a delicate colour and renewed frequently. Old varnish must be removed completely before a new application. It is better to apply two thin coats of varnish than one thick one.

2. *Pedicure.* Particular trouble should be taken to trim the toe-nails correctly with a pair of nail cutters. The toe-nails should be cut straight across so that the nail will grow straight and the corners will not dig into the flesh, causing ingrowing toe-nails. Tired or swollen feet should be bathed in very hot and cold water alternately, and stockings or socks should be washed every day. Cuticle treatment is the same as for the hands. If corns form, a chiropodist should be consulted.

See also SKIN; SKIN, CARE OF.
See also Vol. II: NAILS AND CLAWS.

MANOR. In the Middle Ages the word 'manor' had much the same all-embracing sense as 'farm' has today. But, whereas a farm involves the control of an area of land, a manor also involved legal rights over the people who lived and worked on the land.

The first written laws of the Anglo-Saxons, dating from the early 7th century, show that there were lords who were owed some kind of obedience by other men. The increasing control of the lords over their weaker and poorer neighbours in the same villages was the origin

Lord De L'Isle and Dudley

THE HALL OF PENSHURST PLACE, KENT, *c.* 1341

The courtyard is surrounded with buildings, with a gatehouse opposite the hall

of manorial rights. From the great surveys of lands in France made at the time of the Emperor CHARLEMAGNE (q.v. Vol. V) we know that the same development was taking place on the Continent in the 9th century. A document of the 10th century describes the peasant who must 'pay land-rent, and a swine yearly for grass-rent, and ride and carry with his beasts, and haul loads, work, and provide food for his lord'. By 1086, the date of the DOMESDAY BOOK (q.v. Vol. X), most of England was divided into manors.

A manor was often one of a huge group of estates scattered all over England and owned by a wealthy family or a monastery. The outlying manors of such a group would be administered by reeves or bailiffs. In the early medieval manor the lord held some of the land himself and worked it to provide food which he could eat or sell. This was called the 'demesne'. The rest of the land was rented by tenants either for money or food-rents or for labour services. The labour services provided a large part of the ploughing, reaping, carting, and other work that was necessary on the demesne (*see* OPEN FIELDS AND ENCLOSURES, Vol. VI).

Besides this economic relationship, however, many of the peasants were not legally free men.

The various classes of unfree men, called 'villeins', were not allowed to leave the manor or to marry without the lord's permission, and very often they had other burdens according to the local custom of the manor. In addition, every manor had a court, which all tenants were bound to attend, where the lord or his steward settled the small differences between the tenants, punished small offences, and took the fines for himself.

From the 13th century the lord of the manor came gradually to exercise less control over the tenants and to lease more of his land; peasants acquired their freedom and became either paid labourers or rent-paying tenants. A man who rented land was called a farmer (*see* LAND OWNERSHIP, Vol. VI). During the 18th century the squire took the place of the lord of the manor as the owner of the land to whom the farmer paid rent for his farm. In France and other parts of Europe manorial courts were abolished at the time of the French Revolution (1789) and after, but in England some of these lingered on without any real importance until manorial rights were abolished in 1926.

Early manor houses, like CASTLES (q.v.), were fortified, for in the unsettled conditions of the Middle Ages they had to be able to withstand attack. In the 12th century the manor house consisted mainly of a single large hall, in which the lord and his family and household all lived. At Boothby Pagnell, in Lincolnshire, the hall is on the first floor for greater safety and is approached by an outside stair. The space below was used for storage (*see* Rooms). In the 13th and 14th centuries more rooms were added: kitchens at one end of the hall and private rooms for the lord at the other; these often spread round three sides of a courtyard, with a Gatehouse (q.v.) at the fourth, as, for instance, at Great Chalfield in Wiltshire and Cothay Manor in Somerset. As well as living rooms there were stables and barns for storing the produce of the manor fields. The whole was designed to house a self-contained community with a sharp distinction of status between lord and servant. Outside the walls of the manor, the Village (q.v.) grew up in which the villeins lived.

See also Houses, History of; Rooms.

MARMALADE, *see* Jam.

MARRIAGE, HISTORY OF. This contract
is of very great antiquity. It is doubtful, in fact, if any society has existed, however savage and primitive, without some formal sanctions governing the relations between men and women. The reasons for instituting marriage were many, and love—on which, we like to think, most marriages today are based—had little or no place in them. The human infant needs longer care after birth than the young of any other animal, and this at once introduces the need for the Family (q.v.). Similarly, man and woman naturally supplement one another's labours: while the man hunts, fights, and builds, the woman weaves, cultivates, and cooks. Besides this need for family organization, there was society's need to know who exactly everyone was, partly in order to settle problems of Inheritance (q.v. Vol. X), but still more to prevent marriage between persons too nearly related (*see* Relationships), or, in some cases, between persons who were not related closely enough (*see* Totemism, Vol. I). This involved basing marriage on a formal, publicly recognized tie.

A deep instinct has always governed the choice of marriage partners. Most peoples have been 'exogamous', that is, they allowed marriage only with someone outside the family or clan. Others have been 'endogamous', that is, they have encouraged marriage within the family. In either case the rules governing marriage have been strict, and the penalties for breaking them severe—in some cases death. These rules have varied very greatly. In ancient Persia and Egypt, for example, marriages between brother and sister were common among ruling families, and this was true also of medieval Peru and, more recently, of Hawaii. In ancient civilizations marriage between a brother and his half-sister by a common father was frequent: Abraham, for instance, married his half-sister Sarah. Some Indian castes admit the marriage of uncle and niece, and in Peru and Uruguay, aunt and nephew may marry. Marriage between first cousins is forbidden in some countries, but not in others, including England. (The Table of Affinities in the Anglican Prayer Book shows the attitude of the Church, but not all these rules are enforced by the State.)

The choice of marriage partners has been narrowed not only by the rules concerned with blood-relationships. Occupation, too, was often important. Among the Masai (q.v. Vol. I) of East Africa, smiths were not allowed to marry into families practising other trades. Social Class (q.v.) has been a factor in nearly all societies. If a well-bred Tahitian woman married a plebeian, their children were killed. Race has often restricted choice—a factor that has preserved the national characteristics of the Jews. Sometimes religion has played the same part. The Emperor Constantine forbade marriages between Christians and Jews; and even today the Roman Catholic Church forbids a Catholic to marry a non-Catholic unless the latter promises that the Catholic partner's religious life will not be interfered with, and that all children of the marriage will be baptized and brought up as Catholics. In Europe political marriages have lost their importance only within the last century. In primitive societies such marriages are of extreme importance in reconciling small hostile groups. Both in primitive and in civilized societies, marriages which tend to preserve the economic interests of a given class have been encouraged.

Because marriage was used to cement the traditional order of society, it was treated in a very practical way. Choice was a matter of policy, not love, and marriages were arranged by parents. Often, as in ancient Greece and Rome, very young children were engaged with the aid of professional marriage brokers: in the Latin language there are no words expressing the idea of 'woo' or 'court'. Girls were commonly married between the ages of 13 and 16. The legal minimum age was 14 for men and 12 for women, whereas today the legal minimum age in Britain is 16 for both. In England youthful marriages were very common up to the 17th century: in 1672 the diarist Evelyn watched the Archbishop of Canterbury marry two children of 5 and 7. The motive was usually to protect property interests. In particular, a child marriage sometimes ensured that land did not descend to an unmarried orphan who was a minor, for in this case the Crown managed—and often grievously exploited—the property until the ward came of age. Marriages have been celebrated between children so young that they had to be carried in the arms of the witnesses; but these contracts could be broken, and sometimes were, when the children became 12 and 14.

Other motives have led to child marriage: the Chinese, for example, wanted descendants who, by the proper observance of the rites of ANCESTOR WORSHIP (q.v. Vol. I), would make certain that the ancestor's spirit would be preserved. Hindus, too, believe that their spirits after death know no peace unless a son has been left to pray for them. In both cases, therefore, parents arranged early marriages for their children in the hope of descendants. There has been such general agreement that the married state is desirable that governments have regularly taxed bachelors. The Roman Emperor Augustus fined unmarried men of 24 and over; in England, between 1695 and 1706, bachelors and widowers of 25 and over were taxed 1s. a year if they were commoners, £10 if they were marquesses, and £12 if they were dukes. The bachelor today is to some extent penalized through INCOME TAX (q.v. Vol. X).

Marriage is commonly a religious ceremony (see MARRIAGE CEREMONIES, Vol. I), but in 1836 civil marriage was legalized in England. As early as the reign of Elizabeth I there was discontent with the orthodox Anglican wedding service, and in 1653 a civil ceremony was introduced by Cromwell; this, however, was banned at the Restoration. The dissatisfaction with the service grew to such an extent that during the 18th century nearly one-third of all marriages were contracted irregularly. Apart from the ritual, which offended Dissenters, the causes of discontent were the delay and publicity involved in the publishing of banns, the heavy fees, and the need for consent in the case of minors. All these inconveniences could be avoided by private and more or less illegal ceremonies. Such was the notorious 'Fleet Marriage', which any parson imprisoned for debt in the Fleet Prison could perform for visitors, who could come and go freely; and there were London shops with the sign of clasped hands and the legend 'Marriages performed within'. Hardwicke's Marriage Act of 1753 checked these abuses; but non-Anglicans still protested because only the Anglican Church could legally perform the marriage service. The Act of 1836 introduced the additional system of marriages by a registrar in a registry office or non-Anglican Church. These require 21 days' notice or, with a special licence, notice of one full day only. Private contracts of the Gretna Green variety are still legal in Scotland, but only after 21 days' residence.

Generally speaking, in the last 100 years, marriages have been contracted at a later age than formerly, and dissolved more readily (see DIVORCE LAW, Vol. X). In the eyes of the law, marriage is no longer an unbreakable life-long engagement, with its chief purpose the upbringing of children in an unchanging home: it is now felt to be primarily a union devoted to the happy relationship of man and wife. If either party, by cruelty, desertion, or adultery, injures the other, the law is prepared to see the marriage dissolved in spite of the grave disturbance which may be caused in the lives of the children. Legally, there is no bar to the remarriage of divorced persons, but the Church of England disapproves of its ministers officiating in such circumstances, and the Roman Catholic Church forbids it. Another important change is that the choice of marriage partners has been considerably widened, partly because social barriers and parental authority are less strict than they were, and partly because education often levels out differences of class, race, and religion.

See also FAMILY, HISTORY OF.
See also Vol. I: MARRIAGE CEREMONIES.

MASTOID, *see* EAR STRUCTURE.

MATERNITY CLINICS, *see* FAMILY WELFARE SERVICES, Section 4.

MEALS. To break bread with a man and to share his salt were once actual ceremonies that established friendship. Meals are more than the occasions for consuming food. They are social events and symbols of hospitality, sometimes with a religious significance. By custom special meals celebrate family events, such as a coming-of-age or marriage, and State events, such as coronations, as well as FAMILY FESTIVALS (q.v.) and the great days of the CHRISTIAN YEAR (q.v. Vol. I).

Meals have often been the means of showing by lavish expenditure the generosity and wealth of the donor. Largesse in the form of a splendid meal was once expected of men in important positions, and they, in response, risked ruin in their desire to impress. When Archbishop Nevill was installed at York in 1467 he gave a feast to all who could come. Among the fare were: 330 tuns (large casks) of ale and 100 of wine, 104 oxen, 6 wild bulls, 1,000 sheep, 2,000 geese, 13,500 miscellaneous small birds, 1,500 hot venison pasties, 4 porpoises, 8 seals, and 13,000 dishes of jelly. The great feasts of the 12th to the 16th centuries were popular not only for the food but as great occasions of social intercourse and entertainment. There was music, and often tumbling, juggling, and dancing. There were splendid set pieces of fruit and pastry representing mock battles, castles and palaces, and other such subjects; roast peacocks were served in all their feathers, or gilt or silvered, and there were dishes designed as 'subtleties'—riddles of which the guests had to suggest the meaning. Men and women would travel long distances to such great feasts. The object of these feasts was often a visit by the sovereign to wealthy subjects. When visits of this kind were no longer paid and other forms of entertainment grew up, banquets which were affairs purely of eating and drinking took the place of these great feasts. A feast somewhat of the old style, however, was provided by Queen Salote of Tonga when Queen Elizabeth II visited her in 1953.

Meals, of course, have always been a principal means of ENTERTAINING (q.v.). Sometimes the Church or the State has intervened to limit their luxury, as in the sumptuary laws that regulated the amount that might be spent by people of different classes on meals in 15th-century Venice and Scotland. Till the 17th century, dinner was the meal used for entertainment; in the early

Condé Musée, Chantilly
A MEDIEVAL BANQUET
Illumination from the Calendar of the *Très Riches Heures du Duc de Berry*, early 15th century

18th century breakfast entertainment became fashionable; towards the end of the 18th century, luncheon; and in mid-19th century London elaborate afternoon tea parties became the mode.

Hospitality can involve great depth of feeling. It is significant that when a Roman wished to give a meal of especial importance, he gave it not in his own house but in a temple. And certain meals have, in fact, a crucial religious significance. The central Christian ceremony, the Communion, is a symbolical re-enacting of the Last Supper (*see* SACRAMENTS, Section 2, Vol. I).

Many societies have attached religious or magical ideas to some foods and meals (*see* MAGIC, Vol. I). To the Hindu all meals can have a religious significance, and this leads to severe restrictions on the preparation of meals and the company in which they may be eaten (*see* HINDUISM, Vol. I). These restrictions apply only to food cooked with water, such as rice and broths, but as these make up the main daily diet of an Indian they are of great importance. Only a cook of the man's own CASTE or sub-caste (q.v. Vol. I) may prepare such food (*Kachchi* food), and only members of the same group may eat it with him. This leads to great practical

Bodleian Library

A 17TH-CENTURY FAMILY SAYING GRACE BEFORE A MEAL

5.30 p.m., and was a lighter form of dinner. In the 18th century, when dinner was at 4 p.m., supper retreated to 10–11 p.m., and consisted of cold meats, sweets, fruit, and wine—to which hot dishes might be added if there was company. But by the 19th century, when a full, late dinner was served, supper disappeared. As it vanished, luncheon appeared on the time-table to fill in the long gap between breakfast and the late dinner. In Doctor Johnson's *Dictionary* of 1755 'Nunchin' is defined as 'a piece of victuals eaten between meals', and 'Lunch' as 'as much food as one's hand can hold'. It was then, in fact, no more than a mid-day snack, but as breakfast became earlier and dinner later, lunch became a larger meal, slowly taking the place of breakfast as the meal second only to dinner for ceremony and leisurely ease. During the first half of the 19th century it was fixed at 1 p.m. and was adopted by more and more people, though in 1853 the middle-class householder was warned that 'this meal is admissible only when either the interval between the breakfast and dinner is very prolonged, or when the quantity of food taken at breakfast is very small', and as late as the turn of the century, lunch in the City tended to consist of no more than biscuits and a glass of wine.

A 16th-century breakfast was a casual snack with no fixed menu or social importance; but by the 18th century it was established as a weighty, lengthy meal, to which guests were regularly invited and which might last from 10 a.m. till 1 p.m. Such social breakfasts survived in Oxford and Cambridge into the present century, but in the world at large breakfast tended to become earlier, and to shrink into a purely family affair. Between 1800 and 1850 it gradually got as early as 8 or 8.15 a.m., and acquired a menu of its own, different from that of any other meal.

Afternoon tea did not become habitual until

difficulties when many Hindus of different castes have to live together, as in an army camp or at a university. At a hostel at Allahabad, thirty-seven separate kitchens had to be provided for one hundred students.

The nature of meals varies between town and country, for the rhythm of farm life imposes its own meal times. Among town-dwellers part of England waits for dinner while the rest is eating high tea. Meal times vary from country to country and have also changed from period to period. The following is an account of the changing fashions of meal times among well-to-do English people.

Dinner, the main meal of the day, was at 11 a.m. in the 16th century, but towards the end of the century it was beginning to take place rather later. In an article in *The Tatler* in 1710, Steele noted that 'in my own memory the dinner has crept by degrees from twelve o'clock to three'. By the late 18th century it had moved on to 5 p.m., though many families clung to an earlier hour. By 1800, 7 p.m. was fashionable, but the hour remained a matter of wide choice, some dining at 5, others perhaps at 7.30 p.m. By the 1850s, 7–8 p.m. became a more standard hour, and dinner has remained so ever since.

In the 16th century supper was taken at

the 1860s, when the price of **tea** dropped sharply, and when improved transport made it easier to get about London. (London led the provinces in this as in all matters of polite behaviour.) By the 1880s it usually took place about 5 p.m., and was primarily for ladies. The habit spread rapidly from the wealthy to the poorer, and it was in part to cater for it that the first A.B.C. restaurant was opened in 1880 and the first Lyons in 1894.

The 18th-century working day ended with dinner at 3 p.m., but the Victorian business man had two periods equally devoted to work, 9 a.m. to 1 p.m. and 2 p.m. to 6 p.m. The desire to secure a long working day was the main factor that affected the time-table of meals. Other factors may affect it. In Spain, for instance, the heat of summer afternoons makes it convenient to have a long break in the middle of the day and to work much later in the evening. The mid-day meal, therefore, is about 1.30 p.m. or 2 p.m., and the evening meal as late as 9 p.m. or 10 p.m.

The wide use of sandwiches and portable snacks, the shortage of domestic help, and the rapid growth of facilities for eating out, have all affected the times and nature of meals. Very many families have a late meat tea when working hours are over, and a snack for supper. But the basic pattern of four meals a day remains as it was set by the 1890s, although we probably eat no more than our 16th-century ancestors did in their two meals.

See also TABLE MANNERS; ENTERTAINING; FOOD, HISTORY OF.

MEASLES, *see* INFECTIOUS DISEASES, Section 2.

MEAT. This article is about meat eaten in Britain—that is, from ox, sheep, and pig—but, in fact, horses, goats, water buffaloes, camels, dogs, whales, seals, elephants, and many other mammals are considered wholesome meat in other countries. Various people have religious objections to eating various kinds of meat. For

Picture Post Library

A 19TH-CENTURY FAMILY AT BREAKFAST
Engraving after T. Webster, 1800–86

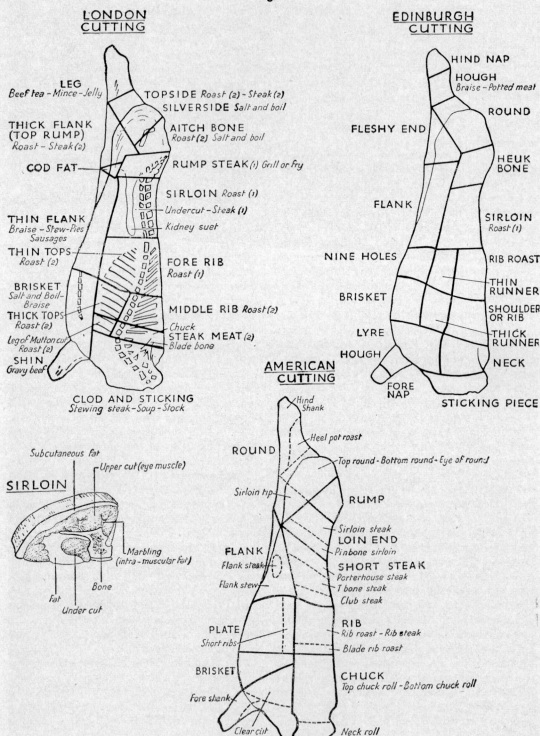

FIG. I. LONDON, EDINBURGH, AND AMERICAN METHODS OF CUTTING BEEF, AND THE PARTS OF THE SIRLOIN

First and second grade joints are marked 1 and 2 respectively

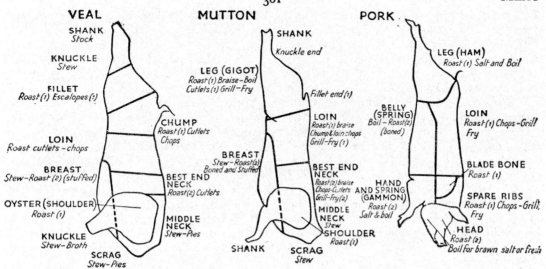

FIG. 2. JOINTS OF VEAL, MUTTON, AND PORK
First and second grade joints are marked 1 and 2 respectively

instance, orthodox Jews and Moslems will not eat pork, nor will Hindus eat beef. Carcase meats derive their English names from the Norman-French words for the whole animal—*bœuf, veau, mouton, porc*—but OFFALS (q.v.) retain their Anglo-Saxon names—oxtail, calf's foot, sheep's tongue, pig's trotter.

To know what to buy it is necessary to know how the butcher cuts up a carcase and how he names the joints. There is a broad general agreement in different parts of the world about the cutting up of a carcase, based on the skeleton of the animal; but the details vary surprisingly, even in different parts of Britain (*see* Fig. 1). The beef carcase diagrams show the London method and the Edinburgh method as a contrast. An example from America is included to show the various American steak cuts.

Everyone is agreed that good beef is marbled with tiny streaks of intra-muscular fat; prime Aberdeen Angus is the best. Beef from 1–2-year-old animals is very tender, that from 2–5-year-old animals is less tender, but fuller flavoured. Cream-coloured fat is usually looked for—not because there is anything wrong with yellow fat (it merely contains accumulated carotene), but because it is a sign either of age or of a Jersey or Guernsey which, though better for dairy purposes, is not so good as beef. Cherry red is usually considered the best colour for the lean, but some people hold that the flavour is richer if the meat is darker—in bull beef, for example.

Veal is softer than beef, pinkish white, and with very scanty white fat. Calves are killed at 3 to 12 weeks old; the veal from younger calves has so little muscle and fat in relation to connective tissue that it is very leathery. It is for this reason that even prime veal needs longer and slower cooking than beef. Because it tends to be tasteless, it needs more seasoning, hence such dishes as veal goulash and stuffed veal. A veal carcase is cut up in the same way as mutton (Fig. 2).

Mutton should have firm, white fat, and juicy, light red lean—darker in some hill breeds. Probably a 3-year-old wether, well hung, has the best flavour. The flavour of any mutton is strengthened by rubbing it lightly with salt and garlic before roasting. Lamb, which comes from animals under one year old, has firm, white fat, and pale pink lean with fine grain and good marbling. 'Milk lamb' comes from the suckling lamb, 'house lamb' from animals fed indoors, 'grass lamb' from those fed out of doors. Lamb needs more cooking than mutton just as veal needs more than beef.

Pork has clear, white fat, and lean which is almost white when young, greyish rose when older. The Large White pig can reach porker weight—about 100 lb.—in 16–18 weeks. Sucking pigs are nowadays encountered only in literature. Bacon and ham are produced by curing pork (*see* FOOD PRESERVING).

The most expensive steaks are cut from parts

of the animal where the muscles are little used and so are fine-grained and tender. They are cooked by the quick methods, GRILLING, FRYING, and ROASTING (qq.v.). Slow, moist methods help to break down the fibres of the tougher cuts. Stewing steak, though not as attractive, is as nutritious as best steak. From along the back come part of the rump, almost all of the tender chops and rib cuts, and the upper cut of the sirloin (the 'sir' is from the French *sur*, 'above', and not, as the old story has it, because this joint was knighted by Charles II). The part beneath the backbone in the loin region is the most prized for steaks; it forms the undercut of the sirloin and when removed whole is called the fillet in England, the tender-loin in America, and in France *le filet*. The uppercut of the sirloin is the French *contrefilet*. Fillet steaks are those cut laterally from the thickest part of the fillet; 1½ inches thick, they weigh about 6–7 ounces. Tournedos are the kernels of the fillet; they are 1½ inches thick, round, and only 3–3½ ounces in weight. Châteaubriand steaks, also from the thick fillet, are two or three times heavier than fillet steaks—1 pound or more each. Châteaubriand's chef, Montmireil, used to place this big steak between two others of the same size, which were burnt black in the grilling and thrown away, leaving the Châteaubriand a beautiful, even pink. *Entrecôte*, known as sirloin steak in America, is cut from the upper-cut. Sirloin, pin bone, porterhouse, T. bone, and club steaks are American steaks cut forward from the sirloin region. The larger ones are carved into wedges at table. The corresponding parts are usually bone roasts in Britain. The part of the pig which corresponds to the beef under-cut is sold separately for grilling, in America as pork tenderloin and in Britain as fillets.

For carving, the knife must be sharp, and the meat platter big enough. The carver should stand to his work, push the fork in, with the guard up, near the top of the meat between bones, and carve across the grain of the meat wherever possible. Bits such as knuckle mutton should be eaten while hot, as they dry up when cold. Beef is cut as thin as possible, and mutton up to ¼ inch thick. Efficient carving means the greatest possible number of meat slices, and it is better to cut enough for all before serving any.

See also OFFAL; POULTRY.
See also Vol. VI: CATTLE; PIGS; SHEEP.
See also Vol. VII: MEAT TRADE.

MEDICINE. Modern medicine has achieved unprecedented success by bringing to its problems the ever expanding scientific knowledge which is characteristic of modern civilization. Scientific method, based on observation and experiment, has enabled us to abolish or reduce considerably the risk of EPIDEMIC DISEASES and TROPICAL DISEASES (qq.v.). These conquests, together with the scientific study of NUTRITION and of the DEFICIENCY DISEASES (qq.v.) arising from malnutrition, have helped to free vast tracts of the earth's surface for development and to bring to their native populations improved health and increased expectation of life, together with the energy and desire for social betterment. An international body, the World Health Organization at Geneva, a branch of the UNITED NATIONS ORGANIZATION (q.v. Vol. X), now helps to bring preventive medicine and modern ideas of public health to 'backward' countries.

In the last resort, however, after all the sciences have made their contributions to medicine, and national and international bodies have organized health campaigns and services, the practice of medicine is a matter between the doctor and his patient. The main lines of treatment are based on scientific methods, but their individual application must vary with the patient's response and the doctor's insight, judgement, and experience. Even with the most advanced scientific techniques, results are not always predictable, especially in the case of the ALLERGIC DISEASES (q.v.). Medicine is not a pure science; it is a synthesis of sciences, and its application is an art, sometimes reaching a very high level, sometimes falling short of the best since its agents are human. This art is today supported by a vast array of scientific specialist studies, extending from such nearly related medical sciences as pharmacology, the science of DRUGS (q.v.), to others which may seem to have little to do with medicine, such as nuclear physics (*see* RADIO-ACTIVE ISOTOPES, Vol. VIII). But however rapidly ideas change with advancing knowledge, the relationship between doctor and patient remains the stable and abiding factor in medicine.

Although medicine was practised by the ancient Egyptians—and we know something of their methods from surviving documents—it is the famous Greek physician HIPPOCRATES (q.v. Vol. V), a contemporary of Socrates in the 5th century B.C., who is regarded as 'the father of medicine'. Although little is known for certain about Hippocrates, he has been for succeeding ages the embodiment of the ideal physician. A mass of Greek medical literature which bears his name—the Hippocratic collection—was probably put together in Alexandria in the 3rd century B.C. It is doubtful whether, in fact, Hippocrates wrote any of it, and much of it was certainly written by various authors at different times, expressing different views. But they all have something in common: their discarding of ancient superstitions and theories which blinded men to the facts. Some of them concen-

Wellcome Historical Medical Museum

A GREEK PHYSICIAN EXAMINING A GIRL

The figure on the right holds the staff of Aesculapius which is still the symbol of the medical profession

trated attention on the sick patient, carefully studying the 'natural history' of particular diseases, and recording it in simple prose so that others could easily recognize similar conditions when they saw them. The course of many diseases is described so accurately that modern doctors can identify them. This method of careful recording and comparison of actual clinical cases is known as the Hippocratic method. The best known of all the Hippocratic writings is the celebrated Hippocratic oath, a code of medical ethics which is still observed by medical men throughout the world. It stresses the fellowship of doctors, the dedication of their lives to healing and goodness. It ends thus: 'whatsoever things I see or hear concerning the life of men, in my attendance on the sick or even apart therefrom, which ought not to be noised abroad, I will keep silence thereon, counting such things to be as sacred secrets. Pure and holy will I keep my life and my art.'

Greek physicians were famous, and after the Roman conquest of Greece, medicine was left almost entirely to Greeks throughout the Roman world, except for public hygiene in which the Romans excelled. At first the Romans regarded medicine as an occupation worthy only of slaves; but in 46 B.C. Julius Caesar gave citizenship to all physicians, and gradually their status improved. The greatest Greek physician of the Roman age was Galen, who became court phy-

sician to the Emperor Marcus Aurelius in the 2nd century A.D. Galen dominated medical knowledge for nearly 1,500 years. He wrote a great number of medical works as well as other books on ethics, logic, and philosophy. His best medical writings, those on anatomy, physiology, and pathology, continued to be standard text-books in the medical schools until the 17th century. So great was his authority throughout the Middle Ages, when medical practice fell to a low ebb, that the patient was almost forgotten in the scholastic discussion of some point of Galen's text.

Throughout the Middle Ages the care of the sick was mainly in the hands of the monasteries (*see* HOSPITALS, HISTORY OF). Qualified doctors were very few, and only the rich and powerful could command their services. Ordinary people were treated by quacks with an illiterate smattering of Galenic knowledge, by 'wise women' skilled in herbs, or, for external wounds and injuries, by 'unlettered surgeons' whose skill and knowledge hardly reached that of a first-aid worker today. Purgation and bleeding were the mainstays of medical treatment, and ASTROLOGY (q.v. Vol. I) was the medieval equivalent of the modern sciences. The theory of 'humours'—an old Greek idea firmly established by Galen— seemed to provide all the answers about the causation and treatment of disease. The four 'humours' were 'blood' and 'phlegm', 'yellow

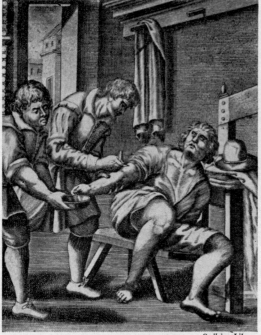

Bodleian Library

A 17TH-CENTURY BARBER-SURGEON BLOOD-LETTING

collection, gave a tremendous impetus to advances in medical knowledge. It is remarkable that within a few days of each other in the year 1543 there were published two great books written by medical men which revolutionized man's thought about his own body and about his place in the universe. One, by the Flemish anatomist Andreas VESALIUS (q.v. Vol. V), described with greater accuracy and detail than had ever been attempted before the anatomical structure of the human body, without a sound knowledge of which medicine must be purely speculative (*see* ANATOMY). The other, by a Polish doctor Nicholas COPERNICUS (q.v. Vol. V), set forth revolutionary ideas about the structure of the universe, implying that man could no longer be regarded as the centre of the universe, for the earth travelled round the sun and not, as men had always believed, the sun round the earth.

Once the structure of the human body was correctly understood, the way was opened to new discoveries about the function of the various organs. The 17th century was notable for new advances in experimental physiology, the most important being the discovery made by William HARVEY (q.v. Vol. V) of the BLOOD CIRCULATION (q.v.). GALILEO's experiments (q.v. Vol. V) led to the introduction of the THERMOMETER (although the clinical thermometer was a later development) and the MICROSCOPE (qq.v. Vol. VIII), which the Dutchman Anton van Leeuwenhoek used for the first time to investigate the previously invisible world of micro-organisms. From the early experiments of the alchemists Robert BOYLE (q.v. Vol. V) evolved the first principles of modern scientific chemistry. Thomas Sydenham, at one time a Cromwellian trooper, founded the modern study of epidemic diseases, and by his careful and accurate clinical observations earned for himself the title of 'the English Hippocrates'. And while Charles I was still king, Jesuits from South America brought to Europe the bark of the cinchona tree, from which, in 1820, two French chemists, Pelletier and Caventou, isolated the drug quinine for use in malaria. This was the first specific drug to be used against any disease.

Meanwhile SURGERY (q.v.), too, stimulated by the new and accurate knowledge of anatomy, was making great advances. Technological advances in the use of metals provided the surgeon with better instruments than any he had

bile' and 'black bile'. Disease occurred whenever the 'good' humours in the body were overcome by the 'bad', so that to be purged of one's humours, or bled, seemed an obvious remedy. Such phrases—originally medical terms—as 'a good humour' and 'a bad humour' still persist in our speech.

Galen's writings were also an important influence in the East, where the flourishing civilization built up by the Arabs after the Islamic conquest (*see* ISLAM, Vol. I) gave a high place to medicine, pharmacy, and chemistry. The Arabs preserved much of the classical knowledge which might otherwise have been lost, and they introduced a number of important drugs into medical use. The most distinguished of the Arabic physicians were Avicenna, sometimes called the Arabic Galen, and Rhazes, who wrote a description of smallpox and measles which is still accepted as basically correct. The first university medical faculty was instituted at Bologna (*see* UNIVERSITIES, Vol. X) about 1150, to be followed by many others from the 13th century onwards.

The intellectual ferment of the RENAISSANCE (q.v. Vol. I), and the publication in 1525–6 of the Greek texts of Galen and the Hippocratic

EMBROIDERY BY MARTHA EDLIN, BORN 1660, WORKED
BEFORE SHE WAS 14 YEARS OLD

At the top is the lid of a trinket box embroidered with beads and silks on white satin in tent and rococo stitches;
below this is a casket embroidered on white satin with coloured silks, metal, and seed pearls. It stands on two
linen samplers, one embroidered with coloured silks in cross, tent, and satin stitches, and the other in cut work.
The small objects are pincushions, needle and bodkin cases, miniature bellows and gloves, and a goose

ever used before. The scope of surgery, however, was still much limited by the lack of a suitable general anaesthetic and by ignorance of the importance of scrupulous cleanliness.

A period of great discovery in medicine is usually followed by one in which the new discoveries and observations are absorbed into a system of medical doctrine. The varied knowledge which had been accumulating throughout the 17th century was organized and directed towards its chief end by one of the greatest of physicians, the Dutchman Hermann Boerhaave (1668–1738). At the medical school at Leyden, where he presided, he organized medical education on the lines which it still follows today, with its emphasis on clinical instruction at the patient's bedside, aided by all the information which the new scientific knowledge provided. One of Boerhaave's pupils, Alexander Monro, founded the Edinburgh Medical School, which became the model for all medical schools in every part of the English-speaking world.

This new system of medical education required good hospitals, which would never have been provided but for the growing social conscience which became more and more active as the 18th century advanced. Many of our most famous HOSPITALS (q.v. Vol. X) were founded at that time, and in them have been established the medical schools where the great majority of doctors are trained today. As opportunities for study became more easily available, the scientific study of the causation of disease made considerable advances. In Italy Morgagni devoted his life to the study of post mortem conditions, and set out the results of his investigations in one of the great classics of medicine, *The Seats and Causes of Disease* (1761). In London at the same time the Scottish surgeon John HUNTER (q.v. Vol. V) changed surgery from a mere craft into a scientific study based on comparative pathology (the study of disease). Hunter's collection of specimens demonstrating diseased organs in man and animals is preserved in the Hunterian Museum in the Royal College of Surgeons of England.

In 1798 one of Hunter's pupils, Edward JENNER (q.v. Vol. V), first introduced the practice of vaccination against smallpox (*see* INOCULATION), and so helped to liberate mankind from one of its most dreaded enemies.

In the 19th century some of the most acute observers medicine has ever known, men such

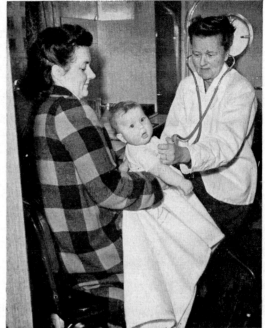

Nursing Mirror

A DOCTOR EXAMINES A BABY WITH A STETHOSCOPE IN THE CONSULTING-ROOM OF A MOBILE HEALTH CLINIC

as Addison, Bright, and Graves, wrote classic descriptions of diseases which still bear their names—for example, 'Graves's Disease', a very severe form of goitre (*see* ENDOCRINE GLANDS). In 1830 the compound microscope came to their aid, invented by Joseph Jackson Lister, a wine merchant and father of the great Lord LISTER (q.v. Vol. V). In 1846 an American dentist, W. T. G. Morton, first used ether as a general ANAESTHETIC (q.v.), and the following year chloroform was introduced. In the 1860s PASTEUR (q.v. Vol. V) made his first investigations which led to his germ theory of disease. Lister was the first to appreciate its importance and to build on it his system of ANTISEPSIS AND ASEPSIS which made possible modern SURGERY (qq.v.). The revolution in PUBLIC HEALTH (q.v. Vol. X) which followed this discovery is not yet concluded, for there are still places—not all of them in 'backward' countries—where the vital importance of cleanliness in preventing disease is not appreciated.

The three great discoveries—anaesthetics, the germ theory of disease, and antiseptics—brought about a transformation in medicine; but a host of minor discoveries, without which medicine would be very different from what it is today, accompanied and succeeded them. The growth of organic CHEMISTRY (q.v. Vol. VII) led scientists to study the effect of certain chemicals on the human body and on the invading organisms which cause disease; and the new science of chemotherapy, of which the founder was the German chemist Paul Ehrlich (1854–1915), has revealed many substances which can be introduced into the body in order to kill the germs without harming the normal tissues. Antibiotics, which are chemical substances extracted chiefly from fungoid growths, are a natural development of this search for specific DRUGS (q.v.), so many of which are now invented and put together in the laboratory.

Another important contribution of the chemists was the discovery in the early years of the 20th century of the VITAMINS (q.v.), elements in our diet essential to health; the absence of these causes 'deficiency diseases', which can now be cured easily and swiftly by administering the required vitamins.

With the phenomenal growth of all the sciences, medicine has itself been divided into a number of specialities, each dealing with the study and treatment of a particular disease or organ. The family doctor, however, remains the 'general specialist', who is highly trained to deal with most conditions which come his way. In cases of doubt or special difficulty he has a whole body of specialists whose particular skill he can call upon.

See also SURGERY, HISTORY OF; MENTAL DISEASES; NURSING.

See also Vol. X: HOSPITALS, HISTORY OF; PUBLIC HEALTH; NATIONAL HEALTH SERVICE.

MEMORY. Memory may be defined as 'the power of retaining and using knowledge or ability acquired in the past'. This definition could be fairly safely shortened to 'the power of learning'.

How many different types of things can we remember? We remember drill-movements (for example, how to present arms), skills (for example, how to play the piano), routes and methods (the way to the station, or how to make a bed), general facts (such as that milk boils quicker than water), particular facts (such as that Germany invaded Belgium in 1914), persons and things we have met with in the past, and, finally, past events in which we played a conscious part.

Philosophers, in particular John LOCKE and David HUME (qq.v. Vol. V), have tended to concentrate on the two last-mentioned types. The result was that they have left to us what may be called the 'album theory' of memory, which they did not intend as a physiological account, but merely as a metaphorical description of conscious processes. It runs something like this: when we see or hear something (have an 'impression of sense') the mind takes a copy of it and stores it up. Later on some new impression, by a mysterious mechanism called 'the association of ideas', causes the album to open at the right page and display to the mind the picture of what we saw or heard long ago.

There are several difficulties in such a theory. Though most of us can form images in our minds of things we have seen, fewer of us can do it with the sounds, fewer still with the tastes, smells, and feelings that we remember. Again, animals undoubtedly remember persons, places, and events, but we do not know whether they form mental images or not, for they cannot tell us. The 'album theory' does not at all fit some types of memory, such as how we remember how to do Latin verses. Finally, a picture, whether it is on paper or 'in the mind's eye', tells us nothing unless we know what it is a picture of. This we can know only by memory; and only by memory can we know that it is a picture of something we have seen, and not a fantasy of our imaginations. Further, we make the picture just as much as if we drew it on paper; and we could not do that unless we already remembered what the thing was like.

Arguments of this sort have convinced most modern philosophers that forming mental pictures is not the essential part of memory, but is, at most, one of the abilities memory confers. In some cases, forming the picture is possible and helpful. For instance, in order to find something you put somewhere, it may help you to visualize your movements when last you had it; though some people would find a description in words easier and just as helpful. In some sorts of memory visualization is, as we have seen, impossible or useless.

What have the physiologists to say about memory? Can they tell us what changes occur in the BRAIN (q.v.) when we see something, and how these changes make us recognize it when we see it again, answer questions about it correctly, draw it accurately, and so on? What is the physical mechanism of learning?

Physiologists answer that at present we know next to nothing about the mechanism, for we cannot observe directly what happens in the brain at the moment of remembering; but they believe more may be learned about it by means of the 'encephalograph', a device which records electrical effects of the activity of the brain. There has, however, been a steady flow of speculation on the subject since before the time of ARISTOTLE (q.v. Vol. V). Experiences, it has been argued, must leave some traces in the brain if they are to be remembered later, and these traces may be pathways, or networks of pathways, through the nerve-fibres of the brain; such trails, 'blazed' by the impulses of the original experiences and of our responses to them, are more easily followed by later impulses from similar sources. So far, the theory seems to explain learning by heart and drill-movements, but little else.

To explain how we are reminded of past experiences by 'association of ideas', it has been supposed that when two pathways are used at the same, or nearly the same, time, connecting links are formed between them, so that afterwards impulses traversing either pathway overflow into the other.

Some theorists, accepting that the memory pathways are identical with those followed by the impulses giving rise to sensation, maintain that in memory the pathways are traversed in the opposite direction, or by impulses entering them through the 'link' channels, or in some other special manner which distinguishes a memory or image from a sensation. Others say that memory traces its own separate pathways, and that this is a part of what happens when we perceive something, when 'a memory is imprinted on the mind'. This view raises the question, in what part of the brain are memory traces located. Cases of brain tumours suggest that the third ventricle has some special connexion with memory, and the results of artificial stimulation of the cortex suggest that the temporal lobes have; but all parts of the brain depend so closely on one another that it is unsafe to infer that either of these regions is the site of the traces.

Such 'trace-theories', however, are little more than physiological versions of the philosopher's 'album theory'. They explain only recall by association of single experiences and mechanical habits. What needs explaining is how a man becomes better and better able to deal with changing circumstances; how, that is, he not only forms useful habits and perfects skills, but also applies them in the light of past as well as present experience.

Therefore Professor Bartlett and others have suggested that experiences, instead of blazing trails, set up patterns of nervous activity, which, like the vibrations of a tuning fork, continue after the experience has ceased. Each such pattern is shaped in part by the preceding patterns, and helps to shape those that follow. These patterns, formed into organized groups corresponding to our various interests and needs, Professor Bartlett calls 'schemata'. Their function is to be a kind of living model of our past which helps to determine how we respond to each new situation.

A different approach to the problem is from the side of 'cybernetics', the study of CALCULATING MACHINES, AUTOMATIC CONTROLS, THERMOSTATS (qq.v. Vol. VIII), and similar devices. Some of these have parts which may be called 'memories', and some theorists claim to find structures and processes in the human brain which look as if they might work in the same way as the 'memories' of the machines.

The above account is the merest outline of a great variety of complex theories, all of them speculative. Two interesting facts about 'traces' are well supported by evidence. The first is that at least some memory traces do not fade with time: even the earliest memories of childhood can be revived by hypnosis, drugs, and other methods. The very vivid recollections of early youth enjoyed by old people even suggest that sometimes traces grow stronger. The second is that the formation of a trace takes some time. It is easier to repeat a memorized sentence after an interval than at once. The trace needs time to mature, or, as we often say, 'sink in'. In cases of concussion the patient often never recovers the memory of what happened immediately before the accident, because, it is suggested, the accident prevented these traces from maturing.

Psychologists in recent years have found out much about why we forget things, and how the memory of what has been forgotten may be recovered. We are all familiar with the tendency to forget what we do not want to remember. We forget to write a tiresome letter, or to give an embarrassing message to a friend; we refer to someone we dislike as 'What-do-you-call-him, never can remember the fellow's name'. FREUD (q.v. Vol. V) claimed to have shown that this phenomenon, 'active forgetting', is much more extensive than we ordinarily suppose, and that the 'repressed' memory can sometimes damage our mental health. It is then the psychologist's business to bring the buried memory back to consciousness. Even if the memory dates back to very early childhood this can sometimes be done by what is called 'deep analysis', involving hypnosis, the interpretation of DREAMS (q.v.), and long and skilful tracing of unconscious associations of ideas.

See also BRAIN; INTELLIGENCE; PSYCHOLOGY.
See also Vol. I: PHILOSOPHY.

MENDING. The same equipment as for SEWING and DRESSMAKING (qq.v.) is necessary for good mending. Darning and patching are the usual methods of repairing garments; but it is better to reinforce a thin place by darning it with yarn of similar colour and texture than to patch it, as a successful darn is almost invisible. Various synthetic preparations—mending glue, glued tape, and rubber tissue—are effective for quick repairs or for mending hems or small tears in mackintoshes.

Reinforcing to strengthen the thin parts of a garment may be done by hand or machine, whichever is more suitable for the article and fabric, by darning new threads in with the worn ones or instead of them. Warp threads unravelled from the seams give the most invisible darns. A darn on thin material consists of parallel rows of small running stitches, worked lengthwise of the material, extending at least $\frac{1}{4}$ inch outside the thin parts, with extra reinforcement by working rows of stitches crosswise. Worn places on woollen garments, for instance, at the elbows or underarms, may be backed with double net, chiffon, or any pliable material, the running stitches being worked through both garment and backing so that they are almost invisible from the right side of the garment. Small tears and holes are bridged lengthwise with matching yarn, held by stitches on either side; then the bridging strands are woven across, over and under (Fig. 1a). Long splits may be fishboned together, with darning or machine stitching for added strength (Fig. 1b). Very long ones are tacked on to paper before mending so as to keep the proper shape. Corner tears should also be tacked on to paper, darned across from one slit to the corner, then across the corner again and down the other slit. Small loops of thread are left at the ends of each line of darning to allow for stretching.

Darning by electric or treadle SEWING MACHINE (q.v.) is strong and quickly done. Fine machine-cotton, 80–100, or mercerized thread gives the best results, and the work must be stretched right side up on the base of an embroidery frame.

In knitted fabrics or stockings, thin places should be darned either to match the weave or diagonally. Coarse ladders can be picked up with a fine crochet hook and the stitches sewn at the top, but fine ones on underwear or stockings may be whipped or machined into narrow seams on the wrong side. When darning holes or mending diagonal tears, each loop must be picked up by the mending thread to prevent ladders, and the cross-wise threads woven under and over until the hole is filled. Stockings should be mended with very fine needles and thread; mesh or net weaves should be darned on a frame with a single fine thread, following the weave of the fabric.

Patches are made in different ways to suit different fabrics, and some patches are better hand sewn, some machined. The patch must be of a similar fabric to the garment, in age, colour, weight, and pattern, and the weaves must match exactly, so that the result is as invisible as possible. The area to be cut away, the centres of the top and bottom of the hole, and the centre line of the patch are marked. The patch is then cut, allowing for necessary turnings. The patch may be of any shape to suit the hole, it may be on the right or wrong side according to the fabric, but it must be flat; for firm plain fabrics, a hemmed patch on the wrong side is usually best (Fig. 2a). The patch is cut 1 inch bigger

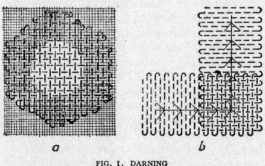

FIG. I. DARNING
a. A hole. *b.* A corner tear

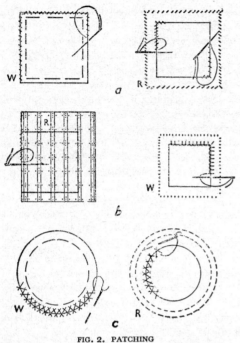

FIG. 2. PATCHING

a. A hemmed patch on plain fabric. *b.* Overcasting a patch on the right side of patterned materials and buttonholing the edges on the wrong side. *c.* Patching a hole in knitted fabric with herring bone stitch. R. Right side. w. Wrong side

than the hole, and, after its edges have been turned under, it is tacked and hemmed to the wrong side of the garment. The worn parts are then cut away, making a square or rectangular hole, the corners are nicked ¼ inch, and the edges turned under and hemmed to the patch. A patterned patch may be placed on the right side for easier matching. For non-fraying fabrics such as flannel, the patch is cut without turnings, and the raw edges are herring-boned first round the hole and then round the patch on the wrong side. A flat patch in a dress is cut as described, and the edges of the hole turned in and tacked over the patch. Then the edge is either overcast from the right side or stitched on the creased, turned-in edges of the patch (Fig. 2*b*). The seams are pressed out flat, and the corners reinforced with overcasting. For knitted or elastic fabrics, patches should be round or oval instead of rectangular, and sewn with herring-bone or buttonhole stitch to give them elasticity (Fig. 2*c*). Worn woven fabric of a very good garment can be rewoven, the work being done in similar yarns and the weave copied exactly.

Many types of repair combine darning and patching; for example, holes left by ripped off buttons should be backed with tape and then darned, before the buttons are replaced. Torn plackets are reinforced under the tear with twill tape, and then the seams are relapped and sewn over the original stitchery. Split ends of buttonholes may be machined or hand darned, and frayed ones whipped all round; if the buttonholes are very worn, they may be re-bound with tape. Foundation garments which split at the seams may be whipped on the right side, and reinforced with twill tape on the wrong; torn elastic should be darned by hand and backed with ribbon or fabric.

See also SEWING; CLOTHES, CARE OF.

MENINGITIS, *see* NERVOUS SYSTEM.

MENSTRUATION, *see* LIFE CYCLE.

MENTAL DISEASES. Among primitive peoples and in ancient times an insane person was considered to be possessed by a god or an evil spirit. Prehistoric man even went to the length of making small holes in the skull with a sharply pointed flint in order to release the demon responsible for mental derangement. The idea of demoniac possession is also well illustrated in the Bible, which contains vivid accounts of the casting out of evil spirits. Some peoples believed that changes of the moon induced insanity, hence the word 'lunatic', derived from the Latin *luna*, the moon. HIPPOCRATES (q.v. Vol. V), the great Greek physician of the 5th century B.C., was the first to maintain that mental diseases have natural causes and should be looked at like any other disease. Following Hippocrates there were a few advocates of rational medical treatment and gentleness in the care of the insane, but until comparatively recent times the lot of the mentally ill was unfortunate in the extreme.

In the Middle Ages the ceremony of 'exorcism', or casting out of a devil from a 'possessed' person, was carried out by a priest, and if this failed, violent measures such as immersion in cold water or whipping were tried. From the 11th century onwards asylums for the insane were founded by the Arabs, who treated the mentally sick in a kindly way; and similar provision was made by religious houses in Europe. Bedlam Hospital in London was founded in

1247, but did not become an institution (or rather a prison) for the insane until about 200 years later (*see* MENTAL HOSPITALS, Vol. X).

Until the end of the 18th century and later, the mentally afflicted were treated with no understanding of their condition and often with great brutality. Any old and friendless woman suffering from mental disorder ran the risk of being treated as a witch. Inmates of lunatic asylums were kept in cages or loaded with chains, and if troublesome they were often beaten and tormented in a variety of ways. Even the great were not exempt from the prevailing brutalities: for example, when King George III was suffering from periodic attacks of madness he was confined in a strait-jacket, and on more than one occasion he was knocked down by his keeper.

The pioneer of reform in the treatment of the insane was Philippe Pinel, who was appointed head of the great Paris asylum, the Bicêtre, in 1793. Pinel wrote that 'the mentally ill, far from being guilty people who merit punishment, are sick people whose miserable state deserves all the consideration due to suffering humanity'. He had the fetters removed from the mad people at the Bicêtre (some of them had been chained up for more than 30 years) and began to treat them as patients rather than as criminals. William Tuke, a Quaker merchant, played a similar part in England; in 1794 he founded The Retreat at York, a mental hospital from which all restraint and all forms of terrorization were banished. It was many years before the ideas of these pioneers were generally accepted. In 1827 a commission was set up by Parliament to inquire into the condition of mental asylums. Lord Shaftesbury served on this, and largely due to his efforts during the next 7 years, drastic reforms were introduced. During the last 100 years the care and treatment of the insane has been increasingly high in standard, and British mental hospitals in particular have a great tradition of humanitarian service.

Before the passing of the Mental Treatment Act of 1930 the law was mainly concerned with safeguarding the sane from the risk of wrongful detention in an asylum; now it is designed to facilitate the entry of the mentally ill into hospital at an early stage and with the minimum of formality, so that they may receive treatment which often leads to a cure. Mental hospitals— no longer called 'lunatic asylums'—are rigor-

ously controlled and inspected. Mental disorder is treated as a disease and not a special affliction marked off from all others. It is also known that there are many forms of mental disease, and that only a relatively small proportion of mental patients are hopelessly 'mad', and only a very few are dangerous. Though segregation is usually necessary at some stage of the illness, increasing numbers of mental patients are being restored to normal life. The modern mental hospital looks after and often mends broken minds just as the orthopaedic hospital cares for and mends broken limbs.

The classification of mental diseases is complicated, because many types of disorder shade off into others; in some conditions the mental changes are associated with physical changes in the brain or in some other organ of the body, but in others no such connexion can be traced. In many organic mental disorders some hereditary or degenerative brain disease is present; in others the mental condition has been brought about by poisons (such as alcohol or cocaine), by changes in the thyroid or other ENDOCRINE GLANDS (q.v.), or following certain infections. The affective disorders (*see* PSYCHOLOGY) are disturbances of feeling or emotion, and are remarkable for the rapidity with which the mood of the afflicted person (or manic-depressive) changes from excitement to depression or from boundless optimism to fear and anxiety. The sufferer from schizophrenia is unable to adjust himself to the strain and stress of life and consequently withdraws from reality into a world of fantasy. The paranoiac suffers from fixed delusions, but his mentality is not otherwise impaired. Deranged mentality is sometimes associated with great intellectual powers and with creative ability, as was expressed by the poet Dryden in the lines:

> Great wits are sure to madness near allied,
> And thin partitions do their bounds divide.

The modern treatment of mental disease is psychological and physical. The doctor who specializes in the treatment of mental disease is called a psychiatrist (Greek *psyche*, 'soul', *iatros*, 'physician'), and his field of study is called psychiatry. Psychotherapy (the healing of the mind) includes such methods as hypnosis, psychoanalysis, persuasion, suggestion, and social rehabilitation. Each of these methods varies a good deal from one physician to another.

ring called a savarin border, and filled with liqueured fruits. The word *Soubise* now suggests onion soup or sauce more readily than it does Charles de Rohan, Prince de Soubise and Marshal of France (1715–87). On the other side of the world, George Washington and General Lafayette bequeathed their names to dishes such as maize soup and chicken with sweet corn.

The 19th century, a period of elaborate meals, produced many new dishes because of new imported materials and new facilities such as refrigeration (*see* FOOD, HISTORY OF). Opera singers and composers now competed with aristocrats and successful generals for the titles of honour. The Italian composer Rossini, a friend of cooks and a great eater, was named again and again, as was the novelist Victor Hugo. The singers Patti, Melba, and Caruso all had new creations named after them, as had several actresses. Carême, the greatest of 19th-century cooks, celebrated many of his employers; for example, he named at least three soups, a canapé, a sole, and a salad in honour of Prince Bagration, who figures in Tolstoy's *War and Peace*. Napoleon's victory over the Austrians at Marengo in north Italy in 1800 is recalled by 'Chicken à la Marengo', said to have been concocted for the first time on the battlefield itself. His wife, Josephine de Beauharnais, is celebrated under her own names and also as 'Malmaison', her little palace outside Paris. Many other 19th-century royalties, including the Empress Eugénie (wife of Napoleon III) and the English Queens Victoria and Alexandra, as well as many aristocratic personages, all were commemorated by special culinary novelties.

In the 20th century new dishes tend to be of a light type, such as 'Waldorf salad' (from a famous New York hotel) or Bircher 'Muesli' (*see* SALADS). Many originally European dishes have come back to Europe from America in a slightly different form, and other dishes have come from the East and the Commonwealth. In whatever language they are written, menus continue to contain hidden in their terms much social history of times past and present.

See also COOKING, HISTORY OF; RECIPES AND COOKERY BOOKS.

MIGRAINE, *see* ALLERGIC DISEASES.

MILK. For centuries men have domesticated animals in order to milk them; and 200 years of scientific rearing have produced herds of milch-cows capable of a large milk-yield (*see* CATTLE BREEDS, Vol. VI). Goats, and in some countries camels, buffaloes, reindeer, asses, mares, and other animals, are also milked.

Milk is often described as the perfect food. It contains all the factors necessary for the body except iron. Its average composition is water 87%, fat 3·5%, protein 3·5% (mainly casein), sugar (lactose) 4·7%, vitamins A, B_1, B_2, C, and D, and traces of calcium, phosphorus, and potassium compounds (*see* FOOD VALUES). Cows fed on good grassland produce milk rich in butter-fat and VITAMINS (q.v.), hence 'summer' milk and butter is superior to that produced by stall-fed cows.

The products of milk are cream, butter, CHEESE (q.v.), curds-and-whey, and butter-milk. Devonshire cream is the thick clotted cream produced by heating fresh milk very slowly in large shallow pans. When cream is churned it solidifies, forming butter. The butter-milk left in the churn contains the lactose, all the mineral salts, and much of the protein, and is therefore a valuable food, but is frequently thrown to the pigs. Milk can be clotted to form junket (curds-and-whey) by warming the milk to blood heat and then adding rennet, prepared from the rennin in the stomach of a calf. 'Clotting' must not be confused with 'souring'; this occurs when micro-organisms in the milk convert the lactose into lactic acid, causing the casein to separate out into a solid curd from which the liquid runs when it is broken up. In warm, thundery weather, which encourages the growth and activity of these micro-organisms, milk sours quickly, but in normal weather it should remain sweet for at least 24 hours after it has been delivered.

Milk is a substance favourable to the growth of BACTERIA (q.v. Vol. II), not only of harmless ones such as those which produce souring, but also of disease germs, especially those which cause TUBERCULOSIS (q.v.). Special precautions must be taken, therefore, to preserve milk from contamination at all stages. Bacteria in milk are killed in two ways. Sterilization, which consists in raising the milk to a temperature of 230° F., alters the flavour, but PASTEURIZATION (q.v. Vol. VII) in which the milk is kept at 145–50° F. for half an hour and then immediately cooled to 55° F., does not have this disadvantage. In hot weather milk should be kept in a refrigerator or scalded and poured into an already scalded and cooled jug, and kept covered in a cool larder (*see* FOOD STORAGE).

Milk can be bought in tins in the forms of condensed, evaporated, or powdered milk (*see* DAIRY INDUSTRY, Vol. VII). Besides being drunk either hot or cold, it is used as a basis for cream SOUPS and white SAUCES, and mixed with cereals or flour, eggs, sugar, and other commodities to make puddings, CAKES, SCONES (qq.v.), and batters. It is indispensable in INVALID COOKERY (q.v.) and in the feeding of infants (*see* BABIES, FEEDING OF).

See also Vol. VI: CATTLE, CARE OF.
See also Vol. VII: DAIRY INDUSTRY.

MIND AND BODY. The influence of scientific method upon MEDICINE (q.v.) has been to concentrate attention on the physical signs of disease which can be demonstrated and classified. A great many diseases are amenable to such treatment; but doctors and scientists, in their efforts to abolish or control the major ills which afflict mankind, have come up against certain acute or chronic disorders which are obscure in origin and difficult to classify or diagnose.

It has long been known that emotions and mental states have a great effect upon the body, the simplest examples being when the shy or embarrassed person blushes, or the person who is afraid feels sick. Conversely, physical well-being or illness often affects the emotional or mental state. The great effect on physical health which mental happiness or unhappiness can have is also generally recognized. Investigations made by modern psychiatrists have extended enormously our knowledge of the range of these interactions of mind and body, from the most everyday and easily observed conditions to the extreme effects seen in people suffering from mental disorders. The study of the ENDOCRINE GLANDS (q.v.) and their effects on the body and the mind has also provided a groundwork for a new approach to those 'difficult' diseases which may arise from and are certainly aggravated by the mind-body relationship. This new branch of medicine is called 'psychosomatic' (mind-body) medicine; and those who practise it use the methods of both the psychiatrist and the general physician, even for illnesses that used to be considered purely physical. They claim that gastric and duodenal ulcer, high blood-pressure, coronary disease, thyroid disease,

migraine, colitis, and asthma are psychosomatic disorders, that they are often caused by the mental condition of the individual, and can often be relieved or completely cured by treating the mental rather than the physical condition. A state of anxiety, irrational fears, nervous tension, and other mental reactions to the stress of modern living are conditions of which the physical disorder is the 'somatic' counterpart.

It is always difficult to prove scientifically any theory connected with something as intangible as 'mind', but the psychosomatic approach seems to be based upon sound scientific knowledge and ordinary common sense. It is also a useful reminder—both to the doctor and to the patient—that a human being is an individual who cannot always be classified and docketed according to the rigid standards of scientific method. The family doctor who knows the life and background of his patient is in the best position to deal with disorders of this kind, but we can all help ourselves and each other by remembering that body and mind need relaxation as well as hard exercise, that the will to succeed, however admirable it may be, must be measured against the powers of the individual personality, and that anxiety and nervous stress must be taken as the warning signs of possible physical ills.

See also PSYCHOLOGY; MENTAL DISEASES.

MIRRORS. Glass was scarcely ever used for mirrors before the 15th century, those of the ancient world being of metal—brass, bronze, gold, or silver. Greek and Roman mirrors, some of which still exist, were usually round, with handles and with engravings on the back. Chinese bronze mirrors, which had a magical significance as well as a practical use, date back several centuries B.C. They were decorated on the back with a variety of patterns in relief and later occasionally also with landscapes.

In Europe in the Middle Ages, although glass was known (*see* GLASS-MAKING, Vol. VII), and also a method of backing it with a metallic substance, the glass was not pure enough to give a clear reflection. Therefore the wealthy used for their toilet small plates of gold, silver, or bronze, polished and set in elaborate frames, and poorer people used polished pewter. In France the royal household had hand mirrors enriched with pearls and precious stones, which were carried in pockets hung from the girdle or in elaborate cases (*see* Vol. IX, p. 126).

Gloucester Museum

Left: A GREEK MIRROR

Centre: BACK OF A CELTIC MIRROR FROM BIRDLIP, 1ST CENTURY, A.D.

Right: 17TH-CENTURY LOOKING-GLASS WITH EMBROIDERED FRAME

Victoria and Albert Museum

In the 15th and 16th centuries most mirrors were made of steel and rock-crystal, though mirrors of glass were occasionally brought to England from Italy. Hanging mirrors were made for the first time. They appear in Flemish paintings: there is a crystal mirror, for example, in van Eyck's portrait of Jan Arnolfini and his wife (*see* Vol. V, p. 162). At the beginning of the 17th century mirrors of glass were still so rare that, when the Republic of Venice presented one to Queen Marie de Medici on the occasion of the birth of her eldest son, it was considered an important gift.

In the 17th century wall-mirrors of steel formed part of house furniture, being enclosed by shutters or curtains to prevent oxidation. Then hanging mirrors began to play a part in decorative schemes. They were framed in soft wood, ebony, silver, coloured enamel, or needlework, the style of frame following closely the furniture fashion of the day. The 17th-century mirrors had elaborately carved, wooden frames or more delicate veneered and inlaid frames; in the 18th century mirrors were introduced as a part of the architectural setting (*see* Vol. XII, p. 377); from 1750 curved mirrors were fashionable, sometimes with Eastern designs painted on the back of the glass or with patterns cut on the surface.

Dressing-table mirrors do not seem to have been in regular use until the late 17th century; from the early 18th century ordinary dressing

Victoria and Albert Museum

CHEVAL-GLASS WITH FRAME AND STAND OF PAINTED SATINWOOD, *c.* 1790

Frank Partridge

SHERATON DRESSING MIRROR, LATE 18TH CENTURY

Victoria and Albert Museum

CIRCULAR MIRROR WITH CONVEX GLASS AND CARVED AND
GILT FRAME, *c.* 1800

glasses were mounted above box stands, often like small bureaux, on supporting uprights. Towards the end of the 18th century, when it was possible to cast single pieces of looking-glass of more than 10 feet, mirrors called 'cheval-glasses', swung on a frame and high enough to reflect the whole person, were made. In the 19th century mirrors were sometimes fixed on to a wardrobe door, or 'pier-glasses' were made to fit the whole area between two windows or between a chimney piece and the ceiling (*see* p. 195).

A glass mirror is produced by painting the back of a piece of glass first with a layer of stannous chloride, then with a thin film of metallic silver mixed with certain chemicals, and finally with a coat of varnish to protect the silver.

See also FURNITURE, HISTORY OF; INTERIOR DECORATION, HISTORY OF.
See also Vol. VII: GLASS-MAKING.

MOTHERING SUNDAY, *see* FAMILY FESTIVALS.

MUFFS seem first to have appeared in France, at the luxurious Court of Henry III (1574–89).

They were made of velvet or satin, lined and trimmed with fur. An engraving in England, at almost the same period, shows an English lady of quality with a small muff hanging from her girdle.

Another engraving of the reign of Charles I shows an Englishwoman with a muff entirely of fur. In the middle of the 17th century muffs were, in winter, universally carried by ladies of any social standing. When Charles II returned from the Continent in 1660 he brought with him the strange fashion of muffs for men. These were quite large and sometimes made of such expensive furs as sable, and were suspended from a band round the waist. Samuel Pepys in his *Diary* (November 1662) writes, 'This day I did first wear a muffe, being my wife's last year's muffe'. A ballad describing the fair on the Thames during the great frost of 1683–4 speaks of a young man of fashion as 'a spark of the bar, with his cane and his muff'.

For a short period, early in the 18th century,

muffs became very small, but by the middle of the century they were large again, as can be seen in the engravings of HOGARTH (q.v. Vol. V). By the 1780s no gentleman's winter attire was complete without one, and the most popular muffs were made of the fleece of Siberian sheep. Men still carried muffs in the 1790s, but soon after that the custom disappeared and has never returned. In France it was the fashion for ladies to carry a lap-dog in the muff: there was even a special breed known as muff-dogs (*chiens de manchon*).

In the early years of the 19th century women's clothes were extremely flimsy, without the capacious pockets of earlier costumes. So ladies carried HANDBAGS (q.v.) instead of muffs. As skirts grew more ample again the muff returned, and small muffs were particularly popular in the second half of the 19th century. The very large fur muff had a considerable vogue during the period of the 'hobble-skirt' (*c.* 1910–11); but muffs disappeared after the First World War and, though attempts have been made to bring them back, they have never regained their former popularity.

See also COSTUME, HISTORY OF; FURS.

MUMPS, *see* INFECTIOUS DISEASES.

MUSCLES. These are bands of tissue-fibres in all parts of the body which, by contracting and expanding, make movement possible (*see* MUSCLE, Vol. II). The 'visceral' muscles, which form a large part of the internal organs of the body, enable them to function; the cardiac or heart muscle makes the heart pump; and the skeletal muscles, with which we are largely concerned here, cover the bones of the skeleton, running from one bone to another, and bring them into movement. The muscle is usually attached to the bone by a tough fibrous tendon; it expands into a thick body of flesh, and then tapers into another tendon as it joins a second bone. When the muscle contracts it draws the two bones towards each other. At the same time the muscles which have an opposite action must relax, whilst other muscles modify the movement in a variety of ways. In a complicated action such as walking, more than a hundred muscles all combine to make a smooth movement, not to mention those involved in swinging the arms.

The most important head muscles are those controlling facial expression. Round the eyes

1. LADY'S MUFF AND FUR, 1644. 2. MAN'S MUFF, 1694. 3. MAN'S MUFF, 1742. 4. LADY'S MUFF, 1817. 5. EDWARDIAN MUFF AND STOLE, 1910

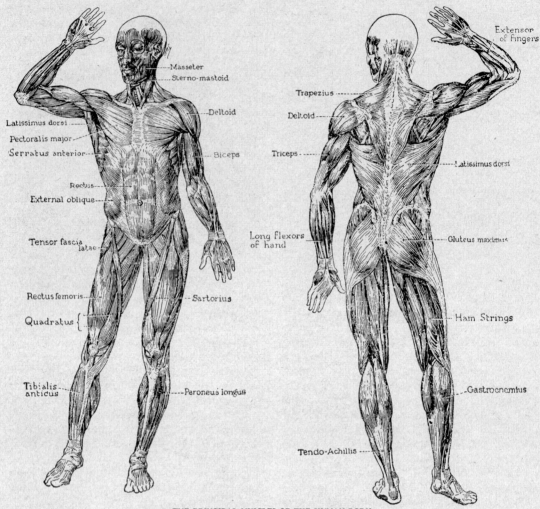

Masseter
Sterno-mastoid
Deltoid
Latissimus dorsi
Pectoralis major
Serratus anterior
Biceps
Rectus
External oblique
Tensor fascia latae
Rectus femoris
Sartorius
Quadratus {
Tibialis anticus
Peroneus longus

Extensor of fingers
Trapezius
Deltoid
Triceps
Latissimus dorsi
Long flexors of hand
Gluteus maximus
Ham Strings
Gastrocnemius
Tendo-Achillis

THE PRINCIPAL MUSCLES OF THE HUMAN BODY
From Logan Clendening, *The Human Body*, Alfred Knopf

and mouth run circular bands of muscle which, on contracting, close the eyes or purse the lips. Smiles or sneers depend on straps of muscle from the cheeks and sides of the nose to the corners of the mouth. Biting, chewing, and clenching the jaws bring into action a strong muscle inserted into the angle of the jaw. Neck muscles move the head on the spinal column.

Many of the muscles arising from the chest are inserted into the humerus or upper arm bone, and so move the arm. Others are concerned with the act of breathing. All down the spine complicated slips of muscle control the various bending and stretching movements which the body continuously needs to perform.

The abdomen is covered with sheets of pro-

tective muscles in layers which keep in place the important organs behind them. The buttocks conceal the main muscle that enables a man to stand upright, the 'gluteus maximus', which acts by pulling the spine into line with the legs. The fleshy muscles in front of the thigh insert their fibres into the knee-cap on their way to the shin-bone or tibia, so keeping the knees straight in standing. The fleshy mass at the back of the leg is largely due to a muscle the tendon of which runs behind the heel as it goes to the heel bone. This is called the 'tendo Achillis' after the Greek hero Achilles who, according to the legend, was vulnerable only at this spot.

See also BONES AND JOINTS.
See also Vol. II: MUSCLE (Animal).

N

NEEDLEWORK, DECORATIVE. Materials are decorated with many types of needlework, using decorative stitches (Fig. 1) as well as those used in plain SEWING (q.v.). Different styles used in the past and in various parts of the world are described in the articles EMBROIDERY, ENGLISH and EMBROIDERY, WORLD. Some of the many techniques are described in this article.

1. APPLIQUÉ (applied work) is the decoration of one material by the sewn-on pieces of another. It has a very long history; it was used by Persians, Egyptians, and Greeks, and in the Middle Ages a knight's surcoat, horse trappings, and banners were appliquéd with his coat of arms to identify him in battle or tournament, when his face was hidden in armour. The Renaissance ladies did appliqué of velvet and damask for domestic hangings, bed curtains and covers, chair seats and backs, and cushions. It has always been a very effective technique for church embroideries. It is popular today, both in bold forms, dramatically coloured, for hangings and curtains, and in fine work for lingerie or handkerchiefs.

The success of appliqué depends very largely on the design, the stitchery being a secondary

Needlework Development Scheme
LINEN TRAY CLOTH EMBROIDERED WITH APPLIQUÉ

consideration. Both form and colour must be well planned, with bold and simple shapes, since the colour is supplied mainly by the fabric pieces. Appliqué does not have to be in colour: interest can be achieved by change of texture. Fine linen with insets of net and with applied pieces of linen, satin, or muslin, and areas of openwork stitching can be effective entirely in white. Fancy braids and trimmings can add to the interest of the design. Pictures of almost any subject may be worked, but naturalistic forms should be avoided.

Most materials can be used for this work—cotton, silk, wool, linen, synthetic fabrics, plain and printed cloth, braids, sequins, beads, buttons, felt, leather, and American cloth. Net is frequently used for finer work, in which case the ground fabric is usually cut away so that the net is really inset. Articles that will have hard wear and frequent washing, such as aprons, cushion covers, or table mats, need a closely woven non-fraying material; care must be taken to match the warp and weft of the patch with those of the background, for a motif on the bias will pull and pucker when washed.

The method is first to transfer the entire design to the ground fabric, and then each shape in the design to its own material. If the applied fabric is one that does not fray, such as felt or American cloth, the shapes are cut out round the outline; otherwise small turnings are allowed, turned under, tacked, and pressed. Then the shapes are placed in position on the ground fabric and hemmed down. When all the pieces are in place, embroidery may be added—for instance, centres of flowers or outlines of petals may be put in with rows of stitching.

2. BRODERIE ANGLAISE. This, also known as eyelet or Swiss work, consists of a pattern of holes punched in the material with a stiletto and then overcast. They are varied in size and shape to represent leaves, petals, or decorative shapes.

This work—nearly always in white—was very popular in the early 19th century for baby clothes, house linen, and dress frills. The designs were entirely of holes with no surface embroidery; nowadays satin stitch is frequently used for stalks, leaves, and so on. Fine-textured and firm materials, such as cambric, linen lawn, or cotton, are worked with cotton or mercerized thread.

Eyelets of $\frac{1}{4}$ inch or smaller are outlined with running stitch, pierced with a stiletto, and

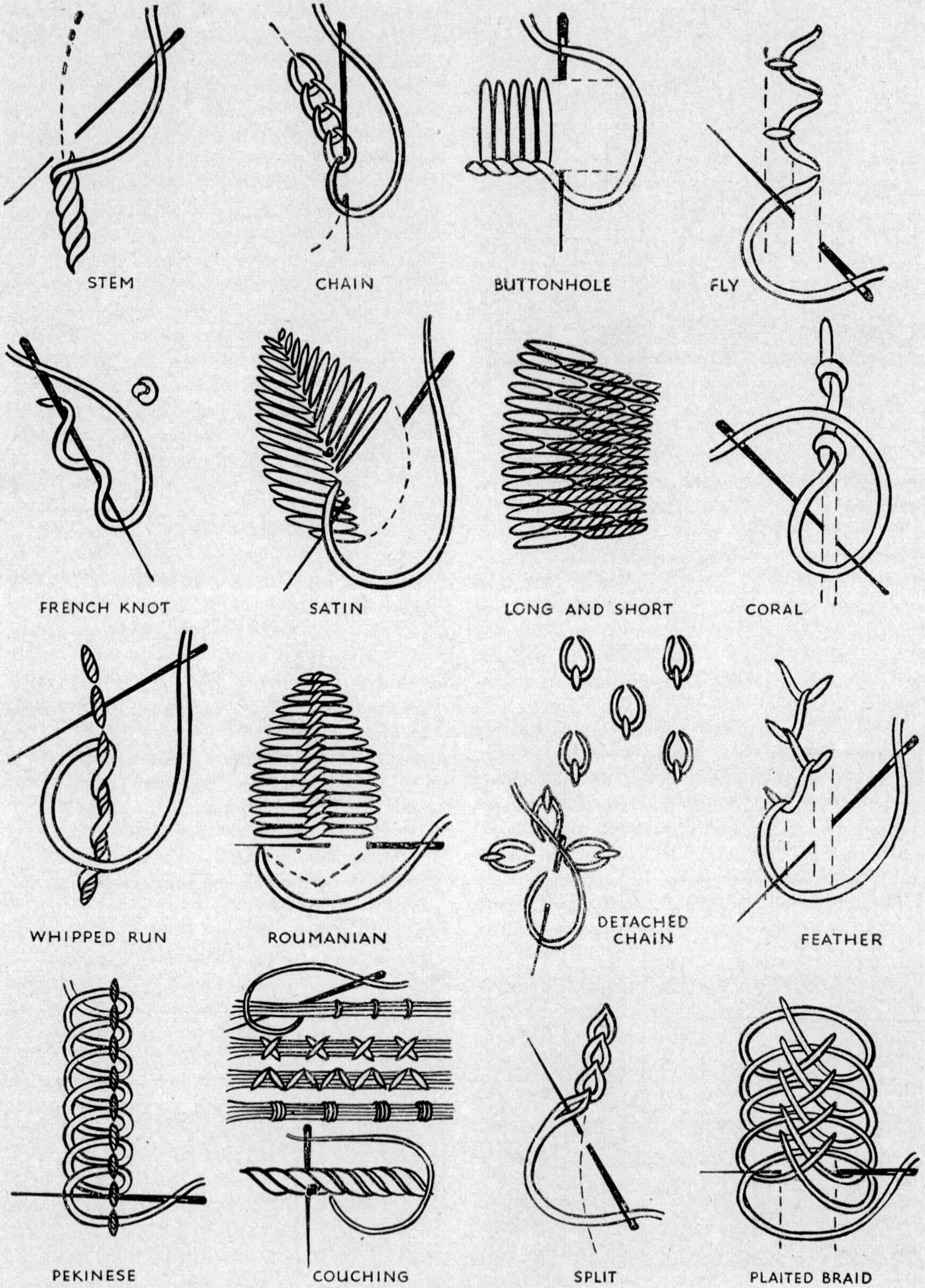

STEM   CHAIN   BUTTONHOLE   FLY

FRENCH KNOT   SATIN   LONG AND SHORT   CORAL

WHIPPED RUN   ROUMANIAN   DETACHED CHAIN   FEATHER

PEKINESE   COUCHING   SPLIT   PLAITED BRAID

FIG. I. EMBROIDERY STITCHES

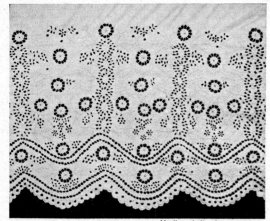

Needlework Development Scheme

BRODERIE ANGLAISE

work pictures depicting Biblical or allegorical subjects, or figures in contemporary dress. Canvas embroidery was at its best in technique and design in the early 18th century when it was used to upholster furniture. The designs were mainly floral, although birds and animals were popular. Sometimes figures and pastoral scenes formed a centre medallion on chair backs or seats, the fine detail worked in tent stitch, and the background in a larger stitch, frequently cross. This work was done on double thread canvas, the fine stitching over one thread, and the coarse over two threads.

Linen canvas is used, worked with good tapestry wools of a thickness suitable for the mesh of the canvas, so as to cover it completely. The work is done in a frame with a blunt needle. The design can be copied from one worked out on squared paper, counting the threads and stitches to match. Sometimes a tracing with a very thick black line taken from a full-scale coloured working drawing is placed behind the canvas so that the outline of the design can be seen through the canvas and painted on it with either oil or water-colour. A wide variety of stitches can be used to produce different textures. The most usual ones are tent (petit point), cross (gros point), double cross, long-armed cross, french, star, rococo, rice, gobelin, encroaching gobelin, and plaited gobelin (Fig. 2).

The finished canvas is stretched by being pinned out on a padded board, covered with a damp cloth and a heavy weight, and left for some hours; or it can be pressed lightly with a warm iron over a damp cloth. It is important to avoid flattening the stitchery too much.

Canvas work is practical as well as decorative since it will stand hard wear. It can be used for

covered with fine overcast stitch. Larger eyelets, after being outlined, are cut from the centre outwards vertically and horizontally; the material is turned back to the running stitch and overcast. The points on the back are cut away afterwards. The work is finished with scalloped edges. The scallops are outlined with running stitch, padded with rows of the same stitch, and then close blanket-stitched with the heading to the outside. Finally, surplus material is cut away.

3. CANVAS WORK. This is embroidery, usually of wool, on a canvas background, the entire surface of which is covered with stitchery. The finished piece somewhat resembles woven TAPESTRY (q.v. Vol. VII), which is probably why it is so often wrongly called 'tapestry work'.

Canvas work was popular in Tudor and early Stuart times for cushions and table CARPETS (*see* p. 134), and in the 17th century for needle-

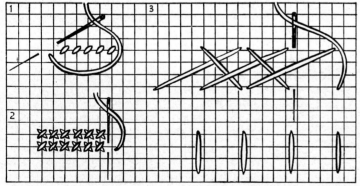

FIG. 2. CANVAS WORK STITCHES

1. Tent stitch. 2. Cross stitch. 3. Long-armed cross stitch. The reverse is shown below. 4. Rococo stitch

Victoria and Albert Museum

ABRAHAM AND THE THREE ANGELS

Part of a picture embroidered in wool and silk tent stitch on canvas, 17th century

many purposes, from handbags and pochettes worked with silk or wool on fine canvas, to hard-wearing rugs worked on large meshed canvas with thick wools.

Needlework Development Scheme

NORWEGIAN EMBROIDERY ON LINEN

The pattern is made with cut work, drawn thread, and woven buttonhole bars, with squares of satin stitch

4. CUT AND DRAWN WORK. Cut work is the name given to embroidery in which parts of the material are cut away, and the holes bound with a decorative stitch. Sometimes the spaces are filled with stitchery, sometimes the solid parts are embroidered to contrast with the open spaces. Designs for this work should be bold and simple, and preferably worked on linen with matching coloured thread. Edges to be cut are first secured with close blanket stitch, and detached blanket-stitched bars are sometimes used. Renaissance and Richelieu, Hardanger and Hedebo embroidery are differing forms of this type of work. In Italian cut work small squares are cut out of the linen, and geometrical patterns are worked into them in close blanket stitch. Other parts of the work are decorated in scrolls and spirals with raised stitches such as bullion knot and overcast stitch.

Drawn thread work is done on good quality linen, preferably hand woven so that the thread can be drawn easily. Hems, which are very important, should be fairly narrow with mitred corners. Threads of the cloth are removed in one direction, and a pattern of holes made by stitching the remaining threads together.

Drawn fabric ('pulled linen') work is a form of openwork embroidery in which a lacy effect is obtained by pulling the working thread tight, so as to draw the threads of the material together to make patterns. It is better to use hand-woven linen, but a good machine-woven linen or linen scrim can be used. The working thread should resemble the threads of the background fabric as nearly as possible, since it is the grouping of threads that should be seen rather than the stitches producing the effect. A fairly large, blunt needle is used to avoid splitting the threads. Designs for this work should be simple with uncomplicated outlines. There are a great number of stitches, each producing a different effect, but all worked by the counted thread.

5. QUILTING is a decorative method of stitching together two or more layers of material. Its effect and usual aim is to increase the warmth of the material. In Tudor days both men's and women's garments—jackets, skirts, and trunks—were quilted. The finest work was done in the reign of Queen Anne, when quilted petticoats became most important and decorative garments, and when bed coverlets were quilted and embroidered with great skill.

There are two forms of quilting: English, the

method used for the articles mentioned so far, and corded or Italian. In English quilting three layers of material are stitched together. The outside material, which is cotton or sateen, or sometimes silk, is sewn into a wooden frame consisting of four strong strips of wood to which a strong braid is nailed. It is then covered with the interlining—washed and carded sheep's or lamb's wool is best, but domette, flannel, old blankets, or wadding can be used. Finally the lining is spread over all. For reversible articles such as bed quilts, the lining fabric is the same as the top, but for cushions or bags which will have another lining when they are made up, a fabric such as buttermuslin can be used. The layers are tacked horizontally, vertically, and diagonally all over the surface. Traditionally the design is scratched with a needle point round a wooden or metal template, the mark staying visible long enough to be stitched. Running, back, or chain stitch is used for the quilting, but they must be done in two separate movements, first downwards, then upwards, through all the layers of material.

Italian quilting consists of two layers of cloth sewn together in a design built up entirely of parallel lines. A padding of soft wool or piping cord is then threaded between the narrow channels.

6. SMOCKING. This stitching takes its name from the smock, a loose-fitting garment of the overall type. Smocks in the 13th and 14th centuries were richly ornamented with coloured embroidery and gold. Later they were worn usually by country workmen and were simply made of holland or coarse linen, elaborately embroidered in white on front, shoulder, and cuff. The back and front were the same, with the neck opening large enough to allow the smock to be put on over the head. The fullness of the garment was gathered into the yoke and decorated with feather, stem, and chain stitch. The colour varied in different parts of England, white or natural in the south, deep blue in the midlands, and olive green in the east, but everywhere white or natural for 'Sunday smocks'. Materials were home-spun and woven, the design of the decoration often showing the occupation of the wearer: churns, butterpats, and hearts for milkmaids; chopping blocks, saws, and choppers for butchers; wheels, whips, reins, and bits for carters; and trees and leaves for woodmen.

In smocking, parallel rows of evenly spaced

Needlework Development Scheme

A SMOCK IN THE TRADITIONAL SHAPE WITH EMBROIDERED DESIGNS USED ON GARDENERS' SMOCKS IN STAFFORDSHIRE AND SHROPSHIRE

running stitches are put in one above the other, the number of rows depending on the depth of smocking required. When all the lines have been run in, the gathers are drawn up—not too tightly so as to leave some 'give' in the work—and tied two and two together to prevent slipping. The tops of the gathers are then worked in a variety of stitches, and finally the running threads pulled out, the stitches holding the gathers in place. Honeycombing is a simple up and down stitch. The best materials are fine linen, cottons, silk, silk substitutes, and fine woollens; the working thread should not be stranded. Too many colours spoil the effect—two tones of one colour look well—and the simplest designs are the best.

See also EMBROIDERY, ENGLISH; EMBROIDERY, WORLD; SEWING.
See also Vol. VII: LACE-MAKING.

NERVOUS SYSTEM. Whenever contact is made between our bodies and the outside world, a stimulus is received by a special receptor organ, and conveyed along a sensory nerve cell to the spinal cord and the brain. Whenever a movement, however slight, has to be made, an impulse is emitted along a motor nerve to a MUSCLE (q.v.) which, in its turn, responds by contracting. Between these two events the incoming message has entered the spinal cord or the brain, and may have passed over one or many connector nerve cells before issuing forth as a message to the muscle for action.

The nervous system of man may be separated

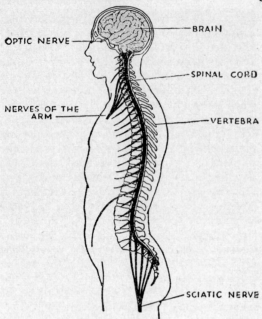

FIG. I. THE CENTRAL NERVOUS SYSTEM

After Logan Clendening, *The Human Body*, Alfred Knopf

into a central system and a peripheral system. The central system is formed by the brain in the skull and the spinal cord, which is contained within the top two-thirds of the back bone, the tissues of the brain merging with those of the cord. The brain and cord are embedded in protective membranes called 'meninges.' A cross-section of the central nervous system shows that it is composed of patterns of grey and white matter. The grey matter consists of multitudes of nerve cells or 'neurons', the shape and substance of which are designed according to their essential work of conducting impulses. These cells have delicate branches or 'dendrites' for receiving impulses, and a specialized elongated nerve fibre which conveys the impulses to the dendrites of the next cell in the chain. The nerve fibres, collected in bundles or 'nerve tracts', form the white matter of the central nervous system.

The peripheral nervous system consists of twelve pairs of cranial nerves supplying the face and head; thirty-one pairs of spinal nerves which are distributed to the limb and trunk muscles and joints and the skin; and a system of nerves and 'ganglia' (small masses of nerve cells) called the 'autonomic nervous system', which influences the actions of the heart and blood-vessels, the glands, and some internal organs.

The spinal nerves originate in the spinal cord. Each arises by two strands or roots, one called the sensory root and the other the motor root. The sensory root is made up of nerve fibres which convey impulses from the skin muscles and internal organs to the central nervous system; the motor root consists of fibres which conduct impulses from the central nervous system to the muscles and glands. The two roots quickly blend and after sending a branch to an autonomic ganglion in the chest, pass on as spinal nerves containing a mixture of motor and sensory fibres.

The nervous system is the main co-ordinator of the activities of the body. The sensory fibres bring to the central nervous system information about the external world from receptors which are sensitive to light, sound, temperature, pressure, or pain. They also convey information about the internal state of the body. Acting on this information the central nervous system sends impulses along the motor nerves to produce appropriate movements of muscle or secretion of glands. The impulses go from cell to cell along pathways which may be either very long and complicated or quite short and simple, until finally they emerge in a motor root. Sometimes the incoming messages reach consciousness; but many of the activities of the body are regulated without our being aware of them; such automatic reactions are called reflexes—for example, blinking, sneezing, swallowing, breathing.

Many of the separate muscle actions involved in the maintenance of the normal postures of the body are controlled reflexly through centres in the spinal cord. The simplest form of reflex known is the knee-jerk. If the tendon running between the knee-cap and shin-bone is stretched suddenly by a sharp tap, sensory nerve cells amongst the muscle fibres send up impulses to the spinal cord. These pass directly to the motor nerves and down to the muscles in front of the thigh, making them contract involuntarily, pull up the knee-cap, and jerk the foot forward.

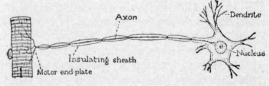

FIG. 2. A NERVE CELL, OR 'NEURON', SHOWING ITS CONNEXION WITH A MUSCLE CELL

From Logan Clendening, *The Human Body*, Alfred Knopf

The white matter of the cord contains bundles of nerve tracts *en route* to cell stations in the brain. The tracts are arranged so that the fibres connected to one type of receptor (that is, those for pain or touch or temperature) are collected together from the different parts of the body. Pain fibres are placed towards the front of the cord. If their tract is divided in this position by a surgeon's knife, the capacity to feel pain disappears from the part of the body whence they came, though other sensations remain. The touch fibres, and the fibres from muscles and joints which signal position and movement of the body, are grouped together in the back tracts of the cord. At the end of the cord the great sensory tracts travel through the bulb of the brain, on up through the mid-brain, to end deep in the substance of the brain, in a walnut-sized mass of grey matter called the 'thalamus'. Here the impulses which travel in the tracts enter consciousness, though still only in a crude, primitive way. They become sensations. The sensations must pass from the thalamus to the surface of the brain, the 'cerebral cortex', before they can be interpreted with judgement and compared with other sensations (*see* BRAIN).

But the nervous system is something more than an apparatus for receiving and responding to stimuli. It also has the function of selection. Stimuli meet various fates. Some are suppressed or inhibited, and fade away producing no response; others create disproportionate effects on the body. Certain forms of stimulation found to be of great importance in EVOLUTION (q.v. Vol. II) have been allotted specially elaborate sense organs—such as the EYE, EAR, and NOSE (qq.v.). Thus light, sound, and smell have their own pathways into the brain. Man's power of finely controlled movement is dependent on the suppression of cruder elements and the perfection of actions by practice. Here the cerebellum has an important role to play.

The cerebral hemispheres are much more highly developed in man than in other mammals. They are responsible for the exercise of thought, judgement, and wisdom, and they control the faculties of speech.

The nervous system, like the rest of the body, is susceptible to invasion by germs called BACTERIA or VIRUSES (q.v. Vol. II). Bacteria most commonly attack the meninges enclosing the brain and spinal cord, producing meningitis, a disease which was particularly deadly before the discovery of the sulphonamide drugs and antibiotics such as streptomycin (*see* DRUGS). Bacteria may reach the brain itself through the blood, or more commonly from infection of the ear—an important reason for not neglecting earache. POLIOMYELITIS (q.v.) is a virus disease which especially attacks that grey matter in the spinal cord composed of motor-nerve cells. Rheumatic fever, besides affecting the heart and joints, sometimes involves the brain, producing the strange movements of face and limbs described as St. Vitus's Dance, or chorea. Perhaps the most common disease of the brain is caused by blocking or bleeding from a blood-vessel, which brings about a 'stroke' (apoplexy). Motor-nerve cells are destroyed, producing paralysis of the opposite side of the body. If the right side of the body is affected, the patient is also unable to speak, for the centre for speech lies on the left side of the brain where the haemorrhage (or bleeding) has occurred.

Tumours or growths may arise in any part of the nervous system, and produce symptoms by interfering with movement or sensation according to their site, and by raising the pressure inside the head—a potent cause of headache.

In general, disease processes destroy nerve cells. When the paths of the motor nerves are affected anywhere between brain and foot, paralysis of a part of the body results, just as any affection of the sensory nerve paths interferes with sensation. Disease, however, can first stimulate the nerve cells to unhealthy activity before killing them. For example, if the motor cells of the brain are involved, fits may occur, followed by paralysis. The commonest kind of fit, EPILEPSY (q.v.), however, is produced by a discharge of nervous energy without any underlying structural disease. Stimulation of sensory nerve cells may produce abnormal sensations, often called vaguely 'neuritis' or 'neuralgia'. In certain conditions of the spine the roots of the sciatic nerve may rub against a projection of cartilaginous substance between the bodies of two lumbar vertebrae, on their way to the spinal cord. This produces 'sciatica', a pain which the patient feels at the back of his leg.

The neurologist, a physician who makes a special study of disorders of the nervous system, is able, by his detailed knowledge of the way nerve cells and tracts are affected in disease, to track down disturbances of movement or sensation to their exact source. This makes it more and more possible to diagnose and then to treat nervous disorders.

See also BRAIN.
See also Vol. II: NERVOUS SYSTEM (Animals).

NEURALGIA, *see* NERVOUS SYSTEM.

NIGHTCLOTHES. Before the 15th century only very wealthy people possessed special garments for sleeping in. Ordinary people did not consider them necessary, and either slept naked or wore their underclothes. By Henry VII's reign, however, it had become usual for men to sleep in shirts and women in shifts which, though practically the same as their day-garments, were strictly kept for night. With them went nightcaps of quilted cotton, wool, or velvet to keep out the cold air or, for women, linen coifs with which forehead-bands, called cross-cloths, were sometimes worn (*see* p. 134).

The nightshirt remained popular until the end of the 19th century. In Tudor and Stuart times it was a rather elaborate garment, with long, full sleeves, lace insertion, and ruffled

A 19TH-CENTURY NIGHTSHIRT AND CAP
From a drawing by George Cruikshank

London Museum
A 16TH-CENTURY LINEN NIGHTGOWN SAID TO HAVE BEEN WORN BY ELIZABETH I BEFORE SHE WAS QUEEN

cuffs. White linen was the most usual material, though black shirts and caps were often worn during periods of mourning. The 'nightgowns' made of rich velvet or lined with fur, that Elizabethan writers mention, were not nightgowns but dressing-gowns worn over the true nightclothes when the wearer was out of bed.

Men's nightshirts gradually became longer and fuller until by the 19th century they were frequently ankle-length—rather cumbersome garments made of longcloth or flannel and worn with jelly-bag-shaped knitted nightcaps usually adorned by a tassel. Nightcaps went out altogether about 1870, and shortly afterwards pyjamas began to replace the nightshirt. These became so popular that the older shirt almost entirely disappeared.

As men's nightwear developed from the shirt, so women's nightdresses developed from the shift, or chemise. The earlier types of nightdresses were all cut low in the neck and were hardly more than knee-length, like chemises. In the 17th century they were longer and usually made of linen or thin silk and lavishly trimmed

Manchester City Art Galleries
WOMAN'S COTTON NIGHTCAP, 1870

with lace and ribbons. In the 18th century a sleeping-jacket tied with ribbons was sometimes worn over them, with a matching mob-cap of finely embroidered dimity or lawn. By Victorian times nightdresses had entirely lost their resemblance to chemises and had become voluminous garments of longcloth or flannel, with long sleeves and high necks, and little trimming beyond featherstitching, plain frills, or narrow insertion. By 1886 this severe fashion had given place to softer styles: nightdresses of this period were commonly made of coloured nun's veiling, zephyr, or silk, with quantities of lace and pink and blue baby-ribbon. The comfortable, cold-resisting, flannel garments were considered old-fashioned. In 1883 pyjamas for women first appeared, but they did not become popular until the First World War.

Feminine nightcaps disappeared about 1860. The lace-and-ribbon boudoir-caps fashionable in Edwardian times were worn for ornament rather than for warmth.

See also COSTUME, HISTORY OF; UNDERCLOTHES.

NOSE STRUCTURE. The most important function of the nose, which forms the first part of the air passage (*see* RESPIRATION), is to cleanse, warm, and moisten the air breathed in. It also contains the specific sense organ of smell, and acts as a resonant chamber in the production of a clear voice.

The framework of the nose is composed of bone and cartilage. The nasal cavity is divided vertically by a partly cartilaginous and partly bony partition, the septum, and each side opens in front at the nostril and behind joins with the nasal part of the pharynx. The sidewall of each nasal cavity has three parallel curved small bones. The floor of the nose is the roof of the mouth.

The olfactory cells and endings of the olfactory nerve serving the sense of smell lie in the upper part of the lining of the nose. The rest of the lining serves the function of breathing. Immediately above the nostril it is covered with coarse hairs which tend to hold up foreign particles carried in with the air. The upper lining contains small hair-like projections—the cilia—which are constantly waving in such a manner as to propel dust, bacteria, and other foreign matter towards the back of the nose into the throat, so that they are swallowed instead of blocking the air-passages. The lining also contains glands which produce phlegm and the moisture necessary for rendering the air breathed in suitable for the lower air-passages. The stickiness of the phlegm causes dust and foreign particles to adhere to the lining and thus to be removed by the action of the cilia.

Under the lining of the nose there are large, thin-walled, communicating blood-vessels, the warm blood from which heats the air as it passes over the lining of the nose. When the lining of the nose is irritated, as, for instance, in colds or in hay fever, these vessels become filled with blood, making the lining thicker and causing obstruction to breathing.

In the bones surrounding the nose there are air-spaces called sinuses. These open into the nose and their lining is continuous with that of the nasal cavity. The 'frontal' sinus lies behind the arch of the eye-brows. The 'sphenoidal' sinus lies behind the upper part of the nasal cavity. The 'ethmoidal' sinus lies in the centre and consists of numerous thin-walled cavities. The 'maxillary' sinus, the largest airspace, is bounded above by the floor of the bony cavity containing the eyeball and below by part of the roof of the mouth (*see* p. 452).

Colds usually inflame the lining of the nose,

and because this is continuous with the lining of the sinuses, they, too, are frequently affected. Conversely, chronic inflammation of the sinuses may cause frequent colds. All the sinuses can be infected from the nasal cavity, and the maxillary sinus can also be infected from septic teeth. In chronic inflammation the lining of both the nose and the sinuses may thicken considerably.

See also THROAT; RESPIRATION; INFLUENZA AND COMMON COLD.
See also Vol. II: SENSES, Section 6.

NURSERY EQUIPMENT. The very young baby in the first 3 months of life usually sleeps in his mother's room, but after that, if possible, he sleeps in his own bedroom.

In England the baby usually has a cot, with a side which pulls down. The bars of the cot are so placed that he cannot push his head in between them and then find himself unable to get it out again. When there is no cot, a drawer, placed on the floor or on chairs, is quite comfortable for a young baby, provided there are plenty of blankets and a baby mattress for him. A more luxurious first bed for a baby is a bassinet, lined with satin or other pretty material. A small canvas cot with two handles is useful,

Victoria and Albert Museum
EARLY 19TH-CENTURY ROCKING CRADLE FITTED WITH A CLOCK SPRING FOR ROCKING

for it can be carried easily from one room to another, with the baby in it, or put on the back seat of a motor-car. Cradles with solid wood sides mounted on rockers used to be popular, because they could be rocked from side to side to help the baby to go to sleep, but such cradles are never used now.

A pillow is not necessary, and only a hair or firm rubber pillow is safe. A baby able to turn may be smothered by a feather pillow. The cot needs small cotton or flannelette sheets, woollen blankets, and a rubber sheet to cover the mattress so that, should the baby wet the bed, the mattress is kept dry and not spoilt. Older babies kick the bedclothes off and then become cold in the night. To prevent this some people put a baby into a sleeping bag, or fasten a clip on the bedclothes to prevent his kicking them off, or fix round him a canvas strap fastened under the mattress.

A young baby can be bathed in the wash basin, care being taken that he does not get scalded by hot water or bump his head on the tap. An older baby may be bathed in an ordinary bath in the bathroom. But it is better to have a baby's portable bath, made of plastic, papier mâché, enamel, or rubber. A folding bath of rubber material has a table top which pulls up over the bath so that baby can be placed on it when he is being dried or dressed. Other toilet necessities are a tray to hold his special soap, sponge, comb, hairbrush, powder, baby cream, and cotton wool, an enamel bucket to hold soiled or wet nappies, and a pottie.

When he is 5 or 6 months the baby will need a well-made high chair, which will not fall over if he jumps about in it. Some high chairs have a rod which fits between the baby's legs so that he cannot slide down; they all have straps which fit over his shoulders and round his body so that he cannot fall over the edge; and they have a tray in front on which he can play with his toys. When he begins to feed himself, he will drop quite a lot of food over the side, and so a piece of plastic material should be put under the chair to protect the floor or carpet. The baby wears a plastic feeder with sleeves to keep his clothes clean when he is learning to feed himself.

After the age of 6 months or so a baby needs a playpen, so that he can roll and crawl about without getting into danger. Many babies, however, when about 1 year old, learn a bad trick of standing up in the playpen and pushing it about the room. Playpens are so made that

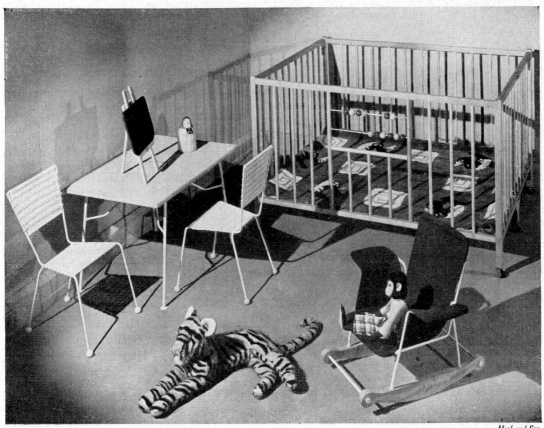

Heal and Son

PLAYPEN, ROCKING CHAIR, AND CHILDREN'S TABLE AND CHAIRS

they can be folded up. Those that have wooden floors can be used in the garden, even when the grass is wet. Some playpens have only three sides, and fit into a corner of the room.

During their first 3 months babies have no use for toys, but soon after this they can play with a rattle if it is placed in their hand, and when they are 5 or 6 months they can pick toys up and play with them. They then like bricks, dolls, bobbins, tins with something inside to rattle, baskets, and boxes. It is important to see that these toys have nothing sharp on them which can hurt the baby, that they are not small enough to be swallowed, and that the colour does not come out of them when they are sucked. All babies at this age take everything they get hold of to the mouth, and so the eyes of dolls, teddies, and golliwogs must be very firmly sewn in, so that the baby cannot pull them out and swallow them.

Children of $1\frac{1}{2}$ to 2 like to play with plastic beakers, bricks, pyramid rings, and toy carts and engines which they can push or pull and put bricks into; toy sweeping brushes, dolls, baskets, and tins which fit into each other; and dolls' tea sets, cooking sets, and books (*see* PLAY). For the young baby the pages of books should be of hard cardboard or of linen which will not tear, but by the time children are about 18 months they can begin using coloured picture books with ordinary paper pages and learn not to tear them.

See also BABIES, CARE OF; BABY TRANSPORT.
See also Vol. IX: TOYS, HISTORY OF.

NURSERY, HISTORY OF. Until the 18th century there was scant interest in children, and little was written about them until comparatively modern times; the history of the nursery, therefore, remains somewhat obscure. Well-to-do families frequently sent babies to be brought up by foster parents until they were 4 or 5, and it was common in medieval times to send both

16TH-CENTURY CHILD'S CHAIR

century. Babies, when they were kept at home, were loved and cossetted; but as soon as the child began to assume a character of his own, he was impatiently forced, with more blows than sympathy, into useful maturity. His very clothes reflected the parents' desire to ignore the gap between baby and young adult: a child might wear baby clothes as late as 4 or 5, and then go straight into clothes modelled on those of his parents (see CHILDREN'S CLOTHES). At home the child was kept out of his parents' way in the nursery. Here he kept his toys—DOLLS' HOUSE (q.v.), drums, tops, and rattles (see TOYS, HISTORY OF, Vol. IX), and here he began, at the age of 3, or even 2, to learn his letters. Just as there was no special style of dress for childhood, there was little idea of a special diet, and the 16th-century child ate in the nursery the breakfast of bread, beer, and mutton his parents were eating in the dining-room. Children were the victims of primitive ideas about hygiene. Fresh air was hurtful, so the windows were kept shut. Young limbs had to be helped to grow straight, so the child was closely bound with bandages until he was sweltering and powerless to move. He was the victim, too, of his parents' fads: a daily dip in cold water, for instance, regardless of weather, or the use of the backboard, to which the child was strapped to improve his carriage.

Traditions of feudal authority made relations between parent and child formal and constrained. Children stood in their parents' presence, knelt to receive their blessing, and addressed them as 'sir' and 'madam'. Absolute obedience was exacted, especially from girls, and regular thrashings and other punishments were dealt out to secure it. When the young Sir Peter Carew (1514–75) ran away from school, his father had him fetched back coupled to a hound, and chained to a dog kennel. The spread of Calvinism, in the late 16th century, intensified the idea that children were prone to wickedness and must be sharply corrected and chastised into

boys and girls away at about 9 or 10 to be pages and maids in great houses to learn good manners (see DOMESTIC SERVICE, HISTORY OF). In some cases, then, the child would be in its parents' house only for 4 or 5 years, and would even then see little of them. For there was no love for the state of childhood; parents, impatient for their offspring to grow up, hurried them quickly through the period from babyhood to maturity and as much as possible kept them out of sight in the nursery. There was no idea that children had any natural rights just because they were children, rights to express themselves or to develop their own interests. There was, too, little attempt to understand their interests or personalities as a guide to their education and future career: they were treated as chattels to be made use of as quickly as possible, and just as the parents saw fit. In 1465 prosperous John Paston wrote angrily about his idle elder son, 'Every pore man that hath browt up his chylder to the age of xii yer wayteth then to be holp and profited be hes chylder.' Daughters were married off early, commonly before they were 15 (see MARRIAGE), and boys were expected to cease being a burden to the family as soon as possible. Although legislation was passed in the 15th century to stop the employment of very young children, its purpose was to protect the quality of craft work done, and not the children's health.

This attitude continued well into the 17th

virtue. Young children received far less individual attention and love than they do today. Families were very large—twenty was not uncommon and deaths were mournfully frequent. The qualities that endeared a child to his parents were not artlessness or simplicity, but precocity, because this showed he was well on the way to becoming an adult. John Evelyn (*see* DIARIES, Vol. XII) was very proud of his son who could read English, French, and Latin at 2½, and who at 4 'had a strong passion for Greeke'. He died when he was 5. Baby talk and childish ways were kept for the nurse and her attendant 'rockers', as nursery maids were called.

A change came in the 18th century. As children were less frequently sent out to foster parents, and as they were not married at so early an age, they spent more time in the home. It was beginning to be recognized that the period of childhood was something to be enjoyed instead of merely hustled through. Discipline remained strict but became less harsh. High spirits came to be regarded as natural in a child, and not simply the devil working in him and requiring to be whipped out. Children began to call their parents 'papa' and 'mamma', and little boys wore clothes designed for their needs, though little girls continued to look like small versions of their mothers. The greater part of the young child's life was still spent in the nursery, but this was rather because it was the only convenient method of organizing large families than because childishness could not be tolerated in adult company. Nursery life, large families, and the attitude that children should be seen and not heard, however, lingered on in fashionable society until late Victorian times, so that a busy hostess might spend very little time with her children until they were in their 'teens. Many parents used to try to reserve a period after tea when the children paid a formal visit to the drawing-room.

The Victorian and early Edwardian nursery was a self-contained and highly organized unit in the household. It was often at the top of the house, where big rooms were set aside as night and day nurseries, and where a regular pattern of life was carried on quite separate from that of the rest of the house. The little children belonged entirely to the nursery, and followed their

Ashmolean Museum

A VICTORIAN NURSERY
Drawing by John Leech for *Punch*, 1869

routine of getting up, meals, nursery walks, and play and rest times under the domination of the nurse and her nursemaids, often little more than children themselves. The older children belonged to the nursery for part of the day, but passed on to governesses or tutors for the rest. The nursery was ruled over by the 'nanny', a person who meant much more to many Victorian children than their own mothers. When the last of the children had grown out of the nursery, the nanny often remained with the family waiting to welcome to her nursery the visiting children of her 'children', and to introduce them in their turn not only to her strict and regular routine but to the joys of the nursery rocking-horse, dolls' house, and box of bricks.

In the 20th century a well-to-do child's life has come to be lived less and less in terms of the nursery. Rising domestic wages have made it difficult to run the nursery as a separate establishment, with its own meals, and with under-servants to wait on the children, nurse, and governess. Smaller families have made the nursery less necessary, few families now have more staff than one nanny, and increasingly mothers look after their young children themselves. Girls as well as boys now usually go to school, so that a governess is unnecessary; and NURSERY SCHOOLS (q.v. Vol. X) provide an excellent environment for children under 5. Some mothers who go to work leave children under 2 in DAY NURSERIES (q.v. Vol. X).

There has been a growing interest in children for their own sake and, as a result, a desire on the part of parents to see more of them. The child has gained greatly in love and parental attention, but his increased emotional dependence on the parent has in some ways complicated his psychological make-up; he is no longer protected by the secure routine of the nursery from the possible insecurity of some home environments. The mother's increasing preoccupation with the children has meant that she has less time to spend on her husband and less energy to share his problems and enter into his life. Generally speaking, nurseries in modern homes exist to cater for children's special needs, not to keep them out of sight and mind until they have been precociously groomed by a special staff to enter their parents' lives again as responsible young adults.

See also BABIES, CARE OF; SOCIAL ENVIRONMENT; CHILDREN, UPBRINGING OF; NURSERY EQUIPMENT.

NURSERY RHYMES, *see* STORY-TELLING; LULLABIES. *See also* Vol. XII: NURSERY RHYMES.

NURSING. In the sense of attention to the elementary needs of the sick, nursing has no doubt existed from the beginning of human history, but as a profession it is little more than a century old. The gradual evolution of the professional nurse can, nevertheless, be traced back for a considerable period. The Hindu physician Charaka laid down minute rules for the conduct of those in attendance on the sick as early as 1000 B.C., but as in oriental countries the women lived secluded lives, it is unlikely that they took much part in this work. The voluminous medical writings of Egypt, Babylonia, and Greece, although they contain descriptions of nursing procedures, are disappointing in that they tell us nothing about the people who had to carry out these procedures. It is probable that nursing the rich was the work of handmaidens and personal slaves, and that the poor were nursed by their wives or mothers.

The origin of organized nursing is closely linked with that of HOSPITALS (q.v. Vol. X), and accounts of the healing temples of Greece and the great military hospitals (*Valetudinaria*) of the Roman Empire are more definite. It seems that there were two grades of priestesses attached to the healing temples, those concerned with the rites and ceremonies, and an inferior class of attendants who waited on the sick.

With the coming of Christianity the care of the sick became a religious duty, and in the early days of the Church this work was carried out by the deacons and deaconesses. They visited patients in their own homes and in the houses of the richer Christians who opened their doors to the sick and suffering. But many leaders of the early Church objected to deaconesses taking part in this work, and in A.D. 533 the Order of Deaconesses was abolished, 'by reason of the frailty of this sex'. There were many efforts at revival and, indeed, at a later period deaconesses played an important part in the development of nursing.

As the monastic system flourished (*see* MONK, Vol. I), the monasteries made provision for the sick; each religious house had its infirmary which cared not only for the regular inmates but also for wayfarers and pilgrims. But as prayer and exhortation played a large part in medical care, the nursing was confined to little more than washing, bed-making, and feeding. The late Middle Ages saw the foundation of the great secular Nursing Orders, among the most famous being the Augustinians, the Misericordia, the Béguines, and the Order of Poor Clares. Although all but the Béguines were Orders of nuns, they were permitted to visit the sick in their homes, to serve in hospitals, and to follow armies in time of war. At the Hôtel Dieu in Paris, founded in A.D. 651, nursing was carried out by Augustinian Sisters for more than 12 centuries.

In the 11th century the famous Order of the Knights of the Hospital of St. John of Jerusalem was instituted, though it was not formally recognized by the Pope until 1113. It was composed of priests and knights, and of serving brothers who acted as nurses and servants. They established a hospital in Jerusalem about 1048 to care for poor pilgrims. The CRUSADES (q.v. Vol. I) inspired the founding of more military orders such as the Knights Templars and the Teutonic Knights, who were also concerned in the nursing of the sick (see KNIGHTS, ORDERS OF, Vol. I). The Knights of St. Lazarus were particularly concerned with the care of lepers. The great Islamic hospitals, at Baghdad, Damascus, Cairo, and Cordova in Spain, which were among the wonders of the world at this period, were staffed by physicians and surgeons of the greatest renown and by male and female nurses.

Nursing was so much in the hands of the religious orders during medieval times that in England, when the monasteries were dissolved in 1536–40, medical and nursing services suffered a decline, from which they did not recover until the 19th century. There is ample evidence of the low state of nursing in the records of our most famous and ancient hospitals. In 1544 the nursing staff of St. Bartholomew's Hospital consisted of five 'Sisters', but these so-called nurses were drawn, so we are told, from a very low class of society. At St. Thomas's, in 1555, 200 sick and aged patients were cared for by one surgeon (there was no physician), one steward, one porter, and two women or sisters 'to attend to the poor and wash their clothes when necessary or convenient'. There is no mention of a matron until 1557. Hospital records of this and succeeding centuries contain frequent complaints of drunkenness and brawling on the part of the sisters. At the London Hospital in the 18th century the nursing staff consisted of elderly and decrepit women, who received a yearly wage of £6 for a nurse, serving hours of duty from 6 a.m. to 10 p.m., and £4 for a 'watcher' or night nurse. As late as 1830 many of the women employed as nurses in hospitals could neither read nor write. They were in general people of low status and doubtful morals, and patients usually had to bribe them in order to obtain the slightest service. It must be remembered, however, that medical and surgical treatment was still so limited that nursing gave little scope for anything but the most elementary attention (see MEDICINE and SURGERY, HISTORY OF).

By the end of the 18th century the efforts of the prison reformer John Howard and others for improving hospital services were beginning to have some effect. The Industrial Revolution accentuated the need for this as people crowded from the country into the insanitary factories and slum dwellings in industrial towns, bringing about a great increase in sickness and in accidents. New hospitals and infirmaries had to be established to meet the need. Medicine and surgery by this time were themselves advancing, and the widening scope of treatment meant that there was more skilled work for nurses to do.

The great turning-point in the history of nursing was reached with the work of Pastor Fliedner, a Lutheran clergyman of Kaiserswerth, Germany. In 1822 Fliedner visited England to study the work which Elizabeth FRY (q.v. Vol. V) was carrying out among the women prisoners in Newgate. He was so much impressed by what he saw that on his return to Germany he bought a house and established a hospital for discharged prisoners and orphans. Here he set to work to train deaconesses to help him and his wife with the nursing. He gave them a good training in the theory and practice of nursing, and in course of time some of them went from Kaiserswerth to work in other hospitals. The success of Kaiserswerth—the first training school for nurses in the world—attracted visitors from many countries, among them Florence NIGHTINGALE (q.v. Vol. V). In 1851 she spent 4 months training at Kaiserswerth—an experience which had a profound influence upon her. Florence Nightingale was the real founder of the modern profession of nursing. Apart from her wonderful work in the Crimea, she reformed the sanitary administration of the British Army and of India and laid

PROBATIONER NURSES ARRIVING AT KAISERSWERTH
From *Jahrbuch für Christliche Unterhaltung, Kaiserswerth*, 1894

down the lines for all future progress in hospital construction and administration. She became a legend in her lifetime and her fame grows with the years. She spent the public subscription of £50,000 which was given her at the end of the Crimean War to found the Florence Nightingale School for Nurses at St. Thomas's Hospital. This school, opened in 1861, became a model for the whole world.

In 1916 the Royal College of Nursing was founded, and this body was responsible for the Nurses Registration Act of 1919. This Act set up a General Nursing Council with powers to lay down standards of education and training, to recognize schools, and to maintain a Register of duly qualified nurses. The Nurses Acts of 1943 and 1949 provided for the enrolment and training of nurses.

The nursing profession offers a very wide field of employment. The NATIONAL HEALTH SERVICE (q.v. Vol. X) is the largest employer, and there is also a constant demand for nurses in the Armed Forces and the Queen Elizabeth Colonial Nursing Service, in Residential Nurseries and Institutions, and in private nursing. The main Nursing Register is for General Nursing, but there are supplementary Registers for Male Nurses, Infectious Diseases' Nurses, Sick Children's Nurses, Mental Nurses, and Nurses for Mental Defectives. All candidates take the same preliminary examination, and then specialize if they wish to in the final examination. Girls who have taken a pre-nursing course at a secondary school or polytechnic approved by the General Nursing Council may take Part I of the preliminary examination before entering hospital. They may enter hospital when they are $17\frac{1}{2}$–18 years, and their training takes from 2 to 3 years according to the branch of nursing they are following. A training in general nursing takes 3 years. There are also special courses of training for nurses specializing in ORTHOPAEDIC work and TUBERCULOSIS (qq.v.). After 2 years' training, including one year in a hospital, a girl can be admitted to the Register of Assistant Nurses. There are now, also, 'cadet schemes' which allow a girl, on leaving school at 15 or 16, to do paid work in a hospital, and at the same time to gain general experience in hospital work, as a prelude to becoming a student nurse.

The present-day nurse has travelled far from the 'watcher' of the 18th century and even from Miss Nightingale's 'young lady'. A nurse's duties and opportunities are vastly increased, largely because of the great advances in medical and surgical knowledge and the increasing possibilities for successful treatment in even the most serious diseases. A skilled nurse must know, among other things, how to use a wide range of complicated instruments, and how to make delicate biochemical tests. She must understand something about the various DRUGS (q.v.) used in modern medicine and their possible effects on her patient. From being a mere attendant and bed-maker, the nurse has become an indispensable member of the medical team, with ample scope for the application of knowledge, training, intelligence, and initiative. If in the past the profession has not been accorded the status which is its undoubted right, that is a fault which is now being corrected.

Full information about nursing as a career and advice in the choice of a training school can be obtained from the Secretary, Nursing Recruitment Service, 21 Cavendish Square, London, W. 1.

See also MEDICINE; SURGERY, HISTORY OF; HOME NURSING; FIRST AID.

See also Vol. X: HOSPITALS, HISTORY OF.

NUTRITION. Nutrition is the science concerned with the nourishment of the human body. Nutritionists have to discover the different needs of our bodies and which foods can best satisfy them.

1. ENERGY REQUIREMENTS. Just as a railway engine requires fuel to supply it with energy, so our bodies require food to keep them going. But whereas an engine, when not working, does not use up fuel, a man, even when resting, still needs energy to keep the heart, lungs, and other organs working and to maintain the body temperature.

As heat and energy are different forms of the same thing, they can be measured in the same units, namely 'Calories'. The Calorie is the amount of heat necessary to raise the temperature of 1,000 grammes of water through 1° Centigrade—which is nearly the same as that needed to raise 1 pint of water through 3° Fahrenheit. (This is one thousand times a 'small calorie'

spelt with a small c, the unit commonly used in physics and chemistry, which denotes the amount of heat required to raise the temperature of 1 gramme of water by 1° Centigrade.) The energy which results from eating any particular food can also be measured in Calories. Foods vary greatly in the amount of energy they will produce on being 'burnt' in the body, that is, in their calorific values.

The scientist can estimate the amount of energy the body uses up in different occupations, the general rule being that the more vigorous the exercise, the greater the amount of energy required. The following table obtained by Professor Rose in America shows the amount of energy an average person needs for various activities:

Form of activity	Calories used per hour
Sleeping	65
Awake, lying still	77
Sitting at rest	100
Standing relaxed	105
Standing at attention	115
Dressing and undressing	118
Dish washing	144
Light exercise	170
Walking slowly	200
Carpentry and metal work	240
Active exercise	290
Fast walking	300
Severe exercise	450
Swimming	500
Very severe exercise	600

2. BODY BUILDING. If the housewife's sole concern were to restore the used-up energy of her family every few hours, the nutritional problem would be an easy one. All she would have to do would be to place before them platefuls of food as tasty and as varied as she could contrive. However, food has to do a good deal more than supply energy. In the first place the muscles, the internal organs, the bones, and teeth must be built up gradually in the growing child, and kept in repair in the grown man and woman. Only certain foods contain the substances necessary for building our bodies and maintaining them in good repair. We need to know, therefore, something of the chemistry of foods in order to understand fully the subject of nutrition.

Foods, in general, are of two types: those derived from animal tissues and those from plant tissues. Either type may contain three classes of chemical compounds, called proteins, fats, and carbohydrates. All three classes supply energy, but the proteins are more especially important for body-building purposes. Fats, carbohydrates, and proteins contain the elements carbon, hydrogen, and oxygen; proteins contain nitrogen as well, and sometimes also sulphur and phosphorus.

3. PROTEINS. The body cannot absorb proteins as they occur in food until they are broken down into simpler substances called 'amino acids'—first into large groups, and then into smaller groups or even individual amino acids. In this state they are absorbed and carried away in the blood-stream to various parts of the body, where they are used in the building up of new protein material. As there are many different amino acids and as they can be used in different combinations, a large number of different proteins is theoretically possible; and, in fact, different parts of the body are found to be made up of different proteins. Since all living matter, both plant and animal, has been found to contain protein material, it is believed that life cannot exist without it. Plants can form proteins by synthesizing amino acids from the simple 'inorganic' substances, water, carbon dioxide in the air, and ammonia and nitrates in the soil (see PHOTOSYNTHESIS, Vol. II); but animals cannot do this. Hence, in order to obtain their protein requirements, animals must feed either on plants or on other animals which have themselves fed on plants. For practical reasons only, foods which contain a considerable proportion of proteins, such as egg white, lean meat, and fish, are suitable for body-building purposes. As has been mentioned, the body can and does use proteins for the production of energy also, in the absence of carbohydrates. The fuel value of proteins is approximately 4·1 Calories per gramme.

4. FATS. These are compounds of glycerol (commonly called glycerine) with organic acids known as the fatty acids. The nature of the fatty acid determines whether the fat is solid when cold (suet or dripping) or liquid oil (such as olive oil). Foods from animal sources generally contain fat; and there are a few vegetable sources such as nuts and soya and cocoa beans. Butter is an example of a fatty food obtained from animal sources, whilst vegetarian margarine is one obtained from vegetable sources. Just as proteins are broken down in the body before they are absorbed, so fats are broken down into glycerol and their fatty acids.

After absorption the body utilizes the glycerol and fatty acids for building up new fats. Fatty foods are good sources of energy, for 1 gramme of fat produces 9·3 Calories when it is oxidized or 'burnt' in the body, while a gramme of sugar or starch produces less than half as much. Fats may be used immediately for the production of energy, or they may be stored in the body tissues and used as a reserve supply.

5. CARBOHYDRATES. As their name suggests, these are compounds of carbon, hydrogen, and oxygen, the last two elements being present in the proportion of 2 to 1, as in water. Carbohydrates may be divided into two groups: the sugars and the starches. There are many sugars known to the biochemist. These are obtained mainly from vegetable sources, for growing plants are continually manufacturing sugar. Ordinary sugar is the same chemically, whether it is obtained from cane or beet. Most fruits contain two closely allied sugars known as fructose and glucose. These can be produced chemically by boiling cane sugar (sucrose) with any dilute acid. They are therefore produced in jam-making, when cane sugar is boiled with fruit. Glucose, also called grape sugar or dextrose, can be made from starch. Lactose, the only sugar present in animal foods, occurs in milk but is far less sweet than the sugars derived from vegetable sources.

Starch, which comes solely from vegetable sources, is the chief constituent of potatoes, bread, and rice. During digestion it is broken down into soluble sugars. Whether carbohydrate requirements are obtained from starch or from sugar, the body will use them to produce glucose, the sugar present in the blood, which transfers energy to different parts of the body. It has been estimated that more than half the energy requirements of the body come from glucose. Carbohydrates have an average fuel value of 4·1 Calories per gramme. They can be stored in the liver as the compound glycogen, which is often referred to as animal starch. If they are eaten in large quantities they are changed into fat and stored as such in the tissues.

6. VITAMINS. Besides supplying energy and body-building materials the food we eat also has to supply substances which, although present in very small amounts, are nevertheless absolutely necessary for good health. These are described in the article VITAMINS (q.v.).

7. MINERAL SALTS. These are also necessary

for the proper functioning and growth of the body tissues. Practically all foods contain mineral salts, though in varying degrees. If a sample of food is heated till the 'organic' parts (that is, the fats, proteins, and carbohydrates) are burned away, a small quantity of white or grey ash remains. This is the mineral part of the food—usually calcium, iron, potassium, sodium, magnesium, or a mixture of these, in the form of one or more of the following salts: phosphate, carbonate, sulphate, or chloride.

Calcium and phosphorus in particular are concerned with the formation of the bones and teeth, since these are largely made up of a calcium phosphate mineral which accounts for their hardness. The absorption of calcium is helped by the presence of vitamin D in the diet; and the ratio of the amounts of calcium and phosphorus present is important—apart from the actual quantities. For good health, iron has to be absorbed from our food because iron is the essential ingredient of 'haemoglobin', the substance in the red BLOOD corpuscles (q.v.) which enables them to do their work of carrying oxygen from the lungs to all the tissues of the body. Iron-deficiency, therefore, produces anaemia of a type which used to be called 'green-sickness'.

8. IODINE. A small quantity of this is also necessary for good nutrition—probably less than one ten-thousandth of a gramme daily. Even so, there are many parts of the world where too little is obtained—in England, for instance, in the Cotswolds, the north of Derbyshire, and the Mendips. Deficiency of iodine results in goitre, an overgrowth of the thyroid gland, which is often called 'Derbyshire neck'. This form of goitre can usually be relieved by taking salts of iodine in extremely small doses or by eating food containing iodine. In New Zealand there is a slogan, 'An oyster a day keeps the goitre away'. As the thyroid gland is active during youth and particularly active during pregnancy, it is important to provide plenty of fish and foods containing iodine in the diet at these times (*see* ENDOCRINE GLANDS).

9. ROUGHAGE. The body also needs some material, often referred to as roughage, which is neither digested nor absorbed, but helps to maintain the muscular activity of the intestines. It is generally some form of cellulose, and is obtained from fruit and vegetables. Cellulose is another type of carbohydrate, quite distinct, however, from the sugars and starches which, as we have already seen, are digested and absorbed.

10. WATER. This is an essential in food, and about two-thirds of every tissue in the body consists of it. However, there is no difficulty in obtaining it. On the average the 'solid' food we eat is about half water, and liquid foods contain an even greater proportion. Besides this, we all have the habit of drinking water, or some other liquid such as tea, which is nearly all water.

These main nutritional requirements of our bodies are supplied by various foods as detailed in the article FOOD VALUES (q.v.).

See also VITAMINS.
See also Vol. II: NUTRITION OF ANIMALS; NUTRITION OF PLANTS.

O

OCCUPATIONAL THERAPY. This has been defined as 'any work or recreational activity prescribed and guided by a medical practitioner for the purpose of furthering recovery from disease or injury'. The idea that occupation or diversion is beneficial to the sick is not new; it was well known to the Greeks, and Galen, a celebrated physician of the 2nd century A.D., wrote that 'employment is nature's best physician and is essential to human happiness'. But although it was used in some mental hospitals in the 18th century, occupational therapy did not come into its own as a recognized branch of rehabilitation (bringing people back to normal health) until the time of the First World War. The first School of Occupational Therapy was opened in Chicago in 1915.

The occupational therapist, usually a woman, is now regarded as an important member of the team of medical auxiliaries, and there is an increasing demand for her services. Professional recruitment, training, and certification are carried out by the Association of Occupational Therapists (founded in 1936). Candidates for entry to the training schools must hold the General Certificate of Education with passes in five subjects, including fine arts or crafts, and a knowledge of music and folk dancing is a further advantage. The courses extend over a period of $2\frac{1}{2}$ to $3\frac{1}{4}$ years and are followed by one year of practical work. At the present time the Association has about a thousand members, of whom 90% are women.

Occupational therapists are employed in mental hospitals, colonies for mental defectives, sanatoria for the tuberculous, the medical, surgical, and orthopaedic wards of general hospitals, convalescent homes, and in curative workshops and rehabilitation centres. Occupational therapists, whose work is very varied, must have a thorough knowledge of the basic crafts of needlework, knitting, and crochet, rug-making, chair-caning, weaving, basketry, leather-work, block printing, painting, and joinery; and a knowledge of gardening, music, team games, and physical exercises is also likely to be useful.

The occupational therapist is not merely concerned with developing hobbies and providing recreation for her patients. In many surgical and orthopaedic cases her work forms an essential part of the curative treatment, and she has to work in close co-operation with the physiotherapist. One of the principal aims of occupational therapy is to restore and improve function, for example, to restore the muscular control of hands and fingers or the co-ordination of hand and brain. That is why the method finds such a wide field of application in cases of fractures and nerve injuries and in chronic disabling diseases such as arthritis.

OFFAL (literally, 'what falls off') comprises the skin, head, entrails, and extremities of animal carcasses. Although much of this is edible, it has not always been considered good to eat. Some societies have had rules against eating offal (*see* FOOD, HISTORY OF), and individuals differ in their attitude to it—for example, tripe is regarded with disgust or with relish by different persons or communities according to their upbringing and traditions.

Brains and tongue of ox, sheep, and pig are fairly generally regarded as delicacies, for instance, as brain fritters with fried bacon, or as tongues in aspic. The head itself is muscled with good meat; in the case of the ox, it is so large that it subdivides into cheek, muzzle, and palate, all of which make fine stews. A 19th-century cookery book gives twenty-eight recipes for calf's head (French *Tête de veau*). Pig's cheek and pig's ears, boiled long with onions, with or without previous pickling in salt, make excellent brawn because they are full of gelatine. Sheep's head holds a 'rare lot of miscellaneous pickings', and also makes a good brawn.

Of the chest organs, the heart, choicest from calves, is usually stuffed and braised. Its characteristic firm, dense texture is not toughness in the ordinary sense but is due to the special kind of muscle of which it is made. The lungs, or 'lights', are spongy in texture and are not fit for use as a separate dish; with the heart and the liver they form what butchers call the 'pluck'. They are the basis of the Scotch haggis, a dish descended from a Roman sausage made in a pig's stomach from minced ham, eggs, and spices. The Romans brought it to Britain where it survived, in England till the 18th century, and in Scotland till the present day. A sheep's or lamb's pluck is minced with onions, mixed with suet, oatmeal, and seasonings, and filled into a sheep's first stomach (the rumen), which is sewn up and boiled well. It is now rarely made at home, owing partly to the difficulty of procuring the right organs; and the shop-made versions are often very inferior, lacking liver and onions, over-peppered, and sewn up in a piece of thick, inedible sausage skin.

Sweetbreads (French *ris*) are the pancreas and thymus (*see* ENDOCRINE GLANDS). Their delicate texture and delicious flavour make them a real gourmet's dish. They may be served creamed, in combination with a white SAUCE (q.v.), or fried, after being dipped in egg and crumb, or in batter as fritters (*see* FRYING).

Skirt steak is meat from the edges of an ox's diaphragm, that is, the horizontal sheet of muscle separating chest from belly. Pig's diaphragms are on sale in every butcher's shop in Denmark. Skirt steak is used in casseroles, stews, and pies.

Of abdominal organs, tripe is made from the first, second, and fourth stomachs of the ox. In Scotland the third stomach is used also. Sheep tripe, from the paunch (the first stomach) and the honeycomb (the second stomach), is eaten in the English Midlands and in Scotland. In Lancashire tripe is eaten 'raw', that is, after it has been scrubbed and boiled by the tripe dresser, cut in strips, and seasoned with vinegar. Elsewhere in Britain it is reboiled and served with onions. New Zealanders fry best pieces of boiled tripe in batter. The French *Tripes à la mode de Caen* is a sort of brown stew with carrots, herbs, and wine cooked in a closely sealed casserole. Spaniards cut their tripe into strips and braise it with tomatoes and garlic.

Livers of calves, pigs, and lambs are the best for frying, and these, as well as the more delicate chicken and goose livers, make good liver pastes and liver SAUSAGE (q.v.). The most famous liver paste, *Pâté de Foie Gras*, is made from goose liver. The liver, heart, and spleen of the pig is known as pig's fry or 'haslet', and faggots, a kind of rissole, are made from it. Kidneys are popular in many forms—as traditional British steak and kidney pie and pudding, kidneys grilled, kidneys devilled, kidney soup. Intestines, on the other hand, are considered inedible by most Western people, though a Saturday night's feed of pig's chitterlings (small intestines) from the pork butcher round the corner used to be a kind of ritual in some English towns. Melt, which is the spleen of ox, sheep, or pig, goes 'off' very quickly and is used mostly as dog meat. The testes, however, sold during the Second World War under the name of sweetbreads, contain first class protein, comparable with that of fish roes, and stand refrigeration well. Udders, salted and boiled, can be stuffed or fried.

Most of the extremities—toes, trotters, tails of ox, pig, and sheep—are well known and widely acceptable. We find fat-tailed varieties of sheep in the Middle East and Central Asia almost everywhere that the Moslem religion is practised, for, as Moslems do not eat pork, these fat tails are a much prized delicacy and are the equivalent of pig fat in our cooking. Blood makes the black puddings of Scotland and Poland and the blood sausage (*Blutwurst*) of Germany.

Offal from birds, known as giblets, includes necks (stuffed goose's neck is a German-Jewish preparation), heart, liver, gizzard, spleen, kidneys, feet, and pinions. Fish offal is not much used in the West, apart from hard and soft roes (ovaries and testes). The Chinese, however, cook up all sorts of things, including shark's fins and fish gills and stomachs.

See also MEAT.

OILS, *see* FATS AND OILS.

OMELETTES, *see* EGG DISHES.

ORIENTAL COSTUME. Before the days of mass-production and large-scale export of cheap garments, the two main factors which determined what kind of clothing people wore were the materials available to them and the sort of lives they led (*see* PRIMITIVE COSTUME). On the steppe lands of Central Asia men very soon learned to ride on horseback, and they made their clothes from the skins and hair of the animals they hunted or reared. Because skins, being partly shaped already, are easy to fit round the body, and because a life spent mostly on horseback requires clothing that allows the

ASSYRIAN, SASSANIAN, AND JAPANESE COSTUME

arms and legs to move freely, these nomad horsemen evolved fitted garments—trousers and jackets—earlier than any other people in the world.

This sort of clothing seems commonplace to us. But the costume worn in the ancient cultures of the Middle East and southern Asia consisted almost entirely of large pieces of cloth folded and draped about the body, often in extremely ingenious ways. The EGYPTIANS,

INDIAN MAN AND BRAHMIN LADY

SUMERIANS, BABYLONIANS, and ASSYRIANS (qq.v. Vol. I) all seem to have dressed in this way. We can see this quite clearly in pictures of the ancient Egyptian male, in which the costume of high and low alike was a sort of kilt made of a single piece of cloth intricately folded about the waist (see Vol. XII, p. 123). It is more difficult to see in the case of Egyptian women, or of the Assyrian kings whose splendid fringed and embroidered robes fit all over the body and look as though they must have been made by a tailor; yet these, too, are simply the result of skilful folding and tying (see Vol. I, p. 41). Doubtless the convention of the sculptors and painters makes them look a little more close-fitting than they really were.

Clothing of this kind is still worn today in many parts of the East, particularly in India, Ceylon, and Burma. Traditional Hindu dress has from time immemorial consisted of two large pieces of cloth; one of them, the *dhoti*, wrapped around the waist as a loin-cloth or skirt, the other worn around the shoulders and sometimes over the head. The beautiful *sari* worn by Indian women is simply a large piece of cloth; so is the skirt-like *sarong* worn in many parts of south-east Asia, often, as in Burma and Ceylon, with a small jacket or bodice (see INDIAN PEOPLES; CEYLONESE; BURMESE, Vol. I).

The Chinese seem to have learned very early

how to cut and sew cloth and make it into garments; but, unlike the people of the steppes, they made garments which were long and loose with wide sleeves, and tied up at the waist with a girdle, somewhat like a voluminous dressing-gown (*see* Vol. I, opp. p. 112). They were also the first to discover the secret of weaving silk (*see* SILK INDUSTRY, Vol. VII), which enabled them to produce very large pieces of material with fine, clear patterns. Like most peoples of the Ancient World, the Chinese hunted and fought in chariots. But, in the 5th century B.C., one of the Chinese frontier states, which was constantly fighting against the raiding nomads, adopted the nomad custom of fighting on horseback. Then they found their long, flowing garments no longer suitable, and the barbarian trousers had to be adopted as well. In time trousers became the standard wear for men and women alike. They were worn even under the long, voluminous robes always considered appropriate for persons of education or consequence. The familiar high 'mandarin' type of collar was a late development. Before its appearance, gowns were generally collarless, and were folded in front in a V-shape, like Western-style coats.

The loose 'dressing-gown' type of costume is found also in Korea, and is the basis of the traditional Japanese costume, the *kimono* (*see* Vol. I, p. 269). Japan imported much of her culture from China in the middle part of the first millennium A.D., and clothing was no doubt influenced by Chinese models. The *hakama*, which in formal male costume was belted on over the *kimono*, was really a pair of trousers so wide as to give the appearance of a rather full skirt. In the Heian period, the *hakama* worn in Court dress were immensely long, with yards of trouser-leg trailing on the ground behind the feet—perhaps the most inconvenient costume which has ever been invented.

During the centuries when the 'barbarian' costume of the steppes was becoming established in China, Scythians (*see* RUSSIANS, Vol. I) and PERSIANS (q.v. Vol. I), who were also peoples of Central Asian origin, were making trousers a familiar costume in northern India and the Middle East. The Persian costume of medieval times is familiar to us from paintings: a full-skirted coat girdled at the waist, trousers bound at the ankle, and a cap or turban on the head. But the costume of the Sassanian kings of Persia, centuries earlier, is really the same sort of thing

CHINESE MAN'S COSTUME

in principle, though its billowing, diaphanous materials and numerous ribbons and furbelows make it a far more fanciful attire. In the 16th century the Moghul emperors made the Persian 'coat and breeches' type of costume familiar throughout India, and it became the characteristic dress of Indian Muslims. In time what had once been features of Muslim dress were copied by Hindus as well. The costume associated with the Mahatma GANDHI (q.v. Vol. V) is the traditional Hindu dress of draped, untailored cloth (*see* Vol. V, p. 181); but the costume worn by Pandit Nehru (also a Hindu) is basically much the same as that worn by Persian kings and Moghul emperors (*see* Vol. V, opp. p. 64).

Fashions in HEADWEAR (q.v.) are often influenced by the way in which people wear their hair. The Chinese, Koreans, and Japanese used to wear their hair in a sort of top-knot. This made a convenient anchorage for hat-pins, and so enabled them to wear extremely elaborate hats—often indicating a person's rank or status. Most Central Asian people, on the other hand, wore their hair in plaits, and did not attach much importance to headwear. The wearing of the 'pig-tail' was forced upon the Chinese by their Manchu conquerors in the 17th century. Then hats became simpler, but more elaborate headwear continued to be worn in Japan and Korea. The quaint Korean hat, rather like an undersized European top hat tied on with strings, persisted into modern times. In all of these countries, however, the women have never taken to hats owing to the complicated nature of their hair arrangement and hair ornaments. In China a woman's hair ornaments used to be the main part of her dowry and often constituted her entire worldly wealth.

With the coming of Western ideas and techniques to the East, clothing has become less picturesque. No longer do officials in India or China or Japan dress in the gorgeous brocades and flowing silks that once seemed suitable. The large-scale export of cheap manufactured articles has made Western-style shirts, trousers, and footwear (and above all, trilby hats) a familiar sight throughout the whole of Asia. Officials and business men often wear European suits. Only women and peasants seem to be somewhat conservative about their dress. Peasant costume has always been simple, practical, and inexpen- sive, and survives for that reason. Thus the situation in Asia is gradually becoming similar to the situation in Europe, where 'national dress' is seldom seen and means, in effect, the costume of an ever-decreasing number of conservative countryfolk (see EUROPEAN PEASANT COSTUME) or a fancy dress for festivals.

See also COSTUME, HISTORY OF.

ORNAMENTS, HOUSEHOLD. These are usually small, movable objects arranged in a house in order to satisfy a sense of display. Some, such as vases or ashtrays, serve another purpose besides decoration. In the past, they were usually miniature works of art, precious materials treated decoratively, and belonged only to the wealthy. A common kind of ornament is some treasure brought home from foreign travel and put, probably, to a use very different from its original one.

The earliest pure ornaments in Western civilization may have been the small TERRA- COTTA statuettes (q.v. Vol. XII), in the 4th cen- tury B.C., of figures from Tanagra in Greece. Later, wealthy Romans delighted in small bronze figures or groups of gods and goddesses, mythical persons, and animals. They also put in their houses life-size portrait busts in marble, as well as smaller ones in bronze, and vases of carved onyx or blue and white glass.

During the Middle Ages hunting trophies and weapons were hung on the walls; but the only real ornaments were the winecups and dishes of gold or silver displayed on the sideboard during feasts in great establishments. On the dais table stood the medieval 'salt' and the 'nef' or ship in richly decorated precious metal such as silver. These at first served an important practical purpose—the 'nef' contained the host's personal table utensils, knife, napkins, and even wine— but later the 'nef' at least became merely orna- mental.

During the Renaissance, TABLE DISHES (q.v.) became very decorative and flower vases of silver, glass, or decorative earthenware began to appear. As the 'salt' and the 'nef' disappeared they were replaced by centrepieces such as the 18th-century silver 'epergne', hung with small baskets, and equipped with vases. Small groups in bronze, wood, or terracotta in imitation of classical types were placed in important rooms in grand houses.

In the later 17th century, as more furniture

Dr. W. L. Hildbrugh, F.S.A.

SILVER GILT 'NEF', GERMAN, c. 1620

came into use, it became fashionable to place Chinese porcelain vases, jars, or bowls in conspicuous places in rooms (see Vol. XII, opp. p. 224). These were soon copied in Europe, together with the dainty porcelain figure groups of Meissen, Sèvres, Chelsea, and Bow (see POTTERY AND PORCELAIN FIGURES, Vol. XII). Staffordshire pottery and earthenware figures (see Vol. VII, p. 349) were popular, as well as the more expensive porcelain. Figures of birds generally followed Eastern models, but animals such as cats, greyhounds, and poodles were original. Bouquets of porcelain flowers or flowers set separately on gilt metal sprays were popular, and some English ladies excelled at making flower bouquets of shells. Busts and statues of marble, white earthenware, or porcelain were set in formal positions, especially in large mansions.

During the prosperous 19th century came a profusion of ornaments, generally of little artistic merit, mostly mere bric-à-brac, fans, shell boxes, realistically coloured piles of wax fruit or flowers under glass domes. Curios, such as glass 'snow scene' balls, Swiss cuckoo-clocks, Benares inlaid brassware, or carved elephants of ebony or ivory from India, were found in most homes, and also sportsmen's trophies, such as skins, heads, horns, and stuffed fish, and engraved silver 'cups' won at sports. For the very rich, Carl Fabergé's workshops made such conceits as exotic small flowers of precious stones

Victoria and Albert Museum

BASKET OF FLOWERS MADE OF SHELLS. ENGLISH, EARLY 19TH CENTURY

(sapphire, ruby, emerald), a single spray, perhaps, being set in crystal 'water' in a crystal vase.

In the early 20th century came the fashion for collecting 'antiques', real or copies, including everything useful or ornamental from English copper warming-pans to fine Chinese jade

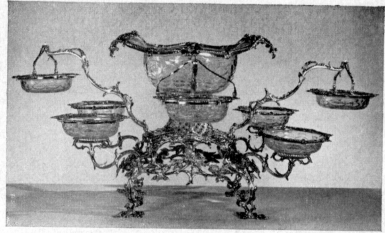

Victoria and Albert Museum

Above: SILVER EPERGNE WITH CUT GLASS BOWLS, ENGLISH, 1764–5

Right: SMALL ENAMELLED EASTER EGG SET WITH DIAMONDS. MADE BY THE RUSSIAN JEWELLER CARL FABERGÉ, 1846–1920

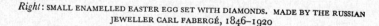

By gracious permission of H.M. the Queen

carvings. After the First World War it was fashionable to have very few or no ornaments in rooms; and today one or two ornaments, carefully selected in style and colour, take their place in modern schemes of INTERIOR DECORATION (q.v.).

ORTHOPAEDICS. The word 'orthopaedic', from two Greek words, *orthos*, 'straight', and *paideia*, 'child rearing', was coined by the French surgeon Nicolas Andry to serve as the main title of a book which he published in 1741 on the prevention and treatment of deformities in children. The term is now used to include the treatment of adults as well as children and is concerned not only with the correction of deformities such as bow-legs, knock-knees, and curvature of the spine, but with every aspect of the surgery of the supporting framework of the body. The orthopaedic surgeon, therefore, deals with the diseases and injuries of bones, muscles, tendons, and ligaments (*see* BONES AND JOINTS) and with lesions of the blood vessels and nerves which are connected with those parts.

Orthopaedic surgery has a long history, although it did not become recognized as a

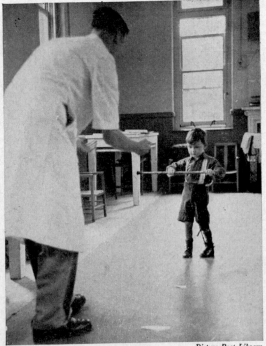

Picture Post Library

A CHILD, PARALYSED BY POLIOMYELITIS, LEARNING TO WALK IN CALLIPERS IN AN ORTHOPAEDIC HOSPITAL

special study until the time of the First World War. Crutches were used in ancient Egypt, and artificial limbs of wood and metal were also known in antiquity. The Greek physicians HIPPOCRATES (q.v. Vol. V) in the 4th century B.C. and Galen in the 2nd century A.D. laid the foundations for the treatment of fractures by traction, manipulation, and splints. The common bone disease, rickets (*see* VITAMINS), was well described by Soranus of Ephesus in the 1st century A.D.

The first orthopaedic hospital with special beds and equipment was opened in Switzerland in 1790, and some 27 years later a similar institution was established at Birmingham. In 1838 Dr. W. J. Little, himself a cripple, founded the Royal Orthopaedic Hospital in London, and from this time onwards the need for special hospitals to deal with long-term orthopaedic cases and for specially qualified surgeons became more and more recognized. A great contribution was made by Antonius Mathijsen, a Dutch surgeon, who invented the plaster-of-Paris bandage in 1852. But before the introduction of ANAESTHETICS and before Lord Lister had established his system of ANTISEPTICS (qq.v.), few surgeons were bold enough to open a joint, because such a procedure would almost certainly have been followed by death from sepsis. The only treatment for a compound fracture was amputation of the limb, and this operation also carried a fearful mortality. But Lister soon showed that by using antiseptic and aseptic methods it was possible to open a joint and to fasten together broken fragments of bone, thus saving innumerable lives and limbs (*see* SURGERY, MODERN).

The vital importance of prolonged rest in the treatment of orthopaedic cases became better understood, especially after 1875, as a result of the teaching of the great orthopaedic surgeon Hugh Owen Thomas of Liverpool, who came from a famous family of bone-setters. Thomas invented most of the fracture splints now in use, including the invaluable Thomas hip splint, used for the treatment of fractures of the femur. The enormous number of bone and joint injuries produced by the First World War and the use of X-RAYS (q.v. Vol. VIII) to diagnose and examine them gave a great impetus to the development of orthopaedics. After the war, in 1919, the Central Council for the Care of Cripples was founded, and this Council did

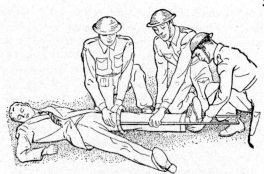

From 'First Aid Manual', H.M.S.O.

FIXING A THOMAS HIP SPLINT TO A BROKEN LEG

much to extend the number of special homes opened for the treatment of crippled children. The ever increasing number of accidents in factories and on the roads has made orthopaedic services essential to modern life, and special accident hospitals and fracture clinics have now been established in many parts of the country.

The orthopaedic surgeon has to carry out complicated techniques such as the transplantation of tendons, the stitching together of divided nerves, and the treatment of fractures by wiring, plating and nailing, and bone grafting. He also often plays a very important part in the treatment of osteomyelitis (inflammation of the bone marrow), arthritis (inflammation of the joints), POLIOMYELITIS, and TUBERCULOSIS (qq.v.).

See also BONES AND JOINTS; SURGERY, HISTORY OF; SURGERY, MODERN.

OSTEOPATHY. This is mainly concerned with the manipulation of the spine and of the other BONES AND JOINTS (q.v.) of the body in order to correct faults and to relieve pressures thought to be causing disease. Osteopathy was discovered and formulated in 1874 by Andrew T.

Still of Baldwin, Kansas, U.S.A. Still's early years were spent in the hard life of the north-west frontier, and he appears to have received little regular medical training. He became interested in some bones dug up in an Indian graveyard and studied them until he could identify each of the bones blindfold. This preoccupation with bones, and especially with those of the spine, was reinforced when he lost three of his children in an epidemic of cerebrospinal fever. It was suddenly 'revealed' to him that the forming cause of every disease is some interference with the blood-supply or nerve functions brought about by a displacement of one of the small bones of the spine, and that if the structural abnormality causing obstruction were located and mechanically adjusted, the curative powers residing in the body would do the rest.

Osteopathic or any other kind of manipulation undoubtedly does give relief at times, and all orthopaedic surgeons make use of manipulation in appropriate cases. But Still and his followers tried to exalt a simple method of manipulative treatment to a complete system of medicine. Like other irregular practitioners, osteopaths have gradually adopted other methods of treatment, such as electricity, massage, hydrotherapy, and surgery.

Osteopathy is widespread in the United States and Canada, but there are not more than 2,000 to 3,000 practitioners in Britain, of whom less than 200 can claim to be 'qualified'. A Bill for the registration and regulation of osteopaths was introduced into the House of Lords in 1935, but this attempt to 'enter medicine by the back door' was heavily defeated, and the Bill was withdrawn. Chiropractice is an offshoot of osteopathy founded by D. D. Palmer in America in 1895.

P

PAINTING AND ENAMELLING. On new or stripped wood, plaster, or metal, three coats of paint are usually necessary for the best result. These are the priming, the undercoat, and the topcoat.

The priming is absorbed by the wood or plaster and gives a surface on metal to which the undercoat can adhere. The undercoat gives the surface an even colour so that the topcoat, which is the real decoration, can be applied more easily and more smoothly. Paint for the priming is made up of red or white lead, linseed oil, and turpentine. An 'aluminium primer' is particularly suitable for resinous woods and metal.

The undercoat must be a 'flat' paint, that is, without shine, as this gives a better 'key' for the topcoat. Either flat or enamel paint may be used for the topcoat, an enamel paint producing the most glossy hard-wearing surface. Plastic emulsion paint gives a mat surface with a soft sheen. It is usually best to buy a paint or enamel with an undercoating to match.

A good finish largely depends on the way the surface is prepared. All nail holes and cracks must be stopped, any roughness smoothed down, and the whole surface made perfectly clean before painting is started. If paintwork is sound and there are no cracks or blisters, complete stripping is not necessary, so long as the surface is washed down with warm water and sugar soap, thoroughly rinsed and dried, and then rubbed down with glasspaper.

A good stopping for holes and cracks can be made from equal parts of white lead and whiting mixed with enough gold size to make a soft putty. This is pressed well into the holes with an old knife, allowed to dry for 24 hours, and then rubbed down with glasspaper. Linseed-oil putty, made from dry whiting and linseed oil, is also suitable but usually takes longer to harden.

Knots in wood, which spoil the painted surface, must be given a coat of 'knotting', a solution of SHELLAC (q.v. Vol. VII) in methylated spirits which prevents resin coming through. After one coat has been applied and allowed to dry, the surface should be rubbed down.

Surfaces which have had a number of coats of paint should first be washed and rinsed to remove the dirt and grease and then sandpapered to strip them. If the old paint is in a bad condition, it is best to strip it off completely. Professional painters use a blowlamp to soften the paint so that it can be peeled off easily with blunt instruments called 'strippers'. There are, however, proprietary liquid strippers which, if the instructions are followed closely, can be satisfactory. It is important to wash down the surface after using the liquid to remove any caustic soda which may be in it and which would spoil the new paint. After stripping, the surface is rubbed down with glasspaper, and holes and cracks are attended to.

The priming coat must be worked well into the grain, allowed to dry for 24 hours, and then rubbed down lightly with fine glasspaper.

The undercoat, one coat of which is usually sufficient, must be applied thinly in order to cover the surface completely and as evenly as possible. If a very dark surface is to be covered with a light paint, a second or even third undercoat may be necessary. Each must be allowed to dry, be rubbed down with glasspaper, and be dusted off before the next is applied.

A gloss paint flows more easily than an undercoat, so brush marks often fade out as the work proceeds. It is best to work from top to bottom of the surface in strips and sufficiently quickly to prevent the edge drying before the next strip is painted. Over a large area there should be no break in the work and the strips should not overlap more than is necessary to give a complete coating.

See also INTERIOR DECORATION; DISTEMPERING; PLASTERING.
See also Vol. VII: PAINTS AND VARNISHES.

PALACE. The word 'palace' derives from the Palatine Hill in Rome on which Augustus, the first of the Roman Emperors, built his home. The most magnificent palaces belonged to those ancient empires in which the powers of kings were more exalted and all-embracing than they have ever been in modern Europe. In the

RECONSTRUCTION OF THE PALACE OF PERSEPOLIS

Ancient World the king's power was generally unchecked. As he was regarded as the protector of gods or even as a god himself, his dwelling had to be magnificent, and remote from ordinary people.

We find these characteristics first in the palaces of the EGYPTIAN, BABYLONIAN, and HITTITE kings (qq.v. Vol. I), in the palace of Minos at KNOSSOS (q.v. Vol. XII) in Crete, and, later, in those of the kings of the ASSYRIANS (q.v. Vol. I) who came to dominate western Asia in the 9th and 8th centuries B.C. The palace of King Sargon at Khorsabad (about 720 B.C.) included not only armouries and halls and living-rooms for the Court but also a huge *ziggurat* or temple for the worship of the god Ashur. The whole complicated group of buildings, covering 25 acres, was raised up on a single platform and defended with towering walls. In the Persian Empire, which succeeded and surpassed the Assyrian and dominated the Middle East in the 6th to 4th centuries B.C., the palaces of Persepolis (*see* Vol. I, p. 354) and Susa were of essentially the same character, though their halls of slender pillars made them appear more open and airy than any Assyrian architecture.

The Greeks and Romans, who had quite different ideas of how the State should be run, allowed their rulers much less wealth and power. After Augustus had established himself as Emperor at Rome (27 B.C.), he built a comparatively modest palace on the Palatine Hill, within the city. Succeeding emperors added to it; Domitian (A.D. 81–96), for instance, added not only living-rooms for the Emperor's many servants and guards but also a great banqueting-room and a hall in which he gave judgements on important disputes. As the Roman Empire became more influenced by Eastern ideas and its Emperors more despotic, the importance of the palace increased. The great palace of Constantinople, founded by the Emperor Constantine when he built the new city in A.D. 330, was very much the centre of the Empire, especially after the Western part, including Rome, had been overrun by the barbarians in the 5th century. Besides the private apartments of the Imperial family, it included many reception rooms and galleries, through which visiting envoys were led with elaborate etiquette to fall finally at the feet of the Emperor.

Medieval kings produced nothing to rival the buildings of antiquity, but they had palaces in which their retainers lived, with great halls for eating and holding court. Halls of English palaces survive at Westminster and at Eltham. In the Italian City States (q.v. Vol. X) of the 14th and 15th centuries, the wealthier merchants built palaces, such as the Strozzi Palace in Florence, which are really private houses on a grand scale, rectangular buildings with a courtyard in the middle from which the rooms around were to be entered. The bare, rugged wall facing on to the street gave safety against fighting in the city. The towns also had communal palaces—there are famous examples at Florence, Siena, and Perugia (see Vol. X, p. 87)—which in the 16th century became larger and more ornamental; the Palazzo Farnese at Rome and the Doge's Palace at Venice have a series of grand rooms, the walls and ceilings of which are decorated with huge paintings.

The great palaces of the Chinese Emperors, especially that of Peking, Forbidden City (q.v. Vol. XII), mostly belong to the Ming Dynasty (see Chinese Civilization, Vol. I).

The greatest palaces of modern Europe were built by the kings of the 16th, 17th, and 18th centuries. As the French kings acquired more wealth and control over their kingdom, they built large palaces in and near Paris to emphasize the magnificence of the monarchy. These immense ranges of buildings and courtyards, set in formal pleasure gardens, were designed partly to house the royal household, even more for the king to hold court in the galleries and halls with the many nobles who surrounded him in his capital. The palace of Fontainebleau was designed for Francis I (1515–47); the Louvre (q.v. Vol. XII) was begun for Francis I but continued by Louis XIII and XIV in the next century. The Tuileries was also built largely in the 17th century; and, greatest of all, Versailles (q.v. Vol. XII) was built for Louis XIV. The more religious tastes of another great despot, Philip II of Spain (1556–98), produced the Escurial near Madrid, only part of which is taken up with royal apartments, the palace

Anderson

THE MONASTIC BUILDINGS OF THE ESCURIAL PALACE, MADRID

THE CLOCK PAVILION OF THE ZWINGER PALACE, DRESDEN

Mansell Collection

being dominated by a church and including both a monastery and a college.

The ostentation of the French kings was copied by other rulers in the 17th and 18th centuries, and magnificent palaces were built, not only by great rulers such as the Habsburg emperors of Austria, who built Schönbrunn Palace in Vienna in the early 18th century, but also by comparatively petty ones such as the Dukes of Saxony, who about the same time built the Zwinger Palace in Dresden. Even wealthy Prince Bishops built magnificent palaces, such as the Bishop's palace at Würzburg. The rulers of Brandenburg–Prussia built a series of palaces at their capital of Berlin. The big square palace in the middle of the city itself was built at the beginning of the 18th century. Later on it was connected by a road running through the Brandenburg Gate with the palaces which Frederick the Great built in the suburb of Potsdam. The most famous of these is the pleasure palace of Sans-souci, which has room after room with delightful, fantastic mouldings on walls and ceilings, and which looks out on to carefully planned gardens.

In England kings were never so powerful and wealthy as on the Continent. The most imposing palace in England is probably Blenheim (*see* Vol. XII, p. 234), built by Vanbrugh (q.v. Vol. V) for the Duke of Marlborough and given him by the nation to commemorate the battle of Blenheim. Hampton Court and St. James's Palace, the king's residences from William III to George III, are unremarkable by Continental standards; the present Buckingham Palace was re-built by George IV in 1821 (*see* Royal Household and Residences, Vol. X).

See also Houses, History of; Castle.

PARALYSIS, *see* Nervous System.

PARTY GAMES, *see* Vol. IX: Party Games.

PASTA. This is a general Italian term, with no precise English equivalent, for the starchy foods of which macaroni, spaghetti, noodles, and ravioli are probably the best-known examples outside Italy. Within Italy, however, where pasta is a staple food, it is found in countless varieties, all stemming from two main types: the

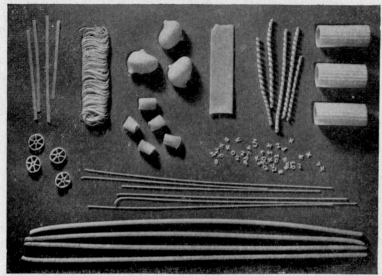

KINDS OF PASTA

Above are a few of the different types used in soup and pasta dishes, and below are spaghetti and macaroni

Naples varieties (*pasta napolitana*), cylindrical in form and bought ready made (spaghetti, macaroni, and vermicelli); and the Bologna varieties (*pasta bolognese*) or noodle type, in flat ribbon form, and made in the home (such as tagliatelle and lasagne). The essential constituents of pasta in any form are very finely ground flour from 'hard' wheat, and eggs. Pasta is eaten either *asciutta* (dry), in which case a meat sauce or a tomato sauce is usually served with it (this is described as *al sugo*); or *in brodo* (in broth), that is, served in a consommé. Many varieties are served with fillings, among them *ravioli*, *agnellotti*, and *tortellini*. Grated parmesan cheese is not only used in the cooking of many forms of pasta, but is almost always served with it at table. Pasta is cooked by BOILING (q.v.).

Besides pasta, Italy provides two related dishes, *risotto* (*see* RICE DISHES) and *polenta*, the latter being a stiff maize meal mash which has for long been the staple dish of the country people of Lombardy and Venetia. It is cut in thick slices and eaten warm with cheese or '*al sugo*'. Left-over slices are very good fried in oil.

PASTRY. Pastes of flour, fat, and water, aerated in various ways, make different kinds of pastry The seven main British types are short crust, suet crust, rough puff, flaky, puff, hot-water crust, and *choux*. They differ chiefly in the proportion of fat and the way it is put in—rubbed into short crust, stirred dry into suet crust, rolled into the dough of puff and flaky types, melted in hot liquid for *choux* and hot-water pastry.

The flour should be 'weak' for short pastry, 'medium' for puff (and strengthened with lemon juice), and 'strong' for *choux* paste which is beaten (*see* FLOUR MILLING, Vol. VII). Lard and modern shortenings give the tenderest pastry, butter the best flavour. For short and flaky pastes a mixture of lard and margarine is satisfactory. Butter is best for puff paste because it is more plastic than the other FATS (q.v.). Packeted suet saves time, but home-grated suet tastes better and is much cheaper. Some cooks use baking powder for short pastry, and it is necessary for suet crust unless self-raising flour is used. Puff and flaky, with no baking powder, are raised almost entirely by the air sandwiched between the many layers of paste. Steam operates in all pastry, especially in *choux* (*see* RAISING AGENTS).

Pastry is baked in a hot oven: short and flaky pastry at a temperature of 425° to 475° F. according to the dish, puff pastries at 470° to 500° F., and suet crusts and hot-water pastes at 350° to 400° F. The time varies according to the size of the dish and the heat of the oven. The best way of learning to make pastry is to watch an expert doing it.

1. *Short Types.* For a basic short crust suitable for pies and tarts 4 oz. of fat are cut up and rubbed into 8 oz. of sieved flour (1 cup), a little salt, and perhaps $\frac{1}{2}$ teaspoon of baking powder. The mixture is moistened to a fairly stiff dough with cold water.

For a biscuit crust suitable for flans and tartlets 2–3 oz. of fat are used, only $\frac{1}{4}$ teaspoon of baking powder, a little sugar, and one egg yolk.

For a suet crust suitable for jam roll, dumplings, or steak pudding, the basic short crust recipe is used, except that 3–4 oz. of suet are used instead of fat, and 1 teaspoon of baking powder.

2. *Flaky Types.* Rough puff for party pies and sausage rolls is quick to make but does not rise as well as true puff; 4–6 oz. of fat are used for 8 oz. of flour. Small marbles of the fat are dropped into the flour, and cold water is added. The dough is rolled, folded, and rotated three or four times.

Flaky, a rich pastry suitable for eccles cakes or mince pies, is made with 5–6 oz. of fat to 8 oz. of flour. The fat is divided into four portions, the first, with flour and water, makes the foundation short-crust dough, and the remaining three, subdivided, are introduced in three further sets of rolling, folding, and rotating operations.

Puff, the lightest paste, suitable for *vol au vent*, patty cases, and horns, contains equal quantities of butter and flour. All the butter, except the bit used for making the foundation dough, is spread on the dough in one flat piece and folded and rolled in up to seven times, the dough being rested between whiles.

3. *Melted-fat Types.* In hot-water paste for pork and other raised pies, the hot water gelatinizes some of the starch in the flour, strengthening it and enabling it to brown; it also oils the fats which later cool and set more firmly, thus helping to prevent the pie from collapsing. 2 oz. of lard and 8 oz. of flour are used, with salt and $\frac{3}{4}$ gill of boiling water.

Choux paste is piped on to a greased tray, in lengths for *éclairs*, in blobs for *choux*. The fabulously light puffs of the professional pastry-cook are baked in steam-tight tins, so that crusting is delayed and the *choux* can rise to their limit; they are also assisted by a pinch of 'vol' (*see* RAISING AGENTS). 4 oz. of flour are stirred into a just-boiling mixture of $\frac{1}{2}$ pint of water and 2 oz. of

MAKING FLAKY PASTRY

Above, left: Rubbing a quarter of the fat into the flour; *right*: folding the paste spread with fat. *Below, left*: sealing the end to include air before rolling into a strip; *right*: folding for the final rolling

butter, and beaten to a fairly stiff paste. When it is slightly cooled, two eggs are beaten in.

4. *Some Exotic Pastes.* Danish pastry is a slightly sweetened yeast and egg dough in which shortening is enfolded, as for puff paste. Curiously enough the Danes, who always produce it, if possible, for visitors, call it *Wienerbrød* (Vienna bread). It is generally coated either with water ICING (q.v.) sprinkled with flaked, roast almonds, or with boiled vanilla custard and nuts. More elaborate kinds contain fruits and are topped with apricot jam or glacé pineapple covered with a transparent glaze of water icing.

German sweet pastry, made by cutting egg and bits of butter into a heap of flour and sugar, adding vinegar or rum, and kneading, is used for fruit tarts and cream-cheese cakes (*Käse Kremtorte*). *Kuchen* pastry is not really pastry, but a sweetened bread dough. Great squares of it, spread with neat rows of sliced apples, pears, or plums, are sugared, baked, and cut up. *Strudel* pastry, the speciality of Austria, begins like German sweet pastry but takes two people to complete the making, as it must be rolled very thinly and then stretched on a clean floured tablecloth until it is so transparent 'that one can read an old love letter through it'. Strewn with, for example, apples, poppy seeds, or cream cheese, rolled up, and baked, it makes all kinds of *strudels*. Canadian or 'crumble' topping may have descended from German *Krümmeltorte* or crumble cake. It is not mixed with liquid. 3 oz. of margarine, rubbed into 6 oz. of flour and 2 oz. of sugar, is sprinkled thickly over prepared fruit and baked at 400° F.

See also BAKING; CAKES; SWEETS AND PUDDINGS.

PATCHING, *see* MENDING.

PENICILLIN, *see* DRUGS.

PERAMBULATOR, *see* BABY TRANSPORT.

PERFUMES. Herbs and aromatic gums must have been used for making perfumes at a very early period in human history, probably largely for religious purposes. The Book of Exodus (xxx. 34) even gives us a recipe: 'And the Lord said unto Moses, Take unto thee sweet spices, stacte, and onycha, and galbanum; these sweet spices with pure frankincense: of each shall there be a like weight. And thou shalt make it a perfume, a confection after the art of the apothecary,

Ashmolean Museum

GREEK PERFUME VASE, *c.* 430 B.C.

tempered together, pure and holy . . . it shall be unto thee holy for the Lord.' Stacte was probably a variety of myrrh, the earliest aromatic gum of which there is any record; galbanum and frankincense are other aromatic gums, and onycha was obtained from a sea-snail.

The Egyptians were using such gums at least by 2000 B.C., but the most famous Egyptian perfume was 'kyphi', an elaborate compound, the recipe for which is given by ancient Greek writers. It gave a pleasant odour when burned, and was used to perfume the body, and also to embalm the dead. The ancient Babylonians and Assyrians made much use of incense in that part of medical treatment which consisted in the exorcism of demons, and they also perfumed their own clothes and persons. The Middle East was for long the region of sweet odours: we hear, for example, of a king of Syria who, during the sacred games, employed 200 women to sprinkle the spectators with perfumes, and everyone who entered the arena was anointed with cinnamon or spikenard. Later, the Persians, as can be gathered from their literature, used musk and ambergris (animal perfumes obtained, respectively, from the musk-deer and the sperm whale), and they had a passion for roses. This they passed on to the Arabs who had the advantage of growing most of the aromatic shrubs in their own territory.

Contact with the Persians introduced the ancient Greeks also to such refinements as the use of perfumes. Fashionable Greek women used different unguents for each part of the body: marjoram for the head, palm oil for the face and chest, essence of ivy for the neck and legs, and mint for the arms. The learned Greek botanist, Theophrastus, made an extensive list and wrote a special treatise *Concerning Odours*. He tells us how to extract the scent from the petals of flowers by steeping them in oil. The Greeks were particularly fond of violets, but they also used rose, gillyflower, crocus, and bergamot. Athenaeus, who wrote *Connoisseurs in Dining*, describes the anointing of the heads of the guests with extract of roses, apples, and iris. Sometimes doves whose wings had been impregnated with scent were allowed to fly about the room. The philosopher, Socrates, was moved to protest against the excessive use of perfumes, especially by men.

By the 1st century A.D. Rome was absorbing the exports of all the perfume-producing countries of the Ancient World. A favourite unguent for anointing the body after bathing, called susinon, contained a mixture of lilies, honey, cinnamon, saffron, and myrrh. Some of these preparations were extremely expensive. The luxurious Emperor Heliogabalus, in the 3rd century A.D., is said to have bathed in a wine of roses. At the games the whole amphitheatre was perfumed by means of burning censers and scent sprinklers. In the end laws were passed limiting the private use of perfumes to prevent there being a shortage of perfumes needed for religious services.

With the fall of the Roman Empire all such refinements ceased, and the DARK AGES (q.v. Vol. I) could not have been a very sweet-smelling period. CHARLEMAGNE, at the end of the 8th century, received from his contemporary HAROUN-AL-RASCHID (qq.v. Vol. V) a gift of perfumes, but this was a rarity. When, however, the Crusaders began invading the Holy Land in the 11th and 12th centuries, they found the Arab civilization much more luxurious than their own. From the 13th century onwards an increasing traffic developed, and perfumes were frequently transported in little crystal boxes, generally of Arab manufacture. We find many

British Museum

ARABIC ROCK CRYSTAL FLASK, 9TH CENTURY
It was probably made as a perfume flask or as a container for eye black

British Museum

SYRIAN PERFUMER MADE OF BRONZE, PIERCED AND INLAID WITH SILVER, 13TH CENTURY
It contained incense and was probably rolled over carpets to perfume them

A SILVER VINAIGRETTE

A sponge soaked with aromatic vinegar was placed beneath the inner perforated cover

examples of these, as well as metal 'pomanders', balls filled with aromatic substances, in the inventories of royal treasures.

In the Middle Ages European countries obtained their perfumes from the Arabs either via Spanish Morocco or from Venice, which was the great mart of spices. In the 15th century, however, with the discovery of the new route to India round the Cape of Good Hope (*see* TRADE ROUTES, Vol. IV), spices and perfumes became easier to obtain and so cheaper. In the 16th century there was a swarm of apothecaries and perfumers in Italy, France, and England, and their efforts were much assisted by the growing technique of DISTILLATION (q.v. Vol. VII).

Alcohol had been unknown to the Ancient World, except in its diluted form as wine; but it had long been known to the Arabs—indeed, 'alcohol' is an Arabic word. Its use facilitated the preparation of perfumes and made many more subtle blends possible. One of the first was the famous 'frangipani', first manufactured in Rome, and much used in the 16th century for perfuming gloves. Ruggiero, the famous astrologer of Catherine de Medici, opened a pharmacy in Paris where he sold perfumes—and also poisons. A hundred years later perfumes were so popular at the Court of Louis XIV that everything was scented: gloves, furs, clothes, cushions, shoes. The austere Madame de Maintenon, however, the wife of Louis's later life, could not endure them. Under Louis XV it was etiquette to use a different perfume each day, and Madame de Pompadour, his favourite, used a prodigious quantity.

The Queen's Closet, printed in England in 1663 after the restoration of Charles II, gives a whole range of recipes for perfumes, including one said to have been invented by Edward VI and another by Elizabeth I. The latter recommended a pomatum made from apples and mixed with the fat of a young dog.

In the 18th century perfume was highly fashionable in England and even more in France; and though for a period during the French Revolution it was dangerous to smell too sweet, the fashion soon returned. The Empress Josephine had a passion for perfumes, and Napoleon himself used a pint of eau-de-Cologne every day. In England George IV had luxurious tastes in perfume, but the leader of fashion Beau Brummell started the idea, which still persists, that a man should smell, and that only slightly, of clean linen. Though perfumes were still much used by ladies during the 19th century, they became less and less used by men.

In 1855 nitrobenzene, now known as essence of mirbane, was first identified as a synthetic perfume. Other discoveries followed, and by the end of the century most perfumes were being made in the laboratory. The old process of making them from the petals of flowers still lingers, however, at Grasse, in France, and elsewhere.

See also COSMETICS, HISTORY OF.
See also Vol. VII: PERFUMERY.

PERSONAL HYGIENE, HISTORY OF. A high degree of personal hygiene usually coincides with an advanced civilization, but it has not always done so. People of the ancient EGYPTIAN and MINOAN CIVILIZATIONS (qq.v. Vol. I) were extremely cleanly in their habits. Public baths, both for men and women, were a Greek innovation, and the Romans carried the development of public bath-houses to a degree that has never been equalled before or since (*see* ROMAN BATHS, Vol. IX). The Roman bath procedure included sweating, a cold bath, massage, oiling, and exercise. The Roman system lingered on in Byzantium, was taken over by the occupying Turks, and reintroduced much later and in a modified form to western Europe as 'Turkish baths'.

After the fall of the Roman Empire standards of hygiene in western Europe deteriorated, but, low as standards were, the people of the Middle Ages were on the whole cleaner than those of the Renaissance and of the 17th and 18th centuries. There were, in medieval times, many public bathing-places, but clerics and moralists continually denounced them as leading to debauchery, and gradually they became fewer. At the end of the 16th century it was quite rare even for royal personages to take a bath. Queen Elizabeth I was considered to be quite advanced in the matter of personal hygiene. A medical writer of the time states that 'Her Majesty hath a bath every 3 months whether she needeth it or no'. Henry IV of France thought bathing a dangerous practice, and usually had a physician in attendance; it was on an unfortunate visit to his minister Sully to see how he had survived the ordeal that the king was assassinated. Louis XIV was certainly no cleaner. On the rare occasions when he washed all over, an official was present with a red-hot shovel on which perfume was thrown to keep the air sweet. Perhaps it was a necessary precaution. In England, in the reign of Charles II, we hear that Mrs. Pepys 'went with her woman to a hot house to bathe herself, after her long being within doors in the dirt'. Her husband said she made him, rather unwillingly, 'clean myself with warm water, because she do herself'.

Ablutions became somewhat easier at this period because of the growing use of soap, which was mostly made at home (*see* SOAP MANUFACTURE, Vol. VII). Castile soap was also used, sometimes as a basis for 'a delicate washing ball', consisting of rose-leaves and lavender, orris root, and various aromatics pounded in a mortar with scrapings of Castile soap dissolved in rose-water. People, at least in the upper walks of life, were beginning to pay more attention to the teeth. They were recommended to rub them with tamarisk bark, or the peel of pomegranates, and to whiten them with cuttle-fish bone, pumice-stone, or powdered brick. Such abrasives must have removed the enamel from the teeth and done more harm than good (*see* DENTISTRY).

The 18th century was far from clean, either in France or England. England can, however, claim one important innovation: when the first Duke of Devonshire was rebuilding Chatsworth in 1694, he installed a real bathroom. It had a magnificent painted ceiling, and the walls and floor were of marble. The bath itself was cut from a single piece, and, most astonishing of all, as we learn from the contemporary Journals of Celia Fiennes, the bath had 'two Cocks to let in one hott ye other Cold water, to attemper it as persons please'. The Duke's bath was, in fact,

A HIP BATH IN A VICTORIAN NIGHT NURSERY

Drawing by John Leech from The Collection of 'Mr. Punch', 1842-64

if not the first, among the first, in the world to be fitted with 'h. and c.'.

During the 19th century in the wealthier homes baths became gradually more the custom, though they were usually taken in portable hip baths in the bedroom. The maids in those times had to carry heavy cans of hot water up many stairs (*see* DOMESTIC SERVICE).

If the standards of personal cleanliness were low among the wealthy, they were hardly likely to be better among the poorer people, who had to contend with an almost total lack of facilities in miserable housing conditions (*see* WATER SUPPLY, HISTORY OF). But bad as was the lack of hygiene, it had not been so disastrous in its results when most people lived more or less in the country, with plenty of fresh air. In the 19th century, however, as the results of the INDUSTRIAL REVOLUTION (q.v. Vol. VII) altered the face of England, and hundreds of thousands of people came to live herded together in insanitary, overcrowded towns, where the air was polluted by the smoke from factory chimneys, the problem became urgent. It was demanding the impossible to expect any standard of personal cleanliness when six or eight people shared a two-roomed house, facing into a tiny court, with little light or air, with probably only one cold water tap between ten or twelve houses and no drainage (*see* SANITATION, HISTORY OF). On top of this there was, until 1852, a tax on soap which made it too expensive for the very poor to buy.

In these circumstances the introduction of

public bath-houses and wash-houses was a great improvement. The first was established by the Liverpool authorities in 1842. The idea sprang from the action of a poor Irish immigrant, Catherine Wilkinson, who during a cholera epidemic arranged for eighty-five families to use her copper for washing their clothes. The neighbourliness of this 'poor helper of the poor' has been commemorated in a memorial window in the Lady Chapel of Liverpool Cathedral.

As the 19th century progressed and standards of sanitation gradually improved, it became more possible for people to keep themselves clean; and the great strides in social welfare that have taken place in the 20th century have roused in people a wish for a more civilized way of living. Not only are modern houses always supplied with water and ways of heating it, but no modern house is now built without a bathroom. That a daily bath should now be considered normal would have seemed a fantastic idea to our great-great-grandfathers, and that underclothes should be changed and washed at least every week was foreign to the ideas of those 19th-century mothers who sewed their

MODERN BATHROOM DECORATED WITH SCENES OF WATER SPORTS BY JOHN ARMSTRONG

children up into their winter woollies and did not unstitch them till the spring.

See also SANITATION, HISTORY OF; WATER SUPPLY, HISTORY OF.
See also Vol. X: PUBLIC HEALTH; SLUMS.

PHYSIOTHERAPY. This is the treatment of disease by physical agents such as heat, light, cold, water, electricity, and by mechanical means such as massage and corrective exercises. RADIOTHERAPY (q.v.), which is a form of physiotherapy, is sufficiently important to be considered separately. Many forms of physical therapy have been practised from time immemorial: the rubbing of an aching part is an instinctive action, and the beneficial effects of heat and water must have been known to the earliest men. The Greeks and Romans were great exponents of physical therapy, but succeeding generations tended to neglect 'natural' methods of healing in favour of drugs, and to consider physiotherapy as a form of 'quackery'—which it often was. In recent years, however, the various physiotherapeutic techniques have come to be recognized as forming an important part of regular medicine, and physiotherapy is now prescribed by doctors. Treatment is carried out by specially trained workers who constitute the new professional body of physiotherapists. In Great Britain the Chartered Society of Physiotherapy prescribes a course of training extending over 3 years and conducts examinations in the different branches. All members of the Society undertake to work only under the direction of qualified medical men. There is an ever-increasing demand for chartered physiotherapists both at home and abroad.

Physiotherapy has its greatest field of application in the rheumatic diseases (*see* BONES AND JOINTS). Scientifically applied movements or exercises are used to bring the limbs back to proper working order after illness or injury, to correct deformities, and to prevent circulatory and other disorders likely to accompany long confinement in bed. The exercises may be active or passive, and they are often carried out in salt-water because when the limbs float less strain is imposed upon the patient. The aim of the various kinds of massage is to soothe and relieve spasm and pain, to improve the circulation, and to break down adhesions and fibrous deposits. Electrical currents are of great use in the treatment of paralysed or weakened muscles.

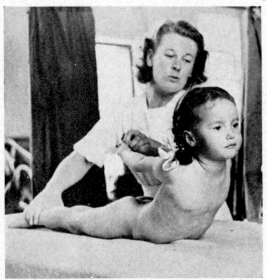

Picture Post Library

A CHILD BEING GIVEN EXERCISES BY A PHYSIOTHERAPIST

The comforting and healing effects of heat can be produced by means of fomentations, hot-water bottles, mud packs and wax baths, infra-red rays or diathermy—that is, the application of heat to the deeper tissues of the body. In surgical diathermy the heat is sometimes used to destroy diseased tissues or to seal bleeding vessels. Ultra-violet rays, which have a general tonic effect, are used in the treatment of skin diseases and of rickets. The value of hydrotherapy or the 'water cure' is attested by the lasting fame of innumerable springs and baths in all parts of the world. Some of these contain minerals, salt or sulphur, for example, which may assist the cure.

See also BONES AND JOINTS; RADIOTHERAPY.

PICKLES, *see* CONDIMENTS AND RELISHES.

PITUITARY GLAND, *see* ENDOCRINE GLANDS.

PLAGUE, *see* EPIDEMIC DISEASES.

PLASTERING. This is the application to the inside walls and ceilings of a building of a material or mixture of materials which is plastic and which hardens after application. Its main purpose is to cover up the unavoidable differences of level in surfaces such as brickwork, and to provide a smooth, joint-free surface suitable for final decoration. Occasionally it has a special purpose, such as the correction of the ACOUSTICS (q.v. Vol. VIII) in a large hall or the fireproofing of steelwork.

The craft was developed over 2,000 years ago in the Middle East, and its technique is much the same today. The basic materials were, and still are, lime and gypsum plasters. Portland CEMENT (q.v. Vol. VII) is a relatively modern addition.

LIME (q.v. Vol. VI) is manufactured by heating limestone or chalk in a kiln to a temperature exceeding 1,000° C. The resulting quicklime was, until the present century, always run to putty with water by the plasterer and was then matured, sometimes for many years, before it was used. It is a very smooth-working, plastic material, highly thought of by old craftsmen. About 1900, hydrators were developed in which the reaction of quicklime with water, or slaking, takes place under controlled conditions to give, not a putty, but a free-flowing fine powder called hydrated lime. This material when mixed with water, though not so plastic as putty, is convenient to use and free from particles of unslaked quicklime which can spoil the look of plaster-work.

Gypsum plasters are prepared from a natural rock, GYPSUM (q.v. Vol. III); this, when heated in open pans or closed 'kettles' to about 160° C., loses three-quarters of its water and becomes plaster of Paris. This sets hard quickly when mixed to a stiff paste with water, and so for plastering purposes it is mixed with a 'retarder' to delay its set. If, however, gypsum is heated to a higher temperature—say 500° C. or more—it loses all its water to give an 'anhydrous' product, which hardens slowly when mixed with water and needs an accelerator to make it into a suitable plaster. When set, it is particularly hard.

In early English plastering, mixtures were used containing only lime and sand with plenty of ox-hair beaten in. Today mixtures may contain lime and cement, lime and gypsum plasters, or gypsum plasters alone. Sand is always used in undercoats but not invariably in finishing coats.

Plasterers use both flat trowels and 'floats' for spreading the wet plaster on walls and ceilings; often several coats have to be applied. After the plaster has been spread evenly over the surface and smoothed with the trowel, it has to be left to dry thoroughly before distemper, paint, or paper can be applied.

THE DOLL'S BIRTHDAY PARTY

Engraving from a 19th-century German children's book

PLAY. The word 'play' is properly used to mean doing something for one's own entertainment, of one's own choice, without outside compulsion. Play is usually associated with childhood, though, in fact, the need for play as relaxation continues throughout life. The term recreation, that is, re-creation, gives a true picture of play as an antidote to boredom and fatigue.

Play is often contrasted with work, but there is no very clear distinction between the two. In the present century play has come to have importance not only as an amusement activity, but as a means of education. As early as 1837 FROEBEL (q.v. Vol. V) opened the first Kindergarten where the children's occupation was to be 'play', which he considered to be 'the highest expression of human development in childhood' and therefore an important vehicle of education. This idea is usually accepted in our Infant Schools today. 'All work and no play makes Jack a dull boy' has little meaning in a modern free-activity school.

There have been many theories about the biological function of play; for example, it has been considered as training of the child for his future roles in adult life, as an outlet for superabundant energy, and as a means of recapitulating the progress of the race. Let us consider these theories one by one.

Perhaps the most obvious example of play as a preparation for adult life is that of the small girl and her DOLLS (q.v.). She dresses the doll, wheels it out in a toy pram, talks to it, puts it to bed—in fact, she rehearses the part she will play in later years as a mother. Another example may be taken from the play of animals. Picture a kitten stalking a piece of paper on the floor. Slowly, with infinite patience, he crawls towards it, every muscle tensed, tail twitching. Then he gathers himself, and with a final spring, seizes the piece of paper between his paws. There is no doubt that, in play of this kind, the kitten is practising the skills necessary in adult life for hunting.

'Play as bodily activity' has various functions and provides various degrees of pleasure. For example, the very young child gets both value and pleasure from trying to move his own body, and later from pushing and pulling his toys. As everyone knows, a child sometimes needs 'to let off steam'. This often consists of muscular activity which has no special aim except the use of the muscles and limbs concerned. Joy of muscular skill prompts various forms of rhythmic play and games, such as knocking skittles down. Play as bodily activity has other functions less obvious than these. It expresses feelings and sensations which are hardly understood even by the child, certainly not by the observer. Examples of these are the sensations of 'hiding'—of being crouched up in a corner while friends, acting as 'enemies', look for him—and the feelings, too, of being in new postures, as in the game of 'statues' and in the pastime of pulling faces. Such muscularly exciting roles lead later to actual personification in dramatic play.

Play of this kind persists into adult life. The bowler, putting down a tricky leg-break; the three-quarter, swerving to avoid a tackle; the oarsman, covering his blade, and kicking back against the stretcher; the runner, winning the 100 yards with half a second to spare; the golfer, crouching over a long putt—all of these are practising muscular activity and muscular skill.

The theory of play as a recapitulation of the history of the race is perhaps more obscure than the other two. It is based on a number of activities which can be observed in children of different ages and which may correspond with the activities of primitive man at successive stages of his development. Examples of these are the delight most children take in climbing trees; their pleasure in being in water, whether the bath or the sea; the way they sometimes fight with one another, and their delight in weapons of any kind.

A child's play begins in babyhood in the

home. The mother knows its importance, and she understands through it what he is feeling and wanting. She begins the first baby games of peep-bo, and later gives him toys and play material suitable to his age. These enable him to use his imagination, and to work out in play the troubles that beset him even at an early age. For example, the little girl who punishes her doll by putting it to bed in the day-time may, in fact, be punishing her mother for spending too much time shopping.

In many families play has a prominent part in the relationship between children and their fathers. With mechanical toys, electric railways, and constructional toys, the father may be not only an invaluable ally, but also an eager participant. The first elaborate brick castles are often achieved with his help, and his superior skill sets a standard for the small child proudly to emulate.

Play is the means by which the child learns about the nature of the world and his place in it. In his play at home he learns about heaviness and lightness, how things fit and balance, what is hard to bump against and what is soft. Later in the NURSERY SCHOOL (q.v. Vol. X) he can share his exciting new discoveries with other children who are likewise discovering. He can also learn about these other children, what they like and dislike, what they demand of him, and what he can demand of them. He can share with them, too, the world of his own imagination. This leads on to more elaborate forms of social play, such as the games of 'let's pretend', and the 'gang' or group activities of 10 and 11-year-

Studio Lisa

A BOY PLAYING WITH PLASTICINE

olds, and various other forms throughout the child's life. The 'let's pretend' games of the boy or girl frequently inspire interests and hobbies which will remain in adult life—such as an interest in railways, painting, carpentry, natural history, acting, or gardening.

Play exists all around us, not only in the human but also in the animal world. Much animal play is preparation for adult life, but some of it seems to be play for its own sake, sheer pleasure in muscular skill and activity, like the gambols of rabbits on a summer's evening. Some animal play, the ritual dances of certain birds, for example, is a part of courtship (see ANIMAL LANGUAGE, Vol. II).

Recently, emphasis on play as a means of psychotherapy has led to more detailed theories about the function of play in the emotional development of the child. In treating maladjusted children (see CHILD GUIDANCE CLINIC), psychotherapists provide opportunities for play in which the children can express their feelings freely, and they then observe the children's play in order to find out about them. The child is enabled to repeat in play situations which have puzzled him in the past; and by thus reliving previously disturbing experiences, he is able to

Studio Lisa

A CHILD PLAYING WITH AN INSTRUCTIONAL TOY

dispose of them and to regain feelings of security and adequacy. The inability to play denotes acute anxiety or a serious condition of mal-adjustment.

See also PSYCHOLOGY; CHILDREN, UPBRINGING OF; NURSERY EQUIPMENT.

See also Vol. IX: TOYS; HIDING GAMES; TRACKING GAMES; TRADITIONAL SPORTS AND CUSTOMS.

PLEURISY, *see* RESPIRATION.

PLUMBING, *see* HOUSEHOLD PLUMBING.

PNEUMONIA, *see* RESPIRATION.

POISONING, *see* FIRST AID; FOOD POISONING.

POLIOMYELITIS. This virus disease used to be called infantile paralysis because it was mis-takenly thought that it attacked only children. It has come into prominence in recent years, but, in fact, case-records have been traced back to the 17th century and it is thought that it may have existed in ancient Egypt. Sir Walter SCOTT and Franklin ROOSEVELT (qq.v. Vol. V) are among those who have suffered from it.

The particular VIRUS (q.v. Vol. II) respon-sible is one which singles out the motor nerves for its attack and causes inflammation and destruction of the grey matter of the spinal cord in its front part, through which messages are relayed from the brain to the muscles (*see* NER-VOUS SYSTEM).

The first signs of infection are a slight cold, fever, a flushed face and furred tongue, and perhaps vomiting and headache. As the illness develops, the headache becomes worse, and the patient may develop a stiffness of the neck and spine so that he tends to keep his back and neck rigid and to resist any attempt to bend his head or his body forwards. After a day or two of this the patient may recover, but in a proportion of cases sudden paralysis of a muscle or a group of muscles occurs.

In Great Britain poliomyelitis occurs through-out the year, but towards the end of July the number of cases increases and continues to do so throughout the autumn. At the end of the autumn the numbers begin to diminish, and by the beginning of December they have generally fallen to the minimum. In districts where polio-myelitis is present, only a small proportion of those who harbour the virus actually become ill,

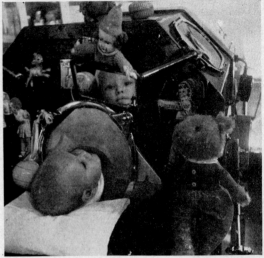

Picture Post Library

A CHILD WITH POLIOMYELITIS IN AN IRON LUNG

and only approximately one-quarter to one-fifth of those who become ill develop serious paraly-sis, and of these a still smaller proportion die or are totally incapacitated. Complete rest in bed during the early stage of the disease is thought to lessen the likelihood of paralysis or to limit the extent of the damage, whereas vigorous exercise or an injury at this time may make paralysis more likely or more severe.

In epidemic times measures of control, such as closing schools and places of entertainment, do not appear to reduce the number of cases as much as might be hoped. The most effective measure, beneficial to the patient as well as to the public, is to isolate every patient who de-velops symptoms which may be poliomyelitis at the beginning of his illness, and to keep him in bed until the danger of paralysis is past, generally a week or 10 days. The adoption of this measure means that many children and adults with simple colds will be somewhat unnecessarily confined to bed while poliomyelitis is prevalent; but this consideration is negligible if the patient who is infected with the virus of polio-myelitis is thereby saved from a serious paralysis and if the spread of the disease is reduced.

There is no certain cure for poliomyelitis, but early and appropriate treatment of the paralysed muscles often does a great deal to mitigate the damage which might otherwise remain. It is characteristic of the paralysis of poliomyelitis that a certain amount of recovery may take place in affected muscles for at least a year after the attack; moreover other groups of muscles may be trained to take on part of the work of the paralysed group and so lessen the patient's disability. The difficult early phase of the patient's convalescence is now greatly helped by skilful medical treatment: for example, the iron lung—a mechanical breathing apparatus—may enable the patient whose breathing muscles have been paralysed to survive long enough to get back his power of breathing. Much can also be done by PHYSIOTHERAPY (q.v.) to prevent deformity and to train other muscles to make the movements formerly made by the paralysed group. Very many patients now recover from a serious condition of paralysis with little permanent disability.

Important work is being carried out both in America and in Britain to develop a vaccine to prevent poliomyelitis.

See also EPIDEMIC DISEASES; PHYSIOTHERAPY.
See also Vol. II: VIRUS.

PORCHES. The doors of the larger medieval houses were protected by stone or wooden porches resembling those of churches (*see* p. 294). In the 15th century there was often a small room above the porch. In the 16th century the porch was the central feature of a symmetrically planned house and was, therefore, elaborately decorated. Columns, niches, swags of fruit and foliage, or heraldic devices were carved about and above the round-headed opening of the porch in imitation of the Renaissance style of Italian architecture, though without much knowledge of its meaning. Inscriptions on the porch, such as 'And yours, my friends' at Montacute House in Somerset, indicate that the porch may have been thought of as symbolic of the welcome offered to guests.

In the 17th century Italian styles were more carefully studied and understood. Doors were sometimes surrounded by mouldings or pilasters which did not break the flat surface of the façade, or were protected by porches consisting of columns supporting an entablature and perhaps a pediment. In town houses a hood projected from above the door, often with the underside shaped like a shell.

Country houses in the 18th century often had large pillared porticos, the pillars running up to the height of two storeys; but town houses had either no porch or a simple one with a column

National Buildings Record

THE PORCH AT BARLBOROUGH HALL, DERBY, 16TH CENTURY

National Buildings Record

A 'SHELL' PORCH ON A HOUSE AT BEWDLEY, WORCESTERSHIRE

PARK CRESCENT, REGENT'S PARK, LONDON
The porches form a colonnade which gives unity and interest to the terrace

at each outer corner. The terrace houses built at the end of the 18th century had a series of such identical porches, the projecting columns and the shadows behind them contrasting with the flat surface of the upper wall. This type of porch remained popular in the 19th century and, topped by a balustraded balcony, was a feature of the Victorian stuccoed villa. Houses built in the GOTHIC REVIVAL style (q.v. Vol. XII) imitated the Gothic porch with its pointed arch.

Many different styles of ornamental porch have been built since then, though modern tastes tend towards simplicity, the porches being merely concrete slabs cantilevered out from the wall or possibly supported by slender metal shafts.

See also HOUSES, HISTORY OF; DOORS.

POTATO DISHES. The potato, which was unknown in Europe until the second half of the 16th century, has now become a staple food in Britain, northern Europe, parts of America, and Australasia (*see* FOOD, HISTORY OF). One of the pioneers in the cooking of potatoes was the Frenchman Antoine Augustin Parmentier (1737–1813), who invented twenty different ways of cooking them. His name is still associated with certain potato dishes such as the well-known soup 'potage Parmentier'.

Potatoes can be cooked in a great variety of ways—indeed, it is possible to draw up menus including potatoes for several weeks and never to use the same recipe twice. It is customary to serve them at lunch, dinner, or supper as a vegetable accompanying a main dish; but they can also be served at breakfast as potato cakes, or at tea as potato scones. Boiled potatoes may be served whole or mashed, cut and dressed in potato salad, surmounting meat or fish in cottage pies, or blended with meat or fish in rissoles. The waxy texture and flavour of new potatoes is enhanced by the addition of mint to the cooking water, and they should be put into boiling water to retain the maximum amount of flavour.

Old potatoes should be put into cold water and brought up to boiling-point slowly in order to avoid overcooking them and breaking the outer layers.

Fried potatoes, which are best cooked in deep fat (*see* FRYING), can be cut into various shapes. For chips and straws potatoes are cut into rectangular strips; for crisps they are sliced into very thin disks; for ribbons thin strips are peeled off. If potatoes are parboiled or partially steamed before they are roasted, they acquire a golden-brown crisp exterior. Baked potatoes are cooked in their skins, which are sometimes brushed with fat, and then served with butter. To make stuffed potatoes the baked interior is removed, mixed with cheese and butter, or meat, and replaced in the skin. Sauté potatoes are made by cooking thin slices in a small quantity of fat in a shallow covered pan, and shaking them frequently to prevent their sticking. To make scalloped potatoes, slices of raw potatoes are mixed with flour, fat, and milk, and baked. Potato anna consists of very thin slices baked in a cake tin and served in the shape of the tin in which they have been cooked. Duchesse potatoes are mashed potatoes mixed with egg and milk into a purée, piped into attractive shapes on to a tin, and baked.

The potato consists mainly of water and starch, but it also contains small amounts of other valuable substances, of which vitamin C (*see* VITAMINS) is the most important. The amount of vitamin C present in new potatoes is 30 milligrammes per 100 grammes, but in potatoes which have been stored all winter it has diminished to 7 milligrammes per 100 grammes. Potatoes also contain some vitamin B, iron, phosphorus, calcium, potassium, and small amounts of protein. Some part of these valuable substances is lost in cooking, the smallest losses occurring if the potato is boiled and eaten in its skin because the skin forms a protective coat preventing the soluble nutrients from escaping. There is a further loss of vitamin C if cooked potatoes are kept hot for any length of time. Where potatoes are a staple food, they contribute a considerable proportion of the vitamin C in the diet, so it is important that none should be wasted. The average amount eaten at a meal, $\frac{1}{4}$ lb., provides about 56 of the necessary daily 70 milligrammes of vitamin C, and 128 Calories. If served as roast potatoes the calorific value is 280 per $\frac{1}{2}$ lb. (*see* FOOD VALUES).

Potatoes are also used to produce a thickening ingredient for SAUCES (q.v.), custard powders, and blancmanges, and to produce glucose or corn syrup (*see* SWEETENINGS). Alcohol is also obtained from the starch in potatoes.

See also VEGETABLES.
See also Vol. VI: POTATOES.

POULTRY AND GAME. Tame birds kept for food are called poultry (from the French *poule*, a 'hen'); they include fowls, ducks, geese, guinea fowl (the 'turkey' of Shakespeare), and turkeys (*see* POULTRY, CARE OF, Vol. VI).

Wild birds fit to eat are called feathered game; but the British sportsman would exclude as VERMIN (q.v. Vol. VI) birds such as rooks and pigeons which are not protected and which may be shot without a game licence. The eating habits and game laws in Continental countries differ. In Spain, for example, an observer recorded eighty-one species of birds on sale in Cordova food market between 1947 and 1949, those most frequently appearing being a large variety of song-birds, such as larks and robins and finches, which in Britain are never eaten. Thrushes and lesser birds used, however, to be eaten in Britain, and in parts of England pies are still made of rook and pigeon fledglings, skinned instead of plucked. The true game birds are PHEASANT, PARTRIDGE and quail, the GROUSE group, which includes ptarmigan and red, black, and wood grouse, wild DUCKS (qq.v. Vol. II), mainly mallard, teal, and widgeon, and two small, long-billed birds, the snipe and the woodcock (*see* WADING BIRDS, Vol. II). Just occasionally a cygnet, that is, a young SWAN (q.v. Vol. II), is served as food, though at one time it was a popular dish for a feast.

Sea-birds have never been widely used for food as their flesh is tough and fishy in flavour, but as late as the 16th century GULLS were netted in England, fattened, and, presumably, sweetened in poultry yards. As late as 1885, the GANNET or solan goose, still occasionally eaten in the Outer Hebrides, used to be sent from the Bass Rock to London markets, where it was known as 'Scotch grouse'. The mutton bird, a quick breeding PETREL (qq.v. Vol. II) of the South Seas, is caught when young by the New Zealand Maoris, smoked, tied up in flax bags, and sold in huge numbers in fish shops; it takes the place of the kipper in the national larder.

Furry game includes all wild mammals fit for

food: in Europe rabbits, hares, wild boar, and deer. Venison (from the Latin *venari*, 'to hunt') used to mean the flesh of any mammal hunted and killed; it is now used only of the meat of any kind of DEER (q.v. Vol. II).

Poultry, being fatty and comparatively tender, should be eaten quite fresh. A young bird has a bright comb, smooth legs, and a pliable cartilage at the end of its breastbone. The young turkey is called a poult. The term 'chicken' should strictly be used only for the young fowl, but in America it is used for fowls of all ages, and a young bird is called a spring chicken, a broiler (*see* GRILLING), or a squab chicken. Capons, choicer than ordinary fowls, are castrated male birds; by a modern technique called chemical caponization the quality of the meat is improved by injecting female sex hormones into the fattening bird.

Game is lean and muscular and has to be hung for up to 10 days in order that its connective tissue should be softened by the action of BACTERIA (q.v. Vol. II); if this process is overdone the game becomes high. In the case of game birds, the hanging is supposed to make them tasty and tender enough to roast—boiled grouse is unheard of.

Dressing and cleaning are usually done by the poulterer, but the cook should always examine the body of a bird carefully to see that the job has been done properly. A good picture cookery book will show how to pluck and draw birds or skin rabbits. The giblets are useful for gravy and forcemeat (*see* OFFAL; SAUCES; STUFFINGS). Stuffing, good gravy, and the proper garnishes add greatly to the excellence of all poultry and game.

Very young birds may be split and sautéed, fried, or grilled; youngish birds, rabbits, and hares (leverets) are suitable for roasting. Old Scottish recipes on how to roast venison and grouse are worth studying. Except for geese and ducks, which have plenty of fat, the main roasting problem is how to keep the flesh moist. Frequent basting may be sufficient for a plump chicken, but most game needs protecting with greaseproof paper, fat bacon, or else with aluminium-foil, or by inserting strips of bacon fat under the skin. Tiny, dry birds, such as quail, plump out if simmered first in milk; big turkeys and joints of venison are improved by being enclosed in, or spread all over with, a paste of flour, fat, and water.

Most poultry and game have their traditional accompaniments. Roast chicken, guinea fowl, or turkey may have herbs, mushroom, chestnut, or sausage stuffing; bread sauce in Britain, and cranberry sauce in America; bacon rolls, or plain green salad with french dressing. Boiled chicken or turkey is served with parsley, celery, oyster, or mushroom sauce, and often with boiled ham or pickled pork. Roast goose, duck, or duckling has sage and onion stuffing and apple sauce or orange salad. Roast or jugged hare or rabbit is often accompanied by forcemeat balls and red currant jelly. Partridge, pheasant, ptarmigan, and grouse are served with herb or red whortleberry stuffing, fried breadcrumbs, delicate chip potatoes, watercress, and red currant or rowan jelly. Snipe, teal, wild duck, and woodcock may have celery stuffing, orange salad, or plain salad and orange sauce, and thin chip potatoes.

See also Vol. VI: POULTRY.
See also Vol. IX: GAME SHOOTING.

PRECEDENCE, *see* SOCIAL PRECEDENCE.

PRESENTS. A natural way to express love or affection is to share what we have with a friend, or to prepare a special present for him. This motive has always prompted giving—for example, in gifts to children which ask no return, or in gifts between members of a family. Such a gift may have a value—both in the eyes of him who gives and him who receives—which bears little relation to its worldly value. The child who gives a well-loved shell to a sister, or the girl who devotes time to knitting a scarf for her father, may be offering with the gift much more than appears, as the recipient probably appreciates. But more public gifts often spring from quite different motives. Their purpose may be a form of show, or even a veiled bargain, expecting some return either in goods or in favour.

Among primitive peoples presents sometimes amounted to a simple form of exchange, akin to barter. The gift of a pig, of which one island had too many, was answered by a gift of coconuts: there may have been a delay between the two transactions, and no mention of payment, but the result was that a pig had been exchanged, or bought, for coconuts. Early Pacific Islanders, when visiting an unfamiliar island, would offer gifts which were, in fact, samples of the goods they were prepared to trade. (This type of gift

National Gallery

THE THREE KINGS BRINGING GIFTS TO THE INFANT CHRIST. PAINTING BY MABUSE (DIED *c.* 1533)

forms quite an important part of commercial advertising today.) Gifts also were looked upon as a pledge of friendship. It was customary in Tonga, for instance, to make a small present to any visitor in order to secure his friendship by placing him under an obligation to his hosts—a custom still followed for commercial reasons by the offering of flower-wreaths, or *leis*, to tourists in the Pacific.

The feeling that a gift places the recipient under some form of obligation to the donor has lain behind much present-giving. Gifts were made to the dead so that they would not return to plague the living, and in medieval times people 'bought off' the fairies by leaving a bowl of milk outside the door. This is only one but an important element in the complex nature of SACRIFICE (q.v. Vol. I). Primitive peoples who thought their gods enjoyed eating offered them corn and animals; those who thought they valued servants, as an earthly king does, offered human sacrifices. But the purpose of the sacrificial gift was to win the favour and protection of the god—the feeling being more often fear than affection.

The traditional occasions for giving presents sometimes suggest that at least originally the idea of a bargain was present. In classical times sacrifices were offered at the New Year to Janus because, as porter to the gods, he might be persuaded by gifts to admit men to the favour of the other gods for the rest of the year. The custom grew up of giving New Year presents to the Emperor, partly as an expression of reverence, but partly with the object of 'buying' his favour for the months to come. The habit persisted in England into the 17th century, and the inventories of Elizabeth I's household contain long lists of the valuable presents she received in the New Year: gold, silver, jewels, and rich dresses, valued at many thousands of pounds.

The purpose of present-giving has often been display, the proving of wealth, and the securing of attention and respect. The giver does not expect a tangible return, but he hopes to impress the recipient and to win his gratitude and good opinion. Among the Plains Indians of North America, lavish gifts to strangers were a sign of the social standing of the donor (see ENTERTAINING). The gifts which in ancient times were sent from one emperor to another were concerned solely with a desire on the part of the giver to increase his own prestige in the eyes of a rival.

Many presents today are given not so much, or at least not only, because of the affection we have for the recipient, but because convention demands that on certain occasions presents should be given—at a coming of age or a marriage, for example. To fail to produce a present would be a social blunder. New occasions for giving presents are always being presented by manufacturers and their advertisers, especially in the United States, where Mothers' Day and Fathers' Day have been made into national festivals, and 'showers'—parties for a bride where all the guests bring 'house-warming' presents for her new house—have been exalted from the custom of an occasional circle of friends into a nation-wide 'tradition'. But apart from this rather artificial type of present-giving, which **varies according to the social conventions of the**

time, there remains the real motive for gifts—a pleasure in supplying a friend's needs and increasing his pleasure, and a generous delight in sharing with a friend the good things which come our way.

PRESSURE COOKING. This is steaming under pressure of 5–15 lb. to the square inch. A pressure cooker is simply a very strongly made saucepan, usually of heavy cast aluminium, with a lid sealed by a rubber ring and topped by a vent which can be closed. The food to be cooked is placed in the pan, with or without a rack, in a very small amount of water. The lid is then sealed on, and the contents heated to boiling-point. When all the air has been driven out of the pan from the vent in the lid, and only steam issues forth, the vent is closed, and the cooking is continued until the steam pressure inside has risen to the required degree (some types of cooker indicate this on a gauge). The heat is then reduced to the minimum needed to keep the pressure steady. At pressures above ordinary atmospheric pressure water boils at a higher temperature than 212° F. Inside a pressure saucepan, when the gauge marks 15 lb. per square inch, the water is actually boiling at about 250° F. This partly explains why food cooks so quickly in a pressure cooker, and also why meat cooks less successfully than in the old-fashioned casserole, for 250° is far above the temperatures at which meat proteins coagulate (see BOILING).

Pressure cooking takes roughly one-third of the time taken by other methods, because of the high temperature involved and the very penetrating quality of pressurized steam. For example, tripe, which needs from 6 hours ordinary boiling, can be done in 2 hours. Also, once pressure has been raised, a very low heat is needed to maintain it. Pressure cooking is, therefore, economical in fuel. It eliminates cooking smells and steam from the kitchen, for, as almost no steam escapes, all the volatile substances are kept inside the pan. This is especially convenient in cooking something with a peculiar smell, such as fresh beetroot. Vitamins and flavours tend to be preserved by the tight seal, the absence of air, and the short cooking time (see BOILING). As there is no loss from evaporation, an exact volume of gravy or stock can be obtained. It is also possible to cook different foods at the same time in bowls **or wire baskets within the cooker without their**

A PRESSURE COOKER WITH BASKETS FOR SEPARATING FOOD

flavours getting mixed up—an obvious advantage in cooking for a small family.

Milk puddings made with barley and rice ($\frac{1}{2}$ cup of cereal to 1 pint of milk) are excellent when pressure cooked, for the water from the milk goes to swell the cereal while the milk solids concentrate to form a thick cream. There is a great danger of overcooking green vegetables in a pressure cooker, however, and the saving in time is negligible. The method is very useful in canning and bottling (*see* FOOD PRESERVING).

A pressure cooker, whether of the saucepan or casserole type, should be easy to clean and amply big enough for the needs of the family. It is easy to handle if the simple instructions accompanying it are accurately followed, and it is perfectly safe, as pressure cookers are designed to withstand pressures far higher than can be built up domestically.

PRIMITIVE COSTUME. What kind of clothes primitive peoples wear depends first on the climate in which they live, and then on the materials at hand. Skins, furs, and leather are available to hunters and cattle-keepers. Garments of cloth, woven from sheep's wool, camel-hair, or goat-hair, are made by more advanced stock-keepers. Strips of palm leaves and grasses are plaited into mats for wear in the South Seas. Native cotton is woven in South America and southern Asia. Strips of the inner bark of certain trees are beaten out to make the bark-cloth of Africa or the *tapa* of Polynesia.

Another influence on costume is provided by the occupation and daily needs of the wearer. A hunter in the jungle must be free from encumbering clothing, but he needs a belt in which to keep a spare arrow or from which to hang his knife-sheath. The rice grower needs a large hat to shield his head from the scorching sun. The fisherman must have loose trousers which he can roll up above his knees. The worker in a hot climate may wear nothing but a loin cloth, while his master, being idle, is swathed in rich robes. Such practical considerations are familiar to us all. The white collar of the city worker, the rough jersey of the fisherman, the flannels of the cricketer, or the crash helmet of the motor cyclist betray the occupation of their wearers no less than the uniforms of policeman or postman.

In the very early history of mankind men and women must have been contentedly naked, as were Adam and Eve in the story of the Garden of Eden; and there are naked peoples still in Australia and New Guinea, the Solomon Islands and New Britain, and among the Nilotic tribesmen of East Africa. But the AUSTRALIAN ABORIGINE usually wears a belt, made of his wife's hair, into which he can tuck odds and ends. The Papuan or MELANESIAN (qq.v. Vol. I) has a belt of plaited grass. The Nilotic Negro probably has a necklace with an amulet and usually something tied round his waist (*see* Vol. I, p. 338).

Pitt Rivers Museum Coll.

A FIJIAN GIRL WEARING BARK CLOTH

Paul Popper

A BOY IN INDO-CHINA WEARING A LOIN CLOTH

The most primitive and universal form of clothing—whether skin, hair, bark-cloth, or woven cloth—is something worn round the waist to hold tools and oddments. The belt can develop into the loin cloth, it can be lengthened into a skirt, and the skirt can be divided to make trousers. For the upper part of the body, skins, mats, or cloth can be worn simply as cloak or toga, or with more trouble and ingenuity fashioned into coat, shirt, or bodice.

Skins have provided the basic material for clothes for all hunting peoples from very early times. The costume of the BUSHMEN (q.v. Vol. I) is merely a belt made of a strip of skin with a little apron in front and a little tail behind. But for cold nights he has his kaross or cloak, generally made of springbok skin most carefully scraped and stretched and worked with fats until it is soft and supple. The American Indian of the plains used to be dressed entirely in skins, mostly deer skins scraped and prepared until they were as soft as chamois leather (see Vol. I, p. 11). The men had shirts and leggings, and the women long chemise-like garments stitched together with sinews, and against the cold weather they had thicker cloaks of bison skins. Elaborate head-dresses of feathers showed the

rank of a warrior or a chieftain and the shape and decoration of his moccasins showed his tribe. Reindeer skins provide the clothing for the tundra peoples of northern Asia (see SIBERIAN PEOPLES, Vol. I), as they did for the LAPPS (q.v. Vol. I) of northern Europe—the softer fawn skins for leggings and the tough hides for coats. The Yukagir of Siberia wear two or three long sack-like coats, one over the other, if the winter is very cold, with a skin apron in front, often decorated with fur and hair, and skin leggings tucked into high boots. The most complete and cosy skin clothing is worn by those who need it most, the ESKIMOES (q.v. Vol. I). Men, women, and children are all clothed in fur coats with hoods, trousers, and high boots. These are of sealskin for summer and of thick caribou skins for winter, made double with fur both outside and inside. The hoods for the women's coats are specially made to hold their babies, who are kept warm against their mothers' backs.

Grass, leaf strips, and bark-cloth provide clothing materials for the Pacific Islanders and the peoples of the warmer parts of Africa and South America. A girdle of leaves is sufficient in Samoa and a 'grass skirt' in Melanesia. The Negro peoples of Uganda used to wear more ample bark-cloth garments. There, though the aristocracy had cow-skins and the kings leopard skins, the ordinary peasant was entirely clothed in a large sheet of terracotta bark-cloth knotted on the right shoulder like a toga, with a belt to keep it in place while he was at work. The women draped the cloth round under their arms, and tied a girdle of contrasting colour round their waists. Some of the AMERICAN INDIANS (q.v. Vol. I) of Central America wear bark-cloth, the men a strip round their waists and the women long skirts, while both men and women have cloaks of bark-cloth to keep off the rain. The Indians in Brazil wear the simplest bark-cloth garment—a length of the stem or branch of a tree called the 'shirt tree' is cut off, soaked, peeled, and hammered, holes are cut for the arms and head, and the shirt is made.

Cloth woven from wool or hair is the basic clothing material for the more advanced stock-keeping peoples. Herdsmen who keep only cows, such as the MASAI (q.v. Vol. I) of East Africa, wear cow-skin capes. Those who breed camels, sheep, and goats, such as the SOVIET CENTRAL ASIAN PEOPLES (q.v. Vol. I), have woven garments. The women spin the thread,

EUROPEAN PEASANT COSTUME

Top left, Finnish; right, Greek woman from Epirus and man in the uniform of the Greek Guards. Bottom left, Flemish; right, Spanish, from Catalonia

Paul Popper

A MAORI WOMAN IN NEW ZEALAND WITH RUSH AND BEAD SKIRT AND WOVEN CLOAK

weave it on a narrow loom, and make the long padded coats and thick trousers which both men and women wear.

In southern Asia the native cotton has been spun and woven for thousands of years; in the warm climates of India and south-eastern Asia a narrow strip supplies the loin-cloth for the peasants, and strips joined together are wrapped round to make skirts for their wives. A shoulder cloth may be added, and lavish draperies denote the idle rich.

See also CLOTHES; COSTUME, HISTORY OF; ORIENTAL COSTUME.

PRIMITIVE DWELLINGS. From the very earliest times men and women have always had two primary needs: the need for food and the need for sleep. And sleepers want protection not only from the weather but from enemies and savage beasts. Hence PREHISTORIC MAN (q.v. Vol. I) was driven to make some form of shelter for himself.

We have no evidence that prehistoric man lived in trees as his less advanced relatives, the apes, did, but tree-houses are certainly not unknown in some primitive societies today. They are mostly used as look-out places to watch

for enemies or to guard crops, but in New Guinea strongly made huts, built in trees and reached by rope ladders, provide a place for retreat in case of a raid. The tree-house, from which the owner can shower down sticks and stones on his foes below, is a very secure dwelling.

We tend to picture our ancestors as living in caves, because it is in caves and rock shelters that the best evidence of their daily lives has been preserved (*see* CAVE MAN, Vol. I). But such ready-made homes are not found everywhere, and in most places some artificial shelters had to be made. We can guess what they were like by looking at some of those made by the wandering peoples of Australia and Africa today. The AUSTRALIAN ABORIGINES (q.v. Vol. I), for example, when camping for the night, stick a few stakes into the ground to prop up some brushwood as a temporary shelter. For a longer stay, a circle of stakes is covered in with a low roof of interlaced branches. Sheets of eucalyptus bark, covered with skins and sometimes with mud-plaster, make a serviceable roof-covering in countries where there is little rain. In the wastes of the Kalahari desert in South Africa, where stakes are scarce, the BUSHMEN (q.v. Vol. I) scoop out holes in the ground to form a sort of nest, preferably in the lee of a thicket or rock, and then cover the hole with a roof of skins, grass, or mats made of reeds. Though the structure is seldom more than 3 feet high, the whole family can curl up inside.

Obviously no prehistoric structures of this kind could still be existing today. There is evidence, however, that fairly snug houses were made with the simplest materials on the simplest plan. Hollows in the ground were scooped

Irish Tourist Board

A BEEHIVE HUT ON THE ARAN ISLANDS, IRELAND

A VILLAGE IN NEW GUINEA

From the Pitt Rivers Museum *Occasional Papers on Technology, No. 3*

out and the earth heaped up all round. Stakes were then stuck into this low wall and a roof formed with branches, the crevices of which were filled in with turf or mud. Where there was plenty of stone, walls could be built by laying the stones evenly in a circle, gradually converging towards the top in the shape of a beehive. Such huts are found in many parts of the British Isles, but it is hard to fix their date for they continued to be built until recently, and are still used as temporary shelters in out-of-the-way parts.

At much the same time, tree trunks were used to make doorways and to support the roof, and even when men had nothing better than stone or flint axes, they built timber-framed houses, filling in the sides with interlaced branches plastered with mud. Timber was also used for the primitive LAKE DWELLINGS (q.v. Vol. I), which were built in parts of Germany and Switzerland as early as 2500 B.C. This 'wattle and daub' type of building has been in continuous use down to the present day, and examples of it can be found in many old stone houses of much more elaborate design.

Primitive house-building has always been influenced by two factors. First, as most back-ward communities depend for their food on the crops and cattle they raise for themselves, they have to be continually moving about from place to place in search of fresh pasture; their houses, therefore, are lightly made and quickly abandoned. Second, they must make use of whatever building materials are available on the spot, or can be carried easily from place to place. The most extreme example of the use of local building materials is the igloo of the ESKIMOES, built of snow and ice. The ANDAMAN ISLANDERS (qq.v. Vol. I), who need no protection from cold, enemies, or savage beasts, prop up plaited palm-leaf mats on poles to keep off the rain. A similar type of lean-to structure, built up from poles and woven mats and strong enough to resist heavy storms, is used by the HOTTENTOTS of south-west Africa. In the Sahara, where protection is needed against sun and wind, the BEDOUIN (qq.v. Vol. I) weave long strips of black goat's-hair cloth, which they support on posts to form an awning. The posts and rolled-up cloth can be easily packed up and carried on the backs of camels when they move camp. Brushwood and sheets of birch-bark covered the wigwams of the North AMERICAN INDIANS (q.v. Vol. I) in the Mississippi valley; and when bison were plentiful, their hides were used to make the tepees of the Plains Indians. The most luxurious tents of all are to be found on the plains of cen-

Paul Popper

INSIDE A CHINESE PEASANT'S HUT

South African Railways

INTERIOR OF A ZULU HUT IN SOUTH AFRICA

be directly recorded by the methods of science. As behaviour is governed by physical no less than by mental conditions, the psychologist is obliged to study the body, in particular the sense organs, the NERVOUS SYSTEM (including the BRAIN) and the ENDOCRINE GLANDS (qq.v.); but he is interested less in the study of the particular organs and systems of the body (whether healthy or diseased) than in the behaviour of the individual as a whole. It is this interest in total behaviour that sets him apart from his colleagues in physiology and medicine. Psychology also shares many problems in common with PHILOSOPHY (q.v. Vol. I). Indeed psychology, like all other sciences, is a child of philosophy; it differs from them mainly in being the youngest science, and still very much in the experimental stage, but its methods are modelled upon those of biology. Psychology, in short, is the scientific study of experience and behaviour.

The simplest forms of behaviour are those which are directly managed by the NERVOUS SYSTEM (q.v.) and seldom, if ever, subject to control or direction by the mind. These are known as 'reflex' actions. The simplest of them, the 'knee-jerk', for example, can neither be started nor stopped by conscious effort. A little more elaborate is the eye-blink, which may be provoked by various agents (technically known as 'stimuli'), ranging from a piece of dust to a loud noise close at hand. Although we cannot prevent ourselves blinking, we are perfectly able to blink at will. Blinking, then, although still a reflex action, is considerably more complicated than the knee-jerk. At an even higher level is the 'startle-pattern'—the sudden jump which we are liable to make if surprised by a loud and unexpected noise. This is a highly complex reflex involving a large number of active muscles in the body; even more than the blink, however, it may be controlled by knowledge and even suppressed altogether by an act of will. Reflexes are probably the simplest kinds of action open

tral Asia (*see* MONGOLS, Vol. I). A framework of light criss-crossed poles is built up, with a stronger pole for the centre, and firmly fixed to withstand the fierce winds. Over the framework is stretched a thick roof of felt made from the hair and wool of the herds; in winter, two extra thicknesses are added. Heavy, richly embroidered cloths line the walls, and a thick curtain, which can be rolled up by day, forms the front door.

See also HOUSES, HISTORY OF.

See also Vol. I: PREHISTORIC MAN; CAVE MAN; LAKE DWELLINGS.

PROTEINS, *see* NUTRITION, Section 3; FOOD VALUES.

PSYCHIATRY, *see* PSYCHOLOGY; MENTAL DISEASES; CHILD GUIDANCE CLINICS.

PSYCHOLOGY. In the simplest terms, this is the study of the mind. But, since MIND AND BODY (q.v.) have enormous influence over each other, it is hardly practicable to consider either without reference to the other. Consequently, psychology is more concerned with the study of people (although animals are also studied) than with mind in the abstract. It gives particular attention to those aspects of behaviour that can

to psychological study; indeed, in the simpler animals, and in very young children, so much of behaviour is reflex that little remains to be explained in terms of the activities of the mind. In the behaviour of older children and adults, on the other hand, the simpler reflex patterns are so overlaid by acquired habits and skills that the concept of reflex action comes to have little explanatory value. Other and more elaborate principles have, therefore, been put forward to account for it.

The concept of 'instinctive action' is widely used in endeavouring to explain these more complex activities of animals and man. An instinct is often defined as a kind of inherited behaviour which is of biological value to the organism or to its species and does not, therefore, depend on experience or practice for its execution. Examples are food-seeking and mating, nesting, rearing of the young, and self-protection in the face of attack. Although common to all animals, instinctive activities are best studied in insects, fish, and birds, where they are usually found to follow a rigid pattern, varying little from individual to individual. In the mammals, on the other hand, instinctive behaviour is much modified by learning, and is therefore often difficult to distinguish. In man this difficulty becomes so great that a few psychologists have rejected the notion of human instincts altogether. Most, however, believe that man's behaviour is founded on a basis of instinctive action, which is so much modified by experience, learning, and social convention that it is sometimes hardly recognizable.

Instinctive behaviour, though often making use of inborn reflex action, is not truly reflex by nature. In fish and birds complex instinctive activities tend to be 'released' by particular stimuli; once 'released', the whole pattern runs itself off without any further control by the sense organs. For example, fighting among male robins is 'released' by perception of the red breast. Once it has begun, its course and outcome are largely independent of further sensory stimulation. Instinctive activity, in the mammals at least, is more highly variable than reflex action, and may give rise to many truly adaptive individual habits and skills. Psychologists have studied this aspect of behaviour, and have revealed ways in which an 'instinctive' need (for example, for food or water) may be used to 'motivate' behaviour such as learning to run a maze or to operate the latch of a cage. In these cases, what is 'learnt' is truly new, but it is made possible only by the existence of an inborn (or 'instinctive') tendency to seek food or water. Behaviour in the higher animals is, therefore, more variable, more highly individual, and adapted to the environment as a result of learning rather than of heredity. Adaptive learning in animals has also been much studied by psychologists (see INTELLIGENCE, Vol. II).

Psychologists are greatly interested in perception—in particular, in how we come to create an orderly and coherent world of objects (or environment) from the fragmentary impressions which we gain through our SENSES (q.v. Vol. II). Our visual impression of objects and their qualities undergoes far less alteration than the physical and physiological properties to which they correspond. Thus if one looks at a penny held a foot away, it appears to possess a certain size; if the distance of the penny is now doubled, the penny undergoes little, if any, change in its apparent size. Yet the size of the image cast on the retina of the EYE (q.v.) is now exactly halved. Again, coal continues to look black in sunshine and paper white at twilight, yet the amount of white light reflected to the eye from the coal may be very much greater than that reflected from the paper. It follows that we must possess some means of maintaining the appearances of objects more or less the same despite wide variations in the actual impressions received by our senses. Effects of this character are known as 'constancy phenomena'. They have been particularly studied by a group of German workers known as *Gestalt* psychologists (from a German word meaning 'shape'), who stress the unity of sensory experience, and the activity of the individual in creating his own sensory world.

Psychologists are interested not only in the ways people resemble one another (that is, in general or universal properties of the mind) but also in the ways in which they differ from one another. In particular, individual differences in intelligence have been much studied, and rough-and-ready methods of measuring them have been devised (see INTELLIGENCE TESTS, Vol. X). Although such tests are limited in what they can tell, they do often give reliable information—for example, as to the relative 'brightness' of different children and their capacity to benefit from different types of schooling. Attempts have also been made to measure differences in temperament and personality by test methods, but these have proved considerably less successful than intelligence tests. So little is yet known about personality that attempts to measure individual differences in qualities such as aggressiveness, laziness, or honesty, are fraught with difficulty.

An important branch of psychology—medical psychology—is concerned with the understanding and treatment of the less severe forms of mental ill-health, including 'nervous breakdown' or neurosis, and widespread relief of mental suffering has resulted from it. This type of treatment is based on an understanding of the patient's history and emotional life rather than on knowledge of his bodily constitution. Medical psychology has also led to new theories of the normal mind in general. In particular, the inquiries of FREUD (q.v. Vol. V)—who introduced the method of psycho-analysis—have made it abundantly clear that things can go on in our minds of which we may be wholly unaware, and which we cannot, therefore, consciously control. To mental activities of which we are unaware the term 'unconscious' has been given. It would seem from the work of Freud and others that unconscious processes (mainly related to emotional stresses) play an important part in causing neurosis. Unconscious processes also play a part in normal dreaming (*see* DREAMS) and day-dreaming, and may perhaps contribute in an important way to the development of individual interests, tastes, and character. At the same time, not all the findings of medical psychology are firmly established by scientific investigation, and some of Freud's theories are decidedly extravagant.

Among other influential psychologists Jung, the Swiss psychiatrist, disagrees with Freud on a number of points. He believes that there is a 'collective unconscious'—a kind of race-memory —and that individuals may be divided into two main types, the 'extravert'—the sociable individual—and the 'introvert'—the dreamy solitary. Adler (1870–1937), a Viennese psychologist, developed what he called 'individual psychology'. He considered that human striving is a will to power and is due to rebellion against inferiority. This idea led to the term 'inferiority complex'. Watson, an American, limits psychology to the study of behaviour, believing that the conduct of an individual is the sum total of a vast number of 'conditioned reflexes'. This idea gave rise to a school of psychology known as 'Behaviourism', which has had great influence on present-day psychology.

Other aspects of psychology are concerned with fitting people to jobs (vocational guidance), fitting jobs to people (vocational selection), and the study of work (in particular, industrial work) from the point of view of the ease and satisfaction of the worker. This is known as INDUSTRIAL PSYCHOLOGY (q.v. Vol. VII). Social psychology studies the behaviour of groups and the effects of society upon the behaviour of the individual. Although this is a most important and developing subject, as yet very little is known about it.

Psychology is still a young science which has won its place as a serious study only in this century. It has yet to justify its promise of providing a scientific explanation of the realities of human behaviour.

See also CHILD GUIDANCE CLINIC; INTELLIGENCE; DREAMS; MEMORY; MENTAL DISEASES.
See also Vol. II: INTELLIGENCE (animals); SENSES.
See also Vol. V: FREUD.

PUDDINGS, *see* SWEETS AND PUDDINGS.

Q R

QUILTING, *see* NEEDLEWORK, DECORATIVE.

RADIOTHERAPY. The discovery of X-RAYS (q.v. Vol. VIII) by Röntgen in 1895 and of radium by Pierre and Marie CURIE (q.v. Vol. V) in 1898 was of profound significance for medicine. It was soon found that constant exposures to X-rays produced burns and chronic skin ulcers on the hands and other exposed parts, and similar effects were seen to follow exposure to radium. These accidents drew attention to the use that the new rays might have when kept under proper control, and very soon astonishing results were obtained in the treatment of disease. But in the early years many doctors working with X-rays and radium suffered severe, even fatal, injuries.

Further research showed that the radioactive elements emit three different kinds of radiation: alpha- and beta-particles and gamma-rays (*see* ATOM, Vol. III). The first two which possess great energy and destructive powers, are unable to penetrate the bodily tissues for more than about $\frac{1}{2}$ inch and are stopped by a number of metals. The gamma-rays, however, the ones chiefly used in medicine, have great powers of penetration and can pass through several inches of lead. Therefore, by using filters or screens of lead, platinum, or silver, it is possible to intercept the harmful alpha- and beta-particles while permitting the gamma-rays to exert their influence on the body.

The biological action of radiations is still not fully understood; but generally speaking it is found that in small doses they tend to stimulate living cells and in large doses to destroy them. It is also known that the cells of the human body react to X-rays and radium in different ways, some organs responding more readily than others. Moreover, diseased or cancerous cells are more sensitive to X-rays and gamma-rays than normal cells; and so it has become possible to apply the gamma-rays to the deep tissues of the body and to reach cancerous growths which were beyond the reach of surgery (*see* CANCER). X-ray therapy was found to be effective in certain SKIN diseases (q.v.) and in some blood disorders which other forms of treatment had failed to cure.

A single gramme of radium used to cost about £12,000 and, although great deposits of radium-bearing ore have been discovered in the Belgian Congo, it is still one of the most valuable of all substances. Fortunately, it is not always necessary to use the radium element itself. When radium disintegrates it is first of all transformed into radon, a gaseous element which can be collected and sealed up in small tubes. Radon itself breaks down quickly into other forms of radioactive matter known as Radium A, B, and C, but while these emanations last they are as effective as the original radium.

For superficial application radium or its salt, radium sulphate, is enclosed in platinum or silver containers which shut off the harmful alpha- and beta-particles. The tubes are fixed to plastic material which is moulded to the part of the body to be treated. For the treatment of internal growths small amounts of the radioactive substances are inserted into hollow platinum needles or into 'seeds'—small gold, silver, or glass capsules—which contain a tiny bubble of radon gas. These needles or seeds are inserted into the growth or into the rectum, bladder, or other natural cavities of the body, and left there for some hours or even days. Some forms of radiotherapy necessitate the use of immensely powerful and costly apparatus, and with these the most stringent precautions have to be observed. The huge radium 'bombs' are completely enclosed in massive containers which may be moved only by mechanical means; and the treatment, carried out in a lead-lined room, is controlled from a distance.

The employment of radon—which can be inhaled, given as a drink, or injected—makes it possible to introduce radioactivity into the blood-stream so that it may be diffused through the body. In 1931 Irene Curie, the daughter of Madame Curie, and her husband, F. Joliot, made the very important discovery that radioactivity could be induced in a number of elements that are not ordinarily radioactive. This discovery has been applied to the treatment of several diseases, for instance, radioactive phosphorus and iodine are widely used in treating diseases of the blood-forming organs and of the thyroid gland. The enormous potential value in medicine of Radioactive Isotopes (q.v. Vol. VIII) is now becoming more and more understood; in the meantime, the older methods of radiotherapy have established themselves as major weapons in the fight against disease.

See also Cancer.
See also Vol. III: Radiation.
See also Vol. VIII: X-rays.

RAISING AGENTS.

RAISING AGENTS. Food in which flour is a main ingredient needs to 'rise' in order that it shall be light. Steam, air, and carbon dioxide all serve this purpose in baking, and usually do so in combination.

Steam is generated in all baked foods and, as water increases its volume 1,600 times when it vaporizes at atmospheric pressure, the raising power of steam is considerable, especially for wet mixtures such as batters and soft scones.

Batters such as Yorkshire Pudding are raised still further by being beaten vigorously until the flour gluten becomes elastic enough to hold large amounts of air; this air expands in a hot oven. Sponges, Angel Food cakes, and meringues are lightened mainly by extra air incorporated in whipped egg foams.

Carbon dioxide can be produced by live Fermentation (q.v. Vol. II), as with yeast, or by the chemical reaction of a carbonate with a weak acid. The fermentation of yeast is described under Breadmaking (q.v.). Other things besides bread are raised with yeast—for example, English buns, muffins, and crumpets (*see* Scones), Danish Pastry (q.v.), German *kuchen* pastry, and Austrian *Kugelhopf* cakes.

Baking powders are mixtures of baking soda (sodium bicarbonate) with a weak acid salt such as cream of tartar (potassium hydrogen tartrate), together with up to 40% of dry starch to keep them from moistening and so reacting in the tin. When wetted and heated they react as follows:

potassium hydrogen tartrate + sodium bicarbonate

→ sodium potassium tartrate + carbon dioxide + water.

Most cakes, short pastry, quick breads, scones, and girdlecakes are raised with baking powder. For cooks who like to mix their own baking powder, the correct proportion, based on molecular weights, is 1 part soda to $2\frac{1}{4}$ parts cream of tartar. Cream of tartar is expensive, however,

and other acid salts are frequently used commercially. Acid sodium pyrophosphate, sold as cream powder, has the advantage of reacting only very slowly in the cold dough and so reserves its puff for the oven. Acid calcium phosphate (A.C.P.) reacts rather too easily in cold solution and its residue leaves a sharp burning taste on the tongue. This is why many shop cakes and cakes made from certain self-raising flours roughen the mouth.

The weak acids in treacle or molasses, sour milk, buttermilk, lemon juice, and vinegar also combine with soda to make carbon dioxide and give an agreeable moist texture especially suited to scones, gingerbread, chocolate, and spice cakes. These are the proportions:

1 cup of really sour milk to $\frac{1}{2}$ level teaspoon of soda;
1 cup of treacle to $\frac{1}{2}$ level teaspoon of soda;
1 tablespoon of vinegar or juice to $\frac{3}{8}$ level teaspoon of soda.

'Vol', used by bakers for biscuits, is ammonium carbonate which breaks down in the oven to ammonia and carbon dioxide.

See also Breadmaking; Cakes; Scones; Pastry.
See also Vol. VII: Baking Industry.

RECIPES AND COOKERY BOOKS.

RECIPES AND COOKERY BOOKS. In the 1st century A.D. a Roman gourmet called Apicius wrote an account of his cookery experiences, but his account has not survived. Some centuries later a collection of recipes, *De Re Coquinaria*, with the famous name of Apicius attached, was compiled; and this is the earliest surviving cookery book.

The next known cookery books belong to 14th-century France. In about 1375 Guillaume Tirel, a chef of Philip VI, produced his *Viandier*. This was followed in 1393 by *Le Menagier de Paris*, a book written by a man of about 60 to guide his young wife of 16, not only in running her large household, but also in her deportment as a wife and as first lady of his house.

From this time a great many recipe books appeared, more than a thousand, for example, being published in England between 1500 and 1850. Many of these early books show the close relationship existing between medicine and cookery—an association which was not new, as eminent physicians in ancient Greece had also been interested in food and cookery. Many of the medical recipes made use of herbs and natural vegetable products, and were later included in special herbal books. Some of these

cuisine and the latter defending the simple and less extravagant methods of England.

Many of the names associated with cookery books, such as Ude, Francatelli, Soyer, Escoffier, Brillat-Savarin, and Senn, are those of famous chefs, but women have also made their contribution. Hannah Wolley produced three books on different aspects of cookery (1661–75), and in 1727 E. Smith published *The Compleate Housewife* or *Accomplished Gentlewoman's Companion* which, reprinted in the American colonies in 1742, is said to be the first cookery book printed there. Hannah Glasse's two notable contributions, *The Art of Cookery made Plain and Easy* (1747) and *The Complete Confectioner* (1770), were still being reprinted in 1803. The most famous domestic book of the 19th century is Mrs. Beeton's *Household Management* (1859–61). This tremendous work, which was compiled by a woman who died at the age of 29 leaving a family of four children, is still in use today, although some of

M. *André L. Simon*

FRONTISPIECE OF DE LA VARENNE, 'THE FRENCH COOK', 1654

were recipes for horrible concoctions, such as snail water or a pint of great earthworms boiled in a gallon of new milk (*see* DRUGS). These early books often contained, too, recipes for different alcoholic drinks, such as mead and beer. In *The Closet of Sir Kenelme Digby Kt. opened* (1669), Sir Kenelme Digby (whose father was concerned in the Gunpowder Plot) gives 100 recipes for mead, metheglin, hydromel, stepany, bragot, strawberry wine, cock ale, and other such drinks.

Another feature of English cookery books from the beginning of the 17th century is the number of recipes from foreign countries, for at that time travel abroad was becoming popular among the wealthy classes. The influence of France, which persists today, was particularly strong, and gave rise to some controversy, as is shown in two books of about 1750 by William Verral and Hannah Glasse, the former recommending the French

BLANCMANGE, JELLIES, CHRISTMAS PUDDING, AND AN EPERGNE WITH FRUIT AND FLOWERS

Coloured plate from Cassell's *Dictionary of Cooking*, 1878

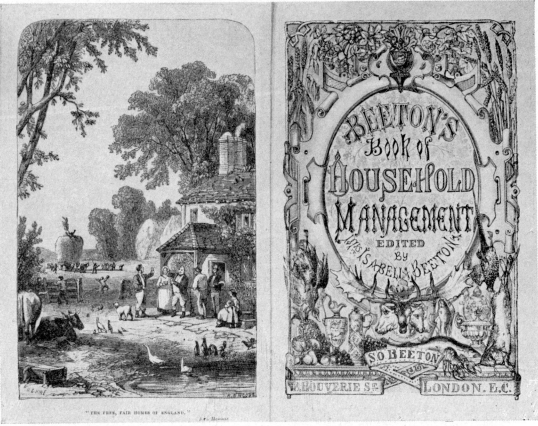

"THE FREE, FAIR HOMES OF ENGLAND."

FRONTISPIECE AND TITLE-PAGE OF 'BEETON'S BOOK OF HOUSEHOLD MANAGEMENT', 1861

the recipes which were suitable for the spacious days of Queen Victoria require adaptation to meet present-day restrictions.

Modern cookery books range from encyclopaedic collections of recipes from all countries down to brief treatments of one foodstuff. Their authors include professional chefs, devotees of particular countries and their cooking, competent housewives, and trained domestic science specialists. There is now generally greater precision of method and measurement, as well as more exact instructions for baking, due in part to the introduction of thermometers and thermostatic control of ovens (see THERMOSTAT, Vol. VIII). Many housewives make their own collections of recipes—perhaps in a loose-leaf notebook.

See also COOKING, HISTORY OF; MENU TERMS.

REFRIGERATOR. Many foods deteriorate when stored at or above the average room temperature of 60° F., but can be kept in good condition for some time if the temperature is lowered to about 45° F. Two centuries ago, people used to line an underground room with blocks of ice during the winter months to make an ice-house for cold storage. The next development was the ice-box, still used in some hot countries; this consists of an insulated box, lined with enamelled metal and with a door. On the top, to hold a block of ice, is a galvanized iron well, covered with an insulated lid, and usually provided with an outlet pipe for water from the melting ice.

In the modern refrigerator a mechanical method is used to maintain a constant low temperature in the refrigerating cabinet, based on the principle that when a liquid changes into a gas it takes up heat from its surroundings (see REFRIGERATOR, Vol. VIII).

In using a refrigerator, the following practical points are important: (1) The coldest part of the refrigerator is immediately under the ice-box, and the next coldest at the bottom of the cabinet, for cold air, being heavier than warm air, falls. (2) Food should not be packed so closely that air cannot circulate freely. This free circulation is necessary because when food at a temperature above that of the containing cabinet warms the air about it, the warm air, being lighter, rises to the top of the cabinet where it is cooled again by the evaporator. (3) All foods containing moisture should be kept in separate air-tight containers, for the air inside the cabinet takes up moisture from uncovered food and deposits it as frost on to the cold surfaces. Not only does this dry up the food, but the ice deposit reduces the efficiency of the evaporator. (4) It is important to cover strong-smelling foods such as fish. (5) All foods should be cooled to room temperature before being put into the cabinet, for if hot food is put in, the inside temperature is raised unduly, and power (usually electricity) has to be used in lowering it again.

The deposit of ice should not be allowed to exceed $\frac{1}{8}$ inch. At regular intervals of about a week, the refrigerator should be defrosted—that is, switched off and left with the door open for half an hour or so. Then, before it is started again, the inside of the cabinet should be washed out and dried.

The insulating cork board between the inner and outer casing of the cabinet only partially prevents the transfer of heat from the surrounding air. Therefore, if the refrigerator stands near a cooker or a fire, there is an additional load on the cooling unit.

Many modern refrigerators have a compartment maintained at temperatures below 32° F. for storing already frozen foods. But such storage of frozen foods is intended to be temporary; for permanent storage, a cabinet kept at 0° F. is essential (*see* FOOD PRESERVATION), and such deep-freeze cabinets may be purchased and installed in the house. In America it is quite common to rent a deep-freeze locker in a warehouse, and such lockers are now available in some rural areas in Britain.

See also Vol. VII: COLD STORAGE.
See also Vol. VIII: REFRIGERATOR.

RELATIONSHIP. The accompanying diagram shows the relationship in which the various members of her family stand to Freda A. But it must be remembered that this diagram holds good only for modern western Europe, and cannot be made valid for all societies in all periods of history simply by translating the relationship terms into other languages. Some of the terms were vague even in 19th-century English, when 'mother-in-law' was sometimes used to describe a step-mother. Some peoples use more words to describe relationships than we do. For example, while we use the word 'uncle' to describe the brothers of both parents, the Anglo-Saxons and the Romans used one word for the paternal uncle and another for the uncle who was the mother's brother. And some societies, Fiji, for example, can distinguish between maternal and paternal grandfathers in the same way, whereas we have to qualify the common term 'grandfather'. Again, in Bulgaria there are special terms for the younger and elder brothers and sisters. On the other hand, some societies use fewer terms than we do. In ancient Egypt there was one word, *senet*, which was used to describe not only a man's wife but also his sister, and 'brother' could also mean 'husband'. This was because, in princely families at least, brother could marry sister, and there was less need to distinguish between the two relationships, wife and sister, than in societies where incest is forbidden. And, similarly, in certain primitive societies where the father's brothers have as much say in the son's upbringing as the father himself, the use of one term to describe both the father and the father's brother is common.

The relationship terms, in fact, and the degrees of relationship which a given term includes, reflect the social organization of a people. In modern England we use the loose term 'uncle', because a father's brothers are no more important than a mother's brothers. The Anglo-Saxons used different words because relationships through women were then thought to be more important than through men, and the relationship between a man and his mother's brother was much closer than his relationship with his father's brother. This is, indeed, a characteristic of all peoples where relationships are affected by some degree of 'mother-right', that is, where a child belongs to the social group of his mother, and may even live with his mother's kin rather than his father's (*see* ASHANTI, Vol. I). In mother-right societies—and they are to be found in fairly primitive societies all over the world—all succession (to land, offices, and

Relationships

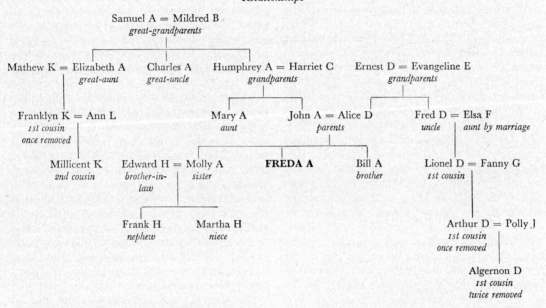

The words in italics give the relationships of all the people in the family to FREDA A.

Millicent K is Freda's *second cousin* because Millicent's father and Freda's father are first cousins.

Arthur D is Freda's *first cousin once removed* because he is the son of Freda's first cousin Lionel and is therefore one generation removed from full cousinship.

If Freda's father marries again, Martha J, who has children by a former husband, Lawrence J and Susan J, Martha A (*née* J) becomes Freda's *step-mother*, Lawrence her *step-brother* and Susan her *step-sister*. If John and Martha then have a son and daughter, Andrew and Pamela, Andrew is Freda's *half-brother* and Pamela her *half-sister* because they have one parent (John) in common.

so on) is through the mother, and order in the family may be kept by one of the mother's brothers. 'Father' and 'uncle', in these circumstances, come to mean something very far removed from the significance we give them. 'Brother' and 'sister', too, have very different associations among some MELANESIAN people (q.v. Vol. I), where brother and sister are not allowed to see or speak to one another.

Blood relationships, such as those shown in this chart, are not necessarily, or universally, the most binding ones. In polyandrous societies (where a woman has more than one husband), as among, for example, the Todas of India, the paternity of a child may be in doubt because so many husbands are involved; and so some ceremony is used to choose who is to be the 'father' for all social purposes—even if this 'father' is a child himself—even if he has never seen the mother. Yet the child will grow up to feel a close tie with this 'father'. In other societies a young man may feel a stronger sense of loyalty towards the companions of his own age

who are undergoing a similar discipline, and living in a common hut, than towards his parents, separated by a generation. The precise significance of relationship terms, their psychological meaning, can be determined only from a close study, for each race, of the mingling of two elements, the blood tie and social convention. In no two races do they mingle in quite the same way, and in each race they are subject to constant change.

See also FAMILY, HISTORY OF.

RELISHES, *see* CONDIMENTS AND RELISHES.

REPRODUCTIVE SYSTEM. Human beings reproduce themselves just as other animals do: the males produce sperms (*spermatozoa*) and the females produce eggs (*ova*); one sperm unites with one egg to form what is called the fertilized egg; and the fertilized egg grows into the young creature (*see* REPRODUCTION IN ANIMALS, Vol. II). In human beings, as in all mammals, the fertilization of the egg takes place inside the body of the female, and the sperm is introduced into her body by the male when the male and the

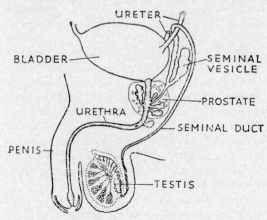

FIG. 1. DIAGRAM OF THE MALE REPRODUCTIVE ORGANS

Sperms are formed in the testes. They pass up the seminal duct to the seminal vesicles, where they remain until expelled through the penis in a fluid produced by the prostate gland

female perform the sexual act together. The egg, when it has been fertilized inside the woman's body, remains inside her womb and develops there, so that the young child is, for the early part of its development, protected inside its mother's body. When a man introduces the sperm into the body of a woman the male sexual organ (penis) enters the outside sexual opening of the woman. This opening is the lower of the two openings inside the female

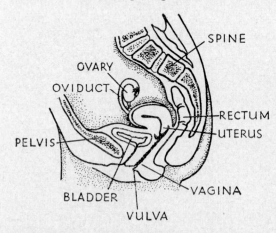

FIG. 2. DIAGRAM OF THE FEMALE REPRODUCTIVE ORGANS

The ova, usually shed singly one each month, are trapped in the funnel-shaped end of the oviduct and so eventually reach the uterus. Figs. 1 and 2 after Bell, Davidson, and Scarborough, *Textbook of Physiology and Biochemistry*, E. and S. Livingstone

external genital organs (vulva), the upper being to pass out the water (urine) made by the KID- NEYS (q.v.). The woman's external genital organs differ in this way from those of a man, whose penis has only one opening at its tip, through which both the urine and the sperms pass out.

The penis, which is normally a soft and pendulous organ, must become stiff and firm before it can be introduced into the external female sexual opening. When a man experiences sexual desire, blood flows into the large blood spaces in his penis, which becomes enlarged and stiff and stands up erect. In a similar manner, when a woman experiences sexual desire, blood flows into the lips of her external genital organs (vulva), so that they also become more swollen. At the same time the glands of the vulva secrete a fluid which lubricates the genital opening so that, when the sexual act occurs, the penis can enter more easily.

The woman's genital opening leads into a canal called the 'vagina', and this canal leads up to the womb, or 'uterus', which is situated in the lower part of the abdomen behind the bladder. Inside the womb the young human child develops.

When the sexual act occurs, the male sperms become very active. They travel, by moving their tails, up the vagina into the womb and, passing through this, they enter one or other or both of two tubes called the 'oviducts', which lead out of the upper end of the pear-shaped womb. These oviducts have funnel-shaped upper ends placed underneath the ovaries which make the eggs. The ovaries are one on each side of the womb and from them the eggs pass into the funnel-shaped mouths of the oviducts. When a sperm meets with an egg in the oviduct, it bores its way into the egg and, throwing off its tail, unites with it, thus fertilizing it. The fertilized egg then passes down the oviduct into the womb, taking about a week to do this, and becomes embedded in the innermost layer of the wall of the womb, where it remains, developing into the child. Usually, when one sperm has fertilized an egg, all the other sperms die without fertilizing eggs. The woman, therefore, has only one child. It sometimes happens, however, that two eggs are fertilized in the same woman at about the same time, and the woman then has two children at the same time (twins). It occasionally happens that more than two eggs are fertilized after a single sexual act, in which case the woman may have three children (triplets), four (quadruplets), or even five (quintuplets). This commonly occurs with many animals, such as dogs and cats. In some cases a single egg has two yolks, both of which are fertilized and develop into two children—identical twins.

The fertilization of the egg of the woman by a sperm of the man is the 'conception' of the child, and when it has occurred the woman is 'pregnant'. If the development of the child is not stopped by disease or by some other means, she will inevitably have, about 9 months after the conception, the baby, which will by then be ready to be born (see BIRTH).

All normal men and women experience sexual desire. The moral code of our society and of most others and the marriage laws of state and church dictate that sexual intercourse should be limited to men and women who are married to each other. The natural consequence of the sexual act is to produce a child, and married people can best provide the child with a FAMILY (q.v.) in which to grow up. All children need to belong to a stable family group where love and security are assured; and this is one basic reason for the growth of the moral law which forbids sexual intercourse outside the marriage bond (see MARRIAGE, HISTORY OF). Among other reasons for this is the fact that precautions taken to prevent conception are not invariably effective, and the woman may yet conceive a child. Contraceptives, for example, a rubber cap fitted, under medical supervision, into the mouth of the woman's womb, are often used by married people (see FAMILY WELFARE SERVICES, Section 3), to enable them to plan their families so that neither is the mother exhausted by too frequent pregnancies nor the family economy unbearably strained. The Roman Catholic Church, however, forbids the use of contraceptives.

See also LIFE CYCLE.
See also Vol. II: REPRODUCTION IN ANIMALS.

RESPIRATION. This is the act of breathing; by it the body takes in a fresh supply of the oxygen essential for its life, and rids itself of carbon dioxide. When we breathe in, fresh air containing oxygen is drawn through the nose and throat and into the lungs by way of the trachea and bronchi; in the lungs the BLOOD (q.v.) takes up the oxygen and gives up carbon dioxide. When we breathe out, the air contain-ing the carbon dioxide passes from the lungs to the outside of the body by the reverse route.

1. *The Respiratory System.* The most important organs concerned in respiration are, of course, the lungs, which are large, soft organs, of the consistency of light dough, shaped like rounded pyramids. With the heart and the great blood-vessels they occupy most of the chest or thorax. They rest on the diaphragm, which is the sheet of muscle separating the thorax from the abdominal cavity (see ANATOMY). Their outside surface is covered by a smooth, glistening membrane, the pleura, which continues on to line the inside of the chest wall, so that each lung lies in a slippery pocket.

When air is drawn through the nose and throat, it passes into a short, flattened tube, the trachea. The walls of this tube are made up of fibrous tissue and muscle, and at intervals there are incomplete circular cartilaginous rings which keep the tube open. The trachea divides into the right and left bronchi, which are similar in structure and carry the air to each lung. The main bronchi run to the roots of the lung, and they divide and redivide into smaller and smaller tubes until eventually the smallest of these end in an air pocket. In each lung there are many hundreds of thousands of such tiny air pockets, or alveoli.

The alveoli are closely surrounded by loops of very small blood-vessels, the capillaries, with walls composed of a single layer of cells. It is between the alveoli and these capillaries that carbon dioxide flows from the blood to the air and oxygen from the air into the blood. The

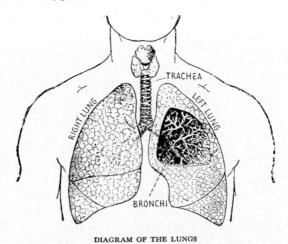

DIAGRAM OF THE LUNGS
From Logan Clendening, *The Human Body*, Alfred Knopf

blood in the capillary loops comes from the pulmonary arteries (*see* BLOOD CIRCULATION), which enter the roots of the lungs along with the bronchi and give rise to smaller and smaller branches. The blood is collected by small veins, which combine to form the large pulmonary veins and these leave the lungs at their roots in company with the bronchi and the pulmonary arteries. The pulmonary veins thus carry arterial blood which has been oxygenated; this flows to the left side of the heart and is distributed to the body tissues (*see* p. 215).

2. *The Mechanics of Respiration.* The chest wall is made up of the ribs, which arise from the vertebrae at the back and are joined to the sternum in front. For breathing in, the ribs are raised by the muscles of respiration attached to

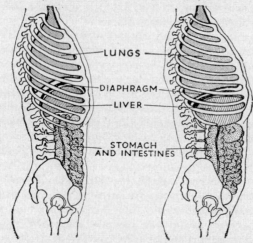

LUNGS

DIAPHRAGM
LIVER

STOMACH
AND INTESTINES

From 'First Aid Manual', H.M.S.O.
LEFT, BREATHING OUT; RIGHT, BREATHING IN

them, and because of their forward and downward angle the volume of the chest cavity is increased. At the same time, the diaphragm, bulging into the chest cavity from the bottom, is drawn downwards, which further increases the volume of the chest. The result is that the lungs, lying freely in the pleural-lined pockets, expand, and air is drawn in through the trachea and bronchi to fill them.

For breathing out, the ribs fall, partly by the action of muscles but mainly by the force of gravity; the diaphragm relaxes; the volume of the chest cavity is reduced; and air flows out from the lungs. At rest, we breathe about eighteen times each minute; when taking exercise, or if we have a fever, we need more oxygen and consequently we breathe more quickly.

3. *Diseases of the Respiratory System.* The common cold or upper respiratory infection is the most frequent disease from which humans suffer (*see* INFLUENZA AND COMMON COLD). The cold infection, if neglected, may obstruct the narrow bronchial tubes; in which case a condition known as bronchitis results and the patient suffers from a hard, dry cough.

In pneumonia there is an invasion of the lung tissues by BACTERIA (q.v. Vol. II), usually pneumococci, and the infected tissue shows reactions similar to those which are seen when a cut on the hand becomes infected. There is an outpouring of white cells from the blood, creating a barrier to the further spread of infection. The patient develops a cough, pain in the chest, and fever. Fortunately, most cases of pneumonia can now be rapidly cured by antibiotics (*see* DRUGS).

An infection of the pleural cavity outside the lungs, or pleurisy, may develop as a complication of pneumonia. The lungs are unable to expand properly because the pleural cavity becomes partially filled with pus. If antibiotics fail to clear this away, it may be necessary to operate. Pleurisy is very often the result of TUBERCULOSIS (q.v.), but in this case the fluid is clear. The lung itself may be infected by the pus or fluid, and a lung abscess may form; in this case an operation is usually necessary.

In recent years lung CANCER (q.v.) has increased to such an extent that it is now the cause of more deaths than pulmonary tuberculosis. The precise cause is still unknown. It is primarily a disease of town-dwellers. There are some grounds for believing that prolonged and heavy cigarette smoking and the inhalation of the exhaust fumes now so heavy in town atmospheres make people more liable to be attacked by cancer of the lung.

The importance of detecting lung cancer or tuberculosis early cannot be over emphasized, and a chronic cough or bronchial trouble should not be neglected.

See also BLOOD CIRCULATION; CANCER; TUBERCULOSIS.

RHEUMATISM, *see* BONES AND JOINTS; ORTHOPAEDICS.

RICE DISHES. 1. Wherever RICE (q.v. Vol. VI) is a main crop and a staple food, the art of cooking it has developed into a tradition. The curries of India, the rice dishes of Chinese restaurants, the *risottos* of Italy are deservedly famous. Less well known, but equally good, are the *pilafs* of Turkey (Indian *pulaos*) and the *arroz* and *paella* of Spain. All these dishes are based on rice, fried or unfried, boiled in water, flavoured or accompanied by a rich savoury sauce, and often augmented with meat, fish, shellfish, vegetables, fungi, or eggs.

There are many opinions about the best way to boil rice. The truth is that there is no one way; the method varies according to the result aimed at and the kind of rice used, and there are at least 25,000 varieties of rice. This is a suitable way for most dishes. The rice, having been washed, is put into a saucepan and covered with water so that the water comes about 1 inch above the rice surface; when it comes to the boil it should simmer undisturbed till the water is all absorbed and the grains dry and separate. Large-grained varieties, such as the American Carolina and Best Chinese (*si mu mai*), need 21–27 minutes in water equal to six times the weight of the rice. Small grains, such as the Italian Originario and the Indian Patna, need only 12–16 minutes in liquid equal to six times the weight of the rice.

2. CURRY. Indians make curry powder at home by grinding on a curry stone spices such as turmeric, ginger, mustard seed, corianders, and chillies (*see* SPICE CROPS, Vol. VI). Most curry dishes begin in the same way; onions and garlic are fried in *ghee* (dehydrated butter), and the curry spices are added and fried too, to get rid of their raw taste. Then a liquid is added, which may be coconut milk, squeezed from grated coconut which has soaked or simmered in hot water, stock (*see* SOUP), or plain water. Vegetables, meat, or fish are then added, and the whole very gently stewed. Sharpening agents such as limes, tamarinds, and tomatoes are put in towards the end of the slow-cooking process. A great deal of plain, dry, boiled rice is usually served with curry, but separately. Real Indian curries are never thickened with flour and never contain apples or raisins.

3. PILAF (*Pulao, Pilau, Pilaw*). Turks, Syrians, Arabs, Persians, Tartars, and the Muslims throughout India look upon this as their national dish. Rich and spicy, but not hot like curry, it is a blend of two components. The rice component (or *Pilaf* proper) is fried in *ghee* or oil with onions, garlic, and spices, and then cooked by slow simmering in stock. Near the end fried almonds and sultanas are thrown in and then all

A SAVOURY RICE DISH WITH PRAWNS

is carefully mixed with the meat dish, or *Korma*, which has been separately, and often very elaborately, prepared. A modified *Pilau*, slightly sweetened, yellowed with turmeric, and dotted with raisins, has become naturalized in South Africa. Kedgeree is a European dish of rice with flaked fish and hard-boiled eggs, which is derived from an Indian dish, *Khichri*, in which lentils or split peas, onions, and eggs are mixed with boiled rice.

4. CHINESE RICE. 'Have you eaten your rice?' is a form of greeting used in China. If the friend answers 'Yes', it means that he is in good health. Although in many poor parts of China maize or bread is the staple food, rice, plainly boiled, with grains dry and separate, forms the basic substance of the better Chinese food. A great variety of savoury preparations may be served with it in separate bowls. Distinctive ingredients of these are pork and chicken (always cut small, because of fuel economy and chopsticks), onions, Chinese mushrooms (such as 'Cloud ears'), bean sprouts, bamboo shoots, and water chestnuts, an aquatic plant of the willow-herb family. Typical seasonings are Soy bean sauce (*see* CONDIMENTS) and root ginger. The well-known chop suey (mixed fragments) contains all or most of these things and, though it is an American invention, unknown in China, it sufficiently resembles genuine Chinese rice dishes to give the Westerner an exciting experience in eating.

5. RISOTTO AND ARROZ. These Italian and Spanish dishes are rather similar in that the rice, often first fried, is cooked in and slowly absorbs a liquid made from onions fried in oil, garlic, herbs, and tomatoes. Red and green peppers, pimentos, green peas, pieces of chicken, rabbit, fish, or whole cooked mussels and prawns may be strewn throughout the rice. The centre of Italian rice growing is north of the River Po, and so risottos are northern specialities. *Risotto alla milanese*, flavoured and coloured yellow with saffron, is a striking example. Italian risottos are often served with grated Parmesan cheese; Spanish rice dishes never. In the north-east of Spain, where most of the local rice is grown, a rice dish is called *paella*, from the Catalonian word for the shallow pan in which the rice is cooked. The celebrated *Paella á la Valenciana* combines chicken with shellfish and rice.

6. SWEET RICE. *Pootoo* is a specially glutinous variety of rice used in India for sweet dishes. Ground rice is popular there, too, for making little crisp cakes and wafers, and it is used to a lesser extent in Britain, mainly for milk puddings. The familiar British rice pudding can be good if a little rice is baked or pressure cooked in a lot of milk, but too often the proportions are the other way round. In Germany and Scandinavia milk rice, sprinkled with sugar and cinnamon, is a Christmas sweet. A similar recipe comes from Galicia in northern Spain. There are some good combinations of milky rice with gelatine, whipped cream, apricots, pineapple, candied fruits, and so forth, especially in America. *Rice à l'Impératrice*, sometimes made in Cambridge college kitchens, is notable among such sweets.

7. OTHER USES. Alcoholic drinks made from fermented rice include the Japanese *saké*, Chinese *samsu*, and Javanese *arrak*. The Japanese make a kind of paper from rice straw, but the delicate, edible 'rice' paper which we associate with the underside of macaroons is not made from rice at all but from the pith of a tree (*Aralia papyrifera*) peculiar to Formosa. Wild rice (*Zizania aquatica*) differs from true rice (*Oryza sativa*) in that it has a greenish grain with a peculiar, slightly smoky taste. It has always been the chief starchy food of some American Indians, and is now widely grown in the southern U.S.A., chiefly as a breakfast food.

See also CEREALS AND PULSES.
See also Vol. VI: RICE.

RICKETS, *see* DEFICIENCY DISEASES.

ROASTING originally meant the grilling of meat—often whole animals—on a revolving spit before an open fire; but it now means moist and

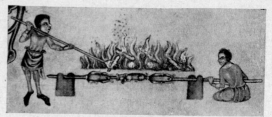

British Museum
ROASTING ON A SPIT IN THE MIDDLE AGES
Marginal drawing from the Luttrell Psalter, *c.* 1340

fatty cooking in an oven, especially of meat and poultry. It is suitable for large, good-quality joints and for whole birds, but not for very small cuts, which expose too much surface and so dry up. Most roasts should be 'seared' by 10–15 minutes at a high temperature (475–500° F.), and then cooked at reduced heat (300° F.) with occasional basting, that is, spooning hot fat over. The crackling of pork needs to be rescored very narrowly with a very sharp knife (the butcher never does it enough), brushed with oil, and seared for 15 minutes at 500° F. Roasting times at 300° F. are: beef, 16, 22, and 30 minutes per lb. for rare, medium, and well done; mutton, 30 minutes; and lamb, veal, pork, and venison, 35 minutes. Birds take different times according to the kind, size, and age; a quail, for instance, needs 15–20 minutes at 400° F.; a 10-lb. turkey, after searing, needs 3 hours at 350° F.

Pot-roasting is gentle stewing in a saucepan after the meat has been browned in hot fat; it is good for poor-quality and small joints, and can be well done in a pressure saucepan (*see* PRESSURE COOKING).

See also BAKING; MEAT; POULTRY AND GAME.

ROOFS. The shape of a roof is determined by the materials of which it is made and, to a lesser extent, by the need to throw off water (*see* HOUSES, TYPES OF). In recent years the technical means of making roofs watertight have so improved that houses in wet climates need not have such steeply sloping roofs as formerly.

In most countries houses usually have sloping timber roofs. A given distance can be spanned by shorter lengths of timber if two sloping timbers are made to meet at an angle than if a single beam is laid flat from wall to wall. To cover a sloping surface with overlapping slates or tiles is also an efficient and economical way of keeping out the water. Flat roofs are economical only when the spans are short or when some stronger material than timber is used for the beams: for instance, steel or concrete. A house with a flat roof can have a plan of any shape, but one with a pitched roof is restricted to fairly simple geometrical shapes or the roof becomes a complicated arrangement of intersecting peaks and valleys.

A house with a pitched roof is more easily kept warm in cold weather and cool in hot weather, as the volume of air within the roof space helps to insulate the rooms below. With flat roofs this insulation is provided by layers of absorbent material beneath the roof. Water tanks, which have to be at the highest point in the house (*see* HOUSEHOLD PLUMBING), are put in the roof space beneath pitched roofs; in flat-roofed houses they have to be on top of the roof where they often look unsightly and are difficult to protect from frost.

The ordinary type of wooden roof consists of sloping timbers, called rafters, spaced about 1 foot apart, with their upper ends resting against the faces of a ridge board, and their lower ends resting on a wall-plate at the top of the wall (Fig. 1). The rafters are covered with boarding (this is omitted in a cheap roof), and then with battens to which the tiles or slates are fixed. Often felt or impregnated paper is laid beneath the battens for extra protection. The lower edge of the roof can project beyond the top of the walls to form eaves, or it can be hidden behind a parapet. To prevent water from the roof running down the walls, it is collected in

M. N. Parry

FIG. 2. A GABLE END WITH A BARGE BOARD AT DINTON, BUCKS.

gutters and carried down a drain-pipe. The sloping side of the roof adjoining the gable can be finished with wooden 'barge boards', which are sometimes painted or carved (Fig. 2).

Different roof-covering materials demand a different pitch, that is, steepness of slope. For ordinary English tiles the best pitch is an angle of about 52°. Slates are best used with a flatter pitch, often as little as 31°; other materials, such as copper sheeting, can have a still flatter pitch.

Shingles—small tiles made by splitting billets of wood, especially cedar—are used to cover roofs where wood is plentiful in America, northern and eastern Europe, and sometimes in England; stone slabs, made by splitting large stones, used to be common in parts of England, particularly the Cotswolds, where stone is plentiful. Their weight demands heavy supporting timbers and they are too expensive to be frequently used nowadays. Straw or reed thatch was, until recently, common in the country (*see* THATCHING, Vol. VI); it is warm in winter and cool in summer, but it needs to be renewed periodically and it harbours vermin. In parts of Scotland and Ireland, and in Scandinavia, cottages have traditionally been thatched with heather or turf; in Scotland, the thatch is held down by ropes weighted with stones. Recently, light synthetic materials have been introduced, such as tiles made from asbestos cement, sheets of corrugated galvanized iron, and bituminized or tarred felt. As they need less support and are

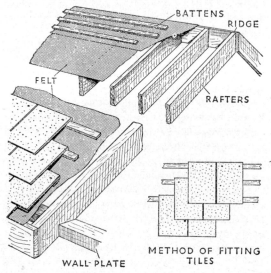

FIG. 1. THE CONSTRUCTION OF A PITCHED ROOF

National Buildings Record

FIG. 3. A HOUSE AT DIDBROOK, GLOUCESTERSHIRE, WITH THE ROOF SUPPORTED BY CRUCKS

R.C.H.M.

FIG. 4. MANSARD ROOFS IN CHEYNE WALK, LONDON

cheap, they are often used for sheds and farm buildings; they are less often used for houses.

The easiest places for water to penetrate are at the lines where a pitched roof meets a chimney-stack or the wall of a higher part of the house. Strips of lead, called flashings, are tucked under the tiles and into the joints of the brickwork to prevent water penetrating through them.

Flat roofs are never actually flat, but have a very slight slope in one or several directions so that water will run off them into gutters. The most usual coverings for flat roofs are asphalt, bituminized felt, zinc, or lead, though lead has lately become very expensive.

All these methods of constructing and covering roofs go back little changed for centuries. In medieval timber-built houses heavier and more widely spaced rafters were used, and sometimes the roof and walls were supported by curved beams rising from the ground to the roof ridge, called 'crucks' (Fig. 3). The complicated plan of late medieval and Tudor houses, with wings iutting out from the main part of the building, produced an irregular-shaped roof line, consisting of peaks and gables running in all directions, further complication being given by dormer windows. Tall moulded or carved CHIMNEYS (q.v.) completed the picturesque effect.

In the 17th century mansard roofs, named after the French architect François Mansart, were introduced into England. In these the pitch of the lower part of the roof is very steep and the upper part is at a flatter angle (Fig. 4). This gives more space beneath the roof and makes it possible to use the roof spaces for attics.

In the 18th and first half of the 19th centuries roofs were low in pitch and often hidden by a parapet, for in GEORGIAN and REGENCY ARCHITECTURE (qq.v. Vol. XII) the interest was concentrated on the horizontal lines of the façade. There was also a fashion in Regency houses for 'hipped' roofs with wide eaves. These are low-pitched roofs which slope back on all four sides so that there are no gables (Fig. 5). Houses built in the mid-Victorian style of the GOTHIC REVIVAL (q.v. Vol. XII) imitated the high-pitched roofs of medieval houses, with ridges and gables at all angles and heights, and with the addition of turrets. The modern tendency is for simple, geometrical roof lines. Some houses have roofs with a one-way pitch so that one side is higher than the other, or 'butterfly' roofs with a double

FIG. 5. A HIPPED ROOF: BROOM HALL, CHWILOG, CAERNARVONSHIRE

slope, highest at the eaves and meeting at a gutter in the middle.

See also HOUSES, HISTORY OF.

ROOMS, HISTORY OF. The shape, size, and number of rooms in a house depend on the way people live and on their skill in planning and building. The history of rooms reflects the development of indoor activities and the growing need for privacy.

Primitive people and those living in warm climates spend much of their time out of doors; they need dwellings for little more than shelter at night, so that one room in which they can sleep suffices (*see* PRIMITIVE DWELLINGS). In the north they need warmth too; the single room of a Saxon hut had a hearth dug out in the centre, and the floor raised round the walls as a sleeping platform. Poor people lived in single-roomed cottages throughout the Middle Ages, and until much later in Ireland and in the poorer parts of Europe. Until quite recently the Scottish peasant's cottage consisted of a 'but and ben', a living-room in front and a bedroom behind. As wealth and indoor activities increased, the number of rooms grew, each with its special purpose. Houses, however, are not always rigidly divided into rooms. In Japan the walls are often thin, movable partitions, and modern European houses are sometimes planned with similar partitions, especially between the dining-room and the sitting-room.

We know little of the houses of ancient peoples. PALACES (q.v.) were large and had many rooms, but these were public buildings and the centres of religious and political rather than domestic life. In the Greek town of Olynthus (early 5th and 4th centuries B.C.) there were houses with separate kitchens, bathrooms, and dining-rooms. The principal living-rooms faced south for, as Aristotle wrote, 'homesteads should be airy in summer and sunny in winter'. In many of the bigger Roman houses there were also a number of rooms for special purposes.

In the north, during the early Middle Ages, when men spent most of the day out of doors, hunting, working on the land, or fighting, the hall was at first the only room, and then the principal room, of the house. In it the master, his family, and his servants ate at long trestle tables and slept on benches or even on the tables. The master's table was raised on a dais at one end of the hall, and at the other end was a screen of wood or stone to stop the draughts from the door. There were often recesses or alcoves in the walls for the ladies' sleeping quarters or for guests, and there were 'garderobes' (*see* SANITATION, HISTORY OF) leading from them.

In the 13th century, as life became more refined, a 'solar'—bed-sitting-room for the master and his lady—was built above the end of the hall. It was reached by a circular stair. A parlour for the ladies was added and, at the other end of the hall, more rooms for domestic purposes. There was little furniture, but the walls were often covered with tapestries or cloth hangings for warmth and decoration; the stone floors were strewn with rushes.

INTERIOR OF A PREHISTORIC HUT AT SKARA BRAE, SCOTLAND
The hearth is in the centre; on either side are stone beds, and at the back a stone dresser

Nordiska Museum, Stockholm

ROOM IN A SWEDISH PEASANT'S COTTAGE

The bed is in a curtained recess on the right

By the 15th century, town houses usually had a number of rooms. Merchants and craftsmen who carried on their business in their houses needed work-rooms and extra rooms for the apprentices and journeymen working for them. During the 16th century more rooms were added —a library as books became more common and, running the length of an upper floor, a long gallery for entertaining. The rooms became lighter as the size of windows increased, and

Cabinet d'Estampes, Amsterdam

INTERIOR OF A 17TH-CENTURY DUTCH COTTAGE

Drawing by A. van Ostade, 1610–85

more furniture was added to their comfort. The chief room, however, was still the hall, divided from the entrance passage by an elaborate screen. The kitchens were on the other side of the passage, and there were more living-rooms beyond the hall.

In Renaissance Italy a new style of architecture, based on the study of Roman buildings, was developed during the 15th century. Rooms were symmetrically planned, and decorated with columns surmounted by an entablature, or painted with frescoes. In the 17th and early 18th centuries the Italian plan, with rooms leading off an entrance hall, was adopted in the north. Rooms became more elegant and their number increased, each having a particular purpose. Among the rich there was much formal entertaining in the 'public' rooms—the dining-room and the withdrawing-room (to which the guests withdrew after dinner and where tea was served). There might also be a music-room, a billiard-room, and a smoking-room, for gentlemen of the 18th century never smoked in the presence of ladies. The lady of the house had her boudoir, and there might be a tiny powder closet for powdering the hair (*see* HAIRDRESSING, HISTORY OF).

In the 19th century, thick walls, dark passages, and a number of highly ornamented and heavily furnished rooms, even in small villas, suited contemporary taste. With the increase in the size of families, nurseries became important. Often a wing of the house was devoted to day nursery, night nursery, schoolroom, and the nurses' and maids' rooms. Several children might sleep in one room (*see* NURSERY, HISTORY OF). The arrangement of the rooms was inconvenient, with long corridors and steep stairs, but this did not matter as servants were plentiful and their wages low (*see* DOMESTIC SERVICE, HISTORY OF).

All this time the houses of the poorer people in town and country remained small and simple. There were perhaps two bedrooms, and one main living-room for cooking, eating, work, and leisure. Even on large farms, the kitchen was the chief room of the house, where the farm workers joined the family for meals and where the family sat by the huge fire in the evenings. Where there was a parlour, it was often used only on Sundays and special occasions. In towns, too, the 'front parlour' was for Sundays only.

Until the end of the 18th century there was very seldom water laid on to the house, except

Lord De L'Isle and Dudley

THE 16TH-CENTURY LONG GALLERY AT PENSHURST PLACE, KENT

F. R. Yerbury

THE 'DOUBLE CUBE ROOM', WILTON HOUSE, NEAR SALISBURY

Built by Inigo Jones in 1647 in the proportion of two cubes. The furniture was designed by William Kent in 1725

A JAPANESE ROOM WITH MOVABLE WALLS, VERY LITTLE FURNITURE, AND A RECESS FOR FLOWERS AND A PAINTING
From Jiro Harada, *The Lesson of Japanese Architecture*, Studio Ltd.

for a pump in the kitchen. Water-closets first became common in middle-class houses in the 19th century, and bathrooms not until the beginning of the 20th century. Nowadays no houses are built in England without a bathroom (*see* Sanitation, History of).

After the First World War the new style of architecture, with its emphasis on simplicity and little decoration, was reflected in the bare rooms with distempered walls and few pictures. As domestic servants have become fewer, everything possible is done to simplify and make more convenient the arrangement of rooms in a house. The kitchen and dining-room are often combined, as the housewife is also cook; or the dining-room may be a part of the sitting-room, so that less fuel is needed for heating. There is no need for a separate nursery when there is no nurse to look after the children, but older children may have their bedrooms furnished with a desk and bookshelf so that they can do their homework in quietness. Rooms are arranged in a less crowded manner, and large windows reaching to the ground often link them with the garden or with Balconies or Verandahs (qq.v.). Some architects, particularly in California, have even tried to do without fixed rooms altogether, and to re-arrange space by moving around their walls and curtains. The house itself can then be treated as one unit rather than as a group of separate rooms (*see* Colour Plate, opp. p. 256).

See also Houses, History of; Houses, Types of; Interior Decoration, History of.

RUPTURE, *see* Hernia.

S

SALADS. 1. The word 'salad' derives from the Latin *sal*, which may indicate that salads were first eaten with salt only, although the Ancient World was well acquainted with oil and vinegar. The dietetic importance of eating raw vegetables and fruit has long been known (*see* NUTRITION); long before the discovery of VITAMINS (q.v.), sailors knew that scurvy could be prevented or cured only by such a diet.

A salad may consist of raw vegetables or fruit, cooked vegetables, fruit, meat, or fish, or combinations of these. For raw salads, any vegetable may be used which does not have an unpleasant taste. The best known is lettuce in all its varieties; but there are also chicory, endive, mustard and cress, watercress, the heart of green or red cabbage, onion, chive, dandelion, sweet corn, cucumber, tomato, celery, celeriac, carrot, swede, turnip, avocado pear, and peppers. Raw fruit salads are made of any kind of raw fruit cut up and sugared or soaked in syrup or liqueurs. *Muesli*, invented by the Swiss diet reformer Dr. Bircher-Benner, consists of raw rolled oats soaked in water or milk overnight and then mixed with raw fruit such as grated apple, sliced oranges or bananas, whole grapes, and chopped nuts. With cream or top milk this makes a breakfast dish which children are certain to enjoy. In some countries sweet and savoury ingredients served together in one salad are popular; for instance, an American salad may consist of lettuce, pineapple, and cream cheese; or of chopped celery, apple, and walnuts in a French dressing (Waldorf salad). Among the more eccentric things used to flavour and decorate salads are chrysanthemum petals in Japan, and rose and nasturtium flowers in Turkey.

Very good salads can be made of such cooked vegetables as asparagus, globe artichoke, potato, peas, carrots, French and broad beans, and beetroot. These combine well with cooked meat or fish; Russian salad is a combination of finely cubed potatoes, beetroot, cooked carrots, turnips, peas, and beans in mayonnaise dressing.

The first part of a Roman dinner consisted of HORS D'ŒUVRES, EGG DISHES, SHELLFISH (qq.v.), and salad; and to this day a green salad is served after the meat course as an integral part of lunch and dinner in all Latin countries. In England 'saladings' were known by Elizabethan times but were not considered serious eating; indeed, a writer in 1846 said, 'The salad is the glory of every French dinner, and the disgrace of most in England.' Salads still tend to be regarded in England as fit only for hot weather or as the inevitable accompaniment of cold meat.

2. SALAD DRESSINGS. Although the main ingredients of a salad, such as lettuce, endive, or tomatoes, do not vary much throughout the world, different regions have very different tastes in dressings. India has *ghee* (clarified butter), *sarsa* (mustard oil), and *narel* (coconut oil). Japan and China have soy sauce (*see* CONDIMENTS AND RELISHES), either by itself or with limejuice and oil; the South Seas use coconut milk with limejuice. Siam's *namphrik* sauce is made from 'high' prawns or shrimps, pounded in a mortar with red peppers, and mixed with brine and ginger, black pepper, onions, and garlic.

The two classic European dressings are French dressing and mayonnaise. French dressing is made by blending two to three parts of best olive oil with one part of vinegar (wine vinegar if possible), and adding salt and pepper to taste. For mayonnaise one fresh egg-yolk is beaten with ½ teaspoon of mustard in a small basin, and about ¾ cup of oil is added very gradually, the beating continuing all the time. The emulsion thickens and lightens in colour the more oil it absorbs; when thick enough to spread, vinegar or lemon juice and salt are added to taste. A mayonnaise which has gone wrong may be salvaged by mixing a little mustard water in a clean bowl and beating the mixture into it drop by drop. To make boiled dressing, ½ oz. of butter is melted in a double saucepan, and ½ oz. of flour is stirred in and cooked for a minute; then one gill of milk is added and the mixture stirred till it thickens. After it has cooled a little, one egg-yolk, sugar, salt, pepper, mustard, and lemon juice or vinegar to taste are beaten in. Last of all the egg-white is whipped till it is stiff,

SALADS OF ORANGE AND WATERCRESS, TOMATO, CABBAGE, AND WALNUTS, AND MIXED VEGETABLES

and folded in. For sour-cream dressing, one cup of sour cream, one egg, $\frac{1}{4}$ cup of vinegar, two teaspoons each of salt and sugar, one teaspoon of mustard, and a shake of pepper are stirred in together and cooked in a double saucepan until the mixture thickens.

Salad ingredients must be as dry as possible, for dressings lose much of their flavour if they become diluted with water. Salads are also more appetizing if well chilled. The choicest and most colourful parts should be kept for decorating. The best bowl for green salads with French dressing is an unpolished wooden one which, instead of being washed, should be wiped out with a little olive oil. For many people a salad is not complete without a slight tang of garlic, easily achieved by rubbing a cut clove of that powerful vegetable once round the bowl.

SALT, see CONDIMENTS AND RELISHES; TABLE-WARE. *See also* Vol. III: SALT. *See also* Vol. VII: SALT MANUFACTURE.

SALTING AND SMOKING, see FOOD PRESERVING.

SANDWICHES. It is now 200 years since the famous occasion when the 4th Earl of Sandwich sustained himself throughout a 24 hours' gambling bout on cold beef laid between slices of bread. The closed sandwiches to which he thus gave his name have steadily increased in popularity ever since. Because they are easy to make, portable, quick and tidy to eat, and can constitute an appetizer, a snack, or a whole meal, they

fill many needs in modern life. The word 'sandwich' has been adopted in all south European languages, as well as in Arabic and Turkish. Scandinavia, Germany, and East European countries, however, have invented their own open sandwiches which they call 'butter breads'. Though these sandwiches, too, are used as luncheon, picnic, and train snacks, they also appear as HORS D'ŒUVRES (q.v.).

A good closed sandwich is moist and tasty, and the filling dominates the bread. American sandwiches are often very large, with several layers, and may contain hot meat and gravy as well as fried eggs and salad; obviously such a sandwich, which is a meal in itself, must be eaten with knife and fork. The Spanish idea of a sandwich is a huge piece of ham or a whole omelette clapped between two vast hunks of dry bread.

Typical English sandwiches are small, thin, and neatly made of white, brown, fancy, or nut bread, old enough to slice well, and preferably square, cut in cross-section. Evenly cut slices are spread smoothly with margarine or butter which has been creamed, and then the filling is put on, right up to the edges and corners. The two slices, when closed, are pressed gently and cut into halves, squares, diamonds, or triangles, the crusts having been cut off. Some of the many fillings are savoury butters (*see* SAUCES); sliced raw apples with honey and walnuts; raw carrot grated, with cooked salad dressing (*see* SALADS) or lettuce; cucumber slices, with flaked kipper and vinegar; cottage cheese (*see* CHEESES) with

OPEN SANDWICHES

strawberry jam, crushed pineapple, or chopped olives; hard cheeses grated, with chutney, lettuce, or tomato; hard-boiled eggs mashed with milk and flavoured with chives, curry powder, or anchovy essence; dates and walnuts with lemon juice; peanut butter with raisins and sliced oranges; ham and mustard or other cold meats with salads or relishes. Rolled sandwiches are made by rolling up a very fresh, crustless, buttered slice, spread with seasoned cream cheese or other soft filling, or containing an asparagus tip. It is best to fasten them with toothpicks and wrap them in a damp cloth till it is time to serve them. To make ribbon sandwiches, alternate slices of white and brown bread are filled, and then wrapped in a damp cloth and pressed under a weight; just before serving they are sliced across $\frac{1}{4}$ inch thick. To make a 'sandwich loaf', a whole pan loaf, the crusts having been cut off, is cut in four slices lengthwise; the slices are put together with butter and fillings, and then pressed under a light weight; the surface is spread with mayonnaise or cream cheese and decorated; after it has been chilled for $\frac{1}{2}$ hour, it is sliced and eaten with a fork. Toasted sandwiches are large sandwiches filled, for example, with mild cheese, bacon, or sliced tomatoes, brushed on the outside with melted butter, and toasted under the griller.

SANITATION, HISTORY OF.

SANITATION, HISTORY OF. Today it is common knowledge that dirt contains germs and that some germs cause disease. We know, too, that an inadequate or impure water supply and poor drains and sewers can lead to disease. A hundred years ago men had no such knowledge: indeed, it was not until the second half of the 19th century that any connexion between dirt and disease was established. Up to the mid-19th century, the main cause of infection was thought to be the stench arising from accumulated dirt rather than the dirt itself. Only when it was seen that the main victims of the cholera epidemics of the early 19th century were the poor, living in insanitary hovels, with no proper WATER SUPPLY (q.v.) or sewage system, did people realize that the disease was a direct result of these insanitary conditions (*see* PUBLIC HEALTH, Vol. X).

Isolated examples exist of ancient communities with a high standard of sanitation. For example, as early as 2000 B.C., at the palace of Minos at KNOSSOS (q.v. Vol. XII) in Crete, there were

Dr. C. Harrison

A GARDEROBE AT BROUGHAM CASTLE, WESTMORLAND
The sewage dropped through a hole in the bottom and fell into the moat below

elaborate domestic sanitary arrangements, including a system of drainage for rainwater quite separate from that for sewage, and latrines which in construction surpass anything built before the 19th century.

The Romans had not only a good water supply but large underground sewers, public latrines of a water-flushing design, and public baths. The houses of richer citizens were well-ventilated and contained baths, though these were not as a rule connected to the main sewers. But even in Rome refuse was thrown into an open gutter in the street, whence it made its way into the sewers. Indeed, Juvenal, in the 1st century A.D., had difficulty in persuading his friend Umbricius to stay in Rome because of the danger of being hit by refuse thrown from the windows.

In medieval Europe there was no drainage system and an insufficient and most unwholesome supply of water. The houses of the rich might possess a courtyard into which all refuse would be thrown, and occasionally collected and removed outside the town, but the general practice was to throw everything into the STREETS (q.v. Vol. IV) where a small stream running down a central gutter served as a sewer. In medieval Paris the cry of '*Garde à l'eau*' usually accompanied the throwing of refuse from the windows into the streets. The cry 'gardy loo' used on similar occasions by the inhabitants of the 18th-century Edinburgh tenements clearly derives from the French cry. In England castles contained closets known as 'garderobes'. A wooden seat was fixed over a stone shaft, down which the sewage fell, passing into the open or into the moat surrounding the castle.

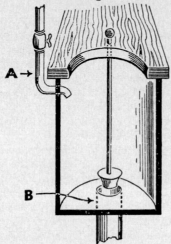

FIG. 1. SIR JOHN HARINGTON'S WATER-CLOSET, 1596
A. Water supply. B. Plug waste operated by a handle in the seat

In Elizabethan times Sir John Harington designed what is considered to be the first British water-closet. The closet was installed in his home near Bath, where, he wrote, it did much to relieve the former stench. He described how, in order to provide sufficient pressure for flushing the closet, water was pumped up into a cistern placed on a high water-tower built on the top of his house. The water was then conducted by a pipe to the pan of the closet, the flow being regulated by a hand-operated tap. The water was retained in the pan by a valve which could be pulled up by a handle in the seat (Fig. 1). When the handle was pulled upwards, the water and sewage were released into a cesspool under or near the house. As there was no kind of trap between the pan and the cess-pool, vents were built into the closet to provide some means of drawing off the evil-smelling gases. Although Queen Elizabeth is said to have had a model of the invention installed at her Richmond Palace, most of Sir John's contemporaries regarded the innovation as a joke, and it was never patented. In general, there was little attempt at this time to keep houses clean or to prevent filth from accumulating.

Although the Great FIRE OF LONDON (q.v. Vol. X), in the 17th century, following upon the Great Plague gave an opportunity for rebuilding the worst of the slums, little permanent improvement in sanitation was seen until the middle of the 18th century. The first patent for a water-closet was taken out in 1755 by Alexander Cumming, a watchmaker. Although this, like Harington's invention, was a valve-type closet, the sewage was now discharged into a lead soil pipe, which appears to have been 'trapped' in order to cut off the smell that rose from the cesspool below. Such 'stink-traps', as they came to be known, often tended to become contaminated with sewage, and so no longer served their purpose. In 1778 another form of valve water-closet was patented by a Yorkshireman, Joseph Bramah. In his model the valve was hinged to the side of the pan so that it shut up against the bottom of the basin (Fig. 2). One great drawback to these valve-type closets was that to be efficient they had to be most carefully made and hence proved very expensive. Other and cheaper forms of water-closets came into use from the end of the 18th century, but until the latter part of the 19th century they all had this drawback—it was impossible to keep them clean. At the same time, the little progress that had been made was largely offset by the rapid erection of shoddily built houses in which no pro-

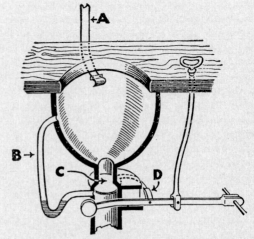

FIG. 2. JOSEPH BRAMAH'S WATER-CLOSET, 1778
A. Water supply. B. Trapped overflow. C. Flap valve. D. Cranked arm to keep valve in position

vision at all was made for sanitation or water supply.

Most people had only an earth-closet or privy-midden, often in a shed or outbuilding at the end of the back garden or yard. A privy-midden consisted simply of a wooden seat built over a brick receptacle or pit, into which all the household rubbish and ashes were emptied. Occasionally, these pits were emptied by buckets, the sewage being carried to carts which deposited their load in the nearest river. More often, the sewage was allowed to seep away into the surrounding earth.

By mid-Victorian times most middle-class homes had indoor water-closets, but an adequate water supply and sewage system was not provided until near the end of the 19th century. Consequently, the installation of water-closets in better-class houses involved the building of cesspools, which usually both leaked and stank, the poisonous fumes rising up into the house, and the sewage soaking away to pollute the surrounding rivers and wells. A cesspool was only a slight modification of the earlier pit. It consisted of a large, bricked-up reservoir, built under the house or near it, but always accessible for cleaning. Although these were, in fact, cleaned from time to time, this did not prevent the sewage filtering into the surrounding earth. When, with the growth of towns, the older cesspools were no longer able to deal with the sewage, they were connected by pipes to the existing town sewers which discharged into the rivers or the sea. The inadequate water supply that was available meant that whenever the plug of a water-closet was pulled a mere trickle of water was released, insufficient for keeping the complicated workings clean. Since closets at this time were invariably housed in cupboard-like spaces beneath the stairs, with no means of ventilation, it is not surprising that the water-closet proved a somewhat mixed blessing, and that many people died from the effects of the foul gases which rose from the cesspools.

Despite the more general use of water-closets in the first half of the 19th century, the chamber pot and the more refined commode, a chair-like object, were indispensable articles in all houses. Water-closets were still unknown in working-class homes, and in some of the worst tenement houses in London there was no sanitary provision and refuse was piled high in the courtyards shared by as many as a hundred people (*see*

SLUMS, Vol. X). Usually there was one privy-midden to a courtyard; though the middens were supposed to be emptied every night, this duty was usually neglected, and they often overflowed into the surrounding courtyard (*see* Vol. X, p. 135). Outside London, the standard method of sanitation in towns was, at best, the pail-closet, and, at worst, the ordinary midden, a huge, wet, unlined hole into which refuse of all kinds was emptied and allowed to rot, and from which a fearful stench arose.

Until well into the 19th century, the water supply was both inadequate and impure. As water cost money, it was used for many purposes before it was finally thrown into the gutters—for washing children, clothes, and floors, for example. Such a shortage of water meant that many people never washed at all; chimney sweeps washed only three times a year, and children were often sewn into their winter clothes and not released until the spring. Fixed baths were hardly known, even in the houses of the rich (*see* PERSONAL HYGIENE, HISTORY OF).

After the serious epidemics of cholera in the early 19th century, improvements slowly began to be carried out. Commissions were appointed to inquire into sanitary conditions, and efforts were made to remove the worst conditions, to improve the water supply, and to build better sewers and drains. Many of the fast-growing industrial towns of the 19th century, however, were little touched by these improvements, and sanitation in the country still remained quite primitive. Even today, in towns in the north of England, and in some country districts where there is no piped water supply, privy-middens are still in use, and where a water-closet is provided, it is by no means always indoors. In some industrial towns, outdoor closets are still sometimes shared between several houses.

The presence of a water-closet in every new house is now taken for granted, and new houses are also provided with a bathroom and a proper hot- and cold-water system (*see* HOUSEHOLD PLUMBING). Local authorities are responsible for seeing that the sanitary arrangements are in perfect order, so that bad sanitation can no longer be the threat to good health that it was for many hundreds of years.

See also WATER SUPPLY, HISTORY OF; HOUSEHOLD PLUMBING.
See also Vol. VIII: SEWAGE DISPOSAL; WATER SUPPLY.
See also Vol. X: DRAINAGE; REFUSE DISPOSAL.

SAUCES. These are used to enrich the flavour of other food, improve its appearance, moisten it, and often, incidentally, to increase its food value. Sauces, which have a very ancient history, probably reached the highest pitch of variety and perfection in the hands of the French from the 18th century onwards—in fact, many of the terms and methods used in sauce-making are French in origin. The flavour and colour are matters of personal choice, but the consistency of a good sauce must be smooth and velvety; once a cook has learnt to make a good white or brown sauce he can make almost any other, for these form the foundation of almost all the rest.

1. SAVOURY SAUCES. (*a*) *Basic white sauce* (for four persons). The first step is to make a *roux*, a smooth paste of 1 oz. of melted butter or fat and 1 oz. of flour with seasonings, in either a double saucepan or a single, thick saucepan, over very gentle heat. This is stirred with a wooden spoon till the *roux* is smooth and can be cleanly lifted up in one even mass. The pan is then removed from the heat, and cold milk is poured in quickly and stirred until the mixture is quite smooth, when the pan is returned to the fire and stirred constantly to thicken. The classic method is to beat the milk into the *roux* gradually over the heat, but it is more difficult for the beginner to avoid lumps this way. In either case, the sauce should be simmered for 5 minutes in order to cook the flour thoroughly. A lumpy sauce can, in the last resort, be put through a sieve, but practice will make this quite unnecessary.

A white sauce can be varied by adding different ingredients to it before serving. Half-a-cup of grated cheese, a chopped, hard-boiled egg and extra seasonings, a large boiled onion, drained and chopped, cooked celery and celery salt, a dessertspoon of finely chopped parsley, or half-a-cup of capers and a spoonful of their vinegar all make tasty sauces.

(*b*) *Basic brown sauce.* 1 oz. of butter or bacon fat is melted, as before, and 1 oz. of flour and seasonings is stirred in. The *roux* should brown slightly before mixing in ½ pint of brown stock. Brown sauces can be varied by adding a purée made from 1 lb. of tomatoes, an onion, seasonings, and a dash of sugar, well simmered and rubbed through a sieve; or a cup of mushrooms sliced and fried in margarine; or four large pickled walnuts chopped small and stirred in with a tablespoon of their vinegar. This can be served with roast mutton. To make Madeira sauce, to serve with grilled gammon or salt pork or tongue, a teaspoon of cornflour or arrowroot is used instead of the flour, as it makes a clear sauce; then two tablespoons of Madeira or any white wine and a dessertspoon of tomato catsup are stirred in.

(*c*) *Fine sauces.* These, which are less frequently made at home because they are expensive, usually include egg-yolks, extra butter or cream, and mayonnaise. *Hollandaise* (or Dutch sauce) is made entirely of butter emulsified with egg-yolks and lemon juice—a sort of butter mayonnaise served warm. *Béarnaise* (from a district in southern France bordering on Spain, and introduced by a Paris chef in 1835) resembles *Hollandaise* but is flavoured with tarragon vinegar instead of lemon juice, and is served with grilled meats. *Tartare* sauce is a sharp, cold sauce for fried fish or steak, made by mixing mayonnaise with capers, chopped raw onion, chopped pickles and olives, and a little extra tarragon vinegar. When served hot, it is more likely to remain stable if made partly with white sauce. Newburg sauce (after a German banker called Neuberg), for lobster, shrimps, and frog's legs, is a white sauce made with cream instead of milk, further enriched with egg-yolks, and flavoured with sherry; it is popular in America. *Béchamel* (named after a steward of Louis XIV) is another fine white sauce thickened with cream, and sometimes made partly with veal or chicken stock. *Mornay* sauce (*see* MENU TERMS) contains egg-yolks and melted cheese and is a correct sauce to serve with fillets of sole. Italian tomato sauce, or *sugo*, can be prepared in many ways, but often begins with onions fried in olive oil and then simmered for a long time with garlic, tomato purée, finely ground meat, and HERBS (q.v.), in particular Italian parsley, marjoram, and basil. Variants of it are met with all over the Mediterranean, especially in Greece.

(*d*) *Savoury butters.* These are excellent alternatives to sauce with grilled steak or fish. Butter is creamed with chopped parsley and lemon juice (*Maître d'Hôtel*), or with chopped onions, horseradish, anchovy, or the coral of lobster.

(*e*) *Gravy* is the natural juice which drips from roast meats or exudes from stewed ones (French = *jus*), usually thickened a little and seasoned, but not artificially concocted. Water and cornflour flavoured and coloured with something out of a bottle or packet is not gravy at all, but only a very poor substitute. If the meat has been roasted properly (*see* Roasting), the pan fat will be rich in tasty, brown meat extractives which make excellent gravy. Continental gravy is usually served unthickened; the British and American way is to pour off the superfluous fat from the pan and then to make a brown *roux* with what is left behind, adding cold stock and seasonings as for brown sauce. The best gravy for roast poultry and game, from which little exudes, is made from the giblets (*see* Offal) fried with onions, minced, then simmered or pressure-cooked with herbs, and finally strained. Gravy to accompany dry-cooked dishes, such as rissoles, is made by first frying chopped onion in fat, enriching it with flour and marmite (which has much more food value than commercial gravy browning), and adding stock or vegetable water. Wheaten flour produces a better flavour and is less sticky than cornflour, although perhaps not so easy to keep smooth. Cornflour produces a semi-transparent gravy.

Certain sauces are traditionally served with certain roast meats—for example, bread sauce and mint sauce (almost the only famous English ones) with chicken and lamb respectively; apple sauce with pork and goose; cranberry with turkey; horseradish with beef (*see* Condiments and Relishes).

2. Sweet Sauces for desserts and steamed puddings taste better thickened with cornflour.

(*a*) *Milky sauces*. A white sauce is made using ½ oz. of cornflour instead of 1 oz. of flour and a tablespoon of sugar instead of the salt. The sauce can be varied by flavouring it with cocoa, coffee essence, brandy, Marsala wine, ginger, or butterscotch (*see* Flavourings). The most common sweet sauce—'custard' made from artificially coloured cornflour sold as 'custard powder'—is greatly over-used in Britain. Real custard is made from fresh eggs, milk, and sugar (*see* Egg Dishes). This mixture, stirred in a double saucepan until thick, is the only proper custard to use for trifles and vanilla creams.

(*b*) *Clear sauces* provide great scope for inventiveness; jam, marmalade, golden syrup, prune juice, syrup from preserved ginger or tinned pineapple, red currant juice, lemon and orange juice (with some grated rind) all make useful hot sauces when diluted with water, thickened with cornflour, and sweetened if necessary. Americans excel at sweet sauces, many of which they use, hot or cold, on ice cream. A genuine Melba sauce is made from crushed, fresh raspberries, strained and cooked to a syrup with sugar, and sometimes slightly thickened. Hot chocolate sauce, easily made by boiling about equal parts of cocoa, sugar, and water until thick, is, like melted chocolate, delicious on ice cream or stewed pears. Mashed bananas or apricots, gently cooked with sugar and lemon juice, make a fine sauce for steamed pudding, ice cream, or milk puddings.

(*c*) *Hard sauces* are sweet versions of savoury butters made (for four people) by creaming 2 oz. of butter (or margarine) with 4 oz. of icing sugar; it is flavoured, for Christmas Brandy Butter, with a teaspoon of brandy. Mocha sauce is flavoured with a teaspoon each of dry cocoa and coffee essence (or two tablespoons of warmed strong coffee). For the American Ohio sauce, soft brown sugar replaces icing sugar, and chopped nuts and dates, lemon essence, and two tablespoons of cream or warmed top milk are added.

SAUSAGES. 1. It is not known when the idea originated of stuffing small pieces of meat into casings to make sausages, but certainly for centuries in China it has been a way of using up scraps of meat and the intestines of animals, and it is known that sausages were popular in ancient Rome. The name itself, from the Latin word *salsus* ('salted'), indicates that sausages were probably made from preserved meat. Today there are a great many varieties, some of which

Picture Post Library

SOME DIFFERENT KINDS OF SAUSAGE IN A FRENCH SHOP

take their name from the place where they were first made—such as Frankfurter, Bologna, Vienna, Braunschweiger, Strassburger, and Lyon sausage.

2. *Types.* There are three main groups of sausages: fresh, cooked, and dry. The fresh ones, made from pork or beef and sold raw to be cooked later, vary in size, the smallest being 'chipolatas' and Paris sausages. Some cooked sausages are eaten cold; others are heated through before serving. In Britain the best known are pork and beef luncheon sausages, saveloy, polony, veal and ham, ham and tongue sausages, and black puddings which include a large quantity of pigs' blood. From the Continent come Bologna, Frankfurter, and Wiener blood sausages, and varieties of liver sausage such as Braunschweiger and Strassburger. All these have been already cooked, either by light smoking or by immersion in water at about 160° F. for up to ½ hour. Of dry sausages, salami is the most common; it is made from beef, pork, and pork fat, cured with sodium nitrate, and then stuffed into skins and dried for about 10 weeks. There are many varieties of dry sausage, made in various sizes and shapes, and they usually include an appreciable amount of garlic together with other seasonings and spices.

3. *Ingredients.* The meats used in commercial sausage-making are those from old animals, too tough to be used in the ordinary way, as well as trimmings and scraps; these latter form the basis of the home-made sausage produced after a farmer's own pig killing. The meat is always minced and then thoroughly mixed with the other ingredients by being chopped in a bowl.

The intestines of the ox, pig, and sheep, after suitable treatment, provide sausage-containers in a variety of shapes and sizes, those of large diameter being used for the bigger cooked ones, such as luncheon sausage and Bologna, the smaller ones for fresh pork or beef sausage, and the bladder (usually that of an ox) for Mortadella, an Italian dry sausage. These materials form a tough casing which protects the meat within, but which on cooking becomes soft enough to be eaten. Synthetic skins made from cellulose are also available today, and these are always used for kosher (Jewish) sausages.

Binders, ingredients added to bind the other ingredients together and to reduce the cost, may be of bread, rusk, rice, or potato flour. In some countries, the amount of binder permitted is limited; for example, in the U.S.A. it is limited to 3·5%. In Britain there is no such restriction, and in fact, during the period of rationing of the Second World War, it was the amount of meat included in the sausage rather than the other ingredients that was controlled; consequently the sausage had a much reduced value as food.

Salt and pepper, and a variety of HERBS AND SPICES (q.v.), are added to sausages for their flavouring and preservative properties. Onions, garlic, and truffles give their special flavour to certain kinds of sausages.

4. *Cooking and serving.* The cooked and dried varieties are used as appetizers in HORS D'ŒUVRES (q.v.), and are served by themselves or mixed with other cold meats for SALADS (q.v.). The fresh ones are cooked by FRYING, GRILLING, or BAKING (qq.v.), and served as a main dish for breakfast and other meals and as an accompaniment to POULTRY AND GAME (q.v.). Two popular dishes are sausage and mash—fried sausages served on a dish of mashed potatoes—and toad in the hole—sausage cooked in batter. Frankfurters, which are cooked by being reheated in water, are very popular served as 'hot dogs'—a hot bread roll with a sausage inside.

SAVOURIES. The savoury course in a formal dinner comes between the sweet and dessert; or it sometimes takes the place of a sweet. It is more commonly met with in Britain than elsewhere. The typical after-dinner savoury is something very tasty served piping hot, on toast

Studio Lisa

COCKTAIL SAVOURIES

or fried bread, or in patty or *choux* cases (*see* Pastry), or in scallop shells. Examples are Welsh rabbit and other toasted cheeses; sardines, anchovies, roes, mushrooms, or *foie gras* on toast; 'angels on horseback', that is, oysters wrapped in bacon and grilled; creamed shellfish; or cheese custards in cases or scallops. Any of these can also come at the beginning of a meal, when they are called hot Hors d'œuvres (q.v.).

In Britain, the Dominions, and America, a savoury may also mean any rather quickly prepared, light supper dish, such as Pasta, Rice Dishes, toasted Sandwiches (qq.v.), and any of the savoury toasts described above. In the U.S.A. hot supper savouries are often cooked at table in electrically heated chafing dishes, grills, or waffle irons.

Savouries can also mean any of the hors d'œuvres served with cocktails or at evening parties—olives, radishes cut in flowers, curled celery, salted nuts, potato crisps, chipolata sausages, shrimps, pickled onions, cheese straws, or savoury rolls. *Canapés* are little round platforms of toast or plain crisp biscuits spread with savoury butters (*see* Sauces), or with caviare, pâté, and so on. Often they are elaborately decorated, and sometimes glazed with aspic (*see* Jellies and Aspics). They are, in effect, tiny open Sandwiches (q.v.), and can be the prettiest and best of all the cocktail savouries.

SCARLET FEVER, *see* Infectious Diseases, Section 5.

SCIATICA, *see* Nervous System.

SCONES. These originated in Scotland where ovens were rare, and 'baking' was done on an iron girdle hung over a peat fire on a little crane which regulated the girdle's height. Scones are made from a milky, flour dough (originally barley flour), shortened by rubbing in fat with the finger-tips, and raised with baking powder, or preferably with soda and buttermilk (*see* Raising Agents). Girdle scones are shaped into round, flat cakes or bannocks, floured, and cut into quarters; then they are baked one side, turned with a knife, and baked on the other. Oatcakes contain oatmeal, melted fat, and water, and the quarters, or 'farls', are very thin and merely crisped on the girdle. Scotch pancakes or drop scones, known in Australia and New Zealand

COOKING SCOTCH PANCAKES ON A GIRDLE

as pikelets, are made by dropping spoonfuls of a raised, sweetened egg-batter on to a hot, greased girdle, and turning them when the top surface bubbles but before it has time to dry; they should be velvety on both sides. A large, thin version, bubbly on one side like an English crumpet, is sold in Scotland under the name of crumpet—but, of course, an English crumpet is made from bread batter. American girdle cakes may be made from wholemeal flour, maize meal, boiled rice, or buckwheat; they are served hot at breakfast with butter and maple syrup.

Oven scones are floured lightly and baked in a very hot oven, but not turned; in America they are known as baking-powder biscuits or hot biscuits and are varied most appetizingly with cheese, minced ham, pecan nuts, or marmalade. Apple scones and date scones seem to be New Zealand inventions.

American muffins and New Zealand gems, made of egg-batter raised with baking powder, are oven-baked in hissing-hot iron gem pans. Popovers rise astonishingly high in gem pans or hot fire-proof cups; the batter is raised by air and steam—like Yorkshire Pudding. Waffles are baked in closed gridded waffle irons, using a light, baking-powder batter. They are eaten hot with butter and syrup.

Quick breads, that is, breads raised not with yeast but with soda or baking powder, include soda bread, nut loaves, and American corn breads or Johnny cakes. They are similar to scone mixtures and not unlike plain luncheon and rock cake which contains little fat, and that

VARIOUS KINDS OF SCONE
In the centre is a bannock cut into 'farls'

melted or rubbed in rather than creamed (*see* CAKES).

On the Continent flour cookery is based on YEAST (q.v. Vol. II) and not on the baking-powder type of raising agents, and tea—the meal at which scones are usually eaten in Britain and the Dominions—does not exist. But many countries, though they do not make scones, make similar small yeast rolls and breads. Yeast breads include not only English buns, muffins, tea-cakes, and crumpets (called 'pikelets' in the north of England), and Scotch baps and cookies, but also French croissants and brioches, Swedish coffee breads, and American doughnuts and crullers. All of these are oven-baked and are eaten split with butter, except for doughnuts and crullers, which are fried in deep fat. In India many unleavened quick breads are eaten: *chupatties*, from whole-wheat or rice flour, are baked on a kind of girdle and are comparable with oatcakes; *parattas* are Deccan wheaten cakes, fried in a pan with oil or *ghee*.

See also RAISING AGENTS; BAKING.
See also Vol. VII: BAKING INDUSTRY.

SENSES, *see* EAR STRUCTURE; NOSE STRUCTURE; EYE STRUCTURE; SKIN. *See also* Vol. II: SENSES.

SEWING. This is the technique of stitching, together with the correct handling of different fabrics, and the methods of assembling and finishing garments (*see* DRESSMAKING). Fabrics are also decorated by stitching (*see* NEEDLEWORK, DECORATIVE).

1. EQUIPMENT. Various-sized needles and types of thread are needed according to the fabric: silk thread is best for silks and linens, cotton thread for cottons, mercerized thread for mixed fabrics, nylon thread for nylon fabric. No. 100–120 thread and No. 10 needles are most suitable for fine material; No. 50–80 thread and Nos. 7–8 needles for medium cotton and mixed materials; and No. 40–60 mercerized thread and Nos. 5–6 needles for heavy cottons and woollens. The work may be done by hand or with a SEWING MACHINE (q.v.). Large scissors or shears are used for cutting out, small, sharp-pointed scissors for unpicking and snipping into corners. A tape-measure with metal ends, a thimble, a 3-foot ruler, tailor's chalk, a stiletto, dressmaker's steel pins, and lillikins (small pins) for fine fabrics are all part of the equipment needed for sewing. In addition, a table for cutting out, an iron and a skirt- and sleeve-board for pressing, and a full-length mirror for trying on are all needed.

2. STITCHES. All stitching is begun and ended with a back stitch into the material. Different stitches are used for different purposes (Fig. 1). Straight tacking, to hold seams together temporarily before stitching, consists of long and short stitches alternately through both pieces of fabric. 'Tailor's tacking', which marks fitting lines through two layers of material, is made with small stitches in double thread, leaving loops on the top. When the layers are pulled apart and the loops cut, short ends remain in each piece of fabric to mark the lines. 'Running', for joining seams, consists of even stitches in and out of the two pieces of fabric. 'Back stitching', which is stronger, is also used for seams. 'Hemming' is used for sewing down edges. 'Slip stitch', for hems or seams, is invisible on the right side but less strong than hemming. 'Herringbone' is used for hems and seams, in particular in locknit garments and to neaten the raw edges of non-fraying fabrics. 'Overcasting', or neatening raw edges, consists of sloping stitches worked from left to right over the edges. 'Oversewing' is similar but worked from right to left, with smaller and closer stitches, and is used for joining two edges together. 'Whipping', not unlike oversewing, is used as a hem edge on very fine fabrics, such as muslins, or for

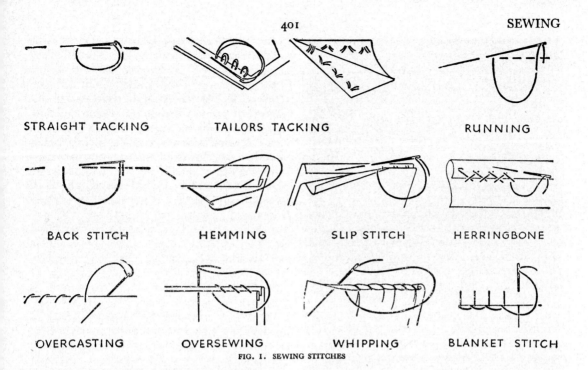

STRAIGHT TACKING   TAILORS TACKING   RUNNING

BACK STITCH   HEMMING   SLIP STITCH   HERRINGBONE

OVERCASTING   OVERSEWING   WHIPPING   BLANKET STITCH

FIG. 1. SEWING STITCHES

applying lace neatly. 'Shell edging' is used for narrow hems on fine material. 'Blanket or loop stitch' neatens raw edges or covers scalloped edges; the stitches may be close together or widely spaced.

3. SEAMS. A garment is put together with seams, the type depending on the garment and the fabric. Lingerie and sheer fabrics are hand-sewn, while heavier ones are machine-stitched. Each seam is tacked before sewing, and the tacking-threads later removed and the seam pressed. The amount of material allowed for the seam depends on the fabric and on the method of seam finishing. A 'flat seam' (Fig. 2) joins two pieces of material with running stitch, back stitch, or machine stitching. The raw edges of the turnings are overcast, or, with thin fabric, turned under once and stitched, or, with non-fraying material, pinked with pinking shears. A 'French seam' (Fig. 2), used for fine fabrics on garments which will be constantly washed, is first stitched on the right side, then, the edges having been trimmed and pressed, the seam is turned to the wrong side, tacked, and stitched again below the first turning. A 'run and fell seam' (Fig. 2) is a strong, flat seam suitable for babies' clothes, shirts, and lingerie. A flat seam is made on the wrong side of the garment; both turnings are pressed to the back, and the under

one cut away very narrow; then the edge of the top one is turned under, pressed, and hemmed flat to the garment. A 'lapped seam' (Fig. 2) is made when one piece of fabric is laid over the other, as for a yoke. The edge of the overlapping piece is turned under on the fitting line, placed over the other piece so that the raw edges and fitting lines correspond, and then stitched down

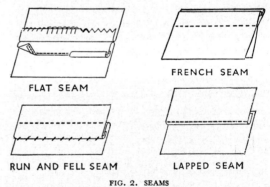

FLAT SEAM   FRENCH SEAM

RUN AND FELL SEAM   LAPPED SEAM

FIG. 2. SEAMS

The flat seam shows different methods of finishing the edges

close to the fold. The raw edges are overcast and, if the seam is curved, they are notched at intervals to make them lie flat.

4. SHAPING DEVICES. (a) *Darts* (Fig. 3a) are used on most garments, chiefly to give a better fit, but sometimes for decoration only; they may be tapered at one or both ends.

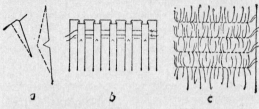

FIG. 3. *a.* DARTS. *b.* GATHERS. *c.* SHIRRING

(*b*) *Gathers* (Fig. 3*b*) are used to give fullness, usually in fine material, the material being cut one and a half times the finished width. To make the gathers flat two or three rows of even running stitches are made, one on the fitting line. The threads are pulled up to the correct length, fastened off, and the gathers stroked into pleats with a pin. They are set into a band with a lapped seam or with a flat seam. Shirring (Fig. 3*c*) is a decoration in which several rows of gathers are spaced below each other at equal intervals; if the stitches in each row are placed exactly under each other so that tubular pleats are formed, the gathers are said to be gauged.

(*c*) *Pleats* may be used on all kinds of fabric to give fullness. They may be pressed or unpressed, stitched flat or slightly raised, and hand- or machine-pleated. Fabric three times the width of the finished pleating is required. The chief types of hand-pleating are box pleats, inverted pleats, and knife pleats (Fig. 4). Box pleats are flat and wide on the right side and make inverted pleats on the wrong side, so that a skirt of box pleats has inverted and box pleats alternately, and each fold meets the next. Knife pleats are folded like box pleats but lie the same way all round. A full pleated skirt is fitted at the hips, with the pleats overlapping at the

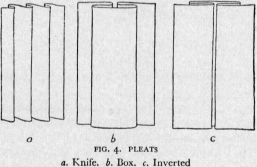

FIG. 4. PLEATS

a. Knife. *b.* Box. *c.* Inverted

waist, the surplus material being cut away inside, and the raw edges bound.

(*d*) *Tucks* (Fig. 5) serve not only a decorative but also a practical purpose on children's clothes, for they may be let out as the child grows. They are measured with a cardboard gauge and sewn on the right side of the garment. Pin tucks, which are very small and placed close together, are effective on thin fabrics for blouses and lingerie.

(*e*) *Frills* may be cut on the straight or on the cross, the latter giving a more fluted appearance.

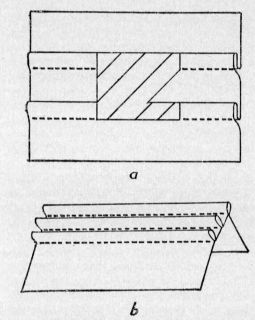

FIG. 5. *a.* TUCKS WITH MEASURING GAUGE. *b.* PIN TUCKS

The material should be one and a half times to twice the finished length, and the right depth plus turnings. The bottom edge is hemmed or bound, the top edge gathered twice, and the frill drawn up to the required length and stitched in place, as for gathers. A top-sewn frill is hemmed on both edges, then gathered, and sewn in place with small running stitches over the gathering thread.

5. FINISHING EDGES. (*a*) *Hemlines* (Fig. 6) are finished according to their shape and the fabric used. For a straight skirt of heavy fabric, the hem is turned up once and either herringboned over the raw edge or bound with Paris binding or straight tape; for a similar shape in thinner fabric, the edge is turned in twice, and hemmed or slip-stitched; hems in very fine material may

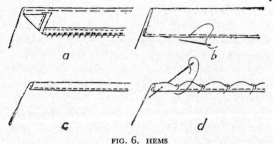

FIG. 6. HEMS

a. Finished with bias binding. *b.* The fabric turned in and slip-stitched. *c.* Narrow hem. *d.* Shell edging

be secured with small running stitches or shell edging. Shaped hems may be faced with self or contrasting material which has been cut on the cross to match exactly the grain of the skirt. A circular hem must have the fullness distributed evenly, on very fine fabrics by gathering, on medium ones by pleating, and on heavy woollens by shrinking. When the top edge of the hem is flat it is covered with bias binding (or net on transparent material), and the lower edge is sewn to the hem, the upper to the garment.

(*b*) *Binding* (Fig. 7*a*), either double or single, is used to cover raw edges. It may be bought, or cut in fabric on the straight for straight edges only or on the exact cross grain. Single binding is cut twice the finished width plus turnings, double binding four times the width. The binding is sewn by machine or back stitched.

(*c*) *Piping* (Fig. 7*b*) is purely decorative. It may be plain or corded, the latter being padded with piping cord which can be obtained in various thicknesses. If cord is used, it is shrunk, then covered with crossway binding, fitted under a lapped seam, and either stitched by hand on the fold or machined close to the edge with a special

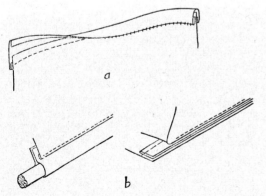

FIG. 7. *a.* BINDING. *b.* PIPING AN EDGE WITH CORDED AND FLAT PIPING

attachment called the cording foot which allows room for the thickness of the cord. A flat piping strip may be inserted into an ordinary seam; the crossway strip is tacked to one edge on the fitting line and the other edge is stitched over it.

See also DRESSMAKING; TAILORING; NEEDLEWORK, DECORATIVE; EMBROIDERY, ENGLISH; EMBROIDERY, WORLD; SEWING MACHINE; MENDING.

SEWING MACHINE. GANDHI (q.v. Vol. V), who learned in prison to use a sewing machine, said 'it is one of the few useful things ever invented', and exempted it from his ban on Western machinery.

The earliest patents for mechanical sewing devices were taken out in England, the first, in 1755, by Charles Weisenthal who devised a double-pointed needle with an eye in the middle, working horizontally. We do not know much about the fate of this invention except that twenty double-ended needles of the Weisenthal type were used in Alsace in 1828 in the first successful mechanical embroidery frame. The second machine, in 1790, by Thomas Saint, a London cabinet-maker, was intended for leather work. The holes were first pierced by a vertically descending awl; then thread was laid over each hole, and a loop of it pushed through by a descending fork-shaped needle. This loop was caught underneath by a hook, and the work moved on one stitch. A second loop through the next hole was formed within the first loop, the first loop being then slipped off the hook, thus making a chain stitch on the underside (Fig. 1). Had Saint thought of combining hole-piercing with sewing by using a sharp needle with an eye in its point instead of his awl and fork, he would have completely anticipated the modern chain-stitch machine. A model constructed from his drawings is in the Science Museum in London.

Nearly 30 years later the problem was again seriously tackled, this time in France by Barthelemy Thimonnier, a tailor of St. Etienne who, although handicapped by poverty and lack of mechanical knowledge, succeeded in 1829 in constructing a machine, mostly of wood, with a needle like a crochet hook which made a chain stitch, presumably on the upper surface of the cloth. Two years later eighty of his improved machines were working in Paris on uniforms for French soldiers. But the garment workers feared that Thimonnier's invention would threaten their livelihood and, in the troubles of 1831, his

SAINT'S SEWING MACHINE, 1790

machines were smashed by angry crowds, and he himself was nearly murdered.

Back in St. Etienne Thimonnier continued to struggle against prejudice and poverty, improving his machine until it would sew at 200 stitches per minute (a good modern speed is 4,000 stitches per minute). But the blind anger of unemployed men in the Revolution of 1848 again wrecked his prospects, and though one of his machines was shown at the Great Exhibition of 1851 in London, nobody seems to have taken it seriously, and Thimonnier died in 1857, disappointed and exhausted.

Meanwhile independent inventive efforts were being made in the U.S.A., where finally, after many false starts and many squabbles over patent-rights, sewing machines were developed and successfully marketed.

The credit for the first lock-stitch machine

HOWE'S LOCK-STITCH SEWING MACHINE

(Fig. 1) belongs to Walter Hunt of New York, although he did not try to patent his invention until too late, and others reaped the benefits. He used an eye-pointed needle which carried a loop of thread through the cloth. A shuttle working to and fro under the cloth passed a second thread through the loop, thus locking it. The needle was curved and worked horizontally. The first patent for a lock-stitch machine was obtained in 1846 by Elias Howe, of Massachusetts. The two important features of his machine were the curved eye-pointed needle and the under-thread shuttle, and both these were essentially Hunt's ideas of 14 years earlier.

While Howe was in England trying to adapt his machine for corset-making, various other people in the U.S.A. had been making sewing machines, chief of whom was Isaac Singer (1811–75) who had come to New York with his parents as an immigrant, probably from Germany. He used a straight, eye-pointed needle and made it work up and down. He took out his first patent for this improved lock-stitch machine in 1851. His subsequent success was due not only to the worth of the machine itself but to the astuteness of Edward Clark, a lawyer and subsequent member of his firm, who fought his patent battles against Howe and pioneered selling by HIRE-PURCHASE (q.v.). Other American contemporaries of Singer designed types of sewing machine still in common use.

Modern lock-stitch machines (Fig. 2) are used in homes in every country of the world. They work by a hand wheel, by treadle, or electrically with foot or knee control. Attachments for turning in hems, for tucking, frilling, piping, darning, and so on make it easy to perform on the machine sewing operations which are laborious and less efficient when done by hand. New developments include the tubular bed, on to which can be slipped a sock for darning, a cuff for stitching, or an awkward shaped patching area, such as a trouser seat or leg; and the swing needle, which can sew in a simple zigzag stitch for covering raw edges or for carrying out a variety of decorative stitches composed of zigzags of different lengths and amplitudes. Furthermore, two needles can be fitted into the needle bar and used simultaneously with different coloured threads. Some modern machines are made of very light and portable materials. Many elaborate industrial machines are now in use (*see* CLOTHING INDUSTRY, Vol. VII), some of

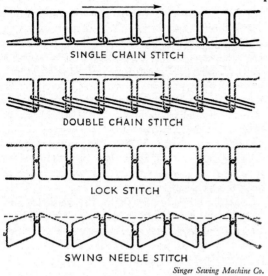

SINGLE CHAIN STITCH

DOUBLE CHAIN STITCH

LOCK STITCH

SWING NEEDLE STITCH

Singer Sewing Machine Co.

FIG. I. DIAGRAMS OF STITCHES
The arrows show the direction of stitching

which can work at the rate of 20,000 stitches per minute.

Embroidery is done mainly on chain-stitch machines, especially in India for decorating Numdah rugs and Jaipur hangings. It is also possible to produce very charming decorative work on the domestic lock-stitch machine. Simple border patterns can be traced on to towel ends or dress hems and carefully followed with plain machine stitch at normal tension in contrasting colours. By using a heavy thread, such as buttonhole twist or metal thread, in the bobbin, loosening the under tension, and working from the wrong side of the material, a kind of beaded thread or cable stitch can be produced.

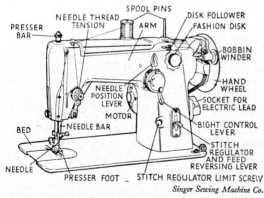

SPOOL PINS

NEEDLE THREAD TENSION

DISK FOLLOWER

PRESSER BAR

ARM

FASHION DISK

BOBBIN WINDER

HAND WHEEL

NEEDLE POSITION LEVER

SOCKET FOR ELECTRIC LEAD

MOTOR

BED

BIGHT CONTROL LEVER

NEEDLE BAR

STITCH REGULATOR AND FEED REVERSING LEVER

NEEDLE

PRESSER FOOT

STITCH REGULATOR LIMIT SCREW

Singer Sewing Machine Co.

FIG. 2. SWING-NEEDLE LOCK-STITCH SEWING MACHINE
Different stitches are produced by changing the 'fashion disk'. The 'bight' is the sideways swing of the needle

Different tension adjustments and lengths of stitch give a variety of effects suitable for stitching simple designs. 'Free embroidery', which is more intricate, is done like darning; the presser foot of the machine is removed, and the material, held taut in embroidery hoops, is guided to and fro until all the outlines of the design have been steered under the needle as it chops up and down. Embroidery can also be done very effectively with a swing-needle machine.

See also SEWING; DRESSMAKING.

SHELLFISH. The better known shellfish, the MOLLUSCS (q.v. Vol. II) of northern waters, are the clams, scallops, oysters, cockles, mussels, whelks, and winkles. Clams, large bi-valve molluscs found on American coasts, are prepared chiefly as chowder (*see* SOUPS). 'Native' oysters from the famous English beds of Whitstable and Colchester are too expensive and too good to eat any other way than raw; but elsewhere in the world—Chesapeake Bay and Long Island (where Blue Point oysters come from) in America, Portugal, and Bluff in New Zealand—oysters are often cooked and made into 'angels on horseback' (*see* SAVOURIES), oyster soup, pies, and fritters. SCALLOPS (q.v. Vol. II) are cooked and served in their shells, creamed or with mayonnaise. A set of scallop shells is useful for serving other foods 'scalloped'. Mussels, rather neglected in Britain, need careful washing and then, after being steamed for 5 minutes in ½ inch of water with chopped parsley and garlic, they are drained and served either plain on the shells with brown bread and butter, or as a scalloped dish with sauce made from the liquid. Cockles, whelks, and winkles are usually washed, boiled for 20 minutes, extracted with a long pin, and eaten with vinegar; they form part of many Mediterranean 'sea fruit' dishes. All of these, and razor shellfish, make good soup when simmered in a thin white sauce. On parts of the French coast acorn barnacles are used for food. Baby squids appear in an Italian mixed fish grill, and slices of octopus tentacle are offered at a South Sea Island feast. Snails should be washed in brine and cooked in bouillon (*see* SOUPS). They can be served in their shells, packed with garlic and parsley butter (*à la Bourguignonne*), or fried, or in a red wine sauce. Abalone steaks are thin slices from the muscular foot of a large, one-shelled mollusc living off the

PREPARING A LOBSTER

Top: slitting it open. *Centre*: removing the inedible parts.
Bottom: breaking the claws

Californian coast. If pounded until tender, and grilled or fried in egg and crumb, their taste and texture resemble those of a very fine escalope of veal. Molluscs of the same genus, Ormers or sea ears, are eaten in the Channel Islands.

The main CRUSTACEANS (q.v. Vol. II) are lobster (French, *homard*), crayfish, crawfish (French, *langouste*), prawns, shrimps, and crabs. They have all to be dug out of their external skeletons after having been boiled. They can then be eaten cold with mayonnaise or hot with various delicious SAUCES (q.v.), such as à l'Americaine, Thermidor, or Newburg. There are no lobsters in southern hemisphere waters but sea crayfish instead. Soft-shelled crabs are American delicacies; so are oyster crabs—baby crabs found in some New England oysters and eaten whole. Scampi are large Italian prawns fried in oil; Mediterranean cooking makes a great feature of crustacea generally.

'Sea foods' include, besides the molluscs and crustaceans, the edible SEA URCHIN (q.v. Vol. II) and the Bêche de Mer (sea spade)—a sea SLUG (q.v. Vol. II) living in the Timor Sea and prized by the Chinese for soup.

See also Vol. II: CRUSTACEANS; MOLLUSCS.
See also Vol. VI: OCTOPUS, CUTTLEFISH, AND SQUID FISHING; SHRIMPING AND PRAWNING.

SHINGLES, *see* INFECTIOUS DISEASES, Section 7.

SHOES, *see* BOOTS AND SHOES.

SIDEBOARD, *see* CHESTS AND CUPBOARDS.

SINUS, *see* NOSE STRUCTURE.

SKIN. The body makes contact with the outside world through the skin, which has, therefore, the double function of protecting the body from harm and acting as a sense organ providing it with information about changes of temperature, touch, and the presence of harmful objects producing pain. A sensitive skin is thus far more valuable than an insensitive plate of armour like that of the lobster. In man the skin, in addition, plays an important part in regulating the balance of the body fluids and controlling heat loss. For these reasons it has a rich supply of both nerves and blood-vessels.

A microscopic section of human skin (Fig. 1) shows two layers, an 'epidermis' at the surface, below which is the 'dermis', or true skin. This is divided into an upper layer of conical projections, or 'papillae', and a deeper layer containing a network of nerves and blood-vessels.

The epidermis consists of layers of cells. The flattened cells on the surface begin to die, gradually becoming horny flakes and being

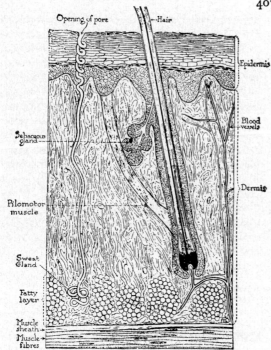

FIG. 1. SECTION OF SKIN AS SEEN UNDER THE MICROSCOPE
From Logan Clendening, *The Human Body*, Alfred Knopf

shed. At the same time new cells are being produced underneath. The upper cells accumulate pigment in the form of small granules in their substance, and in the case of a coloured person's skin the pigment is formed in the lower cells as well.

The dermis is rich in elastic tissue fibres which give the healthy skin its characteristic suppleness. With age, elastic fibres all over the body are gradually replaced by inelastic fibrous tissues which tend to draw the skin into folds, the wrinkles of old age.

Scattered all over the body, except on the palms of the hands and the soles of the feet, are hairs, each lodged in a pit or follicle which penetrates deep into the dermis (*see* HAIR, Vol. II). In older people the pigment of hair gradually disappears and is replaced by colourless vacuoles (pockets of fluid), which reflect light in the same way as the crest of a wave does, so producing the appearance of white hair.

Many kinds of bacteria have their natural home in skin and will invade it through any weak spot, such as an unhealthy hair follicle. Slight injury, from a chafing collar for instance, may give the opportunity for bacteria called

staphylococci to enter. Here they multiply rapidly, killing the cells of the hair sheath and spreading into the surrounding tissue, so forming an abscess called a boil. Other bacteria interfere with the glands which form the natural hair oil, so that the hair, lacking its oil, loses its gloss, becomes dry, and falls out, and the skin forms scales which flake off, making scurf or dandruff. The skin may be invaded by animal or vegetable parasites, as in ringworm or scabies; but there are now effective preparations to destroy them.

The sweat glands of the skin consist of coiled tubes which penetrate into the dermis, opening on the surface by short straight ducts. They occur all over the skin but are most plentiful in the arm-pits, groins, palms of hands, and soles of feet. On the fingertips these glands open at the top in fine curved ridges, arranged in patterns which are peculiar to each person—the FINGERPRINTS (q.v. Vol. X). Three main patterns are known: arches, loops, and whorls. Sweat glands are of great importance because they help to regulate the temperature of the body by pouring out sweat; this, by evaporating, takes heat from the skin beneath. In this process the rich blood supply of the dermis plays an important part. The blood-vessels of the dermis expand, whereby hot blood from below is brought to the surface to be cooled by the evaporation of the sweat. This is the reason for the flushed, red skin of a hot person. When this occurs all over the body, a large part of all the blood in the body is cooled very quickly, and the deep organs as well as the skin get cooler. In cold conditions the skin vessels contract, giving the cold person a pale skin; the sweat glands cease working, so the skin is dry; and heat loss is reduced to a minimum. In still colder conditions, the smallest blood-vessels, the skin capillaries, may be paralysed so that the blood stagnates in them, losing its oxygen; the red haemoglobin changes colour to a purple hue, and the skin becomes 'blue with cold'. Chilblains, which

FIG. 2. FINGERPRINTS
Left, arch; *centre*, loop; *right*, whorl

we associate with cold hands and feet and which result in painful itching and eruptions of the skin, are caused by a sluggish circulation, and can be provoked by exposure to cold. But why some people are more susceptible to chilblains than others is not fully understood.

The horny layer of the epidermis is modified at the ends of the fingers and toes into growing plates which we call nails (*see* NAILS AND CLAWS, Vol. II). Since they are transparent, the blood underneath gives them their pink colour. The nail at its base is embedded in deep layers of skin where the nail cells reproduce themselves, pushing the dead transparent ones towards the edge of the finger so that the nail becomes 'long'. The growing cells which have not yet become transparent form the white 'half moon' at the base of the nail. A whole new nail is made in about 6 weeks, the rate of growth depending somewhat on the general state of health and the local blood-supply. Patients suffering from chest diseases may produce a rounded shape to the nail, known as 'clubbing', and in some types of anaemia the nail becomes spoon-shaped and very brittle.

Should the cells of the horny outer layer of skin fail to rub off and shed in the normal way because local pressure is stimulating continued growth, a small plug of scales, a 'corn', is formed, and this presses into the sensitive skin layers beneath. Under very severe rubbing the skin just under the horny cell layer may break, and a pocket of watery fluid form. This is a blister. If the injury has been severe enough, as, for example, when one hits one's finger with a hammer, the lowest cell layer and the blood-vessels beneath may be broken, and a blood blister results. Warts are formed by an overgrowth of skin cells, but they do not usually last very long.

Most of the rashes which appear with such diseases as measles and scarlet fever (*see* INFECTIOUS DISEASES) are due to poisonous substances reaching the blood-vessels of the skin; these cause small patches of inflammation which raise the epidermis above them into red 'spots' very variable in size, shape, and number, but usually characteristic of the particular disease. Rashes after eating such foods as lobsters and oysters are caused in the same way. They are sometimes called 'nettle rash' because a nettle sting has a similar effect; it penetrates the epidermis, injecting its little dose of formic acid around the blood-vessels beneath; this makes them release fluid, so raising an irritating weal.

The skin is rich in special little organs designed to detect touch; these are connected to nerve-endings and are most plentiful just under the epidermis. Other nerve-endings which convey the sense of pain are also widely distributed. Itching is closely associated with pain; often, after the pain of a sting has subsided, there is a period of intense skin irritation, and many skin diseases are complicated by injury due to scratching. Rubbing and scratching may result in eczema, but this is also often caused by internal disturbance. The sensation of 'tickle', on the other hand, is a matter of touch, not of pain, some areas of skin such as the soles of the feet being much more sensitive than others.

See also SKIN, CARE OF; MANICURE AND PEDICURE; ALLERGIC DISEASES.

See also Vol. II: SKIN; HAIR; NAILS AND CLAWS.

SKIN, CARE OF. The SKIN (q.v.) not only serves to regulate the body's temperature, but acts as a protective covering. It is at once extremely resistant and extremely sensitive. It is essential to keep the outer surface scrupulously clean by bathing the whole body in warm water with soap and drying it with a reasonably brisk friction. The natural process of the shedding of the old skin cells and the renewal of fresh ones is thus stimulated, and the skin is kept free from dirt and sweat. Over the entire surface of the body there are sweat pores or openings of the sebaceous glands which continually give off unwanted fluid and acids from the body. We lose, in fact, several pints of moisture through our skin every day, but, as it evaporates quickly in most areas, we are unconscious of the continued process. It may be helpful, however, to use deodorants, either liquid or cream, under the arms to protect clothing as well as to prevent odour.

The skins of people who are used to an open-air life and who regularly work out-of-doors are conditioned to exposure and suffer little damage from it. But people who normally work indoors, particularly people of fair complexion, need a soothing cream on their skin to serve as a protection if they are going to spend long days out-of-doors in intense sunlight or in stringent weather conditions. Members of the Everest expedition in 1953 took cosmetics with them for just this

THE WAY TO MASSAGE CREAM INTO THE FACE

purpose. Too sudden an exposure of the skin to the sun, in sun-bathing, for example, will damage the skin tissue and subject it to too great a shock. A bad sun-burn makes the outer surface of the skin blister, and is extremely painful. Chapped skin, whether on the face, hands, or the back of the heels, needs attention to avoid cracks through which infection can enter. In intensely cold or windy weather, it is wise to apply softening creams to the exposed skin as a safeguard. Cracks should be covered with an antiseptic dressing containing one of the medicated liquid sealing products, which form a plastic film over the wound, yet do not impede movement.

Pimples or spots tend to be an embarrassment to both girls and boys in their teens. They occur at this period of development largely because the metabolism of the body is changing from its youthful to its mature pattern. Although they are no cause for anxiety, measures can be taken to help them to clear up. The skin should be washed frequently, with gentle but firm friction to remove blackheads. If the blackheads persist, the affected area should be steamed over a bowl of hot water and then massaged with a face cream with little circular movements. If this treatment is repeated regularly and patiently it should free the underskin of the deposits of sebum (fatty secretion) which cause the blackheads; but if some of the blackheads still do not yield, they can be pressed out between the two first fingers which should be covered with antiseptic gauze, care being taken not to damage the surrounding skin. The core of a blackhead or pimple must be removed once it has been tackled or it will become inflamed and be even more unsightly. Once it is out, the

application of some soothing lotion such as witch hazel will close the pores.

Some types of dandruff can be a source of infection for pimples; the shoulders should therefore be covered when the hair is being brushed and combed so that nothing can fall on to the skin which might create trouble (*see* HAIR, CARE OF).

As pimples are often due to internal disorder, a healthy diet with plenty of fresh fruit, salads, and brown bread, enough out-of-door exercise, and plenty of sleep in a well-ventilated room all help to keep a healthy skin. If skin troubles still persist, a doctor should be consulted, as skilled attention may be needed to prevent severe scarring.

Girls who want a skin that is not only healthy and unblemished, but also fine and soft in texture, should use cleansing cream as well as soap and water. The oils of the cream penetrate deep into the pores, and the massage needed to apply the cream ensures that the skin receives beneficial added stimulation. The nightly application, with special soothing massage, of rich types of cream containing both animal and mineral oils is very helpful, particularly to women over 25, when the growth of skin cells is slowed down and the supply of natural oils and moisture diminished. Open pores and general skin coarseness can be lessened if toning and astringent lotions, usually containing cooling herbal solutions, are patted briskly on to the face and neck.

See also SKIN.
See also Vol. II: SKIN (Animal).

SLEEP. The capacity for sleep is very general among living organisms. Most animals have it, although it is not certain whether very lowly animals, such as worms and snails, ever really sleep. Many insects show a marked difference between their day-time and night-time levels of activity: butterflies, for instance, are active only during the hours of daylight and remain hidden and quiescent at night; moths, on the other hand, appear to be 'awake' only after dark. Fishes are much less active in the absence of light, and it is quite probable that they 'sleep' when undisturbed. Birds, too, are active only during hours of light (though owls and a few other night-flying species are exceptions). The time that birds spend asleep is closely related to the length of the night, so that most birds sleep for much shorter periods in summer than in winter, and also tend to awaken earlier on a bright morning than on a dull one. These findings have led scientists to suppose that the duration of sleep in birds is governed by two factors—by the actual brightness of the light to which the bird is exposed, and by seasonal changes in its body chemistry. Not much is known about sleep in the lower animals, but it is probably due to nervous processes similar to those which govern it in the higher animals and man.

The pattern of sleep and wakefulness in the mammals is closely related to their general habits of life and to the importance of their different SENSES (q.v. Vol. II). Animals such as squirrels, dogs, and monkeys, which depend principally upon vision for their food, shelter, and defence, are 'diurnal'—that is, they are for the most part active during the day and sleep at night. But animals such as bats and hedgehogs, that depend mainly on hearing and scent for maintaining themselves, are 'nocturnal'—that is, they are active principally by night and tend to sleep during the day. Some mammals, however, such as lions, horses, and sheep, do not show any clear-cut rhythm in their activities and may sleep at any time, probably because they depend about equally on the senses of sight, hearing, and smell, and the need for a regular 'sleep rhythm' consequently does not arise.

Man is, of course, a diurnal animal, and in the conduct of his life he depends on vision to an overwhelming extent. It is, therefore, not surprising that his sleep habits resemble those of the higher animals, in particular of the apes, to which he is most closely related (see EVOLUTION, Vol. II). The human 'sleep rhythm' is not already established at birth, but is built up gradually during the earliest years of life. The new-born baby spends no less than 90% of his time either dozing or asleep, and his periods of sleep are much more closely related to feeding times than to the alternation of night and day. By his first birthday he sleeps only 50% of the time, and he tends already to sleep more at night than during the day-time. This tendency increases further during the next year of life, and it is probable that both natural growth and regular routine contribute to its establishment. By the age of 3 or 4, indeed, a regular diurnal 'sleep rhythm' is fully established in most children.

The amount of sleep which a person needs to maintain himself in full health has never been ascertained with certainty, and appears to vary considerably with age, with the individual, and even with race. It is generally held that pre-school children need between 10 and 12 hours sleep at night, school children between 9 and 11 hours, and adults between 7 and 9 hours. Adults, however, probably need progressively less sleep as they grow older, and exceptional cases are even known of elderly people who have remained healthy for many years on as little as 2 or 3 hours sleep per night. There is some evidence that the sleep-needs of different peoples differ to some extent; for example, Japanese—both children and adults—are reliably said to sleep less than Europeans. It is uncertain, however, whether this difference is really due to race or to habit. While it is doubtful exactly how much sleep is needed to maintain full health, it is wise to remember the words of a distinguished physiologist, Sir Charles Sherrington, that 'without plenty of sleep the activity of a working-day is like a house built on sand'.

Sleep is generally held to vary not only in duration but in depth. We distinguish between light and heavy sleepers by whether or not they are hard to wake up. Moreover, a man's sleep tends to vary in depth in the course of a single night. Experiments have been carried out to measure its depth by determining how loud a sound is just sufficient to waken the sleeper at different times of the night. The results show that, although the depth of sleep fluctuates considerably right through the night, these fluctuations tend to become smaller, and the general level of sleep lighter, as the night proceeds. It has also been shown that many individuals may awaken sufficiently during the night to carry out a prescribed action, such as pressing a bell, though they have no memory of doing so when they wake in the morning. In general, these experiments bear out the common belief that sleep is deepest in the first few hours of the night.

Inability to sleep is known as insomnia. It is common among older people, especially when they are worried, and it may give rise to considerable fatigue and distress. The doctor usually prescribes hypnotic (that is, sleep-producing) DRUGS (q.v.), and attempts to relieve anxiety and worry. Excessive sleep also occurs, usually as a result of certain nervous diseases. From the study of such diseases (see NERVOUS SYSTEM), doctors have been led to the view that sleep depends on the activity of a small and primitive

Anderson

THE DREAM OF ST. URSULA. PAINTING BY V. CARPACCIO (ACTIVE 1486–1525)

part of the BRAIN (q.v.) known as the 'sleep centre'. If this area of the brain in a dog or cat is artificially stimulated by an electric current, sleep immediately results. It is therefore probable that the normal 'sleep rhythm' in animals and man is governed by a kind of 'nervous clock' situated in the brain.

It is not known for certain whether mental activity (other than dreaming) can take place when one is asleep. It is certainly true that some people can awaken themselves at will at particu-lar times, and this power has sometimes been ascribed to a subconscious time sense which con-tinues to operate during sleep. Stories are also told of mathematicians who have gone to sleep while trying to solve a difficult problem and have awakened to find themselves in possession of the solution. These stories have not, however, been fully confirmed and should be accepted with a grain of salt. On general grounds, it is entirely possible that mental activity may persist to some extent; but the claim that prodigious feats of intelligence may be accomplished during sleep should be dismissed as wholly fanciful.

See also DREAMS.
See also Vol. II: HIBERNATION.

SLEEPING SICKNESS, *see* TROPICAL DISEASES, Section 5.

SMALLPOX, *see* EPIDEMIC DISEASES, Section 3.

SMOCKING, *see* NEEDLEWORK, DECORATIVE.

SMOKING. The Spaniards were the earliest Europeans to sample TOBACCO (q.v. Vol. VI). Accounts of Columbus's first voyage in 1492 speak of the natives of Cuba using 'smoking reeds', which were a kind of primitive pipe. Most of the Indian races of the American mainland were given to smoking, partly purely for pleasure, but partly, also, for ceremonial purposes—as with the celebrated Red Indian 'pipe of peace'. Cortés's men in Mexico found that the Emperor Montezuma was served with a ritual pipe, filled with specially scented tobacco, which he smoked after his state banquets, while dancers performed before him (*see* AZTEC CIVILIZATION, Vol. I).

Once introduced to Europe, the habit of smoking spread rapidly round the world. Barely 50 years after its discovery Portuguese sailors introduced smoking into the East Indies and Japan. When tobacco first reached England is uncertain, but it seems likely that small quantities were imported in the earlier half of the 16th century, many years before the name of Sir Walter RALEIGH (q.v. Vol. V) became associated with it. In Elizabethan and Jacobean times there were two distinct schools of thought about smoking. Some learned men (such as Thomas Marriot, the official geographer to the expedition sent to Virginia by Raleigh) maintained that it had a medical value, that it 'purged excessive humours' and acted as a disinfectant. Others regarded smoking as a badge of immorality, believing that it went with free-thinking and loose-living; indeed, when Christopher Marlowe was arraigned before the Privy Council, tobacco-addiction was listed as one of his 'vices'. King James I held strong views on the subject; he not only wrote a violent pamphlet, *Counter-Blast to Tobacco*, but also imposed heavy duties on imported tobacco. But the tobacco plant was naturalized in southern England and Ireland by Raleigh and other pioneers. At one time in the 17th century there were as many as 6,000 plantations, and from these the needs of the increasing numbers of English smokers were supplied. This home-grown tobacco industry was later

A SMOKER, 1623

stamped out by government authorities in order to safeguard the revenue drawn from import duties; and, by the reign of Charles II, Virginia and other American colonies had become the chief sources of supply.

During its first century in England, tobacco was smoked in short clay pipes. Snuff, however, was introduced from France in the reign of Charles II, and throughout the 18th century it was considered to be the most polite form in which to take tobacco. The long-stemmed pipes known as 'churchwardens' came in from Holland in the reign of William III. During the Napoleonic Wars cigars became popular, originally among Wellington's officers in Spain. After the Crimean War the Russian habit of smoking cigarettes was adopted, though at first only by the more fashionable young men. Their cigarettes were made of Balkan tobacco, and the familiar 'Virginia' cigarette of today became common only during the 20th century.

Until about 1900 smoking was almost entirely a masculine habit, to be indulged in private in special smoking-rooms and smoking-compartments. Many people, including Queen Victoria herself, strongly disapproved of tobacco. The present century has seen a great change in the public attitude to smoking, among women especially, and there has been a corresponding increase in tobacco consumption. In the 200 years following the accession of Queen Anne, the

F. Bruckmann

A GERMAN 19TH-CENTURY PIPE
Detail from a painting by Karl Spitzweg

consumption per head of the population remained at about 2 lb. a year; but since 1900 it has risen to 4 lb. per head. Tobacco duties now account for the second largest contribution to the national revenue, exceeded only by income tax. Though doctors have lately suggested that lung CANCER (q.v.) may be caused by heavy smoking, the amount of tobacco consumed has not diminished.

SOAP, *see* CLEANING MATERIALS; WATER, DOMESTIC. *See also* Vol. VII: SOAP MANUFACTURE.

SOCIAL CLASSES. It is hard to get any agreement on the meaning of the term 'social class'. In ordinary social life, people tend to meet on equal terms those whom they think of as belonging to the same social class, and they may behave differently with those they consider to be of a higher or lower class. In the popular awareness of class, dress, accent, area of residence, education, and manners all play their part.

In ancient civilizations, for example, the SUMERIAN (q.v. Vol. I), social differences were based on birth, status, or rank, rather than on wealth. Four main classes can be recognized: the rulers; the priestly administrators; the freemen (such as craftsmen, merchants, or farmers); and the slaves.

In Greece, after the 6th century B.C., there was a growing conflict between the peasants and the landed aristocrats and a gradual decrease in the power of the aristocracy as something like a middle class of traders and artisans grew up. The population of Athens, for example, was divided into three main classes which were politically and legally distinct (*see* GREEK CIVILIZATION, Vol. I). About a third of the total were slaves who did not count politically (*see* SLAVERY, Vol. X). The next main group consisted of the resident foreigners, the 'metics', who were freemen though they had no share in political life. The third group was the powerful body of citizens, who were themselves divided into sub-classes. In Rome, too, a similar struggle between the *plebs* or working people and the landed families brought about social changes. After the Punic Wars inequalities in wealth were sharpened, and the property and power of the landlord class became very great.

The medieval FEUDAL SYSTEM (q.v. Vol. X) gave rise to a comparatively simple class system based on birth. Many freemen felt that they had to seek the protection of someone more powerful than themselves, and consequently there evolved two main 'classes'—lords and vassals. The vassal owed the lord fidelity, obedience, and aid, especially in the form of military service. The lord, in return, owed his vassals protection and an assured livelihood. The development of a money or exchange economy and the growth of cities and trade led, in the later Middle Ages, to the rise of another class, the burghers, from which ultimately the modern middle classes have come. Gradually office and occupation began also to play an important part in determining social position. A person might still be born to a certain station in life, but it became more and more possible to change to another. This change affected towns more than the country. In country areas remnants of feudalism lasted much longer.

With the break-up of the feudal economy, the increasing division of labour, and the growing power of the burghers of the towns, the middle class became more and more important, and the older privileged upper class, the landed aristocracy, began to lose some of its power. In the

18th century one of the first modern economists, Adam SMITH (q.v. Vol. V), thought that 'the whole annual produce of the land and labour of every country' provided revenue to 'three different orders of people: to those who live by rent, to those who live by wages, and to those who live by profit'. But each successive stage of the INDUSTRIAL REVOLUTION (q.v. Vol. VII) brought a more complicated social structure. A multiplicity of intermediate groupings grew up during the 19th century between the upper middle class and the working class. There were medium-size industrialists as well as large-scale ones, small shopkeepers and tradesmen, officials and salaried employees, skilled workers alongside unskilled, professional men such as doctors and teachers. Farmers and peasants continued in all countries as independent groups.

In spite of this development, one of the most famous writers on social class in the 19th century, Karl MARX (q.v. Vol. V), thought that there was, in the capitalist era, a tendency for society to split up into two huge class camps, the *bourgeoisie* (the capitalists) and the proletariat (the workers). Marx's theory of social class was a very important and influential one, but it is grossly oversimplified. The social make-up of modern societies is much more complex than he suggested.

During the 19th and early 20th centuries the possession of wealth in the long run played a great part in determining class. Industrialists, seizing the opportunities so richly available, made fortunes which lifted them into an economic group far higher than that of their parents. But, though they owed their position to their initiative, they lacked the social training of the 'upper' class and were looked down on by those of aristocratic birth as *nouveaux riches*. In England, however, their wealth enabled them to buy for their sons a PUBLIC SCHOOL education (q.v. Vol. X) which carried with it this social training. The sons mixed with the sons of the upper class and very likely married into this class. The third and fourth generations accepted their social position as their 'birthright'. In the same way, a hard-working and thrifty labourer might win for his son an extended secondary school education in the hopes that he would move into a 'black-coated' occupation carrying with it a higher salary and a move up in the social scale.

The tendency to move down in social class is less obvious, for a claim to an aristocratic birth, at any rate in England, has always carried a certain distinction, and people have made great efforts to obtain for their children the kind of opportunities they have had themselves.

Several factors are considerably altering the social outlook in the 20th century. Perhaps the most important of these are increased taxation of the wealthier classes and the growth of the social services. Another factor is the development of free State education. Generally speaking, the real upper classes are now made up of those holding high official positions, irrespective of birth or wealth—the professional administrators, politicians, industrial managers, military officers, legal experts, and economists.

Many people today are hostile in their attitude towards the effects of class distinctions and privileges and hope that we shall eventually achieve a classless society. But, in fact, as one inequality is removed, another tends to take its place; and perhaps the best that can be looked for is a society in which distinctions are elastic and in which every member has fair opportunities for making the best of his capabilities.

See also Vol. X: FEUDAL SYSTEM; CAPITALISM; SOCIALISM; COMMUNISM; EDUCATION, HISTORY OF.

SOCIAL ENVIRONMENT. Babies at birth can be regarded as animals which learn to be human and social as they grow up with other human beings. One or two cases are known where a baby soon after birth was lost to human kind and, instead of dying of cold and hunger, was brought up by animals. Romulus and Remus, according to the legend, were reared by wolves, and, later, founded the city of Rome. But, in fact, babies reared by wolves or, as in one other example, by gazelles become as like their foster parents as possible, impeded as they are by a human body. Wild children have never been known to become civilized: they usually die because they find the effort of changing their habits too great.

If the process of growing up as members of a family makes us human, there are two questions we must ask ourselves: 'how do we come to be different?' and 'how do we come to be alike?'. Let us take the second question first, for it is by far the more difficult one. There are many ways in which Englishmen are more like Englishmen than they are like Frenchmen or Italians: they speak the same language, wear the same styles of clothes, grow and cook the same sorts of foods, and produce a distinctly English literature or political and industrial system. Amongst primitive peoples, differences in 'national character' such as these are more marked, but within each tribe there is less variety; so it becomes easier to consider our second question—'what is meant by saying that people in one nation or tribe are alike'—if we take our examples from among primitive peoples. In any given tribe there is less variety in the jobs its members do, the tools they use, and the thoughts they think than there is in a large and complicated society such as that of England. Yet so far as we know, the basic stuff of all humanity is biologically the same: an Eskimo baby is not biologically different from an English baby.

Adult persons may differ so much that this simple fact of biological similarity is easily forgotten. For example, among the Arapesh of New Guinea the adult man is a gentle, co-operative, law-abiding creature. He believes that all the difficulties, such as accidents, sickness, death, earthquakes, that trouble the Arapesh come because one of the rules of living has been broken, not, of course, by anybody in his own tribal society, but by the aggression, hate, and anti-social desires of his neighbours. Arapesh men and women are very much alike, for they do not have our ideals that 'men should be men'. By contrast, in another tribe some miles away, the men are given to fighting and to boasting of their prowess in war: they are treacherous, unreliable, and fond of painting themselves. Their women use no make-up but they are good at trading, gardening, and making household equipment: they, and not the men, provide all the household's everyday needs.

If people who live so near to each other, and who are much alike in race, differ so much in temperament and personality, they must have acquired this difference in the process of learning to be good members of their own tribal group. In the same way, European babies become Englishmen, Frenchmen, Germans, or other types of adults because they are taught from different models.

The school for babies is the FAMILY (q.v.). Each mother has ways of showing her affection and her disapproval. Since babies are utterly dependent, the reward for compliance with the orders of parents is life itself. Parents teach children what they ought to want, what they should avoid, when they should feel embarrassed or pleased, according to the code of the society they live in. Thus girls in some primitive societies go naked except for a string of beads around the waist: if the beads are not there, they suffer acutely from shyness and embarrassment. In our society the chief purpose of upbringing in the family is to implant in the child a code of good behaviour, an inclination to want the 'good' things of life, and an internal censor which will make him feel anxious and disturbed when he offends against the code he has learned. This internal regulation follows the model set by the parents, and particularly by the mother: it is sometimes called the 'conscience'. Psychologists who follow the theories of FREUD (q.v. Vol. V) call it the 'super-ego'.

The word used for all the habits and customs, beliefs, and sense of values common to any people is 'culture' (not to be confused with the word 'cultural', used for literature, art, music, and things of beauty). These are parts of culture, but so, too, are everyday things such as the habit of blowing the nose on a handkerchief and using a knife and fork at table. So the answer to our question, 'how do we come to be alike?', is that we have been taught the same culture.

This is not to say that all members of a given society are alike. The fact that one can distinguish by dress, by style of haircutting, or by language an Englishman from an Italian does not prevent one from being able to distinguish between one Englishman and another. For an answer to the question that this sets—'how do we come to be different from everyone else?'—we have to consider two new sets of facts.

The first is about the nature of the family as a social group. The first child usually makes the third member of a group, and the second child makes the fourth member, so that no child experiences exactly the same social conditions as another (though identical twins nearly do). Parents, too, have changed since the birth of the first child, being older and more experienced, and so, while teaching the same culture to the second child, will teach it in different detail. Experiences outside the family with other children in the neighbourhood, with relatives or friends, and at school differ for each child; and so, while broadly speaking each child is taught the same things, no child learns within exactly the same social framework of example, precept, punishment, and reward. In this way every child has special experiences which are enough to make him different from every other child.

There is a second side to this. Thus far we have talked about babies as if they came into this world all exactly alike. Adults may be blond or brunette, tall or short, thin or fat, intelligent or stupid, and such physical and mental traits are due largely to HEREDITY (q.v. Vol. II). Babies come into the world each with a different amount of intelligence and each with a different aptitude for learning: the way in which they will develop these inherited gifts will depend upon the culture of the society into which they are born and the family which interprets this culture to them. We know, from studying primitive tribes in which the amount of variation allowed to the tribesman is much less than that allowed in a complex country such as England, how much alike people can become. This knowledge supports what we have learned from biologists that every child, black or white, with curly hair or straight, comes into this world with more similarities to other babies than differences from them. These two sorts of knowledge about culture and about biology have been used to answer our two important questions.

There remains just one last point. The family is essential to this process by which one generation is trained to be like the last and through which civilization and a life style carries on through the ages. The ways in which the family transmits the cultural heritage are innumerable. Within it should be found love and affection; the mother gives continuous care and supervision, the father provides food and authority; and together with the other children the parents form models from which a style of life may be copied. Of all these elements the most important seem to be love and affection and a sense of being wanted; food, care, hygienic conditions, gifts, and all the rest are of lesser importance. No other social group can provide this setting so well for the growing child.

See also FAMILY, HISTORY OF; CHILDREN, UPBRINGING OF.

SOCIAL PRECEDENCE. The word 'precedence' is derived from the Latin *praecedere*, to 'go before' or 'precede'. The general rule of social precedence, which throughout history has been highly valued by many nations, is that people of greater importance precede those of lesser importance. Even in a fairly democratic society precedence is still observed at many public functions. Its conventions decide the order of priority or superiority of rank both at State ceremonies, such as CORONATIONS (q.v. Vol. X), royal marriages, and State funerals, and on formal social occasions. Precedence is expressed in daily life in a thousand complicated ways. It decides who speaks first at a meeting, who walks first into a dining-room, who is selected to greet an important visitor, and so on. Often, as in a procession, it is the most important people who walk last, not first (*see* ETIQUETTE).

In Britain precedence is based on the royal pleasure (the Crown is the fountain of honour), except in so far as restraints by Act of Parliament have been accepted. In olden days the courts of CHIVALRY (q.v. Vol. X) decided upon questions of precedence, and disputed questions may still be referred by the Crown to the College of Arms, or in Scotland to the court of the Lord Lyon King of Arms (*see* HERALDRY, Vol. IV). Various sovereigns in the past tried to accord special precedence to particular persons. Charles II, for instance, tried and failed on two occasions to accord precedence to the Earl of Banbury and the Viscount Stafford; and this assumption of power was amongst the things condemned in the BILL OF RIGHTS (q.v. Vol. X).

There are different kinds as well as different degrees of precedence. 'Personal' precedence is possessed by members of the royal family and of the PEERAGE (q.v. Vol. X) and certain other people. 'Official' precedence may be conferred by Crown or Parliament on certain dignitaries, such as the Prime Minister, by virtue of their office; as a result, a man of low 'personal' precedence may on public occasions be placed far above others of higher 'personal' precedence. 'Personal' precedence is extended to the family; for example, the wife and children of a peer take precedence according to that of the peer. Official rank, however, gives no precedence to the wife and children of its holder.

The order of precedence has been roughly the same for about 3 centuries, but as the social and political circumstances for which it was framed have completely changed or vanished, there are a number of anomalies. The holders of certain offices of State, which once involved great power, may still have precedence over those who really possess that power today. Some ranks highly esteemed elsewhere—for example, those in any of the armed forces—are not entitled to precedence. The Prime Minister was not recog-

ENGLISH PORCELAIN

The teapot and cup and saucer are Worcester, c. 1770, the cream jug on the right is Bow, mid-18th century. On the left is a
small tureen in the form of asparagus, made at Chelsea c. 1755. The plate, part of a tea service, is Pinxton, early 19th century

nized in the table of precedence until the beginning of this century, and Secretaries of State may rank below certain officials of the ROYAL HOUSEHOLD (q.v. Vol. X).

Here, as an example, is part of the table of precedence for men in Great Britain in 1955 (the Sovereign, of course, takes precedence over all):

The Duke of Edinburgh
The Duke of Cornwall
The Duke of Gloucester
The Duke of Windsor
Archbishop of Canterbury
Lord High Chancellor
Archbishop of York
The Prime Minister
Lord President of the Council
Speaker of the House of Commons
Lord Privy Seal

High Commissioners of Commonwealth countries and ambassadors of foreign States

The five following great officers of State if they are dukes:

Lord Great Chamberlain
Earl Marshal
Lord Steward
Lord Chamberlain
The Master of the Horse

Dukes, according to their creation
Ministers and envoys
Eldest sons of dukes of royal blood

The above five great officers of State if they are marquesses

Marquesses
Eldest sons of dukes

The five great officers of State if they are earls

Earls
The younger sons of dukes of royal blood
Marquesses' eldest sons
Dukes' younger sons

The five great officers of State if they are viscounts

Viscounts
Marquesses' younger sons
Bishops of London, Durham, and Winchester
All other English bishops, according to their seniority of consecration

The five great officers of State if they are barons

Secretaries of State, if barons
Barons

Women take the same rank in personal precedence as their husbands or as their eldest brothers, so that Princess Anne, for example, ranks with the Duke of Cornwall. Daughters of peers come after their elder brothers' wives and before the wives of their younger brothers. If daughters of peers marry peers of lower degree they take the same precedence as their husbands; and they retain their title if they marry a commoner. The ladies of the present royal family have the following order of precedence after the Sovereign: The Queen Mother, Princess Anne, Princess Margaret, the Princess Royal; the Duchess of Kent comes after the Duchess of Gloucester.

See also ETIQUETTE; SOCIAL CLASSES.
See also Vol. X: CROWN, BRITISH; PEERAGE; HONOURS.

SODA, *see* CLEANING MATERIALS; WATER, DOMESTIC. *See also* Vol. VII: ALKALIS.

SOUFFLÉS, *see* EGG DISHES.

SOUP. The practice of taking soup as an appetizer at the beginning of a meal is reasonable because meat and vegetable extracts stimulate the flow of gastric juice; but the more ancient and widespread use of soup is as a main dish of peasant peoples. The many allusions to 'broth' in folk tales and proverbs and the very word 'supper' bear witness to this.

The foundation liquid of most soups is called 'stock'. In old-fashioned kitchens the stock pot or *pot au feu* or soup kettle was an institution. Replenished frequently, it simmered away gently for hours at the side of the fire or coal range. The bones, boiling beef, liver, veal, and vegetables it contained yielded a gelatinous and savoury fluid constantly drawn upon for rich soups and sauces, as well as tender meat which could be served hot or cold and jellied. Nowadays, with high fuel costs, a permanent stock pot is not so practical. A supply of stock in the larder, however, is important. Vegetable water, left over gravy, tough meat scraps, bacon rinds, and so on, while still very fresh, are simmered or pressure cooked with new bones, vegetables, and cereals. The resulting broth makes a very good family soup. For special soups, however, it is necessary to use select materials and take more trouble.

Brown stock is made from beef, mutton, or game; white stock from chicken, veal, or rabbit; fish stock can be made not only from fish, but also from fish scraps—even the shells of shrimps and lobster. Vegetable stock is the water in which VEGETABLES (q.v.) have been boiled; it may replace water in making brown soups, or meat stock in making cream soups.

Bouillon is a clear soup made from brown stock, lightly seasoned, and clarified with egg shells. *Consommé* is made from two or more kinds of meat (such as beef, chicken, or veal), highly seasoned, cleared, and strained. When it contains vegetables cut in match-like strips it is called *Julienne*. *Bisque* is a very smooth, delicately flavoured, cream soup, generally made of shellfish, milk, and seasonings, sometimes with cream or eggs. There can be oyster, clam, shrimp, veal, tomato, and pimento *bisques*.

Oyster soup and the Scots partan bree (crab soup) are the only notable fish soups of Britain, though the great French chef, Carême, who worked for a time for George IV, invented a magnificent concoction of soles, plaice, eels, oysters, crayfish, champagne, truffles, and eighteen other ingredients and called it 'English Fish Soup'. In America, on the other hand, there is a great variety of fish soups. 'Chowder', thick with shellfish (especially clams), cubed potatoes, and 'crackers' soaked in milk, and flavoured with salt pork and onions, has become an American speciality. The south of France provides *bouillabaisse*—a solid, stew-like soup of fish, mussels, shrimps, and white wine, with garlic and herbs, saffron, and a good deal of bread or toast. The varieties of Italian *Zuppa di Pesce* resemble it. A small New Zealand mollusc is ground to provide the basis for the delicious green Toheroa soup which, tinned, is gradually becoming known outside New Zealand.

There are countless substantial meat soups, notable amongst them kidney, oxtail, hare, chicken, and veal. The turtle soup always served at the Lord Mayor's Banquet is a *bouillon*, laced with Madeira wine, in which float gelatinous cubes of turtle flesh. The sheep's head and mutton broths of Scotland, with characteristic leeks, barley, and turnips, are known all over the English-speaking world. Scotch cock-a-leekie is made by boiling an old fowl with leeks and serving the broth with pieces of the bird in it. Mulligatawny (from the Tamil word meaning 'pepper water') or curry soup is derived from an Indian source, while *Kraase Suppe* is the Danish version of the Continental giblet soup.

Vegetable soups vary in consistency according to whether the vegetables are sieved or merely chopped. There are innumerable varieties. Ukrainian *Borsch*, made from beetroot and cabbage and served with a spoonful of heavy sour cream on top, is a picturesque one. The Russian peasant has always lived largely on *Shchi*, a cabbage soup resembling the French *Soupe aux Choux* with cabbage and bacon. Similarly French brown onion soup, poured on to toast or fried bread and sprinkled with grated cheese, was regarded as a meal in itself. Cream soups are made with thickened cream or milk and a sieved vegetable—onions, asparagus, celery, tomatoes, artichokes, mushrooms, and others. Pea soup, called *St. Germaine* in menus, is familiar to most Westerners, and in the Balkans and Middle and Far East thick, peasant-type, bean soups are often eaten as main meals. Italian *Minestrone* is full of vegetables of all kinds, PASTA (q.v.), and cheese as well.

The almost legendary 'Birds' Nest Soup' (*Yen wo*) of Chinese epicures is not nearly so peculiar as it sounds. The nest of the Edible Sea SWIFT (q.v. Vol. II) is built of a fluid resembling isinglass (fish gelatine), which the bird secretes from its salivary glands. Each nest, about the size of a duck's egg, is sufficient to make a quart of soup. It is washed, soaked in water overnight, and then simmered in chicken broth. It comes to table transparent and, to Western palates, almost tasteless, but quite pleasant.

Cold soups, especially *Minestrone*, are eaten in Italy in hot weather, while iced or jellied consommé often precedes a formal English or American dinner.

Fruit soup, hot or cold, is used in Scandinavia instead of a sweet course, but at the beginning of a meal. The commonest kind is a thin purée of red currants, plums, or rhubarb, thickened slightly with potato flour, and sweetened. American fruit soup may be juices from pineapple, orange, grapefruit, or berries, thickened with cornflour and spiced with cinnamon and cloves.

Tinned and packet soups are useful in small households or for emergency meals. An inventive cook will combine tinned varieties, dilute them with milk or stock, add cream, sherry, onion juice, curry powder, and so on, garnish them with fried sippets of bread, chopped parsley, grated cheese, or cubes of egg custard, and serve accompaniments such as tiny fresh rolls, melba toast, or cheese straws.

See also JELLIES AND ASPICS.

SPECTACLES. In the sense of shaped lenses attached by some means to the face, spectacles were unknown to the Ancient World. The Romans knew that a glass vase filled with water magnified objects seen through it. From that it was but a step to the magnifying glass, but it was not until the end of the 13th century that this knowledge was applied to making spectacles. The credit is generally given to a Florentine, Salvino Armato degli Armati, and by the time of his death in 1317 scholars in Italy had already begun to realize the benefits of the new invention. As most people could not read, defective eyesight was not generally much of a handicap, and for many centuries spectacles were the mark of the learned man.

The first portrait showing spectacles being worn is that of Cardinal Ugone in the church of San Nicolo at Treviso. The two lenses are held together by a joint or hinge stiff enough to keep them on the nose (an early form of pince-nez). It was not until the 16th century that this was replaced by a metal spring, and side-pieces came later still.

In England spectacles were in common use among learned men at the beginning of the 16th century. Holbein's portrait of St. Thomas More (in the museum at Aix) shows him wearing them. Shakespeare says of Coriolanus that 'bleared sights are spectacled to see him': an anachronism, of course, as applied to a Roman hero, but true of Shakespeare's own day. With the increase of books and the spread of literacy, the spectacle trade grew rapidly in the 16th century, and by 1600 there were opticians in most of the bigger towns of Europe. The early rims were of horn or leather. Metal ones date from about 1600.

In the 18th century the 'quizzing glass' or monocle with a handle came into fashion, and after the French Revolution there was a brief mode for two glasses mounted in a similar fashion. Some of the examples which have survived are exquisite works of art. Bifocal glasses worn on the nose date from about 1760, when a pair was made for the American statesman Benjamin Franklin. These are spectacles combining distant and near vision lenses.

During the 19th century only the elderly and scholarly made use of spectacles, which took the form of small oval lenses surrounded by gold rims. Short-sighted ladies carried a lorgnette (a pair of eye-glasses held on a long handle), and fashionable men in the second half of the cen-

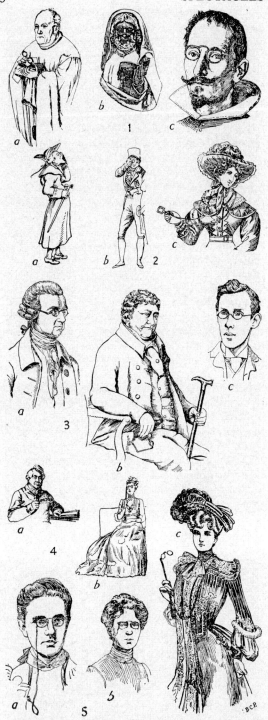

1. *Early spectacles*: *a.* 15th century; *b.* 16th century; *c.* 17th century. 2. *Quizzing glasses*: *a.* 1780s; *b.* 1800s; *c.* about 1825. 3. *18th- and 19th-century spectacles*: *a.* 1770s; *b.* 1800s; *c.* about 1885. 4. *Lorgnettes*: *a.* 1860s; *b.* 1887; *c.* 1901. 5. *Pince-nez*: *a.* 1890s; *b.* about 1895.

Lord De L'Isle and Dudley

THE 14TH-CENTURY CIRCULAR STAIRCASE LEADING FROM
THE GREAT HALL AT PENSHURST PLACE, KENT

N.D. Phot.

THE GREAT DOUBLE STAIRCASE AT CHAMBORD, FRANCE

tury wore a monocle, sometimes solely for show. Now that universal education has brought reading within everybody's reach, spectacles have become common. The gold rims have been abandoned either for rimless lenses or, more commonly, for horn-rimmed. The National Health Service Act (1946) has made spectacles available on a small payment to everyone for whom doctors have prescribed them.

See also EYE STRUCTURE.
See also Vol. VIII: LENS.

SPICES, *see* HERBS AND SPICES. *See also* Vol. VI: SPICE CROPS.

SPINAL CORD, *see* ANATOMY; NERVOUS SYSTEM.

SPIRITS, *see* WINES AND SPIRITS.

STAIRCASES. In medieval CASTLES (q.v.) and houses in which the hall was on the first floor there was usually an outside stone staircase. When the stairs were built inside the building, they often wound in a spiral round a central pillar, called a 'newel', and were built in a turret, like the stairs in many medieval church towers. They were made of stone, brick, or wood, the wooden ones often having steps of solid wooden blocks and being enclosed by panelling in cupboard-like recesses. In the 16th century, as the skill of carpenters increased, wooden stairs were more often built, and were more spacious in design. Elizabethan staircases had short flights of steps separated by square landings surrounding an open well, and they often had elaborately carved newel-posts, handrails, and balusters.

Many continental 16th-century staircases were very elaborate. In the French Château Chambord, for example, one stair encircles another, and the outside wall has an open balustrade which admits light. In Italy the staircase became a feature of the great two-storey hall in the centre of the house. In 17th-century Italy and 18th-century Austria and Germany grand marble staircases in BAROQUE style (q.v. Vol. XII) were elaborately designed and richly carved. In England also, the staircase of stone or wood, sometimes with wrought iron balustrades, was the most important feature of the hall, though it was rarely so elaborate as on the Continent. The high newel-posts and panelled enclosing walls

National Buildings Record

Left: CANTILEVERED STAIRCASE IN THE QUEEN'S HOUSE, GREENWICH, BUILT BY INIGO JONES, 1618–35
Right: 18TH-CENTURY STAIRCASE IN BELTON HOUSE, LINCOLNSHIRE

Crown Copyright

of the 16th century disappeared, and the stairs stood freely out from the wall, either boldly cantilevered (that is, supported only by the wall on one side) or supported on a sloping beam, called a string, forming the outer edge of each flight. In 18th-century GEORGIAN ARCHITECTURE (q.v. Vol. XII) the staircase became more elegant and slender. The staircases of town houses were fairly narrow, ascending round three sides of a staircase-hall with a square quarter landing between the flights, or in two flights of opposite direction joined by a rectangular half-landing and separated by a narrow well. In some houses the stairs curved round a semicircular hall. Often the staircase had an open string, that is, the steps, instead of ending against the inside face of the string, were carried over it and ended in a scroll or other ornament. It was as beautifully finished as a piece of furniture, with turned wooden, or delicately scrolled iron balusters and a moulded handrail.

A plainer version of the Georgian staircase,

usually of painted wood, has been the common pattern ever since, apart from a short period in the 1930s when stairs with enclosing walls or solid balustrades were fashionable. The open plan and small size of many modern houses has led architects to give staircases an appearance of lightness by using steel in their construction, by cantilevering the individual steps out from the wall, and by making the balustrades of lighter looking materials than wood, such as aluminium or glass panels.

Staircases with shallow steps, though dignified, take up a lot of floor-space; but very steep stairs, though they save space, are inconvenient, especially for old people. A comfortable slope for a staircase in an ordinary house is given by a tread (the flat area of the step) 9 inches wide and a rise (the vertical distance from step to step) of 7 inches. This means that the normal ascent of about 10 feet 6 inches from floor to floor is made in two flights of nine steps each. Whatever the slope, the proportion of the tread to the rise is important; the rule of thumb commonly followed is that twice the rise plus the tread should equal 23 inches, that there should not be more than fifteen steps in a straight flight, nor a rise of more than 8 feet without a landing. To save space, triangular steps that go round a corner are sometimes used in place of a flat landing; these are called winders.

See also HOUSES, HISTORY OF.

STEAMING. Cooking over the steam from boiling water is essentially a slow, gentle method, suitable for custards and sauces, for tough meat and for some fish, and for raised sponges containing fat or suet, such as dumplings, steamed puddings, and steamed breads. Its special merits are that it preserves the shape of the food, and that prolonged steaming makes even old chicken or tough steak tender. On the other hand, temperatures for steaming are too low to develop good flavours in protein foods so that they tend to be, although digestible, rather flat and tasteless. Root vegetables, including potatoes, steam well, but green vegetables do not keep their good colour and protective value (*see* VEGETABLES). For reasons of economy, steaming is widely used in hospitals, ships, canteens, and school kitchens, in large-scale apparatus. For the housewife, special-purpose steamers are available; one, like a colander, has several rims to fit several sizes of saucepan. But the old-fashioned bowl, covered with a clip lid, or with greaseproof paper, cloth, and string, is still hard to beat. The double boiler—a saucepan fitting exactly over another containing boiling water—is important for making smooth egg custards or white sauces. An alternative is to stand a jug or basin containing the mixture in the saucepan of water.

See also BOILING.

STEWING. The best method for tenderizing the poorer meat cuts or old chicken is to stew them—that is, to boil them very gently either in a covered saucepan over direct heat, or in a thick, covered earthenware or heat-proof glass casserole in the oven. Stewing, however, is wasteful of gas or electricity, especially when done in an oven, but economical if a HAY-BOX (q.v.) is used.

English stew consists of pieces of meat previously fried with onions, placed in a pot or casserole with cut-up root vegetables, peas, or beans, and cooked slowly in thickened or unthickened gravy until all is succulent and tender. The French, who make stewed meat and vegetables delicious, stress the importance of sealing the casserole with a paste of raw flour and water to prevent the escape of juices and savour. Irish stew, made with mutton layered with onions and sliced potatoes (and sometimes carrots), is cooked in a saucepan. A famous stew from Hungary is the highly seasoned *goulash*. Small pieces of veal or beef are stewed with onions, tomatoes, garlic, and cubed potatoes in a rich juice flavoured and coloured with paprika. American pork and pineapple and Boston baked beans owe their excellence to slow stewing in casseroles.

See also BOILING; BRAISING.

STITCHES, *see* SEWING; NEEDLEWORK, DECORATIVE.

STOCK POT, *see* SOUP.

STORY-TELLING. The aim of story-telling is to give delight. Its value is to stimulate the child's imagination, to help him to know more of the world in which he lives, and to increase his understanding of language. The successful story-teller in the nursery must know how to choose stories which will delight her children and meet their ever-widening interests as they grow from babyhood.

A baby's one absorbing interest is his mother, who satisfies all his needs. His stories are the NURSERY RHYMES (q.v. Vol. XII) and jingles she repeats as she cuddles him on her lap. He does not understand them of course, but he enjoys them for their musical sound and for the play with his fingers and toes that often accompanies them. Most of all, however, he enjoys them as a demonstration of his mother's love for him.

As he approaches the age of 2, the child begins to take an interest in the activities of his daily life, such as washing and dressing, having meals, and going to bed. These will provide themes for endless stories. But as the 2-year-old can understand only what is near to his own experience, his stories have to be made up for him by his mother, or someone living close to him. They can be about the child himself—'I'll tell you a story about Roger. One day . . .'; they can be about his toys or pets—'One day Teddy didn't want his breakfast. I'll tell you all about it . . .';

Fitzwilliam Museum, Cambridge

PAMELA TELLS A STORY
Illustration by Joseph Highmore to Richardson's *Pamela*

and they can be about the pictures in his books—'Look, here is Sheila's own little bed! Every night . . .'. The stories need no plot; they are just brief and faithful descriptions of events in the child's daily life.

At 3 years old, the child's great adventures are still the incidents in his daily routine, but he is now not interested exclusively in his own world as he was at 2. He is becoming aware of other children and enjoys hearing about their adventures, which are so very like his own. He is developing in independence too, and takes great pride in doing everything for himself. He will enjoy being one of a group of children listening to stories, suitably illustrated, about experiences common to all 3-year-olds. In theme and style these stories are similar to the earlier ones, but they contain more detail, and convey the pride children feel in their newly acquired capabilities

—'Every morning when Billy has dressed himself . . .'. In addition to these 'everyday' stories, children of this age enjoy stories about the weather—'A Snowy Day', 'A Rainy Day', and stories about special days such as birthdays and holidays.

Towards the age of 4, the child's interests widen and pass beyond his immediate and very personal environment. His reasoning power increases also, and his ability to form complex ideas (*see* INTELLIGENCE). Stories for 4-year-olds, therefore, may be about people and animals and things familiar to them, but not directly related to them, such as the farmer, milkman, and postman; animals of the farm, and fields, and woods; tractors, trains, and aeroplanes. They may also have a simple plot, and they need to be profusely illustrated because the children's knowledge of language is limited. At this age, too, children begin to enjoy the traditional nursery stories, especially those which contain repetitive phrases in which they can join, such as 'The Gingerbread Boy' and 'The Three Little Pigs'.

By the time the child is 5 he is interested in everything. His outstanding characteristics are his thirst for knowledge, his joy in making things, and his strong desire to be useful. He is ready for stories which explain in a simple way the origin of bread or woolly clothes; the source of the water in the tap, and the coal for the fire; the habits of plants and animals and birds, and the phenomena of night and day. But informative stories are not the only ones that 5-year-olds enjoy. They like stories about themselves, describing their own feelings, and their pride in achievement and in taking responsibility; they enjoy the mischief and fun of traditional stories, and they can enjoy some stories for their beauty of language or rhythm and pattern. Their stories need not be so fully illustrated as those for younger children, but anything unfamiliar should always be explained by an illustration.

It is essential that the story-teller should tell her story simply and clearly. Her voice should be resonant and flexible, and convey by its different tones all the feelings of wonder, joy, and sadness that the stories contain, and all the poetry and rhythm of the words. A story should always sound as if it is the story-teller's own, something delightful which she is sharing with her listeners. It is not sufficient, therefore, to learn a story by rote. The story-teller must meditate on her story until she feels as close to it as if she herself had created it. Then, because she has made it her own, she can re-create it and make it live for her listeners. To tell a story well, even to the youngest children, is not easy. Only by study and effort can the story-teller achieve her aim—to give delight.

See also LULLABIES.
See also Vol. I: FAIRY-TALES AND TRADITIONAL TALES.

STRAINS AND SPRAINS, see BONES AND JOINTS; ORTHOPAEDICS; FIRST AID.

STROKE, see NERVOUS SYSTEM.

STUFFING. 1. Meat, fish, and vegetables taste better if stuffed, and also go farther. Boned pieces of meat are suitable. For example, a right and left flank (breast) of mutton or lamb, boned, spread thickly with any favourite stuffing, fitted

together like a sandwich, and then oversewn neatly round the edges with a curved sack needle and string, makes a cheap, delicious, and easily carved roast. Boned shoulders of mutton and pieces of a steak or veal can be either sewn or rolled up and tied with string. Stuffed rabbit and whole fish need sewing up the middle, but whole chicken and other birds are stuffed through the neck and vent and secured with wooden toothpicks. Hearts are usually served stuffed, and goose's neck stuffed and roasted is a Jewish delicacy.

Vegetables suitable for stuffing include potatoes baked in their skins, tomatoes, braised onions, marrows, and the other GOURD VEGETABLES (q.v. Vol. VI). Some of these need to have their seeds scooped out first. Cabbage can be stuffed by scooping out the heart (which is kept for salad), replacing it by a meat or nut stuffing, and then tying the leaves firmly round with string, before braising it. In Austria blanched, de-ribbed cabbage leaves are spread with stuffing, rolled up into little parcels, and casseroled. In Italy marrow flowers are stuffed with risotto (see RICE DISHES) and fried in batter; in Greece vine-leaves are stuffed.

2. KINDS OF STUFFING. (a) Forcemeats have a basis of minced meat, giblets (see OFFAL), or fish, often mixed with a 'panada', that is, bread and milk or water cooked to a paste, as well as chopped herbs and seasonings. Oyster, salmon, and halibut forcemeats are used for stuffing fish; chicken, veal, and giblet forcemeats for poultry and game; ham and bacon for stuffed hare. English mincemeat, the filling for mince pies, is now made entirely of fruit and suet, but used to contain minced steak. Small forcemeat balls

STUFFED MARROWS

BREAST OF MUTTON STUFFED WITH PARSLEY STUFFING

cooked in boiling stock (quenelles) are used to garnish soups or other dishes.

(b) *Bread Stuffings* are very economical and easy to make, especially if a mincing-machine is available. There are two distinct types: short crumb or American, and moist or British type. For short crumb stuffings, dry, minced crumbs or raspings are mixed with melted savoury fat or margarine in the proportion of 2 cups of crumbs to $\frac{1}{4}$ cup of fat and $\frac{1}{2}$–1 teaspoon of salt. To this is added one of the following: chopped herbs, celery, onion, raisin and walnut, or cheese and nut (especially for stuffing vegetables).

For making moist stuffings, fresh or dry crumbs are seasoned and moistened with egg and milk, or with plain milk, using 2 cups of crumbs to $\frac{1}{2}$ cup of milk and $\frac{1}{2}$–1 teaspoon of salt. Various flavourings are added, such as sage-and-onion for duck, goose, and pork; mixed herbs for chicken; mixed herbs and raisins for mutton; parsley with tomato and a touch of grated lemon rind for mackerel. Moist stuffings usually made without bread are sausage with chestnut or mushroom for turkey; apple and prune for goose; and orange for duck. These are traditional combinations, but a cook with a taste for stuffing will make up her own, remembering that fresh green parsley and garden HERBS (q.v.) look and taste much better than dried ones; that if crusts and heels of bread are left to dry on a shallow pan or in the oven, they will go easily through the mincer; and that it is easier to add the seasonings and mix well before moistening.

See also HERBS AND SPICES.

SUGAR, *see* SWEETENINGS. *See also* Vol. VI: SUGAR CANE; SUGAR BEET. *See also* Vol. VII: SUGAR REFINING.

SULPHONAMIDE DRUGS, *see* DRUGS.

SUMMER-HOUSES, *see* GARDEN BUILDINGS.

SURGERY, HISTORY OF. The beginnings of surgery can be traced back to many thousands of years before the period of recorded history. The most ancient surgical instruments were sharpened flints which were used for extracting thorns, for opening abscesses, for scarifying the skin, and for one far more serious operation, that of 'trephining' the skull. In trephination an artificial opening was made in the skull with a sharpened flint by removing pieces of bone. This extraordinary procedure was carried out in cases of head injury to remove splinters and fragments of bone and also perhaps for magical reasons—to release the demons which were thought to be responsible for disease. Trephining is still practised by some primitive peoples, along with other operations such as scarifying the skin, which are also performed partly for magical purposes.

The earliest written records of surgical operations are found in the clay tablets of ancient Babylonia and in the inscriptions and papyri of Egypt. An Egyptian papyrus, written about 1600 B.C., is a handbook on the treatment of wounds of the head and the chest. A number of surgical instruments were used, and fractures were treated with splints. The ancient Hindus were pioneers in many departments of surgery. Susruta, a Hindu medical writer of the 5th century A.D., describes more than a hundred surgical instruments. The Hindus treated fractures with bamboo splints, and performed many operations including Caesarean section, the excision of tumours, and the extraction of stone from the bladder. Their great speciality, however, was the making of new noses by skin grafting, an operation that was in demand owing to the fact that cutting off the nose was a common form of punishment. The Hindus were thus the pioneers of modern plastic surgery. Hua To, the most famous surgeon of ancient China (A.D. 115–205), is said to have carried out abdominal operations, including removal of the spleen. It is believed that he gave his patients narcotic drugs, such as Indian hemp, before operating on them, in order to produce a state of general anaesthesia.

There are many descriptions of wounds and their treatment in the *Iliad* and the *Odyssey* of Homer, but the most complete picture of Greek

Wellcome Historical Medical Museum

MEDIEVAL SURGEONS

surgery is given in the writings of HIPPOCRATES (q.v. Vol. V). The Greek surgeons drained pus, set fractures, reduced dislocations, and trephined the skull. They were highly skilled in bandaging and dressing wounds; their surgical 'technique' was simple, and they had sufficient idea of asepsis to use boiled water. The Romans had considerable experience of military surgery, but their writers also describe operations for goitre and for hernia, stone in the bladder, the removal of the tonsils, and various eye operations. In the surgeon's house in POMPEII (q.v. Vol. XII) have been found a set of surgical instruments, including forceps, scalpels, scissors, and hooks, not unlike those still in use in the 19th century.

The Arabians and Persians—great doctors in the Middle Ages—were more renowned for their knowledge of DRUGS (q.v.) than for their achievements in surgery, but they were expert operators on the eye. They arrested bleeding by cauterizing with a red-hot iron and also used this harsh method of treatment in various external diseases. The Moslems did not like shedding blood, and their dislike of cutting operations was shared by the medical men of western Europe throughout the Middle Ages. At different periods the Church even forbade the practice of surgery by its members and, as most of the educated doctors of this period were clerics, this meant that surgical operations were left to barber-surgeons and other lowly practitioners. Consequently the practice of surgery became separated from that of internal medicine, and for hundreds of years the status of the surgeon was markedly inferior to that of the physician.

The Church had particularly frowned on the practice of dissection of human bodies, without which an exact knowledge of ANATOMY (q.v.) was impossible. In spite of this the practice of dissection began in the 12th century at Bologna University, and at the beginning of the 13th century Mondino da Luzzi dissected a human body in public. Even in the 16th century, however, the Flemish anatomist, Andreas Vesalius, had to snatch bodies from the gallows or graves in order to write his great work *On the Fabric of the Human Body*. This book led the way to modern surgery and to the practice of the French surgeon Ambroise Paré, who is regarded as the Father of Modern Surgery. In England, the bodies of executed criminals were occasionally handed over to the surgeons for dissection, which was performed publicly in Shakespeare's day. Apart from this, dissection was illegal until the passing of the Anatomy Act in 1832, partly as a result of Dr. Southwood Smith's essay *The Use of the Dead to the Living*.

Most surgical advances have been made as a result of the experience gained in times of war. Ambroise Paré gained his experience in the French religious wars of the 16th century. He was the first surgeon to give up the traditional method of treating amputation stumps by the application of hot irons or boiling oil. He reintroduced the use of ligatures to control bleeding —a method that had been known to the Greeks but had been forgotten or neglected; and he obtained wonderfully good results by treating wounds with simple dressings in place of the obnoxious substances used by his contemporaries. Paré was a surgeon of vast skill and experience. He was surgeon to no less than four successive kings of France and he was idolized by the common soldiers for whom he had done so much. To find his equal we have to turn to the famous Baron Larrey, chief surgeon to the armies of Napoleon, who introduced the 'flying ambulance' service, and was described by the Emperor as 'the noblest man I have ever met'.

By the end of the 18th century surgery had almost reached its technical limits, but the scope of operations was still extremely narrow; it was, in fact, hardly wider than that known to the ancient Greeks and the Hindus. Within their limits, many surgeons had achieved a high degree of skill; amputations and the extraction of stones from the bladder were carried out in a matter of seconds. The Scottish surgeon John HUNTER (q.v. Vol. V) had provided a scientific basis for surgery by explaining the processes of

Wellcome Historical Medical Museum

AN OPERATION ON THE SKULL IN 16TH-CENTURY ITALY

inflammation and repair in wounds and by his profound researches in human and comparative anatomy. Further advance was impossible until two problems had been overcome: these were pain and infection. The problem of pain in surgical operations was conquered in 1846 when W. T. G. Morton of Boston, U.S.A., introduced ether ANAESTHETICS (q.v.). In the following year Dr. James Young Simpson of Edinburgh began to use chloroform.

The second revolution in surgery was the discovery by the French scientist Louis PASTEUR of the part played by germs in the production of sepsis and disease. Pasteur's discoveries were taken up by Joseph (afterwards Lord) LISTER (qq.v. Vol. V), who showed that infection of wounds is caused by microbes which are present on the surgeon's hands, on his instruments and dressings, and in the air. By using ANTISEPTICS (q.v.) Lister showed that it is possible to control infection and to ensure rapid and clean healing of operation wounds. Before this, even if the patient withstood the agony and the shock of operation, he very often succumbed to

post-operative infection. The death-rate of all surgical operations was appallingly high, and admission to a hospital was regarded more or less as a death sentence. No attempt was made at cleanliness, the surgeons usually wearing filthy, blood-sodden coats when they operated, for no one realized where the danger lay.

With the introduction of anaesthesia and antisepsis it became possible for surgeons to operate on the internal organs of the abdomen, the chest, and the head—regions which had hitherto been almost entirely exempt from the surgeon's knife. Also, now that the patient no longer suffered, the imperative need for working at great speed was over. After a few years Lister's method of antisepsis, that is, killing the germs present in the operation area by means of chemical disinfectants—was to a large extent replaced by asepsis, which is excluding germs by sterilization of the air of the operating theatre, draping the operation area with sterile towels, the boiling of all instruments, and the wearing of sterile masks, gloves, and gowns. During the present century the technical efficiency of the surgeon has been

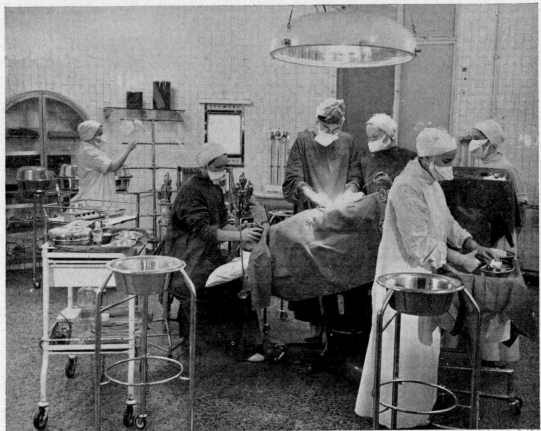

Nursing Mirror

AN OPERATION IN A MODERN HOSPITAL THEATRE

The surgeon, helped by an assistant, works under a bright light, while the theatre sister hands him the instruments he requires. The anaesthetist holds an anaesthetic mask over the nose and mouth of the patient, regulating the amount of anaesthetic given. The tiled walls and floor are made for easy swabbing, surgeon and attendants wear masks and sterile clothing, and the instruments are stored in sterilized containers

supplemented by a number of discoveries and techniques which have helped to make even the most extensive operations safe. These aids include the use of X-rays and radium, modern methods of blood transfusion, the injection of other fluids to maintain the nutrition and chemical balance of the body, new methods of controlling haemorrhage, anti-shock measures, intravenous, local, and spinal anaesthesia, and above all the introduction of penicillin and the other antibiotics. Instead of a surgical operation being a terrible ordeal both for patient and surgeon, it has become a deliberate, planned procedure, carried out without hurry and without pain (*see* SURGERY, MODERN).

See also MEDICINE; ANAESTHETICS; ANTISEPSIS AND ASEPSIS.
See also Vol. X: HOSPITALS, HISTORY OF.

SURGERY, MODERN. The achievements of modern surgery were made possible by the discovery of ANAESTHETICS and the introduction of methods of ANTISEPSIS AND ASEPSIS (qq.v.) in the 19th century. But although the introduction of anaesthetics has made the performance of operations infinitely easier, it did not greatly affect the patient's chance of survival; and even when the adoption of antisepsis had very much reduced the death-rate after operations, the scope of surgery was still extremely limited. In 1873 Sir John Erichsen, one of the greatest surgeons of the day, said that surgery had almost reached its limits: 'There cannot always be fresh fields for conquest by the knife: there must be portions of the human frame that will ever remain sacred from its intrusion, at least in the surgeon's hands.' The great surgeon prophesied wrongly.

By the end of the 19th century surgeons had successfully performed operations for appendicitis and for every type of intestinal obstruction; they had removed the stomach, the rectum, the gall-bladder, the spleen, the bladder, the gullet, the kidney, and the thyroid gland. In 1884 a brain tumour was removed and in 1887 a tumour of the spinal cord. A heart wound was successfully sewn up in 1884. No part of the human body was proving beyond the reach of the surgeon's knife.

These operations were performed by great pioneers who deliberately set out with the intention of exploring new ground in surgery, and in many cases it was years before other surgeons dared repeat such operations. During the present century the techniques of all these operations have become standardized and are carried out as a matter of everyday routine in hospitals all over the world. The present high level of surgical skill is partly due to the extreme degree of specialization which is one of the most striking features of modern medicine. Some of the well-defined special departments of surgery are abdominal surgery, thoracic and neurosurgery (surgery of the chest and nerves), ORTHOPAEDICS, EYE, EAR, NOSE, and THROAT surgery (qq.v.), and plastic surgery. Some surgeons go so far as to confine their practice almost entirely to one organ—the thyroid gland or the breast, for example.

A surgeon needs a profound knowledge of ANATOMY (q.v.) and a high degree of technical skill, but a knowledge of when to operate and what type of operation to perform is quite as vital. Modern surgery is, therefore, largely a matter of teamwork, and the surgeon works in close collaboration with the physician, the pathologist, the biochemist, the radiologist, and, of course, the anaesthetist. This tendency has reached its highest development in the United States, in such world-famous centres as the Mayo Clinic.

At the beginning of this century it was said that surgery had been made safe for the patient, but that it was still necessary to make the patient safe for surgery. This meant that the exact diagnosis had to be established in each case by the use of X-rays and by bacteriological and chemical tests, and that the resistance of the patient had to be built up to the highest possible level in preparation for the operation. Treatment before the operation with sedative drugs and anaes-thetics and methods of making the muscles relax have been brought to an extremely high state of efficiency; pain is abolished, the shock is minimized; the transfusion of blood and other life-giving measures make operation possible in the most desperate cases. After the operation the patient is given exercises and got on to his feet again as soon as possible, a treatment which has greatly reduced post-operation complications. The use of DRUGS (q.v.), in particular the introduction of penicillin and the other antibiotics, has not only made surgery safer but in many cases has made an operation unnecessary.

Surgery is now concerned not so much with removing diseased organs and tissues as with repairing and restoring their function. This tendency is seen in the wonderful operations which have been devised for the cure of congenital abnormalities in, for example, the heart, or in the great vessels as in the so-called 'blue-baby' operations (*see* HEREDITARY DISEASES). The results achieved by plastic surgery in correcting deformities and repairing war wounds; by plating and pinning fractures (*see* BONES AND JOINTS); by treating 'medical' diseases such as high blood-pressure and certain types of MENTAL DISEASE by operations on the NERVOUS SYSTEM (qq.v.); and by transplanting organs and tissues are all examples of modern operations of repair. In spite of these triumphs every surgeon will avoid an operation if he can, and as preventive medicine advances, many of the surgical operations of today may become unnecessary (*see* MEDICINE, HISTORY OF).

See also SURGERY, HISTORY OF; ANAESTHETICS; ANTISEPSIS AND ASEPSIS; ORTHOPAEDICS.

SWEETENINGS. HONEY (q.v. Vol. VI) was the only sweetening agent known in most parts of Europe until late medieval times, when cane sugar (*see* SUGAR CANE, Vol. VI) was imported, at first in small amounts from India and Arabia. Later, during the 15th century, it came in somewhat larger amounts from Madeira and the Canaries; but it was a rare luxury until the 18th century, when trade with the West Indies greatly improved supplies. At the end of the 18th century the processes for extracting sugar from SUGAR BEET (q.v. Vol. VI) were developed in Germany.

Sugar from cane or beet is in the form of crystals or syrup (*see* SUGAR REFINING, Vol. VII). There is a wide variety of crystalline forms: white sugar may be granulated, castor, lump, or icing, which is finely crushed crystals; and brown sugar includes demerara, coffee crystals, and moist or 'pieces'. Besides treacle and syrup derived from cane there are other natural syrups. Maple syrup is obtained by tapping the trunk of the MAPLE TREE (q.v. Vol. VI) in the early spring when the sap is rising, and sorgo syrup is prepared in a similar way to cane syrup. Corn syrup is not a natural syrup but can be prepared from maize and other plants with a high starch content.

Cane sugar consists entirely of sucrose ($C_{12}H_{22}O_{11}$). Other forms of natural sugar are fructose in fruit, lactose in milk, glucose in honey; they have a somewhat less sweet taste than cane sugar.

All the sweetening substances mentioned so far are foods which contribute to the calorific value of the diet (see FOOD VALUES). Another sweetening agent, saccharin, is not a food in this sense, but is invaluable as a sweetening agent for people suffering from DIABETES (q.v.) who may take only a limited amount of carbohydrate. Saccharin, which is 300 times as sweet as cane sugar, is made from coal-tar, a by-product in GAS MANUFACTURE (q.v. Vol. VIII).

SWEET-MAKING. 1. Some home-made sweets do not need cooking at all, and others can be made on a gas-ring with a thick saucepan. As success with cooked sweets depends almost entirely on getting precise temperatures, a sugar thermometer is a great help, but an alternative is to watch the boiling sugar carefully and to test drops of it in cold water. At a temperature of 225° F. a drop of the syrup, if drawn apart between finger and thumb, will form a thread— the consistency needed for ICINGS (q.v.). At 245° F. the syrup, lifted in a cold teaspoon and dipped into cold water, will roll off the spoon into a soft ball—the consistency needed for fudge. At 250° F. the syrup will roll off the spoon as a hard ball—as needed for caramels. At 280° F. the syrup, when dropped into very cold water, will form a hard brittle ball; if at this stage it bends instead of breaking, it needs more cooking for toffees. At a temperature of 300° F. the consistency is even harder and more brittle —as needed for hard toffees.

2. UNCOOKED SWEETS. (a) Fondant. For this, 1 lb. (2 breakfast cups) of sieved icing sugar, ½ tablespoon of cold water, ¾ teaspoon of vanilla,

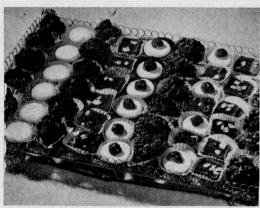

HOME-MADE SWEETS INCLUDING PEPPERMINT CREAMS AND FUDGE

and 1 egg-white are needed. The egg-white, water, and vanilla are beaten together, and then the sugar is added gradually to make a very stiff mixture. This is kneaded with the hands until smooth, then coloured, flavoured, and shaped as desired. Cream, strong black coffee, or lemon juice can be used instead of water. Two tablespoons of coconut can be used with a cream fondant; and six drops of peppermint essence make a good flavouring.

(b) Almond Paste and Marzipan. For almond paste, ½ lb. of ground almonds, ½ lb. of icing and castor sugar mixed, 1 tablespoon of orange juice, and a whipped egg are mixed in the same way as fondant. To make marzipan, ½ lb. of granulated sugar and ½ cup of water are stirred to a soft ball, and then ½ lb. of ground almonds and ¼ cup of orange juice are mixed in. The mixture is beaten till creamy and turned on to a sugar-dusted slab or plate to cool. The marzipan can then be moulded to represent tiny apples, carrots, and so on, and painted with a clean paint brush dipped in food colour bottles, and rolled in castor sugar; potato shapes are rolled in cocoa. Angelica and cloves can be used for stalks and flowers.

(c) Stuffed Dates, Prunes, or Figs. These fruits can be split and filled with marzipan or several kinds of fondant, and topped with a piece of nut. Peanut butter and orange juice, candied ginger, nuts, or quartered marshmallows can be used as stuffings.

(d) Fruit Rolls. ¾ cup of washed raisins or dates and ¼ cup of walnuts are minced and formed into small rolls, dusted with castor sugar, and sliced.

(e) *Candied Orange Peel.* Peel from the sections of four oranges is covered with cold water and boiled slowly until soft. Then, after the white part has been removed with a spoon, the peel is cut in thin strips with scissors and put in a saucepan with a cup of sugar and ½ cup of water, and cooked slowly until the peel is clear (230° F.). After being cooled, the strips are rolled in granulated sugar (being handled with forceps if possible) or dipped in melted chocolate.

(f) *Salted Nuts.* If peanuts are placed on a tray in a moderate oven the skins will soon pop off. Nuts or skinned peanuts are tossed in oil or butter in a frying-pan until delicately browned, drained on brown paper, and sprinkled with salt. They can alternatively be sprinkled with oil and browned in a hot oven (400° F.), being occasionally stirred.

(g) *Sugared Nuts.* ½ lb. of nuts are cooked in a heavy pan in a syrup of 1 cup of sugar and ½ cup of water. They are stirred until the syrup begins to look white and slightly sugary. Then, ½ teaspoon of cinnamon having been added, they are set aside for 10 minutes. Then they are heated over a low flame on an asbestos mat, and stirred constantly until the sugar starts to melt. They are then poured on to a wire cake tray standing on wax paper and separated to dry.

(h) *Pop Corn.* The right sort of corn is sold in America in tins; ½ cup yields 1½ quarts when popped. About 1 tablespoon of corn is put into enough melted margarine to cover the bottom of a thick saucepan and shaken over a low heat until the popping begins; the grains must then be shaken rapidly until popping stops, when they are removed from the fire and salted.

3. COOKED SWEETS. (a) *Turkish Delight.* 1 oz. of gelatine (preferably sheet) is broken up and soaked in ½ cup of cold water till it is soft. 1 lb. of sugar is put into ½ cup of boiling water, stirred, and brought back to the boil. The gelatine is then added and the whole simmered for 30 minutes. Then the juice of one lemon and a little cochineal colouring is added. It is poured, an inch deep, into a small square pan or plate which has been rinsed in water, and left to cool. When it has set, it is cut in cubes and rolled in icing sugar.

(b) *Fudge.* To make a milk fudge, 1 lb. of sugar, ¾ cup of milk, and 1 dessertspoon or more of butter are used. The sugar and milk are boiled to 245° F., being stirred only until the sugar dissolves. The butter is then added, off the heat. This mixture is beaten until it granulates, turned into a greased tin, marked into squares, and cut when cold. The more butter used the tenderer the fudge will be. Evaporated milk can be used instead of plain milk. For chocolate fudge, 2 oz. of cocoa or 2 squares of cooking chocolate are added as the sugar comes to the boil, and vanilla flavouring is added at the end. For coffee fudge, rather more butter is used, and a tablespoon of coffee essence beaten in. For coconut fudge, 2 oz. of coconut are stirred in at the end of the cooking, half the mixture is poured into a buttered tin, and the other half is coloured pink and poured on top. Another variation of fudge can be made by beating in 3 tablespoons of peanut butter, and chopped nuts, ginger, or sultanas.

(c) *Cream Caramels.* 8 oz. of soft brown sugar are dissolved in 2 tablespoons of water; then 3 tablespoons of cream or evaporated milk, 4 oz. of butter, and some vanilla flavouring are added. The mixture is boiled to 250° F., poured into a buttered dish, preferably between oiled caramel bars, and marked into squares when almost cold. It is then cut and wrapped in wax paper.

(d) *Toffees.* 1 lb. of sugar, ¼ cup of water, and a tablespoon of vinegar are stirred only until the sugar is dissolved, and then the temperature is raised, not too quickly, to 280° F. or 300° F. (If the temperature rises too fast, the sugar granulates, and this can be avoided by adding a spoonful of cold water.) The mixture is then poured into a shallow well-greased tin, marked in squares, and, when cool, knocked into pieces.

Barley sugar is made in the same way but the vinegar is omitted, and the juice of a lemon or ½ teaspoon of cream of tartar is added when the temperature reaches 245° F. Towards the end, ¼ teaspoon of lemon essence is added gradually. The mixture is then poured on to a slab, folded sides to middle, and pulled into strips or twists or cut into lengths, or treated like toffee.

For butterscotch, brown sugar replaces white in the recipe, and a tablespoon of golden syrup and 2 oz. of butter are used, and for treacle toffee, 2 tablespoons of treacle and 1 oz. of butter. For nut toffee, the toffee mixture is poured on to browned nuts sprinkled on the greased tin. For hokey pokey, when the toffee mixture reaches 300° F., a level teaspoon each of baking soda and cream of tartar mixed together are stirred in quickly, and the mixture is poured into a deep greased cake tin.

SWEETS AND PUDDINGS. 1. The distinction between puddings and other sweets is somewhat vague. Puddings seem to have originated in Britain as mixtures of forcemeat, cereals, and herbs boiled in animal skins, now represented by haggis and mealy pudding. Sweet puddings boiled in a cloth, such as roly-poly and Christmas pudding, came next, and later the term was extended to boiled or baked mixtures, mainly of cereal and milk, such as rice or bread pudding. Nowadays almost anything of this consistency is called a pudding; the French have adopted the word as *pouding*, the Italians as *budino*.

Because there is plenty of fresh fruit for dessert in the warmer parts of Europe, puddings, or even sweets, in the British sense, are rare. In France the sweet is called *entremets*, because it comes between the roast and dessert, and is most likely to be a tiny *crème caramel* or a few spoonfuls of jam on a saucer. In America it is either ice cream or a wedge of 'pie', that is, open pie or tart, generally cold and often *à la mode*, that is, with ice cream. The British 'pie' is unique; it has to be specially asked for in America as 'deep dish pie', and elsewhere in the world, apart from places with British traditions, it does not exist.

2. HOT SWEETS. (*a*) *Boiled Puddings.* Cereal and milk puddings are frequently boiled and, like custard (*see* SAUCES), are a favourite accompaniment for stewed fruit. The addition of a few spoonfuls of coconut, chocolate, coffee, treacle, or home-made butterscotch makes plain milk puddings more interesting. Pear Condé consists of pears peeled and simmered whole in syrup and served with ice cream on a bed of creamy rice coated with apricot jam. Most English puddings of the suet class are steamed not boiled; but the rich Christmas or plum pudding and the plainer spotted dog are both boiled.

(*b*) *Steamed puddings* (*see* STEAMING) can be very simple mixtures of flour, suet, and water, steamed in a basin lined with jam or syrup—for example, treacle sponge—or they can be egg-and-butter mixtures of the cake type, such as golden marmalade pudding. All demand a SAUCE (q.v.)—for example, lemon for fig or date pudding, or ginger syrup and whipped cream for ginger sponge. Apple (or other fruit) dumplings are little parcels of steamed suet crust (*see* PASTRY) containing the fruit. They can also be baked, or steamed, or fried.

(*c*) *Baked puddings.* Many steamed pudding

PUTTING A BOILED PUDDING INTO THE SAUCEPAN

mixtures can be baked—jam roly-poly, apple sponge, and all the cereal puddings—provided that powdered cereals are first boiled and stirred to avoid lumps. A characteristic of baked milk puddings is the brown milk skin which some people love. Baked custards are often stood in water in the oven to prevent their curdling. Bread-and-butter custard consists of bread thinly sliced and buttered, sprinkled with sugar and raisins or sultanas, and half immersed in custard. 'Queen of Puddings' is a light bread custard spread with jam and topped with meringue, delicately browned. Various batters and sponges are baked with fruit—for example, American pineapple upside-down cake, strawberry shortcakes, and cobblers. Ordinary Yorkshire pudding batter strewn throughout with dates and walnuts or with sugared apple slices, and served with lemon sauce or cream, makes a fine sweet. *Migliaccio* is an Italian sweet of baked chestnuts topped with pine-seed kernels. Throughout Polynesia the common pudding is *Poée* made from the red plantains of the mountains. There are many varieties of pies, of which English apple pie is widely known. It needs crisp, evenly baked pastry and, if the apples have a poor flavour, pieces of quince, lemon rind, or sultanas to make it more interesting. Cloves should be avoided. In Yorkshire cheese is eaten with apple pie. Black currants, gooseberries, apricots, damsons, and blackberry and apple make good pies. Notable English open tarts are Bakewell, an almond-flavoured sponge on top of jam and pastry; Felixstowe, pastry spread with jam, stewed apples, and meringue; and treacle tart filled with breadcrumbs and golden syrup. American pies such as pumpkin and lemon meringue are equally famous.

Soufflés are described in EGG DISHES (q.v.).

(d) *Fried Sweets*. The French version of our Shrove Tuesday pancakes is called *crêpes*. Filled with a sizzling mixture of orange juice, sugar, and butter, they are called *Crêpes Suzette*, named after a maid who carried pancakes in a Comédie française play performed in 1897. Sweet omelettes and apple and banana fritters deserve to appear more often in home cooking.

3. COLD SWEETS. The bases for these are fruit, nuts, JELLIES, milk, cream, mock creams, custard sauces, sponge cake, meringue, liqueurs, and ICES (qq.v.).

Stewed fruit or mixtures of fruits, known in French as *compôtes*, are often served with custard or with junket (curds and whey set with rennet).

Jamaica cream is milk jelly flavoured with treacle. Milk from a newly calved cow, called beestings, makes, when cooked, a firm curd which is the basis of the Welsh *Llo bach* (little calf) and the Scots *beist* cheese. *Pascha* is a Russian sweet made from milk cheese. A 'cream' is a cold sweet made with real cream or with milky sauces in imitation of cream, which has been allowed to set. *Blancmange* or 'shape' is a humble example, and Bavarian cream, thick with eggs, real cream, and gelatine, is a rich one. When such creams are whipped and frozen they are often called *mousses*.

Sponge cake or fingers, soaked in wine and fruit juice and covered with egg custard and cream, makes tipsy cake, trifles, and *Charlotte Russe*. Meringue (*see* EGG DISHES) is served with cream and fruit, and it is the basis of a delicious modern Australasian sweet, Pavlova Cake.

There are many cold sweets made with ice cream, such as parfaits, sundaes, or bombes (*see* ICES). Escoffier, a famous French cook, invented several peach and ice-cream dishes including *Pêches Melba*—skinned ripe peaches on a bed of vanilla ice-cream covered with Melba sauce (*see* SAUCES). Nesselrode pudding, made of cream and eggs, chestnuts, currants, and raisins, was introduced by Count Nesselrode's chef. The Sicilian *cassata* is an ice encrusted with candied fruits and served in slices.

Various cakes and pastries often replace sweets, as do certain sweetmeats—for example, *membrillo*, the flat, square chunks of jellied quince, or *turrón*, the almond and honey nougat of Spain, or one of the many Oriental sweetmeats, of which the most famous is the almond and honey *halva*.

See also EGG DISHES; JELLIES AND ASPICS; ICES; MILK; SALADS.

T

TABLE DISHES. The peoples of ancient civilizations usually possessed a few richly decorated dishes, mostly in precious metals (*see* Vol. I, p. 363), which they used for ceremonial feasts. These, however, as well as the simple, almost crude, pottery dishes which sufficed for everyday use, were generally limited to bowls and flattish circular dishes. Such dishes have been found among the excavations of all ANCIENT CIVILIZATIONS (q.v. Vol. I) whether of the Old World or of Peru and Mexico.

The Greeks used principally bronze dishes, the Romans silver and pewter, as well as

ROUND AND SQUARE WOODEN TRENCHERS, THE LATTER
WITH A PLACE FOR SALT

decorated earthenware. In the great feudal households of medieval Europe fine gold and silver dishes were displayed on the sideboard; but the food was served in 'chargers', large, shallow, pewter bowls or dishes, from which each diner's portion was put onto a smaller bowl or platter. More humble folk used similar dishes of wood, and ate their food from round or square wooden 'trenchers' (a name derived from *tranchoir*, the piece of bread on which portions of meat were served and cut up). A trencher had a slightly sunken and rimmed centre to hold in the gravy, and a small depression in one corner for salt. Towards the beginning of the 16th century many English people owned, or hired for a season, a whole service of pewter chargers and round trenchers—a 'garnish of vessells'; but by the 17th century earthenware was in more general use throughout western Europe.

During the early Renaissance highly decorative pottery dishes were already appearing—fine lustre in Spain (*see* Vol. XII, p. 277), 'majolica' with blue, orange, yellow, and green designs in Italy, and blue-painted 'faïence' in France. A set of plates usually had the owner's coat-of-arms in the rather deep centre of each dish. Besides plates, large dishes with broad flat rims, smaller ones for handing sweetmeats, and saucer-shaped dishes on low feet for holding fruit were common. The large, round, flattish, wooden dishes of 17th-century England, painted with heraldic and floral patterns, were probably for display only. Small wooden roundels, usually in sets of ten or twelve in a box, were painted on one side with 'mottoes' or pictures and comic descriptions of a stock character, such as a wife, bachelor, or merchant; besides being for amusement, they may have been used for serving the course of fruit and sweetmeats with wine, which was known as the banquet or 'banket'.

By the later 17th century Chinese porcelain (*see* Vol. XII, opp. p. 224) and Chinese tea were being imported, and soon European factories, led by Meissen, were making porcelain tea- and coffee-sets, and all manner of dishes for formal meals (*see* PORCELAIN and POTTERY, Vol. VII). One saucer served both for the straight-sided coffee 'can' and the more graceful teacup. Early teacups had no handles, like the original Chinese, and tea-sets had no plates. Teapots and coffee-pots, cream jugs, and sugar-bowls were made in silver and also in pottery or porcelain, often copied from the silver shapes, and usually

Victoria and Albert Museum
MAJOLICA DISH MADE IN FAENZA, ITALY, *c.* 1520

decorated in bright colours, painted or printed (*see* Colour Plate, opp. p. 416).

The Rococo fashion (q.v. Vol. XII) first influenced the design of Meissen porcelain in Germany and then of Sèvres in France. In England the Chelsea, Bow, Derby, and Worcester works all made many beautiful pieces. All sorts of fantastic shapes and designs were used; for example, large tureens might be made in the shape of a swan or rabbit, and smaller ones in the shape of a melon, cauliflower, or bundle of asparagus. Jugs and sauceboats were shaped like folded leaves with a stem or twiggy handle; fruit dishes like large flat leaves painted with bees, butterflies, or flowers; cups like folded strawberry leaves; and salt dishes like shells or crawfish. Plates and dishes were often lobed and

Council of Industrial Design
MODERN CHINA TEA-SET

fluted in imitation of silver, or designed with open trellis borders like basketwork, and had multicoloured decoration, and perhaps some gilding, on a white ground. Sèvres porcelain was richly painted and gilded, Worcester was noted for blue and white designs, and Derby for its rich intense blue with much gilding. Wedgwood of Staffordshire became famous throughout Europe in the later 18th century for a very durable and efficient cream-coloured earthenware (*see* Vol. V, p. 476). The Caughley factory in Shropshire made the well-known printed blue and white 'willow-pattern' pottery dinner service. Sets of pottery or porcelain supper trays were made in various styles, often as open segments on a circular tray incorporating a small covered centre dish. Pink lustre (almost like copper) or silver lustre, with white patterns of scrolls and leaves, was a favourite finish about 1800.

By the mid-19th century Coalport, Derby, Rockingham, and Worcester were well known, and English 'bone china' (*see* PORCELAIN, Vol. VII) was being exported all over the world. Complete matching tea-sets, dinner services, and eventually also breakfast services were made, which included cruet-sets, butter-dishes, large deep soup or porridge plates, egg-cups, toast-racks, preserve jars, and covered cheese and hot muffin dishes. These 19th-century services were very large both in size and numbers. As well, special services for dessert were usual, and the green Wedgwood pottery 'sunflower' and 'vine-leaf' designs have become very well known

In the early 20th century special crescent-shaped individual vegetable salad plates were added, and also soup 'cups' with two small handles and a cover. Oven-ware of strengthened glass or pottery, including casseroles (covered dishes in which the food has been cooked), vegetable dishes and sauceboats, is now so attractive looking that it can be brought to table. Modern table services are much smaller and usually simpler in design. Most of the table 'china' is mass-produced in factories, but a considerable quantity is still produced by individual artist-potters.

See also JUGS AND VESSELS; TABLE GLASS.

TABLE GLASS. Glass is generally agreed to have been an Egyptian discovery, but until the Roman invention of glass-blowing, some time during the first century B.C., it was used mainly to hold cosmetics, oils, and other toilet preparations, and only rarely as table-ware.

The art of GLASS-MAKING (q.v. Vol. VII) spread rapidly through the Roman provinces, and by the end of the 1st century A.D. the manufacture of glass for table use, for jugs, dishes, drinking-vessels, bottles, plates, and lamps, was widely spread over Italy, France, Germany, Belgium, and, in the East, in Egypt and Syria. Indeed, there is evidence that it was made and used in Roman Britain.

During the centuries which followed the final dissolution of the Roman Empire, there was a decline in the art of glass-making in Europe, and although medieval craftsmen never entirely lost the art, their wares were crude and by no means in general use. It is strange that in the latter part of this period the medieval craftsmen should have produced STAINED GLASS (q.v. Vol. XII) superior to any produced in earlier or later centuries.

Outside Europe much fine glass was made in the Middle Ages. Medieval Islamic glass was of the highest quality, and Egypt and the Near East produced plain and decorated glass vessels, splendid both in form and colour, which were highly prized not only in their countries of origin, but also by the then more barbarous peoples of the West.

It was not until the 15th century in Europe, when the Renaissance, with its insistence on beauty, had turned to the antique for inspiration and had discovered among other things the excellencies of Roman glass, that a revival of glass-making began.

In this revival Venice was pre-eminent. Her trading fleets and foreign garrisons gave her contact with the East and knowledge of the Eastern wares, and this she quickly put to use. She obtained almost a monopoly of glass manufacture and, indeed, it still forms a considerable part of the city's industrial life. In spite of every effort to prevent it, emigrant Venetians in a short time carried the art of glass-making throughout Europe. In the 16th century glass factories producing the Venetian type of table glass, mainly under the direction of Venetians, were set up in England, France, Germany, Spain, and in the Netherlands.

After this time the development of table glass in western Europe, except for differences due to varying local materials and national tastes, followed much the same pattern in every country.

GLASS UTENSILS

Ashmolean Museum

From left to right: Roman ewer, 1st–5th century, A.D. Venetian goblet, 17th century. Venetian dish, 16th century
English decanter of glass and lead made by George Ravenscroft, 1618–88

Ashmolean Museum

ENGLISH DRINKING GLASSES

From left to right: Baluster goblet, *c.* 1690. Engraved ale glass, *c.* 1750. Champagne or sweetmeat glass, *c.* 1760. Wine glass with white enamelled decoration, *c.* 1775. Commemorative wine glass engraved with a portrait of the Duke of Cumberland, 1745

Although a 14th-century record speaks of 'bottles, bowls, cups to drink and such like', there was very little table glass in England until the 16th century, when Protestant refugees from Lorraine began its manufacture on a scale which brought glass once more into general use.

In 1575 a privilege to make glass in England was granted by Queen Elizabeth to a Venetian, Jacopo Verzelini, to whom are attributed a small number of goblets and cups with covers still extant, some dated, all enriched with diamond engraved decoration. Verzelini was succeeded by an Englishman, Sir Jerome Bowes; and in 1623 a company, under Sir Robert Mansell, was established by royal proclamation, which gave it the sole right to make 'all manner of drinking glasses, broad glasses, . . . and all other kinds of glasses, bugles, bottles, vials or vessels whatsoever'. It was at this time that the vessels known as decanter bottles, that is, bottles in which wine was brought from the cask to the table, came into use.

In the latter half of the 17th century the discovery, by George Ravenscroft, of introducing lead into the composition of glass produced a hard, less breakable, and more brilliantly lit type of table glass. This proved to be much more serviceable than the thin, brittle Venetian variety, and its surface lent itself to elaborate cutting and other intricate forms of decoration.

For some 80 years after the discovery of 'glass of lead', that is, until about the middle of the 18th century, English table glass attained qualities of form, texture, design, and decoration which have not been equalled (*see* Vol. VII, p. 204). Technical skill and mechanical devices in the 19th and 20th centuries have greatly increased the production of table glass, and some of this machine-made glass is of good design; but no modern glass can compare in beauty of form and texture with that produced in the 18th century.

In an elaborate TABLE SETTING (q.v.) for a dinner party, glasses of different sizes and shapes are set out in a regular order of the wines to be drunk with the different courses, beginning with sherry with the soup and ending with port with the dessert (*see* p. 493). Other types of glasses are used for brandy or liqueurs served with the coffee.

See also WINES AND SPIRITS.
See also Vol. VII: GLASS-MAKING.

TABLE MANNERS. Man does not instinctively behave well at meals. In the absence of rules to the contrary he is concerned principally with satisfying his animal instincts of hunger and thirst. Through the ages, however, conventions of civilized behaviour have gradually grown up, often beginning in monasteries, formulated by upper-class society, and imitated by lower classes (*see* SOCIAL CLASSES). Such conventions were encouraged by the presence of women at meals, and, in 18th-century England, for example, were apt to be forgotten when the women left the table, and the men were free to drink themselves under it.

In early medieval society manners dictated where to sit rather than how to eat: for an inferior to sit 'above the salt' (*see* TABLE-WARE) was a serious offence. Even by the 13th century, when women commonly ate with men and society was refined and even learned, the standard of behaviour at meals was, by present standards, low. We know some of the bad table habits from medieval writings. A 13th-century Italian treatise says: 'He who gets mad-drunk offends in three ways: he harms his body and his soul, and loses the wine which he consumes.' And two centuries later, in England, a girl is warned that she will get a bad name if she is seen habitually drunk. A treatise of 1430 on table manners for English children advised them not to pick their teeth with their knife. The *Babees Boke* of 1475 warned: 'Don't hang your head over your dish or stuff your mouth when it is already full, or pick your nose, teeth and nails'. In the next century, Hugh Rhodes's *Boke of Nurture* contained these suggestions: 'If another shares your dish

ENGRAVING FROM 'THE PRIZE FOR YOUTHFUL OBEDIENCE', 1800

don't crumble bread in it, as your hands may be sweaty; don't dip your meat in the salt-cellar; belch near no man's face; don't scratch your head at meals; don't blow your nose on the napkin; if you must spit, tread it into the ground; don't blow on your soup or drink, your breath may be foul; don't throw your bones under the table.' French books on table manners contain similar rules: 'Don't spit out food in your dish', says a 15th-century one, 'don't drink with a frothy mouth; don't wipe your teeth with the cloth; and don't spit in the washing basin'. In this way a code of social behaviour at the table was gradually established, based on consideration for one's neighbours; practical convenience, such as the need to keep the salt-cellar free from gravy; and artificial rules for purposes of prestige, such as the rule that forbids eating peas off the end of the knife, which is purely a conventional one, based neither on convenience nor consideration for others.

In medieval times there was a great contrast between meals in a monastic refectory, where order, some degree of cleanliness, and silence prevailed, and those in a castle hall where, even when important nobles were present, there was confusion and noise. The standards of the monastery, however, gradually influenced the homes of the nobility, since the sons of nobles were often sent to monasteries to be educated, and monks often became tutors in noble houses. As behaviour in the homes of the wealthy gradually became more orderly, and rules of behaviour were formulated, the influence spread to the tables of more ordinary families. It was the custom from the 12th to the 16th century to send children from the age of 7 or 8 to serve as pages in the households of great men, and there they learnt the best table manners, which they could never have learnt at home. It is significant that the early books on manners stress the need to show reverence to authority. 'Stand until you are told to sit', advises the *Babees Boke*, 'keep your head, hands, and feet quiet; don't scratch yourself or lean against a post; bow to your lord when you answer.' These years in a great house helped to undo the gross habits children learnt in their early years, which they spent almost entirely with the servants (*see* NURSERY, HISTORY OF), mixing very little with their parents; and therefore the books on manners had much to do in checking behaviour learnt from the servants' hall and stables.

Table manners reflect the character of a society, generation by generation, and what is refined behaviour in one age may be gross in another. We no longer wipe our plates clean with our bread, but in the 16th century this was customary. We no longer belch, even in moderation, but the belch was hardly more upsetting to the medieval diner than a hiccough, and is still in some countries, as, for instance, in Arabia, expected by the host as a sign of his guest's approval. We are recommended to rise from the table feeling that we 'could eat a little more'; but the Roman was accustomed to make himself deliberately sick in order to face still further courses. In fact, Roman houses had special departments, called *Vomitoria*, for this purpose.

In England, by the 16th century, table manners, though by no means without rules, were still crude by modern standards. Even in Italy, where society was more elaborately refined than in any other nation, the usual attitude of the eater was to eat quickly as much as possible. Giovanni della Casa, in his widely read work on etiquette, *Galateo* (*c.* 1550), mentioned those who 'thrust their snouts, like pigs, into their broth, and never raise their eyes or hands from the victuals, and gorge rather than eat with swollen cheeks, as if they were blowing at a trumpet or at a fire'. But from this period table manners became increasingly complicated and artificial. The introduction of the fork led to a technique more delicate than fingers had allowed, and gradually the custom was established of having different tools for each course (*see* TABLE-WARE), instead of cleaning the same ones. As TABLE SETTING (q.v.) became more complicated, there were more rules to learn and observe; the sprawling freedom of the medieval diner with his single knife and goblet gave way to the constrained demeanour of the modern diner, hemmed in with a dozen knives, forks, and spoons, and half a dozen glasses, the uses of which he must understand. While the lord and his household and servants all ate in the same hall, though in different parts of it, their manners did not differ strikingly; but as households became more divided, and especially as MEALS (q.v.) came to be valued for the opportunities they gave for refined conversation as well as for eating, differences in standards of table manners between cultured society and the lower classes became great. Elaborate ceremonial developed around the meals of the 19th-century gentry,

'FIDGITY PHIL'

Cautionary tale warning children of the consequences of bad table manners. From *Struwwelpeter*, 1901

especially in London, a striking example of which is the growth of the elaborate ritual of afternoon tea, a meal that involved more etiquette than food. During the later 19th and the 20th century, however, there has been a levelling upwards in all forms of polite behaviour, due greatly to extended popular education and improved standards of living. The habits of upper-class society in London spread outwards into the provinces, and downwards into the middle and lower classes. Today there is a commonly accepted pattern of table manners to a great extent affecting all civilized peoples.

Oriental table manners as a rule pay less attention to the mechanics of eating and more to questions of precedence and honour. Eating may be noisy or even messy, as long as proper attention is paid to elders and guests. In China, where the prepared dishes are common and only the rice or staple food is served individually, a host may pick choice morsels from the common dish with his chopsticks and urge them upon a politely declining guest. Meals tend, in fact, to become a polite and ceremonious warfare between the two. The idea that food must be kept strictly on one's plate seems a peculiarly European one. In China, for example, fish and fowl bones are deposited on the table and swept up afterwards.

There is great economy in the use of tableware, because the same bowl and chopsticks are used for every course. This economy is even greater in India and many other parts of Asia where the right hand is the only implement used. It is used skilfully and tidily, but fairly thorough washing is necessary when the meal is over. In China the hands may be wiped with steamed cloths once or twice during the course of the meal, and it is usual to rinse the mouth after the meal with tea or boiled water. Seating affects table manners almost as much as the implements used. Thus, Chinese sit at tables much higher than ours, with their mouths correspondingly nearer the food. Japanese sit on the floor and have to be served kneeling. In this position the diner's whole body is visible, and so his deportment and the movements of his body are as important as those of his mouth. Drinking, which takes place before the main meal, is even more ceremonious than eating. But the most elaborate and artificial set of manners to be found in all Asia is the Japanese Tea Ceremony, which, with its rigidly prescribed movements and prostrations, resembles a religious ritual more than a tea party (*see* p. 148).

See also ETIQUETTE.

TABLES. Like chairs and chests, tables were among the earliest kinds of domestic furniture. The Egyptians, as early as 1500 B.C., made small, simple wooden tables, with rectangular or round tops, supported on three or four plain legs. The Assyrians also had tables, though they used metal and other materials besides wood in their construction and decoration. The Greeks, like the Egyptians and the Assyrians, used tables almost exclusively for eating off. Instead of sitting (and this is also true of the Romans), they ate their meals reclining on couches, and therefore their tables were low and lightly constructed so that they could be removed when the meal was over. The earliest Greek tables, made of wood, bronze, or marble, and dating from the 5th and 6th centuries B.C., had rectangular tops supported by three, or sometimes four, plain legs. In the 4th century B.C. three-legged round-topped tables became popular, the supports being carved in the form of the legs of an antelope, deer, or lion.

The Romans used tables as permanent pieces of furniture, more important than any others. They therefore introduced both original and handsome designs and decorations. As well as developing the low rectangular and the round-topped tables of the Greeks, they evolved another form of round table, which was supported on only one leg or pedestal, and also a rectangular-topped table, either of wood or marble, supported at each of the shorter ends by an elaborately carved, solid marble slab. Several bronze and marble tables of great beauty and fine workmanship have been found at POMPEII (q.v. Vol. XII).

Throughout Europe during the Middle Ages, when many of the refinements of Roman civilization had disappeared, and furnishing, like life, was extremely simple, tables were used almost exclusively for eating off. They were mostly of trestle construction—long, heavy boards of oak or elm resting on a series of central supports. We know from descriptions in Chaucer and other medieval writers that after meals the table tops were taken off and leant against the wall, leaving the floor of the hall free for entertainments or sleeping. Practically the only remaining examples of the English medieval trestle table are the magnificent pair which still stand in the Baron's Hall at Penshurst Place in Kent, and which date from the late 15th century. Towards the end of the Middle Ages, particularly in France, smaller tables, sometimes with circular tops, which could be drawn close to the fire, were in use, but small tables did not become common until a much later date.

Joined tables, that is, tables with the top fixed permanently to the frame and the legs, though made in the 15th century, did not come into general use until the 16th century. With the introduction of this kind of table, the word 'board', used to mean a table throughout the Middle Ages, was replaced by such phrases as 'joined' or 'framed' tables. At first, these were large and cumbersome, with oblong tops usually about 12 feet long and 2 to 2½ feet wide. These were supported on thick legs joined by wide stretchers, which, being fixed low to the ground, helped to keep off the draught. Towards the end of the 16th century these tables were elaborately decorated, the frames gadrooned, and the legs turned and carved in bulbous shapes, a fashion introduced into England by Dutch pattern-books and immigrant craftsmen. They were so heavy, however, that two could not be easily moved together when a longer table was needed. Consequently, during the 16th century, the 'draw-table' was introduced, which had two extending leaves fitted under the top of the table so that they could be pulled out when necessary to make the table nearly twice as long.

In the late 16th century table legs became grotesquely bulbous, but were soon replaced by simpler baluster-shaped legs. On the Continent table legs were sometimes elaborately carved in the shape of animals or human figures.

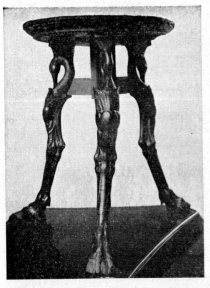

Top: left, GREEK TABLE; *right,*
ITALIAN TABLE, MID-16TH CENTURY.
Centre: ENGLISH DRAW-TABLE, *c.*
1600. *Bottom: left,* ENGLISH GATE-
LEG TABLE, *c.* 1690; *right,* ENGLISH
TEA TABLE, MID-18TH CENTURY

*The Greek table from the Musée du Cinquan-
tenaire, Brussels, and the rest from the Victoria
and Albert Museum*

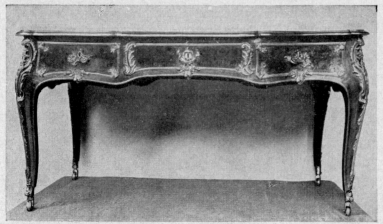

FRENCH ROCOCO TABLE, MID-18TH CENTURY

elaborate turning. Other small tables of the late 17th century had rectangular tops, frequently decorated with elaborate marquetry work, and turned legs joined by flat serpentine stretchers.

During the 18th century the number and variety of tables increased rapidly, and new types were introduced from the Continent. Writing tables, dressing tables, and card tables, and, later, even more specialized types, such as breakfast tables, tea tables, and shaving tables, took their places as everyday items of domestic furniture. The form and decoration of these various kinds changed according to fashion. In the early 18th century the table surface was decorated with beautiful walnut veneer, and the cabriole leg predominated. About 1720 some tables were made of pinewood, carved and gilded, a fashion which continued for a long time. With the introduction of mahogany, a hard wood excellent for carving, the legs and frames of tables were elaborately decorated with Rococo carving (q.v. Vol. XII). Chippendale's *Director*, first published in 1752, provided many designs for different types of tables, some in the rococo style, others in the Chinese and Gothic taste (*see* Vol. VII, p. 196). About 1770, when CLASSICAL styles (q.v. Vol. XII) again became fashionable, furniture as a whole became lighter in design, and tables were made with straight, elegant, tapering legs which were often fluted. Satinwood was widely used, and the place of carved decoration on tables was taken by inlay, painting, and the addition of finely chased gilt brass mounts. Typical of the early 19th-century Regency period was the table with a circular top supported on a central shaft or by three animal legs, a design based on the antique models of classical times which at that time were inspiring furniture designers.

During the late 16th and early 17th century a number of smaller tables were made, notably gaming tables for cards and dice, and various types of small side tables. The earliest example of the gate-leg table, dating from about 1620, had a semicircular flap and a back leg split in two halves; one half could be swung out to support the flap, which, when opened, formed a round-topped table. After the Restoration great numbers of small tables of varying shapes and sizes were made, mostly of walnut which had replaced oak. Many of them had flaps and stood folded against a wall when not in use. A two-flap, oval-shaped, gate-leg table was developed, the legs and stretchers decorated with

REGENCY TABLE, c. 1800

During the 18th century the development of the table on the Continent was as complicated as in England. In France the rococo style of decoration came earlier than in England: the elaborate tables of Louis XV's time were designed in a series of elegant curves and were richly decorated with ormolu mounts. In

Louis XVI's reign, however, the classical revival caused designs to be more severe with rectangular lines and straight legs, though the gilt mounts remained as elaborate as before. French designs for tables as well as for other furniture strongly influenced the whole of western Europe. In America, where the cabinet-making trade was firmly established during the 18th century, designs for furniture followed the English pattern.

In many eastern countries the habit of sitting on the ground limited the need for tables, as the food was put on the floor. Japanese tables, for example, were simple in design and raised only a little from the ground. Most Chinese and Japanese furniture dates from the 16th century and later, and was usually lacquered. Much of the furniture made in the East, including tables, was not typical of the furniture used by the Orientals themselves, being specially made for export to western markets.

See also FURNITURE, HISTORY OF; INTERIOR DECORATION, HISTORY OF.
See also Vol. VII: FURNITURE INDUSTRY; CABINET-MAKING.

TABLE SETTING. The simple table arrangements of the early Middle Ages gradually became more elaborate until they reached the complex magnificence of Victorian banquet tables. Today, owing partly to a change in fashion and partly to the shortage of domestic staff, table setting is simpler—even for special functions. In Norman castles the only utensils provided were a plate and drinking-vessel; nobles and servants ate at the same table, with a tall 'standing salt' marking the dividing line between the two classes of society (see TABLE-WARE). Knives and spoons were the only pieces of cutlery used in England before the 17th century, but by the 19th century, each place at a formal dinner table carried a range of spoons, forks, and knives designed for each of the many different courses, with a variety of glasses for different wines. All were set out on a fine linen cloth, with other silver and glass appointments for condiments, wine, water, fruit, and flowers. Today the formal table, though similar, is less elaborate, because fewer courses and wines are served.

The set table, besides looking attractive, should be arranged so that the things on it are conveniently placed. A dinner table is covered either with a cloth or with individual place mats and serving mats. A cheese plate is put on the left of each place or 'cover', and the cutlery is then arranged in order of its use—the soup spoon on the outside of the right hand, then the fish knife and fork, meat knife and fork, and finally cheese knife. The dessert spoon and fork are usually laid across the top of the cover, the spoon on top, but sometimes they are put with the other cutlery, in the innermost position. If there is only one glass, it is placed opposite to the end of the long knife; if two, the white wine glass occupies this position and the red wine glass is placed to the left of it (see TABLE GLASS). On the dinner table are also placed cruets, water jugs, decanters, and plates and cutlery for serving—though in some households these latter remain on the sideboard, where the carving is done, and are handed to the table by maids. FLOWER DECORATIONS (q.v.) should be in low vases so as not to impede the view across the table. Table napkins are sometimes folded in a decorative way and each is placed on an individual place mat.

A 19TH-CENTURY TABLE ARRANGEMENT
From Garrett's *Encyclopaedia of Cooking*, 1891

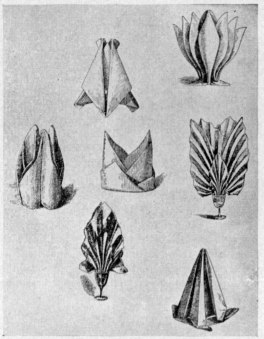

SOME WAYS OF FOLDING TABLE NAPKINS
From Garrett's *Encyclopaedia of Cooking*, 1891

Embroidered and lace-trimmed cloths, fine china, and silver are traditional on the tea table. If tea is to be handed around, a trolley often replaces the table nowadays and a number of small tables are used.

See also TABLE DISHES; TABLE GLASS; MEALS, HISTORY OF; TABLE MANNERS; HOUSEHOLD LINEN.

TABLE-WARE. In the later Middle Ages each person probably possessed a personal knife and spoon which they brought to table with them. The knives were of various shapes, with sharp steel blades and plain or ornamental handles. The spoons were made of bone, brass, pewter, or silver, and they had fig-shaped bowls and thin, hexagonal handles, with a device or figure at the end—the apostles being a common motif. Forks were not yet in use.

The most important object on a medieval table was a large standing-salt, a few of which still survive in the possession of university colleges and city companies. The lord's family and guests together with the whole household ate at a long table in the hall. The salt was placed so that the lord, his family, and his guests sat 'above the salt' and the servants sat 'below the salt'. The salt was shaped like an hour-glass with a circular depression beneath a tall cover, and it was often gilt and enamelled.

With the RENAISSANCE (q.v. Vol. I) and the revival of classical styles, the standing salts were generally shaped as square or round pedestals, sometimes nearly 2 feet high though often very much smaller, and usually gilt. The most famous of all salt-cellars is Cellini's golden one of about 1540 (*see* Vol. V, p. 78). Sometimes they were made in elaborate architectural forms, and by the end of the 16th century bell shapes were common. Castors for pepper and spices were sometimes incorporated in the top of the salts.

During the 17th century, when the lord's family no longer ate in the hall but in a private dining-room, the large salts began to disappear, except for a few still made for ceremonial use, and were replaced by small salt-cellars. Typical of the mid-17th century was a low, waisted salt-cellar, with three or four scrolled arms to support a plate of fruit, and with a shallow depression to hold the salt. Later, the pedestal was supported by spreading feet.

About this time, spoons with oval bowls and plain flat handles appeared, though after the Restoration (1660) the handles were often ornamented. Table forks, other than the two-pronged silver sweetmeat forks, also began to appear on English tables. They had three or four prongs (four became standard by the end of the 18th century), and their handles matched those of contemporary spoons.

Table-ware, like other features of the domestic arts, developed very much in the 18th century. Two principal sizes of spoons and forks appeared, 'table' and 'dessert', as well as a variety of spoons for special purposes, such as teaspoons and spoons for basting, separating, ladling, and serving, some more than 12 inches long. Curiosities appeared, such as folding spoons, spoon-forks, and 'mote-skimmers'—teaspoons with attractively pierced bowls, and long, tapering handles, for dealing with the tea-leaves in either the cup or pot. 'Marrow-scoops' had blunt gouges at each end for extracting the soft marrow from bones. Sets of knives with silver blades and forks to match were introduced for dessert and later for fish, because the taste of either is spoilt by contact with ordinary steel. The modern use of stainless steels has removed this difficulty.

Some very beautiful designs for spoons and forks were made. About 1700 the elegant heavier

TABLE PLATE

From left to right: Castor, 1703; salt-cellar and spoon, 1726; fruit plate, 1734; castor, 1707; salt-cellar, 1737

CUTLERY

From left to right: Apostle spoon, St. John the Evangelist, 1504; fork, 1689; spoon with 'lace' ornament in relief, 1691; fork, knife, and spoon with chased ornament, the knife with pistol grip handle, *c.* 1725

PATTERNS OF SPOONS AND FORKS

Ashmolean Museum

From left to right: Hanoverian spoon, 1737; King's fork, 1837; Old English spoon with threaded edge, 1806; Fiddle fork with threaded edge; Fiddle spoon, 1818

spoon with an egg-shaped bowl, much like those in use today, was introduced, and early in the 19th century the heavy Regency 'King's' pattern and the 'fiddle' pattern appeared. Modern table silver is for the most part made in imitation of these designs.

At the beginning of the 18th century plain, small, rectangular salt-cellars were the most common; at the end, glass liners, usually blue, were placed in silver frames, because salt corrodes silver severely. A pierced oval frame on four legs was the most common of the many shapes then made. Salt-spoons were introduced for the first time—shaped as hearth shovels, little teaspoons, or flattened ladles. Drum-shaped castors in pairs or threes for pepper, spices, and mustard appeared, and many slender and light shapes with bulged sides were designed.

During the late 18th and the 19th century cruet-frames, originally only for oil and vinegar, were made to hold smaller castors as well, and were known as 'Warwick' frames. In the 19th century these sometimes held as many as ten different sauces. Egg-cup stands of similar design also began to appear.

Silver table-baskets for bread or fruit were made as early as the 16th century, and became common in the 18th century, especially oval baskets, at first with a handle at each end and later with a swing handle. Miniature ones were made for sweetmeats. During the Rococo period (q.v. Vol. XII), in the late 18th and early

19th centuries, elaborate centre-pieces, called 'epergnes', held several baskets or glass dishes. Silver or silver-gilt dinner services were made, especially for royal use, and soup tureens and sauce-boats (double-lipped, double-handled boats on moulded bases) were widely used. With the introduction of SHEFFIELD PLATE (q.v. Vol. VII), entrée dishes with covers, as well as soup- and sauce-tureens with ladles, were common table-ware in well-to-do houses.

In the 19th and early 20th centuries the equipment of a dinner table in all such houses was very elaborate and included a great deal of silver. With the more simple, labour-saving habits of modern times, much less table-ware is used, and silver and plate which has to be cleaned is put away in favour of stainless steel and fire-proof pottery and glass. The elaborate table-ware of the past is now rarely used in private houses.

See also TABLE DISHES; TABLE SETTING.

See also Vol. VII: GOLD AND SILVER WORK; SHEFFIELD PLATE.

TAILORING. Factory tailoring is described under CLOTHING INDUSTRY, Vol. VII; this article is concerned only with home tailoring. Many processes of soft tailoring are similar to those of

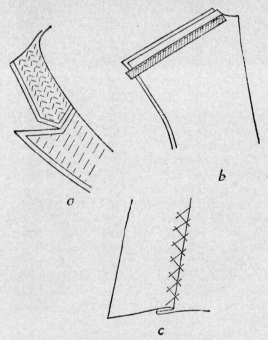

FIG. I. *a.* LAPEL DIAGONAL TACKED AND COLLAR PAD-STITCHED. *b.* TAPE STITCHED ALONG SEAM TO PREVENT ITS STRETCHING. *c.* LINING DART HERRINGBONED

A 17TH-CENTURY TAILOR WORKING IN HIS HOME
Painting by Brekelenkam, *c.* 1620-68

DRESSMAKING (q.v.), but there are some additional ones which give a coat or suit a professional appearance.

Facings, collars, cuffs, pockets, and belts have a firmer, neater appearance if they are interlined—most usually with tailor's canvas. This interlining material, which must be shrunk before use, can be obtained in white or natural colouring, and in various weights, stiff or soft. A synthetic stiffening material, which has no grain and washes without wrinkling, can also be obtained in several weights. This interlining may be pressed in place with a hot iron, but the thicker ones must be tacked in place with diagonal tacking or pad stitching (Fig. 1*a*).

To prevent seams from stretching and losing shape, narrow cotton tape is stitched along them at the back (Fig. 1*b*); and the fold lines of revers,

lapel edges, armholes, shoulder seams, and neck edges can also be taped. All unlined seams are bound, or their edges are turned under and stitched. Darts (*see* SEWING, Section 4) in thick fabrics are cut and pressed flat. In unlined garments, they are bound; on interlining they are either cut out and herringboned flat over a muslin strip, or slit and overlapped flat with zigzag stitching; lining darts are often just pleated or herringboned (Fig. 1*c*). Sleeve hems are stiffened with bias canvas to keep them from wrinkling.

Most coats have a lining, which is usually of shiny material to make the coat slip on more easily. Linings are cut from the garment pattern, but extra fullness is allowed in the centre back and the front facings are omitted. The darts and pleats are sewn, and the back pleat herringboned at the neck and waistline. The lining may then either be pinned in place, right side out, and slip-stitched all round; or it may be machined to the facings, and the shoulder and neckline slip-stitched. It will be easier to fit if the lining is tacked round the armholes and down the underarm seams before slip-stitching. The sleeve linings are sewn in last; the wrist edges of the lining are placed over the sleeve wrists, about 1¾ inches up, and slip-stitched in place; the armhole edges are then turned in and hemmed over the armhole lining. The hem of a coat is usually catch-stitched, and the lining pinned just over it and lightly slip-stitched; but if the coat is of very heavy cloth, its hem is bound, and the lining, also hemmed, is attached only at the seam lines with bar tacking. Tailored skirts are lined from waist to below the hip line with a lining slightly tighter than the garment to prevent the skirt 'sitting out'.

See also SEWING; DRESSMAKING; DRESS DESIGN.

TALLBOY, *see* CHESTS AND CUPBOARDS.

TAPESTRY, *see* FURNISHING MATERIALS. *See also* Vol. VII: TAPESTRY.

TARTANS. The Highland clans and regiments of Scotland (*see* SCOTS, Vol. I) have each a traditional tartan, with its own individual pattern of coloured checks. No special loom is needed to weave tartans. The numbers of threads of the different colours are arranged when the weaver sets the warp (the threads running the length of the fabric); and an exactly similar sequence of threads is woven through it to form the weft (the threads crossing the stuff). The 'sett' of a tartan is always symmetrical, and generally has two wider bands of different colours divided by narrower ones. The colours used are green, blue, often red, sometimes yellow, white, or black. In the past the dyes were made from natural plants and lichens. Red was very difficult to make, blue even more so until indigo, long known in the East, was imported (*see* DYES, Vol. VII).

We know that from the earliest times the Gaels of Scotland loved bright colours and check patterns for clothes. There were two reasons for the use of checks. The Highlanders liked the complicated, symmetrical patterns, for they appealed in the same way as interlaced 'Celtic' patterns, the elaborate metres of old Highland poetry, and the complex arrangements of ancient

National Gallery of Scotland

COLONEL ALASTAIR MACDONELL OF GLENGARRY
He wears the plaid and kilt of Macdonell tartan. Painting by Raeburn, 1756–1823

pipe music. Secondly, without large vats, only small quantities of yarn and not lengths of stuff could be dyed.

The introduction of particular tartans for each clan seems to have been gradual. In many cases, a 'dress' tartan with a good deal of red and a 'hunting' tartan, largely green, were evolved. Some patterns distinguished different districts rather than clans. After the Jacobite Rising of 1745, a law was passed forbidding the wearing of Highland dress and of tartan and, by the time the law was repealed in 1782, many of the old traditions were lost.

Regimental tartans were introduced when, in 1740, the first Highland regular regiment, the Black Watch, was established. The regimental tartan was of green, blue, and black; and this tartan was adopted by many of the Highland regiments that were raised during the American and Napoleonic Wars. In some cases an additional stripe was added, such as the yellow stripe of the Gordons. The Camerons, on the other hand, adopted an entirely different tartan.

The wearing of tartan by civilians had become fashionable when George IV visited Edinburgh in 1822, and was no longer purely a Highland custom. The number of tartans now worn is well over a hundred. With the use of aniline dyes and of fluffier fabrics, much of the charm of the older tartan fabrics has been lost.

See also Vol. I: Scots.
See also Vol. VII: Wool Weaving.

TATTING. This is a kind of knotted lace made with a small shuttle and cotton thread. Its origin is unknown but it seems likely from the form of the Knots (q.v. Vol. IV) that it has been derived from netting. Tatting was very popular on the Continent in the elegant second half of the 18th century, and was called in France and Germany by the charming name of *frivolité*. When it was revived in England in the mid-19th

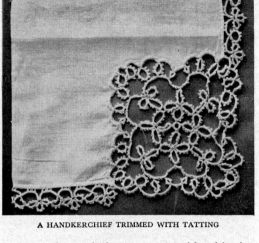

A HANDKERCHIEF TRIMMED WITH TATTING

century, the technique was considerably improved, but the delightful lace went by the less attractive name of 'tatting'. Tatting shuttles, usually about 2 inches long, are made of bone, tortoise-shell, steel, or plastic (Fig. 1*a*). The cotton thread is wound on to the shuttle until it is full. The tatter takes the shuttle in the right hand, makes a ring of the thread round the fingers of the left hand, and forms alternate under and over knots, like button-holing, along the thread (Fig. 1*b–f*). The part of the thread in the right hand is kept taut, and the knots are made on it by the thread in the left hand, so that the taut thread can be drawn up to form a ring (Fig. 1*g*). Spaces can be left at intervals between the knots. When the ring is drawn up, such spaces are pulled into loops or 'picots'. Rings and picots together form the basis from which the lace stitches can be made. In the more complicated stitches an additional ball of cotton is used, or even two shuttles. The shuttle threads alone make the rings, and the other thread makes straight chains of knots. Rings are joined to one another at their picots by using a fine crochet hook to pull the thread of the new ring through a picot of the made ring (Fig. 1*h*). Tatting has become fashionable once again and is used for decorating household linens and for delicate lacy trimmings for clothes.

See also Crochet; Knitting.
See also Vol. VII: Lace-making.

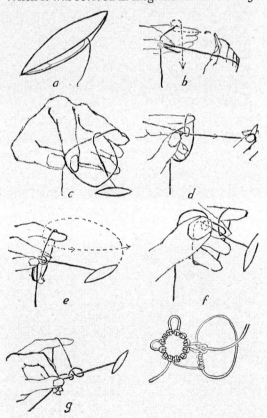

FIG. 1. TATTING
a. The shuttle. *b–f.* Making a stitch. *g.* Forming the ring.
h. Joining one ring to another

TATTOOING. An Egyptian mummy of 2000 B.C. has tattoo marks on the shrivelled

Picture Post Library

AN AMERICAN INDIAN WITH HIS BODY TATTOOED
Drawing by John White, 1585-90

manders of concentration and labour camps in totalitarian countries in this century. The early Christians, many of whom had been slaves, sometimes tattooed themselves with the sign of the Cross, but the first Christian Emperor, Constantine, forbade the practice. Tattooing fell out of use during the Dark and Middle Ages, and so much out of memory that when, during the early voyages of discovery, the Spanish found tattooed men in Mexico and Peru, it seemed like a new discovery. The North-American Indians were much tattooed, the boys probably being marked at the period of INITIATION into the tribe (q.v. Vol. I).

Later, travellers found the faces and bodies of the South Sea Islanders elaborately embellished. It is, indeed, from the Tahitian word *tatau*, 'to mark', that we obtain our word 'tattoo'. A tattooed South Sea Islander was brought to Europe by DAMPIER in the closing years of the 17th century and provoked great interest; later Captain COOK (qq.v. Vol. V) brought over another and displayed him all over England. The most elaborate examples of the art of tattooing can be found amongst the MAORIS (q.v. Vol. I) of New Zealand.

High Commissioner for New Zealand

A MAORI WITH TATTOOING ON HIS FACE

skin, and other mummies dating from the first millennium are patterned with figures which, strangely enough, are still used in North Africa today. In the Far East tattooing existed almost as early, for records of it in Japan date back to the 6th century B.C. Shortly afterwards the practice was brought from the mainland of Asia to the South Sea Islands.

In Europe tattooing was practised by the Germans, Gauls, and ancient Britons. The Greeks regarded it as the mark of the barbarian, and the Romans deliberately used it to mark criminals and slaves, as, indeed, did the com-

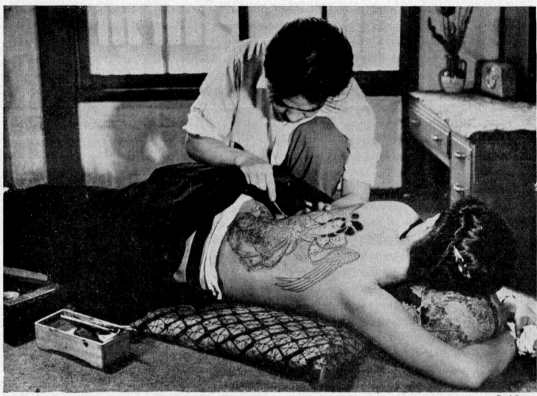

Paul Popper

A JAPANESE TATTOOER AT WORK

In the 19th century some Europeans began to have themselves tattooed all over and to be exhibited at fair-grounds, usually claiming that they had been captured by savages and forcibly decorated. This proved such a profitable line that a number of women began to exhibit themselves covered with tattoo markings. A certain Mr. and Mrs. de Burgh were exhibited in the 1890s, the latter with Leonardo da Vinci's 'The Last Supper' tattooed right across her back, and the former with 'The Crucifixion' similarly applied. In the late 1890s, and in the first decade of the 20th century, tattooing became so fashionable that professional tattooists could hardly meet the demand. Some of these experts, known by courtesy as 'professors', were extremely skilful, and they used an electric tattooing machine which was invented in 1891. The skin was pricked by a needle dipped in coloured inks, driven by electricity. Sailors of all nations are often tattooed, especially on their arms and chests, and so are some members of the criminal classes. It is supposed to be a sign of 'toughness'.

TEA, *see* HOT DRINKS. *See also* Vol. VI: TEA.

TEETH, *see* DENTISTRY. *See also* Vol. II: TEETH

THROAT. Separate anatomical structures, namely the airway and the swallowing apparatus, are combined in the throat, or pharynx. The pharynx is a muscular tube behind the nose and the mouth, which is a passage both for the air from the NOSE (q.v.) and mouth to the windpipe, and for food and drink to the gullet. At the end of the pharynx and below the level of the mouth, the airway and food-way separate. The airway, which lies in front, becomes the larynx, or voice box, and from it runs the windpipe (trachea) which conducts air into the lungs. The food passage, which lies behind, runs into the gullet (oesophagus) which leads into the stomach. During swallowing, breathing stops automatically, and the airway is tightly shut off by the epiglottis to prevent food from entering it.

The adenoids and tonsils are placed at the entrance of these two passages, as 'filters' to keep out infection. The adenoids are placed in the nasal part of the pharynx, above the soft palate. If they become so enlarged that they obstruct the entrance to the pharynx, they may interfere

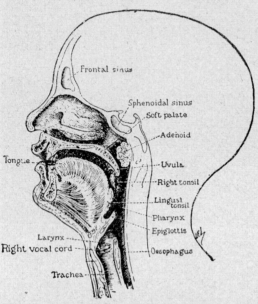

THE NOSE AND THROAT OF A CHILD

From Logan Clendening, *The Human Body*, Alfred Knop

with breathing through the nose. The tonsils are visible through the open mouth as a pair of almond-shaped bodies in the lower part of the pharynx. Bacteria passing down the throat must come into contact with the surface of the tonsils, and may even work their way into them. Healthy tonsils keep out the bacteria; but if they do not, and the bacteria congregate there, their poisons are absorbed into the bloodstream. However, this provokes the creation of protective substances, called antibodies, which make the bacteria inactive. It is easy to appreciate, therefore, that normal tonsils are important in protecting the body from germs entering through the mouth. Diseased tonsils, however, may themselves become breeding-places for germs.

Acute inflammation of the pharynx is common in colds. Chronic inflammation is the result of prolonged irritation due, perhaps, to smoking, to over-use of the voice, or to infection of the nose and sinuses, when the pus is swallowed and so inflames the throat. In diphtheria the pharynx and the tonsils are especially involved.

See also RESPIRATION; NOSE STRUCTURE; INFECTIOUS DISEASES.

THYROID GLAND, *see* ENDOCRINE GLANDS.

TONSILS, *see* THROAT.

TOWN PLANNING, HISTORY OF. TOWNS (q.v.) have seldom been the subject of deliberate design. Most of them have grown as the result of a number of accidental, unrelated factors, and only during the present century has the importance of town planning been recognized (*see* TOWN AND COUNTRY PLANNING, Vol. X).

A Greek, Hippodamus of Miletus, who was born about 480 B.C., made plans for laying out towns systematically with the streets at right angles to each other. The Romans followed Greek principles of planning. Their military camps, which were designed with careful forethought and discipline, and which formed the sites of many cities of the Roman Empire, had an unvarying rectangular layout, based on a pair of main roadways intersecting at right angles and connecting four gateways, one on each side of a fortified square. This layout can be traced today in numerous English cities, of which Chichester is typical.

By contrast, medieval cities grew in an informal, accidental way. Yet the plan of many of them, as with the Roman camp-cities, was largely determined by military requirements. Cities were also strongholds, and were surrounded by walls and other FORTIFICATIONS (q.v. Vol. X) arranged according to the way the ground lent itself to defence. As building was confined to the space within the walls, streets were generally narrow, and the buildings densely packed. When a city was forced to expand, it generally did so by building a new series of fortifications outside the first; the growth of many cities, therefore, can be seen as a number of concentric rings, marked by the roadways that so often follow the lines of earlier fortifications.

Those medieval cities which did not originate as fortresses generally grew up round important cross-roads, bridges or fords across rivers, harbours, or the walls of a palace, monastery, or cathedral. Cities were trading-places, and so a market-place was their central feature; but even such towns were surrounded by defensive walls which restricted and controlled their growth. The few medieval towns that were designed all at one time show variations of the Roman chessboard type of planning. In Renaissance

Aerofilms

AIR VIEW OF CHICHESTER

The two chief roads (one running beside the Cathedral) follow the original Roman plan. Part of the medieval city wall can be seen on the left, and the line of it can be followed by the roads and houses encircling the centre of the city

Co. Aérienne Française

AIR VIEW OF PARIS SHOWING THE LAYOUT OF THE STREETS PLANNED BY HAUSSMANN

At the bottom right is the Seine with the Place de la Concorde, and in the centre the Church of the Madeleine

towns too, where the practice of designing a whole street or even a complete quarter of a town as a single architectural unit was revived, formal planning on some kind of geometrical pattern was generally the rule. Important buildings were made focal points in the design of streets and squares and at the end of vistas, and parks and gardens were introduced into the plan of the town. The most celebrated example of large-scale geometrical planning, however, took place after the French Revolution, when PARIS (q.v. Vol. III) was replanned under NAPOLEON I (q.v. Vol. V), and was largely rebuilt some 70 years later by Baron Haussmann, working for Napoleon III.

During the later part of the Renaissance period, military considerations still often dictated the plans of towns. The great French designer of fortifications, Vauban (1633–1707), laid out numerous towns (called *bastides*) in an octagonal or star shape, the shape determining the pattern of the streets. The flat unobstructed space outside the walls (called the *glacis*), which was needed

for military purposes, helped to maintain the abrupt separation of the town from the surrounding countryside.

During the 18th century, when long periods of peace made fortifications less necessary, and improvements in artillery made them less effective, towns spread outwards, and new residential areas in the form of squares and gardens grew up on their fringes. In England there was often a town square planted with trees and grass, and a whole street was treated as one unit. This sometimes led, as in the Bloomsbury quarter of London, to an informal sequence of squares, streets, and terraces, combining dignity of architectural effect with ease and convenience. But few examples of large-scale formal planning exist in England, and most of the older English towns are either haphazard medieval growths with Georgian additions, or Georgian ribbon towns that grew up along the great coach routes. Notable exceptions are the sequence of squares and crescents laid out on the hill-sides of Bath by the younger John Wood (1728–75) and, to a lesser degree, those parts of London which were replanned by John NASH (q.v. Vol. V) for George IV, especially Regent Street and the terraces surrounding Regent's Park. Soon after this scheme was completed, the wave of building that followed the INDUSTRIAL REVOLUTION (q.v. Vol. VII) smothered most English cities in a shapeless growth of unplanned, hasty development, consisting of factories, densely packed houses, and, later, widely scattered suburbs.

The worst results of this rapid and unplanned growth of towns were overcrowded and insanitary SLUMS (q.v. Vol. X), a lack of open spaces, STREETS (q.v. Vol. IV) that are now mostly inadequate for modern traffic, and an inconvenient mixture of industrial and residential buildings. Large numbers of streets were built in accordance with the 'model by-laws', contained in the Public Health Act of 1875, which prescribed a minimum size for roofs, a minimum width for roads, and a minimum distance between rows of houses. Though this Act ensured a certain amount of light and ventilation for all houses, and thus prevented the worst type of slum from being built, it resulted in mile upon mile of monotonous streets, all keeping to these minimum dimensions, and with no provision for open spaces, schools, and public buildings.

In 1898, in protest against these ugly and unhealthy conditions, the social reformer Ebenezer Howard produced the first scheme for a garden city. Howard's ideas and experiments aroused wide interest, and by 1920 two garden cities, at Letchworth and Welwyn in Hertfordshire, had been founded, as well as industrial garden suburbs, such as Bournville, near Birmingham, and many municipal housing estates on similar lines (see GARDEN CITIES AND NEW TOWNS, Vol. X). These have had a great influence abroad, but in England they represent only small and isolated attempts to solve an immense problem. The fashion they set for widely scattered housing had the unfortunate result that the suburbs of big towns tended to spread still farther into the country, especially along the main roads in what is called 'ribbon development'.

After the Second World War the Government adopted many of Howard's ideas in its plan for fourteen new 'satellite' towns, eight near London, two in Durham, and others in Scotland and the Midlands, each of which will eventually house some 50,000 people from badly overcrowded areas in the larger cities. These towns are planned as independent communities, with public buildings, schools, shops, and cinemas to satisfy all the needs of the people. Sites are provided for factories so that workers do not have to travel long distances. Houses are of different sizes, suitable for young people with families or for the old, and variety in planning is given by different types of building, tall blocks of FLATS (q.v.) contrasting with small houses with their individual gardens.

See also TOWNS, HISTORY OF.
See also Vol. X: TOWN AND COUNTRY PLANNING; GARDEN CITIES AND NEW TOWNS.

TOWNS, HISTORY OF. The saying 'God made the country, man made the town' expresses the old rivalry between urban and rural life. Towns are products of human effort and of human organization; their origins can be traced far back to the distant ages of antiquity. The need for protection and defence, the claims of religion, and the growth of trade were the three main factors involved, and as soon as towns passed a certain stage of development they became centres of culture as well.

The need for protection was obvious in communities where a band of settled inhabitants sought to keep out their semi-nomadic brethren or enemies, such as the Assyrians who, in the words of the poet, descended on the Jews 'like a wolf on the fold'. For purposes of defence there were advantages in choosing certain sites for a town: the old Sanskrit word for 'high rising ground' is the origin of our English word 'borough' and of the French '*bourg*'. Given a good site, such as a hill or bend of a river, towns could be defended by fortified walls. As early as the 6th century B.C., Babylon was a large city surrounded by great walls and a moat; the Greeks and Romans constructed walls also, many of which still survive, and so did the various barbarian tribes after the fall of the Roman Empire. The great number of British towns ending in 'burgh' or 'chester' (from the Latin for 'camp') bears witness to the importance of defence in determining the site of settlements.

The claims of religion were also of major importance, particularly in the first towns and cities of the Ancient World, which were rich enough to have temples and provide for a professional priesthood. In the SUMERIAN cities (q.v. Vol. I), which grew up in the river valleys of the Middle East, the existence of temples was one of the distinguishing features of urban life; and big cities such as Ur and Kish had their local gods as well as their local despotic ruler. Even in Christian times, cities in Europe have grown up round the seats of bishoprics and their cathedrals, and have been regarded as centres for ecclesiastical administration and organization.

TRADE (q.v. Vol. VII), both local and international, has played an essential part in the history of towns. Merchants needed docks, markets, and offices, and they had to congregate together in reasonably large groups. In ancient Crete, where there was a highly organized town life in 2000 B.C., many large towns, such as KNOSSOS (q.v. Vol. XII), were built at the end of valleys linking the north and south coasts. While towns of this type were defended by the Cretan fleet, the inland towns were generally encircled with great walls. They all had crowded groups of houses within their boundaries, well-planned streets with pavements and gutters, and an adequate drinking-water and drainage system. At their central point there would be a market place, which was the trading centre of the town, and a small palace, which served as the centre of administration and of artistic life. The same basic town pattern existed in the Europe of the Middle Ages, although the high administrative standards of the Cretans (see MINOAN CIVILIZATION, Vol. I) were not equalled, and in remoter parts of Europe the towns were rough and ill-kept. In medieval England only London and York had a population of over 10,000. The richest towns of Europe were those which had grown with the increasing trade of the 12th and 13th centuries, such as Bruges, Cologne, Genoa, and Venice (see CITY STATES, Vol. X); there was a marked distinction between towns of this kind, which were closely bound up with international trade, and those towns which merely served as market centres for a surrounding rural district and lived off the food surplus which that district produced.

The growth of modern towns introduced two further factors. In the 15th and 16th centuries it became the fashion for kings and princes to display their wealth and power by improving their cities and making them as magnificent as possible. From this period onwards many of the great capital cities became centres of concentrated power and influence. Out of the rather cramped alleys and courts of the medieval towns were carved formal squares, often surmounted

CARCASSONNE, A MEDIEVAL WALLED TOWN IN THE SOUTH OF FRANCE

AIR VIEW OF OLDHAM, AN INDUSTRIAL TOWN IN LANCASHIRE

with parades and flanked with great new churches. Sometimes old walls were pulled down, as in VIENNA (q.v. Vol. III), where a new ring road, the Ringstrasse, was constructed to fill the open spaces left where the walls had been destroyed. In other places new towns were created, such as MADRID (q.v. Vol. III) or VERSAILLES (q.v. Vol. XII), often with elegant palaces and boulevards; in one of them, Karlsruhe in Germany, the whole town was designed to revolve about and radiate from the king's palace. LONDON (q.v. Vol. III), which grew rapidly in Tudor and Stuart times, escaped most of this formal planning. It was essentially a

trading city and when, after the Great Fire of 1666, Christopher WREN (q.v. Vol. V) drew up a symmetrical plan for rebuilding it which cut across existing property rights and boundaries, the plan was rejected because in a city without an all-powerful prince the people would not agree on the necessary readjustments. Formal planning in London was left to the 18th century when dignified classical squares were built in the West End outside the limits of the city.

The second factor in the modern history of towns has been the rise of industry. The enormous increase in man's power over nature, made possible by the invention of the STEAM

City Engineer, Birmingham

PLAN FOR THE REDEVELOPMENT OF DUDDESTON, BIRMINGHAM

New housing estates, replacing slums, are planned as a 'neighbourhood', with schools, community centres, libraries, and churches surrounding open spaces

ENGINE (q.v. Vol. VIII), permitted a rapid rise in population and a greater growth of towns than ever before in human history. Industrialization made for the concentration of a working population in towns which usually lacked the beauty and style of the capital city or even of the medieval town. These towns were soon associated with smoke and waste. The new urban landscape, completely man-made, was dominated by the grey walls of the factory, the long rows of small houses stretching round the workshop or mills, and by the tall chimneys, 'out of which', in Charles Dickens's phrase, 'interminable serpents of smoke trailed themselves for ever and ever, and never got uncoiled'. Dickens was one of the many 19th-century writers to attack the monotony of this new urban environment: in his novel *Hard Times* (1854), for instance, he says of the industrial town, Coketown, which is modelled on a Lancashire town, 'it contained several large streets all very like one another, and many small streets still more like one another, inhabited by people equally like one another, who all went in and out at the same houses, with the same sound upon the same pavements, to do the same work, and to whom every day was the same as yesterday and tomorrow and every year the counterpart of the last and next'.

Such gloomy pictures were not completely true representations of the new industrial towns. Without the concentration of economic activity in busy, smoky places there would have been no revolutionary increase in national income, and without this the remarkable social progress made in the 19th century could not have taken place. The very deficiencies of urban organization in the first decades of the century stimulated increased popular awareness of the complicated problems of PUBLIC HEALTH (q.v. Vol. X) and public order. Later on in the century, it stimulated the first modern experiments in TOWN PLANNING (q.v.) and the first attack on the SLUMS (q.v. Vol. X). By that time many of the industrial towns had grown to enormous size; their original industrial core was flanked with residential suburbs, and often the boundaries touched those of neighbouring towns and cities with no country at all between them. Planning became a necessity, and in England and almost every other industrialized country steps were taken to ensure a better balance between town and country and a closer control over unrestrained urban expansion.

One of the most interesting aspects of the recent history of towns has been the increase in the number of towns outside Europe and the rapid growth of some of those which already existed. In the middle of Africa, for example, the native population of Leopoldville, the capital of the Belgian Congo, increased from 46,000 in 1940 to 250,000 in 1953. During the same period the Negro population of Elisabethville, the main city of the uranium and copper-mining province of the Congo, jumped from 30,000 to 130,000. Such rapid rates of growth, very much more pronounced than in English cities in the 19th century, have created enormous social problems, and are striking examples of the changes in modern world economy. In the U.S.S.R., to take a second example, there were in 1939 no less than forty-nine 'boom cities' of more than 50,000 people, which had more than trebled in size during the previous 12 years; some of them, such as Magnitogorsk, had not existed at all in 1926. In consequence of this great growth of towns, the proportion of town-dwellers to country-dwellers in the total world population has altogether altered; in Britain, for example, the seven largest groups of built-up urban areas account for almost 40% of the total population. Within 50 years the world total is likely to be even higher than it is today. Most of the increased world population will be gathered together in towns, and will consist very largely of non-Europeans. We are in the midst of an urban revolution, far more dramatic in its implications than any previous urban revolution in history.

See also TOWN PLANNING, HISTORY OF.
See also Vol. X: TOWN AND COUNTRY PLANNING.

TOYS, see DOLLS; DOLLS' HOUSES. *See also* Vol. IX: TOYS, HISTORY OF.

TROPICAL DISEASES. 1. There are some diseases which are especially prevalent in hot countries, chiefly because of the undeveloped nature of many of those regions and because of certain climatic, geographical, and social factors which favour their spread. Some of the most important are carried by insects and injected into the bloodstream of human beings when the insect bites. One kind of mosquito is the 'vector', or carrier, of the parasite which causes malaria, and another kind carries the virus of yellow fever. Plague is carried by the rat flea, typhus by body lice, and sleeping sickness, or 'trypanosomiasis', by the blood-sucking tsetse fly.

Other diseases persist in the tropics because the knowledge and practice of hygiene and sanitation are in many parts still below the Western standard. Cholera and typhoid fever are examples of these, for both result from swallowing food or water contaminated by the disease organisms (*see* EPIDEMIC DISEASES).

2. LEPROSY is now almost entirely a tropical disease, though it used to be common in medieval Europe, and there were many leper houses then in England. It was gradually stamped out by strict isolation and improved hygienic measures, and is now found chiefly in Asia and Africa, where there are many millions of sufferers. Leprosy is a disease of the nerves and certain other tissues of the human body, the leprosy bacillus (*mycobacterium leprae*) being present in the diseased parts.

The disease takes two main forms. The so-called 'benign' type affects mainly the skin and the nerves. It makes certain areas of the skin unable to feel or to sweat, and it disturbs the nerve supply of the skin and bones, which affects their nutrition. Consequently, painless ulcerations arise, and the muscles waste, causing distortion of the hands and feet or even loss of fingers and toes, or blindness. This form of the disease is essentially chronic, but eventually burns itself out. The malignant type is more acute and considerably more fatal. It causes swellings in the skin and on the nerves, and the patient generally dies of exhaustion or the poisonous accumulation of infection.

It is now realized that leprosy is contagious only by prolonged and intimate contact with a leper who is in an infectious stage of his illness. Many healthy infants are born of leprous mothers but remain free from infection if they are separated from the mother after birth. Segregation of infectious lepers is practically universally recognized as being the only means of controlling the disease. At one time segregation meant segregation for life, but now that we know that lepers are not continually infectious, it is possible to release uninfectious lepers from isolation and allow them to return to their homes under medical surveillance. This greatly mitigates the hardship of the lepers' existence.

Modern methods of treatment appear to be effective if the disease is treated in the early stages, but not so effective once the disease has taken hold. A population subject to leprosy, therefore, should be under continual surveillance so that victims can be detected in the early curable stages, isolated, and brought under treatment before they have spread their infection.

3. MALARIA, or ague, occurs mostly in lands lying between 45° N. and 40° S. latitudes. It is perhaps the disease which causes more suffering and disablement than any other, and which afflicts the greatest number of people. It is caused by a certain type of the minute living organisms called PROTOZOA, which are transmitted to healthy persons from those infected

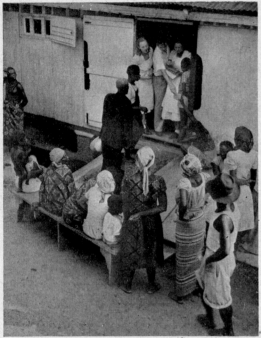

Camera Press

PATIENTS WAITING FOR TREATMENT AT THE LEPER HOSPITAL AT LAMBARÉNÉ, FRENCH EQUATORIAL AFRICA, FOUNDED BY DR. ALBERT SCHWEITZER

with malaria by a particular species of female MOSQUITO (qq.v. Vol. II). The organisms must undergo a stage of development in the mosquito's body before they can establish themselves in another human being.

About a fortnight after being bitten by an infected mosquito, the patient begins to suffer from attacks of fever and profuse sweating. One kind of malaria causes the fever and sweating to occur every third day, and another every fourth day. Yet another type, known as malignant malaria, causes a more or less continuous fever, and is associated with dangerous complications. In the early stages of 'typical' malaria the patient feels quite well between the attacks of fever and sweating, but as these continue, he gradually becomes anaemic and debilitated. In the malignant type he may experience vague ill health and fever for some days before the acute stages of his illness appear, or he may mystify his physician by presenting symptoms suggestive of pneumonia or appendicitis.

A person whose malaria has not been treated may continue to have intermittent attacks even after he has left the tropics. Malaria may complicate and so add to the risk of other diseases, such as dysentery or pneumonia, or a surgical operation may cause a hidden malarial infection to flare up, perhaps with serious results. Sometimes malaria causes severe damage to the red blood corpuscles, giving rise to the dangerous complication known as blackwater fever.

Drugs called 'anti-malarials' are used in treating malaria and are successful in the great majority of cases. The earliest known of these was quinine. The best means of prevention is to attack the mosquitoes, which may involve drainage of swamps and stagnant waters where they breed, as well as attacks with poisonous sprays or smoke. Protective measures can also be taken, such as mosquito-proofing houses or rooms, wearing mosquito-proof clothing, and using mosquito nets over beds.

4. YELLOW FEVER, the notorious 'yellow jack' of the old sea-stories, is a virus disease, which, like malaria, is carried from infected persons to healthy persons by female mosquitoes of another species. Primarily a disease of monkeys, it became established in humans many centuries ago and was probably carried from Africa to the West Indies when African slaves were first taken there. There have been many severe epidemics in America, notably that at Philadelphia in 1793, and there were many outbreaks in African ports during the last century. Modern methods of prevention and control, however, have almost eliminated epidemics. One of the greatest risks is that infected mosquitoes may be imported in aircraft to a country where the population has no immunity, and so cause an epidemic. This is one reason for the stringent sanitary regulations relating to aircraft which land in tropical regions in the course of their journey (see QUARANTINE REGULATIONS, Vol. X).

The method by which yellow fever is spread was first suggested by Carlos Finlay, a Havana doctor, in 1881, but it was definitely proved only in 1901 by an experiment for which some members of the American army heroically volunteered to be infected with the disease. One of them, J. W. Lazear, died as a result, becoming one of many hundreds of martyrs who have given their lives so that knowledge may advance and life be made safer and healthier for all.

The early symptoms of yellow fever are much like those of influenza, but in cases of yellow fever an almost intolerable headache develops, especially behind the eyes, together with backache and general muscular pain, and then nausea and vomiting of blood. Other complications follow, and death usually occurs within a week. As there is no satisfactory cure for yellow fever once it has been contracted, prevention and control are all-important. Vaccination, which is compulsory for all those travelling in or through yellow fever regions, gives protection for 4 years. D.D.T. and other modern INSECTICIDES (q.v. Vol. VI) have been very effective in reducing the numbers of the virus-carrying mosquito.

5. SLEEPING SICKNESS is caused by the protozoan trypanosomes which are injected into the victim's blood by the TSETSE FLIES (q.v. Vol. II). Sleeping sickness may cause fever, a rash on the skin, enlargement of certain lymphatic glands, followed by loss of appetite, great physical weakness, wasting of the body, mental derangement, and death. Before death occurs patients are often completely stupefied. In the absence of treatment death may occur within a few months of the onset of the disease.

Vast numbers of people in tropical Africa have been killed by the disease; the best-known epidemic took place along the northern shore of Lake Victoria, Uganda, at the beginning of the 20th century, when in 7 years the disease killed two-thirds of the estimated population of 300,000.

The areas where sleeping sickness occurs are known as fly belts, and in tropical Africa they are very extensive. The characteristic feature of these areas is a dense shade cast by thickly growing small trees and shrubs, such as may be found on the banks of water courses and watering holes. There the fly flourishes. One of the principal control measures is to eliminate such vegetation, especially around villages, fords, and other places where people congregate. Insecticide dusts and smokes are used to render fever-stricken areas healthy, and then steps are taken to resettle these areas and to encourage settled agriculture which will keep the land clear. In fly-infected areas the population is kept under continual observation so that cases of the disease can be identified early and treated immediately with drugs to kill the protozoa in the blood.

Trypanosomes which cannot be distinguished from those causing sleeping sickness are found to be existing harmlessly in the blood of game animals; but in domestic stock they cause a very fatal wasting disease known as 'nagana'. This has led some experts to believe that the reservoirs of the trypanosomes are the game animals, especially antelope, and that if these were exterminated, sleeping sickness in man and nagana in domestic animals might be eliminated.

6. DYSENTERY is an inflammation of the colon (part of the large intestine) with some ulceration which causes pain, diarrhoea, and the passing of small quantities of blood and mucus. It is caused by one of several parasitic organisms—bacilli or protozoa—which are swallowed in contaminated food or drink. Bacillary dysentery, usually spread by flies alighting on food, may occur in any part of the world, but it and other types of dysentery are more common in hot countries, partly because of low standards of hygiene. The most common form of dysentery in the tropics is caused by protozoa which invade the lining of the caecum and the colon and produce ulcers. There is, however, a combination of drugs which will kill the invading protozoa. Dysentery is best prevented by scrupulous cleanliness, especially in the handling of food, and by thorough protection of food from flies. The earlier the disease is treated the more effective the drugs.

See also EPIDEMIC DISEASES.

TUBERCULOSIS. This disease occurs throughout the world and has grave social importance because some 2 million people die from it each year and many more suffer a long and incapacitating illness. Primitive races are extremely vulnerable to tuberculosis; it has practically exterminated the AMERICAN INDIANS (q.v. Vol. I) and has decimated many African tribes.

The most common form is tuberculosis of the lungs, popularly called 'consumption'. The lungs are invaded by bacteria known as tubercle bacilli, first identified by the German bacteriologist, Robert Koch, in 1882. Consumptives who harbour these bacilli in their lungs expel them into the atmosphere when they talk or cough, thus endangering others who may breathe the contaminated air. The tubercle bacilli are very tough and can linger dried up in dust for long periods and flourish again when they find a suitable home in the human lungs after being breathed in with the air.

In the early stages the symptoms are usually so slight that the infected person is able to continue working and taking part in social life. At this stage he may be unknowingly spreading the disease wherever he goes—a state of affairs which

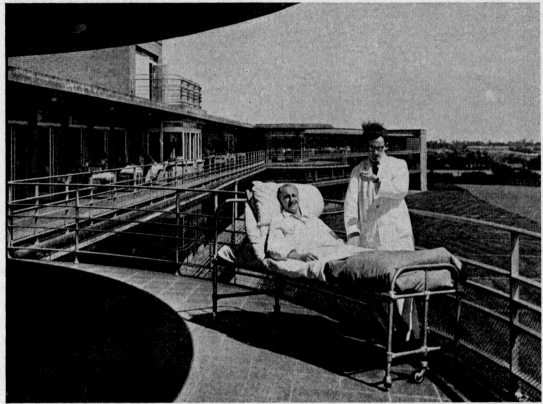

Nursing Mirror

BROOMFIELD TUBERCULOSIS HOSPITAL, CHELMSFORD

Fresh air is an important element in the treatment, and patients spend much of their time out of doors

may last for months before he feels ill enough to go to a doctor.

Tuberculosis, once called the 'white plague', used to be considered incurable; but modern methods of treatment, which include complete rest, the use of new drugs such as streptomycin, sometimes used with P.A.S. (para-amino-salicylic acid), and isoniazad, as well as operations which can now be performed on the lungs, can arrest the disease completely and restore the patient to normal health. In consequence the death-rate from tuberculosis, especially among civilized peoples, has been dramatically reduced. But the decline is certainly also due to the greatly improved standard of living and hygiene, for tuberculosis always flourishes among the over-crowded and the underfed. A good standard of general health is the best defence against it. Its control by public health authorities is one of the finest examples of the success of a carefully planned and well-directed campaign against a disease.

King Edward VII, when Prince of Wales, on being told that tuberculosis was a preventable disease, reasonably asked why it was not being prevented. With his encouragement, the National Association for the Prevention of Tuberculosis was founded in 1898. In subsequent years voluntary bodies, and in some cases local health authorities, established and maintained dispensaries for the diagnosis and treatment of tuberculosis. The idea of the dispensary was to bring the patient under proper treatment before irreparable damage had been done to his lungs, and so not only to make him less dangerous to his fellows, but also to bring him back to normal health. In addition, sanatoria were established where, with the conditions of fresh air and rest, the special treatments required in tuberculosis could be obtained.

The establishment in 1907 of the school medical service made it much easier to detect the disease among children in good time and, consequently, the death-rate among children has been reduced to a fraction of what it was. In 1912 tuberculosis was added to the list of 'notifiable diseases' (*see* PUBLIC HEALTH, Section 2, Vol. X), so that medical officers of health could find out how much tuberculosis there was in their areas and where it occurred, and could study how to remove the conditions favourable to its spread. After the establishment of the Ministry of Health in 1919, all these local schemes were co-ordinated and directed by a special department of the Ministry, and all local authorities were compelled to adopt schemes, improve measures of notification and prevention, and increase provision of hospitals and sanatoria (*see* SPECIAL HOSPITALS, Vol. X).

The early diagnosis of the disease has been made much easier by radiography, or X-RAY photography (q.v. Vol. VIII), which reveals diseased conditions of the lungs at a very early stage. It was recently found that by using a special camera such photographs could be made very quickly on a 35 mm. film, so that large numbers of people could be examined in a short time. This method of mass miniature radiography is now well established, and since it was first begun as a regular procedure in 1943 over 12 million people have been examined. Those whose radiographs showed no disease have been reassured, and those whose radiographs suggested disease have been re-examined by the larger apparatus which shows finer detail than the small film. Of all those examined 5% have been found to need treatment—a treatment which, given at an early stage, can arrest the disease.

Another important modern development has been the use of a vaccine consisting of tubercle bacilli specially modified for the purpose and known as B.C.G. ('Bacille Calmette-Guérin') after the French bacteriologists who first evolved the method (*see* INOCULATION AND VACCINATION). This is now used throughout the world to increase the resistance to tuberculosis of children and groups of persons at special risk, such as nurses, medical students, and others working in sanatoria. The World Health Organization and the United Nations Children's Emergency Fund have collaborated with national governments in this campaign, and more than 20 million children have already received this protective inoculation.

Tuberculosis can affect not only the lungs but other parts of the body, in particular the BONES AND JOINTS or the central NERVOUS SYSTEM (qq.v.). There is also a type known as bovine tuberculosis which attacks cattle, and the milk of infected cows can cause tuberculosis of the intestine and abdominal cavity in human beings. A great reduction in the amount of abdominal tuberculosis has been made by eliminating tuberculosis from dairy herds, and by disinfecting milk by heating it in the process known as PASTEURIZATION (q.v. Vol. VII).

TYPHOID, *see* EPIDEMIC DISEASES, Section 5.

TYPHUS, *see* EPIDEMIC DISEASES, Section 6.

U

UMBRELLAS. Some scholars think that the umbrella was first regarded as a kind of portable tree, and that as early kings and other important personages sat under trees, so they sat, or rode, under umbrellas, not only to protect them from the heat of the sun but as a mark of their dignity. Ancient Assyrian and Persian sculptures indicate this use of umbrella-like canopies, and modern African chiefs use umbrellas to mark their importance. In ancient China the size and splendour of the umbrella was carefully regulated according to rank, and in comparatively recent times the King of Siam had a four-storied umbrella (canopies of diminishing size one above the other on the same stick), a device which could have served no practical purpose.

In ancient Greece the ceremonial use of umbrellas still lingered (there was even a feast of the *skirophores* or umbrella-bearers); but by the time of the Roman Empire ladies carried them for the practical purpose of protecting their complexions. In the Middle Ages they served a ceremonial purpose again, being carried over the heads of popes and bishops; the Doge of Venice had one, as well as other important persons. It was not until the Renaissance that they were reintroduced to Europe, probably from the East, as a protection against the sun.

The English word 'umbrella' means a shade, that is, a protection against the sun. The French are more logical in distinguishing between the *parasol*, a protection against the sun, and the *parapluie*, a protection against the rain—a word which first occurs early in the 17th century. Jonas Hanway created a sensation in 1750 by walking about London with an umbrella, but by the end of the century umbrellas had become

1. SIAMESE 7-DECK UMBRELLA, 17TH OR 18TH CENTURY. 2. CHINESE UMBRELLA, 1655. 3. INDIAN UMBRELLA, 18TH CENTURY. 4. MODERN INDIAN STATE UMBRELLA. 5. FRINGED PARASOL, 1809. 6. METHOD OF CARRYING PARASOL, 1809. 7. HINGED PARASOL, 1808

common among the dandies. By the middle of the 19th century they were used by the middle classes, and indeed had become the very symbol of respectability. When used as parasols they were in general rather small, and were sometimes provided with a jointed stick which could be bent at any angle. In England, however, umbrellas are more practical possessions than parasols, which are now hardly ever seen. Women have umbrellas of different colours to suit their costumes, and a carefully rolled umbrella adds much to the appearance of a well-dressed man when he walks abroad.

See also WALKING-STICKS.

UNDERCLOTHES. These were not amongst man's earliest garments but were a luxury invented by civilized peoples. They were probably first worn to protect the skin from rougher outer garments, and to save outer garments from being soiled by contact with the body. That they gave extra warmth can have been only a secondary consideration, for in the beginning they were few in number and usually of thin material.

Roman ladies wore a sleeveless undergarment —*tunica interior*—and some such chemise or smock continued to be worn in one form or another until superseded by the vest in our own day. This was at first the only feminine undergarment. Cloth stockings, reaching to the knee and held up by ties or garters, were known in the 9th century. Petticoats came in some time before the 15th century, and have been worn ever since, in greater or lesser number, according to the width of the skirt. The term 'petticoat' is now used solely for underskirts, but in the 17th and 18th centuries there was a distinction between the under- and the dress-petticoat. The latter, often made of quilted satin, was intended to show, the dress being looped back to display it.

Drawers, of Oriental origin, were worn by Frenchwomen as early as the 16th century, but Englishwomen did not adopt them until 200 years later, about 1806. They were at first considered rather indecent. One variety reached only to the knee and was consequently hidden by the dress, but another type, known as pantalettes, extended almost to the ankle and showed beneath the skirt (*see* p. 60). This fashion did not last long for women, but little girls continued to wear pantalettes until about 1830. As

London Museum

PALE BLUE SILK VEST WORN BY KING CHARLES I AT HIS EXECUTION IN 1649

London Museum

POLONAISE DRESS WITH THE SKIRT LOOPED UP, SHOWING A QUILTED PETTICOAT

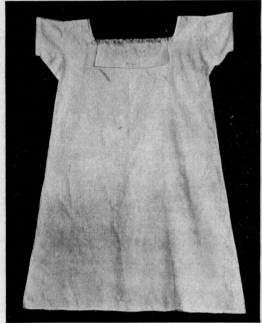

Manchester City Art Gallery

A CHEMISE, 1857

real undergarments, drawers became usual from 1841 onwards. They were of two main types—the closed knickerbocker, afterwards called 'knickers', and the open-leg type, known as 'French drawers'. Towards the end of the 19th century the latter became almost as wide as petticoats, frilled, and elaborately trimmed. The most usual materials for both types were longcloth, nainsook, white or scarlet flannel, and, occasionally, silk lined with flannel. About 1920 the open-leg drawers disappeared.

Knickers remained fashionable, but by 1924 they were often shortened to 'panties', and by 1930 to 'trunks', from which developed the 'briefs' we know today. Combinations, which joined chemise and drawers in a single garment, appeared by 1877, and their briefer, more elegant descendants, cami-knickers, towards the end of the First World War.

Masculine underwear developed chiefly from the brief linen shirts and the baggy drawers, or braies, worn during the Middle Ages. Shirts, at first short and plain, became elaborate in the 16th and 17th centuries when, like feminine petticoats, they were allowed to show above the top-clothes. Half-shirts, reaching to the hip and worn under the ordinary shirt, were also usual at this period, together with waistcoats, then known as vests. Woollen or flannel under-vests appeared about 1840, and a few years later men, as well as women, took to combinations. The modern singlet, which came into fashion in the 1930s, is derived from the vest, which it has partly replaced.

'Braies' were originally part of the top-clothes, and became true under-garments only in the 12th century. These loose breeches were replaced in the 16th century by close-fitting 'strossers'. These in their turn were superseded by silk trunks tied with ribbons, or by long, tight pantaloons held down by a band under the foot, and eventually by woollen underpants and the more modern shorts and trunks.

See also FOUNDATION GARMENTS; COSTUME, HISTORY OF.

UPHOLSTERY, *see* BEDS; CHAIRS. *See also* Vol. VII: UPHOLSTERY.

V

VACCINATION, *see* INOCULATION AND VAC-
CINATION.

VACUUM CLEANER, *see* CLEANING EQUIP-
MENT.

**VARICOSE VEINS AND HAEMOR-
RHOIDS.** A varicose condition (derived from
the Latin *varus*, 'crooked') can occur in any vein,
but is most commonly seen in the superficial
veins of the leg, where the veins show up as dark
blue knots and swellings. In a severe case the
swollen vein may be as thick as a finger. Animals
do not suffer from varicose veins, and the condition is probably a remote result of man's adopting an upright posture.

At every beat of the heart, blood is pumped
into the arteries, which convey it to all parts of
the body. When it reaches the end of the arteries
it passes into minute channels known as capillaries, and from these into the veins, which
return it to the heart, thus completing the
BLOOD CIRCULATION (q.v.). Blood flows freely
through the smooth walls of the arteries because
it has the force of the heart's thrust behind it,
and the contraction of the arteries' muscular
coats helps along the stream. On its return
journey via the veins the blood has a much
harder passage with but little thrust from the
heart-beat, and against the force of gravity. To
prevent blood from flowing the wrong way, the
veins contain valves which allow the blood to
flow in the direction of the heart but open out
and stop up the bore of the vein if the blood tries
to flow back. If the walls of the vein degenerate,
the veins lose their elasticity and become dilated;
the valves then hold up the continuous flow of
blood, which stagnates in pools, causing the
typical blue, swollen, varicose vein. If the
sufferer has to stand a great deal, the fatigue
aggravates the condition, and the veins, as well
as being unsightly, cause much discomfort or
even severe pain. The complications of varicose
veins may include the formation of blood-clots,
dropsical swelling of the leg, eczema, and ulceration.

If not too severe, varicose veins can be relieved
by rest and by means of elastic bandages and
stockings. It is also possible to inject into the
vein a chemical solution which causes a mild
inflammation of its wall, leading to the formation of a blood-clot; this blocks up and puts out
of action the vein concerned. When a superficial
vein is blocked, the blood will find another route
back to the heart by way of the deeper veins of
the leg. It is sometimes better to remove the
affected veins by a surgical operation known as
'stripping': incisions are made in the thigh and
the ankle, and the superficial veins are pulled
out of the leg. This operation can result in a
permanent cure.

Haemorrhoids or piles is a varicose condition
affecting the veins round the anus and the lower
part of the rectum. Though there is probably
an hereditary factor in its cause, this disorder
is aggravated by strain, by constipation, and
by the use of too violent laxative medicines.
Haemorrhoids can be treated by compresses and
drugs, by injection, or by tying up or pulling out
the vein, according to the severity of the condition.

See also BLOOD CIRCULATION.

VEGETABLES. 1. The moment a vegetable is
gathered it begins to deteriorate in flavour and
protective food value; therefore far the best
vegetables are those picked fresh from the garden
or allotment (*see* VEGETABLE GARDEN, Vol. VI).
If, however, the vegetables have to come from
the shop, only enough for one day should be
bought, and those, if possible, from a shop that
gets fresh supplies daily, or sells vegetables kept
fresh in a 'deep freeze.' There are about
fifty different vegetables available in Britain—
many more than are used in most kitchens.
Some of the less well-known ones are well worth
trying.

2. HISTORY. The oldest cultivated vegetables
in Europe and Asia are gourds, peas and beans,
the onion tribe, globe artichokes, cabbages, and
the commoner root vegetables such as carrots.
From Bronze Age times down to the fall of
the Roman Empire all these vegetables were

STUFFED CABBAGE LEAVES SERVED WITH CARROTS AND RICE

popular. But when there swept over Europe hordes of barbarian peoples whose tradition was hunting rather than agriculture, vegetables were not grown. From the 14th century onwards they began to be cultivated again in monastery gardens, and so they slowly became more popular, and varieties were exchanged from land to land. They regained popularity on the Continent earlier than in Britain where, even by the end of the Tudor period, banquets would still consist of endless courses of meat, poultry, and game, but no vegetables. The introduction of the POTATO (q.v.), the Jerusalem artichoke, and, later, the tomato widened the range, but change was slow (*see* FOOD, HISTORY OF). Even Victorian and Edwardian dinners seem to us now to have been overloaded with meat and very light on vegetables. No doubt the poorest people always eked out their miserable meals with nettles and charlock and whatever they could grow, but we know little about the diet of the really poor.

Vegetables used to be strictly seasonal, and some months of the year were almost barren. Nowadays glass houses, exotic imports, and deep freeze have increased the general supply and variety of vegetables, and made a vegetarian diet possible (*see* NUTRITION).

3. COOKING. (*a*) *Root vegetables.* Carrots, turnips, and beets are best boiled (*see* BOILING). They can then be buttered, sautéed, or creamed. Parsnips, one of the few dishes known to northern Europe but not to the Romans, need sharpening with lemon or vinegary sauces after boiling and lubricating with butter or fat. Parboiling them and then roasting them under beef or mutton brings out their best flavour. The roots of salsify

and scorzonera can be treated like parsnips, as can also skirrets (Scottish, crummock). Celeriac is boiled and served in sauce or sliced raw and fried in butter. Radishes, rampion, and chervil roots can be boiled. Dasheens or taro root are eaten boiled, in the hot, wet lands where they grow.

(*b*) *Tubers.* The various ways in which potatoes can be served are described in the article POTATO DISHES. Jerusalem artichokes are boiled lightly, being either scraped before boiling or skinned afterwards. They are served with butter or grated cheese, or creamed and baked with tomatoes and cheese, or roasted under the joint, or puréed as soup. Yams (*see* TROPICAL ROOT CROPS, Vol. VI), now obtainable in England, and New Zealand kumaras can be boiled, or parboiled and then roasted. Sweet potatoes if further sweetened and glazed, as they are in America, are good though rather gluey.

(*c*) *Bulb vegetables.* Onions, shallots, and leeks can be boiled and creamed, served cold with salad dressing, stuffed and braised, or fried, or scalloped. Chives and garlic are used as seasonings. Onions are essential vegetables in the kitchen for flavouring a great many dishes.

(*d*) *Stem vegetables.* Asparagus is tied in bundles, boiled with the tips above the water, and served with Hollandaise, Béchamel, or Béarnaise sauce, or with melted butter. Celery is cut into 6-inch lengths and boiled like asparagus, then braised in the oven in brown sauce or with a cheese sauce. Seakale, a peculiarly English vegetable, is cooked and served like asparagus. Fennel has thick round leaf stalks which are treated like celery and served in a rich parmesan sauce. Cardoons (American, chard), the leaf stalks of a thistle like the globe artichoke, need blanching to remove their woolly skins; they are boiled, 'stringed', and then simmered in stock. Kohl rabi, the bulbous stalk of a kind of cabbage, is cooked like turnips. Hop shoots are served like asparagus or cold in salad. Bamboo shoots are a standard vegetable of Chinese cookery (*see* RICE DISHES).

(*e*) *Leaf vegetables.* Cabbage, kale, spinach, and leafy beet varieties, and also endive, chicory, and lettuce should be either braised or boiled in as little water as possible and no soda. They can be puréed after boiling. 'Greens' can indicate many leaf vegetables, including turnip tops, brussels sprouts, curly kale, and spring cabbage. Nettle tops and mercury (or 'Good King Henry')

STUFFED TOMATOES WITH PASTA

are not to be despised whenever green vegetables are scarce; they should be cooked like spinach. The taro leaf is the staple green vegetable of many tropical lands.

(*f*) *Flower vegetables*. White and purple sprouting broccoli and cauliflower should be boiled no longer than is needed to make them tender, and should be served with bland SAUCES (q.v.). Globe or French artichokes, which are the flower heads of a large thistle, are boiled and eaten hot with melted butter, or cold with French dressing; or they are braised with ripe olives, or stuffed. Their bottoms (*fonds*), boiled till tender, may be served with sauce or sautéed (*see* FRYING).

(*g*) *Fruit vegetables*. These are chiefly the gourd vegetables, and tomatoes and egg-plant which belong to the potato family. Pumpkin, squashes, and marrows make delicious spiced custards for pies, or they can be braised, and the smaller ones stuffed. Cucumber, the little speckled French *courgettes*, and egg-plant are sliced and fried after being peeled and de-seeded, or stuffed and baked. Tomatoes are excellent fried, baked, or stuffed, as are red and green or sweet peppers, which have almost as many uses as tomatoes. Olives, especially the ripe, black kind, play a big part in Italian cooking.

(*h*) *Seed vegetables*. Green peas, if boiled for a short time when young and fresh, are delicious; if old, tinned, processed, or overcooked, they are rather dull. Of pod beans, scarlet runners are the most popular in Britain, while dwarf or French beans—*haricot verts*—are used much more on the Continent. Both need slicing or snapping, stringing if old, and very fast cooking. Broad beans should be picked much younger than they usually are; when bigger than a trouser button they should have the skin blanched off. Butter or Lima beans, very common in America, are sold loose or in tins. The soya bean is the most nutritious and has the most uses. Special soft-shelled peas called sugar peas and the pods of very young broad beans make a useful and economical change. Dried legumes need soaking overnight and boiling for a long time. Okra or gumbo are the young pods and seeds of a mallow plant much used both as a vegetable and for soup in New Orleans, U.S.A. Indian or sweet corn, long popular in America, is beginning to gain popularity in Britain. It is boiled and served either on the cob or creamed. It is the basis of the Mexican dish *tamales*. Chestnuts, as purée, stuffing, sauce, or whole with brussels sprouts, are particularly valued in France.

The cultivation of most of the vegetables mentioned in this article is described in separate articles in Volume VI. Raw vegetables are considered in the article SALADS in this volume.

See also SALADS; SOUPS.
See also Vol. VI: VEGETABLE GARDEN.

VENEREAL DISEASES. These diseases—so called from Venus, the goddess of love—are contagious and are usually contracted through sexual intercourse with an infected person. The most common diseases in this group are syphilis and gonorrhoea, and of these two syphilis is the more serious.

Although it was probably known in ancient times, some historians have maintained that syphilis was brought to Europe from the New World by the sailors of Columbus, basing this theory on the fact that the first recorded outbreak occurred in Europe very shortly after their return. It swept through the French army then fighting in Italy and was spread rapidly in France by the returning troops. It was therefore called 'morbus gallicus' (the 'French disease', 'French pox', or simply 'pox', often referred to in 16th-century literature). In France, for obvious reasons, it was called the Neapolitan or Italian disease. An account of it was written in 1530 by the Italian physician Fracastoro in the form of a pastoral poem with a shepherd-boy hero named Syphilus, from whom the disease took its name.

In past centuries syphilis was probably the commonest of all the many diseases which then plagued mankind. The opportunities for PERSONAL HYGIENE (q.v.) were much less than they are now, and the avoidance of infection and scrupulous cleanliness are the chief means of prevention. The disease is caused by a corkscrew-shaped microbe of the PROTOZOA class (q.v. Vol. II) called a spirochaete.

The first sign of infection is usually a small ulcer at the site of entry of the germ, together with a swelling in the groin, which appears between 2 and 4 weeks after contact. This often disappears without treatment, but is followed by the secondary stage of the disease, marked by fever, rash, swelling of the glands all over the body, and sores in the mouth and around the genitals.

Without proper treatment there follows a latent period of anything up to about 20 years before the grave complications of the third stage appear. These include affection of the brain and spinal cord, and occasionally paralysis, deafness, and blindness.

Syphilis can now be diagnosed in its early stages by suitable blood and other tests. In both the primary and secondary stages the disease can be cured by a course of penicillin. Every untreated person is a source of danger to others, and the children of an infected mother may suffer from congenital syphilis. It is, however, rare for a person who has had congenital syphilis to pass it on to the next generation.

Gonorrhoea, caused by the bacterial microbe gonococcus, has been known since very ancient times. It affects both sexes, and its chief sign is a discharge from the genitals. It may now be speedily cured by injections of penicillin.

The need for expert medical advice and treatment is as important for these as for any other diseases. Ignorance and false modesty have helped to perpetuate them and to prolong much needless suffering. A doctor can often relieve unnecessary anxieties, and if a disease has been contracted it can easily be cured in its early stages.

VENTILATION, DOMESTIC. The proper VENTILATION (q.v. Vol. VIII) of a room, which is essential for health and comfort, depends mainly on regulating the temperature, moisture, and carbon dioxide content of the air in it. To do this there must be some means of letting in fresh air and removing stale air.

Houses are ventilated naturally by the cold air outside the building, which is rarely still, entering through WINDOWS, DOORS, CHIMNEYS (qq.v.), and cracks in the fittings of doors and windows. As warm air is lighter than cold air, the stale air inside the building rises and finds its way out through the chimney or some other upper opening. Indeed, the open coal fire plays a most important part in the ventilation of most British homes. The column of hot air in the chimney is being continually replaced by air from inside the room, producing perhaps as many as ten air-changes an hour.

The amount of fresh air that should be let into a room depends on its size and on the number of people in it. The following is the minimum amount recommended:

Living-room (4 persons) .	2,400 cu. ft. of air per hour
Bedroom (2 persons) .	1,200 ,, ,,
Bedroom (1 person) . .	600 ,, ,,
Kitchen (cooking for not more than 6 persons) .	1,000 ,, ,,
Halls and passages . .	1 air change ,,
Bathrooms and w.c.s .	2 air changes (or more) per hour

In practice, this means that more air must be admitted to a small room containing several people than to a large room with few people. It is important to remember this when arranging the ventilation of bedrooms, where fresh air is important not only for general health but for reducing chances of infection. Ventilation of kitchens presents a special problem because of the presence of steam, the smells of cooking, and the heat generated by cooking-equipment (*see* KITCHEN DESIGN).

See also HEATING SYSTEMS, DOMESTIC.
See also Vol. VIII: VENTILATION.

VERANDAHS. These are covered terraces attached to one or several sides of the ground floor of a house, giving a sheltered place in which to sit in the sun, and also protecting the rooms from the direct rays of the sun. Verandahs are common in hot countries—the name comes from the Portuguese. Tropical bungalows often have verandahs on all sides of the house, which serve as outdoor living- or sleeping-rooms. In England villas of late GEORGIAN and REGENCY ARCHITECTURE (q.v. Vol. XII) often had verandahs with

National Buildings Record

VERANDAH OF AN EARLY VICTORIAN HOUSE AT SIDMOUTH, DEVONSHIRE

slender iron columns and lead or copper roofs; later, the romantic taste of the Victorians led to a fashion for rustic verandahs.

When a verandah is given a more classical form, with columns supporting arches or a cornice and entablature in brick or stone, it is called by its Italian name, a loggia. A loggia is often recessed into the structure of the house, whereas a verandah projects in front of it.

See also BALCONIES.

VILLAGES, HISTORY OF. Some villages have an unbroken history of several thousand years. England is particularly rich in them, and each one of the some 10,000 in existence claims to be different from the rest. It is for this reason that it is extremely difficult to generalize about the development of the village apart from certain aspects—particularly smallness of population in relation to the town and nearness to the country-side and to agricultural pursuits. In many cases an absence of adequate surviving records makes the task of the historian even more difficult.

There were village settlements in prehistoric times, some of which remain villages today. When early men began to construct shelters of boughs and leaves they were taking the first step towards the establishment of settled village life. When they went on to cultivate plants, to domes-ticate animals, and to introduce agriculture, they were moving on a step farther. The enjoy-ment and use of such possessions as crops, ani-mals, and tools depended upon co-operation and protection from hostile forces outside. In conse-quence, families would collect into friendly groups and form the first villages. These villages were often constructed in places which offered natural protection—islands, peninsulas, or high ground—or at communication points in the middle of fertile agricultural areas. One of the earliest known villages was built upon piles in a Swiss lake (*see* LAKE DWELLINGS, Vol. I). The site of some of these prehistoric villages can be traced on the ground in air photographs (*see* ARCHAEOLOGY, Vol. I). Usually they were built of perishable materials, wood or wattle and daub, but in Scotland, at Skara Brae, where there is no wood, a village has been excavated which consisted of stone huts closely packed together. Even the furniture in the single rooms was made of stone (*see* p. 387). Sometimes a near-by hill-top camp provided shelter for the villagers and their animals in times of danger, and later, in Scotland, tall circular buildings called 'brochs' were built as refuges.

The Saxons surrounded their villages with wooden stockades, the gates of which could be closed at night to keep out enemies or wild animals. The chief building within the stockade was the lord's hall (*see* HOUSES, HISTORY OF), and round it were grouped his kitchens and store-rooms and the huts of the villagers. The land around the village was cultivated by the people to supply his needs and their own. An elaborate system grew up in which the land was divided into strips, a number of which were allotted to each villager. In addition there were meadows for hay and grazing and forest land, which were common to all. This system lasted throughout the Middle Ages. Laxton in Nottinghamshire still retains its 'open fields' and many of its ancient customs of management (*see* OPEN FIELDS AND ENCLOSURES, Vol. VI).

Manorial villages in Norman England were dominated by the MANOR (q.v.) and the church. The villagers were greatly dependent on the lord of the manor; they could not leave the village or even marry without his consent, and they had to accept his terms, however unjust they might be (*see* FEUDAL SYSTEM, Vol. X). Some gradually won the right to pay rent in money instead of labour; and these independent farmers were called 'yeomen'.

The church was not only geographically in the middle of the village but was the centre of its spiritual and social life. People met their friends or did business in the church, and their entertainments started with a service, though they might continue with dancing on the green. The priest was a power in the village second only to the lord of the manor, for besides his clerical duties he was usually the only schoolmaster and doctor.

The church and the manor were the only buildings of any size, often the only stone buildings. The tiny cottages, with walls of wattle and daub on a timber frame or of 'cob' (clay, gravel, and straw), seldom had more than one room. The earliest surviving cottages date from the 15th and 16th centuries when greater

CORFE CASTLE, DORSET, WITH THE VILLAGE AT ITS FOOT

Aerofilms

AIR VIEW OF LAXTON, NOTTINGHAMSHIRE, AND THE SURROUNDING FIELDS
The village is built along the road, with the church in the centre. Round it can be seen 'open fields', which are still
cultivated as they were in the Middle Ages

wealth had begun to make larger houses possible. These were built of stone where it was available, with mullion WINDOWS and thatched or stone-tiled ROOFS (qq.v.). Where stone was lacking, the walls were timber framed (*see* p. 241). The smaller houses were built in groups, each with one or two rooms downstairs and bedrooms above; in poorer districts, such as in Scotland and Ireland, there was seldom an upper floor.

In Tudor England and later on, during the 18th century, there was a movement towards enclosing the open fields and common land, first for sheep grazing and subsequently for corn

farming. Many of the villagers came to work on a farmer's land for a money wage and to own no land of their own; and the farmers paid money rents to the landlord. The social structure of the village changed as the number of landless agricultural workers increased, men who were as dependent on the farmers (who were in turn dependent on the landlords) as the factory workers were dependent on their employers.

But, though the system of farming had changed, the village itself had changed little by the early 19th century. The same families often lived there from generation to generation. Most

Reece Winstone

CASTLE COMBE, WILTSHIRE

In the centre of the village are the medieval market cross, the church, and the inn

people still worked on the land, though now as labourers, or were craftsmen—carpenters, wheelwrights, and blacksmiths—supplying the farmers' needs. The people made their own furniture and wove their own cloth; they needed little from outside and had little money with which to buy luxuries. Each village was responsible for looking after its own poor and sick, for guarding its property, and for keeping the roads in repair. Few people went farther afield than the nearest market town. Miss Mitford in *Our Village*, written in 1824, described the closely knit character of the village:

Of all the situations for a constant residence [she wrote], that which appears to me most delightful is a little village far in the country; a small neighbourhood, not of fine mansions finely peopled, but of cottages and cottage-like houses . . . with inhabitants whose faces are as familiar to us as the flowers in our garden; a little world of our own, close-packed and insulated like ants in an ant-hill, or bees in a hive, or sheep in a field, or nuns in a convent, or sailors in a ship; where we know everyone, are known to everyone, interested in everyone, and authorised to hope that everyone feels an interest in us.

Even during the 19th century, when the population as a whole increased greatly, villages did not as a rule grow much larger. Indeed, the agricultural labourers were so poor that as many as could began to drift to the towns to work in factories. The 20th century, however, has brought a remarkable change in village life. Improvements in transport and the development of education have brought the village into closer contact with the town and widened its outlook. Between the two wars the mechanization of agriculture meant that fewer men were needed on the land and they had to find work elsewhere. So more and more villagers drifted to the towns. But at the same time townspeople began to move to the villages, buying week-end cottages or settling in the country and travelling daily to work in the towns. The size of many villages has increased enormously, the people living in the new houses often travelling some distance to their work. As a counter-movement, many workers on the land now travel to the towns for their pleasures. The control of village affairs has largely passed from the villagers themselves to urban, county, and national bodies who are responsible for the organization of social services, education, and planning and house building, though the PARISH council (q.v. Vol. X) still looks after the welfare of its village in matters of purely local importance. Over most of the country the self-sustaining village community has ceased to exist.

This position has not been reached in all parts of the world, although the process has gone much further in the United States than in England. In peasant societies, where land-ownership is concentrated in the hands of small farmers themselves, village life is often intense and isolated. In non-industrialized countries, several villages are usually centred on a market town. In most countries with rising populations, however, there is an increasing rate of urbanization which changes the nature and importance of the village, no matter what the villagers themselves wish. It is true, therefore, to say that the village can never hope to be able to regulate the pace of social change which most affects its own stability or development. Only in times of war and of dearth can the food-grower in the village call the tune: in normal conditions it is the townsman who gives the orders.

See also TOWNS, HISTORY OF.
See also Vol. VI: AGRICULTURAL HISTORY.

VINEGAR. If wine, beer, or cider is allowed to stand for some time in contact with air it becomes sour; in other words, vinegar (*vin-aigre*, 'sour wine') is produced. The sourness is due to the formation of acetic acid from the combination of alcohol and oxygen, as shown in the formula:

$$CH_3CH_2OH + O_2 \rightarrow CH_3COOH + H_2O$$
(alcohol) + (oxygen) → (acetic acid) + (water).

Commercially, the reaction is usually accelerated by allowing the liquid to drip over beech twigs impregnated with vinegar. This increases the surface area over which the liquid trickles, and also ensures an adequate concentration of the acetic acid bacteria which bring about the oxidation of alcohol.

In wine-producing countries vinegar is made from either red or white wine. In other countries it is made from either cider or malt, and in this case the first stages in its making are similar to WHISKY DISTILLING (q.v. Vol. VII). Another type, a distilled vinegar, is not itself distilled but is made from a distillate (mainly ethyl alcohol) of fermented grain and molasses (*see* INDUSTRIAL ALCOHOL, Vol. VII).

Vinegar is used in the home as a preservative (*see* CONDIMENTS), as a flavouring, particularly in SAUCES and SALAD dressing, as the acid constituent of the RAISING AGENT in some cakes, and as a tenderizer in the cooking of MEAT (qq.v.).

VITAMINS. These are complex organic chemical compounds which are present in very small amounts in most foods. They are essential, though in minute quantities, for normal growth and maintenance of life; and their presence or absence in the diet makes all the difference between health and disease, both to man and animals.

The first vitamin was recognized in 1911 when a Polish chemist, Casimir Funk, extracted from rice polishings a crystalline substance which could cure the Oriental disease 'beriberi'. He called this extracted substance 'vitamine'—the root 'vita' indicating that the substance is essential to life. After several years of experiment by scientists such as Sir Frederick Gowland Hopkins at Cambridge, several different 'vitamines' were identified, and were called vitamins A, B, C, D, and so on—the terms by which we know them today.

1. *Vitamin A* assists our general health and enables us to see better in dim light. It is one of the essential constituents of a substance called 'visual purple', a peculiar colouring matter, which forms part of the retina at the back of the EYE (q.v.). Carrots are rich in it, and so, during the Second World War, people were urged to eat carrots to enable them to see in the blackout. People who are seriously short of vitamin A develop a disease of the eye called xerophthalmia—a disease practically unknown in Britain, but in India still the chief cause of preventable blindness in children. Mild vitamin A deficiency causing partial 'night-blindness' is, however, fairly common in Britain. An early reference to a deficiency of this vitamin occurs in the Old Testament (Jeremiah, xiv. 6), where the wild asses are described as being unable to see because there was no grass: the latter would have supplied them with the vitamin.

Vitamin A itself is found only in certain animal foods such as halibut and cod liver oils; but another substance called carotene, which is found in many vegetables, especially carrots, can be converted in the body into vitamin A—in fact, this 'pro-vitamin', as it is called, is an equally important source of vitamin A. Men and animals store this vitamin in their liver; hence animal liver as a food is a rich source of it.

2. *Vitamin B.* This is the substance which Funk discovered would cure beriberi, a widely prevalent disease in the Far East, especially where the husk of the rice (the staple food) has been removed in the process of milling. It first causes numbness in the legs, and then pain in the calf muscles, followed eventually by exhaustion and paralysis, which will kill the victim unless he is treated with the vitamin. In 1925 it was discovered that vitamin B was a mixture of at least two vitamins, Funk's anti-beriberi vitamin B_1 and a new anti-pellagra vitamin B_2. Pellagra, a disease from which thousands of people died yearly in the southern States of the U.S.A., where the people live largely on maize, is characterized by ulcerations of the mouth and inflammation of the tongue and skin. Vitamin B_1, now called thiamine (and formerly known as aneurin in Britain), and vitamin B_2 are often found together in the same foods, for example, in fresh yeast which is effective in preventing both beriberi and pellagra. It was later found that vitamin B_2 contains the substances 'riboflavin' and 'nicotinic acid', and that it is the nicotinic acid, or 'niacin' as it is now frequently called, which prevents pellagra. Riboflavin is concerned with the way the body obtains energy from food. Deficiency of another compound, pyridoxine or vitamin B_6, causes dermatitis in rats: this vitamin is also required by humans. Pantothenic acid, another B vitamin, is concerned in preventing a skin disease in POULTRY (q.v. Vol. VI). The most recent of the vitamins to be discovered in this group is known as vitamin B_{12}. It is remarkable in being the most highly active of all the vitamins. It forms a very effective cure for Addisonian pernicious anaemia in man.

Unlike vitamin A, the various B vitamins are all soluble in water (vitamin A is soluble only in oils and fats). Early signs of a deficiency of vitamin B are a check in the growth of children and the development of a special type of neuritis.

3. *Vitamin C* is the anti-scorbutic vitamin, that is, it prevents scurvy, a disease which causes bleeding in different parts of the body, particularly in the gums, makes the teeth become loose, and causes pain in the joints and softening of the bones. For centuries it affected sailors and also large portions of the population of northern Europe, causing thousands of deaths every year. Besides preventing scurvy, vitamin C helps to heal wounds and is, like the other vitamins, necessary for general health.

The citrus fruits, oranges and lemons, are rich in the vitamin; in the early 1600s they were provided by the East India Company on their vessels for the purpose of preventing scurvy. Captain Cook saw that his men ate fresh fruit whenever possible during his famous trip round the world. In 1804 the Royal Navy introduced a compulsory daily ration of lemon juice when fresh vegetables were not available. This is now usually replaced by a drink made from lemon powder which has been fortified by the addition of the synthetic vitamin, ascorbic acid.

At the beginning of this century scurvy was becoming prevalent amongst babies because they were being fed on too much artificial food which did not contain the vitamin; but now this is prevented by the allowances of orange juice provided for young babies and infants (*see* BABIES, FEEDING OF). Rose-hip syrup and blackcurrant juice also supply vitamin C.

Vitamin C was the first vitamin to be synthesized—that is, made artificially from its constituent parts—in 1933. It is, in fact, one of the simplest vitamin compounds, which all animals except man, monkeys, and guinea pigs are able to make for themselves in their bodies.

4. *Vitamin D* is concerned with the laying down of calcium and phosphorus in the bones, and is therefore of especial importance to infants and expectant mothers. An insufficiency of vitamin D causes rickets in children. Rickets used to be the vitamin deficiency disease most frequently encountered in Britain, where, only 50 years ago, it was common in big cities to see children suffering from crippling deformities such as curved arm- and thigh-bones, bow legs, or knock knees. A similar disease called osteomalacia develops in adults who are deficient in vitamin D, and this disease is still common in many parts of India and the Far East.

Vitamin D can be supplied to the body either by food or by sunlight. Sunlight acting on the skin causes the formation of the vitamin in the body. Hence, if children receive sufficient sunlight on their bodies, they will need less vitamin D from their food. Sunbathing in summer and also summer clothes which allow the sun to reach the skin are most beneficial—for example, shorts are more beneficial to growing boys than long trousers and should be worn all the year round.

Sunlight is made up of waves of different wavelength, and it is the short waves, the ultra-violet waves (*see* RADIATION, Vol. III), which are concerned with the formation of vitamin D. These rays can also cause the formation of vitamin D in certain foodstuffs which do not already contain it. The substance in such foodstuffs which is turned into vitamin D is called 'ergosterol' before it has been irradiated, and 'calciferol' afterwards. The best natural sources of vitamin D are certain animal products, notably halibut and cod liver oil. The vitamin exists in several different chemical forms, the form occurring naturally in cod liver oil being not exactly the same as calciferol. All varieties, however, are effective in curing rickets.

5. *Vitamin E.* This is a vitamin concerned with reproduction. It is not yet proved whether it is required by humans, but Professor Evans of California established in 1922 that rats cannot breed without it. This vitamin, which is soluble only in fats, is chemically fairly stable, and may be heated to high temperatures without destruction. Its chemical name is 'tocopherol', from the Greek words *tokos*, 'offspring', and *phero*, 'I bear', the final 'ol' indicating that the substance is an alcohol. Vitamin E acts as an antioxidant —a substance which prevents decomposition by oxidation. It is a normal constituent of fish-liver oils. Its absence from the feed of farm animals is probably responsible for poor muscular development (*see* FOODS, FARM ANIMAL, Vol. VI). In chickens its absence also causes a characteristic abnormality of the brain known as 'crazy chick' disease.

6. *Other vitamins.* Vitamin K is concerned with the clotting power of the blood, the letter 'K' being the initial of the German word *Koagulation*. It has been found, for example, that young chickens deficient in vitamin K have a much reduced power of coagulation of the blood. Vitamin K is now used in the treatment of patients who are undergoing operations for certain internal complaints. It is also sometimes administered to new-born babies. In fact, however, anybody receiving sufficient vitamins A, C, and D from the usual food sources is unlikely to suffer from a deficiency of vitamin K.

Another vitamin-like substance is 'folic acid', which is a growth stimulant and a blood generator, used in the cure of certain types of anaemia (*see* BLOOD). Two further substances must also be mentioned, 'inositol' and 'para-aminobenzoic acid'. Inositol, which is concerned with the way fat is absorbed in the body, was recognized as a vitamin in 1928. Para-amino-benzoic acid (or P.A.B.A) was not recognized as a vitamin until 1941. Other vitamins are vitamin H, or 'biotin', and vitamin M, which is required by monkeys and which may be identical with folic acid.

See also NUTRITION; FOOD VALUES.

W X Y

WALKING-STICKS. The staves which old men from the earliest times used for support must generally have been long, like the 'palmer's staff' of the Middle Ages. The walking-stick with a pommel held in the hand seems to have been introduced during the 15th century. In an inventory of the possessions of Henry VIII we find 'six walking staves, one covered with silke and golde'; and another one, 'garnished with golde, havinge a perfume in the toppe, under that a diall'. It was not, however, until the 17th century that the cane, or walking-stick, became an essential part of the dress of a fine gentleman. Charles I in Mytens's portrait is holding a stick, and the canes of Louis XIV are known to have been especially magnificent. French sticks with ribbons and tassels were brought to England by Charles II, and by the 18th century all kinds of materials were being used—oak, bamboo, malacca, kingwood, whalebone, and ivory; for the handles, bone, horn, shell, ivory, metal, agate, glass, and porcelain were used. Some of the finest of this period have porcelain handles, sometimes mounted in gold, and opening to reveal a snuff-box or pomander. Doctors in particular were in the habit of concealing a perfume or antiseptic in the heads of their canes.

Long gold-headed canes known as *cannes à la Voltaire* were carried by old men, magistrates, and notable people. Footmen also had long canes emblazoned with the arms of their masters. In the 1790s Frenchmen made a point of carrying rough, knobbly sticks as a sign of their advanced opinions. In the early 19th century walking-sticks were notably fashionable, having entirely replaced swords which were no longer carried. In the mid-19th century the fashion of UMBRELLAS (q.v.) rivalled that of sticks, but sticks remained popular up to the beginning of the First World War. The practice lingered for

1. WALKING-STICK DECORATED WITH GOLD, WITH PERFUME IN THE HEAD, 1587. 2. WALKING-STICK WITH GOLD, BLACK, AND RED HEAD, 1597. 3. CANE WITH METAL HEAD, c. 1660. 4. PORCELAIN HEAD OF CANE, 17TH CENTURY. 5. MID-18TH-CENTURY CANE. 6. CANE COVERED WITH TORTOISESHELL, WITH PORCELAIN HEAD, c. 1760. 7. PORCELAIN HEAD OF CANE CONTAINING A PERSPECTIVE GLASS, 1760–70. 8. CRUTCH-HEADED CANE, 18TH CENTURY. 9. CANE WITH 'CROQUET MALLET' HEAD, 18TH CENTURY

a time after the war, but now the traditional 'stick and gloves' of the man-about-town have almost completely vanished.

See also Costume, History of.

WALLPAPERS, HISTORY OF.

WALLPAPERS, HISTORY OF. Paper as a wall decoration was preceded by mural painting (*see* Painting Methods, Section 4, Vol. XII), plaster moulded in relief, Mosaics (q.v. Vol. XII), ornamental Tiles, Tapestry (qq.v. Vol. VII) and painted cloth, and elaborate hangings of embossed leather or patterned fabrics. Wallpaper designs have imitated all of these at various times. Paper-Making (q.v. Vol. VII), known in the East for 2,000 years, spread to western Europe in the 13th century. Decorative papers were first used in Italy and France for covering books or lining chests and boxes, but from the early 16th century they were being used to decorate walls in England. One 16th-century wallpaper which has survived has a red distemper ground, printed with a black pattern and green and blue flowers. Other papers surviving from the early 17th century imitate embroidery patterns, even to copying the stitchery. Black printed on white was common. These early wallpapers were canvas-backed, and were nailed or later pasted to the plaster of half-timbered buildings. Sometimes the paper was fixed to a large canvas-covered framework attached to the wall but not flat against it. Until the mid-18th century wallpaper was usually backed with either canvas or strong Chinese ricepaper, and so could be removed with little fear of damage.

By the late 17th century painted papers had become popular. They were made in sheets, not as yet in continuous rolls, and the outline designs were printed from wood blocks (*see* Textile Printing, Vol. VII); the colour was painted on afterwards with a brush in tempera or watercolour. Sometimes a stencil was used. A 17th-century wallpaper from East Anglia shows a hunting scene in full colour. A special wallpaper known as 'flock', which looked like velvet or brocade and usually had a plain colour on a plain ground, appeared about this time in England and became exceedingly popular on the Continent during the 18th century. The design was first drawn on the white or coloured paper with varnish, thick glue, or oil; very fine particles of wool were then blown or sprinkled on to the sticky surface of the design, where

Victoria and Albert Museum

ENGLISH FLOCK WALLPAPER IN TWO SHADES OF RED, *c.* 1735
From the offices of H.M. Privy Council

they stuck. Chinese wallpaper, with designs of flowers, birds, and figures not arranged in any repeating patterns, was also popular, and skilful English imitations were made in panels. Other papers imitated marble, wood panelling, or embossed leather hangings, and designs such as masks, knots, or festoons of ribbon were often made as cut-outs and pasted on separately.

In France wallpapers ranged from imitation Chinese designs to small pictorial sheets printed with sacred or comic subjects—very popular among the country people. The designer, Jean Papillon, was noted for diaper, stripe, and foliage patterns, and by the mid-17th century, he was successfully imitating tapestry, using brush and stencil methods.

In 18th-century England it was fashionable to fix printed pictures all over a wall and paste round each a printed paper 'frame'. Some wallpapers imitated the new printed calicoes coming from India; indeed, both the paper and the

In France the designers copied the mural paintings excavated at POMPEII (q.v. Vol. XII), or reproduced, in grey or sepia, paintings by artists such as Boucher and Fragonard (*see* Vol. XII, opp. p. 161). The most fashionable designs, however, were those of scenic papers which formed a continuous picture round the room, the subjects being taken from contemporary events, books, or scenery.

Whereas in France great attention was paid to design and drawing, the tendency in late 18th- and 19th-century England was towards technical improvements; for instance, by John Baptist Jackson in the use of oil colour, and by Eckhardt in printing or ornamenting with gold and silver and in giving a final varnish to make a washable surface. When in 1830 the making of continuous rolls began, developments in machine production followed. Engraved rollers instead of blocks were used for printing, and these made possible refinements in embossing and finishing. Synthetic DYES (q.v. Vol. VII), improved drying processes, and aerograph tinting were introduced. Altogether, the change from handcraft methods to those of mass production was more notable in England than taste and artistic quality. Most designs were large, all-over patterns, usually crude adaptations of

Victoria and Albert Museum

PANEL OF CHINESE WALLPAPER PAINTED IN WATER-COLOUR

Victoria and Albert Museum

'SUNFLOWER' PATTERN WALLPAPER DESIGNED BY WILLIAM MORRIS, 1879

linen furnishings were sometimes printed from the same blocks, blue on white being a favourite combination. Plain, unprinted papers were also used, especially blue, as these made a good background to mahogany furniture. Other designs in white, imitating plaster relief and carried out on a specially manufactured coarse paper, were chosen for ceilings or walls of halls and corridors. Throughout the Georgian era, wallpaper was taxed and had to be stamped by the Excise before any colouring was done.

textile prints. The famous exception was the work of William MORRIS (q.v. Vol. V) and his followers, which was refined in design, drawing, and colouring.

Wallpaper went out of fashion during the revolt from ornament in the 1930s (*see* INTERIOR DECORATION, HISTORY OF) but with the 1950s, after the austerity of wartime, it has come again into favour. Some traditional designs have been revived in modified forms; others show the influence of contemporary abstract art (*see* MODERN ART, Section 5, Vol. XII).

See also INTERIOR DECORATION, HISTORY OF.
See also Vol. VII: PAPER-MAKING.

WALLS. The walls of a house have four functions: to protect the interior from the weather, to support the upper floors and roof, to enclose the space of the rooms, and to give privacy.

The style and appearance of a house of any date depends largely on the treatment of the materials of the wall and on the design of the WINDOWS and DOORS (qq.v.) pierced in it. Until recently, the materials depended very much on what were available in the district, so that distinctive styles have grown up and remained in use for centuries in different places (*see* HOUSES, TYPES OF). Nowadays concrete and other materials are used for walls, and these may be taken ready made from factories to the site where the house is to be built.

Immensely thick stone walls were built in the 12th century to give strength to CASTLES and MANORS (qq.v.). In the later medieval buildings the walls were less thick but were strengthened by buttresses placed between the windows (*see* p. 294). The late Tudor and Jacobean builders were so skilful that they could build stone walls strong enough to support several storeys, although much of their surface was taken up by windows. The finest stone walls have always been built of ashlar (square hewn stones), but those of small houses and cottages were generally of the rough hewn type of MASONRY (q.v. Vol. VIII) known as rubble. Ashlar combined with 'rustication'—that is, stones bevelled at their edges or roughened—is characteristic of GEORGIAN ARCHITECTURE (q.v. Vol. XII).

Medieval walls were often topped by battlements from which soldiers could defend the building from attack. The wall was often marked horizontally at the level of each floor with a moulding called a 'string course' (Fig. 1);

G. F. Webb

FIG. I. LITTLE WENHAM HALL, SUFFOLK, 1260–80

The walls are built of rough hewn stone with ashlar corners, buttresses, and windows. A 'string course' marks the level of the first floor. The walls are topped with battlements

in the 17th century it was finished at the top with a moulded cornice; and in Georgian and later houses the wall was often carried above the roof line and finished with a solid moulding or open parapet (Fig. 2).

Throughout the Middle Ages and 16th and 17th centuries walls were constructed on a framework of heavy vertical and horizontal timbers, with occasional diagonal pieces to give added

FIG. 2. HEYTHROP HALL, OXON., 1705

The walls are built with rusticated ashlar and are surmounted by a parapet

G. N. Kent

FIG. 3. CROWN HOUSE, NEWPORT, ESSEX, 1692
The walls are plastered and decorated with pargeting

FIG. 4. THE OLD MERMAID INN, RYE, SUSSEX
The front of the house is half timber, and the upper part of the side wall has tile hanging and weather boarding

strength (*see* Vol. XII, p. 23). The spaces between the frame were filled in with 'wattle and daub' (interlaced willow or hazel covered with mud), or 'lath and plaster' (small strips of wood split the way of the grain and nailed close together across light wooden posts, giving a surface against which plaster will cling). Bricks were also used to fill in the space between the wooden beams.

The timbers were sometimes covered all over with plaster to protect them and the filling material. In East Anglia the plaster was often moulded into patterns, called pargeting (Fig. 3). Half-timbered walls have the timbers uncovered, making a pattern of black lines against the light plaster or brickwork, which was sometimes arranged in a herringbone pattern (*see* p. 385). Timber walls were sometimes covered with overlapping tiles, called tile-hanging, or with horizontal boards, called weather-boarding (Fig. 4). The use of these materials in Britain was encouraged by a tax on bricks imposed in 1784.

Bricks, which were introduced into England from Holland in the late 15th century, were used for many large houses, sometimes with stone at the corners and surrounding the doors and windows (Fig. 5). The 16th- and 17th-century bricks were smaller than modern ones, and they were sometimes moulded to give interest to the wall. In East Anglia flint arranged in geometrical patterns, set in cement, was sometimes com-

National Buildings Record

FIG. 5. THE VYNE, HAMPSHIRE
The walls are of brick with stone quoins and window and door surrounds

bined with BRICKWORK (q.v. Vol. VIII). In the 19th century brick walls were covered with stucco, a kind of plaster, and painted.

In south-west England cottage walls were often made of 'cob', that is, clay pressed down and allowed to dry so that it formed a solid wall. It was usually built on a stone foundation, and the surface was colour washed.

Modern cavity walls have two thin skins of brick or similar material with an air space between (Fig. 6). This makes them lighter than a solid wall and keeps out cold, damp, and noise.

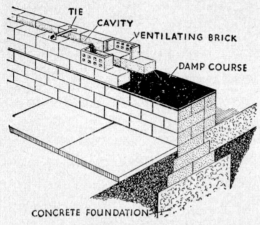

FIG. 6. DIAGRAM OF A CAVITY WALL

They have a damp course of damp-resisting material, such as slate, laid across the bricks just above ground-level to prevent damp from rising up the wall.

Brick walls are still the most common, but the walls of many modern houses and blocks of FLATS (q.v.) have frames of reinforced concrete or steel which carry the upper floors and roof (see CONCRETE CONSTRUCTION and STRUCTURAL STEELWORK, Vol. VIII). These may be filled in with light prefabricated panels, usually in two thicknesses with an air space between. Since they have no structural purpose, the walls of frame-built houses can be made to vary in shape much more than load-bearing walls, and can have WINDOWS (q.v.) of any size and in any position (see p. 243).

Interior walls are lighter than exterior ones because they carry little weight and have no protective function. In medieval houses they were of stone or wattle and daub and, later, frequently of lath and plaster. Nowadays they are of light materials such as breeze blocks. The walls of rooms are usually plastered and decorated with paint, distemper, or wallpaper; in earlier houses they were frequently panelled with wood (see INTERIOR DECORATION, HISTORY OF).

See also HOUSES, HISTORY OF; HOUSES, TYPES OF; ROOMS, HISTORY OF.

WASHING UP. The food particles adhering to the china, glass, or metal-ware used in preparing and serving a meal are of three types: those which, like caramel, are soluble in hot water; fats, which are emulsified by a detergent such as soap or a washing powder; and some, such as dried egg yolk, which can be removed only by friction. Since used dishes often have all three types of soiling, water, detergent, and friction are used together. Washing up is very much easier in really hot water as this increases solubility and also melts the fat. Friction is applied in varying degrees, by means of a soft brush, mop, or dish cloth for cutlery and plates, and a hard brush or metal scraper for pans and tins. The labour of washing up is eased if dishes and pans are filled with water as soon as they have been used, so that the dirt on them loosens instead of drying hard.

Washing up consists of four processes. The articles are first cleared of scraps, sorted into groups of the same sort, and stacked in piles—silver-ware being kept away from knives which might scratch it. They are then washed in water as hot as the hands can bear (about 120° F.), to which a detergent has been added. The least soiled articles are washed first, beginning with glass and silver and finishing with tins and pans. Knives with bone handles should not be soaked in hot water as this loosens the blades. The water is changed when it becomes too dirty or greasy. Thirdly, the articles are rinsed in hot water to remove the greasy washing water, and finally they are dried with a clean, dry cloth, preferably of linen because it is absorbent; a special fine glass cloth is used for silver and glass. An alternative, recommended as hygienic and labour saving, is air-drying china and pottery in a rack, but this is satisfactory only if the rinsing water is about 150–160° F., so that the things dry quickly.

Two bowls are needed for washing and rinsing. The bowls may be portable and made of enamelled iron, zinc, papier mâché, or plastic; but the most satisfactory equipment for

A STAINLESS-STEEL UNIT WITH TWO SINKS, A SINK TIDY AND
WASTE GULLEY BETWEEN THEM, AND DRAINING BOARDS ON
EITHER SIDE

a modern kitchen consists of two fixed sinks
with sink tidy, waste gulley, and grooved draining boards. Instead of one of the draining
boards, a table covered with a plastic material
may be used for stacking. The materials commonly used for sinks are glazed fireclay, ena-

Hurley Manufacturing Co.

AN ELECTRIC WASHING MACHINE FOR CLOTHES OR DISHES
The stacked container is put into the machine, and hot
water is sprayed out to the dishes

melled iron, aluminium, and stainless steel; and
for draining boards, any of the last three, or
wood. One advantage of the metal sinks and
drainers is that they can be manufactured in
one piece, thus avoiding crevices between the
separate components which harbour dirt.

There are several kinds of mechanical dishwashers. In one type, electrically driven rotating brushes fixed on an inside wall of the sink
supply the friction; in another, jets of hot water
are played on to the dishes. Most catering
establishments are equipped with dishwashers,
but they are not used so much in British private
houses as they are in those of some overseas
countries, including North America and New
Zealand.

See also CLEANING MATERIALS; CLEANING EQUIPMENT.

WATER-CLOSET, *see* SANITATION, HISTORY
OF; HOUSEHOLD PLUMBING.

WATER, DOMESTIC. Though all public
WATER SUPPLIES (q.v. Vol. VIII) are safe for
drinking and cooking, domestic water is very
rarely absolutely pure because it dissolves small
amounts of calcium and magnesium salts while
running over and through the ground on its way
to rivers and reservoirs. Water with these
dissolved salts is called hard water because the
salts react chemically with soap, which therefore
lathers less readily than in soft water, that is,
water which is free from salts.

The hardness of water is expressed in degrees,
each degree corresponding to 1 grain of calcium carbonate (chalk or limestone) per gallon.
Hardness varies greatly in different parts of the
country: in London, for example, most water is
16°, in Liverpool it is about 4°, and in Glasgow
less than 1°.

Hardness is of two types, depending on
whether it can be removed by boiling ('temporary hardness') or only by adding chemicals
('permanent hardness'). Temporary hardness is
due to the presence of calcium and magnesium
bicarbonate. If water containing these salts is
heated, carbon dioxide is driven off, and the salts
become calcium carbonate, which is insoluble
and is 'precipitated' (that is, deposited in solid
form), making the water cloudy and leaving
behind a chalky deposit. Most kettles show
evidence of this.

Permanent hardness is due to the presence of
calcium and magnesium sulphates and chlorides

which are not precipitated with boiling. One method of removing these is by adding another salt which reacts with them, producing an insoluble salt which is precipitated. For example, if sodium carbonate (washing soda) is added to permanently hard water, calcium carbonate is produced and precipitated, and also sodium sulphate and sodium chloride (common salt), both of which are soluble but do not react with soap.

The addition of soda will also remove temporary hardness, as it forms calcium carbonate and sodium bicarbonate (baking soda); the calcium carbonate is precipitated, and the sodium bicarbonate which remains in solution does not react with soap. The time that soda takes to react with hardness in water varies greatly with the temperature of the water. At 212° F., for example, the precipitation of calcium carbonate takes 5 seconds; at 140° F., 1 minute; and at 60° F., 1 hour. The amount of soda required to soften 1 gallon of water of 15° hardness is 1 oz.

When soda is used to soften water for washing, it is important to wait for the soda to react before adding soap. If soap is added too soon it will react before the soda and produce a scum (lime soap), a sticky substance which gradually turns the washing grey in colour. Soap itself softens water, but because of the lime soap which it produces, and because it is more expensive than soda, soda should be used first. Many washing powders contain soda as well as powdered soap; when these are put into hard water, the soap softens the water, while the soda remains unchanged. Too much soda in the water can be harmful to the skin; the best soap and detergents, therefore, contain little soda (*see* CLEANING MATERIALS).

Another method of softening water is to use a domestic water softener. This consists of a cylinder packed with zeolite, a substance which replaces the calcium and magnesium salts in the hard water, as it runs through the cylinder, with sodium and aluminium salts. After a certain quantity of water has passed through, the zeolite must be regenerated by adding a solution of common salt. While the salt solution is in contact with the zeolite, the reverse action takes place and the calcium and magnesium compounds are replaced by sodium compounds.

See also WATER SUPPLY, HISTORY OF.
See also Vol. VIII: WATER SUPPLY.

WATER SOFTENER, *see* WATER, DOMESTIC. *See also* Vol. VIII: WATER SUPPLY.

WATER SUPPLY, HISTORY OF.

Early man had to live close to some natural supply of fresh water—a river, lake, or spring; consequently these natural sources of water largely determined the sites of ancient cities. Even in the Stone Age man knew how to dig WELLS (q.v. Vol. III), and wells of considerable depth and size are recorded. One of the deepest (372 feet) was 'Joseph's Well' in Cairo, and even deeper wells existed in ancient China—one of them was reputed to be 1,500 feet. But these wells, which had to be dug by hand, could be made only where the soil was suitable, and not until men had iron tools could they cut long tunnels or build aqueducts. Some ancient cities, however, built cisterns for storing rainwater; Carthage, for example, had a system of underground reservoirs.

Once the cutting of tunnels and the building of aqueducts had become possible, towns no longer depended on local supplies. Indeed, in ancient Assyria and Persia, Egypt and Babylonia, water was conveyed to towns over considerable distances. Two of the earliest water tunnels, or conduits, were built in the 10th century B.C. by Mesha, King of Moab; and since there were no cisterns in his city, the king ordered the inhabitants to place cisterns in each house to be linked with the conduits. By another ancient tunnel, built in Judaea, water was brought

THE WELL AT CARISBROOKE CASTLE, ISLE OF WIGHT
The water was drawn up by the donkey turning the large wheel

THE 15TH-CENTURY CONDUIT AT SHERBORNE, DORSET

THE VILLAGE PUMP AT SHADOXHURST, KENT, 1887

from the Virgins' Pool in the Kedron Valley to the Pool of Siloam.

The Romans, of all the ancient peoples, paid most attention to water supply, and their system was by far the most important of any known before the 19th century. By a series of remarkable aqueducts they were able to bring water in quantity from such distances that cities could expand to a much greater size than their own poor resources would have allowed. Between 312 B.C. and A.D. 305 fourteen aqueducts were built throughout the Roman Empire with a total length of 359 miles (see Vol. I, p. 412). These aqueducts carried a total volume of water equivalent to 300,000 gallons a day. Water engineering works extended over much of the Roman Empire—particularly in France, Germany, and Spain. Water brought from the mountains was stored in the cities in small reservoirs or cisterns with numerous outlets supplying public fountains and baths. A few of the richer citizens had water connected directly to their houses. The daily consumption of water per head in Rome is estimated to have been 50 gallons, a figure comparing very favourably with the daily consumption in many European cities today (see ROMAN CIVILIZATION, Vol. I).

During the Middle Ages most of the Roman waterworks fell into ruin, and most cities had to rely once again on local sources. This meant an insufficient and often dangerously polluted supply, and all of it had to be drawn by hand. By the 16th century the increase in commerce and industry was bringing with it a notable growth in towns and, consequently, new problems of water supply. This was to some extent answered by the introduction of heavy pumping machinery; Augsburg, for example, had a water pumping plant by 1550, and this was probably true of other German cities.

The history of water supply in London is not typical of cities in general. From the late 13th century conduits had been built to carry water; the first ran from Tyburn (present-day Oxford Street) to Cheapside, where it ended in a fountain-head. In general, water was either pumped by hand pumps from shallow wells or led into streets and delivered at fountains, from which it could be drawn off and carried away in buckets. No attempt seems to have been made to bring the water above ground-level. The poorer inhabitants drew water for themselves, while those who could afford it had their water

By gracious permission of H.M. the Queen

SERVANTS PUMPING WATER AND WASHING DISHES IN A COUNTRY HOUSE KITCHEN, 1754
Water-colour by Paul Sandby

carried into their houses for them. In the late 15th century it is recorded 'that it was the custom of all apprentices in London to carry water tankards to serve their masters' houses with water fetched from the Thames or the common conduits'. There were also, in London and in many other European cities, professional water-carriers who earned a living by carrying supplies to houses at perhaps a halfpenny a pail. These water-carriers became so large and influential a body that in early Tudor England they formed a guild called 'The Brotherhood of Saint Cristofer of the Water Carriers'.

From the end of the 16th century private schemes for water supply began to take the place of public water conduits. The first of these coincided with the introduction of the first water-power PUMPS (q.v. Vol. VIII) in London. In 1582 a 500-year lease was granted to a Dutchman, Peter Morice, to enable him to erect a

water-wheel harnessed to a pump. During the next 300 years many such private water-supply schemes came into existence.

It was not until the 19th century, after several outbreaks of cholera had roused public concern, that much attention was paid to improving public water supply and SANITATION (q.v.). By this time the invention of the steam-engine had solved the main problem of supply—how to make water flow uphill; and in the last half of the century many waterworks were built or extended. Since the 17th century some individual houses had been supplied with water, and during the second half of the 19th century this became common. Enterprising water companies began to lay pipes in the streets and to bring the water under such pressure that it would rise to the highest house in the area. Those who could not afford to pay, however, still had to draw and carry their water from public wells, and even those who had water laid on to their houses usually had only one cold tap, probably in the kitchen or scullery. In the present century private companies have given way to PUBLIC UTILITIES (q.v. Vol. VII); though even today quite considerable areas of England are still served by private enterprise. The provision of an efficient water supply to meet modern needs has become a major engineering task (*see* WATER SUPPLY, Vol. VIII).

In England the average daily consumption of water per head now varies between 15 gallons in villages without waterborne sanitation to 60 gallons in large cities. Over 90% of the population of England and Wales have a piped supply of water (*see* HOUSEHOLD PLUMBING), though this still sometimes consists of only a single tap. In the majority of large towns perhaps as many as half the houses have neither baths nor hot-water systems. In remote and isolated rural communities the supply system is still sometimes very primitive. If all houses in both town and country had hot-water systems and baths, the provision of adequate water might well become a serious problem.

See also SANITATION, HISTORY OF; HOUSEHOLD PLUMBING; WATER, DOMESTIC.

See also Vol. VIII: WATER SUPPLY; METROPOLITAN WATER BOARD; NEW YORK WATER SUPPLY.

See also Vol. X: PUBLIC HEALTH.

WHOOPING COUGH, *see* INFECTIOUS DISEASES, Section 4.

WIGS. One of the many ways in which human beings, especially women, have sought to improve upon Nature has been by cutting off all their own hair and wearing somebody else's instead. Some nations have indulged in this practice more than others. The ancient Egyptians, both men and women, shaved their heads, and the upper classes wore wigs of real hair, while poorer people wore wigs of black lamb's wool.

Neither in ancient Greece or Rome nor in the Middle Ages did people wear wigs, except to conceal the loss of their natural hair; but in the 16th century, for a short period in Elizabeth I's reign, the fashion for wigs as an admittedly artificial adornment came in. Stowe the historian says that the 'periwig' was first brought to England from France by Huguenot refugees, and that the fashion had become so general by

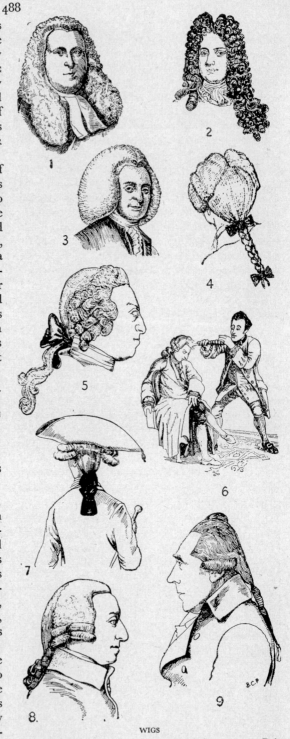

WIGS

1. Full-bottomed wig, *c.* 1666. 2. Periwig, 1714. 3. Bob wig, *c.* 1725. 4. Ramillie wig, 1735. 5. Tie wig, *c.* 1736. 6. Wig being powdered, *c.* 1773. 7. Bag wig, *c.* 1776. 8. Scratch wig, 1787. 9. Pigtail queue, *c.* 1780

about 1595 that tricksters frequently lured children away in order to rob them of their hair. Wigs vanished again in the 17th century until soon after the Restoration of Charles II, when the fashion was copied from the French of shaving the head and wearing an elaborate structure of curls descending to the shoulders and even below.

Before long no fashionable man would have been seen wearing his own hair, although the periwig, this indispensable article of the toilet, was often extremely expensive, as Pepys in his *Diary* tells us. The officers of MARLBOROUGH's armies (q.v. Vol. V) went into battle in periwigs which it was usually impossible to keep on the head (*see* Vol. V, opp. p. 256). It was, therefore, a profitable undertaking for the camp-followers after a battle to scour the field for wigs, which they could sell.

The male wig attained its largest proportions in the early years of the 18th century, the stereotyped 'Judge's wig' of today being derived from the wigs of this period (*see* Vol. X, opp. p. 320). These full-bottomed wigs were extremely inconvenient and hot, and so they were looped up in various ways; the ends could be tied into tight little plaits, or the back curls could be twisted into a pigtail. The Ramillie wig (named from the battle of Ramillies, 1706), had a long, gradually diminishing, plaited tail, which was tied with a large bow at the top and a smaller one at the bottom. There were bag-wigs, the back curls being confined in a bag; black riding-wigs; and bob-wigs, in which the hair, instead of being curled, was frizzed and gathered into two lumps over the ears. By the 1740s bob-wigs were replacing the long curled kind for everyday use, and during the rest of the century the wig became gradually smaller. Soon after the accession of George III gentlemen began wearing their own hair again, but they dressed it and even powdered it like a wig, and it was considered an eccentricity in a man like John WESLEY (q.v. Vol. V) to wear his own hair loose about his shoulders. By the end of the 18th century wigs had been generally abandoned, pigtails had been cut off (except by naval and military men who retained them into the next century), and the hair was worn fairly short. Before the beginning of the 19th century hair-powder also had gone out of fashion.

Throughout the 18th century, though some fine ladies wore periwigs, in general women wore their own hair elaborately dressed and powdered (*see* HAIRDRESSING, HISTORY OF). Although various fashions since then have required the introduction of auxiliary hair, such as 'switches', full wigs have not been worn except as substitutes for natural hair.

See also COSTUME, HISTORY OF; HAIRDRESSING, HISTORY OF; BEARDS AND MOUSTACHES.

WINDOWS. The date of a house can often be judged by the windows because they reveal changing methods of construction and their proportion and decoration are characteristic of their period.

The size of windows partly depends on the amount of light and air required in a room. In southern countries too much sun would make the rooms too hot; in the north large windows would make a room too cold unless it were efficiently heated. Windows weaken the wall, so their size depends also on the skill of builders and on the material available.

National Buildings Record

FIG. I. 13TH-CENTURY WINDOW AT THE MANOR HOUSE, BOOTHBY PAGNELL, LINCOLNSHIRE

National Buildings Record

FIG. 2. ORIEL WINDOW IN THE GATEHOUSE AT WEST TANFIELD, YORKSHIRE, LATE 15TH CENTURY

'dripstone', over the head of the window prevented water from running down into it.

As the need for defence lessened and the skill of builders increased, larger windows were built. Their shape resembled that of contemporary church windows, though they were less elaborate (see CHURCH ARCHITECTURE, ENGLISH, Vol. XII). The pointed head was often filled with tracery, and the main part was divided vertically by stone shafts, called 'mullions'. In the 15th century the larger windows were further subdivided by horizontal stone bars, called 'transoms'. Small oriel windows were sometimes built out of an upper wall (Fig. 2); and large bay windows were built at the end of the hall beside the high table (Fig. 3). The head of each light was a flattened arch, beneath the horizontal lintel running across the top of the whole window.

During the 16th century windows increased further in size, and in Elizabethan and Jacobean houses they were larger than at any time until the 1930s. There was little wall left between the large rectangular windows, divided into many lights by mullions and transoms (see p. 361). STAINED GLASS medallions (q.v. Vol. XII), with

In the earliest stone houses remaining in England, built in the 12th century, the windows are very narrow, partly for defensive reasons and partly because there were no window-panes and wider openings would have made the rooms too cold. The walls were very thick, and the openings were splayed inwards to admit as much light as possible (Fig. 1). In the Middle Ages glass was so rare that wealthy people who possessed glass windows would carry them with them when they travelled from one of their houses to another. Unglazed windows continued to be common up to the end of the 16th century. Occasionally thin pieces of horn were used instead of glass. Glass could be made only in small sizes so the windows were made up of rectangular or diamond pieces joined together by strips of lead. Often only the upper part of the window had glass, the lower part being protected by wooden shutters. Window frames were of iron or wood, and the windows had vertical oak bars and hinged or sliding shutters. A moulding, called a

FIG. 3. BAY WINDOW AND MULLION WINDOWS WITH DRIPSTONES AT COMPTON WYNYATES, WARWICKSHIRE, EARLY 16TH CENTURY

heraldic designs or mythological scenes painted by German glass-painters, sometimes enriched the glass, which still had to be composed of small leaded panes. The windows were set in iron frames and hinged to open outwards—the type called a casement window. Inside the window the thickness of the wall made room for a window seat.

The Renaissance style of architecture, first properly used in England by Inigo JONES (q.v. Vol. V) in the 17th century, called for windows carefully proportioned in relation to the façade. They had precisely defined rectangular shapes, with moulded jambs and a cornice or pediment above the lintel (*see* p. 241). At first, a central mullion and transom were retained and also leaded panes.

In the late 17th and early 18th century there was a fashion for the Venetian or Palladian window, adopted from the architecture of the Italian architect PALLADIO (q.v. Vol. V). This had three lights, the centre one having a semicircular head and the narrower side lights being rectangular (Fig. 4).

Towards the end of the 17th century the double-hung sash window was invented in England. It is divided horizontally into two equal halves which slide over one another. Counter-balancing weights, running up and down inside the frame of the window and attached to each half by cords, keep it in the required position (*see* p. 235). The sash window regulates the VENTILATION (q.v.) of the room without making a draught better than the casement window, for it can be made to open at the top alone.

Sash windows have wooden frames and are divided by wooden glazing bars into equal rectangular panes. These were small in Queen Anne and early Georgian houses, but later, as GLASS-MAKING (q.v. Vol. VII) improved, they became larger and the bars became more slender—especially in Regency houses. Shutters folded back during the day into the splay of the window, and there was sometimes a window seat (Fig. 5).

Casement windows continued to be used, particularly in the country. French windows, that is, casement windows which open to the ground, are most usual on the Continent; where the windows open inward, the shutters are outside. Dormer windows, projecting from a sloping roof with their own tiled or lead-covered roof, were frequently used for attic windows.

National Buildings Record

FIG. 4. 18TH-CENTURY PALLADIAN WINDOW (ABOVE THE DOOR), PERRET HOUSE, PERSHORE, WORCESTERSHIRE

Country Life

FIG. 5. SASH WINDOWS WITH SHUTTERS AT HINTON AMPNER, HAMPSHIRE, 18TH CENTURY

Crown Copyright

FIG. 6. REGENCY BAY WINDOWS, MADEIRA COTTAGE, LYME REGIS, DORSET

Bay windows, round and square, were popular from the mid-18th century onwards. Round bays were a feature of the Regency houses built in watering places, such as Brighton, at the time when these were becoming fashionable resorts; they allowed visitors to watch the people promenading in the street (Fig. 6). The glass was curved to the same shape as the window; curved glass was also used in terraces and crescents with a curved façade.

The surrounds of Georgian windows gradually became simpler, and the face of the glass was brought nearer to the face of the wall, giving an effect of a continuous flat surface. Later this trend was partially reversed and the recessed sides, or 'reveals', of the windows were painted white, thus giving sparkle to the façade of terraces and streets when seen in perspective.

In 1696 houses were taxed according to the number of windows. The tax was increased on six occasions in the late 18th century, and was not repealed until 1851. To avoid paying too much tax many people had some of the windows bricked up, and these blind windows, often with glazing bars represented in paint, can still sometimes be seen.

Windows in the 19th century followed the various revivals of styles of different periods. With the GOTHIC REVIVAL (q.v. Vol. XII), pointed windows became fashionable. As the century progressed, and plate glass could be manufactured more cheaply and in larger sheets, it was used in all types of window, glazing bars being omitted. Most window glass now is sheet glass, which is cheaper.

In the 20th century new building techniques have made possible a much greater freedom in the design of windows. With frame construction (*see* BUILDING, PRINCIPLES OF, Vol. VIII), WALLS (q.v.) no longer have to support the upper floors and roofs, and so they can be pierced at any place by windows as large as are wanted. Steel or concrete lintels, as well as large sheets of plate glass, make possible windows of any width and efficient methods of HEATING (q.v.) compensate for extra cold. Windows can even be made to slide back or fold like a concertina so that the whole width can be opened; or they can be pivoted so that they are easy to clean from inside. Double windows, common in cold countries such as Scandinavia, are sometimes also used in England to keep out noise and cold.

Metal-framed windows are now made in factories to standard sizes, and their uniform shapes largely dictate the appearance of the façades of small houses. They either have hinged casements or they are fixed with a small opening to provide ventilation.

See also HOUSES, HISTORY OF; WALLS; VENTILATION.

WINES AND SPIRITS. 1. Wine is made by fermenting the juice of the grape; spirits by distilling the fermented juice of fruits and other substances. In countries where GRAPES (q.v. Vol. VI) are generally grown, wine is an inevitable part of a meal. In Britain wine is served with meals only on special occasions, and then only for the well-to-do, whereas in the south of France almost everyone ordinarily drinks wine with meals. Wine assists digestion, by making the meal more attractive, and by stimulating the digestive juices.

2. WINES FOR MEALS. The art of serving wines with food has many refinements, but there are certain fundamental principles which are easily grasped. Before the meal begins, an apéritif may be served to stimulate the appetite. Dry, white, fortified wines (see WINE TRADE, Vol. VII), such as sherry, Marsala, and vermouth, are most appropriate, but champagne and other dry white wines are also suitable. Cocktails, which are mixtures containing spirits, are not considered so suitable if wine is to be served at the meal. In some northern countries undiluted spirits accompany the hors d'œuvres, for example, vodka in Russia, schnapps in Denmark. Dry white wines and red wines are most appropriate with the entrée, white wines such as those of Burgundy, Germany, and Italy being best with fish, and the red ones, claret, Burgundy, Rhône, or Italian wines, with meat. With the sweets and dessert, the sweeter white wines taste best; the best known, Sauterne, Barsac, and Graves, come from the Bordeaux country, but other sweet wines come from Germany, Italy, and other parts of France. After the sweet, or in place of it, cheese or another savoury may be served, and with this a red wine is most appropriate. At the end of the meal, dessert wines, such as port, Madeira, and brown sherry, may be served with fruit and nuts; and finally, with black coffee, brandy (Cognac or Armagnac) or liqueurs. There are one or two other general points. Champagne and *vin rosé*, unlike other wines, suit any food with which wine can be drunk. Strongly flavoured foods, such as curry, and dishes containing vinegar, such as dressed salads, tend to spoil the appreciation of a delicate wine. With shellfish, and particularly oysters, spirits are not suitable, Chablis being the traditional wine to drink with oysters.

3. SERVING. White wines are best served cold at about 45° F., and should therefore be put in a refrigerator or on ice for about half an hour before the meal. Red wines, on the other hand, are not at their best unless slightly warm, 65°–70° F., and should be kept in a warm room for an hour or so before serving, a process known as 'chambering'. If the warming is done too suddenly, the quality of the finer wines is impaired. Red wines should also have the cork drawn some time before being served to allow them to 'breathe', which assists in developing the full quality and bouquet of the wine. At the bottom of red wine, particularly if it is old, there is a deposit called the 'lees' which, if allowed to mix with the rest, will make the wine cloudy and unpalatable. The bottles, therefore, must not be

WINE GLASSES

Back row, left to right: hock, brandy, champagne. *Front row*: white wine, red wine, port, sherry, liqueur

shaken and, if decanted, the wine is pour gently without disturbing the sediment. Fine glass decanters and wine-glasses, which have long stems show off the wine to advantage (see TABLE GLASS). There are different kinds of glasses for each kind of wine, small for the apéritif and liqueur, and larger for red and white wines. Certain conventional shapes have been established for special wines. A champagne glass has a shallow bowl, which allows the carbon dioxide to blow off harmlessly; for brandy, a balloon-shaped bowl brings out the bouquet; and a hock glass traditionally has a long stem. Whatever the size or shape of the glass, the rim should turn inwards rather than outwards if there is a bouquet to be savoured, and the glass should not be more than two-thirds filled (see GLASS-MAKING, Vol. VII).

4. CHOICE AND STORAGE. A great deal of experience is needed to choose wines well, and most amateurs have to rely on a good wine merchant for the finer points. Some wines travel well, some can be fully appreciated only where they are made. The grapes in certain years, known as vintage years, produce better wine than in other years, though this does not apply to fortified wines, such as sherry, which by a special process of blending are maintained the same from year to year. The place of origin and the name of the shipper are guides in selecting these wines. It is not always possible to predict what will happen to a wine as it matures; some vintage wines will keep for 20 or more years, improving year by year. After a certain point,

WINE BOTTLES

Left to right: champagne, Grand Marnier (a liqueur), hock, burgundy, Chianti, claret

however, they deteriorate. Only the best vintage Burgundies and a few exceptional other wines will keep for more than 25 years; Burgundies of poorer years will not last so long.

Bottles for different wines have by tradition different shapes; the high shoulders of the claret bottle, the sloping ones of the Burgundy bottle, and the long neck of the hock bottle are well known. The larger bottles are less commonly seen. The two- and four-bottle sizes are called magnum and double magnum respectively, and the larger sizes still are known by various names such as the Imperial, the Rehoboam, the Jeraboam, and the Nebuchadnezzar. These are used only for first-class wines, and because the wine matures more slowly in these than in small bottles the wines are usually of finer quality. Many of the best wines, including those in these large bottles, are bottled at the vineyard where they are produced. In the case of claret these are called 'château bottled', and bear the label *mis en bouteille au château*. Another statement sometimes appearing on the label in Britain describes the alcoholic content in degrees proof. (This method of assessment is based on primitive methods adopted in the past when the only proof of the amount of alcohol present lay in whether it would burn or not.) Proof spirit contains $57 \cdot 1\%$ alcohol by volume, and therefore a wine which is $25°$ Proof (or $75°$ Under Proof) contains $\frac{25}{100} \times 57 \cdot 1$ alcohol, or about 14%. In the U.S.A. 14% would be on this label, for there the alcoholic content is expressed directly in percentages.

It has been found that wine matures best if kept where it is free from vibrations at a steady temperature of $55°$ F. Such conditions exist in underground rooms; hence the common practice of keeping wines in cellars. If wine-bottles are stored lying on their sides in a rack, the cork is always kept moist and in sound condition. If the cork deteriorates, it will cause the wine to have the unpleasant taste known as 'corked'. Spirits, however, are better kept upright because the concentrated alcohol would in time damage the cork.

See Vol. VII: WINE TRADE; WHISKY DISTILLING.
See also Vol. VI: GRAPES.

WINES, HOME-MADE. Home-made wines are not generally made from grapes, and are not therefore true wines, although they have approximately the same alcoholic content. In a true wine this is produced by FERMENTATION (q.v. Vol. II) of the natural sugars of the grape, but in home-made wines the natural sugars present are insufficient and cane sugar is usually added. Few people in Britain now make wines at home, but frequent references in literature and song and numerous recipes found in old cookery books prove that it was a common practice in former centuries, particularly in the country.

Home-made wines may be made from fruit, flowers, and vegetables of various kinds, each of which gives a characteristic flavour—gooseberries, black currants, elderberries, plums, dandelions, elderflowers, cowslips, herbs, nettles, carrots, turnips, parsnips, potatoes. Flowers and fruit supply sugar in varying amounts; vegetables give starch which is converted to sugar and then to alcohol in the process of fermentation. The general method consists of mixing the fruit with water and sugar and then adding yeast, which slowly converts the sugar present into alcohol and carbon dioxide. The latter is allowed to escape, except in a few cases, such as elderflower wine, when a sparkling drink is required.

A typical wine can be made from dandelion heads in the following way. Three quarts of flower heads are steeped in 1 gallon of boiling water for 24 hours, and then strained. To each gallon of liquid obtained is added 3 lb. of sugar, 1 sliced lemon, and 1 sliced orange, and all is boiled for half an hour and allowed to cool. When cool, a slice of toast covered with yeast is added, and the mixture set aside to ferment.

When fermentation has almost ceased, in about 2 days, the liquid is bottled and corked lightly.

Another alcoholic drink which has been known in England for many centuries is made from honey and is called mead, or hydromel. Three to four lb. of honey is boiled in a gallon of water, and then fermented with yeast, and left to mature for 1–5 years. Small amounts of different substances, such as cream of tartar, phosphate of ammonia, lemons, herbs, or hops, are added to give flavour and to ensure satisfactory fermentation.

To prepare drinks with an alcoholic content higher than wines it is necessary to distil them, a practice which is illegal in Britain without an Excise licence. In many foreign countries, however, *eau de vie* is prepared in the home from various natural products such as plums, greengages, apples, potatoes, and grain. Sloe gin and cherry brandy are strong drinks made not by distilling a spirit but by steeping the fruit in gin and brandy respectively for several months.

See also WINES AND SPIRITS.

WOODWORK, *see* FURNITURE, CARE OF; HOUSEHOLD REPAIRS. *See also* Vol. VII: WOODWORK, HISTORY OF. *See also* Vol. VIII: WOODWORKING MACHINERY.

X-RAYS, *see* RADIOTHERAPY. *See also* Vol. VIII: X-RAYS.

YELLOW FEVER, *see* TROPICAL DISEASES, Section 4.